Interdisciplinary Studies in Human Rights

Volume 9

Human rights are one of the normative cornerstones of contemporary international law and global governance. Due to the complexities of actual or potential violations of human rights and in light of current crises, new and interdisciplinary research is urgently needed. The series Interdisciplinary Studies in Human Rights recognizes the growing importance and necessity of interdisciplinary research in human rights. The series consists of monographs and collected volumes addressing human rights research from different disciplinary and interdisciplinary perspectives, including but not limited to philosophy, law, political science, education, and medical ethics. Its goal is to explore new and contested questions such as the extraterritorial application of human rights and their relevance for non-state actors, as well as the philosophical and theoretical foundations of human rights. The series also addresses policy questions of current interest including the human rights of migrants and refugees, LGBTI rights, and bioethics, as well as business and human rights.

The series editors are Members of the Centre for Human Rights Erlangen-Nürnberg (CHREN), an interdisciplinary research center at Friedrich-Alexander-University Erlangen-Nürnberg. The Advisory Board brings together human rights scholars from a wide range of academic disciplines and regional backgrounds. The series welcomes suggestions for publications of academic research falling into the series subject matter.

Ricarda Rösch

Negotiating Norms

The Right to Free, Prior, and Informed Consent in Liberia and Beyond

Springer

Ricarda Rösch
Nürnberg, Germany

ISSN 2509-2960 ISSN 2509-2979 (electronic)
Interdisciplinary Studies in Human Rights
ISBN 978-3-031-45909-2 ISBN 978-3-031-45910-8 (eBook)
https://doi.org/10.1007/978-3-031-45910-8

This Springer imprint is published by the registered company Springer Nature Switzerland AG
The registered company address is: Gewerbestrasse 11, 6330 Cham, Switzerland

Acknowledgments

Given the duration of this book project, I owe thanks to many persons who accompanied me on this lengthy journey. As my supervisor, Markus Krajewski has offered me a lot of support and guidance along the way. I am thankful to Anne Griffiths, who has agreed to act as the second reviewer and provided valuable comments for finalizing the project. I am also grateful for the enriching discussions with my former colleagues at the Chair in Public Law and Public International Law at the Friedrich-Alexander University of Erlangen-Nuremberg. Moreover, I greatly benefitted from several research visits at the Max-Planck-Institute for Social Anthropology in Halle and the exchanges with other researchers working at the intersection of law and anthropology. Therefore, I would like to thank Marie-Claire Foblets for the kind invitations.

Moreover, without funding from the Heinrich Böll Stiftung, this research would not have been possible. Particularly worth mentioning are the exchanges with fellow Ph.D. students on research methods, parenthood, and many other topics. These exchanges provided a lot of inspiration and encouraged me to look beyond the confines of my discipline.

During my research in Liberia, I also met many people providing invaluable support. I am thankful to the Kofi Annan Institute for Conflict Transformation, ACDI/VOCA, and the Sustainable Development Institute that hosted me as a visiting researcher. I am most grateful to the approximately 180 interviewees who were willing to share their time and knowledge with me. Notably, the exchanges with Liz Alden Wiley, Peter Aldinger, David Brown, Felix Gerdes, Abraham Guillen, Chris Kidd, James Otto, Silas Siakor, Jonathan Yiah, and David Young provided important starting points and/or helped me make sense of my data. Gbangaryisi Johnson and Marthaline Boma opened many doors during my research in the two community forests and helped me get in touch with the right people. I also owe thanks to the Sehzueplay and Beyan Poye communities for hosting me—just like the Joghbahn community, even though I ended up not using the data I gathered there. Moreover, I would like to thank Samuel Flanjay Cooper for his excellent translation and transcription of my Bassa interviews. I owe gratitude to Nora Bowier and her colleagues from the Sustainable Development Institute, who regularly helped me out with new information after my return to Germany.

In addition, I would like to thank Hannah Franzki for her feedback on my theoretical framework and Erika Stewart-Finkenstaedt for her scrupulous proofreading. Ultimately, I am incredibly grateful for my family, which supported and encouraged me along the way.

Contents

Abbreviations

ADRIP	American Declaration on the Rights of Peasants
ACHPR	African Commission on Human and Peoples' Rights
ACtHPR	African Court on Human and Peoples' Rights
CBD	Convention on Biological Diversity
CEDAW	Convention on the Elimination of all Forms of Discrimination Against Women
CEDAW Committee	Committee on the Elimination of All Forms of Discrimination Against Women
CERD	Convention on the Elimination of all Forms of Racial Discrimination
CERD Committee	Committee on the Elimination of Racial Discrimination
CESCR	Committee on Economic, Social and Cultural Rights
CFMB	Community Forest Management Body
CLDMC	Community Land Development and Management Committee
COP	Conference of Parties
CRL	Community Rights Law with Respect to Forest Land
CSO	Civil Society Organization
FAO	Food and Agricultural Organization
FCNM	Framework Convention for the Protection of National Minorities
FDA	Forestry Development Authority
FIFES	Forest Incomes for Environmental Sustainability
FPIC	Free, Prior and Informed Consent
FSC	Forest Stewardship Council
IACHR	Inter-American Commission of Human Rights
IACtHR	Inter-American Court of Human Rights
ICCPR	International Covenant on Civil and Political Rights
ICESCR	International Covenant on Economic, Social and Cultural Rights
ICJ	International Court of Justice

ILO	International Labor Organization
LGSA	Land Governance Support Activity
LLA	Liberia Land Authority
LRA	Land Rights Act
LRCFP	Land Rights and Community Forestry Programme
MoU	Memorandum of Understanding
NFRL	National Forestry Reform Law
NGO	Non-Governmental Organization
OSCE	Organization of Security and Co-operation in Europe
PIC	Prior and Informed Consent
PoWPA	Program of Work on Protected Areas
PROSPER	People, Rules, and Organizations Supporting the Protection of Ecosystem Resources
PUP	Private Use Permit
Ramsar Convention	Convention on Wetlands of International Importance especially as Waterfowl Habitat
RSPO	Roundtable on Sustainable Palm Oil
SDI	Sustainable Development Institute
SER survey	Socio-economic resource reconnaissance survey
SSAHUTLC	Sub-Saharan African Historically Underserved Traditional Local Communities
UN	United Nations
UNDRIP	United Nations Declaration on the Rights of Indigenous Peoples
UNDROP	United Nations Declaration on the Rights of Peasants and Other People Working in Rural Areas
UNGP	UN Guiding Principles on Business and Human Rights
UNESCO	United Nations Educational, Scientific, and Cultural Organization
UNMIL	United Nations Mission in Liberia
UNSCR	United Nations Security Council Resolution
USAID	United States Agency for International Development
VGGT	Voluntary Guidelines on the Responsible Governance of Tenure of Land, Fisheries and Forests in the Context of National Food Security
VPA	Voluntary Partnership Agreement
WHC	Convention Concerning the Protection of the World Cultural and Natural Heritage
WLRTF	Women's Land Rights Taskforce
WORTH	Women Organizing Resources Together

Chapter 1
Introduction

The right to free, prior and informed consent (FPIC) is a central claim of the transnational Indigenous movement.[1] It is discussed in a growing number of contexts and it currently most prominently appears in debates about the human rights footprint of extractive industry projects on Indigenous lands.[2] It is assumed that the state and companies are, in some form, obliged to consult with Indigenous peoples before launching a project. However, beyond that, there exists little consensus about what exactly FPIC entails.[3] An Indigenous non-governmental organization (NGO), a human rights lawyer, a World Bank employee, a conservation professional, and a government official quite likely differ in their understanding of FPIC. Open questions pertain to who has the right to grant it, whether a community's no must be respected, and in which situations it applies. Potentially relevant contexts include all types of projects on customary land, legal or administrative measures that may interfere with communities' cultural rights, forced resettlements, and activities impacting Indigenous traditional resource rights.

This book seeks to disentangle the various understandings of FPIC floating around in different socio-legal spaces at different scales, from global, over national, to local time-spaces.[4] It takes a particular interest in the processes at play when FPIC gets transplanted into new geographical contexts. It will be shown that legal transplantation processes are norm negotiation processes taking place in specific semi-autonomous fields.[5] Within these fields, actors struggle to determine the meaning of a norm that is aligned with their interests and values. Thereby, they are regularly

[1]E.g. Papillon and Rodon (2020), Henriksen (2020) The Saami Council Supports Appeal from Indigenous Leaders Regarding NorNickel. https://www.saamicouncil.net/news-archive/saami-council-support-indigenous-leaders-nornickel. Accessed 7 Aug 2023; Indigenous Environmental Network, Free, Prior and Informed Consent. www.ienearth.org/fpic. Accessed 7 Aug 2023.

[2]E.g. Owen and Kemp (2014), p. 91; MacInnes et al. (2017), pp. 152–53; Doyle (2019), p. 171.

[3]For an excellent overview of these controversies, see Doyle (2015).

[4]de Sousa Santos (2002b), p. 85.

[5]Falk Moore (1973), p. 719; see also Hellum (1995), p. 15.

R. Rösch, *Negotiating Norms*, Interdisciplinary Studies in Human Rights 9,
https://doi.org/10.1007/978-3-031-45910-8_1

located in several and not just in one field. Taking the Liberian field of post-conflict law-making as an example, donors like the United States Agency for International Development (USAID) are part of the national legislative field. At the same time, they are also part of the field of development cooperation and, if the projects they fund have a conservation earmark, they may simultaneously be located in the field of conservation. The negotiations of FPIC thus take place in specific fields constituted by specific actors at a specific point in time.

Discourses are a central tool in the negotiation of norms. Actors can draw from different discourses for shaping the law. Power, knowledge, and networks determine whether one can influence the negotiation of a norm.[6] Notably, the construction of social and legal identities, in the case of FPIC, those of the *community* and the *state*, is a strategy for altering the meaning of the law.

With FPIC being under negotiation, the *one* right to FPIC does not exist. While there may be an emerging understanding of FPIC as a human right, questions remain. By focusing on the legal and social identities to which FPIC is attached, its scope and meaning, and the question of who may consent, the differing conceptualizations of FPIC will be demasked, contributing to a better understanding of FPIC as a right, principle, or best practice. Besides questions pertaining to the rights- or stakeholders of FPIC and its scope, FPIC also touches upon issues of culture and gender, which remain underexplored in much of the literature.[7] Who has the right to consent? Is it the chiefs (given their questionable legitimacy in many postcolonial contexts), should it be other customary institutions (if existing), or does the participation of *all sectors* of the community need to be ensured (potentially contributing to the further decline of customary decision-making)?[8] And how about the participation of women and other gender identities in consultation processes? It will be shown that the norm FPIC remains fragmented.

Besides that, geographical research gaps persist: FPIC's application has been explored most often in South American countries.[9] Given the absence of research on FPIC in Africa, the prevalence of land grabs, and the controversies surrounding the concept of Indigeneity, there is a strong need to shed light on the recognition and operationalization of FPIC in sub-Saharan Africa.[10] Despite a few FPIC-related cases of the African human rights institutions and non-binding (sub)regional initiatives, African states have been reluctant to embrace and operationalize FPIC.[11]

---

[6] Chouliaraki and Fairclough (1999), p. 124.

[7] The right to self-determination and gender are discussed by a few authors (e.g. Napoleon (2009); Kuokkanen (2016)).

[8] For a good overview of the different positions on traditional decision-making in the African context see Aikins (2016), p. 68.

[9] E.g. Rodríguez-Garavito (2010); Verbeek (2012); Flemmer and Schilling-Vacaflor (2016); de Casas (2019); Schilling-Vacaflor and Flemmer (2020).

[10] Exceptions include Greenspan (2014); Roesch (2016); Manirakiza (2019), pp. 219ff; Mitchell and Yuzdepski (2019).

[11] Roesch (2016); Roesch R (2 May 2018) Skype Interview with a Lawyer of an International Human Rights Organization, para 50; examples for (sub)regional initiatives include African Union

Many African states only require weaker versions of FPIC, such as consultations with traditional decision-makers for land transactions or stakeholder consultations under their environmental legislation.[12]

More recently, community consent found its way into the legal systems of more African states such as the Republic of Congo,[13] South Africa,[14] and Zambia.[15] Moreover, case law has begun to emerge.[16] The Democratic Republic of the Congo is negotiating an Indigenous Peoples' law, although little progress has been made in recent years.[17] It has, however, adopted an FPIC Regulation for forest conservation projects under REDD+.[18] Other countries with FPIC Regulations under the REDD+ framework include Kenya and Cameroon.[19] In some cases, like the Kenyan Community Land Act, the language of FPIC is not used, but a majority decision is a precondition for investments in community land.[20]

(2009) Africa Mining Vision, p.12; Directives Sous-Regionales sur la Participation des Populations Locales et Autochtones et des ONG à la Gestion Durable des Forêts d'Afrique Centrale (2017) (COMIFAC).

[12]Legal Resources Centre and Oxfam (2018), p. 10; see also Organic Law Determining the Modalities of Protection, Conservation and Promotion of the Environment in Rwanda (2005) (Republic of Rwanda), art 63.

[13]Loi n°5–2011 du 25 février 2011 portant Promotion et Protection des Droits des Populations Autochtones (2011) (Republic of Congo), art. 3.

[14]While the so-called Interim Protection of Informal Land Rights Act (IPIRLA) requires consent before the extinction of informal tenure, this was interpreted as being superseded by the mining legislation in the past (Interim Protection of Informal Land Rights Act (1996) (Republic of South Africa), s 2(1)). More recently, a High Court ruled that the IPIRLA transforms the mining legislation's consultation in a consent requirement when traditional communities are affected (Baleni and Others v Minister of Mineral Resources and Others (2018) North Gauteng High Court, Pretoria. ZAGPPHC 829 (North Gauteng High Court), para 76). The Constitutional Court took the same position (Maledu and Others v Itereleng Bakgatla Mineral Resources (Pty) Limited and Another (2018) BCLR 55 (Constitutional Court of South Africa), para 105).

[15]Draft National Land Policy (2017) (Republic of Zambia), obj 34.

[16]E.g. Meru ELC Case No. 163 of 2014, formerly Nairobi ELC No. 1330 of 2014 (2021) Environment and Land Court at Meru. paras 154ff.

[17]Proposition de Loi Organique Portant Principes Fondamentaux Relatifs Aux Droits des Peuples Autochtones Pygmées (2014) (République Démocratique du Congo), art 2(2); Environnement Ressources Naturelles et Developpement (2020) Contributions à l'Etude du Mécanisme d'Experts sur les Droits des Peuples Autochtones. www.ohchr.org/Documents/Issues/IPeoples/EMRIP/RightToLand/ERNDonDRC.pdf. Accessed 21 Mar 2023.

[18]Arrêté Ministeriel No 016/CAB/MIN/EDD/AAN/KTT/04/2017 du 8 Novembre Fixant le Cadre de Directives Nationales sur le Consentement Libre, Informé et Préalable (CLIP) dans le Cadre de la Mise en Oeuvre de la REDD+ en République Démocratique du Congo (2017) (République Démocratique du Congo),

[19]E.g. Carodenuto and Fobissie (2015); National REDD+ Strategy (2021) (Republic of Kenya), p. 81.

[20]The Community Land Act (2016) (Republic of Kenya), part 3, art 15(5).

Liberia, which assumes a central role in this book, is thus unique: civil society organizations have regularly addressed the lack of respect for FPIC in the past 15 years and it has been made part of the national legal system as early as 2007.[21]

Consent is also a central component of many African communities' customary law. As one Liberian activist explained:

> [If] you went back to the communities, FPIC is not new [. . .] They have practiced FPIC all these years. We have not had the chance to go back to understand how they have practiced it [. . .] From where [you are allowed] to make the farm to how you want to harvest a particular crop, along the way, you need to consult and get the people to agree.[22]

Hence, while not necessarily using the terminology of FPIC, consultation and consent rights are certainly not new to the continent. However, they remain insufficiently recognized or underutilized by African governments.[23]

The negotiation and adaptation of FPIC also highlight some of the dangers of mainstreaming emancipatory concepts and the negative impacts of a centralistic understanding of the law that fails to recognize other legalities and forms of knowledge. Neglecting the self-determination and cultural dimensions of FPIC can result in the legitimized extinction of land or natural resource rights and the further marginalization of communities and the women within these communities.

1.1 Methodology

By linking legal analysis with social science methods, the book's transdisciplinary perspective provides an enriching perspective and shows that legal questions should not be answered in isolation from the social environment in which they emerge. The following section explores the methodology, including my positionality, research methods, and methods of data analysis, before outlining the theoretical framework.

1.1.1 Positionality

The identification of research questions, the data production, and the data analysis are not objective, reproducible processes but reflect the researcher's positionality

[21] E.g. Ten Core Regulations (2007) Reg No 102-07 ss 22(j)(1), 61(c)(3); Roundtable on Sustainable Palm Oil (2020) Green Advocates on Behalf of the Communities in Greenville, Butaw & Kpanyan Districts of Sinoe Country, Forest Peoples Programme, Sustainable Development Institute, Kulu United Development Association v Golden Veroleum (Liberia) Inc. (GVL). https://askrspo.force.com/Complaint/s/case/50090000028ErzuAAC/detail. Accessed 7 Aug 2023.

[22] Roesch R (21 Mar 2018) Interview with Several Staff Members of a Liberian NGO, Monrovia, para 34.

[23] Note that the implementation in settler states on the continents is similarly difficult; Legal Resources Centre and Oxfam (2018), p. 14.

and identity. Recognizing the 'objective limits of objectivism'[24] and the 'embodied nature of all vision',[25] reflexivity is an important tool for dismantling one's own positionality. Reflexivity has three dimensions.[26] The first dimension is social positioning. The need for self-positioning or positionality is now well-recognized in much of the social sciences. In the following section, I will explore my positionality in more detail.

The second dimension is the researcher's location in the academic field.[27] On the one hand, my academic background as a legal researcher (and not a social scientist) certainly played a role. I had to reflect on legal centralism, which had been a central component of my training. Realizing the gaps between the law on the books and the law in practice, I had to question the impulse to label the phenomenon as non-compliance, unwillingness, or inability but to recognize that more complex social and legal processes were at play. On the other hand, my lack of methodological training enabled me to look at research designs and methods in an unprejudiced way—even though my sympathy for legal anthropology and fear of statistics guided me more towards qualitative methods. The outcome is undoubtedly a work that cannot be located within the confines of one discipline but is rather an inter- or even transdisciplinary project.[28]

And, as a third dimension, the 'intellectualist bias'[29] detaches researchers from the actual practice as they perceive the world as a spectacle and field of analysis. It is a challenge to understand the objects of research as actors and, at the same time, to acknowledge that, as a researcher, one becomes part of the study field.[30] Charmaz argues that researchers' make assumptions about what is real, possess stocks of knowledge, occupy social statuses, and pursue purposes that influence their respective views and actions into the presence of each other'.[31] Moore, therefore, describes fieldwork as 'simultaneously a discursive practice and a located labor process'.[32] Particularly during my research in Liberia, I was confronted with the intellectualist bias.

---

[24] Bourdieu (1977), p. 1.

[25] Haraway (1988), p. 581.

[26] Wacquant (1992), p. 39.

[27] Ibid., p. 39.

[28] See also Madsen and Dezalay (2002), p. 191.

[29] Wacquant (1992), p. 39.

[30] Haraway (1988), p. 592.

[31] Charmaz (2014), p. 27.

[32] Moore (2005), p 26.

1.1.2 *Research Approach and Methods*

My research approach was inductive. Inductive research can be defined as 'building patterns, categories, and themes from the bottom up by organizing the data into increasingly more abstract units of information'.[33] Particularly Charmaz's reflexive grounded theory informed my data production and data analysis.[34]' Still, my research was not entirely free from theoretical considerations, which informed my data production, including the choice of cases and interview partners.[35] Legal anthropology's assumptions about legal plurality, the semi-autonomous legal field, and legal transplants influenced how I approached the research project.[36] During the data production, I engaged with the collected data and moved back and forth between data production and data analysis.[37]

The determination of the research unit in Liberia occurred empirically.[38] Three questions guided the early stages of my research: What does FPIC mean in international law? How and why was it incorporated into the Liberian legislation, and what does it mean in practice?

While I first assumed that FPIC as a right was relatively clear-cut, I noticed during my research in Liberia that even though many actors used the language of FPIC and saw it as something vaguely international, it meant different things to them, and served different purposes. This led me to assume that there must be more than one understanding of FPIC on the transnational plane and made me revisit my understanding of FPIC.

Based on the second question, I identified the Liberian fields of post-conflict law-making, which changed considerably over time.

The third question made me explore the *forest-owning community* having the right to FPIC in Liberia as a research unit. These research questions determined the methods I used, which I then adapted to the practical circumstances on the ground.[39]

1.1.2.1 Research on Transnational Law

To understand the meanings of FPIC in the fields of transnational law, I mainly relied on legal documents. I focused on materials with a certain reach in the transnational space and decided to exclude those with smaller-scale implications, such as the law of bilateral development cooperation, NGO reports, and corporate social responsibility commitments of individual companies. Moreover, given the number of

---

[33] Creswell and Creswell (2018), p. 257.

[34] Charmaz (2014).

[35] Ibid., p. 59.

[36] E.g. Falk Moore (1973); Engle Merry (2006); von Benda-Beckmann and Turner (2019).

[37] Charmaz (2014), p. 41.

[38] Bourdieu and Wacquant (1992), p. 100.

[39] Charmaz (2014), pp. 26, 42.

development banks, I focused on those with a track record in engaging with Indigenous peoples or communities.

I also did not try to map the flows of FPIC in detail, which has been done by other authors, but focused on identifying tendencies towards a fixed meaning in each of the fields.[40] Countering my intuition as a person with legal training, the explored documents were not seen as conveying the right or wrong understanding of FPIC but rather as an expression of the field's value and hegemonic discourse.[41]

1.1.2.2 Research in the Fields of Post-Conflict Law-Making

Upon my arrival in Liberia, I knew that the Community Rights Law mentioned FPIC but had no idea how and why it was introduced, in which situations it applied, and how. Therefore, I intuitively started collecting 'rich data'.[42]

The reconstruction of the legal reform processes was mainly based on donor (USAID and World Bank) and NGO reports and various legal drafts (Community Rights Law[43] and the Land Rights Act[44]).

I contextualized these legal drafts through interviews with the actors involved in the legal reforms.[45] I conducted more than 40 semi-structured interviews during two research visits in Liberia from October 2017 to January 2018 and February to March 2018.[46] These were complemented by video interviews after the passage of the Land Rights Act in September 2018. Through these interviews, I aimed to understand the legal framework and identify the actors of the legal reform process, their relationships, and the different positions and discourses with respect to FPIC. While I prepared interview guides for each interview with topics I intended to cover, I also left space for my interview partners to bring up new topics.[47] Besides that, I took extensive field notes to link the interview transcripts with the impression I had of my interview partners, additional information about their positionality, and comments

---

[40] E.g. Corntassel (2008); Barelli (2016).

[41] Charmaz (2014), pp. 48–49.

[42] Ibid., p. 23.

[43] Seven drafts of the Community Rights Law.

[44] Five drafts of the Land Rights Act.

[45] Charmaz (2014), p. 53.

[46] Those include, amongst others, interviews with (former) staff members of the Sustainable Development Institute (5), Green Advocates (1), the Land Commission and the Liberia Land Authority (3), the Forest Development Authority (4), former staff members of the USAID Land Rights and Community Forestry Programme (2), (former) staff members of the USAID-funded project Land Governance Support Activity (2), the Environmental Law Institute (1), the Environmental Protection Agency (2), the National Bureau of Concessions (1), the National Investment Commission (1), international NGOs (5), the World Bank (3), the Liberia Timber Association (2), donor representatives (2), Liberian lawyers (2) and the EU VPA Unit (3).

[47] Charmaz (2014), p. 63.

they made off-record.[48] Thereby, I identified different discourses related to the *community* and the *state*.

One limitation of my research was that interviewees could often not remember the details of the drafting processes—the legal reforms began in 2006—and regularly contradicted each other. Moreover, widespread narratives of participation and inclusivity made it challenging to identify the different actors' interests and positions at times. Together with the lack of written documentation, this rendered the reconstruction of events difficult.

Moreover, given the fact that the Land Rights Act Regulations were only adopted in late 2022, the drafting process will not be explored in this book. However, the impact of the Regulations on the emerging understanding of FPIC will be analyzed.

My positionality also impacted how my informants interacted with me, as government and company officials often tended to be very reluctant to share any information, fearing negative publications. The easiest way of accessing information was via foreign experts and development professionals working for transnational NGOs, donors, or international organizations. This means that their views may be overrepresented compared to other perspectives. The Liberian NGO Sustainable Development Institute (SDI) also provided valuable information and connected me with informants.

1.1.2.3 Research in Two Community Forests

Under the Liberian forest legislation, FPIC only applies primarily to community forestry and not to other sectors such as agriculture or the extractive industries.[49] Therefore, this book explores Liberian community forests as fields.[50] I chose a case study design with two cases, i.e., two community forests.[51] Even though the case study research design informed my case selection, my research approach departs from the largely (post)positivist research paradigm in which case study research is often grounded.[52] The goal was to make sense of the situation on the ground and see how different actors impacted the negotiation of FPIC.

Both community forests—Beyan Poye and Sehzueplay—had completed their community forest registration and had entered into logging contracts with companies. The vast majority of community forests will likely enter into such agreements, making the two forests typical cases.[53]

---

[48] Fischer (2008), p. 298.

[49] A shorter description of my research methods has already been published in Roesch (2021), pp. 140–42.

[50] Falk Moore (2000), p. 78.

[51] Linos (2015), pp. 479–80.

[52] E.g. George and Bennett (2005); Yin (2018).

[53] Global Witness (2018), p. 41; Agyeman et al. (2022) p. 149.

Assuming that different actors renegotiate traveling norms, the actors involved in the negotiation were the variable distinguishing the two cases with a similar outcome ('positive method of difference'[54] or 'most similar cases'[55]). I chose one community forest which had received ongoing financial and technical support from successive forest conservation projects funded by the United States Agency for International Development (USAID). The USAID-funded project—Forest Incomes for Environmental Sustainability (FIFES)—worked with eleven community forests. Three of them had entered into commercial use contracts with companies at the time of my field research. In one of them, Martro, conflicts between different community members on a larger scale were ongoing, rendering research overly difficult. Hence, I selected one of the other two forests: Sehzueplay. Sehzueplay is a typical case and has been classified by staff members of the USAID project as neither the most successful nor the most unsuccessful in terms of sustainable forest.[56]

The other community forest, Beyan Poye, had not seen any ongoing external support. Only the Forestry Development Authority (FDA) facilitated their application process. At the time, I was given the information that only two community forests had entered into commercial use contracts (Beyan Poye and Garwin), even though the number was very likely higher in reality.[57] As the mismanagement of the Garwin community forest had already been made public in newspapers contributing to the presence of journalists and NGOs, I picked Beyan Poye.[58]

On the ground, I conducted semi-structured interviews with most members of the forest management bodies, local decision-makers, and other community members to understand how the community forest registration process was implemented in practice and how FPIC was accommodated.[59] I made sure to cover various towns and hamlets in each community forest, as well as different ethnic groups, where applicable.[60]

I conducted two focus group discussions within the different towns, one with the so-called stakeholders and one exclusively with women.[61] Focus group discussions are interviews involving several participants who discuss topics determined by the

[54] George and Bennett (2005), p. 153.

[55] Hirschl (2005), pp. 133ff.

[56] Liberia Strategic Analysis (2018) p. 3.

[57] It is extremely challenging to access updated information of the status of community forests in Liberia.

[58] Mukpo (29 Nov 2016) Corrupt Logging Practices in Liberia Could Mar New Era in Community Forestry. https://news.mongabay.com/2016/11/corrupt-logging-practices-in-liberia-could-mar-new-era-in-community-forestry/. Accessed 7 Aug 2023.

[59] 45 interviews with elders, women leaders, youth leaders, local USAID-funded project staff, members of the Community Assembly, the Community Forest Management Body, and the Executive Committee.

[60] In the first community forest, I walked to six different villages in a radius of 3 h walking distance. In the second one, I managed to cover all villages (eight plus four smaller settlements).

[61] 15 general focus groups with 6–10 participants and 12 women's focus groups (6–8 participants).

researcher.[62] The rationale behind the women's focus group discussion was to avoid essentializing the *community* and to get the perspective of community members that did not belong to the so-called stakeholders or the forest governance structure.[63] I assumed that gender would be a good starting point, as I knew that very few women were represented in the governance structure. Still, I did not view rural Liberian women as a uniform category.[64] By talking to women with different backgrounds, I tried to avoid essentializing gender.[65] Women from different families and different age groups participated in the discussions. In this way, I could, to some extent, take class, formal education, and age into consideration. In some instances, the focus group format made social relations visible (i.e., who was outspoken, who did not talk at all). Often, the women were much more open in discussion with each other than when talking to me individually.[66] I developed the interview guide, and my research assistants asked the questions in either Liberian English or the local language. I recorded the discussions and, when necessary, a Liberian translation agency translated and transcribed them.

My research still had several limitations. Firstly, most community forests were still in the process of registering their community forests, and very few of them had been authorized by the Forestry Development Authority. Thus, it is possible that shortcuts were taken in the authorization of these first community forests and that the registration procedure may be different in community forests that proceed at a slower pace. On top of that, the adoption of the Land Rights Act in 2018 will very likely impact those community forests that have not been authorized yet.

Secondly, while in the third chapter, I identified different discourses and interdiscursive encounters, the lack of documentation and my positionality prevented me from doing the same in the two community forests. Instead, I only managed to identify the current hegemonic discourse prevailing in the community forest and contestations of that discourse.

Thirdly, my research assistants' and my positionality played a role in my research. In the community forest that did not receive external support, I depended on the goodwill of the community forest management body, whose members walked me to the different towns and acted as interpreters. Yet, these members were also individuals who had granted the logging license to a company. While this helped to render some of the tensions between community members and the managers of the community forest visible, it also impaired people's willingness to share their concerns. My identity as a woman further complicated the situation. The Forestry Development Authority, whose authorization I needed to conduct my research, instructed the community members to ensure my safety. They took this very literally, meaning that I could not take a step away from them. Their undoubtedly good

[62] Wilkinson (1999), p. 222.

[63] Starblanket (2018), p. 3.

[64] See also Mihesuah (2003), p. xii; Mohanty (2003), p. 335.

[65] See also Lowenhaupt Tsing (1993), pp. 33–34.

[66] Stewart et al. (2007), pp. 9ff; Wilkinson (1999), pp. 224ff.

intentions interfered with my free choice of interview partners and allowed only for limited interaction with other community members. Moreover, after a few days, the logging company convinced the management body to stop cooperating with me, bringing my field research to an end.

In the second community forest, I was supported by a field facilitator of the USAID-funded project. This, too, impacted how I was perceived as a researcher, even though the facilitator coped well with criticism voiced by community members.

On top of that, my presence as a young white foreigner certainly raised certain (primarily monetary) expectations in many places, which interfered with the way people interacted with me and the information they provided.[67] I did not always manage to sufficiently explain what the purpose of (my) research was. My privileges impacted how I interacted with people and read situations and vice versa. It also gave me access to spaces and people that would otherwise not have spoken to me. Faria and Mollett, therefore, describe whiteness in data production as a 'structural advantage, standpoint and a set of historical and cultural practices'.[68]

Fourthly, community forestry's technical nature made it very difficult to reconstruct specific events and processes. I received contradictory claims about what happened (or not) at which point in time. One woman had to remind me that 'we don't remember things [like dates]. We are not Kwi[69] [educated, civilized]'.[70] While I tried my best to triangulate all information, the absence of documentation, the politicization of community forestry with negative NGO reporting, and my positionality were challenges. Simultaneously, the competing claims also highlighted the subjectivity of experiences and put into question whether the community forestry program has sufficiently (or at all) been Indigenized and is compatible with local epistemologies.

1.1.3 Data Analysis

Following the data production, I analyzed my data, again drawing from Charmaz's grounded theory approach.[71] I imported my audio files and other documents into the MaxQDA software and transcribed them. Subsequently, I coded my data in four steps. Charmaz describes coding as providing 'the tools for interrogating, sorting, and synthesizing hundreds of pages of interviews, field notes, documents, and other texts'.[72] It is thus the link between data and theory development.

[67] Other researchers in Liberia made very similar experiences (e.g. Utas 2003, p. 54).

[68] Faria and Mollett (2016), p. 81.

[69] See also Brown (1982), p. 287.

[70] Borma M (10 Dec 2017) Focus Group Discussion with Women from Gays Town, Gays Town, para 35.

[71] Breuer (2010); Charmaz (2014).

[72] Charmaz (2014), p. 113.

Given the large quantity of data (approximately 180 interviews), I added a step usually not foreseen by grounded theory: a rough sorting of my data by topic. I reread all interviews and documents and sorted interview passages by topic (i.e., forest governance, land governance, forest legislation) and actors that were mentioned (i.e., government, Forestry Development Authority, NGOs, chiefs). The latter helped me understand the relations between the different actors and was complemented by my field notes.

Afterwards, I did the initial coding.[73] Initial coding is the process whereby codes are extracted from the text, ideally using active language. In this respect, I used a line-by-line coding approach (i.e., 'claiming that the land belongs to the elders'; 'feeling that the government never asked us in forest matters'). The next step is called focused coding. Focused coding is when the initial codes are compared and patterns are identified (i.e., 'community forestry as a tool for reclaiming forest ownership').[74] These codes were not fixed but were revisited when new ideas emerged in the research process.

The last step of the data analysis is theoretical coding. Theoretical codes enable the theorizing of the focused codes and link them to existing theory.[75] At this point, I familiarized myself with theoretical concepts such as legal plurality, discourses, fields, and power in more detail. I identified theoretical concepts that were strongly aligned with my codes and used them as sanitizing concepts.

1.2 Fields, Power, and the Meaning of Law

Methodology and theory are intertwined.[76] During the theoretical coding, I started engaging with theory in more detail. In terms of epistemology, a mildly constructivist approach was adopted, which assumes that social practices and objective structures produce the social world.[77] Social practices and social structures are mutually constitutive.[78] Discourses are one form of social practice and exist in a dialectal relationship with other moments of social practice.[79]

As I tried to understand the transplantation of FPIC to different fields in Liberia, I struggled to comprehend the unique post-conflict legislative practices. In this respect, legal anthropology provided important concepts. Many legal anthropologists take legal plurality, history, space, and scale into consideration; critically reflect on the context and the positionality in the interpretation of legal practices; and

[73] Ibid, p. 116.

[74] Ibid, p. 138.

[75] Ibid, pp. 150–51.

[76] Bourdieu (1992), p. 225.

[77] Wacquant (1992), p. 11; Chouliaraki and Fairclough (1999), p. 4.

[78] Fairclough (1989), p. 37.

[79] Ibid, p. 17; Jørgensen and Phillips (2002), p. 19.

ground theory-building in in-depth research on the ground.[80] The following sections shed light on some key theoretical concepts in more detail. More specifically, they will explore fields as the research unit, the relevance of power, and the law as the subject of my research.

1.2.1 *Fields*

Not only legal anthropologists stress that the law is inherently spatial and entangled with its environment.[81] Particularly, Moore Falk's understanding of the semi-autonomous field and some aspects of field and discourse theory will be used for theorizing the spatiality of law. These concepts provide a useful analytical lens for understanding the dynamics of norm negotiation in different fields at different scales.

Fields are networks of relations between actors and institutions in a larger social space.[82] They follow a logic and necessity that is 'specific and irreducible'[83] to other fields and they can create norms and enforce them.[84] Thereby, they are 'to a significant extent self-regulating, self-enforcing, and self-propelling within a certain legal, political, economic, and social environment'.[85] Simultaneously, fields are not free from external influences but located in a 'larger social matrix which can, and does, affect and invade it'.[86]

However, fields are not only characterized by a specific logic but, more importantly, by the struggles of different actors.[87] Through these struggles, they are susceptible to change.[88] The perspectives and interests of the actors constituting the field are 'embedded in different normative perspectives, social realities, and economic concerns'.[89] Bourdieu's concept of reflexivity is a way of uncovering the values, location, and power of different actors, which shape their practice and habitus.[90]

---

80 de Sousa Santos (2002b), pp. 353ff; von Benda-Beckmann and von Benda-Beckmann (2007a), p. 18.

81 Silbey (1997), p. 209.

82 Wacquant (1992), p. 15.

83 Bourdieu and Wacquant (1992), p. 97.

84 Falk Moore (1973), p. 722.

85 Ibid, p. 728.

86 Ibid, p. 720.

87 Teubner (1997), p. 8; Lahire (2015), p. 63.

88 Bourdieu and Wacquant (1992), p. 102.

89 Bavinck (2005), p. 806.

90 Madsen and Dezalay (2002), p. 190.

1.2.2 Power

Fields are closely entangled with power. Power relations shape the structure of the field. At the same time, the structure is consolidated by the logic and functioning of the field.[91] Power has two characteristics: it is distributional and power relations are both enabling and constraining. Santos describes the latter as the boundary-setting and pathbreaking modes of power that do not necessarily function simultaneously or with the same intensity.[92]

Actors within a field are subjected to 'multiple matrices of power'.[93] The power of actors or institutions is determined by their capital and is susceptible to change'.[94] Capital functions only in relation to a field.[95] It is embedded in the social relations constituting the field.[96]

Bourdieu distinguishes between different types of capital: economic capital, cultural capital, social capital, and symbolic capital.[97] Economic capital is self-explanatory and refers to the financial resources of an actor. Economic capital can be transformed into other types of capital.[98] Cultural capital includes the social assets of a person and mechanisms of social mobility inscribed in institutions and cultural goods.[99] Mastering the rules of a specific field is also a form of cultural capital.[100] Social capital refers to the social network an actor has. It is 'an aggregate of the actual and potential resources which are linked to possession of a durable network of more or less institutionalized relationships of acquaintance and recognition'.[101] Symbolic capital is the 'power of constructing reality'[102] and 'constituting the given through utterances'.[103] Through recognition, every type of capital can be transformed into symbolic capital.[104] The endowment with symbolic capital thus depends on the representation that others have of it.[105] It resides in the relation between the powerful and the powerless. Symbolic power is inscribed in discourses through the 'belief in the legitimacy of words and those who utter them'.[106] For

[91] Bourdieu (1986a), p. 816.
[92] de Sousa Santos (2002b), p. 359.
[93] Moore (2005), p. 21.
[94] Bourdieu and Wacquant (1992), p. 99.
[95] Ibid, p. 101.
[96] See also Ewick and Silbey (2003), p. 1333.
[97] Bourdieu and Wacquant (1992), p. 119.
[98] Bourdieu (1986b), p. 252.
[99] Ibid, p. 243.
[100] Davis (2010), p. 206.
[101] Bourdieu (1986b), p. 248.
[102] Bourdieu (1991), p. 166.
[103] Ibid, p. 170.
[104] Chouliaraki and Fairclough (1999), p. 101.
[105] Bourdieu et al. (1994), p. 8.
[106] Bourdieu (1991), p. 170.

example, political and juridical capital are forms of cultural capital and, at the same time 'objectified and codified form of symbolic capital'.[107] By following the rules of the field, actors can enhance their capital, or they can use their power to change the rules of the field. Yet, in their actions, they are limited by the habitus.[108]

Gender relations play a role in most fields, regularly intersecting with other 'structural axes'.[109] Gender is a characteristic of identity and inscribed in power relations. It is a 'lived social relation'[110] by being embedded in the structure (i.e., in the field), internalized by individuals (i.e., in their habitus), and justified and reproduced through discourses.[111] Moreover, gender is contextual, with gender relations being 'both constituted and reinscribed in and through the discourses, practices, and policy implementation associated with specific local environments'.[112] Thus, gender relations are neither fixed nor homogenous.

While not being the only source of power, the law constitutes and legitimizes power.[113] It does so by setting and justifying the rules of the game and by differentiating between actors with access to legal expertise—juridical capital—and those without.[114] Stories of law are also stories of power, as powerful actors have easier access to different legal orders and have the capacity of forum shopping at the intersection of legalities.[115]

1.2.3 Law

The law is an important aspect of fields. The law of a field expresses and reproduces communities' underlying worldviews. It is not objective but reflects the values of the broader field. However, the law and social practices do not fully mirror each other, with the law being a 'distinctive way of imagining the real'.[116] It represents a distortion of other social practices, and 'the social practices are equally based on a distorted version of the law.[117]

[107] Bourdieu et al. (1994), p. 9; see also Bourdieu (1991), p. 192.

[108] Madsen and Dezalay (2002), pp. 192–93.

[109] Lugones (2008), p. 4.

[110] McNay (2005), p. 175.

[111] Agarwal (1995), p. 51; Reay (1995), pp. 359, 366; Chouliaraki and Fairclough (1999), p. vii; Reay (2004), p. 437.

[112] Altamirano-Jiménez and Parker (2016), p. 88.

[113] von Benda-Beckmann et al. (2009a), p. 1.

[114] See also Foucault (1971), p. 17.

[115] von Benda-Beckmann (1992), p. 314; Falk Moore (2000), p. 64; von Benda-Beckmann et al. (2009a), p. 13.

[116] Geertz (1983), p. 173; see also Falk Moore (1969), p. 283; Bourdieu (1986a), p. 814; Rosen (2006), p. 12.

[117] de Sousa Santos (1987), p. 286; see also Silbey (2005), p. 335.

In the following, the meaning of the law—based on a 'moderate social constructionist vision of the law'[118]—will be explored in more detail. Thereby, the following five assumptions play a central role: (1) The law is more than norms created by the nation-state; (2) the law constitutes the field's rules of the game; (3) the law is a powerful discourse creating, among other things, identities and normalizing power relations.; and (4) the law is pluralistic and multiscalar. As a consequence, (5) legal transplantation processes occur frequently and influence preexisting law.

1.2.3.1 The Sources of Law

The meaning of the law and its sources are highly controversial. During my research in Liberia, different actors regularly mentioned *international best practices* that influenced their understanding of FPIC. In its transplantation, FPIC was thus confronted with more legalities than just the law created by the nation-state.

Anthropology has recognized for a long time that law exists beyond the normative order of the state.[119] State law is seen as one form of law with other normative orders equally yielding power over social practices.[120] Generally speaking, the law refers to norms that restrict actors in a given space in their behavior and in their conception of what is permissible.[121] Legal systems or orders are broader and include not only norms but also organizational structures and authorities enforcing these norms.[122] They include state-based systems like courts and judges but also 'non-legal forms of ordering'.[123]

The law thus patterns behavior in specific fields.[124] It can be created by different types of actors, comes in different forms, and draws from various sources of legitimacy.[125] While state law may be potent in some fields, it can still be superseded or amended by other law-like normative orders. Such other normative orders may include, among other things, global (soft) law or project law.[126] For example, the UN Global Compact may create a strong sense of obligation on corporate actors when competitors, clients, and non-governmental organizations perceive it as the key socioenvironmental standard. A lack of commitment could then have a negative reputational effect. At the sub-state level, state law may coexist with production law (the law of the factories), domestic law (the law existing within households), and

[118] Mertz (1994a), p. 1245.

[119] Woodman (2001), p. 30; von Benda-Beckmann (2002), pp. 61–62; von Benda-Beckmann et al. (2005), p. 6.

[120] Michaels (2009), p. 19; Tobin (2014), pp. 29ff.

[121] von Benda-Beckmann (2002), p. 48.

[122] Bavinck (2005), p. 811; Bavinck and Woodman (2009), p. 206.

[123] Engle Merry (1988), p. 870.

[124] Engel (1980), p. 428; Falk Moore (2000), p. 62.

[125] von Benda-Beckmann et al. (2009c), p. 4.

[126] Ibid p. 4.

religious law.[127] Engel describes these other types of law as customary law or 'interactional law',[128] Ehrlich as living law.[129]

Hence, even though states remain powerful lawmakers, their role is contested.[130] Griffiths also emphasizes that it is often impossible to attribute a social effect to state law, as the effect could as well have been caused by the underlying political decision.[131] Law can thus come in the form of reciprocal obligations, the law created by the state, or best practices.[132] Whilst acknowledging the power of state law in many fields, the formal status of norms is of little importance as long as actors feel bound by them and non-compliance usually has negative consequences.[133]

Moreover, the law can come in several forms: it can be written like a judgment or a regulation, it can exist in the form of legal knowledge, it can be inscribed in statuses, social relationships, and institutions, and it may play a role in social processes and interactions.[134] Thereby, it does not exist independently from other social practices.

Griffiths concludes that 'the "law" which is actually effective on the "ground floor" of society is the result of enormously complex and usually in practice unpredictable patterns of competition, interaction, negotiation, isolationism, and the like.'[135] This book thus understands law as all norms, by which the actors of a field feel bound while also recognizing that state law can oftentimes draw from a specific kind of legitimacy. The use of the terminologies like *soft law* or *customary law* shall not be constructed as accepting a higher legitimacy or social power of (state) law.[136] To get a clearer understanding of the law, it is helpful to look at it in two different ways: law in the processual or functional sense and law as a construction.

---

[127] de Sousa Santos (2002b), p. 389.

[128] Engel (1980), p. 428.

[129] See Griffiths (2003), p. 22; Ehrlich (2022).

[130] de Sousa Santos (2002b), p. 94, 118; Slaughter (2002), p. 18–19.

[131] Griffiths (1979), p. 358.

[132] Falk Moore (1969), p. 257.

[133] Falk Moore (1973), p. 720; Griffiths (1986), p. 38; see also Berman (2007), p. 1178.

[134] von Benda-Beckmann (2002), pp. 66–67.

[135] Griffiths (1986), p. 39.

[136] Tobin (2014), p. 1; Giacomini (2020) Traditional Knowledge and Customary Law: Recognizing Indigenous Peoples for Environmental Conservation. https://voelkerrechtsblog.org/traditional-knowledge-and-customary-law/. Accessed 7 Aug 2023.

1.2.3.2 Law as a Process

The law is processual in the sense of field's rules of a game.[137] The actors of a field generally abide by those rules. Thereby, those rules contribute to the stability of the field and lay the foundation for its autonomy.

However, fields are also permeable and susceptible to external normative and other influences.[138] Due to this permeability and the struggles occurring in fields, the law is always contested and can change. For instance, it would be difficult to argue that tax law is not law because not everybody abides by it and the authorities struggle to prosecute tax offenders.[139] Instead, the law through 'repeated interaction'[140] is a cluster of shared behavioral expectations situated in an interplay between resistance and compliance.

The differing agendas, value systems, and discourses of different actors lay the foundation for legal and political incoherence. The law is not a clear-cut and static system, but it is comprised of 'residues of ongoing struggles'.[141] It 'contains both elements of domination and seeds of resistance'.[142] Norms' exist in the knowledge of people, in the programs and strategies and struggles of social movements and individual movements, in political philosophies of the powerful and the oppressed'.[143] Consequently, 'the law can be understood as encompassing a constant interplay, pulling apart, or mutual checking, or maybe even harmonization between multiple factors and voices.[144]

The law as a process also has a power dimension: different actors may show different degrees of creativity in playing with the law.[145] Depending on their capacities, actors may manage to resort to the legalities that best suit their interests and, thereby, shape the rules of the game.[146] Griffiths speaks of legal eclecticism when actors 'fashion [...] a patchwork composed of bits and pieces'[147] of various laws to foster their vision of society and what the law should be.[148] Bavinck describes the different legal systems applicable to one territory as a map with several transparent overlaying uses: each actor chooses the overlay which best suits their interests.[149]

---

[137] Griffiths (1986), p. 38.

[138] Falk Moore (1973), p. 720.

[139] See also Griffiths (1979), p. 352; Griffiths (2003), p. 3.

[140] Engel (1980), p. 429.

[141] Kidder (1979), p. 296.

[142] Engle Merry (1990), p. 8.

[143] von Benda-Beckmann (2009), p. 121.

[144] Lustig and Kingsbury (2006), p. 407.

[145] See also Silbey (2005), p. 340.

[146] Hendawy and Lindbekk (2022), p. 63.

[147] Griffiths (2015), pp. 758–59.

[148] See also Ewick and Silbey (2003), p. 1346; Klug (2005), p. 296.

[149] Bavinck (2005), p. 811.

Powerful actors may make use of strategies such as creative compliance or identifying and using gaps or indeterminacies in the law.[150] Other strategies include legal historicizing, i.e., the 'search for origins which justify or debunk claims',[151] or using a higher good to justify a version of the law. However, often, such strategies often operate under the cloak of neutrality and impartiality.[152] In line with that, the law may also not have the same effect on everybody. For example, wealthy people may ignore no-parking rules just because they can afford to pay the fine.

Emerging hegemonic norms are the result of power relations between the different actors involved.[153] Engle Merry describes hegemony, in the legal context, as the capacity to 'shape meanings and values by which the whole social world is organized and understood'.[154] Compliance with hegemonic norms can either be enforced through discourses constructing the existing social order as inevitable or just or by force. However, hegemonic norms are never fully stable but remain contested. While the law can thus serve as a tool of resistance for marginalized groups, it still tends to work best for white, middle-class men in many fields.[155]

1.2.3.3 Law as a Construction

Besides the rules of a game, the law is also a social construction and implicated in the construction of fields.[156] It is constituted through everyday actions, such as discourses, but also through semiotic and visual practices.[157] It is an 'imagination, representation, and description of reality'.[158]

Simultaneously, the law is a particularly 'powerful form of social expression'.[159] While this applies to all types of law, this holds particularly true for state law in many fields: it classifies only some institutions or norms as *official* or *legal* and functions in a bureaucratic way.[160] Moreover, many fields attribute a particular competence to lawyers as opposed to other people.[161] Griffiths also finds that law is *more legal*

---

150 Swainger and Backhouse (2003), pp. 2–3; Tamanaha (2008), pp. 409–10; Szablowski (2011), p. 125.

151 Holston (1991), p. 696.

152 Moreton-Robinson (2005), p. 67.

153 See also von Benda-Beckmann and von Benda-Beckmann (2007b), p. 58; Holston (1991), p. 696.

154 Engle Merry (1990), p. 7.

155 Smart (1989), p. 138; see also von Benda-Beckmann (2022), p. 24.

156 Silbey (2005), p. 332.

157 Ibid p. 337.

158 de Sousa Santos (1987), p. 281; see also Teubner (1991), pp. 1452–53; Bourdieu et al. (1994), 3; Madsen and Dezalay (2002), p. 189.

159 von Benda-Beckmann et al. (2005), p. 2.

160 Ewick and Silbey (2003), p. 1347; Silbey (2005), p. 336.

161 Griffiths (1979), p. 358.

when it is differentiated to a stronger extent from the rest of the field and delegated to special functionaries.[162] Moreover, state law derives additional legitimacy from (usually) existing in written form and being tangible—'imparting to [legal texts] a greater fixity and truth value within the epistemological sphere of the law'.[163] Additionally, it enjoys a 'near monopoly on the legitimate use of force'.[164] So not only but particularly state law is characterized by a form of legal legitimacy in many fields.

The power of law is derived from its claim to objectivity, universality, and neutrality.[165] It constructs itself as being detached from its environment.[166] For example, international law as a *global project*—even though historically created by the states that considered themselves *civilized*—benefits from a narrative of universality.[167] Thus, the law legitimizes the social field and ensures its functioning.[168] It is a source of power by constraining and enabling social practices and by creating or reinforcing social categories and mechanisms of in- and exclusion.[169] Power, in turn, needs legalities for it to transform into sovereign authority.[170]

However, the use of the terminology *legal discourse* shall not indicate that legal discourse in itself is homogenous. The discourses of social and economic law, for instance, certainly differ. This is also due to overlaps with discourses from other fields. Moreover, disagreements about legal interpretations are 'part of the dynamic of legal conversation'.[171]

Taking a step back, the question arises: what are discourses? On a very fundamental level, discourses are grounded in a social field and are the field's specialized language.[172] They are 'a particular way of talking about and understanding the world (or an aspect of the world)'.[173] They reflect identities, social relations, and systems of knowledge and meaning.[174] Engle Merry defines them as 'aspects of culture, interconnected vocabularies, and systems of meaning located in the social world'.[175] Thus, they are linked to social processes and actions, determined by

---

162 Griffiths (1986), p. 38.

163 Ewick and Silbey (2003), p. 1360.

164 Falk Moore (1973), p. 721.

165 Bourdieu (1986a), p. 819.

166 Griffiths (1979), p. 361.

167 Riles (2001), p. 280.

168 Griffiths (1986), p. 38; Holston (1991), p. 696.

169 Fairclough (1989), p. 28; von Benda-Beckmann et al. (2005), p. 2.

170 Comaroff and Comaroff (2009), p. 39.

171 Dane (1991), p. 993.

172 Foucault (1980), p. 119; Bourdieu (1986a), p. 839; Engle Merry (1990), p. 110; Jørgensen and Phillips (2002), p. 73; Madsen and Dezalay (2002), p. 189.

173 Jørgensen and Phillips (2002), p. 1.

174 Ibid, p. 67.

175 Engle Merry (1990), p. 110.

their history and context, and are subjective.[176]

Fields have an order of the discourse, which includes different discourses and discourse genres.[177] Within the order of the discourse, different discourses coexist. Through articulation, discourses can be detached from the order of the discourse and 'circulate as free-floating elements capable of being articulated together in new ways'.[178]

More precisely and drawing from Laclau and Mouffe, discourses will be understood as the partial fixation of meaning within a given domain.[179] Within discourses, signs exist. The partial fixation of meaning occurs through so-called nodal points, central signs that attribute meaning to other signs.[180] Moreover, discourse theory distinguishes between elements and moments: elements are floating signifiers with multiple potential meanings.[181] Moments, in contrast, have a fully fixed meaning. Elements can never be fully transformed into moments laying the foundation for the floating character of discourses and their social identities.[182]

Discourses determine what is thinkable and what is not. All the unthinkable possibilities are located in the field of discursivity. The field of discursivity contains all the meanings that signs may have in other discourses but which are excluded in the particular discourse to ensure the relative fixation of meaning.[183] Even though Laclau and Mouffe are not unequivocal in this respect, it will be assumed that the field of discursivity is the place where other competing discourses are located, which attribute a different meaning to signs.[184] To summarize,

> The practice of articulation, therefore, consists in the construction of nodal points, which partially fix meaning; and the partial character of this fixation proceeds from the openness of the social, a result, in its turn, of the constant overflowing of every discourse by the infinitude of the field of discursivity.[185]

The meaning of discourses for social life remains controversial. Bourdieu understands communicative exchanges, i.e., discourses, only as an expression of the structure.[186] However, the data gathered rather corresponds to Fairclough's understanding that discourse and social structures are in an internal and dialectical relationship.[187] Discourses are spaces of interaction that are, to some degree,

---

[176] Jørgensen and Phillips (2002), pp. 5–6.
[177] Chouliaraki and Fairclough (1999), p. 114.
[178] Ibid, p. 116.
[179] Laclau and Mouffe (2001), p. 105.
[180] Ibid, p. 112.
[181] Ibid, p. 113.
[182] Ibid, p. 110.
[183] Jørgensen and Phillips (2002), p. 27.
[184] Ibid, p. 27.
[185] Laclau and Mouffe (2001), p. 113.
[186] Bourdieu (1992), p. 256.
[187] Fairclough (1989), pp. 23, 38.

determined by the field and the positionality of the actors within that field. However, through 'their own generative force',[188] they may transform other discourses and the practice of the field. As discourses reproduce and legitimize power relations, they are both a stake in and sites of social struggle.[189]

Discourses do not necessarily remain within the confines of their field.[190] The phenomenon whereby different discourses meet is called interdiscursivity.[191] Through interdiscursivity, discourses may link various fields and change the order of the discourse. This 'interdependent articulation of many different social fields'[192] is another reason for the semi-autonomy of fields.

Interdiscursivity can occur by accident but also as a strategy, and it can either disrupt or stabilize the dominant order of the discourse.[193] Interdiscursivity can thus be a catalyst for social change. For example, non-legal discourses can be used to promote a certain vision of the law. Translating non-legal social discourses into legal language—and vice versa—results in discursive hybrids.[194] Bourdieu describes this phenomenon as the 'appropriation effect'.[195]

Legal discourses play a central role in the creation of social identities. Linguists and discourse analysts have explored how identities are translated into legal language and how legal identities, in turn, impact the social sphere.[196] Legal discourses not only mirror preexisting social categories and relations but also 'forge, renew, shift, and break social bonds'.[197] They have strong formative effects by granting 'actors a secure identity, a status, and above all a body of powers'.[198] This symbolic power is what Engle Merry calls the 'power of naming'.[199] For example, a US district court in Mashpee Tribe v. Town of Mashpee rejected the land claims of an Indigenous group, applying a very narrow definition of *tribe*.[200] By subsuming the Mashpee political organization under Western categories of sovereignty and property, non-Indigenous experts played a central role in rejecting the Mashpee's legal identity and legitimizing the taking of their land.[201]

---

[188] Chouliaraki and Fairclough (1999), p. 105.

[189] Fairclough (1989), p. 172; Jørgensen and Phillips (2002), p. 65.

[190] Bourdieu (1992), p. 257.

[191] Jørgensen and Phillips (2002), p. 73.

[192] Falk Moore (1973), p. 722.

[193] Jørgensen and Phillips (2002), p. 73.

[194] Mertz (1992a), p. 182.

[195] Bourdieu (1986a), p. 819.

[196] Mertz (1994b), p. 980.

[197] Mertz (1992b), p. 414; see also Delaney et al. (2001), p. xv.

[198] Bourdieu (1986a), p. 838; see also Mertz (1992b), p. 427.

[199] Engle Merry (1990), p. 130.

[200] Mashpee Tribe v Town of Mashpee (1978) United States District Court, D. Massachusetts. 447 F Supp 940 (United States District Court, D. Massachusetts), p. 950.

[201] Torres and Milun (1995), pp. 135–36.

However, the law and its identities are not absolute and stable but relational, and the 'ambiguities, inconsistencies, and contradictions provide multiple opportunities for interpretation and contest'.[202] According to Hall, identities 'are never unified and, in late modern times, increasingly fragmented and fractured; never singular but multiply constructed across different, often intersecting and antagonistic discourses, practices, and positions'.[203] A single person can thus have multiple identities.[204] Those seeking to enforce their rights can make strategic use of this multiplicity. Legal identities may be re-appropriated and imbued with new meaning, either intentionally or unintentionally.[205] Barker describes how Indigenous women aligned themselves as 'racialized Indians, as tribal, as women, as women of color, as feminists, as international and civil rights activists',[206] depending on their agenda. Actors thus have a choice of discourse and its identities.[207] While they are, to some extent, bound by the order of the discourse and their habitus, they can still be active and creative in their communicative practice.[208] The category under which groups subsume themselves impacts real life: 'the categories according to which a group envisages itself, and according to which it represents itself and its specific reality, contribute to the reality of the group'.[209] Finnemore and Sikkink call this process' strategic social construction'.[210] Grewal similarly suggests understanding the legal field as a 'creative space even within highly restrictive hegemonic discourses and structures'.[211]

Discourses are also entwined with power. Difference is both a matter of distribution and representation. In addition to gender, class, ethnicity, and other power relations are inscribed in social representations.[212] Kapur describes fields as a 'site of discursive struggle, where the role and place of the world's cultural Others who are peripheral subjects [. . .] have been and continue to be fought for'.[213]

Power translates into how well actors can navigate discourses. Communicative differences regularly exist between a field's actors. The foundation for communicative differences in the positionality within the field is the 'linguistic capital'[214] somebody holds.[215] Linguistic capital describes the social and communicative skills

---

[202] Engle Merry (1990), p. 9; see also Hall (1997), pp. 23–24; Laclau and Mouffe (2001), p. 106.
[203] Hall (1996), p. 4; see also Jørgensen and Phillips (2002), p. 17.
[204] Schilling-Vacaflor (2009), p. 73.
[205] Benhabib (2006), p. 67.
[206] Barker (2006), p. 129.
[207] Jørgensen and Phillips (2002), p. 17.
[208] Fairclough (1989), p. 28.
[209] Bourdieu (1991), p. 133.
[210] Finnemore and Sikkink (1998), p. 910; see also Sikkink (2002), p. 38.
[211] Grewal (2016), p. 41.
[212] McNay (2005), p. 183.
[213] Kapur (2005), p. 3.
[214] Chouliaraki and Fairclough (1999), p. 101.
[215] Bourdieu (1992), p. 258.

to find the right words at the right time and allows for the appropriation of discourses.[216] Drawing from different discourses, actors work towards the reconfiguration of categories, identities, or values. The following chapters will show how discourses, and particularly the creation of identities, are used by different actors in their competition for power and the meaning of the law.

1.2.3.4 The Multiscalarity and Plurality of Law

Another characteristic of the law—and a logical consequence of the plurality of legal sources—is its plurality and multiscalarity. For example, the normative orders in the different Liberian fields included norms with a global reach like human rights law, national statutory law, and local legalities. The section explores the plurality and multiscalarity of law.

Firstly, and as a consequence of the broad anthropological understanding of the law, fields are not monolegal. In virtually every social field, a web of norms, legal systems, and institutions of different characters coexist.[217] These different legalities interact in different ways. Some authors refer to the phenomenon as 'legal plurality',[218] 'legal polycentricity',[219] or 'legal pluralism'.[220] For example, even within the state administration, different government agencies can have different institutional designs and competing goals while overlapping legally and administratively.[221] Actors or authorities within a legal system play a crucial role in the fabrication and negotiation of legal pluralism by 'tying the normative body together'[222] and ensuring some degree of legal coherence. However, this coherence never fully succeeds as 'divergence is not random or haphazard but systematic'.[223]

But it is not only institutions that create law. Law can also be the result of societal or environmental change that contributes to the emergence of new norms or the amendment of existing norms.[224] Such change may subsequently be incorporated into the legal system. Moreover, a field's law changes through the interaction between the different legalities and through actors navigating legal plurality in different and creative ways.[225] Hence, this book looks at legal pluralism rather

[216] Foucault (1971), p. 19; Schilling-Vacaflor (2009), pp. 37–38.

[217] See also Engel (1980), p. 426; Griffiths (1986), p. 12; Engle Merry (1988), pp. 870, 873; Telesetsky (2017), p. 117.

[218] de Sousa Santos (2002b), p. 89.

[219] Petersen (1995), p. 171.

[220] Griffiths (1986), p. 38.

[221] de Sousa Santos (2002b), p. 95; McCarthy (2002), p. 81.

[222] Bavinck and Woodman (2009), pp. 207–208.

[223] Engel (1980), p. 427.

[224] Falk Moore (2000), p. 58.

[225] Engel (1980), p. 431.

from a social science than from a juristic perspective—based on a broad understanding of the law.[226]

Secondly, in addition to its pluralistic nature, the law is scalar and rooted in 'time-space'.[227] Santos identifies three time-spaces: local, national, and world legalities.[228] Legal frameworks of different scales may apply to the same social event. Yet, they tend to describe the object in varying detail, establish different networks of facts, and create different legal realities.

World or global law is the law that applies to a territory bigger than that of one nation-state. Its authors can be international organizations, governments, transnational corporations, or multi-stakeholder fora. Often, it is deterritorialized and claims to have cosmopolitan validity.[229] In contrast, national law refers to the law created at the state level by governments, parliaments, or specialized agencies. NGOs or citizens may also influence these law-making processes. National law does not necessarily apply to the state's whole territory, as evidenced by the state-sponsored customary law existing in many post-conflict states.

The field of community forestry, in this book, is a local time-space. While local legalities have the most limited geographical scope, their scale is the biggest, and they tend to provide the most details. However, scale is not absolute. The local time-space of community forestry is a field where the community forestry concept based on state law and international best practices meets customary governance arrangements. It concurs with Santos' argument that 'every social action is framed by three time-spaces, one of them being dominant' thereby providing the general profile of the action'.[230]

Moreover, time-spaces have a temporal dimension. Fields are rooted in time. As cultural constructions, they exist at a specific point in time, change over time, and may even disappear.

The law created in one space does not necessarily remain there, but it can move to other time-spaces. The literature on globalization sheds some light on the interrelationship between normative orders located at different scales—often suggesting that this is a new phenomenon. However, law-making beyond the state is not new.[231] Neither is the overlap of normative orders originating from different scales. Only the space-time-compression, i.e., the speed of the movement of norms, people, and

[226] Griffiths distinguishes between the juristic and social science perspective on legal pluralism. The juristic understanding focusses on legal systems, in which the 'sovereign commands [...] different bodies of law for different groups in the population' (Griffiths 1986, p. 5), while the social science perspective sees plurality as an 'empirical state of affairs in society' (ibid, p. 8).

[227] de Sousa Santos (2002b), p. 85.

[228] de Sousa Santos (1987), p. 287.

[229] von Benda-Beckmann et al. (2009b), p. 5.

[230] de Sousa Santos (2002b), p. 85.

[231] von Benda-Beckmann et al. (2009c), p. 2.

values, linked to globalization, is novel.[232] The 're-scaling dynamics'[233] of law, i.e., the increasing flow of ideas, norms, and people around the world causes more friction between normative orders at different scales.[234] For example, activists may use human rights law in local natural resource conflicts.[235] All time-spaces are thus characterized by some degree of legal multiscalarity and multiscalar networks.[236]

To conclude, legal fields can be described as 'different legal spaces operating simultaneously on different scales and from different interpretative standpoints'[237] whilst overlapping and interacting with each other. The result is a 'porous legality',[238] 'interlegality',[239] or the 'messiness of hybridity'.[240] The von Benda-Beckmanns and Griffiths summarize it as

> The legal repertoire embracing multiple legal orders is not necessarily governed by a hierarchical structure with clearly defined boundaries forming a linear progression up the chain of command from local to regional, to national, and international and global arenas. Rather a more porous form of legal pluralism from the conjunction of an interrelated range of domains and associations.[241]

Hence, the diffusion of normative orders and specific norms blurs the different scales.[242] The global partly inhabits the national and the local and vice versa.[243]

1.2.3.5 Traveling Norms

As evidenced by FPIC, norms can cross fields. These norms can be referred to as traveling or 'boundary-crossing'[244] norms or legal transplants,[245] contributing to 'norm diffusion'.[246]

The law generally does not travel in a straightforward way. The von Benda-Beckmanns describe norm flows as 'chains of interdependent social practices of

[232] von Benda-Beckmann et al. (2005), p. 1.

[233] Sassen (2007), p. 93.

[234] Berman (2007), p. 1162.

[235] See also von Benda-Beckmann (2001), p. 34; Sikkink (2002), p. 41; Slaughter (2002), pp. 18–19.

[236] Berman (2007), p. 1159.

[237] de Sousa Santos (1987), p. 288.

[238] Ibid, p. 298.

[239] von Benda-Beckmann et al. (2009a), p. 13.

[240] Berman (2007), p. 1236.

[241] von Benda-Beckmann et al. (2005), p. 21.

[242] Zumbansen (2010), p. 55.

[243] Sassen (2007), p. 76; Krisch (2008), pp. 215–16; von Benda-Beckmann and Turner (2019), p. 11.

[244] Kingsbury (2000), p. 34.

[245] Legrand (1997).

[246] Winston (2017).

actors or networks of actors, which are the channels through which laws are communicated and received transnationally'.[247] Legal transplantation usually involves 'processes of discursive translation, adjustment, negotiation'.[248] The reasons for the transplantation of norms are manifold—it may be their high legitimacy, their power, validity, or their usefulness.[249]

Traveling norms can move both horizontally and vertically. Even though norm transplantation is not a one-way road, norms certainly flow more easily in some directions than in others.[250] Access to the various socio-legal fields and mobility play a decisive role in this respect. Privileged actors can benefit from the 'time-space compression'[251] and 'transnational norm entrepreneurs'[252] can trigger transplantation processes and the enforcement of norms originating from another space'.[253] In contrast, marginalized communities tend to remain at the receiving end of legal transplantation processes.[254] Nevertheless, as evidenced by the international Indigenous movement, transnational alliances can be a way for local time-spaces to influence the global.[255]

The power of the respective actors also impacts the way legal transplants are accommodated.[256] When norms move from one socio-legal space to another, they are not only translated to render them legible but also transformed.[257] Earlier literature on legal transplants theorizes them as fixed norms, which may be internalized or contested. The diffusion of norms was then described as a norm cascade, moving towards a world culture and spiral models of norm change.[258] This book, however, takes a different angle.

It is assumed that both the space of origin and the receiving space are not homogenous but characterized by legal plurality. When a human rights norm moves, it is not *the human right* moving but rather one version of a norm existing in the pluralistic field of transnational law. Krook and True take a similar stance, assuming that 'the norms that spread across the international system tend to be vague, enabling their content to be filled in many ways and thereby to be appropriated for a variety of different purposes'.[259] Or, in Sandholtz's words: norms 'never stand still'.[260] Legal plurality may open 'spaces for contestation, creative adaptation,

---

[247] von Benda-Beckmann and von Benda-Beckmann (2007b), p. 61.

[248] von Benda-Beckmann (2022), p. 13.

[249] Miller (2003), p. 869.

[250] de Sousa Santos (2002a), p. 41.

[251] Ibid, p. 42.

[252] Sarfaty (2005), p. 1810.

[253] Szablowski (2011), pp. 120–21.

[254] de Sousa Santos (2002a), 43.

[255] Brysk (2000), p. 19.

[256] Miller (2003), pp. 873ff.

[257] Zerner (2003), p. 3.

[258] True (2019), p. 137.

[259] Krook and True (2010), p. 104.

[260] Sandholtz (2008), p. 101.

and innovation'.[261] Thus, legal transplantation can be described as a process or 're/enactment of the normative structure of "meaning in use"'.[262]

When norms are restated in a different field, new hybrid norms may emerge.[263] According to Koh, interaction occurs between the originating and the receiving field; prevailing norms and values tend to structure how norms are accommodated and translated into practice.[264] This process has been described as negotiation, interaction, interpretation, or mutual constitution.[265]

Engle Merry argues that norm transplantation involves appropriation and translation.[266] Appropriation is the process whereby a norm developed in one field is transplanted into another field.[267] Translation is (ideally) the second step of the transplantation and describes the 'process of adjusting the rhetoric and structure'[268] of the norm to adapt it to the local circumstances. Thereby, 'the global limits and constrains the local, but the local appropriates and transforms the global for its own needs'.[269]

Whether and how a transplanted norm is appropriated again depends on the actors involved in the process. The power of the actor in question has an influence on the appropriation.[270] Often in transplantation processes, national or local actors fight for a vision of the norm aligned with their values and interests. Their power determines how well they can navigate the multiscalarity and plurality of normative orders.[271] Moreover, alliances between different actors from different spaces may impact how a legal transplant is negotiated. For example, funders, allies, and clients influence how local feminist NGOs use human rights language.[272] Thus, different actors attempt to manipulate, appropriate, or subvert the transplanted norm.[273] This struggle can be described as norm negotiation.

Additionally, the accommodation of the norm depends on the receiving field, its legal system, its values, and its discourses.[274] Silbey emphasizes the 'contests of signification with diverse and competing discourses that take place in most aspects of ordinary life'.[275] It will be shown in the following chapters that, for example,

[261] Berman (2007), p. 1237.
[262] Wiener (2009), p. 176.
[263] von Benda-Beckmann (2002), p. 70.
[264] Szablowski (2011), p. 122.
[265] Teubner (1991), p. 1456.
[266] Engle Merry (1997), p. 30.
[267] Engle Merry (2006), p. 135.
[268] Ibid, p. 135.
[269] Engle Merry (2000), p. 129.
[270] Miller (2003), pp. 873ff.
[271] See also Falk Moore (2000), p. 64; von Benda-Beckmann et al. (2005), p. 11.
[272] See also Engle Merry and Levitt (2017), p. 215.
[273] von Benda-Beckmann et al. (2005), p. 20.
[274] Ibid, p. 8.
[275] Silbey (2005), p. 338.

conservation discourse and its vision of forestry strongly influenced the negotiation of FPIC. Thus, discourses can legitimize a particular vision of the law or the incorporation of legal transplants.

In cases where internal norms collide with the new norm, the reinterpretation can be particularly radical ('discourse-content-decoupling'[276]). Discourse-content decoupling describes situations in which the official discourse does not correspond to the original content and may result in a so-called 'resonance dilemma'.[277] Alternatively, the norm is endorsed but not applied.[278]

When a norm is appropriated, the transplantation process essentially results in the emergence of a new norm and legal practice, which, to varying degrees, overlaps with the norms circulating in the socio-legal field of origin. These emerging norms are sometimes characterized as 'hybrid',[279] 'vernacularised',[280] 'creolized',[281] or 'legal symbiosis'.[282] The hybrid norm is then internalized.[283] Internalization or institutionalization is the process by which norms' come to take on a rulelike status in social thought and action'.[284]

1.3 Structure of the Book

The book traces the journey of FPIC from a claim of the Indigenous movement to various global time-spaces (transnational human rights, development, and environmental law), national time-spaces (the Liberian post-conflict forest and land sector reform), and local time-spaces (Liberian community forests).[285]

The second chapter focuses on FPIC in global time-spaces. The fact that the book goes from the global to the national and local shall not indicate the superiority of transnational law.[286] Instead, it is attributable to FPIC being a well-recognized concept on the transnational plane, while transplantations to the national and local level are a more recent phenomenon and remain the exception rather than the rule. National and local actors also regularly referred to the *international* character of FPIC.

---

[276] Cabrera Ormaza and Ebert (2019), p. 487.

[277] Resonance dilemma refers to the observation that the more a human rights norm gets adapted, the less it can be used for challenging the status quo (Engle Merry and Levitt 2017, p. 216).

[278] Cabrera Ormaza and Ebert (2019), p. 487.

[279] Klug (2005), p. 296; Berman (2007), p. 1162.

[280] Engle Merry and Levitt (2017), p. 213.

[281] Hannerz (1987).

[282] von Benda-Beckmann (1992), p. 313; see also von Benda-Beckmann et al. (2005), p. 10.

[283] Koh (1998), p. 626; Klug (2005), pp. 277–78.

[284] Meyer and Rowan (1977), p. 341.

[285] See also de Sousa Santos (2002b), p. 85.

[286] Cf Griffiths (1986), p. 3; Anders (2009).

The first part of the second chapter will outline the contours of the fields of transnational law. After briefly exploring the origin of FPIC, its meaning will be examined. This includes the exploration of its potential theoretical underpinnings (dependent on the legal identity to which it is attached), the situations in which it applies, and the question of FPIC's internal dimension: who exactly may consent on behalf of a group? This touches upon the institutional autonomy of communities and women's right to FPIC.

Transnational human rights law first transformed FPIC from a claim of the Indigenous movement into a human right. However, within human rights law, different legal identities with different rights vis à vis the state coexist. Those legal identities include minorities, Indigenous peoples, and, more recently, peasants. I will examine how these legal identities impact the meaning of FPIC.

Subsequently, FPIC has been vernacularized on the transnational plane and incorporated into other transnational legal fields. Those include development law and environmental law. The logic of development law greatly differs from that of human rights law and it recognizes other group identities. Human rights legalities thus intersect with economic legalities and discourses, contributing to the adaptation of FPIC. Similarly, transnational environmental law is based on different premises than human rights law, impacting the accommodation of FPIC. It will be explored how FPIC was adapted to the logic of these fields.

In the third chapter, the evolving understanding of FPIC in two Liberian fields of post-conflict law-making—that are predominantly national time-spaces—will be explored. After the Liberian civil war, a coalition of national and international NGOs, donor project representatives, and government officials started reforming the Liberian forest and land legislation from scratch. The two fields are located at the intersection of law and politics and are characterized by a unique, evolving practice of law-making. They are legally pluralistic fields in the sense that national law already existed. Moreover, various external actors, such as NGOs and donors, imported their normative orders, such as project law or human rights law, and national actors amended them to fit their agenda. Their visions of FPIC strongly differed, as well as their perspective on the right-holders of FPIC and their vision of the state. It will be shown how evolving alliances and power relations changed the practice and laid the foundation for an emerging hegemonic understanding of FPIC corresponding to the fields' logic.

The fourth chapter focuses on the so-called implementation of FPIC—or rather its 'social working'[287]—in two local time-spaces: the Beyan Poye and the Sehzueplay community forest. The vision of FPIC embedded in the national legislation is attached to a certain vision of community, the role of the state, forests, and forest management. It was subsequently transplanted into the legally pluralistic local time-spaces, in which (neo)customary modes of forest governance already existed. The fields were also strongly influenced by their history of governmental land alienation and characterized by a multiplicity of meanings of the forest: during the war, the

---

[287] Griffiths (2003), p. 19.

forest served as a hiding place, now it is a home, a place of work, a pharmacy, and a supermarket for many community members. In other places, it is no more than a buffer zone delineating the farmland of different communities. At the same time, logging companies and donors, with their understanding of forestry, were involved in the norm negotiation. Through the construction of the forest as an environmental and economic resource, the meaning of FPIC changed again. FPIC thus crossed several multiscalar and legally pluralistic fields, causing the emergence of new legal hybrids.

References

Agarwal B (1995) A field of one's own: gender and land rights in South Asia. Cambridge University Press, Cambridge

Agyeman VK et al (2022) Sustainable forest management (SFM) in Liberia - the 4Cs approach. United Nations

Aikins JK (2016) Indigenising democracy? Renegotiating the role of Indigenous political authorities in Ghana's constitution review. In: Dhawan N et al (eds) Negotiating normativity: postcolonial appropriations, contestations, and transformations. Springer, Cham, pp 61–78

Altamirano-Jiménez I, Parker L (2016) Mapping, knowledge, and gender in the Atlantic coast of Nicaragua. In: Kermoal N, Altamirano-Jiménez I (eds) Living on the land: indigenous women's understandings of place. AU Press, Edmonton, pp 85–106

Anders G (2009) The new global legal order as local phenomenon: the special court for Sierra Leone. In: von Benda-Beckmann F et al (eds) Spatializing law: an anthropological geography of law in society. Ashgate, Farnham, Burlington, pp 137–156

Barelli M (2016) Seeking justice in international law: the significance and implications of the UN Declaration on the Rights of Indigenous Peoples. Routledge, London, New York

Barker J (2006) Gender, sovereignty, and the discourse of rights in native women's activism. Meridians 7:127–161

Bavinck M (2005) Understanding fisheries conflicts in the South: a legal pluralist perspective. Soc Nat Resour 18:805–820

Bavinck M, Woodman GR (2009) Can there be maps of law? In: von Benda-Beckmann F et al (eds) Spatializing law: an anthropological geography of law in society. Ashgate Publishing, Farnham, pp 195–218

Benhabib S (2006) Democratic iteration: the local, the national, and the global. In: Benhabib S (ed) Another cosmopolitanism. Oxford University Press, Oxford, pp 45–82

Berman PS (2007) Global legal pluralism. South Calif Law Rev 80:1155–1238

Bourdieu P (1977) Outline of a theory of practice. Cambridge University Press, Cambridge

Bourdieu P (1986a) The force of law: toward a sociology of the juridical field essay. Hastings Law J 38:805–813

Bourdieu P (1986b) The forms of capital. In: Richardson JG (ed) Handbook of theory and research for the sociology of education. Greenwood Press, New York, pp 241–258

Bourdieu P (1991) Language and symbolic power. Polity Press, Cambridge

Bourdieu P (1992) The practice of reflexive sociology (the Paris workshop). In: Bourdieu P, Wacquant LJD (eds) An invitation to reflexive sociology. Chicago University Press, Chicago, pp 217–260

Bourdieu P, Wacquant LJD (1992) The purpose of reflexive sociology (the Chicago workshop). In: Bourdieu P, Wacquant LJD (eds) An invitation to reflexive sociology. Chicago University Press, Chicago, pp 61–216

Bourdieu P et al (1994) Rethinking the state: genesis and structure of the bureaucratic field. Sociol Theory 12:1–18
Breuer F (2010) Reflexive grounded theory: Eine einführung für die forschungspraxis. VS Verlag for Sozialwissenschaften, Wiesbaden
Brown D (1982) On the category "civilized" in Liberia and elsewhere. J Mod Afr Stud 20:287–303
Brysk A (2000) From tribal village to global village: Indian rights and international relations in Latin America. Stanford University Press, Stanford
Cabrera Ormaza MV, Ebert FC (2019) The World Bank, human rights, and organizational legitimacy strategies: the case of the 2016 Environmental and Social Framework. Leiden J Int Law 32:483–500
Carodenuto S, Fobissie K (2015) Operationalizing free, prior and informed consent (FPIC) for REDD+: insights from the national FPIC guidelines of Cameroon. Carbon Clim Law Rev 9: 156–167
Charmaz K (2014) Constructing grounded theory. Sage Publications Ltd., London
Chouliaraki L, Fairclough N (1999) Discourse in late modernity: rethinking critical discourse analysis. Edinburgh University Press, Edinburgh
Comaroff JL, Comaroff J (2009) Reflection on the anthropology of law, governance and sovereignty. In: von Benda-Beckmann F et al (eds) Rules of law and laws of ruling: on the governance of law. Ashgate, Farnham, pp 31–60
Corntassel J (2008) Toward sustainable self-determination: rethinking the contemporary Indigenous-rights discourse. Alternatives 33:105–132
Creswell JW, Creswell JD (2018) Research design: Qualitative, quantitative, and mixed methods approaches. London, Sage
Dane P (1991) The maps of sovereignty: a mediation. Cardozo Law Rev 12:959–1006
Davis A (2010) Forms of capital and mobility in the political field: Applying Bourdieu's conceptual framework to UK party politics. Br Polit 5:202–223
de Casas CI (2019) The corporate duty to respect consultation rights in the Americas: how the inter-American system can better promote free, prior, and informed consent. In: Feichtner I et al (eds) Human rights in the extractive industries: transparency, participation, resistance. Springer, Cham, pp 247–279
de Sousa Santos B (1987) Law: a map of misreading. Toward a postmodern conception of law. J Law Soc 14:279–302
de Sousa Santos B (2002a) Toward a multicultural conception of human rights. In: Hernández-Truyol BE (ed) Moral imperialism: a critical anthology. New York University Press, New York, pp 39–60
de Sousa Santos B (2002b) Toward a new legal common sense. Butterworths, LexisNexis, London
Delaney D et al (2001) Preface: where is law? In: Blomley N et al (eds) The legal geographies reader. Blackwell Publishers, Oxford, pp xiii–xxii
Doyle CM (2015) Indigenous peoples, title to territory, rights and resources: the transformative role of free, prior and informed consent. Routledge, Abingdon
Doyle CM (2019) The evolving duty to consult and obtain free, prior and informed consent of Indigenous peoples for extractive projects in the United States and Canada. In: Feichtner I et al (eds) Human rights in the extractive industries: transparency, participation, resistance. Springer, Cham, pp 169–218
Ehrlich E (2022) Grundlegung der Soziologie des Rechts. Duncker & Humblot, Berlin
Engel DM (1980) Legal pluralism in an American community: perspectives on a civil trial court. Am Bar Found Res J 5:425–454
Engle Merry S (1988) Legal pluralism. Law Soc Rev 22:869–896
Engle Merry S (1990) Getting justice and getting even: legal consciousness among working-class Americans. The University of Chicago Press, Chicago
Engle Merry S (1997) Legal pluralism and transnational culture: the ka ho'okolokolonui kanaka maoli tribunal, Hawai'i, 1993. In: Wilson RA (ed) Human rights, culture & context. Pluto Press, London, pp 28–48

Engle Merry S (2000) Crossing boundaries: ethnography in the twenty-first century. Polit Leg Anthropol Rev 23:127–133
Engle Merry S (2006) Human rights & gender violence: translating international law into local justice. The University of Chicago Press, Chicago
Engle Merry S, Levitt P (2017) The vernacularization of women's human rights. In: Snyder J et al (eds) Human rights futures. Cambridge University Press, Cambridge, pp 213–236
Ewick P, Silbey S (2003) Narrating social structure: stories of resistance to legal authority. Am J Sociol 108:1328–1372
Fairclough N (1989) Language and power. Longman Group UK Limited, New York
Falk Moore S (1969) Law and anthropology. Bienn Rev Anthropol 6:252–300
Falk Moore S (1973) Law and social change: the semi-autonomous social field as an appropriate subject of study. Law Soc Rev 7:719–746
Falk Moore S (2000) Law as process: an anthropological approach. LIT, Hamburg
Faria C, Mollett S (2016) Critical feminist reflexivity and the politics of whiteness in the field. Gend Place Cult 23:79–93
Finnemore M, Sikkink K (1998) International norm dynamics and political change. Int Organ 52: 887–917
Fischer H (2008) Dokumentation. In: Beer B (ed) Methoden ethnologischer Forschung. Dietrich Reimer Verlag, pp 293–322
Flemmer R, Schilling-Vacaflor A (2016) Unfulfilled promises of the consultation approach: The limits to effective indigenous participation in Bolivia's and Peru's extractive industries. Third World Q 37:172–188
Foucault M (1971) Orders of discourse. Soc Sci Inf 10:7–30
Foucault M (1980) Power knowledge: selected interviews and other writings 1972–1977. Pantheon Books, New York
Geertz C (1983) Local knowledge: further essays in interpretative anthropology. BasicBooks, New York
George AL, Bennett A (2005) Case studies and theorie development in the social sciences. MIT Press, Cambridge
Global Witness (2018) Power to the people? How companies are exploiting community forestry in Liberia. Global Witness
Greenspan E (2014) Free, prior and informed consent in Africa: an emerging standard for extractive industry projects. CEPIL and Oxfam America
Grewal K (2016) Can the subaltern speak within international law? Women's rights activism, international legal institutions and the power of "strategic misunderstanding". In: Dhawan N et al (eds) Negotiating normativity: postcolonial appropriations, contestations, and transformations. Springer, Cham, pp 27–44
Griffiths J (1979) Is law important? N Y Univ Law Rev 54:339–374
Griffiths J (1986) What is legal pluralism? J Leg Plural Unoff Law 18:1–55
Griffiths J (2003) The social working of legal rules. J Leg Plural 2003:1–48
Griffiths J (2015) 'Legal pluralism'. International Encyclopedia of the social & behavioral sciences, vol 13, 2nd edn, pp 757–761
Hall S (1996) Introduction: who needs identity? In: Hall S, du Gay P (eds) Questions of cultural identity. Sage, Los Angeles, pp 1–17
Hall S (1997) Representation: cultural representations and signifying practices. Sage, Thousand Oaks
Hannerz U (1987) The world in creolisation. Afr J Int Afr Inst 57:546–559
Haraway D (1988) Situated knowledges: the science question in feminism and the privilege of partial perspective. Fem Stud 14:575–599
Hellum A (1995) Actor perspectives on gender and legal pluralism. In: Petersen H, Zahle H (eds) Legal polycentricity: consequences of pluralism in law. Dartmouth Publishing Company Aldershot, Brookfield, pp 13–30

Hendawy M, Lindbekk M (2022) With the best of intentions: divorced custodian mothers negotiating access to housing in Egypt. J Leg Anthropol 6:49–72
Hirschl R (2005) The question of case selection in comparative constitutional law. Am J Comp Law 53:125–155
Holston J (1991) The misrule of law: Land and usurpation in Brazil. Comp Stud Soc Hist 33:695–725
Jørgensen MW, Phillips L (2002) Discourse analysis as theory and method. SAGE Publications, London
Kapur R (2005) Erotic justice: law and the politics of postcolonialism. Glasshouse Press, London
Kidder RL (1979) Toward an integrated theory of imposed law. In: Burman SB, Harell-Bond BE (eds) The imposition of law. Academic Press, New York, pp 289–306
Kingsbury B (2000) Reconstructing self-determination: a relational approach. In: Aikio P, Scheinin M (eds) Operationalizing the right of indigenous self-determination. Institute for Human Rights, Åbo Akademi University, pp 19–37
Klug H (2005) Hybrid(ity) rules: creating local law in a globalized world. In: Dezalay Y, Garth BG (eds) Global prescriptions: the production, exportation, and importation of a new legal orthodoxy. The University of Michigan Press, Ann Arbor, pp 276–305
Koh HH (1998) The 1998 Frankel lecture: bringing international law home. Houst Law Rev 35: 623–681
Krisch N (2008) The open architecture of European human rights law. Mod Law Rev 71:183–216
Krook ML, True J (2010) Rethinking the life cycles of international norms: the United Nations and the global promotion of gender equality. Eur J Int Rel 18:103–127
Kuokkanen R (2016) Indigenous women's rights and international law: challenges of the UN Declaration on the Rights of Indigenous Peoples. In: Lennox C, Short D (eds) Routledge handbook of Indigenous peoples' rights. Routledge, pp 129–145
Laclau E, Mouffe C (2001) Hegemony and socialist strategy: towards a radical democratic politics. Verso, London
Lahire B (2015) The limits of the field: elements for a theory of the social differentiation of activities. In: Hilgers M, Mangez E (eds) Bourdieu's theory of social fields: concepts and applications. Routledge, London, pp 62–101
Legal Resources Centre, Oxfam (2018) Free, prior and informed consent in the extractive industries in Southern Africa: an analysis of legislation and their implementation in Malawi, Mozambique, South Africa, Zimbabwe, and Zambia. Oxfam America
Legrand P (1997) The impossibility of 'legal transplants'. Maastricht J Eur Comp Law 4:111–124
Liberia Strategic Analysis (2018) Forest incomes for environmental sustainability midterm performance evaluation. USAID
Linos K (2015) How to select and develop international law case studies: lessons from comparative law and comparative politics. Am J Int Law 109:475–485
Lowenhaupt Tsing A (1993) In the realm of the diamond queen: Marginality in an out-of-the-way place. Princeton University Press, Princeton
Lugones M (2008) The coloniality of gender. Worlds & Knowledges Otherwise, pp 1–17
Lustig D, Kingsbury B (2006) Displacement and relocation from protected areas: International law perspectives on rights, risks and resistance. Conserv Soc 4:404–418
MacInnes A et al (2017) Free, prior and informed consent: How to rectify the devastating consequences of harmful mining for Indigenous peoples. Perspect Ecol Conserv 15:152–160
Madsen MR, Dezalay Y (2002) The power of the legal field: Pierre Bourdieu and the law. In: Banakar R, Travers M (eds) An introduction to law and social theory. Hart Publishing, Oxford, pp 189–207
Manirakiza P (2019) Asserting the principle of free, prior and informed consent (FPIC) in sub-saharan africa in the extractive industry sector. In: Feichtner I et al (eds) Human rights in the extractive industries: transparency, participation, resistance. Springer, Cham, pp 219–246
McCarthy JF (2002) Power and interest on Sumatra's rainforest frontier: clientelist coalitions, illegal logging and conservation in the Alas valley. J Southeast Asian Stud 33:77–106

McNay L (2005) Agency and experience: gender as a lived relation. In: Adkins L, Skeggs B (eds) Feminism after Bourdieu. Blackwell Publishing, Boston, pp 175–190
Mertz E (1992a) Creative acts of translation: James Boyd White's intellectual integration. Yale J Law Hum 4:165–185
Mertz E (1992b) Language, law, and social meanings: linguistic/anthropological contributions to the study of law. Law Soc Rev 26:413–445
Mertz E (1994a) Conclusion: a new social constructionism for sociolegal studies. Law Soc Rev 28: 1243–1265
Mertz E (1994b) Introduction: legal loci and places in the heart: community and identity in sociolegal studies. Law Soc Rev 28:971–992
Meyer JW, Rowan B (1977) Institutionalized organizations: formal structure as myth and ceremony. Am J Sociol 83:340–363
Michaels R (2009) Global legal pluralism. Annu Rev Law Soc Sci 5:1–35
Mihesuah DA (2003) Indigenous American women: decolonization, empowerment, activism. University of Nebraska Press, Lincoln
Miller JM (2003) A typology of legal transplants: using sociology, legal history and argentine examples to explain the transplant process. Am J Comp Law 51:839–885
Mitchell MI, Yuzdepski D (2019) Indigenous peoples, UNDRIP and land conflict: an African perspective. Int J Hum Rights 23:1356–1377
Mohanty CT (2003) "Under Western eyes" revisited: feminist solidarity through anticapitalist struggles. In: McCann CR, Kim S-k (eds) Feminist theory reader: local and global perspectives. Routledge University Press, New York, pp 446–462
Moore DS (2005) Suffering for territory: race, place, and power in Zimbabwe. Duke University Press, Durham
Moreton-Robinson A (2005) Patriarchal whiteness, self-determination and Indigenous women: the invisibility of structural privilege and the visibility of oppression. In: Hocking BA (ed) Unfinished constitutional business?: rethinking Indigenous self-determination. Aboriginal Studies Press, Canberra, pp 61–73
Napoleon V (2009) Aboriginal discourse: gender, identity, and community. In: Richardson BJ et al (eds) Indigenous peoples and the law: comparative and critical perspectives. Osgoode Readers, Oxford, pp 233–256
Owen JR, Kemp D (2014) 'Free prior and informed consent', social complexity and the mining industry: establishing a knowledge base. Resources Policy 41:91–100
Papillon M, Rodon T (2020) The transformative potential of indigenous-driven approaches to implementing free, prior and informed consent: Lessons from two Canadian cases. Int J Minor Group Rights 27:314–335
Petersen H (1995) Reclaiming 'juridicial tact'? Observations and reflections on customs and informal law as (pluralist) sources of polycentric law. In: Petersen H, Zahle H (eds) Legal polycentricity: consequences of pluralism in law. Dartmouth University Press, Aldershot, pp 185–200
Reay D (1995) 'They employ cleaners to do that': habitus in the primary classroom. Br J Sociol Educ 16:353–371
Reay D (2004) 'It's all becoming a habitus': beyond the habitual use of habitus in educational research. Br J Sociol Educ 25:431–444
Riles A (2001) The view from the international plane: perspective and scale in the architecture of colonial international law. In: Blomley N et al (eds) The legal geographies reader. Blackwell Publishers, Oxford, pp 276–284
Rodríguez-Garavito C (2010) Ethnicity.Gov: global governance, Indigenous peoples, and the right to prior consultation in social minefields. Indiana J Glob Leg Stud 18:1–44
Roesch R (2016) The story of a legal transplant: The right to free, prior and informed consent in sub-Saharan Africa. Afr Hum Rights Law J 16:505–531

Roesch R (2021) Under the disguise of participation: community forestry as a new form of land rush in Liberia. In: Cochrane L, Andrews N (eds) The transnational land rush in Africa: a decade after the spike. Springer International Publishing, Cham, pp 139–172
Rosen L (2006) Law as culture: an invitation. Princeton University Press, Princeton
Sandholtz W (2008) Dynamics of international norm change. Eur J Int Rel 14:101–131
Sarfaty GA (2005) The World Bank and the internalization of Indigenous rights norms. Yale Law J 114:1791–1818
Sassen S (2007) The places and spaces of the global: an expanded analytical terrain. In: Held D, McGrew A (eds) Globalization theory: approaches and controversies. Polity, Cambridge, pp 79–105
Schilling-Vacaflor A (2009) Recht als umkämpftes Terrain. Die neue Verfassung und Indigene Völker in Bolivien. PhD thesis, Universität Wien, p 73
Schilling-Vacaflor A, Flemmer R (2020) Mobilising free, prior and informed consent (FPIC) from below: a typology of Indigenous peoples' agency. Int J Minor Group Rights 27:291–313
Sikkink K (2002) Transnational advocacy networks and the social construction of legal rules. In: Dezalay Y, Garth BG (eds) Global prescriptions: the production, exportation, and importation of a new legal orthodoxy. The University of Michigan Press, Ann Arbor, pp 37–64
Silbey SS (1997) "Let them eat cake": globalization, postmodern colonialism, and the possibilities of justice. Law Soc Rev 31:207–235
Silbey SS (2005) Everyday life and the constitution of legality. In: Jacobs MD, Hanrahan N (eds) The Blackwell companion to the sociology of culture. Blackwell Publishing, Malden, pp 332–345
Slaughter A-M (2002) Breaking out: the proliferation of actors in the international system. In: Dezalay Y, Garth BG (eds) Global prescriptions: the production, exportation, and importation of a new legal orthodoxy. The University of Michigan Press, Ann Arbor, pp 12–36
Smart C (1989) Feminism and the power of law. Routledge, London
Starblanket G (2018) Complex accountabilities: deconstructing "the community" and engaging feminist research methods. Am Indian Cult Res J 42:1–20
Stewart DW et al (2007) Focus groups: theory and practice. Thousand Oaks, Sage Publications
Swainger J, Backhouse C (2003) Introduction. In: Swainger J, Backhouse C (eds) People and place: historical influences on legal culture. UBC Press, Vancouver, pp 1–10
Szablowski D (2011) Operationalizing free, prior, and informed consent in the extractive industry sector? Examining the challenges of a negotiated model of justice. Can J Dev Stud 30:111–130
Tamanaha BZ (2008) Understanding legal pluralism: past to present, local to global. Sidney Law Rev 30:375–411
Telesetsky A (2017) Legal pluralism - linking law and culture in natural resource co-management and environmental compliance. In: Nafziger JAR (ed) Comparative law and anthropology. Edward Elgar Publishing, Cheltenham, pp 116–132
Teubner G (1991) The two faces of Janus: rethinking legal pluralism. Cardozo Law Rev 13:1443–1462
Teubner G (1997) Global Bukowina: legal pluralism in the world society. In: Teubner G (ed) Global law without a state. Aldershot, Dartmouth, pp 3–28
Tobin B (2014) Indigenous peoples, customary law and human rights: why living law matters. Routledge, Milton Park
Torres G, Milun K (1995) Stories and standing: the legal meaning of identity. In: Danielsen D, Engle K (eds) After identity: a reader in law and culture. Routledge, New York, pp 129–142
True J (2019) Gender research and the study of institutional transfer and norm transmission. In: Sawer M, Baker K (eds) Gender innovation in political science: new norms, new knowledge. Palgrave Macmillan, London, pp 135–152
Utas M (2003) Sweet battlefields: youth and the liberian civil war. PhD thesis, Uppsala University, p 54
Verbeek CY (2012) Free, prior, informed consent: the key to self-determination: an analysis of "the Kichwa people of Sarayaku v. Ecuador". Am Indian Law Rev 37:263–282

von Benda-Beckmann F (1992) Symbiosis of Indigenous and Western law in Africa and Asia: an essay in legal pluralism. In: Mommsen WJ, de Moor JA (eds) European expansion and law: the encounter of European and Indigenous law in 19th and 20th century Africa and Asia. Berg, Oxford, pp 307–326

von Benda-Beckmann K (2001) Transnational dimensions of legal pluralism. In: Fikentscher W (ed) Begegnung und Konflikt - eine kulturanthropologische Bestandsaufnahme. Verlag der Bayerischen Akademie der Wissenschaften, München, pp 33–48

von Benda-Beckmann F (2002) Who is afraid of legal pluralism. J Leg Plural Unoff Law 34:37–82

von Benda-Beckmann F (2009) Human rights, cultural relativism and legal pluralism. In: von Benda-Beckmann F et al (eds) The power of law in a transnational world: anthropological enquiries. Berghahn Books, New York, pp 115–136

von Benda-Beckmann K (2022) Trajectories of legal entanglement examples from Indonesia, Nepal, and Thailand. Leg Plural Crit Soc Anal 54:13–30

von Benda-Beckmann K, Turner B (2019) Legal pluralism, social theory, and the state. J Leg Plural Unoff Law 50:1–20

von Benda-Beckmann F, von Benda-Beckmann K (2007a) Gesellschaftliche Wirkung von Recht: Rechtsethnologische Perspektiven. Reimer Verlag, Berlin

von Benda-Beckmann F, von Benda-Beckmann K (2007b) Transnationalisation of law, globalisation and legal pluralism: a legal anthropological perspective. In: Antons C, Gessner V (eds) Globalisation and resistance: law reform in Asia since the crisis. Hart Publishing, Oxford, pp 53–80

von Benda-Beckmann F et al (2005) Mobile people, mobile law: an introduction. In: von Benda-Beckmann F et al (eds) Mobile people, mobile law: expanding legal relations in a contracting world. Ashgate, Aldershot, pp 1–26

von Benda-Beckmann F et al (2009a) Introduction: the power of law. In: von Benda-Beckmann F et al (eds) The power of law in a transnational world: anthropological enquiries. Berghahn Books, New York, pp 1–32

von Benda-Beckmann F et al (2009b) Space and legal pluralism: an introduction. In: von Benda-Beckmann F et al (eds) Spatializing law: an anthropological geography of law in society. Ashgate, Farnham, pp 1–30

von Benda-Beckmann F et al (2009c) Rules of law and laws of ruling: law and governance between past and future. In: von Benda-Beckmann F et al (eds) Rules of law and laws of ruling. Ashgate, Farnham, pp 1–30

Wacquant LJD (1992) Toward a social praxeology: the structure and logic of Bourdieu's sociology. In: Bourdieu P, Wacquant LJD (eds) An invitation to reflexive sociology. The University of Chicago Press, Chicago, pp 1–47

Wiener A (2009) Enacting meaning-in-use: qualitative research on norms and international relations. Rev Int Stud 35:175–193

Wilkinson S (1999) Focus groups: a feminist method. Psychol Women Q 23:221–244

Winston C (2017) Norm structure, diffusion, and evolution: a conceptual approach. Eur J Int Rel 24: 638–661

Woodman GR (2001) Customary law in common law systems. IDS Bull 32:28–34

Yin RK (2018) Case study research and applications: design and methods. Sage Publications, Thousand Oaks

Zerner C (2003) Introduction. Moving translations: poetics, performance, and property in Indonesia and Malaysia. In: Zerner C (ed) Culture and the question of rights: forests, coasts, and seas in Southeast Asia. Duke University Press, Durham, pp 1–23

Zumbansen P (2010) Transnational legal pluralism. Comp Res Law Polit Econ 6:3–57

Chapter 2
The Global Time-Space: FPIC in the Fields of Transnational Law

This chapter explores the right to free, prior and informed consent (FPIC) in the *global time-space of transnational law* and its sub-fields.[1] The sub-fields of the global time-space are (legal) fields of imagination sharing values or interests.[2] FPIC and consultation rights have been discussed in the sub-fields of transnational law for several decades now. However, it will be shown that FPIC does not originate there and its meaning remains highly contested. While activists and Indigenous peoples see it as a tool for challenging power relations and curbing state sovereignty, it is a thorn in the flesh of those who do not want the international order to change. According to Szablowski, it 'represents an attempt to reform governance on a global scale'.[3] It touches upon no less than the '(re)negotiation of the relationships between the states and the Indigenous peoples, including [. . .] questions of resource sovereignty and the control of territories and resources'.[4]

Given FPIC's potential power and the multiplicity of actors and interests involved in the various sub-fields constituting the global arena, there does not exist one FPIC.[5] Instead, different versions of FPIC have emerged. FPIC was first endorsed by the field of human rights law. It subsequently spilled over to other fields of transnational law—including environmental law and development law. Rodríguez-Garavito observes 'a true explosion of hard and soft law norms at both the international and national levels, which incorporate different versions of Indigenous peoples' right to FPIC'.[6] Following FPIC's transplantation, actors within those fields embedded FPIC in the logic and legality of their field, imbuing it with new meaning. The result of this

[1]de Sousa Santos (2002), p. 85.

[2]Bourdieu and Wacquant (1992), p. 117.

[3]Szablowski (2011), p. 112; see also Kingsbury (2000), p. 28.

[4]Schilling-Vacaflor and Flemmer (2020), p. 293.

[5]See also Szablowski (2011), p. 113.

[6]Rodríguez-Garavito (2010), p. 6.

R. Rösch, *Negotiating Norms*, Interdisciplinary Studies in Human Rights 9,
https://doi.org/10.1007/978-3-031-45910-8_2

negotiation and reframing are hybrid norms.[7] It will be shown that the legal identity to which FPIC is attached is strategically used for altering its meaning. FPIC is thereby neither 'self-interpreting nor self-implementing'.[8] Thus, currently, different understandings of FPIC coexist within the global time-space. The coexistence of these different FPIC norms in a given space is a corollary of legal plurality and can be described as legal fragmentation.[9]

Firstly, the meaning and scope of the *time-spaces of transnational law* as research units will be explored. Following a brief description of FPIC's origin and its conceptualization, the emerging understandings of FPIC in the fields of human rights law, development law, and environmental law will be examined. Within each field, I will identify the legal identity on which FPIC is contingent and its theoretical underpinning, the meaning of consent, including the situations in which it is required, and FPIC's internal dimension, notably the protection afforded to customary forms of decision-making (institutional autonomy) and the accommodation of a women's right to FPIC.

As other authors have already explored the alliances of actors and institutions at the global scale, this chapter will refrain from mapping the power relations, actors, and institutions of each field in detail.[10] Instead, the focus will be on the preliminary result of these struggles: the emerging hybrid norms.

2.1 Mapping the Fields

First of all, what is the global time-space examined in this chapter? The global 'time-space'[11] comprises several fields with a specific logic. The fields have in common that they are predominantly global, transnational and pluralistic, and legal.

Regarding the first component, the legal fields produce norms circulating at the scale above the state and include norms with a global and regional reach. Even though it is a predominantly global time-space, it is also characterized by some degree of multiscalarity.[12] Community-based organizations increasingly participate in the drafting of international legal documents but also corporate actors yield influence over legislative processes.[13] A recent example is the transnational peasant

[7] Berman (2007), p. 1159; Rodríguez-Garavito (2010), p. 8; Rombouts (2014), p. 408.

[8] Franco (2014) p. 5.

[9] Kingsbury (1999), p. 342; de Moerloose (2020), p. 243.

[10] Bourdieu and Wacquant (1992), pp. 104–105; on Indigenous advocacy, see also Engle (2010), pp. 102ff; on human rights networks, see also Keck and Sikkink (1998) and Goodale (2009), pp. 96ff; on transnational law-making, see also Riles (2001), pp. 145ff and Engle Merry (2006), pp. 36ff.

[11] de Sousa Santos (2002), p. 85.

[12] See also Ashby Wilson (2007), p. 345.

[13] See also von Benda-Beckmann (2001), p. 34; Sikkink (2002), p. 41; Slaughter (2002) pp. 18–19.

movements that pushed states towards recognizing peasants' rights.[14] Therefore, Engle Merry describes the global as an 'amalgam of multiple national and local legalities'.[15]

With respect to the second component, legal plurality and transnationalism, the time-space's global location does not mean that it comprises a single legal order produced by states. Its norms include not only law in the strict sense created by states but also non-binding frameworks created by state and non-state actors that may influence behavior in different ways.[16] One example of such a framework is the World Bank safeguards, which are non-binding and apply only to specific projects. Still, they are part of an 'international normative process' and influence the behavior of corporations or donors.[17] Similarly, soft law like the United Nations Declaration on the Rights of Indigenous Peoples (UNDRIP) has considerable 'governing weight',[18] particularly when it intersects with binding international law. The influence of such non-binding norms is emblematic of the increasingly pluralized legal authority in the fields of transnational law.[19]

Moreover, it is a time-space characterized by the coexistence of 'a variety of institutions, norms, and dispute resolution processes located, and produced at different structured sites around the world'.[20] The global time-space is thus transnational and not merely international. The actors involved in transnational law-making processes include courts, parliaments, and governments entering into international treaties but also international institutions, activists, and business enterprises.[21] It is 'non-territorially confined, functionally differentiated and constituted by the co-evolution of conflicting societal rationalities'.[22] Still, it should be noted that—despite this multiplicity—the history of the global has for a long time been characterized by the 'deliberate exclusion [of Indigenous peoples] and correlating silences in international law'.[23]

Hence, the global time-space is inherently pluralistic—not only in terms of actors but also in terms of normative orders.[24] With respect to the third component, the time-space of transnational law is a legal field. However, it will be shown that it also intersects with other non-legal fields and their discourses and logic. Those other fields, such as economics or environmental protection, co-determine the sub-fields' logic and, thereby, influence the emerging FPIC norms.

---

[14] Heri (2021), p. 285.

[15] Engle Merry (2005), p. 216.

[16] See also Trubek and Trubek (2007).

[17] Kingsbury (1999), p. 342.

[18] Fredericks (2017), p. 436.

[19] See also Lobel (2004), p. 343.

[20] Snyder (1999), p. 15.

[21] Slaughter (2002), p. 13; Cotterrell (2008), pp. 5–6.

[22] Zumbansen (2010), p. 8.

[23] Stimac (2022), p. 249.

[24] von Benda-Beckmann (2001), p. 35; Michaels (2009), p. 4.

2.2 Tracing FPIC's Origin

Having explored the spatial context, in which FPIC is embedded at the global scale, FPIC's origin will be explored. FPIC is often mentioned in conjunction with the notion of Indigenous sovereignty or the right to self-determination. Hence, this section first examines the concepts of sovereignty and self-determination in international law. Secondly, Indigenous peoples' right to self-determination will be illuminated, and thirdly, consent as a central principle of international law and its appropriation by the Indigenous movement. It will be shown that the Indigenous movement has used elements of positivist international law, including consent as an expression of sovereignty, to challenge the extinction of their nationhood.

2.2.1 *Sovereignty and Self-Determination*

Sovereignty underpins both the national and the international legal system: the sovereign holds 'supremacy in the collective interest'[25] and has the power to create rules and enforce them.[26] Internationally, the sovereign has power beyond its territory by creating agreements or establishing practices with other sovereigns. In this respect, the so-called chunk theory of sovereignty prevailed until quite recently: 'sovereignty may only be possessed "in full or not at all", being represented as a monolithic chunk of identical stones, any one of which is possessed by a sovereign entity'.[27] Statehood is usually understood to be a precondition for sovereignty. This leaves little space for recognizing the sovereignty of Indigenous peoples and other minorities.

However, preceding the emergence of the *terra nullius* doctrine in the mid-nineteenth century, the sovereignty of Indigenous peoples was recognized by the colonizing powers to some extent. Naturalists like di Vitoria argued that the colonizers could only establish sovereignty over foreign territories by concluding (international) treaties with the Indigenous population.[28] However, Indigenous sovereignty was not seen as absolute, and its extinction was justified by the supposed moral superiority of the Christian civilizers.[29] Cultural difference served as a legitimization for differing qualities of sovereignty.[30] For example, in the United States, Indigenous nations were transformed into domestic dependent nations.[31] However, with the emergence of legal positivism and the doctrine of *terra nullius*,

[25] Lenzerini (2006), p. 157.

[26] Wiessner (2008), p. 1146.

[27] Lenzerini (2006), p. 158; see also Shrinkhal (2021), p. 72.

[28] Anghie (1999), p. 24.

[29] Doyle (2015), pp. 20–21.

[30] Anghie (2006), p. 742.

[31] Porter (2002), p. 81; Wiessner (2008), p. 1168.

colonial powers increasingly took the position that Indigenous peoples lacked sovereignty and that colonial sovereignty over their territories could be imposed without their consent.[32]

In the past decades, the emergence of a growing corpus of international norms, including the right to self-determination, has limited the states' sovereignty.[33] The right to self-determination is one of the United Nations' founding principles and traditionally refers to the right of the people of a territorially defined unit to determine its political future.[34] Initially, and as evidenced by the *travaux préparatoires* of the UN Charter, self-determination was seen as dormant within sovereignty and vesting only in states.[35]

However, in the second half of the twentieth century, self-determination increasingly became a way of challenging state sovereignty. It was incorporated into human rights law, played a crucial role during decolonization, and minorities and Indigenous peoples began claiming it. The right to self-determination can be found, amongst others, in art 1 of the International Covenant on Economic, Social, and Cultural Rights (ICESCR) and the International Covenant on Civil and Political Rights (ICCPR).[36] It has also become a norm of customary international law and, arguably, even *ius cogens*.[37] Today, many authors understand it as 'a practical enunciation of a right that ostensibly underpins all other rights',[38] 'the river in which all other rights swim',[39] and 'a standard of governmental legitimacy within the modern human rights frame'.[40]

Despite this, the meaning of self-determination remains controversial. In comparison to other *ius cogens* norms, Niezen describes it as a 'recent inductee with no Hollywood credentials, a kind of highly attractive and mysterious dark stranger, commanding respect through charisma and promise'.[41] In discussions about the meaning of self-determination, a distinction is often made between internal and external self-determination.[42] Internal self-determination, on the one hand, describes self-determination within the state's constitutional framework and is a continuous

[32] Lenzerini (2006), p. 164; Tahvanainen (2005), p. 400.

[33] Anaya (2000), p. 76.

[34] Charter of the United Nations (entered into force 26 Jun 1945) 1 UNTS XVI, art 1(2); Kingsbury (2000), p. 20.

[35] Koskenniemi (1994), pp. 246ff; Anaya (2000), pp. 77–8; Xanthaki (2005), p. 16.

[36] International Covenant on Civil and Political Rights (adopted 16 Dec 1966, entered into force 23 Mar 1976) 999 UNTS 171, art 1; International Covenant on Economic, Social and Cultural rights (adopted 16 Dec 1966, entered into force 3 Jan 1976) 999 UNTS 171, art 1.

[37] McCorquodale (1994), p. 858.

[38] Castellino and Gilbert (2003), p. 161.

[39] Dodson, as cited in: de Costa (2006), p. 137.

[40] Anaya (2000), p. 81.

[41] Niezen (2010), p. 109.

[42] McCorquodale (1994), p. 864; Anaya argues that secession is just one potential remedy and not an element of substantive self-determination (Anaya 2000, pp. 84–85).

process that should ideally encompass the 'right to democratic governance'.[43] External self-determination, on the other hand, comprises the right to freedom from alien rule. Some scholars reject the distinction and understand secession only as a potential remedy for the worst kinds of human rights violations, while autonomy is the more appropriate response in most cases.[44]

The right to external self-determination, i.e., secession, became particularly relevant during the decolonization period.[45] Even though Indigenous peoples have equally experienced colonialism, subjugation, and other severe human rights abuses, many states—not only those in the Global North with an Indigenous population but also many African states—were and are eager to preserve the integrity of the nation-state and the principle of *uti possidetis iuris*.[46] The reason behind this is that the founding myth of most settler and formerly colonized states is based on their attainment of independent statehood.[47] Therefore, to prevent secessions, colonialism was defined in a very narrow way, requiring sea-based conquest.[48] This so-called blue water or saltwater thesis prevented the applicability of the external right to self-determination to Indigenous peoples living within a nation-state. It found its way in the 1960 Declaration on the Granting of Independence to Colonial States and Peoples, according to which 'any attempt aimed at the partial or total disruption of the national unity and the territorial integrity of a country is incompatible with the purposes and principles of the Charter of the United Nations'.[49]

Hence, until recently, self-determination was seen as a privilege of states and colonized peoples. Neither the 1989 ILO Convention 169 on Indigenous and Tribal Peoples (C 169) nor the United Nations Declaration on the Rights of Persons Belonging to National or Ethnic, Religious and Linguistic Minorities (United Nations Declaration on Minorities) recognize the right to self-determination of minorities and Indigenous peoples.[50]

---

[43] Thürer and Burri (2008), para 33; see also McCorquodale (1994), p. 865.

[44] Kingsbury (2000), p. 23; Tomaselli (2015), p. 508.

[45] HRC (1984), CCPR general comment No 12: Article 1 (the right to self-determination of peoples), UN Doc HRI/GEN/1/Rev.9 (Vol. I), para 6; McCorquodale (1994), pp. 850–60; Wiessner (2008), p. 1149.

[46] See also Organisation of African Unity (1964) Border disputes among african states, AHG/Res.16 (1), para 2; Case concerning the frontier dispute (Burkina Faso v Republic of Mali) (1986) International Court of Justice. ICJ Rep 554, para 26; Anaya (2000), p. 83; Corntassel (2008), pp. 111–12; Robbins (2015), p. 56; Barelli (2016), p. 22.

[47] de Sousa Santos (2002), p. 247.

[48] UNGA (1960) Principles which should guide members in determining whether or not an obligation exists to transmit the information called for under article 73e of the Charter, UN Doc A/RES/1541, principle v; Robbins (2015), p. 48.

[49] Declaration on the granting of independence to colonial countries and peoples (1960) UNGA Res 1514(XV), para 6.

[50] Convention (No 169) concerning Indigenous and Tribal Peoples in Independent Countries (adopted 27 Jun 1989, entered into force 5 Sep 1991) 1650 UNTS, art 1(3); United Nations Declaration on the Rights of Persons belonging to National or Ethnic, Religious and Linguistic Minorities (1993) UNGA Res 47/135, art 8(4); see also Lenzerini (2006), p. 179.

2.2.2 *Indigenous Perspectives on Self-Determination*

The section above indicates that sovereignty and self-determination are historically and spatially contingent. Besides the evolving understandings in international law—i.e., of states—different Indigenous peoples, minorities, or local communities may have strongly differing perspectives on sovereignty and self-determination, and those understandings have also changed over time.[51] Despite states' 'territorial approach to self-determination',[52] self-determination has arguably become the *leitmotiv* of the global Indigenous movement.[53]

However, Indigenous claims to sovereignty and self-determination are no recent phenomenon.[54] Indigenous peoples governed their territories according to their own laws in pre-colonial times. Already in the early twentieth century, some of them tried to gain access to international fora. In the 1920s and 1940s, the Six Nations Confederacy appealed to first the League of Nations and later the United Nations to assert their sovereignty and to claim correction of injustices 'as a nation'.[55] They felt that sovereignty was more than a theoretical concept but an 'articulate and forceful international right'.[56] In the 1970s, when the transnational Indigenous movement began to grow, Indigenous groups started advocating for their sovereignty and self-determination on a greater scale.[57] They pressured states through the building of transnational alliances, and collective rights, step by step, became a 'part and parcel of critical legal plurality'.[58] Many Indigenous groups—particularly those from countries of the Global North—envisioned self-determination as including their right to form an independent state and viewed the draft UN Declaration on the Rights of Indigenous Peoples as a way of continuing the process of decolonization.[59] The slogan 'if you act like you're a sovereign, eventually you will be treated as one'[60] reflects this thinking. However, some Indigenous peoples reject the concept of sovereignty as such as it would amount to an inadequate generalization of histories, governance and epistemologies.[61] Others stress that sovereignty is not absolute and needs to be balanced with Indigenous sovereignty;[62]

In response to Indigenous transnational activism, states had to make some concessions, and the applicability of self-determination to groups within the state,

[51] Barker (2005), p. 1; Eichler (2019), p. 153.

[52] Barten (2015), pp. 3–4.

[53] Brysk (2000), p. 191; Rodríguez-Garavito (2010), p. 18.

[54] Barker (2005), p. 18.

[55] Six Nations Confederacy, as cited in: Johnston (1986), p. 23.

[56] Ibid p. 23.

[57] Wiessner (2008), p. 1153.

[58] de Sousa Santos (2002), p. 244.

[59] Engle (2010), pp. 68–69; Engle (2011), pp. 151–52.

[60] Deloria Jr (1998), pp. 26–27.

[61] Shrinkhal (2021), p. 73.

[62] Inuit Circumpolar Council (2009) Circumpolar Inuit declaration on arctic sovereignty.

including Indigenous peoples, was affirmed.[63] The international turning point, in this respect, was the adoption of the United Nations Declaration on the Rights of Indigenous Peoples (UNDRIP) in 2007. 143 states, at the time, acknowledged that the right to self-determination was not confined to states and colonized peoples.[64] Moreover, treaty bodies, like the UN Committee on Economic, Social, and Cultural Rights, affirmed Indigenous peoples as holders of the right to self-determination.[65] Additionally, a growing number of states, including Canada, New Zealand, the United States, Norway, and South Africa, recognize Indigenous self-determination, though its scope varies.[66]

In light of these developments, Wiessner and other authors conclude that the Indigenous rights to self-determination have become a principle of customary international law.[67]

However, in the practice of states and international organizations, Indigenous self-determination only includes the right's internal dimension and has been described as 'cultural accommodation'.[68] States and international institutions found a reduced right to self-determination coated in human rights law to be an acceptable compromise.[69] It runs parallel to the sovereignty of the nation-state.[70] Some prerogatives of sovereignty have been transferred from the state to Indigenous peoples even though the supreme sovereignty and its prerogatives continue to vest in the state. To put it in Alfredsson's words, 'minority and Indigenous and tribal rights are about keeping groups happy within the state'.[71]

While some see this as an essential development for Indigenous peoples, others argue

> that the rights-based discourse has resulted in the compartmentalization of Indigenous powers of self-determination by separating questions of homelands and natural resources

[63] The hesitance of governments to recognize Indigenous peoples as rights-holders is reflected in the discussion about whether to call them Indigenous peoples (with a right to self-determination) or Indigenous people or populations (no right to self-determination) (Thornberry 2002, pp. 40–41); See also Koskenniemi (1994), pp. 241; Motoc and Tebtebba Foundation (2005) Legal commentary on the concept of free, prior and informed consent, UN Doc E/CN.4/Sub.2/AC.4/2005/WP.1, paras 34ff; Wiessner (2008), p. 1151.

[64] Quane (2011), pp. 259–60.

[65] ECOSOC (2003) Considerations of reports submitted by state parties under articles 16 and 17 of the covenant: Concluding observations of the Committee on Economic, Social and Cultural rights, UN Doc E/C.12/1/Add.94, para 11.

[66] Lenzerini (2006), pp. 167ff; Corntassel (2008), pp. 106–107.

[67] Wiessner (2008), pp. 1157ff; International Law Association (2012) Resolution No. 5/2012: Rights of Indigenous peoples, para 4.

[68] Lixinski (2019); see also UN Committee on the Elimination of Racial Discrimination (1996) General recommendation XXI on the right to self-determination, UN Doc A/51/18, para 6; Xanthaki (2005), pp. 17–18.

[69] Engle (2011), p. 161.

[70] Lenzerini (2006), p. 189.

[71] Alfredsson (2005), p. 164.

from those of political/ legal recognition of a limited Indigenous autonomy within the existing framework of the host state(s).[72]

So even though equality is a 'central precept of self-determination',[73] the quality of the states' and the Indigenous right to self-determination and sovereignty strongly differs in practice. Other authors, like Gilbert, still assert an Indigenous 'appropriation of self-determination [that] bring together notions of ethnicity and territoriality'[74] and could provide a space for negotiation between Indigenous peoples and states. Parts of the Indigenous rights movement accepted the more limited understanding of self-determination as a compromise; others still understand self-determination as a synonym for their full sovereignty.[75]

2.2.3 *Consent in International Law*

The right to free, prior and informed consent (FPIC) is intrinsically linked to the question of self-determination and sovereignty. Often it is portrayed as a new right.[76] Yet, consent has always played and continues to play a central role in international relations and international law.[77] Moreover, consent is also a key concept in other legal fields, such as contract law and medical law.[78]

With the emergence of legal positivism in the late nineteenth century, state consent became a cornerstone of the law of nations.[79] It became the basis for creating international legal obligations and submitting to the jurisdiction of international courts.[80] In the early colonization period, when the colonizing powers still recognized Indigenous sovereignty, it was common to obtain the consent of Indigenous peoples before taking their land and extinguishing their sovereignty.[81] Later, occurring hand in hand with the extinction of their sovereignty, Indigenous peoples were not seen as capable of rational decision-making, and their consent to the imposition

---

[72] Corntassel (2008), p. 107.

[73] Anaya (2000), p. 76.

[74] Gilbert (2006), p. 248.

[75] Moreton-Robinson (2005), p. 65.

[76] For example, it has only recently been endorsed by the World Bank (World Bank 2017). The world bank environmental and social framework; see also Doyle (2015), p. 5.

[77] Doyle (2015), pp. 13ff.

[78] Shrinkhal (2014), p. 57.

[79] Anghie (1999), p. 2; Brunnée (2022), s A.1; Doyle (2015), p. 46.

[80] E.g. Status of the Eastern Carelia (1923) Permanent Court of International Justice. PCIJ Rep Series B No 5, para 27; S.S. Lotus (France v Turkey) (1927) Permanent Court of International Justice. PCIJ Rep Series A No 10, para 44; Western Sahara (1975) International Court of Justice. ICJ Rep 12, para 32.

[81] Cheyns and Thévenot (2019), para 6.

of European sovereignty became obsolete.[82] The 1885 General Act of the Berlin Conference, where Africa was divided between the European powers, was the culmination of that trend.[83]

Consent, until the 1960s, remained a privilege of states.[84] This is also reflected in the Vienna Convention on the Law of Treaties. According to its preamble, the 'principles of free consent and of good faith [...] are universally recognized'.[85] The consent of states to international treaties is thus a central principle of international law.[86] However, the understanding of consent as an exclusive privilege of states began to crumble in the second half of the twentieth century. In its Western Sahara Advisory Opinion, the International Court of Justice (ICJ) found that the principle of self-determination applied to the Indigenous Peoples of Western Sahara 'through the free and genuine expression or the will of the peoples of the Territory'.[87] The Western Sahara decision laid the foundation for the re-recognition of consent rights of groups within the state.

Indigenous groups strongly advocated for the recognition of their right to FPIC.[88] For many Indigenous peoples, consent and FPIC 'form part of an attempt to redefine notions of national sovereignty, citizenship, and the nation-state'.[89] States, in turn, were and continue to be reluctant to recognize FPIC. They object to broad collective rights as 'obstructing the exercise of sovereign prerogatives and, ultimately, as undermining the survival of the nation-state itself'.[90] Yet, they are increasingly under pressure to recognize collective rights and a 'territorially-based plurality of legal orders'.[91] However, if they do, they tend to have a different and more limited understanding of FPIC.

Today, FPIC is a vital component of transnational human rights law, and it also increasingly penetrates other legal fields, such as environmental law and development law. The following section will explore how FPIC can be conceptualized to make it a more tangible right.

---

[82] Doyle (2015), pp. 24, 29.

[83] General Act of the Berlin Conference on West Africa (1885).

[84] Wilson (1918).

[85] Vienna Convention on the Law of Treaties (adopted 23 May 1969, entered into force 27 Jan 1980) 1155 UNTS 331, preamble.

[86] Ibid arts 11–18.

[87] Western Sahara (1975) International Court of Justice. ICJ Rep 12, para 162.

[88] Sanders (1989), p. 432.

[89] Szablowski (2011), p. 114.

[90] de Sousa Santos (2002), p. 244.

[91] Ibid p. 247.

2.3 Conceptualizing FPIC

When conceptualizing FPIC, different questions arise. First of all, who are the (rights)holders of FPIC? Laclau's and Mouffe's concept of articulation is useful for understanding how the meaning of FPIC differs in different fields. Articulation describes 'any practice establishing a relation between elements such that their identity is modified as a result of the articulary practice'.[92] The legal identity to which FPIC is attached determines FPIC's meaning. The legal identities, which tend to be relatively fixed in a given field, thus serve as nodal points.[93] In contrast, FPIC is an element—a floating signifier without fixed meaning—that has different meanings in different legal fields.[94]

Based on the legal identity, FPIC is filled with meaning: firstly, is the question of FPIC's legal foundation, rationale, and legal status. Secondly, the implications on the meaning of FPIC will be very briefly touched on. And, thirdly, how are customary forms of decision-making and the participation of women accommodated? These questions should be examined together, as they are relational and contingent upon the legal identity.[95]

2.3.1 A Matter of Naming

Discourses create worlds. Among other ways, they do so by constructing identities. According to Bourdieu, the law is 'the quintessential form of the symbolic power of naming that creates the things named and creates social groups in particular'.[96] Identities may be fragmented across different fields and their discourses.[97]

FPIC is a collective right, i.e., a right of groups. In the fields of transnational law, various group concepts coexist with differing legal frameworks attached to them. Those groups include Indigenous peoples, tribal peoples, minorities, local communities, peasants, and peoples.[98] They are 'transnational abstract categories of

---

[92] Laclau and Mouffe (2001), p. 105.

[93] Ibid p. 110.

[94] Ibid p. 113.

[95] Jørgensen and Phillips (2002), p. 28.

[96] Bourdieu (1986), p. 838.

[97] Hall (1996), p. 4.

[98] E.g. African Charter on Human and Peoples' rights (adopted 27 Jun 1982, entered into force 21 Oct 1986) 21 ILM 58; Organization of African Unity (2000) African model legislation for the protection of the rights of local communities, farmers and breeders, and for the regulation of access to biological resources; Convention (No 169) concerning Indigenous and Tribal Peoples in Independent Countries (adopted 27 Jun 1989, entered into force 5 Sep 1991); United Nations Declaration on the Rights of Indigenous Peoples (2007) UNGA Res 61/295; United Nations Declaration on the Rights of Peasants and other People Working in Rural Areas (2018) UNGA Res 73/165.

belonging'[99] that have been or are still in the process of being given meaning. While some tendencies can be identified, no clear-cut definitions of these groups exist.

The underlying idea of specific rights for specific groups is that of a 'differentialist egalitarianism'[100]: special protection needs to be afforded to (particularly vulnerable) groups. The foundation for becoming a rights-holding group is the recognition of the group's difference, the naming of their difference, and the attribution of normative significance to their difference.[101] The law thus creates identities.

FPIC is strongly tied to Indigeneity. As a claim of the Indigenous rights movement, it has become a central element of the Indigenous rights catalog.[102] However, preceding the recognition of Indigenous rights, the minority rights regime already knew some consultation rights. Moreover, with the emergence and growing recognition of more groups in the fields of transnational law and non-Indigenous groups seeing the benefits of FPIC, the scope of the rights to consultation and consent is again under negotiation.[103] It will be shown that the naming of a group is crucial for determining their rights, including FPIC, and for giving FPIC meaning.

2.3.2 *Theoretical Underpinnings*

It has been demonstrated that consent has historically been tied to sovereignty and self-determination. However, at the global scale, FPIC derives its status from different rights or concepts, depending on the group's identity.[104] Those rights include (1) Indigenous self-determination, (2) internal or 'territorial self-determination',[105] and (3) the right to culture or the collective right to property as usually afforded to minorities.[106] Moreover, (4) consultation rights can also be grounded in concepts like stakeholder participation or 'participatory development'.[107]

The first option is a broad self-determination-based approach, which recognizes the sovereignty of Indigenous peoples. It would clearly include the right to veto projects or other activities affecting communities' land or resources.[108] Moreover, aspects of sovereignty such as eminent domain and the sovereignty over natural

[99] Niezen (2010), p. 115.

[100] Jovanovic (2015), p. 7.

[101] Heinze (1999), p. 34.

[102] As evidenced by the UNDRIP.

[103] Goodland (2004), p. 69.

[104] Petkar (2017) Conceptualizing free, prior and informed consent: Interpreting interpretations of FPIC. MA thesis, Columbia University, p. 16.

[105] As opposed to national self-determination (Hannum 2011, p. 454).

[106] Wiessner (1999), p. 116; Suksi (2008), p. 158.

[107] Tomlinson (2019), p. 890.

[108] Jacobsen (2016), p. 282.

resources would be transferred to the Indigenous community.[109] Such a broad understanding of Indigenous self-determination prevails among some Indigenous peoples and is rooted in their historical struggles for decolonization.[110]

The second option is the internal right to self-determination ('less than sovereign-self-determination'[111]), which includes the transfer of more limited powers to groups within the state.[112] Some authors see it as coinciding with the right to autonomy and the right to participation.[113] It does not necessarily imply autonomy, but it can be realized through autonomy arrangements. In practice, it often entails the recognition of Indigenous peoples' or minorities' legislative power within their territory.[114] In this case, FPIC is more limited and may only include a veto right under exceptional circumstances.

A third option derives FPIC from the right to culture or the right to property. Under the right to culture, the group's rights are usually more limited and tend to be realized within self-administration or self-management arrangements based on the central government's legislation and policies.[115] Self-administration is generally considered to be more limited than self-government.[116] Very similar to that is the approach whereby FPIC is derived from the collective right to property.[117] Land-owners do not have jurisdiction over their property, and sovereignty remains an exclusive privilege of the state.[118] Such an approach has been applied to both Indigenous peoples and minorities. FPIC then tends to get reduced to negotiations or appropriate engagement.[119]

As a fourth option, FPIC can also be derived from (stakeholder) participation. In this capacity, FPIC is usually framed as a principle and not a right.[120] Moreover, participation is often not tied to a specific identity but requires the involvement of different stakeholders. In that sense, participation often is closer to information than to negotiation.

Even though the line between the four approaches is blurred, they indicate that the collective identity, to which a specific legal and theoretical framework is attached, functions as a nodal point and determines FPIC's meaning.

---

[109] See also Doyle (2015), pp. 182, 185.

[110] Merino (2018), p. 131.

[111] Hannum (2011), p. 469.

[112] Suksi (2013), para 23.

[113] Hannum (2011), pp. 473–74.

[114] Imai (2009), p. 293.

[115] Ibid p. 297.

[116] See also Cornell (2006), p. 10.

[117] Errico (2006), p. 381; Haugen (2016), pp. 255–56.

[118] Gilbert (2006), p. 115.

[119] Hales et al. (2012), p. 14.

[120] E.g. Green Climate Fund (2018) Indigenous peoples policy, s III(11)(j).

2.3.3 *FPIC's Internal Dimension: Institutional Autonomy and Gender*

Having explored FPIC's relevant group identities and theoretical underpinnings, this section focuses on the question of who may grant consent or be consulted within groups. Often, this internal dimension of collective rights is neglected.[121] It touches upon the so-called 'own institutions' aspect'[122]: Do consultation and consent procedures need to respect community institutions and decision-making processes?[123]

Oftentimes, consultation or consent processes are state-controlled that are shaped by a state's (or sometimes a company's) vision of what legitimate decision-making means.[124] As a result, there is a high risk that these processes are internally exclusive and "skew Indigenous representations or fail to make sense of them".[125] Already in 1985, the Working Group on Indigenous Populations stressed that 'all Indigenous peoples have the right to determine the form, structure and authority of its institutions'.[126] Yaffe, therefore, describes institutional autonomy as the 'sine qua non of a self-determination-respecting process'.[127]

And how about the right of women to consent? According to the Working Group on Indigenous Populations, Indigenous institutions and their decisions 'must be in conformity with internally human rights both collective and individual'.[128] Yet, gender hierarchies persist in most, if not all, fields. Bourdieu describes gender domination as a 'paradigmatic form of symbolic violence'.[129] Gender is normalized to an extent within social structures and habiti, and through discourses that it needs no justification. If one transfers the gender question into the participation debate, the question arises of how women from Indigenous and other communities can participate in consent and consultation processes. As Tsosie puts it: 'what if [Indigenous] customs and traditions are not gender-neutral? What if they are perceived as discriminatory toward Native women?'[130] It is often argued that the community, as the

[121] With a few exceptions: e.g. Napoleon (2009); Kuokkanen (2016).

[122] Thornberry (1998), p. 118.

[123] See also Errico (2009), p. 67.

[124] Eisenberg (2020), p. 278.

[125] Ibid p. 280.

[126] ECOSOC (27 Aug 1985), Study of the problem of discrimination against Indigenous populations. Report of the working group on Indigenous populations on its fourth session, UN Doc E/CN.4/Sub.2/1985/22, annex III principle 6.

[127] Yaffe (2018), p. 6; see also HRC (10 Aug 2018), Free, prior and informed consent: A human rights-based approach. Study of the Expert Mechanism on the Rights of Indigenous Peoples, UN Doc A/HRC/39/62, para 17.

[128] ECOSOC (27 Aug 1985), Study of the problem of discrimination against Indigenous populations. Report of the Working Group on Indigenous Populations on its fourth session, UN Doc E/CN.4/Sub.2/1985/22, annex III principle 7.

[129] Bourdieu and Wacquant (1992), p. 170.

[130] Tsosie (2010), p. 217.

holder of the right to self-determination, can be both a source of and a threat to individual autonomy.[131] However, this is not to say that Indigenous institutions and ways of decision-making necessarily discriminate against women—quite the contrary is the case. Moreover, it will be shown that in government- or company-facilitated consultation and consent processes, the facilitators' understanding of what constitutes legitimate decision-making often causes the emergence of new forms of decision-making that may negatively interfere with women's right to FPIC.

The first three approaches explored above—sovereignty, internal self-determination, and the rights to culture and collective property—have a cultural or institutional dimension. From an Indigenous sovereignty perspective, one could argue that nobody should be allowed to interfere with customary ways of decision-making, just like nobody can prevent the winning political party in a sovereign state from designating only male ministers. Moreover, respecting the Indigenous institutional autonomy would be a way of avoiding the further colonization of their culture and the fragmentation of autonomies.[132] Under the right to culture or collective property framework, however, one might come to a different conclusion. Moreover, it will be examined whether and how the internal dimension of consent and consultation processes is negotiated in the stakeholder participation framework.

FPIC's internal dimension is also tied to the question of what kind of institutions are protected in the fields of transnational law. While gender relations in pre-colonial societies are highly controversial, there is a growing consensus that *traditional* customary institutions no longer exist in most places.[133] Today's institutions are a 'hybrid of experiences of mythologies that are the result of displacement, dysfunction, and dispossession, as well as "tradition"'.[134] Contemporary patriarchal forms of decision-making are, in many cases, a legacy of colonialism and an expression of 'colonial heteropatriarchy'.[135] Oyěwùmí, for example, explains how colonialism contributed to the emergence of four hierarchical groups: 'men (European), women (European), native (African men), and Other (African women)'.[136] Nigerian women were 'dominated, exploited, and interiorized as Africans together with African men and then separately inferiorized and marginalized as African women'.[137] This translated, for example, into the exclusion of women from the chieftaincy system, which was introduced by the colonizing powers in many parts of Africa. It interfered

---

[131] Starblanket (2018), p. 12.

[132] Friedmann (2003), p. 179; Barker (2006), p. 144; Ladner (2009), p. 68; UNGA (2019) Rights of Indigenous peoples, Note by the Secretary-General, UN Doc A/74/149, para 20.

[133] Napoleon (2002), p. 161; Snyder (2014), p. 378.

[134] Davis (2008), p. 145.

[135] Starblanket (2018), p. 1; see also Mikaere (1999), p. 20; Ladner (2000), pp. 45, 49; Jaimes Guerrero (2003), pp. 65–66; Banda and Chinkin (2004) pp. 20, 25–26; Denetdale (2006), p. 13; Tsosie (2010), p. 201; Sunseri (2011), p. 151; Kuokkanen (2016), p. 134.

[136] Oyěwùmí (1997), p. 122.

[137] Ibid p. 122.

with customary ways of decision-making and contributed to the decline of female leadership among the Yorùbá.[138] Aikins makes similar observations on the interactions between Indigenous and Western-style institutions in Ghana, characterized by 'a continued coloniality of gender and of power'.[139] While the causes for the exclusion of Indigenous women from decision-making structures and political processes are complex and closely entwined with the colonial and post-colonial history of Indigenous communities, the question of how to deal with potential clashes between gender equality and the right to self-determination or culture remains.

The gender-sovereignty-nexus also remains a contentious issue in many Indigenous communities and among scholars. Given the oppression that many Indigenous peoples continue to face, some Indigenous women prioritize the fight against racial discrimination over the gender question.[140] Some of them fear 'that any critique can be used to diminish hard-won advances in the area'.[141] Trask describes her own experience as 'given our national context, feminism appeared as just another haole [white] intrusion into a besieged Hawaiian world. An exclusive focus on women neglected the historical oppression of all Hawaiians and the large force field of imperialism'.[142]

Others challenge the prioritization of Indigenous claims over Indigenous women's interests.[143] To address the 'disconnect between gender and Indigenous sovereignty',[144] Napoleon calls for a gender analysis to be 'applied to the larger political projects of self-determination and self-government'.[145] The individual and the collective should no longer be dichotomized.[146] Instead, the individual component of self-determination—i.e., categories of identity intersecting with Indigeneity—should be taken into consideration as well.[147]

In the Zapatista Women's Revolutionary Law movement in Mexico, Indigenous women have not been reluctant to claim political participation and leadership.[148] They have criticized the labeling of feminism as *white:* 'that presumes that Native women weren't active in shaping our identity before white women came along. And that abusive male behavior is somehow traditional, and it's absolutely not. So I reject that. That's a claim against sovereignty'.[149] DaLuke also cautions against men using

---

[138] Ibid pp. 124, 154.

[139] Aikins (2016), p. 62; see also Mamdani (2012), p. 49.

[140] Sunseri (2011), pp. 152ff.

[141] Kuokkanen (2016), p. 133; see also Barker (2006), p. 127.

[142] Trask (1996), p. 909; see also St. Denis (2007), pp. 34ff.

[143] Starblanket (2018), p. 7.

[144] Ladner (2009), p. 63.

[145] Napoleon (2009), p. 255; see also Imai (2009), p. 313; Snyder (2014), p. 377.

[146] Napoleon (2002), pp. 163–64; Barker (2006), p. 152.

[147] McIvor (1995), p. 36; Napoleon (2005), p. 37.

[148] Nash (2001), pp. 181ff.

[149] Indigenous woman, as cited in Smith (2005), p. 120.

sovereignty as a way of undermining the rights of women in their community.[150] Thus, Kuokkanen concludes that 'the situation whereby the feminist movement overemphasizes gender discrimination, and the Indigenous movement focuses on colonialism reflect the failure of identity politics to attend to intragroup difference or oppression'.[151]

On a practical level, those advocating for reading gender and self-determination together tend to suggest finding intra-community solutions. Instead of state solutions for advancing Indigenous women's rights, Ladner calls upon deconstructing masculinist ideas that dominate many Indigenous institutions today.[152] To prevent further erosion of Indigenous autonomy, gender equality should be realized from within communities.[153] In the following sections, I will explore how FPIC's internal dimension is negotiated in the different fields and whether it is also contingent upon the legal identities to which FPIC is linked.

2.4 FPIC in Transnational Human Rights Law

Human rights law was the first field in the global time-space to engage with the protection of group rights and FPIC. Contemporary human rights law emerged in response to the atrocities committed during World War II.[154] Its rationale is to restrict the power of states and to protect the human dignity of individuals.[155] Particularly since the end of the Cold War, states have signed a growing number of human rights treaties.[156]

Moreover, the field of human rights law has increasingly moved from state-centered international to transnational human rights law. Goodale defines transnational human rights law as a human regime consisting of 'connections, social relations, economic network and so on that transcend the boundaries of the nation-state'[157] and 'in which human rights consciousness, discourse, practices (if not law) unfold in terms of starkly different logics'.[158] Although Goodale understands the transnational and the international as separate legal regimes, I perceive the field of transnational human rights law as one field constituted of different actors (including, for example, advocacy networks), but in which states still remain central and powerful.

---

[150] LaDuke (2002), p. 192.

[151] Kuokkanen (2016), p. 137.

[152] Ladner (2009), p. 72.

[153] Imai (2009), pp. 311–12; Ladner (2009), p. 72; Tsosie (2010), p. 223.

[154] Moyn (2010), p. 2.

[155] Universal Declaration of Human Rights (1948) UNGA Res 217 A(III), preamble.

[156] Kingsbury (1998), p. 425.

[157] Goodale (2009), p. 97.

[158] Ibid p. 97.

While human rights treaties generally limit states in their actions, they do not fundamentally interfere with their sovereignty. Many treaties focus on individual civil and political rights, making them compatible with Western legal systems.[159] States have been more reluctant to recognize the rights of peoples or nations within the state. Therefore, many Indigenous peoples have refrained from framing their claims as human rights issues.[160] Human rights law was sometimes even seen as a potential threat to their culture, and many Indigenous peoples preferred to claim treaty-based rights, such as the Treaty of Waitangi concluded between the Māori and the government of New Zealand in 1840.[161]

In the past decades, human rights have become increasingly transnationalized. This occurred, among other things, through the increasing participation of non-state actors in the drafting and negotiation of legal documents. Particularly worth mentioning, in this respect, is the creation of the Working Group on Indigenous Populations in 1982, which was replaced by the Expert Mechanism on the Rights of Indigenous Peoples in 2008.[162] The Expert Mechanism provides advice to the Human Rights Council. Moreover, a Special Rapporteur on the Rights of Indigenous Peoples was introduced in 2001 by the Human Rights Commission and the United Nations Permanent Forum on Indigenous is in existence since 2000 as the advisory body to the ECOSOC.[163]

Hand in hand with this transnationalization, human rights law has come to recognize a growing number of collective identities. These groups include Indigenous peoples and tribal peoples, minorities, peoples, and peasants. Most groups are not authoritatively defined.[164] They are not 'hermeneutically sealed categories',[165] but the boundaries between them are 'blurred, porous and shifting'.[166] While the legal identities created by human rights law are fluid, states 'do care about who holds and who exercises right',[167] particularly when their sovereignty may be at stake. Consequently, the legal frameworks attached to these groups vary greatly, as well as the consultation or consent rights incorporated in them. It will be shown that depending on the labeling of a group, a different understanding of FPIC may apply. In the following section, I will explore FPIC in relation to the three most common collective identities in human rights law: minorities, Indigenous peoples, and peasants. After presenting the different collective identities and the potential

---

[159] Wiessner (1999), pp. 120–21.

[160] Kingsbury (2001), p. 190; Engle (2010), pp. 100–101.

[161] Treaty of Waitangi (1840) https://waitangitribunal.govt.nz/treaty-of-waitangi/te-reo-maori-version/. Accessed 10 Aug 2023.

[162] HRC (15 Jul 2009) Report of the Special Rapporteur on the situation of human rights and fundamental freedoms of Indigenous peoples, A/HRC/12/34, para 8.

[163] Ibid para 8.

[164] Wiessner (1999), p. 114.

[165] Castellino and Doyle (2018), p. 7.

[166] Ibid p. 7.

[167] Thornberry (1998), p. 121.

theoretical underpinning of their right to FPIC, I will examine how the legal identity impacts the scope of their consultation or consent rights and the negotiation of institutional autonomy and the participatory rights of women.

2.4.1 *Minority Rights*

Minorities are rights-holders under general human rights law and the specialized minority rights regime, which is the oldest rights regime catering to a group. First attempts to protect the rights of minorities were made as early as the thirteenth century.[168] A minority protection regime was formalized under the League of Nations. However, the international interest in and commitment to the rights of minorities waned after World War II.[169]

It was only in the 1990s that different actors on the international plane began adopting new legal instruments pertaining to minorities.[170] In 1993, the Declaration on the Rights of Persons Belonging to Ethnic, Cultural, and Religious Minorities was adopted. However, it had a minimal impact.[171] Later, the Organization of Security and Co-operation in Europe (OSCE) endorsed the Lund Recommendations on the Effective Participation of National Minorities in Public Life (Lund Recommendations), and the Council of Europe adopted the Framework Convention for the Protection of National Minorities (FCNM).[172] Moreover, under general human rights law, the rights of minorities are protected by art 27 of the International Covenant on Civil, Cultural, and Political Rights (ICCPR). The following sections explore the legal identity of *minorities*, the theoretical underpinning of consultation rights grounded in the relationship between minorities and states, the scope of their consultation rights, and the internal dimension of these consultation rights.

2.4.1.1 Minorities and the State

No generally agreed definition of minorities exists.[173] Characteristics of minorities include membership of an ethnic, language, and/or religious group, a vulnerable position in the state where they live, a long-time presence in the territory, that the

---

[168] Kingsbury (2001), p. 202; Socha (2017), pp. 14ff; Castellino and Doyle (2018), p. 14.

[169] Kymlicka (1999), p. 283.

[170] Gilbert (2004), p. 139.

[171] Castellino and Doyle (2018), p. 32.

[172] Organization for Security and Co-Operation in Europe (1999) The Lund Recommendations on the Effective Participation of National Minorities in Public Life; Framework Convention for the Protection of National Minorities (adopted 1 Feb 1995, entered into force 1 Feb 1998) ETS 157.

[173] Capotorti (1979) Study on the rights of persons belonging to ethnic, religious and linguistic minorities, UN Doc E/CN.4/Sub.2/384/Rev.1, paras 566–67; Alfredsson (2005), p. 165.

group does not make up more than 50% of the state's population, and the principle of self-identification.[174] Comparing the characteristics of Indigenous peoples and minorities, similarities and overlaps are easily detectable. According to Alfredsson, the key difference is the time dimension.[175] While groups may already claim minority status after two generations, Indigenous peoples have a more long-standing relationship with their territories. They often lived there before the arrival of the settlers.[176] With respect to the personal scope of art 27 ICCPR protecting minority rights, Scheinin similarly argues that it applies to 'most tribal groups in the world, in the sense of being in a situation of dispossession analogous to [Indigenous] peoples but not qualifying as [Indigenous] under the strict application of the criterion of "being first"'.[177] Kymlicka finds that national minorities are often those groups that lost the struggle for political power within the state.[178] Therefore, their rights are not protected to the same extent.[179] Indigenous peoples, in contrast, existed outside of the system of European nation-states. Still, the understanding of minorities is not universal. Socha observes that, while the Human Rights Committee has embraced a broad understanding of minorities, a narrower concept is common within the European framework.[180] Hence, even though minorities and Indigenous peoples overlap, the 'story of minority rights as an early conception of international law is not the same story as for [Indigenous] peoples, nor is the rights content'.[181] However, the legal identities created by human rights law do not necessarily correspond to existing social identities. For example, given the long-time absence of a *lex specialis* for Indigenous peoples, Indigenous peoples have sought minority protection in some instances.[182] This highlights how groups may use legal identities in strategic ways and that the distinction between 'minorities and Indigenous peoples is one of fuzzy edges rather than bright lines'.[183]

Given FPIC's entanglement with sovereignty, the question arises: do minorities have a right to self-determination under human rights law? The answer is a clear no.[184] They are generally neither considered to be peoples nor holders of the right to self-determination.[185] However, they are holders of cultural rights.[186] Under art 27 ICCPR, minorities 'shall not be denied the right [. . .] to enjoy their own culture,

---

174 Alfredsson (2005), pp. 165–67.

175 Ibid pp. 165–67.

176 Ibid p. 169; Barten (2015), pp. 8–9.

177 Scheinin (2005), p. 12.

178 Kymlicka (1999), p. 282.

179 Yupsanis (2013), p. 376.

180 Socha (2017), pp. 92–93.

181 Thornberry (2002), p. 34.

182 Castellino and Doyle (2018), p. 14.

183 Thornberry (2002), p. 54.

184 Thornberry (1998), p. 107.

185 Carvosso (2020), p. 683.

186 Thornberry (1998), p. 107.

to profess and practice their own religion, or to use their own language'.[187] It is a right of persons belonging to minorities, i.e., an individual right, even though it has a collective dimension.[188] The Human Rights Committee, the treaty body in charge of monitoring the implementation of the ICCPR, has interpreted art 27 in a broad way.[189] It affirmed not only the existence of a positive obligation of states towards minorities, but also embraced a comprehensive understanding of culture as a particular way of life associated with the use of land or natural resources, especially in the case of Indigenous peoples.[190]

However, art 27 ICCPR explicitly does not 'prejudice the sovereignty and territorial integrity of a State party',[191] thus detaching it from the right to self-determination. Therefore, many Indigenous peoples have been reluctant to claim a violation of minority rights, 'as the protection of their rights cannot be adequately considered under article 27'.[192] Some Indigenous peoples still have filed complaints to the Human Rights Committee under art 27. The Human Rights Committee has also been willing to interpret art 27 broadly—and in the light of the right to right to self-determination (art 1 ICCPR)—when certain types of groups were affected.[193] Simultaneously, it is generally agreed that art 1 ICCPR does not apply to minorities.[194]

The *lex specialis* pertaining to minorities focuses on their cultural rights. Attempts to include a right to autonomy in the United Nations Declaration on the Rights of Minorities failed. Opponents stressed the individual nature[195] of the Declaration and the need to safeguard the sovereignty of states.[196] Similarly, the Council of Europe's Framework Convention neither provides for cultural nor territorial autonomy and employs a fairly individualistic language.[197]

In contrast, the OSCE's Lund Recommendations understand self-governance as one method for ensuring the effective participation of minorities. However, the recommendations emphasize that self-governance does not necessarily imply

[187] International Covenant on Civil and Political Rights (adopted 16 Dec 1966, entered into force 23 Mar 1976), art 27.

[188] HRC (1994) CCPR general comment No 23: Article 27 (Rights of minorities), UN Doc CCPR/C/21/Rev.1/Add.5, paras 1, 3.1; Yupsanis (2013), p. 368.

[189] Jacobsen (2016), p. 280.

[190] HRC (1994) CCPR general comment No 23: Article 27 (Rights of minorities), UN Doc CCPR/C/21/Rev.1/Add.5, para 3.2.

[191] Ibid para 3.2.

[192] Voices of the Earth Congress (1993), para 2.

[193] HRC (1994) CCPR general comment No 23: Article 27 (rights of minorities), UN Doc CCPR/C/21/Rev.1/Add.5, para 3.2; Kingsbury (2001), pp. 241ff.

[194] Xanthaki (2005), p. 17.

[195] As evidenced by the language of 'persons belonging to minorities'.

[196] Thornberry (1998), p. 110.

[197] Ibid p. 116; Council of Europe (2008) Commentary on the effective participation of persons belonging to national minorities in cultural, social and economic life and in public affairs, para 133.

exclusive jurisdiction but only a 'measure of control by a community over matters affecting it'.[198]

Practical considerations, particularly that the number of Indigenous peoples is a lot lower than that of minorities, have driven many states into accepting the Indigenous right to self-determination while refusing to grant the same right to minorities.[199] Even though many scholars question the distinction between minorities and Indigenous peoples, the quality of the protection afforded to Indigenous peoples and minorities strongly differs.[200] FPIC and consultation rights of minorities can only be derived from the right to culture.

2.4.1.2 More than Participation?

The minority rights regime contains some consultation rights under the right to culture framework, while FPIC is usually not recognized. The Human Rights Committee acknowledged that the cultural rights of minorities 'may require measures to ensure the effective participation of members of minority communities in decisions which affect them'.[201] The participation requirement was, in the Human Rights Committee's view, only triggered by matters with a particularly strong impact on the lifestyle of the whole community, and the threshold for finding a lack of effective participation has been high.[202] The Human Rights Committee also viewed effective participation more as an opportunity and not as a right.[203] However, after the adoption of the UNDRIP in 2007, the Human Rights Committee changed its position on consultations and FPIC—at least for cases where Indigenous peoples were concerned. The landmark Poma Poma v. Peru decision will, therefore, be explored as an Indigenous peoples case.[204]

The United Nations Declaration on the Rights of Minorities builds upon art 27 ICCPR but goes further in some respects.[205] According to the Declaration, minorities have the right to effectively participate in cultural, religious, social,

[198] Organization for Security and Co-Operation in Europe (1999) The Lund Recommendations on the Effective Participation of National Minorities in Public Life, p. 26.

[199] Kymlicka (1999), p. 288.

[200] Barten (2015), p. 20.

[201] HRC (1994) CCPR general comment No 23: Article 27 (Rights of minorities), UN Doc CCPR/C/21/Rev.1/Add.5, para 7; see also Länsman et al. v Finland (1994) HRC. UN Doc CCPR/C/52/D/511/1992, para 9.6; Anni Äärela and Jouni Näkkäöäjärvi v Finland (2001) HRC. UN Doc CCPR/C/73/779/1997, para 7.6.

[202] Länsman et al. v Finland (1994) HRC. UN Doc CCPR/C/52/D/511/1992, para 9.4; Henrard (2007), p. 123; Yupsanis (2013), pp. 390–91.

[203] Apirana Mahuika et al. v New Zealand (1993) HRC. UN Doc CCPR/70/D/547/1993, para 9.5.

[204] Ángela Poma Poma v Peru (2009) HRC. UN Doc CCPR/95/D/1457/2006.

[205] Thornberry (2002), p. 175.

economic, and public life and in decisions on the national and, where appropriate, regional level affecting them or the region where they live.[206]

The Council of Europe's Framework Convention protects the right of minorities to effectively participate in cultural, social, and economic life and in public affairs, particularly in cases where they are affected.[207] With respect to land, this means that 'the representatives of [Indigenous] peoples should be closely involved in any decision-making affecting the use of land in their traditional areas of residency'.[208] This implies that the consultation standards for Indigenous peoples are more comprehensive than those for minorities. Still, the language of involvement is weaker than that of consent.

In relation to cultural policies affecting minorities, the member states shall adequately consult with them and involve them in decision-making processes.[209] Concerning the participation of minorities in public life, the member states have different options for realizing the effective participation of minorities. However, 'mere consultation, as such, [are] not a sufficient means to be considered effective participation'.[210] The Advisory Board is, however, skeptical about granting minorities veto rights in legislative processes fearing that this may paralyze the state.[211]

The OSCE's Lund Recommendations stipulate that 'inclusive processes may comprise consultation, polling, referenda, negotiation and even the specific consent of those directly affected'.[212] They thus go a step further than the other documents, being the only ones mentioning consent.

To summarize, with consent remaining linked to self-determination, the consent of minorities, which are not recognized as holders of the right to self-determination, is usually not required.

2.4.1.3 Institutional Autonomy, Gender, and Minorities

Given the fact that states are reluctant to recognize the autonomy of minorities, their institutional autonomy tends to be neglected as well.

The United Nations Declaration on the Rights of Minorities stipulates that 'persons belonging to minorities have the right to establish and maintain their own

---

[206] United Nations Declaration on the Rights of Persons Belonging to National or Ethnic, Religious and Linguistic minorities (1993), arts 2(2), 2(3).

[207] Framework Convention for the Protection of National Minorities (adopted 1 Feb 1995, entered into force 1 Feb 1998), art 5.

[208] Council of Europe (2008) Commentary on the effective participation of persons belonging to national minorities in cultural, social and economic life and in public affairs, para 53.

[209] Ibid para 66.

[210] Ibid para 71.

[211] Ibid paras 98–99.

[212] Organization for Security and Co-Operation in Europe (1999) The Lund Recommendations on the Effective Participation of National Minorities in Public Life, explanatory note, p. 20.

associations'[213] without recognizing their right to be represented by their own institutions in participation processes. It does also not consider gender in relation to participation.

The Council of Europe's FCNM only protects religious institutions and does not mention gender or the rights of minority women.[214] However, the commentary on political participation stresses both the importance of inclusive and representative consultative bodies and the participation of minority women. Attention should be paid to the 'balanced representation of women and men belonging to national minorities'[215] in public affairs. Appointment procedures for consultative bodies should be designed 'in close consultation with national minorities'.[216] Women shall also be represented in these consultative bodies.[217] However, the consultative bodies shall integrate all minorities of a country and do not need to reflect customary decision-making structures.[218]

The OSCE's Lund Recommendations, the only document recognizing that minorities could have a right to consent under certain circumstances, stipulate that 'when institutions of self-governance are needed or desirable, the equal enjoyment by everyone of their rights requires application of the principle of democracy within these institutions'.[219]

Hence, it is only the United Nations Declaration on the Rights of Minorities that mentions customary institutions. Simultaneously, only the commentary on the European FCNM considers gender with respect to decision-making.[220] To conclude, the embeddedness of consultation rights in the right to culture framework reduces FPIC to some degree of participation. Neither minorities' institutional autonomy nor participatory rights of minority women are well recognized. Thus, the power imbalance between states and minorities translates into the failure to fully recognize their consultation and consent rights, including the institutional autonomy and gender dimension.

---

[213] United Nations Declaration on the Rights of Persons Belonging to National or Ethnic, Religious and Linguistic Minorities (1993), art 2(4).

[214] Framework Convention for the Protection of National Minorities (adopted 1 Feb 1995, entered into force 1 Feb 1998), art 8.

[215] Council of Europe (2008) Commentary on the effective participation of persons belonging to national minorities in cultural, social and economic life and in public affairs, p. 6.

[216] Ibid para 111.

[217] Ibid para 111.

[218] Ibid para 112.

[219] Organization for Security and Co-Operation in Europe (1999) The Lund Recommendations on the Effective Participation of National Minorities in Public Life, para 16.

[220] Banda and Chinkin (2004), p. 17.

2.4.2 *Indigenous and Tribal Peoples*

Today, Indigeneity is the collective legal identity to which the broadest and most well-recognized catalog of rights is attached. Indigenous concerns have become 'a large and permanent part of the intergovernmental human rights agenda'[221] in the past decades. Indigenous rights are a part of general human rights, as well as a separate sub-field.[222]

However, this is a relatively new development and Indigenous rights remained at the fringe of the field of human rights for a long time. The International Labour Organization (ILO) was the first organization of the UN system to take an interest in protecting the rights of Indigenous peoples. In 1957, the ILO's Indigenous and Tribal Populations Convention (C 107) entered into force, which was replaced by the Convention on Indigenous and Tribal Peoples (C 169) in 1989.[223]

The other UN treaty bodies were more reluctant to recognize Indigenous peoples' rights at the time. Following the emergence of the transnational Indigenous movement, the Working Group on Indigenous Populations was established as a subsidiary organ of the Sub-Commission on the Promotion and Protection of Human Rights in 1982.[224] It strongly contributed to the emergence of transnational Indigenous law by, among other things, drafting the United Nations Declaration on the Rights of Indigenous Peoples (UNDRIP), which was finally adopted in 2007.[225] Even though the UNDRIP is not legally binding, it is characterized by a high degree of legitimacy and a 'satisfactory degree of effective compliance by states'.[226] Even though Indigenous rights are based on existing human rights norms, they go, in some instances, beyond the existing human rights and minority rights regime.[227] They also reflect the 'aspirations and self-understandings'[228] of Indigenous peoples to a greater extent. It has been recognized that at least some of the UNDRIP's provisions now have the status of customary international law.[229] Moreover, several treaty bodies recommend interpreting the human rights conventions in light of the UNDRIP and refer to

---

[221] MacKay (2002), p. 535.

[222] Castellino (2005), p. 59; Barelli (2010), p. 953.

[223] Convention (No 107) concerning the Protection and Integration of Indigenous and other Tribal and Semi-Tribal Populations in Independent Countries (adopted 16 Jun 1957, entered into force 2 Jun 1959) 328 UNTS 247; Convention (No 169) concerning Indigenous and Tribal Peoples in Independent Countries (adopted 27 Jun 1989, entered into force 5 Sep 1991).

[224] ECOSOC (1982) Study of the problem of discrimination against Indigenous populations, UN Doc ECOSOC Res 1982/34, para 1.

[225] Barelli (2016), pp. 49–50.

[226] Lenzerini (2019), p. 55; see also Barelli (2016), pp. 49–50.

[227] Kingsbury (2001), p. 237.

[228] Ibid p. 238.

[229] Rombouts (2014), p. 21.

the UNDRIP in their reports.[230] Thereby, the *lex specialis* pertaining to Indigenous peoples influenced general human rights law. Relevant norms of general human rights law are the right to self-determination (art 1(1) ICCPR and International Covenant on Economic, Social, and Cultural Rights (ICESCR)), the right to take part in cultural life (art 15 (1)(a) ICESCR), and the protection of minorities (art 27 ICCPR). Several treaty bodies—the Committee on Economic, Social and Cultural Rights (CESCR), the Human Rights Committee, the Committee on the Elimination of all Forms of Discrimination Against Women (CEDAW Committee), and the Committee on the Elimination of Racial Discrimination (CERD Committee)—have clarified the relevance and scope of these provisions.

Moreover, case law exists in the African and American regional human rights systems. For example, in 2017, the American Declaration on the Rights of Indigenous Peoples (ADRIP) was adopted. The regional human rights systems considerably contributed to clarifying and operationalizing Indigenous law.[231]

The following sections explore the collective identity of Indigenous peoples and their relationship to the state, their consent and consultation rights, and FPIC's internal dimension.

2.4.2.1 'Indigenous and Tribal Peoples' and the State

To begin with, the concept of Indigeneity and the legal foundation of FPIC and consultation will be examined. Indigenous law knows two main legal identities: Indigenous peoples and tribal peoples or populations.

Indigeneity as a legal identity has become a 'concept with considerable power as a basis for group mobilization, international standard-setting, transnational networks and programmatic activity of intergovernmental and non-governmental organizations'.[232] Just like minorities, Indigenous peoples are not a clear-cut group. Instead, a 'constructivist approach'[233] has become accepted, assuming that Indigeneity as an evolving concept does not need a universal definition. However, certain characteristics are employed to fill Indigeneity with meaning and provide some degree of legal certainty to states and Indigenous peoples.[234] In this respect, the 1986 working definition of then-Special Rapporteur Cobo Martinez functions as a 'vague gatekeeper'.[235] His characteristics of Indigeneity include ancestry, cultural

[230] E.g. UN Committee on the Elimination of Racial Discrimination (2008) Consideration of reports submitted by states parties under article 9 of the convention: Concluding observations of the Committee on the Elimination of Racial Discrimination (USA), UN Doc CERD/C/USA/CO/6, para 29; Committee on the Rights of the Child (2009) General comment no 11: Indigenous children and their rights under the Convention, UN Doc CRC/C/GC/11, para 82.

[231] Barelli (2010), p. 953.

[232] Kingsbury (1998), p. 414.

[233] Ibid p. 415.

[234] Ibid pp. 456–57.

[235] Thornberry (2002), p. 33.

distinctiveness, language, group consciousness, and acceptance by the Indigenous community.[236] Notably, the criterion of a 'historical continuity with pre-invasion and pre-colonial societies that developed on their territories'[237]—i.e., aboriginality—narrows the scope of Indigeneity and makes the concept difficult to apply, for instance, in many parts of Africa and to Black communities in South America.[238]

For that reason, a second group concept has emerged: that of tribal peoples or populations.[239] Castellino and Doyle understand tribal peoples as a sub-category of Indigenous peoples.[240] But do tribal peoples have the same right to FPIC as Indigenous peoples? The following section will explore the legal identities in Indigenous law and general human rights law, as well as their relationship with the state. A particular focus will be on whether these collective rights-holders possess sovereignty, have the right to self-determination, or only the more limited rights to culture and collective property.

2.4.2.1.1 Indigenous Law

The legal identity of tribal peoples, in addition to Indigenous peoples, has its origin in the ILO system. C 107 addresses 'tribal and semi-tribal populations in independent countries',[241] while C 169 applies to Indigenous and tribal peoples.[242] The C 169 defines tribal peoples as peoples 'whose social, cultural and economic conditions distinguish them from other sections of the national community, and whose status is regulated wholly or partially by their own customs or traditions or by special laws or regulations'.[243] Often, the term is used to describe groups not living in settler states.[244] It has thus become a 'catch all-category'[245] for groups who are

[236] ECOSOC (1982) Study of the problem of discrimination against Indigenous populations, final report (supplementary part), UN Doc E/CN.4/Sub.2/1982/2/Add.6; see also ECOSOC (2001) Prevention of discrimination and protection of Indigenous peoples and minorities, Indigenous peoples and their relationship to land, UN Doc E/CN.4/Sub.2/2001/21, para 69.

[237] Martínez Cobo (1986) Study of the problem of discrimination against Indigenous populations, UN Doc E/CN.4/Sub.2/1986/7/Add.4, para 379.

[238] See also Ndahinda (2011), p. 59.

[239] E.g. in the ILO system and the Interamerican human rights system. The African human rights system equally recognizes the existence of non-Indigenous *peoples.*

[240] Castellino and Doyle (2018), p. 11.

[241] Convention (No 107) concerning the Protection and Integration of Indigenous and other Tribal and Semi-Tribal Populations in Independent Countries (adopted 16 Jun 1957, entered into force 2 Jun 1959), art 1(a).

[242] Convention (No 169) concerning Indigenous and Tribal Peoples in Independent Countries (adopted 27 Jun 1989, entered into force 5 Sep 1991), art 1(1).

[243] E.g. ibid. art 1(1)(a).

[244] Barten (2015), p. 12.

[245] Niezen (2010), p. 120.

marginalized but are not aboriginal in the traditional sense.[246] Moreover, the recognition of the principle of self-identification, i.e., the right of communities to determine their own status, indicates that it is up to communities to determine their status and the applicability of Indigenous law.[247] However, the ILO complaints committee has adopted a very narrow understanding of self-identification and found, for instance, that the Uummannaq could not self-identify as Indigenous as they were not distinct from other Greenlandic communities.[248] Moreover, in a report on the implementation of C 169, the ILO declared to rely on 'existing government recognition of Indigenous or tribal groups'.[249] However, in many cases, Indigenous peoples dissent with state-led identification processes.[250]

The ILO framework thus applies to Indigenous and tribal peoples. However, does the legal identity of *Indigenous and tribal peoples* have a right to self-determination? During the drafting of the C 169, experts and states advocated against the recognition of the right to self-determination and the usage of the terminology of peoples in the Convention, as it was assumed that peoples have a right to self-determination.[251] As a result, the recognition as a rights-holder under the C 169 does explicitly not include the recognition of the right to self-determination.[252] According to the ILO Office, the Convention only 'provides for rights to participation, consultation, and self-management for [Indigenous peoples]'.[253] Thus, *Indigenous and tribal peoples* can only derive consultation rights from the right to culture or property.

With the adoption of the 2007 United Nations Declaration on the Rights of Indigenous Peoples (UNDRIP), states—albeit grudgingly—recognized that 'self-determination is the fundamental principle from which [Indigenous] peoples' rights emanate and are based upon'.[254] While the Working Group on Indigenous Populations and the ILO had advocated for an unlimited right to self-determination during the drafting of the UNDRIP, their proposal did not meet widespread

---

[246] However, the negative connotation of 'tribal' has prompted, amongst others, African states to reject the term (Thornberry (2002), p. 39).

[247] Convention (No 169) concerning Indigenous and Tribal Peoples in Independent Countries (adopted 27 Jun 1989, entered into force 5 Sep 1991), art 1(2).

[248] Report of the committee set up to examine the representation alleging non-observance by Denmark of the Indigenous and Tribal Peoples Convention, 1989 (No. 169), made under article 24 of the ILO Constitution by the National Confederation of Trade Unions of Freenland (Sulinermikinuussutissarsiuteqartut kattuffiat-sik) (sik) (2001) ILO, para 33.

[249] International Labour Organization (2019), p. 48.

[250] E.g. Joona (2020), p. 249.

[251] Barsh (1987), p. 760.

[252] Convention (No 169) concerning Indigenous and Tribal Peoples in Independent Countries (adopted 27 Jun 1989, entered into force 5 Sep 1991); International Labour Office (2013) Handbook for ILO tripartite constituents: Understanding the Indigenous and tribal peoples' convention, 1989 (no. 169), 10; Engle (2011), p. 157; Sambo Dorough (2020), pp. 293–94.

[253] International Labour Office (2013) Handbook for ILO tripartite constituents: Understanding the Indigenous and tribal peoples' convention, 1989 (no. 169), p. 10.

[254] Kuokkanen (2012), p. 228.

support.[255] Nevertheless, art 3 UNDRIP reproduces the wording of common article 1 of the two Covenants indicating that Indigenous peoples are put on a par with states.[256] However, art 3 is limited by art 46(1), according to which the UNDRIP shall not be interpreted as impairing 'totally or in part, the territorial integrity or political unity of sovereign and independent states'.[257] Moreover, the preambular distinguishes between states and Indigenous peoples, indicating that Indigenous peoples are not seen as holders of the full right to self-determination.[258] The Indigenous right to self-determination has thus become 'a collective human rights demand rather than a claim for statehood'.[259] It translates into two interrelated principles: autonomy and participation.[260] FPIC thus becomes a tool for the operationalization of this more limited Indigenous right to self-determination.[261]

In the 1990s, the Inter-American Commission on Human Rights began drafting and negotiating the American Declaration on the Rights of Indigenous peoples (ADRIP), adopted in 2016.[262] It only addresses Indigenous peoples and also recognizes their right to self-determination.[263] Unlike the UNDRIP, the ADRIP does not reference the Covenants' common art 1, indicating that the drafters did not see Indigenous peoples as the holders of the full right to self-determination.[264] Instead, self-determination is mainly understood as giving rise to the right to autonomy and self-government.[265] Moreover, the ADRIP detaches FPIC from the right to self-determination. Instead, it derives it from the right to cultural identity and integrity, the right to health, the right to participation, the protection of cultural heritage and intellectual property, and the right to development.[266] However, in its 2021 report on the self-determination of Indigenous peoples, it declared FPIC to be a precondition and a tool for the realization of Indigenous self-determination.[267]

Hence, even though both the UNDRIP and the ADRIP only address Indigenous peoples, the principle of self-identification could very well allow for the

---

[255] Corntassel (2008), p. 113.

[256] See also Anaya (2009), p. 71.

[257] United Nations Declaration on the Rights of Indigenous Peoples (2007), art 46(1).

[258] Ibid preambular, paras 2, 16; for a dissenting opinion see Castellino and Doyle (2018), p. 33.

[259] Engle (2011), p. 148.

[260] Errico (22 Jun 2017) The American Declaration on the Rights of Indigenous Peoples. www.asil.org/insights/volume/21/issue/7/american-declaration-rights-indigenous-peoples. Accessed 10 Aug 2023.

[261] Haugen (2016), p. 254.

[262] Wiessner (1999), pp. 104–105.

[263] American Declaration on the Rights of Indigenous Peoples (2016) AG/RES. 2888 (XLVI-O/16), arts 3, 4.

[264] Errico (22 Jun 2017) The American Declaration on the Rights of Indigenous Peoples. www.asil.org/insights/volume/21/issue/7/american-declaration-rights-indigenous-peoples. Accessed 10 Aug 2023.

[265] American Declaration on the Rights of Indigenous peoples (2016), art 22.

[266] Ibid arts 13(2), 18(3), 23(2), 28(3), 29(4).

[267] IWGIA and Comisión Interamericana de Derechos Humanos (28 Dec 2021) paras 331, 365(12).

subsumption of tribal peoples under the legal identity of Indigenous peoples. The legal identity of *Indigenous peoples+*– i.e., Indigenous and tribal peoples—has become the norm in the field of human rights law. However, perhaps with the exception of the UNDRIP, Indigenous and tribal peoples are neither seen as sovereigns nor as holders of the right to self-determination. Consequently, both the ILO Conventions and the ADRIP do not derive FPIC from the right to self-determination.

2.4.2.1.2 General Human Rights Law

General human rights law also recognizes different types of groups, including peoples, Indigenous peoples, and tribal peoples. The different human rights institutions and treaty bodies in charge of monitoring the implementation of the human rights conventions have not always been consistent in their use of terminology regarding groups.

Generally, there is a tendency to apply the right to self-determination only to Indigenous peoples. The two human rights covenants—the ICCPR and the ICESCR—recognize the right to self-determination in their common art 1. Since the 1990s, in its reports and concluding observations, the Human Rights Committee has confirmed the applicability of the right to self-determination to Indigenous peoples, including their right to FPIC.[268] Moreover, the Human Rights Committee recognizes its importance for interpreting other provisions such as art 27 ICCPR, which protects the cultural, religious, and linguistic rights of members of minority groups.[269] Art 27, interpreted in the light of art 1 and the UNDRIP, 'enshrines an inalienable right of Indigenous peoples to freely determine their political status and freely pursue their economic, social and cultural development'.[270]

The Committee on Economic, Social, and Cultural Rights (CESCR), the treaty body of the ICESCR, uses the right to culture (art 15(1)(a)) for deriving FPIC.[271] Consequently, it does not see FPIC as an exclusive privilege of Indigenous peoples.

[268] HRC (1999) Considerations of reports submitted by state parties under article 40 of the Covenant: Concluding observations of the Human Rights Committee (Canada), UN Doc CCPR/C/79/Add.105, paras 7–8; HRC (1999) Consideration of reports submitted by state parties under art. 40 of the covenant: Concluding observations of the Human Rights Committee on Mexico, UN Doc CCPR/C/79/Add.109, para 19; HRC (1999) Consideration of reports submitted by state parties under art. 40 of the covenant: Concluding observations of the Human Rights Committee on Norway, UN Doc CCPR/C/79/Add.112, para 17; Yupsanis (2013), p. 374; UNGA (2018) Right of peoples to self-determination, report of the Secretary General, UN Doc A/73/329, para 47.

[269] The HRC can only examine complaints by individuals and art 1 is a collective right; see also Lubicon Lake Band v Canada (1990) HRC. UN Doc A/45/40, para 32.1; Apirana Mahuika et al. v New Zealand (1993) HRC. UN Doc CCPR/70/D/547/1993, para 9.2; HRC (1994), CCPR general comment No 23: Article 27 (Rights of minorities), UN Doc CCPR/C/21/Rev.1/Add.5, para 3.1; Rehoboth Baster Community et al. v Namibia (1997) HRC. UN Doc CCPR/63/D/760/1996, para 10.3.

[270] Tiina Sanila-Aikio v Finland (2018) HRC. UN Doc CCPR/C/D/2668/2015, para 6.8.

[271] Jacobsen (2016), p. 275.

It stresses the relevance of the principle of FPIC for Indigenous peoples with respect to their territories, resources, and cultural and traditional heritage and expressions, but it also calls upon states to obtain the FPIC of persons 'belonging to minority groups, [. . .] or to other communities'[272] in the design and implementation of policies affecting them.[273] However, even though the right to culture and the ICCPR's minority rights provision open an avenue for applying FPIC to a broader range of groups, the two treaty bodies see FPIC primarily as a right of Indigenous peoples, and only exceptionally of other sub-state groups.[274]

The other treaty bodies usually do not explore the right to self-determination, as it is not explicitly included in the treaties they monitor, and derive FPIC from other rights. The Committee on the Elimination of Racial Discrimination (CERD Committee) views Indigenous peoples' rights as a matter of non-discrimination. In its General Comment 23, it only refers to Indigenous peoples and recognizes their right to FPIC.[275] While in some concluding observations, the CERD Committee was also concerned about the land rights of persons of African descent, it mentioned FPIC only in relation to Indigenous peoples.[276] In other cases, it recommended obtaining the consent of both Indigenous peoples and persons of African descent.[277] Given the Committee's focus on combatting racial discrimination, it would only be natural to broaden the scope of FPIC and apply it to other marginalized communities.

The Convention on the Elimination of all Forms of Discrimination Against Women (CEDAW) explicitly protects the rights of rural women, including their right to participate in and benefit from rural development.[278] According to General Recommendation 34, exposure to harmful chemicals requires the 'explicit consent of rural women and their communities'.[279] Moreover, development projects, land acquisitions, and projects affecting rural lands and territories shall only be

[272] ECOSOC (2009) General comment 21: Right of everyone to take part in cultural life (art. 15, para 1(a), of the International Covenant on Economic, Social and Cultural rights), UN Doc E/C.12/GC/21, para 55(e).

[273] Ibid paras 36, 37.

[274] Jacobsen (2016), p. 286.

[275] UN Committee on the Elimination of Racial Discrimination (1997) General recommendation No 23: Indigenous peoples, UN Doc A/52/18, annex V, paras 4(d), 5.

[276] UN Committee on the Elimination of Racial Discrimination (2019) Concluding observations on the combined eighteenth and nineteenth periodic reports of El Salvador, UN Doc CERD/C/SLV/CO/18–19, paras 20, 22.

[277] UN Committee on the Elimination of Racial Discrimination (2017) Concluding observations on the combined twenty-third and twenty-fourth periodic reports of Ecuador, UN Doc CERD/C/ECU/CO/23–24, para 19(a); UN Committee on the Elimination of Racial Discrimination (2019) Concluding observations on the combined sixth to eight periodic reports of Honduras, UN Doc CERD/C/HND/CO/6–8, paras 18, 19(a).

[278] Convention on the Elimination of all Forms of Discrimination against Women (adopted 18 Dec 1979, entered into force 3 Sep 1981) 1249 UNTS 1, art 14.

[279] UN Committee on the Elimination of Discrimination Against Women (2016) General recommendation No 34 on the rights of rural women, UN Doc CEDAW/C/GC/34, para 52(e).

implemented after 'obtaining their [rural women's] free, prior and informed consent'.[280]

The Committee on the Elimination of Discrimination Against Women (CEDAW Committee) has also addressed the rights of Indigenous peoples in its concluding observations.[281] However, in many cases, it lumped Indigenous women together with women from other vulnerable groups like rural or local women.[282] For example, it called upon the Ecuadorian government 'to systematically consult [Indigenous], Afro-Ecuadorian and Montubio women and seek their free, prior and informed consent'.[283] It has also recommended implementing large-scale development and extractive industry projects 'with the prior informed consent of the local women affected'.[284] Only in a few cases, it referred to Indigenous women alone. For example, it has recommended state parties to 'recognize the rights of Indigenous women, in particular, their right to self-determination'.[285] Moreover, following calls by Indigenous organizations, the Committee issued General Recommendation 39 on Indigenous women and girls in 2022.[286] The General Recommendation stresses that Indigenous women and girls have a right to self-identify as stipulated by the

---

[280] Ibid paras 54(e), 62(d); UN Committee on the Elimination of Discrimination Against Women (2017) Concluding observations on the combined eighth and ninth periodic reports of Guatemala, UN Doc CEDAW/C/GTM/CO/8–9, para 41(c).

[281] UN Committee on the Elimination of Discrimination Against Women (2017) Concluding observations on the combined eighth and ninth periodic reports of Guatemala, UN Doc CEDAW/C/GTM/CO/8–9, para 41(c); UN Committee on the Elimination of Discrimination Against Women (2018) Concluding observations on the seventh periodic report of Chile, UN Doc CEDAW/C/CHL/CO/7, para 47(c); UN Committee on the Elimination of Discrimination Against Women (2018) Concluding observations on the ninth periodic report of Mexico, UN Doc CEDAW/C/MEX/CO/9, para 46(c); Clerc and Gómez (2019) Indigenous world 2019: The work of the UN treaty bodies and Indigenous peoples rights. www.iwgia.org/en/ip-i-iw/3673-iw-2019-treatybodies.html#_edn42. Accessed 10 Aug 2023.

[282] UN Committee on the Elimination of Discrimination Against Women (2017) Concluding observations on the combined eighth and ninth periodic reports of Guatemala, UN Doc CEDAW/C/GTM/CO/8–9, para 41(c); UN Committee on the Elimination of Discrimination Against Women (2018) Concluding observations on the seventh periodic report of Chile, UN Doc CEDAW/C/CHL/CO/7, para 47(c); UN Committee on the Elimination of Discrimination Against Women (2018) Concluding observations on the ninth periodic report of Mexico, UN Doc CEDAW/C/MEX/CO/9, para 46(c).

[283] UN Committee on the Elimination of Discrimination Against Women (2015) Concluding observations on the combined eighth and ninth periodic reports of Ecuador, UN Doc CEDAW/C/ECU/CO/8–9, para 39.

[284] UN Committee on the Elimination of Discrimination Against Women (2018) Concluding observations on the eighth periodic report of Australia, UN Doc CEDAW/C/AUS/CO/8, para 30(a).

[285] UN Committee on the Elimination of Discrimination Against Women (2018) Concluding observations on the sixth periodic report of Nepal, UN Doc CEDAW/C/NPL/CO/6, para 41(a).

[286] Permanent Forum on Indigenous Issues (2004) Report on the third session (10–21 May 2004), UN Doc E/2004/43; E/C.19/2004/23, para 6.

UNDRIP.[287] It also identifies the lack of implementation of their right to self-determination as one of the root causes of discrimination against Indigenous women and girls. The treaty practice thus indicates that self-determination is seen as an Indigenous right, while FPIC can be derived from the rights of rural women and applied to a broader range of groups.

Moreover, under the auspices of the United Nations Food and Agricultural Organization (FAO), the Voluntary Guidelines on the Responsible Governance of Tenure of Land, Fisheries, and Forests in the Context of National Food Security (VGGT) were drafted and promulgated in 2012.[288] The VGGT is a non-binding multilateral agreement, which pursues the 'goal of food security and progressive realization of the right to adequate food [. . .]'.[289] It does not recognize a right to self-determination. However, the agreement protects legitimate tenure rights, including those of '[Indigenous] peoples and other communities with customary tenure systems'.[290] FPIC is thus indirectly framed as a derivative of the collective right to property. Still, it is only mentioned in relation to Indigenous peoples.[291]

In the regional human rights systems, FPIC is also not seen as exclusively applying to Indigenous peoples in the narrow sense. In the American human rights system, FPIC has been applied to both Indigenous and tribal peoples. The American human rights institutions affirmed the collective dimension of the right to property and derived FPIC from it.[292] Moreover, in some instances, consent has also been linked to the right to cultural integrity.[293] The Inter-American Court on Human Rights (ACtHR) recognizes the concept of tribal peoples without the criterion of aboriginality and has applied rights from the Indigenous rights framework to them.[294] In the Moiwana case, it argued that given the N'djuka tribal people's 'all-encompassing relationship to their traditional land'[295] and their collective sense of ownership, they were holders of the right to property, just like Indigenous communities. This was confirmed in the Saramaka judgment, where the ACtHR found that

---

[287] UN Committee on the Elimination of Discrimination Against Women (31 Oct 2022) General recommendation No. 39 (2022) on the rights of Indigenous women and girls, CEDAW/C/GC/39, para 8.

[288] Kapstein (2018), p. 173.

[289] Committee on World Food Security (2012) Voluntary guidelines on the responsible governance of tenure of land, fisheries and forests in the context of national food security, obj 1.1.

[290] Ibid part 3.

[291] Ibid obj 9.9.

[292] E.g. Mary and Carrie Dann v United Sates (2002) Inter-American Commission on Human Rights. IACHR Doc 5 rev 1 at 860, paras 165, 172; Moiwana Community v Suriname (2005) Inter-American Court of Human Rights. IACtHR Series C No 124, paras 209–11.

[293] Kichwa Indigenous people of Sarayaku v Ecuador (2012) Inter-American Court of Human Rights. IACtHR Series C No 245, para 217.

[294] Ndahinda (2011), p. 203.

[295] Moiwana Community v Suriname (2005) Inter-American Court of Human Rights. IACtHR Series C No 124, para 133.

the Saramaka people were a 'tribal community'[296] with specific social, cultural, and economic characteristics and a particularly close relationship to their land.[297] Especially communities of African descent are recognized as tribal peoples, as evidenced by a 2019 Resolution of the Organization of American States.[298] Some authors describe this as the 'ethnicization of the Afro-descendants under the model of Indigenous ethnicity'.[299] The notion of tribal peoples has been appropriated by non-Indigenous marginalized groups, which found bringing their claims as a form of racial discrimination was less promising than Indigenizing their claims.[300]

The African human rights system recognizes the collective identity of *peoples* and several collective rights.[301] A definition of peoples is lacking, and the terminology of peoples, minorities, and Indigenous peoples is regularly used interchangeably in the case law.[302] Whether a group is a people under the African Charter on Human and Peoples' Rights is largely determined on a case-by-case basis and depends on the right in question. Usually, aboriginality is not a requirement for being a people.[303] The concept of peoples thus overlaps with tribal peoples even though it has a more comprehensive rights framework attached to it. The African Commission on Human and Peoples' Rights (ACHPR) also recognized the applicability of the right to self-determination to intra-state groups as long as the territorial integrity of the state is not jeopardized.[304] Self-determination is seen as an 'enabling right',[305] which serves to facilitate the participation of vulnerable communities in shaping the economic, legal, and political order.

---

296 Saramaka People v Suriname (2007) Inter-American Court of Human Rights. IACtHR Series C No 172, paras 84, 86.

297 See also Kichwa Indigenous People of Sarayaku v Ecuador (2012) Inter-American Court of Human Rights. IACtHR Series C No 245, para 146; Comunidad Garífuna Triunfo de la Cruz y sus miembros v Honduras (2015) Inter-American Court of Human Rights. IACtHR Series C no 204, para 153.

298 General Assembly (2019) Effective participation of Indigenous peoples and people of african descent in OAS activities, AG/RES. 2934 (XLIX-O/19).

299 Dulitzky (2010), p. 77.

300 Anderson (2007), pp. 387, 392ff.

301 African Charter on Human and Peoples' Rights (adopted 27 Jun 1982, entered into force 21 Oct 1986), arts 19, 20, 21, 22, 23, 24.

302 Salomon (2017), p. 226.

303 Advisory opinion of the African Commission on Human and Peoples' Rights on the United Nations Declaration on the Rights of Indigenous Peoples (2007), para 12; Centre for Minority Rights Development (Kenya) and Minority Rights Group (on behalf of Endorois welfare council) v Kenya (2009) African Commission on Human and Peoples' Rights. Comm 276/2003 (ACHPR), para 151.

304 Advisory opinion of the African Commission on Human and Peoples' rights on the United Nations Declaration on the Rights of Indigenous Peoples (2010), p. 32.

305 Salomon (2017), p. 236.

However, FPIC has only been derived from the right to a healthy environment, the right to development, and the right to property.[306] In their jurisprudence, the African institutions at times did not even dwell on the Indigenous status of a group but just affirmed their right to FPIC as a people.[307] Moreover, FPIC's applicability to local or affected communities has also been affirmed in the (soft) law of other African regional organizations.[308]

Hence, it is increasingly recognized that communities do not necessarily have to meet the aboriginality criterion to hold the right to FPIC.[309] However, when Indigenous peoples are mentioned together with tribal peoples, their rights seem to be more limited and possibly closer to those of minorities. FPIC then tends to be derived from the right to culture or the collective right to property.

2.4.2.2 Consent: Yes, But Under Which Circumstances?

Given the emerging tendency to frame FPIC as a derivative of the right to culture or the collective right to property and to apply it beyond Indigenous peoples in the traditional sense, it seems likely that its meaning differs from the FPIC envisioned by the Indigenous movement. This section explores the situations in which FPIC is applied and the scope of the consent requirement.

FPIC has proliferated in the past decades in the jurisprudence of the treaty bodies. The Human Rights Committee introduced a Special Rapporteur on the Rights of Indigenous Peoples in 2001, who called upon the respect of FPIC in relation to the extinction of customary land rights, law-making, development projects, economic activities, removals, and relocations.[310] Moreover, the subfield of Indigenous law

---

[306] Social and Economic Rights Action Center & the Center for Economic and Social Rights v Nigeria (2001) African Commission for Human and Peoples' Rights. Comm 155/96 (ACHPR), para 53; Centre for Minority Rights Development (Kenya) and Minority Rights Group (on behalf of Endorois welfare council) v Kenya (2009) African Commission on Human and Peoples' Rights. Comm 276/2003 (ACHPR), para 290; African Commission on Human and Peoples' Rights v Republic of Kenya (2017) African Court on Human and Peoples' Rights. Application No 006/2012 (ACtHPR), paras 131, 210.

[307] Social and Economic Rights Action Center & the Center for Economic and Social Rights v Nigeria (2001) African Commission for Human and Peoples' Rights. Comm 155/96 (ACHPR), para 53.

[308] Organization of African Unity (2000) African model legislation for the protection of the rights of local communities, farmers and breeders, and for the regulation of access to biological resources; Economic Community of West African States (2009) Directive on the harmonization of guiding principles and policies in the mining sector, art 16(3); Resolution on a human rights-based approach to natural resources governance (2012) African Commission on Human and Peoples' Rights. ACHPR/Res.225(LI)2012 (ACHPR), para 4; United Nations Economic Commission for Africa, About AMV. www.africaminingvision.org/about.html. Accessed 10 Aug 2023.

[309] Committee on the Rights of Indigenous Peoples (2012) pp. 2–3.

[310] ECOSOC (2001) Prevention of discrimination and protection of Indigenous peoples and minorities, Indigenous peoples and their relationship to land, UN Doc E/CN.4/Sub.2/2001/21, paras 42, 45, 67, 69, 71.

has contributed to the mainstreaming of FPIC. FPIC is most prominently discussed in relation to (1) the land and natural resources of communities and (2) relocations as the gravest form of the extinction of their land rights. Moreover, FPIC is considered when it comes to (3) the adoption of legal and administrative measures affecting them.

2.4.2.2.1 Indigenous Law

The sub-field of Indigenous law witnessed a move from consultation to consent in the past decades. Earlier legal documents, like the ILO Conventions, mainly recognize a duty to consult with Indigenous peoples. The ILO framework mentions consultations or consent in three different contexts: in the application of the Conventions, for legal and administrative measures directly affecting Indigenous and tribal peoples,[311] and for relocations.

Under C 107, the member states should 'seek the collaboration of these populations and their representatives' in the implementation of the Convention.[312] This weak terminology prescribes neither a duty to consult with Indigenous people nor to obtain their consent.[313] Instead, the implementation of the Convention remains in the hands of the state. Moreover, Indigenous peoples should not be relocated 'without their free consent from their habitual territories except in accordance with national laws and regulations relating to its national security, or in the interest of national economic development or of the health of the said populations'.[314] The state's interests clearly takes priority over the land and natural resource rights of Indigenous peoples. The Convention thus 'did relatively little to restrict state power'[315] and the integrationist approach or 'palliative philosophy'[316] failed to acknowledge Indigenous self-determination.[317]

Under C 169, communities that may be directly affected by legislative or administrative measures 'should be able to participate and be consulted [...] with the

[311] Only part of C 169.

[312] Convention (No 107) oncerning the Protection and Integration of Indigenous and other Tribal and Semi-Tribal Populations in Independent Countries (adopted 16 Jun 1957, entered into force 2 Jun 1959), art 5(a).

[313] Doyle (2015), p. 77.

[314] Convention (No 107) oncerning the Protection and Integration of Indigenous and other Tribal and Semi-Tribal Populations in Independent Countries (adopted 16 Jun 1957, entered into force 2 Jun 1959), art 12(1).

[315] Barsh (1987), p. 757.

[316] Doyle (2015), p. 92.

[317] As reflected in the references to 'less advanced' population (Convention (No 107) oncerning the Protection and Integration of Indigenous and other Tribal and Semi-Tribal Populations in Independent Countries (adopted 16 Jun 1957, entered into force 2 Jun 1959), art 1(a)); see also MacKay (2009) p. 7.

objective of achieving agreement or consent'.[318] The ILO complaints commission has further elaborated on the meaning of consent. It pointed out that art 6 does not stipulate that consent must be obtained for the consultations to be valid.[319] As long as the government has the objective of obtaining consent but fails to do so, no violation of art 6 can be found.

In relation to the exploitation of natural resources, states shall only consult to ascertain whether Indigenous peoples' interests may be prejudiced.[320] Moreover, consultations are mandated when the state considers the alienation of Indigenous land.[321] When relocations are necessary, these 'shall take place only with their free and informed consent. Where their consent cannot be obtained, such relocation shall take place only following appropriate procedures established by national laws and regulations [. . .]'.[322]

However, when no consent is obtained, the state must still respect the substantive rights enshrined in the C 169. The graver the potential consequences for Indigenous peoples, the more critical is consent.[323] Doyle argues that in light of the C 169's overarching objective to protect Indigenous peoples' way of life, 'it logically prohibits rights' infringements which pose a threat to their current and future way of life'.[324] Göcke, in contrast, finds that the C 169 fails to recognize FPIC.[325] The state parties to the C 169 tend to only recognize consultations and not FPIC in their national legal systems.[326]

More recently, the UNDRIP has become the reference point for FPIC. It requires FPIC for five types of situations: (1) legislative and administrative measures, (2) development projects, (3) relocations, (4) the disposal of hazardous waste, and (5) military activities. However, the FPIC terminology within the UNDRIP is inconsistent and debates relating to its content persist.[327] Relocations and the storage and disposal of hazardous waste are not permitted without FPIC.[328] This

318 Convention (No 169) concerning Indigenous and Tribal Peoples in Independent Countries (adopted 27 Jun 1989, entered into force 5 Sep 1991), art 6(1)(a).

319 Report of the committee set up to examine the representation alleging non-observance by Argentina of the Indigenous and Tribal Peoples Convention, 1989 (No. 169), made under article 24 of the ILO Constitution by the Education Workers Union of Río Negro (UNTER), local section affiliated to the Confederation of Education Workers of Argentina (CTERA) (2008) ILO para 81.

320 Convention (No 169) concerning Indigenous and Tribal Peoples in Independent Countries (adopted 27 Jun 1989, entered into force 5 Sep 1991), art 15(2).

321 Ibid art 17(2).

322 Ibid art 16(2).

323 International Labour Office (2013) Handbook for ILO tripartite constituents: Understanding the Indigenous and Tribal Peoples' Convention, 1989 (No. 169), p. 16.

324 Doyle (2015), p. 91; see also Barelli (2018), p. 264.

325 Göcke (2010), p. 360.

326 Haugen (2016), p. 251.

327 Newman (2020), p. 234.

328 United Nations Declaration on the Rights of Indigenous Peoples (2007), arts 10, 29(2).

terminology indicates that consent is mandatory and that Indigenous peoples may also refuse to consent.[329]

Weaker language is employed with respect to projects affecting Indigenous land and natural resources and legislative and administrative measures. States shall only 'consult and cooperate in good faith [. . .] in order to obtain their free and informed consent prior to the approval of any project affecting their lands or territories and other resources'[330] and for legislative and administrative measures affecting Indigenous peoples.[331] Anaya has outlined that these provisions apply to proposed measures, which may produce a 'differentiated effect'[332] for Indigenous peoples and that they do not entail a general right to veto.[333] Instead, the intensity of the consultation depends on the risk of the measure for Indigenous peoples. Only in the case of a 'significant, direct impact'[334] does the obligation to consult harden into the prohibition of a project or measure without Indigenous consent.

In light of the other provisions and state practice, the International Law Association concludes that art 19 may not be interpreted 'as a general right of veto in favor of the [Indigenous] communities concerned to block the adoption or implementation of the governmental measures which may affect them per se'.[335] Similarly, Jacobsen argues that the phrase 'in order to obtain consent' refers to the state's intention rather than actual consent.[336]

Moreover, according to art 30(2) UNDRIP, states shall effectively consult with Indigenous peoples prior to using their land for military activities. However, military activities do not necessarily require consent: either public interest or the free agreement of Indigenous peoples is mandated.[337] The language is thus weaker than in the other cases explored above.

Barelli takes the position that while the UNDRIP does not grant a general veto right to Indigenous peoples, Indigenous peoples may still refuse to consent under exceptional circumstances.[338] While states are not always obliged to obtain the consent of Indigenous peoples, they must obtain consent if a failure to do so would result in a human rights violation and jeopardize the Indigenous peoples'

[329] See also HRC (2009) Report of the special rapporteur on the situation of human rights and fundamental freedoms of Indigenous peoples, James Anaya, UN Doc A/HRC/12/34, para 47; Committee on the Rights of Indigenous Peoples (2012) p. 7.

[330] United Nations Declaration on the Rights of Indigenous Peoples (2007), art 32(2).

[331] Ibid art 19.

[332] HRC (2009) Report of the Special Rapporteur on the Situation of Human Rights and Fundamental Freedoms of Indigenous peoples, James Anaya, UN Doc A/HRC/12/34, para 43.

[333] Barelli (2018), p. 253.

[334] HRC (2009) Report of the Special Rapporteur on the Situation of Human Rights and Fundamental Freedoms of Indigenous peoples, James Anaya, UN Doc A/HRC/12/34, para 47.

[335] Committee on the Rights of Indigenous Peoples (2012) p. 4.

[336] Jacobsen (2016), p. 283.

[337] United Nations Declaration on the Rights of Indigenous Peoples (2007), art 30(1).

[338] Barelli (2012), p. 11.

cultural integrity.[339] The UN Expert Mechanism on the Rights of Indigenous Peoples goes a step further by explaining that withholding consent would be, inter alia, legitimate if the community finds that a proposal is not in its best interest because of deficiencies in the process, or because of legitimate distrust in the process.[340] However, it also refers to the sliding scale approach and a proportionality assessment with respect to FPIC: the scope of FPIC depends on the expected direct impact of a project.[341]

According to the American Declaration on the Rights of Indigenous Peoples (ADRIP), FPIC is relevant in the following situations: administrative or legislative measures and measures affecting their cultural heritage, intellectual property, and land and natural resources.[342] Unlike under the UNDRIP, states are neither obliged to seek the FPIC for military projects on Indigenous territories nor is FPIC explicitly required for relocations and the storage and disposal of hazardous materials.[343] The ADRIP follows the UNDRIP's terminology to a large extent; in some cases, actions may not be taken 'without their consent'.[344] In relation to development projects, the right to cultural heritage and intellectual property, and legal and administrative measures, states shall 'consult and cooperate in good faith with [Indigenous] peoples [...] in order to obtain their free and informed consent'[345] prior to the project or action.[346]

The situation requiring FPIC thus remains controversial, with the UNDRIP adopting the most comprehensive approach. However, the right to not consent tends to be seen as applying only in extraordinary circumstances, while in most cases, good faith consultations suffice.

2.4.2.2.2 General Human Rights Law

The developments in Indigenous law strongly influenced general human rights law. However, a consistent understanding of FPIC is yet to develop.[347]

Following the adoption of the UNDRIP, the Human Rights Committee endorsed FPIC in the decision Poma Poma v Peru. It held that

> the participation in the decision-making process must be effective, which requires not mere consultation but the free, prior and informed consent of the members of the community. In

[339] Wiessner (2011), pp. 139–40; Committee on the Rights of Indigenous Peoples (2012) p. 7.

[340] HRC (10 Aug 2018) Free, prior and informed consent: A human rights-based approach. Study of the Expert Mechanism on the Rights of Indigenous Peoples, UN Doc A/HRC/39/62, para 26.

[341] Ibid para 35.

[342] American Declaration on the Rights of Indigenous Peoples (2016), arts 23(2), 28(3), 29(4).

[343] See United Nations Declaration on the Rights of Indigenous Peoples (2007), arts 10, 29(2), 30(1).

[344] Right to health (art 18(3)) and right to cultural identity and integrity (art 13(2)).

[345] American Declaration on the Rights of Indigenous Peoples (2016), art 29(4).

[346] Similar terminology in arts 28(3), 23(2).

[347] See also Barelli (2018), p. 295.

addition, the measures must respect the principle of proportionality so as not to endanger the very survival of the community and its members.[348]

In view of Peru's failure to consult, it found a violation of art 27 ICCPR but not of art 1(2) as claimed by the applicant.[349] The decision constituted a move from effective participation to FPIC.[350] Yet, the threshold for FPIC remains high. Moreover, Jacobsen argues that consent does not include the right to veto a specific project or measure but rather refers to the acceptance of the decision-making process.[351]

The CESCR also uses the language of consent in the context of land rights, cultural and traditional heritage and expression, and the design of policies and laws. In its earlier reports, it called upon states to seek the consent of Indigenous peoples in accordance with ILO Convention 169.[352] In its General Comment 21 on the right to culture, it demanded taking steps to return lands and territories that have been taken or used without free, prior, and informed consent.[353] States shall furthermore respect the *principle* of FPIC in the context of their cultural and traditional heritage and their traditional and cultural expressions.[354] They shall also ensure the participation of persons belonging to minority groups, Indigenous peoples, and other communities in the design and implementation of policies and laws affecting them. This may include FPIC, particularly when their cultural resources, including their way of life, are at risk.[355] In more recent recommendations, the CESCR references both the UNDRIP and the ILO C 169 and affirms the right of Indigenous peoples to 'prior consultation with a view of obtaining free, prior and informed consent'.[356] While the CESCR's language with respect to FPIC is not always consistent, it increasingly sees FPIC as a legal obligation and not only a principle.[357]

The CERD Committee has been the most radical of the treaty bodies with respect to FPIC. In 1997, the CERD Committee issued a General Recommendation on the Rights of Indigenous Peoples. It demanded 'that no decisions directly relating to

---

348 Ángela Poma Poma v Peru (2009) HRC. UN Doc CCPR/95/D/1457/2006, para 7.6.

349 Ibid para 7.7.

350 Yupsanis (2013), p. 396.

351 Jacobsen (2016), p. 281.

352 Committee on Economic Social and Cultural Rights (2001) Considerations of reports submitted by states parties under articles 16 and 17 of the Covenant: Concluding observations of the Committee on Economic, Social and Cultural rights (Colombia), UN Doc E/C.12/1/Add.74, para 33; Committee on Economic Social and Cultural Rights (2004) Consideration of reports submitted by state parties under articles 16 and 17 of the covenant: Concluding observations of the Committee on Economic, Social and Cultural rights (Ecuador), UN Doc E/C.12/Add.100, para 35.

353 ECOSOC (2009) General comment 21: Right of everyone to take part in cultural life (art. 15, para 1(a), of the International Covenant on Economic, Social and Cultural Rights), UN Doc E/C.12/GC/21, para 36.

354 Ibid para 37.

355 Ibid para 55(e).

356 UNGA (2018) Right of peoples to self-determination, report of the Secretary General, UN Doc A/73/329, paras 41–46.

357 Jacobsen (2016), pp. 283–84.

their [Indigenous peoples'] rights and interests are taken without their informed consent'.[358] Land that has been alienated without their free and informed consent shall be returned, or, if that is impossible, they shall receive just, fair and prompt compensation.[359] It also affirmed the relevance of FPIC to legal and administrative measures.[360] During the drafting of the General Recommendation, most experts involved understood the FPIC requirements as including a right to veto in cases where it would serve the protection of other human rights.[361] Moreover, the CERD Committee has called upon states to use the UNDRIP as an interpretative guide for the obligations under the Convention on the Elimination of Racial Discrimination (CERD).[362] Therefore, it may be assumed that it embraced a right to say no, at least in some situations.

However, the terminology applied by the CERD Committee in more recent concluding observations also varies. It sometimes refers to 'seeking consent',[363] 'consultations with a view of obtaining consent',[364] or 'good faith consultation and cooperation',[365] indicating that consent does not necessarily have to be obtained if the state has consulted in good faith.[366] In some instances, the CERD Committee has

[358] UN Committee on the Elimination of Racial Discrimination (1997) General recommendation No 23: Indigenous peoples, UN Doc A/52/18, annex V, para 4(d).

[359] Ibid para 5.

[360] UN Committee on the Elimination of Racial Discrimination (2019) Concluding observations on the combined eighteenth and nineteenth periodic reports of El Salvador, UN Doc CERD/C/SLV/CO/18–19, para 23; UN Committee on the Elimination of Racial Discrimination (2019) Concluding observations on the combined sixth to eight periodic reports of Honduras, UN Doc CERD/C/HND/CO/6–8, para 19(a).

[361] Doyle (2015), p. 167.

[362] UN Committee on the Elimination of Racial Discrimination (2008) Consideration of reports submitted by states parties under article 9 of the convention: Concluding observations of the Committee on the Elimination of Racial Discrimination (USA), UN Doc CERD/C/USA/CO/6, para 29.

[363] UN Committee on the Elimination of Racial Discrimination (2017) Concluding observations on the twenty third and twenty fourth periodic reports of the Russian Federation, UN Doc CERD/C/RUS/CO/23–24, para 25.

[364] UN Committee on the Elimination of Racial Discrimination (2019) Concluding observations on the combined eighteenth and nineteenth periodic reports of El Salvador, UN Doc CERD/C/SLV/CO/18–19, para 23; UN Committee on the Elimination of Racial Discrimination (2019) Concluding observations on the combined eighteenth to twenty-first periodic report of Mexico, UN Doc CERD/C/MEX/CO/18–21, para 20; UN Committee on the Elimination of Racial Discrimination (2019) Concluding observations on the combined sixth to eight periodic reports of Honduras, UN Doc CERD/C/HND/CO/6–8, para 19.

[365] UN Committee on the Elimination of Racial Discrimination (2008) Consideration of reports submitted by states parties under article 9 of the convention: Concluding observations of the Committee on the Elimination of Racial Discrimination (USA), UN Doc CERD/C/USA/CO/6, para 29.

[366] UN Committee on the Elimination of Racial Discrimination (2003) Considerations of reports submitted by states parties under article 9 of the convention: Concluding observations of the Committee on the Elimination of Racial Discrimination (Ecuador), UN Doc CERD/C/62/CO/2, para 16; see also Committee on the Rights of Indigenous Peoples (2012), p. 5; Jacobsen (2016), p. 284.

also used the stronger language of 'ensuring'[367] the right to consultations and consent and that no decisions affecting Indigenous peoples are 'taken without their informed consent'.[368] The CERD Committee has thus aligned itself with the practice of the other treaty bodies.

The CEDAW Committee is also ambiguous in its understanding of consent: in some instances, it refers to 'obtaining consent',[369] in other cases, it calls upon states to 'seek consent'.[370] It also recommended that the governments of Guatemala and Mexico implement FPIC in accordance with ILO C 169 without mentioning the UNDRIP.[371] However, with the countries in question belonging to the few signatories of C 169, this does not necessarily mean that the CEDAW Committee endorses the same narrow understanding of FPIC. The 2022 General Recommendations emphasize the need for 'effective participation and obtaining consent'.[372]

The FAO's Voluntary Guidelines on the Responsible Governance of Tenure (VGGT) recognize an FPIC requirement only for Indigenous peoples. Projects or legislative or administrative measures affecting the resources of Indigenous peoples 'should be based on an effective and meaningful consultation with [Indigenous] peoples [...] to obtain their own consent'[373] as mandated by the UNDRIP. For non-Indigenous groups, the applicable standard is 'active, free, meaningful and informed participation'.[374] States shall consult with '[Indigenous] peoples and other communities with customary tenure systems, smallholders and anyone else who could be affected'[375] when intending to recognize or allocate tenure rights.

[367] E.g. UNGA (2011) Report of the Committee on the Elimination of Racial Discrimination, UN Doc A66/18, para 39.

[368] Ibid para 27.

[369] UN Committee on the Elimination of Discrimination Against Women (2016) General recommendation No 34 on the rights of rural women, UN Doc CEDAW/C/GC/34, paras 54(e), 62(d).

[370] UN Committee on the Elimination of Discrimination Against Women (2015) Concluding observations on the combined fifth and sixth periodic reports of the Plurinational State of Bolivia, UN Doc CEDAW/C/BOL/CO/5–6, para 35(a); UN Committee on the Elimination of Discrimination Against Women (2017) Concluding observations on the combined eighth and ninth periodic reports of Guatemala, UN Doc CEDAW/C/GTM/CO/8–9, para 41(c).

[371] UN Committee on the Elimination of Discrimination Against Women (2017) Concluding observations on the combined eighth and ninth periodic reports of Guatemala, UN Doc CEDAW/C/GTM/CO/8–9, para 41(c); UN Committee on the Elimination of Discrimination Against Women (2018) Concluding observations on the ninth periodic report of Mexico, UN Doc CEDAW/C/MEX/CO/9, para 46(c).

[372] UN Committee on the Elimination of Discrimination Against Women (31 Oct 2022) General recommendation No. 39 (2022) on the rights of Indigenous women and girls, CEDAW/C/GC/39, para 11.

[373] Committee on World Food Security (2012) Voluntary guidelines on the responsible governance of tenure of land, fisheries and forests in the context of national food security, part 3 para 9.9.

[374] Ibid part 2 para 3.B.6.

[375] Ibid part 3 para 7.3.

As has been explored above, in the American human rights jurisprudence, consultations and FPIC are derived from the collective right to property.[376] Thereby, the American institutions have embraced a 'culturally driven approach to land rights',[377] locating FPIC at the intersection of the right to property and the right to cultural identity. However, it remains controversial in which situations FPIC applies. While the Inter-American Commission on Human Rights (IACHR) takes the position that the consent requirement is triggered by any project or activity interfering with customary property rights, the Inter-American Court on Human Rights (IACtHR) has adopted a narrower understanding.[378] The IACtHR understands prior or effective consultations as the norm—and a principle of general international law.[379] FPIC is only required in exceptional circumstances when the impact is particularly severe and threatens the group's survival.[380] It developed the following test for the legitimate extinction of customary property rights: compliance with the national legal system, proportionality, a legitimate objective, a participatory process that guarantees the right to consultation, an environmental impact assessment, and, as appropriate, a benefit-sharing agreement.[381] In the Sarayaku judgment, the Court avoided the language of FPIC altogether and mentioned the UNDRIP only in footnotes.[382] However, the fact that in some instances FPIC has not only been linked to the right to property but also the right to cultural identity, for which derogations are harder to justify, could indicate that the FPIC requirement may be triggered even when the survival of the group is not at stake.[383] Barelli reads this as a sliding scale approach similar to the jurisprudence of the Human Rights Committee—the graver the expected human rights violations, the stricter the consent requirement has to be interpreted.[384]

In the African human rights system, the African Commission on Human and Peoples' Rights (ACHPR) found that the right to a healthy environment (art 24 African Charter) required providing 'meaningful opportunities for individuals to be heard and to participate in the development decisions affecting their

[376] Errico (2006), pp. 382f.

[377] Xanthaki (2019), p. 278.

[378] Doyle (2015), pp. 148–51; Reguart-Segarra (2019), p. 115.

[379] Kichwa Indigenous People of Sarayaku v Ecuador (2012) Inter-American Court of Human Rights. IACtHR Series C No 245, para 164.

[380] Saramaka People v Suriname (2007) Inter-American Court of Human Rights. IACtHR Series C No 172, paras 127, 129, 137.

[381] Ibid para 128–29; Kichwa Indigenous People of Sarayaku v Ecuador (2012) Inter-American Court of Human Rights. IACtHR Series C No 245, para 157.

[382] Kichwa Indigenous People of Sarayaku v Ecuador (2012) Inter-American Court of Human Rights. IACtHR Series C No 245, paras 185ff.

[383] Ibid para 217; Doyle (2015), p. 130.

[384] Barelli (2012), p. 14.

communities'.[385] Moreover, it called upon the Nigerian state to ensure 'meaningful access to regulatory and decision-making bodies to communities likely to be affected by oil operations'.[386] In the Endorois decision, the ACHPR also stressed that the threshold for encroaching upon Indigenous property rights in the public interest is higher than for individual property.[387] In the case where a project has a major impact on a community's territory, the state 'has a duty not only to consult with the community, but also to obtain their free, prior, and informed consent'.[388] The African Court on Human and Peoples' Rights, in contrast, avoided the terminology of consent. Instead, it found that the failure to effectively consult with the Ogiek constituted a violation of the right to development, and the lack of 'prior consultations'[389] constituted a breach of the right to property.[390]

To conclude, it remains controversial whether FPIC includes the right not to consent. While most actors assume that no general right to veto exists, there is an emerging consensus that, at least in cases where the project of activity has severe consequences on the group in question, the community has the right to withhold its consent.[391] The International Law Association also concludes that the practice of the treaty bodies 'seems to be oriented towards recognizing the existence of a duty to actually obtain the consent of the [Indigenous] communities concerned'.[392] With respect to non-Indigenous groups or tribal peoples, the scope of FPIC remains even more controversial. Under the current frameworks, if at all, they only seem to be the holders of a right to FPIC *light*. Hence, the FPIC of Indigenous and tribal peoples in the field of human rights law is clearly more reduced than the sovereignty-based understanding.

2.4.2.3 Institutional Autonomy, Gender, and Indigeneity

The rationale behind Indigenous law is to protect Indigenous peoples' 'right to be different and to determine how this difference manifests itself in the future'.[393] In this respect, the question arises of how their institutional autonomy can be reconciled

---

[385] Social and Economic Rights Action Center & the Center for Economic and Social Rights v Nigeria (2001) African Commission for Human and Peoples' Rights. Comm 155/96 (ACHPR), para 53.

[386] Ibid appeals to the government.

[387] Centre for Minority Rights Development (Kenya) and Minority Rights group (on behalf of Endorois welfare council) v Kenya (2009) African Commission on Human and Peoples' Rights. Comm 276/2003 (ACHPR), para 212.

[388] Ibid para 291.

[389] Ibid para 131.

[390] African Commission on Human and Peoples' Rights v Republic of Kenya (2017) African Court on Human and Peoples' Rights. Application No 006/2012 (ACtHPR), para 210.

[391] Diergarten (2019), p. 45.

[392] Committee on the Rights of Indigenous Peoples (2012) p. 6.

[393] Castellino and Doyle (2018), p. 36.

with the right to equality and non-discrimination of human rights law. In the following sections, FPIC's internal dimension will be explored in Indigenous and general human rights law.

2.4.2.3.1 Indigenous Law

While the UN Expert Mechanism on the Rights of Indigenous Peoples incidentally noted in 2011 that Indigenous women have the 'right to participate in both internal and external decision-making processes and institutions',[394] gender remains at the periphery of the sub-field of Indigenous law. In the work of earlier Special Rapporteurs on the Human Rights of Indigenous Peoples, a consistent gender angle was lacking. While recognizing the particular vulnerability of women and children, they failed to explore 'how gender and [Indigenous] status intersect'.[395] Only more recently have Special Rapporteurs examined the situation of Indigenous women.[396]

According to ILO C 169, the governments shall 'consult the peoples concerned, through appropriate procedures and in particular through their representative institutions'[397] in the application of the Convention. Moreover, Indigenous peoples have the right to their customs and institutions.[398] The ILO Committee has affirmed that the 'principle of representativity is a vital component of the obligation of consultation'.[399] Therefore, the consultation procedure has to be designed together with the customary institutions representing the Indigenous community. However, the right to self-determined decision-making is limited by the criterion of compatibility with 'fundamental rights defined by the national legal system and with internationally recognized human rights'.[400] Indigenous peoples' institutional autonomy is limited by the requirement that it must comply with national and international law.[401] If women are not part of customary institutions, the ILO deems it necessary to go

[394] HRC (2011) Final report of the study on Indigenous peoples and the right to participate in decision-making, report of the Expert Mechanism on the Rights of Indigenous Peoples, UN Doc A/HRC/18/42, para 36.

[395] Banda and Chinkin (2004) p. 16.

[396] HRC (2015) Report of the Special Rapporteur on the Rights of Indigenous Peoples, Victoria Tauli Corpuz, UN Doc A/HRC/30/41.

[397] Convention (No 169) concerning Indigenous and Tribal Peoples in Independent Countries (adopted 27 Jun 1989, entered into force 5 Sep 1991), art 6(1)(a).

[398] Ibid art 8(2).

[399] Report of the Committee set up to examine the representation alleging non-observance by Ecuador of the Indigenous and Tribal Peoples Convention, 1989 (No. 169), made under article 24 of the ILO Constitution of the ILO Constitution by the Confederación Ecuatoriana de Organizaciones Sindicales Libres (CEOSL) (2001), para 44; see also Tomaselli (2020), p. 132.

[400] Convention (No 169) concerning Indigenous and Tribal Peoples in Independent Countries (adopted 27 Jun 1989, entered into force 5 Sep 1991), art 8(2).

[401] Xanthaki (2019), p. 296.

beyond those institutions to ensure their participation:[402] '[Indigenous] customs cannot be justified if these are in violation of international human rights'.[403]

The UNDRIP contains very few references to women, and its language is largely gender-neutral.[404] The participation of women is not mandated in the context of FPIC, and it has been criticized that women are characterized as a vulnerable group, along with children and disabled persons.[405] Other authors object to the lack of 'explicit protection against intragroup oppression within [Indigenous] communities'[406] and 'consideration [...] given to the question of the capacity of Indigenous women for economic and political empowerment, given their limited opportunities to participate in decision-making'.[407]

The only indirect reference to the institutional autonomy of a group and the human rights of women is art 34 UNDRIP. It grants Indigenous peoples the right to their own institutions, juridical systems, and customs. Art 34 is seen as the expression of the Indigenous right to self-determination in conjunction with the right to cultural autonomy.[408] Indigenous institutions and laws may only be restricted by international law. They must be 'in accordance with international human rights standards'.[409] Even though the priority of Indigenous law lies in the protection of vulnerable groups, this provision may be interpreted as prioritizing (individual) international human rights over Indigenous laws and institutions.[410] It thus acts as limiting the autonomy of Indigenous peoples.[411] Yet, limitations to the rights of Indigenous peoples must be 'non-discriminatory and strictly necessary solely for the purpose of securing due recognition and respect for the rights and freedoms of others and for meeting the just and most compelling requirements of a democratic society'.[412] Together with art 44, according to which all rights of the UNDRIP apply to both men and women, this indicates that women's human rights may potentially trump the Indigenous right to culture and self-determination.[413] Still, also the silence of the UN Expert Mechanism on women's right to FPIC is striking.[414]

[402] International Labour Office (2013) Handbook for ILO tripartite constituents: Understanding the Indigenous and Tribal Peoples' Convention, 1989 (No. 169), p. 14.

[403] Ibid p. 3.

[404] See also Gunn (2019), p. 57.

[405] Iorns (1993).

[406] Kuokkanen (2016), p. 141.

[407] Davis (2008), p. 146.

[408] Xanthaki (2019), p. 294.

[409] United Nations Declaration on the Rights of Indigenous Peoples (2007), arts 34, 46(2).

[410] Xanthaki (2019), p. 296.

[411] Committee on the Rights of Indigenous Peoples (2012), p. 3.

[412] United Nations Declaration on the Rights of Indigenous Peoples (2007), art 46(2).

[413] Ibid art 44.

[414] HRC (10 Aug 2018) Free, prior and informed consent: A human rights-based approach. Study of the Expert Mechanism on the Rights of Indigenous Peoples, UN Doc A/HRC/39/62, para 23.

2.4.2.3.2 General Human Rights Law

The relevant human rights treaties—ICCPR, ICESCR, and CERD—are equally formulated in a gender-neutral way.[415] However, the treaty bodies tend to reject aspects of culture not compatible with gender equality. General Comment 28 of the Human Rights Committee clarifies that art 27 ICCPR does not authorize any violations of the human rights of women and calls upon states 'to report any legislation or administrative practices related to membership in a minority community that might constitute an infringement of the equal rights of women'.[416]

The CERD Committee urges state parties 'to take into account the traditions and cultural characteristics of each people'[417] in the development of FPIC procedures. However, it also explicitly recommends ensuring the participation of Indigenous women in the 'decision-making processes, particularly in prior consultation processes'.[418]

According to the CEDAW, states shall 'modify the social and cultural patterns [. . .] with a view to achieving the elimination of prejudices and customary and all other practices which are based on the inferiority or the superiority of either of the sexes or on stereotyped roles for men and women'.[419] The CEDAW Committee, in its Concluding Observations, did not address the issue of institutional autonomy. However, it demanded states to respect the FPIC of Indigenous, local, minority, and rural women.[420] More recently, it also called upon states to recognize the right of Indigenous women and girls to FPIC 'in and through their own representative institutions'.[421] In that respect, it seems to have departed from its critical stance towards customary institutions and acknowledges both the right to FPIC of women and the institutional autonomy of communities.[422]

The VGGT also have a strong emphasis on inclusive decision-making. The FPIC of Indigenous peoples shall be obtained 'through their own representative

415 Banda and Chinkin (2004) p. 8.

416 HRC (2000) CCPR general comment No 28: Article 3 (the equality of rights between men and women), UN Doc CCPR/C/21/Rev.1/Add.10, para 32; see also ECOSOC (21 Dec 2009) General comment No 21, UN Doc E/C.12/GC/21, para 25.

417 UN Committee on the Elimination of Racial Discrimination (2018) Concluding observations on the combined twenty-second and twenty-third periodic reports of Peru, UN Doc CERD/C/PER/CO/22–23, para 21(b); UN Committee on the Elimination of Racial Discrimination (2019) Concluding observations on the combined sixth to eight periodic reports of Honduras, UN Doc CERD/C/HND/CO/6–8, para 19(a).

418 UN Committee on the Elimination of Racial Discrimination (2019) Concluding observations on the combined sixth to eight periodic reports of Honduras, UN Doc CERD/C/HND/CO/6–8, para 37.

419 Convention on the Elimination of all Forms of Discrimination against Women (adopted 18 Dec 1979, entered into force 3 Sep 1981), art 5.

420 See Sects. 2.4.2.1.2 and 2.4.2.2.2.

421 UN Committee on the Elimination of Discrimination Against Women (31 Oct 2022) General recommendation No. 39 (2022) on the rights of Indigenous women and girls, CEDAW/C/GC/39, para 6.

422 See also Engle Merry (2003), p. 60.

institutions'.[423] However, in the development of policies, laws, and procedures, states shall ensure 'that both men and women are included from the outset'.[424] Moreover, the VGGT call upon states to ensure that women and girls have equal tenure rights and access to land, fisheries, and forests.[425] All members of a community, including women, shall participate in decisions relating to their tenure systems.[426]

In the regional human rights systems, the reconciliation of gender and customary decision-making has barely been addressed. The Inter-American jurisprudence stresses that consultations shall be in accordance with the 'customs and traditions'[427] of the Indigenous or tribal community and 'through culturally appropriate procedures'.[428] In the Sarayaku case, the IACtHR criticized that the consultation process did not respect the 'form of political organization'[429] of the community.[430] More recently, the IACHR has recognized the key role of women in the realization of the Indigenous right to self-determination and their vulnerability to development projects.[431] It calls upon ensuring that women can participate in internal decision-making processes in adequate ways.[432] Yet, the recommendations on FPIC only emphasize the respect for community protocols and the institutional autonomy of communities while remaining silent with respect to the FPIC of Indigenous women.[433]

The ACHPR, in its Endorois decision, similarly called upon obtaining the FPIC of the Endorois in accordance with 'their customs and traditions'.[434]

Hence, the legal documents examined above tend to focus on either women's participation or customary decision-making, while the intersection of gender, culture, and self-determination is rarely addressed. Moreover, none of them provides any suggestions on how potential tensions can be resolved. The former UN Special Rapporteur on the Rights of Indigenous Peoples Tauli Corpuz, therefore, concludes that not enough attention had been paid to the 'nexus between individual and

423 Committee on World Food Security (2012) Voluntary guidelines on the responsible governance of tenure of land, fisheries and forests in the context of national food security, part 3 para 9.9.

424 Ibid part 2 para 5.5.

425 Ibid part 2 para 3.B.4.

426 Ibid part 3 para 9.2.

427 Saramaka People v Suriname (2007) Inter-American Court of Human Rights. IACtHR Series C No 172, para 133.

428 Ibid para 133.

429 Kichwa Indigenous People of Sarayaku v Ecuador (2012) Inter-American Court of Human Rights. IACtHR Series C No 245, para 203.

430 Ibid para 178.

431 IWGIA and Comisión Interamericana de Derechos Humanos (28 Dec 2021), paras 215, 365(17).

432 Ibid para 216.

433 Ibid paras 365(2), 365(12).

434 Centre for Minority Rights Development (Kenya) and Minority Rights Group (on behalf of Endorois welfare council) v Kenya (2009) African Commission on Human and Peoples' Rights. Comm 276/2003 (ACHPR), para 291.

collective rights'.[435] Thereby, she creates a dichotomy between the right to self-determination and autonomy on the one hand and the individual rights of women on the other hand, instead of recognizing the right to self-determination of (Indigenous) women.[436]

2.4.3 *Peasants*

Recently, a new collective legal identity has emerged in human rights law: peasants. In response to the agrarian crisis in the 1970s, farmers' organizations began lobbying for their rights.[437] The recognition of their rights went hand in hand with the growing support for the right to food and the right to development on the international plane.[438] According to Germann, 'linked up with the principle of self-determination, the idea of a fundamental right to food holds out the potential for constituting new political communities'.[439] The following passage will explore the relationship between peasants and the state, their consultation rights, and the nexus between institutional autonomy and gender equality.

2.4.3.1 Peasants, Food Sovereignty, and the State

After 17 years of negotiations, the Human Rights Council adopted the United Nations Declaration on the Rights of Peasants and Other People Working in Rural Areas (UNDROP) in 2018.[440] The farmers' organization La Vía Campesina provided the first draft, and farmers, Indigenous activists, NGOs, and diplomats were involved in the subsequent negotiations. During the negotiations, it was controversial whether *being a farmer*, i.e., an economic activity, could be the foundation for a group identity and collective rights.[441] While La Vía Campesina tried to construct local agriculture as culture to make peasantness a group identity, the final definition stresses the economic connection between peasants and their land. Peasants are defined as

> any person who engages or who seeks to engage alone, or in association with others or as a community, in small-scale agricultural production for subsistence and/or for the market, and

[435] HRC (2015) Report of the Special Rapporteur on the Rights of Indigenous Peoples, Victoria Tauli Corpuz, UN Doc A/HRC/30/41, para 8.

[436] Ibid paras 75, 79(c).

[437] Edelman and James (2011), p. 85.

[438] Raghu (2018), p. 331.

[439] Germann (2009), p. 129.

[440] Claeys and Edelman (2020), p. 1.

[441] Jovanovic (2015), pp. 12ff; see also Errico and Claeys (2020), p. 7.

> who relies significantly [...] on household labor, and who has a special dependency on and attachment to the land.[442]

It includes persons in 'artisanal, small-scale agriculture, crop planting, livestock raising, pastoralism, fishing, forestry, hunting or gathering, and handicraft related to agriculture or a related occupation in a rural area',[443] including their family members, Indigenous peoples and local communities, and hired and seasonal workers.

Peasants have no right to self-determination. Thus, the UNDROP's consultation rights are not derived from the right to self-determination or the right to culture but from the economic significance of the land for rural land users.[444] However, with many Indigenous peoples also being farmers, the social identities (may) overlap.[445] Yet, the implicit focus on class instead of ethnicity may make the framework less appealing to many Indigenous people. Class and ethnicity are grounded in very different premises. While class-based claims build on uniform interests, ethnicity-based claims focus on legitimate diversity.[446] Moreover, the legal protection afforded to peasants lags behind the minority and Indigenous rights framework, making the decision to identify as a peasant (or not) also a matter of strategy.

However, sovereignty still appears as an important buzzword in the debates surrounding the UNDROP: food sovereignty. Many peasant activists and NGOs saw food sovereignty—and particularly its land tenure dimension—as a way of subverting the state's sovereignty and establishing an alternative trade framework.[447] Some states shared that understanding.[448] For that reason, they argued that the language of food sovereignty should not be used in the UNDROP, with sovereignty belonging exclusively to the state.[449] They also objected to granting a right to territory to peasants, as foreseen by earlier drafts. With territory linked to sovereignty in the mind of many states, the terminology had to be dropped.[450] This strongly indicates that food sovereignty differs from sovereignty, and its scope is considerably more limited. Food sovereignty, according to the UNDROP, entails the

---

[442] United Dations Declaration on the Rights of Peasants and other People Working in Rural Areas (2018), art 1(1).

[443] Ibid art 1(2).

[444] Jovanovic, therefore, conclude that peasantness is not qualified marker of identity giving rise to a collective identity (Jovanovic 2015, p. 18); Edelman and James (2011), p. 95; Diergarten (2019), p. 51.

[445] de Sousa Santos (2002), p. 246.

[446] See also Comaroff and Comaroff (1992), pp. 61–62; Ramos (1999), p. 15.

[447] Claeys (2014) From food sovereignty to peasants' rights: An overview of la via campesina's rights-based claims over the last 20 years. https://www.tni.org/en/briefing/food-sovereignty-peasants-rights. Accessed 10 Aug 2023 7; Raghu (2018), pp. 332, 338.

[448] Raghu (2018), p. 332.

[449] Golay (2018), p. 3.

[450] HRC (2013) Draft declaration on the rights of peasants and other people working in rural areas, UN Doc A/HRC/WG.15/1/2, art 4; Montón (2019), p. 43.

right to 'determine their own food and agricultural systems'.[451] It does not include any right to autonomy and only marginally interferes with the governmental prerogatives.[452]

2.4.3.2 From Consent to Consultations

Peasants thus have no right to self-determination. But what kind of consultation or consent rights can be derived from food sovereignty?

During the drafting of the UNDROP, FPIC was discussed in relation to land acquisition and relocations. The first draft granted 'peasants (women and men) the right to reject all kinds of land acquisition and conversion for economic purpose',[453] and the 2013 version stipulated that relocations require FPIC.[454] Following pressure from states, which saw FPIC as only applicable to Indigenous peoples, it was removed from the text.[455]

The UNDROP still recognizes some participation and consultation rights. Derived from the right to food sovereignty, peasants 'have the right to participate in decision-making processes on food and agricultural policy'.[456] Furthermore, peasants have the right to participate in decisions related to the sharing of benefits from the utilization of plant genetic resources and the definition of priorities and the undertaking of research and development.[457] In the adoption and implementation of policies and legislation, states 'shall consult and cooperate in good faith with [affected] peasants and other people working rural areas'[458] and 'ensure their free, effective, meaningful and informed participation'.[459] Moreover, if states intend to interfere with the rights of peasants to their natural resources, they shall consult in good faith with the affected communities.[460] Thus, the right to food sovereignty only includes a right to participate or be consulted in certain situations but not to consent. Thereby, it is closer to the rights of minorities than those of Indigenous and tribal peoples.

[451] United Dations Declaration on the Rights of Peasants and other People Working in Rural Areas (2018), art 15(4).

[452] See also Golay (2018) p. 4.

[453] La Vía Campesina (2008) Declaration of rights of peasants—women and men, arts 4(9), 4(10).

[454] HRC (2013) Draft declaration on the rights of peasants and other people working in rural areas, UN Doc A/HRC/WG.15/1/2, art 4(5).

[455] Golay (2019), p. 23; Errico and Claeys (2020), p. 19.

[456] United Dations Declaration on the Rights of Peasants and other People Working in Rural Areas (2018), art 15(4).

[457] Ibid arts 19(1)(c), 19(7).

[458] Ibid art 2(3).

[459] Ibid art 2(3).

[460] Ibid art 5(2)(b).

2.4.3.3 Institutional Autonomy, Gender, and Peasantry

Given the presence of many women's rights organizations in the drafting of the UNDROP, women's rights were, from the onset, an important aspect of the Declaration. The title of earlier versions was Declaration on the Rights of Peasants Women and Men.[461] But even the final version contains a much more detailed section on women's rights than the other human rights documents.

The UNDROP references the CEDAW in the preamble.[462] States shall furthermore eliminate all forms of discrimination against peasant women and rural women so that they can benefit from economic, social, political, and cultural development.[463] This also includes the right to 'equal access to use of and management of land and natural resources, and to equal or priority treatment in land and agrarian reform and in land settlement schemes'.[464]

Yet, due to the lack of recognition of cultural rights, the institutional dimension of consultation rights is not among the UNDROP's priorities. It still calls upon states to consult with 'representative institutions'[465] before adopting and implementing administrative and legislative. In light of the gender provisions in the preamble and elsewhere, this indicates that institutions should be both representative and include rural women, even though a stronger focus is on gender equality. However, details are lacking.

2.4.4 *Emerging Understanding*

To summarize, the field of human rights law is characterized by the coexistence of different collective legal identities. The minority protection regime continues to be individualism-centric and does not recognize the right to self-determination.[466] Even though minorities have a right to culture, their consultation rights remain underdeveloped.[467] Moreover, both gender and institutional autonomy continue to be blind spots.

In the sub-field of Indigenous law, the distinction between Indigenous and tribal peoples has become porous. In relation to Indigenous peoples, many documents pay lip service to their right to self-determination. Indigenous peoples as an alone-

---

[461] La Vía Campesina (2008) Declaration of rights of peasants—women and men; Claeys and Edelman (2020), p. 7.

[462] United Dations Declaration on the Rights of Peasants and other People Working in Rural Areas (2018), preamble.

[463] Ibid art 4(1).

[464] Ibid art 4(2)(h).

[465] Ibid art 2(3).

[466] Heinze (1999), p. 40.

[467] Diergarten (2019), p. 39.

standing category are 'closer to peoples in the continuum between minorities and peoples'.[468] FPIC then has a remedial dimension and is not an end in itself but a step towards realizing the Indigenous right to self-determination.[469] Some authors praise the evolution of Indigenous self-determination as an example of the Indigenization of international law.[470] However, the Indigenous right to self-determination, as generally recognized, is a much tamer version of the right to self-determination than envisioned by many Indigenous peoples. The recognition of the sovereignty of Indigenous peoples is usually considered to be off the table and—if the external dimension of self-determination is discussed at all—it is seen as amounting to a right to enter into dialogue with other international actors and to participate in international fora.[471] The creation of the United Nations Permanent Forum on Indigenous Affairs was an essential milestone in this respect, and Indigenous peoples play an increasing role in drafting and negotiating international law, as evidenced by the UNDRIP, the UNDROP, and the Nordic Sami Convention.[472] Yet, their participation frequently depends on the accreditation of their governments, and they do not have the right to consent.[473] Moreover, the UN Expert Mechanism on the Rights of Indigenous Peoples, which reports to the Human Rights Committee, has a very limited mandate.[474] Hence, Indigenous peoples are far from having equal standing as states.

The right to FPIC is most commonly recognized in relation to their land and natural resources, and Indigenous peoples usually only have the right to dissent under exceptional circumstances.

This tendency has been reinforced by the emergence of Indigenous and tribal peoples—or *Indigenous peoples+*—as a single collective identity.[475] Several influential actors in the field of human rights law—like the ILO, the CEDAW Committee, and the African and Inter-American human rights systems—seem to be shifting away from the aboriginality requirement to the so-called 'distinctive connection doctrine'[476]: rights-holders are communities with a special connection to their land.[477] One result of this doctrine is that the right to self-determination, as a

[468] Castellino and Doyle (2018), p. 36.

[469] Petkar (2017) Conceptualizing free, prior and informed consent: Interpreting interpretations of FPIC. Master of Arts MA thesis, Columbia University, p. 108.

[470] Ibid p. 113.

[471] HRC (4 Aug 2021), Efforts to implement the United Nations Declaration on the Rights of Indigenous Peoples: Indigenous peoples and the right to self-determination, UN Doc A/HRC/48/75, paras 16–17.

[472] Tahvanainen (2005), pp. 416–17; Tennberg (2010), p. 267.

[473] Venne (2018), pp. 151ff.

[474] United Nations Human Rights Office of the High Commissioner (2021) Expert Mechanism on the Rights of Indigenous Peoples. www.ohchr.org/en/issues/ipeoples/emrip/pages/emripindex.aspx. Accessed 10 Aug 2023.

[475] Engle (2010), p. 102.

[476] Diergarten (2019), p. 46.

[477] See also Engle (2010), p. 163.

privilege of Indigenous peoples, is often not seen as the legal basis for FPIC. Instead, an understanding has emerged according to which communities whose culture is closely attached to their territories have a right to FPIC.[478] FPIC is then derived from the right to property, which is—im- or explicitly—interpreted in the light of the right to culture.[479] Diergarten even argues that the distinctive connection doctrine has transformed the right to property into a collective right to cultural identity.[480]

Nevertheless, many Indigenous groups have come to see grounding their claims in the right to culture as a promising strategy. According to Engle, 'the focus on the human right to culture [. . .] has functioned to move much of the Indigenous rights discourse to a new terrain and, for the most part, to defer the question of self-determination and autonomy'.[481] This results in the reduced scope of FPIC. For both Indigenous and tribal peoples, the sliding scale approach to FPIC has increasingly been accepted: the graver the potential impact, the more say communities have.[482] A full consent right only exists in the most exceptional circumstances.

Moreover, FPIC's internal dimension, i.e., the question of who from the rights-holding group may provide consent, is also no longer a matter of Indigenous sovereignty. Given the indivisibility of human rights, a compartmentalized approach that views Indigenous self-determination and gender equality as separate human rights issues is not tenable under the human rights logic.[483] In both theory and state practice, this tension translates into the weighing of different rights, namely individual and collective rights. Most states do not see the right to cultural autonomy as absolute.[484] Similarly, many scholars take the positions that in the case of a conflict between the rights of a group and the rights of an individual, the rights of the individual should prevail.[485] Hence, 'in assuming autonomous control over its own internal affairs, the minority group must do so in conformity with international human rights standards'.[486] The state correspondingly has human rights obligations towards both the group and individuals within the group.[487] Other authors are more critical of this approach. Engle argues that the qualification that customs must not

[478] Engle (2011), p. 151.

[479] Doyle argues that subsuming FPIC under the right to property can also be an expression of the right to self-determination (Doyle 2015, p. 172).

[480] Diergarten (2019), p. 48.

[481] Engle (2010), p. 133.

[482] HRC (2009) Report of the Special rapporteur on the Situation of Human Rights and Fundamental Freedoms of Indigenous peoples, James Anaya, UN Doc A/HRC/12/34, para 47; HRC (2011) Final report of the study on Indigenous peoples and the right to participate in decision-making, report of the Expert Mechanism on the Rights of Indigenous Peoples, UN Doc A/HRC/18/42, annex, para 22.

[483] McKay and Benjamin (2010), pp. 159–60.

[484] UNGA (2019) Rights of Indigenous peoples, note by the Secretary-General, UN Doc A/74/149, para 27.

[485] Gilbert (2004), p. 149.

[486] Ibid p. 151.

[487] Ibid p. 161.

violate human rights law is a continuation of the so-called 'repugnancy clause',[488] which served to limit customary law and decision-making during colonialism.[489] Moreover, it does not recognize that Indigenous women also have a right to self-determination and culture, including their institutional autonomy.

Hence, given the tendency to derive FPIC from the rights to culture and property, interferences with the decision-making processes of the collective identity of *Indigenous and tribal peoples* are easier to justify than under the Indigenous self-determination framework.[490] Still, it is striking that the rights of Indigenous women are rarely mentioned in relation to FPIC and decision-making. The women's rights movement has attracted much criticism for mainly reflecting the experiences of Western women and focusing on the right to equality in the public sphere.[491] Since the 1990s, UN organizations have been mainstreaming gender—or, more accurately, women's rights—throughout the system, enhancing the influence of the field of women's human rights on other fields of transnational law. However, gender continues to be in a niche position with respect to collective rights. The absence of a comprehensive gender angle in the fields of minority and Indigenous rights reflects the reluctance of states, NGOs, and Indigenous groups to engage with the issue.[492] Parisi and Corntassel flesh out that, to date, 'both rights movements [women's and Indigenous rights] often require Indigenous women to make trade-offs [. . .] rather than make space for the more fully intersectional frameworks that Indigenous women have been lobbying for'.[493]

Peasants, in contrast, are neither holders of the right to self-determination nor of the right to culture. However, their food sovereignty is recognized, laying the foundation for more limited consultation rights. As the rights of rural and peasant women were a central claim of peasant organizations, the participation of women is well recognized. Simultaneously, given the detachment from the right to culture, the institutional autonomy of peasants is not well protected.

To summarize, the FPICs of the field of human rights law differ from the principle of state consent in international law and claims of parts of the international Indigenous movement. Attaching FPIC to the right to property and culture is evidence of the 'territorial turn'[494] and the 'cultural approach to territory'.[495] These terms refer to the trend toward understanding property as a 'jurisdictional space often materialized

---

[488] The repugnancy clause existed (and continues to exist) in many (former) colonial legal systems. According to it, the customary law had to meet certain minimum standards to be accepted as valid (e.g. Griffiths 1986, p. 7).

[489] Engle Merry (1988), p. 870; Engle (2011), p. 162

[490] Engle (2010), p. 135.

[491] Kuokkanen (2016), p. 136.

[492] Napoleon (2009), p. 235.

[493] Parisi and Corntassel (2007), p. 81.

[494] Bryan (2012), p. 215.

[495] Dulitzky (2010), p. 33.

in terms of rights'.[496] While the culture-property-nexus is very persuasive for a wide range of actors, it also contributed to the decline of self-determination as a political claim. Moreover, it gave rise to an essentialized understanding of cultural identity, which may exclude some groups.[497] It also establishes rights only to that land and natural resources that are critical to a group's culture and have traditionally been used.[498] Moreover, the lack of intersectionality resulted in very limited engagement with FPIC's internal dimension.

The emerging version of FPIC is grounded in 'transnational consensus-building'[499] and the continuous power of states in the field of transnational law.[500] The human right to FPIC is essentially a renegotiated version of Indigenous peoples' sovereignty claims adapted to the logic of transnational human rights law. It questions the assumption that 'the norms [...] generated in the mythical space known as 'the international' [...] are inherently radical and progressive'[501] compared to local understandings of justice.

2.5 FPIC in Transnational Development Law

It has been shown that FPIC has been renegotiated in transnational human rights law. But to what extent did it spill over to other fields of transnational law and did this cause the emergence of even more versions of FPIC? This section explores consultation and consent rights in transnational development law.

Development law is not entirely clear-cut.[502] Instead, it is characterized by 'constant traversal and blurring of conceptual, institutional, and disciplinary distinctions and categories'.[503] In this book, transnational development law will be understood as law that applies to large-scale development projects. It focuses solely on norms applicable in the transnational business context, including three legal sub-fields: (1) the law of development finance, (2) transnational business and human rights regulation, and (3) standards created by major sector-specific multistakeholder platforms and company associations. All these regulatory frameworks are relevant in the context of economic development projects.

The law of development finance is the law created by international financial institutions such as the World Bank, the Inter-American Development Bank, and the Asian Development Bank. As financial institutions, they primarily provide loans to

---

496 Bryan (2012), p. 216.

497 Wainwright and Bryan (2009), p. 155; Dulitzky (2010), pp. 42ff.

498 Dulitzky (2010), p. 47.

499 Engle Merry (2006), p. 19.

500 See also Engle Merry (2005), p. 217.

501 Grewal (2016), p. 40.

502 For an overview see Dann (2013), pp. 1ff.

503 Rittich (2016), p. 826.

states for development projects. The business and human rights frameworks to be explored include, among other things, the UN Guiding Principles on Business and Human Rights (UNGP) and the UN Global Compact. Moreover, I will examine major sector-specific standards like those of the International Council on Mining and Metals (ICMM), the Roundtable on Sustainable Palm Oil (RSPO), and the Forest Stewardship Council (FSC).

Transnational development law is powerful, and its norms permeate many fields, particularly the economic field.[504] The actors creating development law often dispose of considerable economic capital, have a common vision of economic development, and share 'special interest formations [that are] already installed at the heart of development governance'.[505] The market governance paradigm and the corporate social responsibility paradigm play a central role, while human rights are not genuinely part of its logic.[506] Instead, a so-called 'neo-liberal legality'[507] dominates it.

However, with the adoption of the 1987 Brundtland report, it became increasingly recognized that the meaning of development should not solely be determined by the market and states.[508] The idea of Indigenous peoples' rights spilled over from the field of human rights law.[509] 'Ethnodevelopment',[510] 'development with identity',[511] and 'participatory development'[512] became important concepts in this respect. These concepts may not be law in the traditional sense but are a type of 'proto-law'[513] floating around in the field. Due to the pressure from international human rights institutions and activists and because of the lobby work of 'welfarists'[514] within institutions such as the World Bank, it became increasingly recognized that companies are obliged to consult with project-affected communities.[515] Other important actors include non-governmental and international organizations

[504] Bourdieu and Wacquant (1992), p. 98; Trubek et al. (1994), pp. 409–10.

[505] Baxi (2001), p. 1514.

[506] Filer et al. (2020), p. 71.

[507] Rodríguez-Garavito (2010), p. 20.

[508] Engle (2010), p. 191.

[509] ECOSOC (2003) Economic, social and cultural rights: Commentary on the responsibilities of transnational corporations and other business enterprises with regard to human rights, UN Doc E/CN.4/Sub.2/2003/38/Rev.2, para 10(e).

[510] Stavenhagen (2013), pp. 81ff.

[511] Inter-American Development Bank (2006) Operational policy on Indigenous peoples and strategy for Indigenous development, foreword.

[512] Fujita (2013), p. 147.

[513] von Benda-Beckmann (2001), p. 38.

[514] Pahuja (2007), p. 176.

[515] Hale (2005), p. 17; Owen and Kemp (2014), p. 92; Davis (2021), p. 200; see also Weiss (2021).

that put development banks under pressure.[516] Consequently, companies increasingly see FPIC as part of their social license to operate.[517]

Even though actors like the World Bank have consultation standards only for their own projects, these internal standards regularly influence the practice of other companies and development banks.[518] This has contributed to a noteworthy degree of harmonization.[519] Boisson de Chazournes describes this phenomenon as an emulation effect promoting the emergence of a *droit commun*.[520] Similarly, sector-specific multistakeholder platforms regularly have an impact on standards in other sectors.[521]

In the following, it will be explored how FPIC, as an element of the human rights legality, was appropriated and amended to render it compatible with the logic of development law. After exploring the legal identities, the scope of the consultation and consent requirements will be examined, as well as the question of FPIC's institutional autonomy and gender dimension.

2.5.1 *Indigenous Peoples+ as Stakeholders*

For a long time, development law has been reluctant to accommodate human rights, including collective rights. The concept of rights and rights-holders is hard to fit into business logic. Instead, stakeholder engagement is the context in which FPIC is being translated. The following sections explore the legal identities recognized by international financial institutions, business and human rights regulatory frameworks, and sector-specific multistakeholder initiatives.

2.5.1.1 International Financial Institutions

The World Bank and its sister organization, the International Finance Corporation, are particularly powerful actors, yielding considerable influence over economic and development practices. For a long time, they neglected the human rights dimension

[516] Bankwatch Network. Policy engagement delivers for Indigenous peoples. https://bankwatch.org/success-stories/indigenous. Accessed 11 Jul 2023; Office of the High Commissioner for Human Rights. Financial sector: OHCHR and business and human rights. https://www.ohchr.org/en/business-and-human-rights/financial-sector. Accessed 11 Jul 2023.

[517] Goodland (2004), p. 66.

[518] Cariño and Colchester (2010), p. 425; Villela Nunes Antunes (2018) Are multilateral development banks protecting Indigenous peoples? A comparative analysis. MPGI thesis, Escola de Administração de Empresas de São Paulo, p. 31; see also African Development Bank Group (2023) Updated integrated safeguards system, p. 4.

[519] See also Akermark (2005), p. 93; Tomlinson (2019), p. 884.

[520] Boisson de Chazournes (2012), p. 174.

[521] Cariño and Colchester (2010), pp. 431–32.

of the projects they funded.[522] Only more recently, the World Bank has shown a greater commitment to human rights.[523] It was the first international lending institution to introduce safeguards for Indigenous peoples.[524] In the 1980s, after considerable pressure from human rights NGOs, it adopted the Operational Manual Statement 2.34 on 'Tribal People in Bank-Financed Projects'.[525] It was based mainly on ILO C 107's integrationist approach, and Indigenous peoples had no say in the drafting.[526] In 1991, the World Bank replaced it with the Operational Directive 4.20 on Indigenous Peoples and ushered in the 'participation era'.[527] It applied to 'social groups with a social and cultural identity distinct from the dominant society that makes them vulnerable to being disadvantaged in the development process'.[528]

In 1994, the World Bank initiated a revision process of Operational Directive 4.20, amounting to the adoption of Operational Policy 4.10 (OP 4.10) in 2005. During the revision process, consultations with internal and external stakeholders were held.[529] OP 4.10 applied to 'distinct, vulnerable social and cultural groups possessing certain characteristics'.[530] The enumerated characteristics did not include aboriginality but (1) self-identification, (2) a collective attachment to their territories, (3) separate customary institutions from those of the dominant society and culture, and (4) an Indigenous language.[531] OP 4.10's scope of application was thus quite broad, including not only Indigenous peoples but also Indigenous ethnic minorities, Aboriginals, hill tribes, minorities, and tribal groups.[532]

In 2018, OP 4.10 was replaced by the Environmental and Social Framework (ESF). The ESF contains consultation rights applying to 'affected Indigenous Peoples/ Sub-Saharan African Historically Underserved Traditional Local Communities'[533] (IP/SSAHUTLC). Just like the OP 4.10, this terminology means to include '[Indigenous] ethnic minorities, [Aboriginals] hill tribes, vulnerable and marginalized groups, minority nationalities, scheduled tribes, first nations or tribal groups'.[534] The notion of SSAHUTLC was introduced to include communities in countries not recognizing Indigeneity.[535] To identify such groups, the same characteristics as

---

522 Goodland (2004), p. 70

523 van Genugten (2015), p. 5.

524 Kingsbury (1999), p. 324.

525 Akermark (2005), pp. 95–96.

526 Errico (2006), p. 368; Davis (2021), p. 194.

527 Akermark (2005), p. 99.

528 World Bank (1991) Operational directive 4.20, para 3.

529 Errico (2006), p. 371.

530 World Bank (2005, revised April 2013) Operational manual 4.10—Indigenous peoples, para 4.

531 Ibid paras 4(a)–4(d).

532 Barten (2015), p. 9.

533 World Bank (2017) The World Bank environmental and social framework, ESS 7.

534 Ibid ESS 7 para 1.

535 Cabrera Ormaza and Ebert (2019), p. 498.

outlined in OP 4.10 are used.[536] However, the World Bank defines collective attachment to land as requiring 'a physical presence in and economic ties to land and territories'.[537] The group may not meet the criteria if the land is not economically used but only of cultural or spiritual value to the community.[538]

The World Bank's sister organization, the International Finance Corporation, has been even more reluctant to recognize obligations stemming from international human rights law than the World Bank.[539] In 2012, it adopted its revised Performance Standard 7 on Indigenous peoples, which also applies to private entities receiving IFC funding.[540] It only mentions Indigenous peoples, but the International Finance Corporation adopts the same broad understanding of Indigenous peoples as the World Bank.[541] The Performance Standards also contain provisions related to affected or local communities.[542] What is eye-catching in Performance Standard 7 is that FPIC is not grounded in international human rights law.[543] Instead, the macro goal is to alleviate the 'vulnerability' of Indigenous peoples.[544]

Together with nine financial institutions, the International Finance Corporation also adopted the voluntary Equator Principles in 2002 to address development projects' environmental and social risks. They provide guidance for internationally financed projects, project finance advisory services, project-related corporate loans, and bridge loans exceeding ten million USD. They build upon the International Finance Corporation's Performance Standards and address affected communities as a stakeholder group while also recognizing the particular vulnerability of Indigenous peoples.[545] It is up to the finance institution to identify affected Indigenous peoples—based on the national legal framework but also beyond.[546]

The African Development Bank developed new safeguards on land acquisition and vulnerable groups in 2023. More specifically, the Integrated Safeguards System affords specific protection to 'highly vulnerable rural minorities',[547] which may be called Indigenous in some countries. They are defined as rural groups whose culture

---

[536] World Bank (2017) The World Bank environmental and social framework, ESS 7 para 8.

[537] World Bank (2018) Guidance note for borrowers: ESS 7 Indigenous peoples/ Sub-Saharan African historically underserved traditional local communities, p. 3, footnote 6.

[538] See also Cabrera Ormaza and Ebert (2019), p. 498.

[539] van Genugten (2015), p. 5.

[540] Baker (2012), p. 2.

[541] International Finance Corporation (2012) Guidance note 7: Indigenous peoples, p. 3.

[542] International Finance Corporation (2012) Performance standards on environmental and social sustainability, p. i.

[543] Petkar (2017) Conceptualizing free, prior and informed consent: Interpreting interpretations of FPIC. Master of Arts. MA thesis, Columbia University, p. 80.

[544] International Finance Corporation (2012) Performance standard 7: Indigenous peoples, para 1.

[545] Baker (2012), p. 18; Equator Principles Financial Institutions (2020) Equator principles, principle 5.

[546] Equator Principles Financial Institutions (2020) Guidance note on evaluating projects with affected Indigenous peoples, p. 5.

[547] African Development Bank Group (2023) Updated integrated safeguards system, para 65.

and life depend on their and natural resources and whose cultures and quality would be threatened by the deterioration of the aforementioned.[548] This understanding is aligned with that of other international financial institutions. The Integrated Safeguards system furthermore explicitly references the African Charter on Human Peoples Rights.[549] However, it does not frame FPIC as a right. Instead, and under certain conditions, the *principle* of FPIC needs to be implemented.[550]

The Asian Development Bank's approach to Indigenous peoples has strongly evolved in the past years and was informed by the practice of the other lending institutions. While its 1998 Policy on Indigenous Peoples clearly distinguished between Indigenous peoples and other minorities, it has come to accept a broader understanding of Indigeneity in 2009.[551] The characteristics correspond to those of the World Bank and include self-identification, a collective attachment to their territories, separate institutions, and a distinct language.[552] While those characteristics are understood to be cumulative but may be fulfilled in varying degrees, it is mandatory that the community is distinct and vulnerable.[553] This may include Indigenous ethnic minorities, cultural communities, aboriginals, hill tribes, and other groups, making the safeguards applicable beyond the aboriginality criterion.[554]

The European Bank for Development and Reconstruction embraces a similar understanding of Indigenous peoples. The cumulative characteristics of Indigenous peoples include self-determination, a collective attachment to their territory, descent from a population with non-wage subsistence strategies and separate customs, traditions, or laws, separate cultural, economic, social, or political institutions, and a distinct language.[555] Thereby, it is aligned with the practice of other development banks.

The Inter-American Development Bank adopted an Operational Policy on Indigenous Peoples in 2006, which was updated in 2020.[556] While initially addressing Indigenous peoples in the classical sense, the new Environmental and Social Performance Standard (ESPS) 7 uses the common characteristics of self-identification, a collective attachment to the land, customary institutions, and a distinct language that may be fulfilled in varying degrees.[557] ESPS 7 applies to Indigenous peoples whose

548 Ibid footnote 46.

549 Ibid OS 7 para 23.

550 Ibid OS 7 para 35.

551 Asian Development Bank (1998) The Bank's policy on Indigenous peoples, paras 8, 12.

552 Asian Development Bank (2009) Safeguard policy statement, Safeguard Requirements 3 para 6.

553 Asian Development Bank (2013) Indigenous peoples safeguards. A planning and implementation good practice sourcebook: Draft working document, para 31.

554 Asian Development Bank (2009) Safeguard policy statement, Safeguard Requirements 3 para 5.

555 European Bank for Reconstruction and Development (2014) EBRD performance requirement 7: Indigenous peoples, para 3.

556 Inter-American Development Bank (2006) Operational policy on Indigenous peoples and strategy for Indigenous development.

557 Ibid p. 5; Inter-American Development Bank (2020) Environmental and social policy framework, ESPS 7 para 5.

identity is entwined with the land or the natural resources which are affected by a project.[558] It also applies when the link between the land and the community has been destroyed. This understanding is closer to Indigenous peoples+ even though the margin of appreciation in identifying Indigenous peoples is high.

The International Fund for Agricultural Development is often touted as the leading multilateral development bank with regard to the recognition of Indigenous rights. It was the first lending institution to recognize FPIC and the 2022 update of the Policy on Engagement with Indigenous Peoples was elaborated together with Indigenous peoples.[559] Moreover, it introduced an Indigenous Peoples Forum in 2011, has a specific funding program for Indigenous peoples, and adopted specific and timebound indicators for empowering Indigenous peoples.[560] It sticks to the aboriginality criterion in relation to Indigenous peoples.[561] However, its handbook on FPIC applies beyond Indigenous peoples: rights-holders are rural communities and Indigenous peoples.[562] Moreover, it frames FPIC as an operational principle or instrument.[563] Petkar argues that this is not a negation of its status as a right but rather a strategy for affirming its applicability beyond the Indigenous rights catalog.[564] This is supported by the fact that the FPIC of Indigenous peoples is seen as an expression of their right to self-determination.[565] For local communities, the IFAD understands that transnational environmental law, the right to land, standards of public participation and equity, and the right to development provide a foundation for FPIC.[566]

One problem that the safeguards examined above share is that the banks—often taking the national legislation into consideration—determine whether a group is

---

[558] Inter-American Development Bank (2020) Environmental and social policy framework, ESPS 7 para 6.

[559] Petkar (2017) Conceptualizing free, prior and informed consent: Interpreting interpretations of FPIC. Master of Arts. MA thesis, Columbia University, p. 82; International Fund for Agricultural Development (2022) IFAD policy on engagement with Indigenous peoples: 2022 update, p. 1.

[560] International Fund for Agricultural Development (2022) IFAD policy on engagement with Indigenous peoples: 2022 update, pp. 2, 9.

[561] Ibid p. 3.

[562] Ibid p. 7.

[563] International Fund for Agricultural Development (2015) How to do: Seeking free, prior and informed consent in IFAD investment projects, p. 1; International Fund for Agricultural Development (2021) How to do note: Seeking free, prior and informed consent in IFAD investment projects, p. 1.

[564] Petkar (2017) Conceptualizing free, prior and informed consent: Interpreting interpretations of FPIC. Master of Arts. MA thesis, Columbia University, p. 83.

[565] International Fund for Agricultural Development (2022) IFAD policy on engagement with Indigenous peoples: 2022 update, p. 21.

[566] International Fund for Agricultural Development (2021) How to do note: Seeking free, prior and informed consent in IFAD investment projects, p. 26.

Indigenous and whether a project triggers the safeguards for Indigenous peoples.[567] For example, World Bank experts determine whether to apply the ESF and its safeguards for Indigenous peoples and other groups.[568] These experts are often put under pressure by borrowing states to decrease the burden on them.[569] In the past, even in cases where communities met the criteria, the World Bank decided that they were not Indigenous for political reasons and did not oblige the borrower country to respect the safeguards.[570] The non-recognition of Indigenous peoples' self-identification is emblematic of the focus on the sovereignty of states and the negligence of the Indigenous right to self-determination and culture.[571]

2.5.1.2 Business and Human Rights Standards

In the past years, the human rights obligations of companies have increasingly become subject to regulatory attempts on the transnational plane. One example of this is the UN Global Compact, a non-binding corporate social responsibility initiative. In 2013/4, the Global Compact issued a report on Indigenous peoples and FPIC and a reference guide for implementing the UNDRIP. The reference guide refers to and endorses the ILO's understanding of Indigenous and tribal peoples.[572] FPIC may thus be applied to non-Aboriginal communities. Simultaneously, even though the Global Compact references international human rights law, it also repeatedly constructs FPIC as an element of the social license to operate.[573] Thereby, it detaches FPIC from the rights framework.

Moreover, in 2008, the non-binding OECD Guidelines for Multinational Enterprises were adopted. They were amended in 2011 and 2023. They recognize a heightened due diligence obligation for groups like Indigenous peoples and refer to the UNDRIP.[574] Yet, despite calls by civil society organizations, the new version does not include more detailed provisions with respect to Indigenous peoples and

[567] Villela Nunes Antunes (2018) Are multilateral development banks protecting Indigenous peoples? A comparative analysis. MPGI thesis, Escola de Administração de Empresas de São Paulo, p. 39.

[568] World Bank (2017) The World Bank environmental and social framework, ESS 7 para 54.

[569] Güven (2017), p. 497; Cabrera Ormaza and Ebert (2019), p. 486.

[570] Sarfaty (2005), p. 1804; Cabrera Ormaza and Ebert (2019), p. 497.

[571] See also HRC (4 Aug 2021), Efforts to implement the United Nations Declaration on the Rights of Indigenous Peoples: Indigenous peoples and the right to self-determination, UN Doc A/HRC/48/75, para 35.

[572] United Nations Global Compact (2013) A business reference guide: United Nations Declaration on the Rights of Indigenous Peoples, pp. 8–9; OECD (2023) OECD guidelines for multinational enterprises on responsible business conduct, para 72.

[573] See also Petkar (2017) Conceptualizing free, prior and informed consent: Interpreting interpretations of FPIC. Master of Arts. MA thesis, Columbia University, p. 71.

[574] OECD (2023) OECD guidelines for multinational enterprises on responsible business conduct, paras 45, 72.

FPIC but points to existing guidance notes.[575] The OECD Due Diligence Guidance calls upon identifying and appropriately engaging with Indigenous peoples.[576] It also recognizes that stakeholders whose human rights are at stake 'can be referred to as rights-holders'.[577] It does not define Indigenous peoples, though, and refers to both the UNDRIP and the ILO C 169 in a footnote on stakeholder engagement.[578] The Guidance for the extractive sector stresses the importance of self-identification and mentions the characteristics of cultural distinctness, a differing lifestyle, and separate institutions.[579]

The 2011 UN Guiding Principles on Business and Human Rights (UNGP) are another important document. They have been praised for reinforcing the discourse of human rights in relation to business activities.[580] However, they do not specifically address Indigenous peoples or communities and do not reference the UNDRIP. Still, they recognize 'the specific challenges that may be faced by [Indigenous] peoples, women, national or ethnic minorities, religious and linguistic minorities, children, persons with disabilities, and migrant workers and their families'[581] and refer to relevant United Nations instruments.[582] However, they only contain consultation rights of 'stakeholders'[583] and not specifically of Indigenous peoples or other communities.

Hence, even though it would not be far-fetched to assume that the business and human rights regulations overlap strongly with the field of human rights, this does not materialize. Instead, both the UNGP and the OECD Guidelines subsume consultation rights under stakeholder engagement without fully recognizing collectiverights.

[575] E.g. OECD (2023) OECD guidelines for multinational enterprises on responsible business conduct, p. 26 para 45; OECD (2023) Targeted update of the OECD guidelines for multinational enterprises. Public consultation. 10 January 2023—10 February 2023, CEMSOJ's and ENIP's submissions.

[576] OECD (2018) Due diligence guidance for responsible business conduct, p. 38.

[577] Ibid p. 48; see also OECD (2017) OECD due diligence guidance for meaningful stakeholder engagement in the extractive sector, p. 20.

[578] OECD (2018) Due diligence guidance for responsible business conduct, p. 50.

[579] OECD (2017) OECD due diligence guidance for meaningful stakeholder engagement in the extractive sector, p. 94; see also OECD and FAO (2016) OECD-FAO guidance for responsible agricultural supply chains, p. 78.

[580] Owen and Kemp (2014), p. 92.

[581] United Nations Office of the High Commissioner of Human Rights (2011) Guiding principles and human rights: Implementing the United Nations "protect, respect and remedy" framework, pp. 5–6.

[582] Ibid p. 14.

[583] Ibid para 18(b).

2.5.1.3 Sector-Specific Standards

Besides the regulatory attempts examined above, sector-specific standards have been endorsed in many sectors, often in the form of multistakeholder initiatives.

The International Council on Mining and Minerals (ICMM), whose members are mining and metal companies as well as regional and commodities associations, has adopted standards for 'interested and affected stakeholders'[584] and Indigenous peoples. The 2013 statement on Indigenous peoples applies to Indigenous peoples as defined in ILO C 169.[585] However, tribal peoples are separately defined in C 169.[586] Moreover, members may choose to extend their commitment to non-Indigenous peoples when both Indigenous and non-Indigenous groups are affected.[587] This indicates that the ICMM version of FPIC applies to Indigenous peoples in the traditional sense. The ICMM's position statement on Indigenous peoples also does not recognize the Indigenous right to self-determination but stresses the power of the state: states may be involved in determining whether a group is Indigenous and shape the FPIC process.[588]

The Roundtable on Sustainable Palm Oil (RSPO) is another multistakeholder platform and has adopted standards for the sustainable production of palm oil. In 2018, it adopted a revised version of its Principles & Criteria.[589] Moreover, it endorsed updated FPIC guidelines in 2022, which shed light on the Principle and Criteria's FPIC requirement.[590] The Principles & Criteria recognize different stakeholder groups, including communities, smallholders, and workers.[591] Even though they reference the international law on Indigenous peoples and the definition section only includes Indigenous peoples and not communities, FPIC also applies to *communities*:[592] 'FPIC is the right of Indigenous peoples, local communities, and other

[584] International Council on Mining and Minerals (2020) Mining principles: Performance expectations, principle 4.1.

[585] International Council on Mining and Minerals (2013) Indigenous peoples and mining: Position statement, 1.

[586] Convention (No 169) concerning Indigenous and Tribal Peoples in Independent Countries (adopted 27 Jun 1989, entered into force 5 Sep 1991), art 1(b).

[587] International Council on Mining and Minerals (2013) Indigenous peoples and mining: Position statement, 1.

[588] Ibid 3.

[589] Roundtable on Sustainable Palm Oil (2018) Principles and criteria for the production of sustainable palm oil (2018).

[590] Roundtable on Sustainable Palm Oil (2022) RSPO free, prior and informed consent (FPIC) guide (2022).

[591] Roundtable on Sustainable Palm Oil (2018) Principles and criteria for the production of sustainable palm oil (2018), principles 4, 5, 6.

[592] Ibid Annex 1: Definitions; Annex 3: Key International Laws and Conventions applicable to the production of palm oil.

users to give or withhold their consent to any project affecting their lands, livelihoods and environment'.[593]

The Forest Stewardship Council (FSC) is a multistakeholder framework for sustainable timber production. Since 1994, it recognizes FPIC and, in 2012, it adopted a detailed guidance document for implementing FPIC.[594] Moreover, it introduced a Permanent Indigenous Peoples Committee in 2013, which provides advice to the International Board of Directors, and launched the FSC Indigenous Foundation in 2020.[595]

While the FSC's 2021 FPIC guidelines affirm that 'Indigenous peoples, local communities, and traditional peoples' hold a right to FPIC, under the updated Principle and Criteria, local communities no longer have a right to FPIC.[596] Indigenous peoples, among other things, have a 'historical continuity with pre-colonial and/or pre-settler societies',[597] while local communities do not have to fulfill any other criteria besides living in or adjacent to management unit or living close enough to have a significant impact on the management unit, or whose lifes may be significantly affected by the management unit.[598] A third group is traditional peoples, which are seen as a specific type of local community.[599] They are defined as communities that do not self-identify as Indigenous but with long-established land or natural resource rights.[600] This understanding bears strong resemblance to the concept of tribal peoples in human rights law.[601] If they are treated as Indigenous peoples under national law, the standards on Indigenous peoples apply.[602] If not, they are classified as local communities. Yet, with their right to FPIC being explicitly recognized, it may be assumed that this right exists independent of their recognition by the state.[603]

Most documents explored above thus do not ground FPIC in the right to self-determination or the right to culture. Instead, it is derived from stakeholder participation—sometimes in light of human rights. Often, FPIC is referred to as a

---

[593] Roundtable on Sustainable Palm Oil (2022) RSPO free, prior and informed consent (FPIC) guide (2022), p. 12.

[594] Rombouts (2014), p. 346.

[595] Forest Stewardship Council. Indigenous peoples. https://fsc.org/en/indigenous-peoples. Accessed 12 Jul 2023.

[596] Forest Stewardship Council (2021) FSC guidelines for the implementation of the right to free, prior, and informed consent (FPIC), p. 14; Forest Stewardship Council (2023) FSC principles and criteria for forest stewardship, principle 4.

[597] Forest Stewardship Council (2021) FSC guidelines for the implementation of the right to free, prior, and informed consent (FPIC), p. 23.

[598] Forest Stewardship Council (2023) FSC principles and criteria for forest stewardship, p. 28.

[599] Ibid principle 4.

[600] Ibid p. 33.

[601] See also Forest Stewardship Council (2021) FSC guidelines for the implementation of the right to free, prior, and informed consent (FPIC), p. 61.

[602] Forest Stewardship Council (2023) FSC principles and criteria for forest stewardship, p. 10.

[603] Ibid principle 4.

principle. While a few legal documents still attach FPIC to the collective identity of Indigenous peoples, most of them do not. Instead, the principle of FPIC applies to the stakeholder groups *Indigenous peoples+*.

2.5.2 From Consultation to Consent

But what consequences does this emergence of the broader collective identity of the stakeholder group *Indigenous peoples+* have for the meaning of FPIC? The next sections explore which situations require FPIC or consultations and whether communities may decide not to consent.

2.5.2.1 International Financial Institutions

Similar to the tendencies observed in the field of human rights law, the World Bank counteracts its broad understanding of Indigeneity with a more limited understanding of FPIC. Until recently, it avoided the terminology of FPIC altogether and used the language of 'free, prior and informed consultation'[604] instead. The 2018 Environmental and Social Framework departs from the language of prior consultation and requires FPIC in certain circumstances. Those include projects negatively impacting the customarily owned or used land and natural resources, Indigenous cultural heritage, or that require relocations.[605] FPIC is to be established 'through good faith negotiations'.[606] If FPIC cannot be ascertained, 'the aspects of the project relevant to those affected Indigenous Peoples/ Sub-Saharan African Historically Underserved Traditional Local Communities [. . .] will not be processed further'.[607] While this seems to be in line with the UNDRIP, the World Bank sees FPIC as the borrower's task and not as the right of the community in question.[608] The borrower determines whether a project has a negative impact on a community and not the community.[609]

Another potential concern is the World Bank's understanding that 'FPIC may be achieved even when individuals or groups within or among affected Indigenous Peoples explicitly disagree. In and of itself, such disagreement does not necessarily constitute a veto'.[610] This can contribute to the outvoting of community members

[604] World Bank (2005, revised April 2013) Operational manual 4.10—Indigenous peoples, para 1.

[605] World Bank (2017) The World Bank environmental and social framework, ESS7 para 24.

[606] Ibid ESS7 para 25(c).

[607] Ibid ESS7 para 27.

[608] Ibid ESS7 para 24.

[609] Cabrera Ormaza and Ebert (2019), p. 494.

[610] World Bank (2018) Guidance note for borrowers: ESS 7 Indigenous peoples/ Sub-Saharan African historically underserved traditional local communities, GN 25.6.

who are particularly affected. Moreover, good-faith negotiations require, among other things, the willingness of all parties 'to engage in a process and availability to meet at reasonable times and frequency'.[611] There is, however, a risk that this results in rushed consultations instead of respecting customary ways of decision-making.[612] Ormaza and Ebert, therefore, argue that under the Environmental and Social Framework, FPIC is not understood to be a potential veto right but rather as a form of 'collective support'.[613]

The International Finance Corporation has two standards of participation for Indigenous peoples: *informed consultation and participation* and FPIC.[614] In this respect, it draws a clear line between Indigenous peoples and affected communities. As for affected communities, 'the client will conduct an Informed Consultation and Participation process that will [...] result in the Affected Communities' informed participation'.[615] Recognizing the particular vulnerability of Indigenous peoples, Performance Standard 7 also stresses the importance of the Informed Consultation and Participation process but goes a step further by requiring FPIC under certain circumstances[616]: if the project impacts the land and natural resources of Indigenous peoples; if it requires the relocation of Indigenous peoples; or if it significantly impacts critical cultural heritage.[617] FPIC will be established through 'good faith negotiations'[618] in a mutually accepted process and with evidence of an agreement. FPIC 'builds on and expands the process of informed consultation and participation'[619] but does not necessarily require unanimity. The International Finance Corporation also takes the position that FPIC does not confer veto rights to individuals or sub-groups.[620] Thus, the understanding of consent even lags behind the World Bank's approach by only requiring good faith negotiations but no broad community support.[621]

Moreover, Performance Standard 7—and, for that matter, also the Equator Principles—only apply when the bank in question has already approved the funding. At that point, the government has entered into a contract, and the investor has invested considerable resources in the project.[622] Given the severe consequences

---

[611] Ibid GN 25.3(a).

[612] See also Cabrera Ormaza and Ebert (2019), pp. 494–95.

[613] Ibid p. 494.

[614] International Finance Corporation (2012) Performance standard 7: Indigenous peoples, objectives.

[615] International Finance Corporation (2012) Performance standards on environmental and social sustainability, p. 8.

[616] International Finance Corporation (2012) Performance standard 7: Indigenous peoples, para 2.

[617] Ibid paras 15, 16.

[618] Ibid para 12.

[619] Ibid para 12.

[620] Ibid para 12.

[621] See also Cariño and Colchester (2010), p. 425.

[622] Lehr and Smith (2010) p. 30.

of a community's no, it is unlikely that it would be respected and the project canceled.[623]

In addition, in cases where the location and impacts of a process are not foreseeable, the Guidance Note recommends a 'sequencing of achieving FPIC'.[624] However, this is quite obviously in contrast with the *informed* in FPIC and may lure communities into agreements for which the impacts are still unclear or get them involved too late in the process.[625] When the decision-making process is not advanced enough to have obtained FPIC at the time of project approval, 'the overall principles and process, and criteria for obtaining FPIC, should be agreed on before project approval'.[626] This obviously does not make much sense and highlights the confusion about FPIC's time dimension.

The Equator Principles refer to the International Finance Corporation's Performance Standard 7 with respect to the circumstances that require FPIC.[627] Only where 'special circumstances exist',[628] FPIC becomes obligatory. If no agreement can be reached, the client can still decide to finance the project.[629] Moreover, in the case of projects with a potentially significant impact on affected (non-Indigenous) communities, an 'informed consultation and participation process'[630] suffices. Hence, both the International Finance Corporation and the Equator Principles promote an understanding of FPIC that is actually closer to consultations than to consent. Baker labels it as 'consultation plus'.[631]

Given the African Development Bank's long-time lack of safeguards for Indigenous peoples or local communities, there was also no consent requirement until recently.[632] However, the new Integrated Safeguards Systems is largely aligned with the practice of other development banks: FPIC is required when projects have adverse impacts on the land or natural resources of vulnerable rural communities, for relocations, and for projects impacting the cultural heritage of communities.[633] Similarly, FPIC is understood as a good faith negotiation, which does not require unanimity. Consent is seen as forthcoming when collective support is given through a culturally appropriate process.[634] When FPIC cannot be obtained, the project—or

[623] Baker (2012), p. 21.

[624] International Finance Corporation (2012) Guidance note 7: Indigenous peoples, GN29.

[625] See also Baker (2012), pp. 26–27.

[626] International Finance Corporation (2012) Guidance note 7: Indigenous peoples, GN30.

[627] Equator Principles Financial Institutions (2020) Equator principles, principle 5.

[628] Equator Principles Financial Institutions (2020) Guidance note on evaluating projects with affected indigenous peoples, p. 9.

[629] Ibid p. 13.

[630] Equator Principles Financial Institutions (2020) Equator principles, principle 5.

[631] Baker (2012), p. 28.

[632] African Development Bank Group (2016) p. 22.

[633] African Development Bank Group (2023) Updated integrated safeguards system, OS 7 para 36.

[634] Ibid OS 7 para 39.

aspects of it—will not be processed further.[635] In that sense, the safeguards are more aligned with the World Bank's understanding of FPIC than that of the IFC.

The Asian Development Bank also increasingly recognizes a consent requirement. While 'meaningful consultations'[636] with affected communities and persons are the standard, consent is required for three types of situations: the commercial development of cultural resources and knowledge, physical relocations, and the commercial development of natural resources within customary lands, which would impact the lives of Indigenous peoples.[637] Consent is understood to be the 'expression of broad community support for the project activities'.[638] The lack of consent of some individuals or groups is not irreconcilable with broad community support, though. Moreover, it is the bank that determines the magnitude of a project's impact on the Indigenous peoples as well as their vulnerability.[639]

The European Bank for Development and Reconstruction requires good faith negotiations and informed and inclusive participation for all projects affecting Indigenous peoples.[640] FPIC only needs to be obtained under certain conditions: when a project has a negative impact on Indigenous territories and interferes with livelihoods or cultural, ceremonial, or spiritual uses, entangled with their culture and identity; when it requires their relocation; when it proposes to commercially use their cultural resources, knowledge, innovations, or practices.[641]

The Inter-American Development Bank distinguishes between Indigenous peoples and project-affected people. For project-affected people, the standard is 'meaningful consultations'.[642] In cases where the impact is potentially significant, an 'informed consultation and participation process'[643] is required that results in informed participation. Where Indigenous peoples are affected, an informed consultation and participation process is to be carried out and 'in certain circumstances, the Borrower is required to obtain their FPIC'.[644] These circumstances include three types of situations: an impact on land and natural resources, relocations, and cultural heritage. However, an obligation to obtain consent is only explicitly mentioned for relocations and impacts on the cultural heritage.[645] This suggests that FPIC—

[635] Ibid OS 7 para 40.

[636] Asian Development Bank (2009) Safeguard policy statement, Involuntary Resettlement Safeguard principle 2, Environmental Safeguards principle 5, Indigenous Peoples Safeguards principle 3.

[637] Ibid para 33.

[638] Ibid para 33.

[639] Ibid para 52.

[640] European Bank for Reconstruction and Development (2014) EBRD performance requirement 7: Indigenous peoples, para 29.

[641] Ibid paras 31, 33, 35.

[642] Inter-American Development Bank (2020) Environmental and social policy framework, ESPF 1 paras 32ff.

[643] Ibid ESPF 1 para 34.

[644] Ibid ESPF 1 para 35.

[645] Ibid ESPF 7 paras 19, 20.

including the right to withhold consent—is only implemented for Indigenous peoples and in the most serious situations. In other cases, the consultations just need to be more culturally sensitive and more time intensive than in the case of other communities.[646]

The International Fund for Agricultural Development has different scopes of FPIC based on the group in question: if local communities are concerned, the project needs to have a likely impact on land access and use rights; in the case of Indigenous peoples, it suffices when they live in the project area—independent of the expected impact.[647] As a consequence, Indigenous peoples must already be involved during the project design, while local communities' participation is only required during the project implementation.[648] The International Fund for Agricultural Development understands consent as 'the outcome of the consultation, participation and collective decision-making process'.[649] It has clear FPIC requirements for each step of the project cycle and understands FPIC as a process and not as a yes or no referendum.[650] This participatory approach—together with the Fund's focus on rural development—certainly enhances local ownership of projects and minimizes the risk of dissent. Yet, it remains unclear what happens if a community still wishes to not participate in a project: according to the Fund's guidelines, dissent 'may [in most cases] lead to an adjustment of proposed project activities to communities' rights and priorities'. If dissent persists, this 'should be clearly documented and communicated to IFAD and the borrowing government'.[651]

To summarize, most development banks apply FPIC to *Indigenous peoples+* while at the same time transforming FPIC into a form of broad-based community support.

2.5.2.2 Business and Human Rights Standards

The business and human rights standards are more reluctant to recognize FPIC. Only the UN Global Compact recommends applying FPIC in the following situations: impacts on the land and natural resources, relocations, a significant impact on the cultural heritage, and the use of cultural heritage for commercial purposes.[652] The

---

[646] Ibid ESPF 7 para 13.

[647] International Fund for Agricultural Development (2015) How to do: Seeking free, prior and informed consent in IFAD investment projects, p. 3; International Fund for Agricultural Development (2021) How to do note: Seeking free, prior and informed consent in IFAD investment projects, p. 7; International Fund for Agricultural Development (2022) IFAD policy on engagement with Indigenous peoples: 2022 update, p. 10.

[648] International Fund for Agricultural Development (2021) How to do note: Seeking free, prior and informed consent in IFAD investment projects, pp. 9ff.

[649] Ibid p. 6.

[650] Ibid p. 10.

[651] Ibid p. 10.

[652] Lehr (2014) p. 13.

UN Global Compact's UNDRIP business guide goes a step further, citing the situations enumerated in the UNDRIP.[653] For FPIC to be free, Indigenous peoples must need to feel able to reject the project.[654] It thus goes beyond consultations.

The OECD Guidelines for Multinational Enterprises only mentions stakeholder engagement as a 'key component of the due diligence process'[655] and refers to its guidance notes.[656] The OECD Due Diligence Guidelines also understand FPIC to be a form of stakeholder engagement. Only in some cases, 'stakeholder engagement or consultation is a right in and of itself'.[657] In a footnote, they refer to the UNDRIP's FPIC norms and the ILO C 169's requirement to consult with the objective of reaching an agreement or consent.[658] Thereby, it remains unclear whether the UNDRIP's or the ILO's understanding of FPIC applies. The guidance for the extractive sector mentions FPIC only in relation to Indigenous peoples.[659] It references international instruments and national law as the legal basis for FPIC and stresses that enterprises should also consider local expectations—as long as this does not 'place them in violation of domestic law'.[660] Where a company finds that consent is required but has not been granted, the activity shall not proceed.[661]

The UNGP only call upon companies to meaningfully consult 'with potentially affected groups and other stakeholders, as appropriate to the size of the business enterprise and the nature and context of the operation'.[662] In contexts where consultations are not possible, companies should consider 'reasonable alternatives, such as consulting credible, independent expert resources, including human rights defenders and others from civil society'.[663]

Hence, in the business and human rights standards, seeking the consent of Indigenous peoples or communities remains the exception.

---

[653] United Nations Global Compact (2013) A business reference guide: United Nations Declaration on the Rights of Indigenous Peoples, p. 26.

[654] Lehr (2014) p. 14.

[655] OECD (2023) OECD guidelines for multinational enterprises on responsible business conduct, p. 20 para 28.

[656] Ibid p. 20 para 28, p. 26 para 45.

[657] OECD (2018) Due diligence guidance for responsible business conduct, p. 50.

[658] Ibid footnote 8.

[659] OECD (2017) OECD due diligence guidance for meaningful stakeholder engagement in the extractive sector, pp. 95ff.

[660] Ibid p. 97.

[661] Ibid p. 98; see also OECD, FAO (2016) OECD-FAO guidance for responsible agricultural supply chains, p. 81.

[662] United Nations Office of the High Commissioner of Human Rights (2011) Guiding principles and human rights: Implementing the united nations "protect, respect and remedy" framework, para 18(b).

[663] Ibid p. 20.

2.5.2.3 Sector-Specific Standards

The International Council on Mining and Mineral's mining principles apply to interested and affected stakeholders and mandate consultations in the context of environmental and social risk assessments.[664] Companies should 'work to obtain the consent of Indigenous peoples'[665] in the case of relocations or the disturbance of the land, territories, or cultural heritage with likely significant adverse impacts. The mining principles also acknowledge that, in most countries, Indigenous peoples have no veto rights, so FPIC 'should be regarded as a principle to be respected to the greatest degree possible'.[666] While Indigenous peoples can give or withhold their consent based on a process of good faith negotiation as defined by the International Finance Corporation, the position statement also stipulates that 'consent processes should focus on reaching agreement on the basis for which a project [. . .] should proceed',[667] and that they do not confer a veto right to individuals or subgroups nor do they require unanimous support.[668] If consent is not forthcoming and the government decides to proceed with the project, the companies may determine whether they want to remain involved.[669] Thereby, it endorses a very limited understanding of FPIC. Even though it uses the language of consent, dissent can be overridden and FPIC is constructed to be a principle as opposed to a right.[670] This understanding is closer to *consultation+* than to the human right to FPIC.[671]

According to the Roundtable on Sustainable Palm Oil's Principles & Criteria, FPIC is required in three situations: for the extinction of customary, legal, or use rights, for plantings on local peoples' land, and for compensation when relinquishing land rights.[672] Moreover, FPIC includes 'consultation and discussion in good faith',[673] and communities should understand that they have the right to say no prior to the operations and withhold consent.[674] This includes not only land rights in the plantation area itself but also the buffer zones that oftentimes surround plantation

---

[664] International Council on Mining and Minerals (2020) Mining principles: Performance expectations, principle 4.1.

[665] International Council on Mining and Minerals (2013) Indigenous peoples and mining: Position statement, p. 1; International Council on Mining and Minerals (2020) Mining principles: Performance expectations, principle 3.7.

[666] International Council on Mining and Minerals (2013) Indigenous peoples and mining: Position statement, p. 4.

[667] Ibid commitment 4.

[668] Ibid commitment 4.

[669] Ibid commitment 6.

[670] See also Petkar (2017) Conceptualizing free, prior and informed consent: Interpreting interpretations of FPIC. Master of Arts. MA thesis, Columbia University, p. 57.

[671] See also on earlier ICMM standards: Hanna and Vanclay (2013), p. 151.

[672] Roundtable on Sustainable Palm Oil (2018) Principles and criteria for the production of sustainable palm oil (2018), criteria 4.4, 4.5, 4.7.

[673] Ibid indicator 4.4.2.a.

[674] Ibid indicators 4.4.2.b, 4.5.3.

areas.[675] Moreover, since 2018, members should no longer acquire land that has been expropriated by the government without consent unless the smallholders benefit from agrarian reform or anti-drug programs.[676] Even though it is remarkable that eminent domain alone is no longer seen as sufficient, benefits from agrarian reform seem to be quite broadly applicable and could, therefore, become a common substitute for consent. Yet, the explicit recognition that dissent needs to be respected is noteworthy.

The Forest Stewardship Council's Principles & Criteria equally use the language of consent, without which land rights, traditional knowledge, and intellectual property rights cannot be limited.[677] The FPIC guidelines clarify that FPIC includes the right 'to grant, modify, withhold or withdraw approval'.[678]

As for Indigenous peoples, in principle, they shall retain their customary land rights. The delegation of control over management activities and the utilization of intellectual property rights requires FPIC.[679] To traditional peoples, FPIC applies in the same way.[680] Departing from earlier versions and the FPIC guidance, the updated Principles and Criteria no longer contain an FPIC requirement for local communities.[681] Even though their land and traditional resource rights shall also be upheld, only *engagement* is mandated with respect to activities contributing to development, the identification and mitigation of risks, and grievance mechanisms.[682]

2.5.3 Women as Stakeholders

In the field of development law, there is a tendency to endorse a broad understanding of Indigenous peoples as a stakeholder group in conjunction with an understanding of FPIC that is actually closer to consultations and largely detached from the rights

---

[675] Roundtable on Sustainable Palm Oil (2022) RSPO free, prior and informed consent (FPIC) guide (2022), annex 1.

[676] Roundtable on Sustainable Palm Oil (2018) Principles and criteria for the production of sustainable palm oil (2018), indicator 4.5.7.

[677] Forest Stewardship Council (2023) FSC principles and criteria for forest stewardship, principles 3, 4.

[678] Ibid p. 26.

[679] Ibid principle 3 paras 3.2., 3.6.

[680] Ibid principle 4 paras 4.X., 4.8.

[681] Forest Stewardship Council (2015) FSC principles and criteria for forest stewardship, principle 4 paras 4.2, 4.8; Forest Stewardship Council (2021) FSC guidelines for the implementation of the right to free, prior, and informed consent (FPIC), p. 8, Annex A; Forest Stewardship Council (2023) FSC principles and criteria for forest stewardship, principle 4.

[682] Forest Stewardship Council (2023) FSC principles and criteria for forest stewardship, principle 4 paras 4.4., 4.5., 4.6.

framework. This section explores the consequences of this understanding for the institutional autonomy of communities and women's right to FPIC.

2.5.3.1 International Financial Institutions

In its previous engagement with Indigenous peoples, the World Bank has put little emphasis on the participation of Indigenous women.[683] Today, it recognizes the differing roles of Indigenous men and women.[684] In consultations concerning resettlements, 'women's perspectives are obtained, and their interests factored into all aspects of resettlement planning and implementation'.[685] Simultaneously, the engagement process with Indigenous peoples should be 'culturally appropriate and gender and inter-generally inclusive'.[686] This means that 'representative bodies and organizations and, where appropriate, other community members' are involved and that sufficient time for Indigenous ways of decision-making is provided.[687]

The International Finance Corporation's standards stipulate that Informed Consultation and Participation processes with affected communities shall '(i) capture both men's and women's views, if necessary, through separate forums and engagements, and (ii) reflect men's and women's different concerns and priorities'.[688] However, in relation to Indigenous peoples, clients shall 'involve Indigenous Peoples' representative bodies and organizations [...] as well as members of the Affected Communities of Indigenous Peoples'.[689] The International Finance Corporation thus appears to respect the consultation rights of women while also acknowledging the institutional autonomy of Indigenous peoples.

The Equator Principles provide little insight into FPIC's internal dimension. The Informed Consultation and Participation process will take the 'language preferences of the Affected Communities, their decision-making processes, and the needs of disadvantaged and vulnerable groups'[690] into consideration.

The new safeguards of the African Development Bank pursue a gender-sensitive approach to managing the environmental and social impact of projects.[691] They

683 Davis (2002), pp. 237–38.

684 World Bank (2017) The World Bank environmental and social framework, ESS 7 para 3.

685 Ibid ESS 5 para 18.

686 Ibid ESS 7 para 23.

687 Ibid ESS 7 para 23.

688 International Finance Corporation (2012) Performance standards on environmental and social sustainability, p. 8.

689 International Finance Corporation (2012) Performance standard 7: Indigenous peoples, para 10.

690 Equator Principles Financial Institutions (2020) Equator principles, principle 5.

691 African Development Bank Group (2023) Updated integrated safeguards system, OS 7 para 11.

mandate that 'women's perspectives are obtained in an equitable manner'.[692] Yet, it appears to see women and vulnerable rural communities as separate groups.[693]

The Asian Development Bank mandates that prior and informed consultations should be gender-inclusive and responsive as well as tailored to the needs of particularly vulnerable groups.[694] The borrowers should identify 'appropriate [Indigenous] peoples' representatives, and consultation methods appropriate to the social and cultural values [and] pay special attention to the concerns of [Indigenous] women and youth'.[695] This is also echoed in the Involuntary Settlement Safeguards.[696] The Indigenous Peoples Safeguards, however, do not mention gender in relation to meaningful consultations and FPIC.[697] Consent may be expressed 'through individuals and/or their recognized representatives'.[698] However, a sourcebook clarifies that both representatives should be involved and vulnerable sub-groups, such as women.[699] It is suggested to hold separate meetings with sub-groups to ensure their participation.

For the European Bank for Reconstruction and Development, meaningful consultations mean that clients should involve Indigenous peoples' representative bodies, organizations, and affected individuals.[700] The client should familiarize themselves with Indigenous peoples' customary laws, provide sufficient time for their collective decision-making, and facilitate the expression of their views, concerns, and proposals. However, consultations and participation 'must [also] be inclusive of gender, generational and excluded groups',[701] and the clients should ensure the participation 'by all parts of the community'.[702]

The Inter-American Development Bank stresses that consultations with Indigenous people should be through 'representatives chosen by themselves or any other form of their decision-making structure'.[703] Moreover, consultation protocols shall be respected.[704] In a footnote, it goes on to specify that 'specific spaces to obtain

[692] Ibid OS 5 para 23.

[693] E.g., ibid. OS 7 para 18.

[694] Asian Development Bank (2009) Safeguard policy statement, para 32.

[695] Ibid Indigenous Peoples Safeguard principle 11.

[696] Ibid Involuntary Resettlements Safeguards principle 2.

[697] Ibid Indigenous Peoples Safeguard principle 3.

[698] Ibid Indigenous Peoples Safeguard principle 4.

[699] Asian Development Bank (2013) Indigenous peoples safeguards. A planning and implementation good practice sourcebook: Draft working document, p. 72.

[700] European Bank for Reconstruction and Development (2014) EBRD performance requirement 7: Indigenous peoples, para 23.

[701] Ibid para 23.

[702] Ibid para 21.

[703] Inter-American Development Bank (2020) Environmental and social policy framework, ESFP 7 para 15.

[704] Ibid ESFP 7 para 13.

consent'[705] shall be created for Indigenous and peoples of diverse sexual orientations and gender identities.

The International Fund for Agricultural Development's FPIC guide mandates that Indigenous peoples and communities can conduct 'their own independent and collective discussions and decision-making'.[706] Moreover, traditional and customary protocols shall be respected.[707] At the same time, 'there may be a need to go beyond traditional institutions, for example, to ensure participation of women, youth and people with disabilities in decision-making'.[708] This is reinforced by the recent Policy on Engagement with Indigenous Peoples, which seeks to strengthen women's participation in community-level decision-making and local institutions.[709]

The International Fund for Agricultural Development and the European Bank for Reconstruction and Development's safeguards are thus the ones that most explicitly address the balance between respecting customary decision-making and the rights of women. However, it remains unclear how this would be implemented and whether communities would have a say in establishing gender-sensitive consent processes. Generally, it seems unlikely that international financial institutions would enable truly self-determined decision-making.[710]

2.5.3.2 Business and Human Rights Standards

The business and human rights standards tend to have a stronger focus on women's rights than on respecting the institutional autonomy of communities. According to the UN Global Compact guidelines, the FPIC process 'will likely reflect the community's traditional decision-making approach'[711] and 'ensure that it includes marginalized groups, such as women and youth'.[712] It does not include an obligation to respect customary decision-making structures but just assumes that those will have a role to play in the process. The Business Reference Guide to the UNDRIP, in contrast, calls upon business enterprises to negotiate with the legitimate representa-

[705] Ibid ESFP 7 footnote 165.

[706] International Fund for Agricultural Development (2021) How to do note: Seeking free, prior and informed consent in IFAD investment projects, p. 9.

[707] Ibid p. 10.

[708] Ibid p. 9.

[709] International Fund for Agricultural Development (2022) IFAD policy on engagement with Indigenous peoples: 2022 update, p. 8.

[710] de Moerloose (2020), p. 239.

[711] Lehr (2014) p. 17.

[712] Ibid p. 17.

tives of Indigenous peoples while also ensuring that consultations are inclusive of women and other potentially disenfranchised groups.[713]

The OECD Guidelines on Multinational Enterprises regard women as a vulnerable group—just like Indigenous peoples.[714] The Due Diligence guidance call upon enterprises to take into account that risks affect different groups in different ways and suggest that this can involve 'applying a gender perspective to due diligence'.[715] They also suggest 'supporting women's equal and meaningful participation in consultations'.[716] Given the little engagement with FPIC, the institutional autonomy of communities is overlooked. An exception is the OECD guidance for the extractive sector, which stresses the importance of self-governance in decision-making processes.[717]

Due to the UNGP's lack of engagement with FPIC, the guidance document also only calls upon companies to pay special attention to the human rights impact on particularly vulnerable individuals and groups, 'and bear in mind the different risks that women and men may face'.[718]

Except for the Global Compact's Reference Guide to the UNDRIP, the transnational business and human rights regulations thus have a stronger women's rights than institutional autonomy focus.

2.5.3.3 Sector-Specific Standards

The sector-specific standards generally take a stronger interest in the internal dimension of consultation and consent rights than the documents explored above. The International Council on Mining and Metals mandates that stakeholder consultations should 'be gender-sensitive and inclusive of marginalized and vulnerable groups'.[719] The position statement on Indigenous peoples, in contrast, neither mentions gender nor women. However, the FPIC process shall be 'consistent with their traditional decision-making processes while respecting internationally recognized human rights'.[720]

[713] United Nations Global Compact (2013) A business reference guide: United Nations Declaration on the Rights of Indigenous Peoples, p. 22.

[714] OECD (2011) OECD guidelines for multinational enterprises, para 40.

[715] OECD (2018) Due diligence guidance for responsible business conduct, p. 17.

[716] Ibid p. 41.

[717] OECD (2017) OECD due diligence guidance for meaningful stakeholder engagement in the extractive sector, p. 93.

[718] United Nations Office of the High Commissioner of Human Rights (2011) Guiding principles and human rights: Implementing the United Nations "protect, respect and remedy" framework, p. 20.

[719] International Council on Mining and Minerals (2020) Mining principles: Performance expectations, footnote 2.

[720] International Council on Mining and Minerals (2013) Indigenous peoples and mining: Position statement, p. 1.

The Roundtable on Sustainable Palm Oil's Principles & Criteria stipulate that stakeholders should express their views through their own representative institutions.[721] Companies must provide evidence that 'communities are represented through institutions or representatives of their own choosing'.[722] Moreover, information should be provided 'in appropriate forms and languages'.[723] The FPIC guidance also calls upon companies to enable the development of FPIC protocols and to ensure that nothing undermines 'communities' collective, self-determined and autonomous control and decision-making'.[724] However, companies should also ensure that 'vulnerable, minorities' and gender groups'[725] are consulted and informed as part of the FPIC process. If these groups do not have access to the decision-making process, the companies should 'exercise caution on how inclusivity is approached in the FPIC process'[726]—while also taking cultural sensitivities into consideration in each step of the FPIC process.[727]

The Forest Stewardship Council's guidelines call upon companies to identify representative institutions and make sure that all community members are included.[728] Rights-holders have the right to identify their institutions and representative structures.[729] For Indigenous peoples, this right is also derived from the UNDRIP and the right to self-determination.[730] Simultaneously, it shall be ensured that engagement processes also include women and particularly vulnerable subgroups.[731] The role of women, youth, and elders shall be documented 'keeping in mind UNDRIP [...] and ILO 169'.[732]

While not all the documents examined above call for respecting customary decision-making, some of them do—albeit to varying degrees. The rights of women are taken into consideration to a greater extent than in the field of human rights law, and some of the documents, like the Forest Stewardship Council, even

[721] Roundtable on Sustainable Palm Oil (2018) Principles and criteria for the production of sustainable palm oil (2018), principle 4.5.

[722] Ibid indicator 4.4.5.

[723] Ibid indicator 4.4.4.

[724] Roundtable on Sustainable Palm Oil (2022) RSPO free, prior and informed consent (FPIC) guide (2022), pp. 15–16.

[725] Roundtable on Sustainable Palm Oil (2018) Principles and criteria for the production of sustainable palm oil (2018), indicator 4.4.2.a.

[726] Roundtable on Sustainable Palm Oil (2022) RSPO free, prior and informed consent (FPIC) guide (2022), p. 17.

[727] Ibid p. 26.

[728] Forest Stewardship Council (2012) FSC guidelines for the implementation of the right to free, prior and informed consent, p. 28.

[729] Forest Stewardship Council (2021) FSC guidelines for the implementation of the right to free, prior, and informed consent (FPIC), p. 17.

[730] Ibid p. 31.

[731] Ibid p. 21.

[732] Ibid p. 31.

include suggestions on how to reconcile the institutional autonomy of communities with the participation of women.

2.5.4 Emerging Understanding

In transnational development law, a lack of clarity remains on what exactly FPIC entails. FPIC continues to be a slippery objective, with Indigenous peoples' desire to be respected on the one side and corporations' desire to obtain the social license to operate on the other.[733]

Still, certain tendencies can be identified: the discursive frame, in which FPIC gets embedded, is one that essentially views 'development as a fait accompli'.[734] However, the meaning of development has evolved in the past decades, partly because of the spilling over of human and Indigenous rights. FPIC became attached to the broader framework of 'responsible development'[735] and, more specifically, 'ethnodevelopment'[736] or 'development with identity'[737] that recognizes the cultural rights of certain groups.[738] Cultural rights—as applicable to a broader range of groups—are easier to reconcile with the neoliberal development model.[739]

Even though ethnodevelopment is implicitly grounded in the right to culture, FPIC gets divorced from human rights discourse and is transformed into a principle or practice. It becomes a tool of risk mitigation or an investment.[740] The rationale of the business case for FPIC is that it may minimize conflicts with communities.[741] The UN Global Compact's Business Reference Guide to the UNDRIP highlights this by stressing that '[for] example, for a world-class mining operation, a cost of between $20 million and $30 million per week accrues due to operational disruptions by communities'.[742] Besides the reduction of financial risks, human rights and FPIC

---

[733] Petkar (2017) Conceptualizing free, prior and informed consent: Interpreting interpretations of FPIC. Master of Arts. MA thesis, Columbia University, p. 21.

[734] Baker (2012), p. 4.

[735] Tomlinson (2019), p. 881.

[736] Stavenhagen (2013), pp. 81ff.

[737] Inter-American Development Bank (2006) Operational policy on Indigenous peoples and strategy for Indigenous development, foreword.

[738] See also Hanna and Vanclay (2013), p. 150.

[739] Engle (2011), p. 142.

[740] Kemp and Owen (2017), p. 168; Yaffe (2018), p. 5.

[741] United Nations Global Compact (2013) A business reference guide: United Nations Declaration on the Rights of Indigenous Peoples, p. 7.

[742] Ibid., p. 4.

[743] Baxi (2001), p. 1527.

also have the function of whitewashing large-scale development projects by 'add [ing] dissent and stir'.[743]

However, FPIC can only do so when it is made 'business-friendly'[744] and compatible with the ultimate goal of development.[745] Thereby, FPIC gets detached from Indigeneity, Indigenous sovereignty, and self-determination and gets transformed into 'a process that generally safeguards *all* communities' human rights'.[746] It is no longer a part of the remedial or redistributive justice framework.[747] Pahuja describes this appropriation of human rights by development actors as facilitating the 'juridification and instrumentalization of law and rights to expressions of normative orthodoxy—a negation of the political contestation which the symbolic valence of those concepts may otherwise carry'.[748] Rights are then no longer about doing good but about doing good business.[749] Consent gets transformed into a process whose deficiencies 'can be cured by signing on a dotted line'.[750]

The construction of the legal identity of *Indigenous peoples+* enables this transformation of FPIC into more business-friendly *consultations+*: Thereby, the nodal point *Indigenous peoples+* get close to becoming a moment and transforms the meaning of the element FPIC.[751] The multistakeholder documents thus tend to use the language of FPIC—also thanks to the involvement of NGOs in their drafting—but usually fall short of accepting the consequences of dissent. The same applies to the safeguards of international financial institutions. While the terminology of FPIC is increasingly common, the banks, together with governments, determine whether the safeguards apply. Moreover, most international financial institutions stress that FPIC does not mean that everybody has to agree, replacing actual consent with a form of broad-based community support at best. Generally, consultations+ or a 'negotiated process'[752] are the norm in the field of development law.

In development law, consultation rights and FPIC are particularly seen as relevant with respect to economic activities affecting Indigenous territories. Moreover, in light of the field's logic, the broad understanding and unclarities surrounding FPIC are used as means for further reducing FPIC's scope of application. An evaluation of the IFC's FPIC processes shows that the safeguards for Indigenous peoples are rarely applied: only 29 out of 2116 projects between 2012 and 2020 triggered the

[743] Baxi (2001), p. 1527.

[744] Rodríguez-Garavito (2010), p. 23.

[745] Hale (2005), p. 18; Owen and Kemp (2014), p. 93.

[746] Tomlinson (2019), p. 881.

[747] Petkar (2017) Conceptualizing free, prior and informed consent: Interpreting interpretations of FPIC. Master of Arts. MA thesis, Columbia University, p. 108.

[748] Pahuja (2007), p. 182.

[749] Sarfaty (2007).

[750] Yaffe (2018), p. 9.

[751] Laclau and Mouffe (2001), p. 113.

[752] de Moerloose (2020), p. 240.

application of Performance Standard 7.[753] Projects were classified as either too early or too late for FPIC, the existence of communal title was seen as a hindrance, the land was declared to be too degraded, the Indigenous community as too rich, or the national legal framework was considered to be sufficient.[754]

While not all business standards recognize the importance of respecting customary decision-making, many do. However, the community institutions are usually identified by the state, the company, or the international financial institution in question and are only respected as long as the decision-making processes are compatible with the project timeframes. This is a clear departure from Indigenous sovereignty and the Indigenous right to self-determination under transnational human rights law.[755] Simultaneously, many standards acknowledge the necessity to involve Indigenous and local women. While the economic discourse seems to defuse the necessity of respecting culture in participation processes, the stakeholder approach to consultations makes it easier to take women as a stakeholder group into account. Whether this translates into intersectional participation, which respects both the institutional autonomy of communities and the right to FPIC of women, is another question.

2.6 FPIC in Transnational Environmental Law

Transnational environmental law is another legal sub-field in the global time-space. The *raison d'être* of transnational environmental law is the 'conservation of certain plants, certain animals, certain "ecosystems"'[756] and the protection of the environment is among the 'proper and important objectives governments are put in place to serve'.[757]

The fields of environmental law and development law often overlap. For example, international financial institutions are involved in funding projects with an environmental or climate change focus. In contrast, human rights law and environmental law are legal fields with historically less interaction.[758] Exceptions include the recognition of so-called traditional, Native, or subsistence resource uses in some environmental treaties.[759] However, with the emergence of the notion of sustainable

[753] Salcito (2020), cover page.

[754] Ibid. p. 14.

[755] See also Yaffe (2018), p. 37.

[756] Humphreys and Otomo (2016), p. 798.

[757] Lustig and Kingsbury (2006), p. 407.

[758] Cittadino (2020), p. 15.

[759] For example, the International Convention for the Regulation of Whaling (adopted 24 Sep 1931, entered into force 16 Jan 1935) 155 LNTS 349, art. 3; Agreement on the Conservation of Polar Bears (adopted 15 Nov 1973, entered into force 26 May 1976) 2898 UNTS 243, art III(1)(d); Convention on the Conservation of Migratory Species of Wild Animals (adopted 23 Jun 1979, entered into force 1 Nov 1983) 1651, art III(5)(c).

development, it has been increasingly acknowledged that governments should protect vulnerable groups within their territory from majoritarianism and safeguard their rights.[760] In this respect, consultation rights are particularly relevant: access to natural resources raises questions about whether and how to negotiate with the owners of these resources. However, with many treaties predating these developments, it is not uncommon that human rights were a non-issue during the *travaux préparatoires* and do not appear in the treaty texts—making it at times challenging to accommodate consultation and consent rights.[761] In some cases, like in the Convention on the Prohibition of International Trade in Endangered Species of Wild Fauna and Flora (CITES), community consultations remain underrecognized to date—even though many Indigenous territories are characterized by a high degree of biodiversity and listing decisions can have tangible negative consequences on communities 'by restricting access to income, employment and other resources, such as food, materials and medicines'.[762]

FPIC is often discussed with respect to protected area creation and management in the context of so-called 'people in the parks'[763] conflicts: Communities get evicted for the creation of protected areas.[764] After the 1968 International Biosphere Conference and the 1972 Stockholm Conference, the states began seeing conservation and development as interconnected.[765] This laid the foundation for the creation of protected areas throughout the Global South, which often did not take the land or natural resource rights of the communities living there into consideration. In response, cross-fertilizations with the field of human rights law occurred.[766]

Today, conservation organizations and states increasingly take the social dimension of conservation into consideration, as evidenced by the strategy of 'voluntary resettlements',[767] requiring consent for interfering with communities' land rights. Moreover, protected area co-management schemes have become popular.[768]

Hence, environmental law has undergone significant changes in the past decades, ranging from the emergence of the rights-based approach to the increased participation of new actors, such as Indigenous rights organizations, NGOs, and international

[760] See, for example, Adebowale et al. (2001).

[761] Disko and Sambo Dorough (2022), p. 492.

[762] Conference of Parties to CITES. Cites and livelihoods, Conf. 16.6 (Rev. CoP18), preamble; Estrada et al. (2022); Recently, the Standing Committee was charged with the development of non-binding guidelines that 'proponent parties may use, as appropriate, in consulting with Indigenous and local communities as part of the consultations that may take place on proposals to amend the Appendices (Conference of Parties to CITES (2022), Decisions of the conference of parties to cites in effect after its 19th meeting, decision 18.31 (Rev. CoP19).

[763] Telesetsky (2017), p. 118.

[764] See also Mombeshora and Le Bel (2009).

[765] Khan (2016), p. 226; Sellheim (2018), p. 80.

[766] Razzaque (2019), p. 197.

[767] Schmidt-Soltau and Brockington (2007), p. 2183.

[768] Khan (2016), p. 226; Sellheim (2018), pp. 82–83.

financial institutions, in negotiating and implementing environmental law.[769] The International Indigenous Peoples Forum on Climate Change played a central and creative role in including reference to human rights and the rights of Indigenous peoples in the Paris Agreement's preamble.[770] Another example is the creation is the Local Communities and Indigenous Peoples Platform under the United Nations Framework Convention for Climate Change (UNFCCC) and the input of the Permanent Forum on Indigenous Issues to the drafting of the operational guidelines for the nomination of World Heritage sites.[771] Moreover, the Permanent Forum has done considerable lobbying work concerning specific listing decisions affecting Indigenous rights.[772] Moreover, the 2022 Global Biodiversity Framework incorporates Indigenous and human rights perspectives to a greater extent than earlier legal documents.[773] International environmental law has also been transnationalized and is now a 'multi-actor governance system that includes international institutions, treaty bodies, non-governmental organizations, the scientific community and the private sector'.[774]

This section explores the accommodation of consultation rights in climate change law, the law of biological diversity protection, and other legal regimes with an environmental dimension such as the law of cultural heritage protection. The legal sources to be examined include only a few environmental law treaties like the Convention on Biological Diversity (CBD) and the Ramsar Convention on the Protection of Wetlands (Ramsar Convention). Other international treaties like the Convention Concerning the Protection of the World Cultural and Natural Heritage (WHC) do not focus exclusively on the environment but operate in part under a very similar 'conservation paradigm'.[775] Many documents related to the environment are so-called soft law.[776]

Firstly, the collective identities recognized in environmental law and their relationship to the state will be examined. Secondly, the impact on the scope of consultations and consent rights will be explored, and, thirdly, the recognition of institutional autonomy and women's consent rights will be discussed.

---

[769] Bosselmann (1997), pp. 11–12; see also Ong (2010); Conference of the Parties to the Convention on Biological Diversity (2022) Recommendations from the United Nations Permanent Forum on Indigenous Issues to the Convention on Biological Diversity, CBD/COP/DEC/15/21.

[770] Suiseeya and Zanotti (2019), p. 53.

[771] Larsen and Buckley (2018), p. 101; Riedel and Bodle (2018) pp. 10ff.

[772] Disko and Sambo Dorough (2022), pp. 504ff.

[773] E.g. Conference of the Parties to the Convention on Biological Diversity (2022) Kunming-Montreal Global Biodiversity Framework, CBD/COP/DEC/15/4, Annex Target 22; see also Suiseeya and Zanotti (2019), p. 40.

[774] UNGA (2018), Gaps in international environmental law and environment-related instruments: Towards a global pact for the environment. Report of the Secretary-General, UN Doc A/73/419, para 77; see also Heyvaert and Etty (2012), p. 4.

[775] Lixinski (2019), pp. 14–15.

[776] Humphreys and Otomo (2016), p. 798.

2.6.1 'Indigenous Peoples and Local Communities' and the State

The sovereignty of states—and particularly the states' sovereignty over natural resources—plays a central role in transnational environmental law.[777] According to the Convention on Biological Diversity, for example, 'states have sovereign rights over their own biological resources'.[778] Similarly, the United Nations Convention on the Law of the Sea affirms the states' sovereignty over the adjacent belt of the sea and the management of marine resources.[779] Environmental law also recognizes the states' right to consent and requires, for example, the prior informed consent of states to actions with an environmental impact on their territories.[780]

Still, already before World War II, environmental law afforded some protection to Indigenous peoples' rights in certain contexts.[781] Indigenous peoples have also advocated for the recognition of their right to self-determination and, among other things, the full protection of their traditional resource rights in environmental law.[782] However, with natural resource management being tied to sovereignty, states were hesitant to recognize the land and natural resource rights of sub-state groups for a long time. Just like in human rights law, the Indigenous peoples (with an s) controversy interfered with the recognition of collective legal identities in environmental law.[783] States were reluctant to use the terminology of peoples for non-state actors, as they feared that this could be interpreted as the recognition of their sovereignty.

Today, several frameworks address Indigenous peoples. The Ramsar Convention framework has been praised for being the first environmental framework to use the

---

[777] Corpuz et al. (2006) p. 79; Marauhn (2007), p. 730; Green and Colgan (2012), p. 494; Nagoya Protocol on access to genetic resources and the fair and equitable sharing of benefits arising from their utilization to the Convention on Biological diversity (adopted 29 Oct 2010, entered into force 12 Oct 2014) 3008 UNTS 1, art 6(1); Laltaika (2022), p. 711.

[778] Convention on Biological Diversity (adopted 6 Jun 1992, entered into force 29 Dec 1993) 1760 UNTS 69, preamble; see also Ekpere (2000), p. 12.

[779] Convention on the Law of the Sea (adopted 10 Dec 1982, entered into force 16 Nov 1994) 1835 UNTS 3, art 2(1).

[780] Convention on the Control of Transboundary Movement of Hazardous Wastes and their Disposal (adopted 22 Mar 1989, entered into force 5 May 1992) 1673 UNTS 126, art 6(4); Cartagena Protocol on Biosafety to the Convention on Biological Diversity (adopted 29 Jan 2000, entered into force 11 Sep 2003) 2226 UNTS 208, art 10(a); Rotterdam Convention on the Prior Informed Consent Procedure for Certain Hazardous Chemicals and Pesticides in International Trade (adopted 10 Sep 1998, entered into force 14 Feb 2004) 2244 UNTS 337, art 10(a).

[781] E.g. International Convention for the Regulation of Whaling (adopted 24 Sep 1931, entered into force 16 Jan 1935), art 3.

[782] Working Group on Indigenous Populations (1993), The Mataatua Declaration on Cultural and Intellectual Property Rights of Indigenous Peoples, UN Doc E/CN.4/Sub.2/AC.4/1993/CRP.5, preamble; Co-ordinating Body of Indigenous Organisations of the Amazon Basin (1994) Coica statement, p. 107.

[783] See also Sect. 2.4.2.1.1.

language of Indigenous peoples in official documents.[784] Moreover, the 2002 Johannesburg Declaration on Sustainable Development reaffirms 'the vital role of [Indigenous] peoples in sustainable development',[785] and the outcome document of the Rio + 20 conference references not only the UNDRIP but also stresses that sustainable development needs to 'enhance the welfare of [Indigenous] peoples and their communities, [as well as] other local and traditional communities and ethnic minorities'.[786] The Agenda 21, the UN program on environment and development, equally mentions Indigenous peoples without recognizing their right to self-determination.[787]

However, a much greater number of environmental law documents law refer°to *Indigenous peoples and local communities* as one collective legal identity.[788] Those include, for instance, the Rio Principles, the Forest Principles, and the Ramsar Convention's manual.[789] The regulatory framework based on the Convention on Biological Diversity avoided the terminology of Indigenous peoples until recently.[790] Only in 2014, at the COP 12 meeting, the terminology of *Indigenous peoples and local communities* was adopted.[791] The Operational Guidelines of UNESCO's Geoparks Program use the terms local communities and Indigenous peoples interchangeably.[792]

Under the Convention on the Trade in Endangered Species of Wild Fauna and Flora (CITES), communities within the state were neglected for a long time. Since the early 2000s, some engagement has taken place with rural communities and their

784 Oviedo and Ali (2018) pp. 8, 17.

785 UN (2002) Johannesburg Declaration on sustainable development, UN Doc A/Conf.199/20, para 25.

786 UNGA (2012) Resolution adopted by the general assembly on 27 July 2012: The future we want, UN Doc A/RES/66/288, paras 49, 58(j); see also paras 43, 71, 131, 229, 238.

787 UN (1992) United Nations conference on environment & development, Rio de Janeiro, Brazil, 3 to 14 june 1992: Agenda 21, s 26.3.a.ii; Bosselmann (1997), p. 30.

788 Socha (2017), p. 3.

789 UNGA (1992) Non-legally binding authoritative statement of principles for a global consensus on the management, conservation and sustainable development of all types of forests, UN Doc A/CONF.151/26 (Vol. III), principle 1(d); UNGA (1992) Report of the Nnited Nations conference on environment and development, UN Doc A/CONF.151/26 (Vol. I), principle 22; Ramsar Convention Secretariat (2010) Participatory skills: Establishing and strengthening local communities' and Indigenous people's participation in the management of wetlands.

790 Convention on Biological Diversity (adopted 6 Jun 1992, entered into force 29 Dec 1993), preamble, art 8(j); Secretariat of the Convention on Biological Diversity (2004) Akwé: Kon voluntary guidelines for the conduct of cultural, environmental and social impact assessments regarding developments proposed to take place on, or which are likely to impact on sacred sites and on lands and waters traditionally occupied or used by Indigenous and local communities, e.g. art 1; Nagoya Protocol on access to genetic resources and the fair and equitable sharing of benefits arising from their utilization to the Convention on Biological Diversity (adopted 29 Oct 2010, entered into force 12 Oct 2014), e.g. art 5(2).

791 Parks et al. (2019), p. 23.

792 UNESCO (2015) Operational guidelines for UNESCO global geoparks, paras 1, 3(v).

use of plants and wildlife.[793] In 2004, the terminology evolved to 'local people'.[794] More recently, the Conference of Parties decided to conduct a survey on the engagement with 'Indigenous peoples and local communities',[795] it invited state parties to engage Indigenous people and local communities in CITES decision-making at the national level, and created a working group on CITES and livelihoods that shall monitor these engagements.[796] This indicates that the CITES framework aligns itself with the terminology commonly used in environmental law.[797]

Climate change law pursues a similar approach in this respect: some documents refer to 'Indigenous peoples and forest-dependent communities',[798] some to 'Indigenous peoples and local communities',[799] and other standards—particularly those overlapping with the field of development law—apply to Indigenous and tribal peoples.[800] The 2000 model legislation on access to biological resources of the Organization of African Unity, in contrast, mentions farmers and breeders as well as local communities.[801] Hence, there is a tendency to merge Indigenous peoples with other communities.

Socha traces the success of this broader legal identity back to the resistance of states to embrace the concept of Indigenous peoples with its full body of rights, including the right to self-determination.[802] Moreover, it marks a departure from the romanticized image of Indigenous peoples and the recognition that the lifestyle of a group and not necessarily their aboriginality should determine whether they are rightsholders. Additionally, the legal identity facilitates the geographical applicability beyond settler states. It includes groups living in a relationship of interdependence with their environment and whose way of living (and particularly their subsistence farming) contributes to biological diversity.[803] Still, debates about

793 Sellheim (2018), p. 92.

794 Conference of Parties to CITES (2004) Recognition of the benefits of trade in wildlife, Conf. 8.3. (Rev. CoP13), para 1.

795 Conference of Parties to CITES (2019) Engagement of Indigenous peoples and local communities, Rev. CoP 19, decision 18.32.

796 Conference of Parties to CITES (2019) Livelihoods, Rev. CoP19, decisions 18.33, 18.34.

797 See also Conference of Parties to CITES (2022) Decisions of the conference of parties to cites in effect after its 19th meeting, p. 32.

798 UN-REDD Programme (2013) Guidelines on free, prior and informed consent, p. 12.

799 UNFCCC (2011) Report of the Conference of Parties on its sixteenth session, held in Cancún from 29 November to 10 December 2010: Decisions adopted by the Conference of Parties, UN Doc FCCC/CP/2010/7/Add.1, para 4; Paris agreement (adopted 12 Dec 2015, entered into force 4 Nov 2016) UN Doc FCCC/CP/2015/10/Add.1, 2.

800 Adaptation Fund Board (approved in November 2013, revised in March 2016) Environmental and social policy, para 14; Green Climate Fund (2018) Indigenous peoples policy, s IV(16).

801 Organization of African Unity (2000) African model legislation for the protection of the rights of local communities, farmers and breeders, and for the regulation of access to biological resources, part 1(a), (b).

802 Posey (1997), pp. 256–57; Socha (2017), pp. 104–106.

803 Jonas et al. (2013) p. 26; Socha (2017), p. 112.

whether communities are environmental predators or guardians of nature are ongoing.[804] States often try to entrench their sovereignty by arguing that communities are unwilling or unable to protect the environment. Despite peasant and Indigenous organizations claiming to have a right to self-determination, the field of environmental law does not recognize this right.[805] Instead, *Indigenous peoples and local communities* are a stakeholder group whose privileges are grounded in the right to culture. Moreover, the right to culture tends to get tied to the condition that their culture is environmentally beneficial.

2.6.2 *Participation instead of Consent*

While in human rights and development law, FPIC is mostly debated with respect to land and natural resources, consultation and participation rights appear in different contexts in the field of environmental law: firstly, in the drafting and implementation of policies and legal frameworks, secondly, in the context of traditional resource rights[806] and benefit-sharing, and, thirdly, in the establishment and management of protected areas.[807] Moreover fourthly, climate change projects such as hydroelectric dams or tree plantations may impact Indigenous peoples' land and natural resources.[808] As the regulatory frameworks applicable to these contexts tend to differ, they will be explored separately.

2.6.2.1 Law-Making

The right of non-state groups to participate in law-making is contentious in most legal fields. In environmental law, the *effective participation* of communities in drafting and implementing policies is the norm. According to the 1992 Rio Principles, '[Indigenous] peoples and their communities and other local communities have a vital role in environmental management and developments [...]. States should [...] enable their effective participation in the achievement of sustainable development'.[809]

The Forest Principles state that governments should provide opportunities for local communities to participate in developing, implementing, and planning forest

[804] Tennant (1994), pp. 16, 41; Engle (2010), pp. 169ff.

[805] Posey (1997), p. 249.

[806] See also Posey and Dutfield (1996).

[807] Cittadino (2020), pp. 264ff.

[808] HRC (2017) Report of the Special Rapporteur on the Rights of Indigenous Peoples, UN Doc A/HRC/36/46, para 92.

[809] UNGA (1992) Report of the United Nations conference on environment and development, UN Doc A/CONF.151/26 (Vol. I), principle 22.

policies.[810] National forest policies shall recognize and support the rights of '[Indigenous] peoples, their communities and other communities and forest dwellers'[811] to ensure that they can achieve and maintain their cultural identity.

The UN Convention to Combat Desertification (UNCCD) mandates the participation of local communities in the implementation of the Convention.[812] It also encourages policies of decentralization, devolving management and decision-making responsibilities to local communities, and the establishment of local structures.[813] In the framework of the WHC, 'the effective, inclusive, and equitable participation of the communities, Indigenous peoples and other stakeholders concerned with the property'[814] should be ensured with respect to legislation, policies, and strategies affecting World Heritage sites.

Indigenous organizations have been heavily involved in the 2022 COP 15 meeting in Montreal, where the Kunming-Montreal Global Biodiversity Framework was adopted.[815] Governments shall ensure the participation of Indigenous peoples and local communities in the implementation of the framework.[816] Moreover, it calls for 'their full and effective participation in decision-making, in accordance with relevant national legislations, international instruments, including the United Nations Declaration on the Rights of Indigenous Peoples, and human rights law'.[817]

However, when mechanisms are foreseen for ensuring the participation of Indigenous peoples and local communities in the drafting and implementation of environmental law, these have a consultative function at best—like the Local Communities and Indigenous Peoples Platform of the United Nations Framework Convention on Climate Change.[818] In the framework of the Convention on Biological Diversity (CBD), non-state actors, including Indigenous groups and NGOs, only

[810] UNGA (1992) Non-legally binding authoritative statement of principles for a global consensus on the management, conservation and sustainable development of all types of forests, UN Doc A/CONF.151/26 (Vol. III), s 2(d).

[811] Ibid s 5(a).

[812] United Nations Convention to Combat Desertification in those Countries experiencing serious Drought and/or Desertification, particularly in Africa (adopted 14 Oct 1994, entered into force 26 Dec 1996) 1954 UNTS 3, art 3(a).

[813] Ibid art 8(3)(c).

[814] UNESCO (2019) Operational guidelines for the implementation of the World Heritage Convention, UN Doc WHC.19/01, para 119.

[815] Cultural Survival (2022) Securing Indigenous peoples' rights and protecting biodiversity at COP 15. https://www.culturalsurvival.org/news/securing-indigenous-peoples-rights-and-protecting-biodiversity-cop15. Accessed 13 Jul 2023; ESCR-Net (2023) Collective advocacy on biodiversity and land rights—cop 15 outcomes. https://www.escr-net.org/news/2023/collective-advocacy-biodiversity-and-land-rights-cop-15-outcomes. Accessed 13 Jul 2023.

[816] Conference of the Parties to the Convention on Biological Diversity (2022) Kunming-Montreal Global Biodiversity Framework, CBD/COP/DEC/15/4, para 6.

[817] Ibid Annex sec C para 7(a).

[818] Riedel and Bodle (2018) pp. 10ff; see also Larsen and Buckley (2018), p. 90; Sellheim (2018), p. 77; Cittadino (2020), pp. 57–58.

have observer status.[819] Moreover, in 2001, due to the member states' objections, the World Heritage Committee did not approve the establishment of a World Heritage Indigenous Peoples Council of Experts within the UNESCO system and also denied funding for future meetings.[820] However, in 2017, the International Indigenous Peoples' Forum on World Heritage was created in Krakow to engage the World Heritage Committee as a standing body.[821] Yet, it does not have a formal advisory function, does not receive any funding, and only has the status of an NGO.[822] Indigenous peoples also have problems getting heard by the Committee.[823] Similarly, the proposal to create a Rural Communities Committee under the CITES framework was dismissed by the state parties.[824]

Hence, with respect to law-making, transparency and participation or consultation and not FPIC are the norm, even though some progress has been made in the past years.[825]

2.6.2.2 Traditional Resource Rights

Consent plays a more prominent role in relation to the traditional resource rights of communities. The Convention on Biological Diversity (CBD) is the key transnational framework with respect to traditional resource rights. Its art 8(j) has subsequently been concretized by the binding Nagoya Protocol on Access to Genetic Resources and the Fair and Equitable Sharing of Benefits Arising from their Utilization to the Convention on Biological Diversity and soft law, notably the Mo' otz Kuxtal Voluntary Guidelines on Prior and Informed Consent, the Rutzolijirisaxik Voluntary Guidelines for the Repatriation of Traditional Knowledge and the Kunming-Montreal Global Biodiversity Framework.

While the CBD does not explicitly mention FPIC, it calls upon states to

> respect, preserve and maintain knowledge, innovations, and practices of Indigenous and local communities relevant for the conservation and sustainable use of biological diversity

---

[819] See also Suiseeya and Zanotti (2019), p. 39; Cittadino (2020), pp. 57–58.

[820] Meskell (2013), p. 165; Coombe and Baird (2015), p. 340.

[821] World Heritage Committee (2017) Decisions adopted during the 41st session of the World Heritage Committee (krakow, 2017), WHC/17/41.COM/18, para 41; UNESCO (2018) Indigenous peoples launch forum on World Heritage. https://whc.unesco.org/en/news/1841. Accessed 17 Jul 2023.

[822] Disko and Sambo Dorough (2022), p. 501; IWGIA et al. (2022), para 20; Stimac (2022), p. 271.

[823] Disko and Sambo Dorough (2022), pp. 501, 516.

[824] Sellheim (2018), p. 95; Conference of Parties to CITES (2022) Strategic matters. Participatory mechanisms for rural communities in CITES, CoP 19 Doc. 15 (Rev.1), para 2.

[825] See also Aarhus Convention on Access to Information, Public Participation in Decision-Making and Access to Justice in Environmental Matters (adopted 25 Jun 1998, entered into force 30 Oct 2001) 2161 UNTS 447, preamble.

and promote their wider application with the approval and involvement of the holders of such knowledge.[826]

In 2001, the Working Group on art 8(j) interpreted the provision as including the FPIC of Indigenous peoples.[827]

In 2011, the Nagoya Protocol on Access to Genetic Resources and the Fair and Equitable Sharing of Benefits Arising from their Utilization to the Convention on Biological Diversity entered into force, noting the UNDRIP.[828] It also contains a provision protecting Indigenous knowledge and genetic resources: states shall take measures 'as appropriate, with the aim of ensuring that the prior informed consent or approval and involvement of [Indigenous] and local communities for access to genetic resources where they have the established right to grant access to such resources'.[829] Moreover, 'genetic resources that are held by [Indigenous] and local communities [should be] accessed with the prior and informed consent or approval and involvement of these [Indigenous] and local communities'.[830] States shall furthermore ensure that traditional knowledge associated with genetic resources 'has been accessed in accordance with prior informed consent or approval and involvement of [Indigenous] and local communities [...] as required by domestic access and benefit-sharing legislation or regulatory requirements [...]'.[831] According to the CBD's 2016 Mo' otz Kuxtal Voluntary Guidelines on Prior and Informed Consent, access to traditional knowledge requires 'prior and informed consent', 'free, prior and informed consent,' or 'approval and involvement' depending on the national circumstances.[832] FPIC is thus not always mandated, but states can determine whether its application is appropriate, leaving them a considerable margin of appreciation.[833]

Moreover, the scope of (F)PIC is limited: it only applies to traditional knowledge for which Indigenous and local communities 'have the established right to grant

---

[826] Convention on Biological Diversity (adopted 6 Jun 1992, entered into force 29 Dec 1993), art 8 (j).

[827] UNEP (2001) Background to the draft guidelines or recommendation for the conduct of cultural, environmental and social impact assessments regarding developments proposes to take place on sacred sites and on lands and waters occupied or used by Indigenous and local communities, UN Doc UNEP/CBD/WG8J/2/6/Add.1, para 12.

[828] Nagoya Protocol on access to genetic resources and the fair and equitable sharing of benefits arising from their utilization to the Convention on Biological Diversity (adopted 29 Oct 2010, entered into force 12 Oct 2014), preamble.

[829] Ibid art 6(2).

[830] Ibid art 7.

[831] Ibid art 16(1).

[832] Secretariat of the Convention on Biological Diversity (2019) Mo' otz Kuxtal Voluntary Guidelines to ensure the prior and informed consent, para 6.

[833] Nagoya Protocol on access to genetic resources and the fair and equitable sharing of benefits arising from their utilization to the Convention on Biological Diversity (adopted 29 Oct 2010, entered into force 12 Oct 2014), arts 6(2), 7, 16(1); Razzaque (2019), p. 209; for a differing opination see Morgera et al. (2015), p. 176.

access to such resources',[834] PIC must only be sought for traditional knowledge currently held by Indigenous and local communities,[835] and its application in the context of benefit-sharing depends on whether national legislation is in place.[836] Consequently, it has been argued that the FPIC as part of the Nagoya Protocol is not derived from the Indigenous right to self-determination but closer to the right to cultural identity as enshrined in the two Covenants.[837] Particularly the terminology of *approval and involvement* is weaker than that of PIC/FPIC.[838]

The terminology used in the Rutzolijirisaxik Voluntary Guidelines for the Repatriation of Traditional Knowledge concurs with that of the earlier documents. It stresses that 'whenever possible'[839] Indigenous peoples and local communities should be entitled to repatriation of their knowledge. Repatriation 'may include efforts to restore Indigenous peoples' and local communities' governance of their traditional knowledge, and may involve prior and informed consent, free prior and informed consent or approval and involvement, as appropriate'.[840]

In line with that, the 2022 Kunming-Montreal Global Biodiversity Framework stipulates that 'traditional knowledge, innovations, practices and technologies of Indigenous peoples and local communities should only be accessed with their free, prior and informed consent, in accordance with national legislation'.[841]

According to the Model Law of the Organization of African Unity (OAU), 'any access to biological resources, knowledge and or technologies of local communities shall be subject to the written prior informed consent'[842] of both the national agency

[834] Nagoya Protocol on access to genetic resources and the fair and equitable sharing of benefits arising from their utilization to the Convention on Biological Diversity (adopted 29 Oct 2010, entered into force 12 Oct 2014), art 6(2).

[835] Ibid art 7; Morgera et al. argue that threshold for triggering the PIC requirement is lower than in the case of art 6(2) as they do not have to have 'an established right' (Morgera et al. 2015, p. 172).

[836] Convention on Biological Diversity (adopted 6 Jun 1992, entered into force 29 Dec 1993), art 8 (j); Secretariat of the Convention on Biological Diversity (2002) Bonn Guidelines on access to genetic resources and fair and equitable sharing of the benefits arising our of their utilization, art 26 (d); Nagoya Protocol on access to genetic resources and the fair and equitable sharing of benefits arising from their utilization to the Convention on Biological Diversity (adopted 29 Oct 2010, entered into force 12 Oct 2014), art 5(5).

[837] Secretariat of the Convention on Biological Diversity (2011) Tkarihwaié:Ri: Code of ethical conduct to ensure respect for the cultural and intellectual heritage of Indigenous and local communities relevant to the conservation and use of biological diversity, para 11; Morgera et al. (2015), p. 171; Razzaque (2019), p. 209.

[838] Richardson (2009), p. 355; Morgera et al. (2015), p. 152; Parks et al. (2019), p. 25.

[839] Secretariat of the Convention on Biological Diversity (2019) The Rutzolijirisaxik Voluntary Guidelines for the repatriation of traditional knowledge, para 11(a).

[840] Ibid para 11(k).

[841] Conference of the Parties to the Convention on Biological Diversity (2022) Kunming-Montreal Global Biodiversity Framework, CBD/COP/DEC/15/4, Annex Target 21.

[842] Organization of African Unity (2000) African model legislation for the protection of the rights of local communities, farmers and breeders, and for the regulation of access to biological resources, para 5(1).

and the concerned local communities.[843] Without consent, the access is invalid, indicating that consent is indeed mandatory.[844]

With the exception of the OAU Model Law, FPIC thus remains a privilege to be granted by states in recognition of the cultural rights of certain groups. It is thereby detached from sovereignty and self-determination.

2.6.2.3 People in the Parks

Indigenous consent is also a major issue in relation to the creation and management of national parks and territories of particular ecological importance, such as wetlands,[845] world heritage sites,[846] biosphere reserves,[847] geoparks,[848] and marine protected areas.[849] According to estimations, half of the world's protected areas were once inhabited by Indigenous peoples.[850] Yet many, if not most, were designated without the consent of the people who owned and used them. As a result, Indigenous peoples lost access to their territories and livelihood sources.[851] Various actors involved in conservation, such as the International Union for Conservation of Nature and the World Wildlife Fund, have come to recognize the right to FPIC.[852]

However, hard law obligations are still lacking. The Convention on Biological Diversity (CBD) encourages the creation of *in situ* protected areas in forest, coastal and marine, and other areas of high biodiversity value.[853] To date, it has failed to clarify how to reconcile this objective with the customary land and natural resource rights of communities.[854] Both CBD member states and the CBD Secretariat have

---

[843] Ibid para 5(1).

[844] Ibid para 5(2); Ekpere (2000), pp. 18–19.

[845] Under the Convention on Wetlands of International Importance especially as Waterfowl Habitat (adopted 2 Feb 1971, entered into force 21 Dec 1975) 996 UNTS 245.

[846] Under the Convention concerning the Protection of the World Cultural and Natural Heritage (adopted 16 Nov 1972, entered into force 17 Dec 1975) 1037 UNTS 151.

[847] Under the UNESCO's Man and the Biosphere Program.

[848] Under the UNESCO's International Geoscience and Geoparks Program.

[849] See also Secretariat of the Convention on Biological Diversity (2012) Quick guide to the Aichi Biodiversity Targets: Protected areas increased and improved, provided in UN Doc COP/10/INF/12/Rev.1.

[850] Beltrán (2000), p. xi; Colchester (2014), p. 41; Schaaf and Clamote Rodrigues (2016), p. 58.

[851] Permanent Forum on Indigenous Issues (2018) International expert group meeting on the theme "sustainable development in the territories of Ondigenous peoples", note by the secretariat, UN Doc E/C.19/2018/7, para 35.

[852] WWF International (2008) Indigenous peoples and conservation: WWF statement of principles para 30; IUCN (2019) Environmental & social management system (ESMS): Standard on Indigenous peoples, para 22.

[853] Convention on Biological Diversity (adopted 6 Jun 1992, entered into force 29 Dec 1993), art 8 (a).

[854] Cittadino (2020), p. 63.

been reluctant to recognize FPIC in creating and managing protected areas.[855] The 2004 Akwé: Kon Guidelines for cultural, environmental, and social impact assessments adopted by the Conference of Parties (COP) to the CBD affirmed the relevance of FPIC for projects on Indigenous territories.[856] However, FPIC only needs to be obtained when it is part of the national legal system.[857]

The CBD's 2004 Programme of Work on Protected Areas (PoWPA) goes a step further: resettlements require Indigenous peoples' prior, informed consent 'according to national legislation and applicable international obligations'.[858] For other communities, the standard of FPIC does not apply. States shall only ensure the 'full and effective participation [...] of Indigenous and local communities'[859] in consistency with national and international law in the establishment and management of protected areas. Hence, the Conference of Parties (COP) appears to increasingly understand the UNDRIP as a relevant source of international law.[860] Yet, this tendency has not been translated into a binding framework, and, in practice, most states do not feel obliged to seek the consent of communities in the creation of protected areas.[861] Moreover, the COP adopted a technical guidance document stating that protected areas shall be 'established and managed in close collaboration with, and through equitable processes that recognize and respect the rights of [Indigenous] and local communities [...]. These communities should be fully engaged in governing and managing protected areas'.[862]

The commitment to transform 30% of all terrestrial and marine areas into protected areas was reaffirmed at the COP 15 meeting in Montreal.[863] Yet, and probably as an effect of the strong lobby work of Indigenous organizations, this target is tied to the commitment to 'recognizing Indigenous and traditional territories'[864] and that the sustainable use of these areas also recognizes and respects the

---

[855] Corpuz et al. (2006), p. 81.

[856] Rombouts (2014), p. 323.

[857] Secretariat of the Convention on Biological Diversity (2004) Akwé: Kon Voluntary Guidelines for the conduct of cultural, environmental and social impact assessments regarding developments proposed to take place on, or which are likely to impact on sacred sites and on lands and waters traditionally occupied or used by Indigenous and local communities, para 53.

[858] Secretariat of the Convention on Biological Diversity (2004) Programme of Work, goal 2.2.5.

[859] Ibid goal 2.2.

[860] Cittadino (2020), p. 288.

[861] Enyew (2019), p. 67.

[862] Conference of the Parties to the Convention on Biological Diversity (2011) Strategic plan for biodiversity 2011–2020: Further information related to the technical rationale for the Aichi Biodiversity Targets, including potential indicators and milestones, UN Doc UNEP/CBD/COP/10/INF/12/Rev.1, p. 15.

[863] ESCR-Net (2023) Collective advocacy on biodiversity and land rights—COP 15 outcomes. https://www.escr-net.org/news/2023/collective-advocacy-biodiversity-and-land-rights-cop-15-outcomes. Accessed 13 Jul 2023.

[864] Conference of the Parties to the Convention on Biological Diversity (2022) Kunming-Montreal Global Biodiversity Framework, CBD/COP/DEC/15/4, Annex Target 3.

rights of Indigenous peoples and local communities.[865] Moreover, the use, harvesting, and trade of wild species shall respect and protect customary sustainable uses by Indigenous peoples and local communities.[866] In this respect, the Global Biodiversity Framework goes a step beyond the earlier frameworks.

While the United Nations Convention on the Law of the Sea has been interpreted in light of international human rights law, neither the treaty itself nor its comments recommend Indigenous peoples' participation in the management of marine resources, let alone their consent. States also do usually not involve Indigenous peoples in the creation of marine protected areas, as evidenced by the Papahānaumokuākea Marine Protected Area in Hawaii, which was created by a presidential decree without consultations.[867]

The United Nations Educational, Scientific and Cultural Organization (UNESCO) is also active in protected area management under the 1971 Man and Biosphere Programme, the 1971 Ramsar Convention on Wetlands of International Importance, the 1972 WHC, and, since 2004, the Global Geoparks program. The Man and Biosphere Programme applies to terrestrial and coastal/ marine ecosystems or a combination thereof'[868] and seeks to bridge the divide between conservation and development.[869] The management of biosphere reserves should be based on a 'pact between the local community and society as a whole'.[870] However, the statutory framework only refers to the 'involvement and participation of a suitable range of inter alia public authorities, local communities, and private interests'.[871] In practice, co-management arrangements are increasingly common, yet the recognition of customary governance arrangements and FPIC does not seem to be the norm.[872]

In the past, the designation of World Heritage sites, i.e., sites of outstanding universal value, has often ignored Indigenous peoples' rights.[873] The relevant treaty body, the World Heritage Committee, has traditionally pursued a vision of conservation without involving affected communities.[874] Only since 2015 has it increasingly become concerned about the rights of Indigenous peoples. It has criticized the lack of participation of Indigenous peoples in the management of national parks, as

---

[865] See also Reyes-García et al. (2022), p. 85.

[866] Conference of the Parties to the Convention on Biological Diversity (2022) Kunming-Montreal Global Biodiversity Framework, CBD/COP/DEC/15/4, Annex Targets 5, 9.

[867] Bennett et al. (2017), p. 412; Farran (2019), pp. 335–36.

[868] UNESCO (1995) The statutory framework of the world network of biosphere reserves, art 1.

[869] Flikke (2014), p. 175.

[870] UNESCO (1996) Biosphere reserves: The Sevilla strategy & the statutory framework of the world network, p. 6.

[871] UNESCO (1995) The statutory framework of the world network of biosphere reserves, art 4(6).

[872] Stoll-Kleemann et al. (2010), pp. 235–36; Schultz et al. (2011), pp. 668–69; Colchester (2014), p. 44.

[873] Disko and Ooft (2018), p. 105; Vrdoljak (2018), p. 246; Disko and Sambo Dorough (2022), pp. 498ff.

[874] Cittadino (2020), p. 273.

well as the relocation of communities for the creation of protected areas.[875] Moreover, the member states acknowledged that they should 'ensure adequate consultations, the free, prior and informed consent and equitable and effective participation of [Indigenous] peoples where World Heritage nomination, management and policy measures affect their territories, lands, resources and ways of life'.[876]

In its jurisprudence, the World Heritage Committee also increasingly refers to the recommendations of the High Commissioner of Human Rights and recommends state parties not to resume projects until 'due process has been ensured to achieve Free, Prior and Informed Consent by [Indigenous] communities having territorial rights in the affected lands'.[877] It particularly reiterates the obligation to respect FPIC in the case of resettlements, as well as in the designation and management of protected areas and environmental impact assessments.[878] Moreover, the Operational Guidelines now encourage states to consult and cooperate in good faith with the Indigenous peoples concerned 'in order to obtain their free, prior and informed consent before including the sites on their Tentative List'.[879] They shall furthermore demonstrate, 'as appropriate',[880] that the FPIC of Indigenous peoples has been obtained in the nomination process. However, Cittadino criticizes that the proof of FPIC is still not a precondition for the application, and the World Heritage Committee does not have to verify whether consultations and consent have been realized in their evaluation of the application.[881] The UNESCO still hailed the reform and particularly the inclusion of FPIC as a milestone.[882]

[875] World Heritage Committee (2015) Decisions adopted by the World Heritage Committee at its 39th session (bonn, 2015), WHC-15/39.COM/19, paras 23, 81.

[876] General Assembly of State Parties to the World Heritage Convention (2015) Policy document for the integration of a sustainable development perspective into the processes of the World Heritage Convention, Res. 20 GA 13, para 22(ii).

[877] World Heritage Committee (2015) Talamanca Range-la Amistad reserves/ la Amistad national park (Costa Rica/ Panama), 39 COM 7B.28, para 7(c); see also World Heritage Committee (2016) Examination of nominations of natural properties to the World Heritage list: Thailand, 40 COM 8B.11, para 4.

[878] World Heritage Committee (2015) Talamanca Range-la Amistad reserves/ la Amistad national park (Costa Rica/ Panama), 39 COM 7B.28, para 8(b); World Heritage Committee (2016) Examination of nominations of natural properties to the World Heritage list: Thailand, 40 COM 8B.11, para 4; World Heritage Committee (2018) Inscriptions on the World Heritage list: Fanjingshan (China), 42 COM 8B.6, para 4(a); World Heritage Committee (2019) Inscriptions on the World Heritage list: Paraty and Ilha Grande—culture and biodiversity (Brazil), 43 COM 8B.10, para 4(e); World Heritage Committee (2019) Salonga national park (Democratic Republic of the Congo), 43 COM 7A.10, para 6.

[879] UNESCO (2021) Operational guidelines for the implementation of the World Heritage Convention, WHC.21/01, para 64.

[880] Ibid para 123.

[881] Cittadino (2020), p. 307; see also UNESCO et al. (2011), p. 58; Hales et al. (2012), p. 2; Stimac (2022), p. 270.

[882] UNESCO (2020), p. 24.

The Ramsar Convention, which was also drafted under the auspices of UNESCO, remains silent with respect to the participation of Indigenous and local communities in wetland management. However, since the 1980s, the UNESCO has increasingly promoted community-based wetland governance.[883] In 2002, the COP encouraged states to take 'as appropriate, intellectual property rights, customary law, and the principle of prior informed consent'[884] into account in the designation of new wetlands of international importance. However, the manual on participatory management only requires the participation of local communities and Indigenous peoples.[885] Most member states do not read the Ramsar Convention as requiring the FPIC of local communities and Indigenous peoples. In 2017, only 52.7% of member states 'specifically involve[d] local stakeholders in the selection of new Ramsar sites'.[886] A 2017 report on Indigenous peoples and wetland governance thus recommended, among other things, to acknowledge the UNDRIP in the implementation of the Ramsar Convention.[887]

Another type of protected area under the auspices of the UNESCO is global geoparks. Geoparks are defined as geological areas of international value with the objective of realizing a sustainable approach to development.[888] They 'should actively involve local communities and Indigenous peoples as key stakeholders'.[889] However, this does not include an obligation to seek FPIC but translates only into the recommendation to ensure the 'full and effective participation of the local communities and Indigenous peoples in planning and implementing the management and development of the Geopark'.[890]

Hence, while FPIC has not become a mandatory requirement for the designation and management of protected areas—with the shaky exception of the World Heritage sites—the 2018 UNESCO Policy on Engaging with Indigenous Peoples recognizes the right to FPIC of Indigenous peoples.[891] In the policy, the UNESCO commits to implementing the UNDRIP. It recognizes the Indigenous right to self-determination and the right to free, prior and informed consent of Indigenous peoples in the contexts defined by the UNDRIP.[892] It also affirms the relevance of FPIC for climate change mitigation or adaptation projects and states that 'the UNESCO does

883 Oviedo and Ali (2018) pp. 8, 17.

884 Conference of Contracting Parties to the Convention on Wetlands (2002) Guiding principles for taking into account the cultural values of wetlands for the effective management of sites, Resolution VIII.19, para 19(a).

885 Ramsar Convention Secretariat (2010) Participatory skills: Establishing and strengthening local communities' and Indigenous people's participation in the management of wetlands, p. 5.

886 However, it should be noted that not all member states have Indigenous populations (see also Oviedo and Ali 2018, p. 22).

887 Ibid p. 43.

888 UNESCO (2015) Statutes of the international geoscience and geoparks programme, part B art 1.

889 UNESCO (2015) Operational guidelines for UNESCO global geoparks, art 3(v).

890 UNESCO Global Geopark Council (2022) Report of the 7th session, p. 47.

891 UNESCO Executive Board (2018) UNESCO policy on engaging with Ondigenous peoples.

892 Ibid paras 5, 7, 8.

not support the removal of [Indigenous] peoples from their lands and territories in any conservation or sustainable development project or program in which UNESCO is involved'.[893] How the policy will be implemented is yet to be seen. Until recently, Indigenous peoples were still viewed as one stakeholder group among many, and FPIC as a principle at best, contributing to a low degree of protection of their rights.[894]

2.6.2.4 Climate Change Law

FPIC is also relevant in the context of climate change mitigation, adaptation, and geoengineering measures, which can heavily interfere with the rights of Indigenous peoples.[895] Compared to other areas of environmental law, FPIC is relatively well-established in climate change law, likely because of its overlaps with the field of development.

The 1994 United Framework Convention on Climate Change (UNFCCC) and its mechanisms focus on abating greenhouse gas emissions while remaining silent on human rights.[896] This changed to some extent with the adoption of the 2015 Paris Agreement when the state parties committed to considering their respective obligations towards Indigenous peoples, local communities, and other vulnerable groups.[897] Adaption actions should follow a 'country-driven, gender-responsive, participatory and fully transparent approach, taking into consideration vulnerable groups, communities, and ecosystems'.[898]

An important program in the climate change law framework is REDD+: **R**educing **E**missions from **D**eforestation and Forest **D**egradation and the role of conservation, sustainable management of forests and enhancement of forest carbon stocks in developing countries.[899] REDD+ seeks to reduce emissions from deforestation and forest degradation using carbon stocks. Many countries are still in the so-called readiness phase, during which they adopt and implement national REDD+ policies and international donors fund pilot projects. The 2010 Cancún Safeguards that were adopted at the COP16 summit apply to REDD+ readiness activities.[900] They do not

[893] Ibid para 44(b), see also para 53.

[894] Disko et al. (2014), p. 22.

[895] Burger and Wentz (2015) p. viii.

[896] Schade and Obergassel (2014) p. 2.

[897] Paris Agreement (adopted 12 Dec 2015, entered into force 4 Nov 2016), p. 2.

[898] Ibid para 5.

[899] United Nations Framework Convention on Climate Change (adopted 9 May 1992, entered into force 21 Mar 1994) 1771 UNTS 107.

[900] UNFCCC (2011) Report of the conference of parties on its sixteenth session, held in Cancún from 29 november to 10 December 2010: Decisions adopted by the conference of parties, UN Doc FCCC/CP/2010/7/Add.1, appendix 1.

mention FPIC but reference the UNDRIP.[901] Moreover, the Guidelines on Stakeholder Engagement in REDD+ activities focus more on consultation and information than FPIC.[902]

With some REDD+ readiness activities being funded by the UN-REDD program and others by the World Bank's Forest Carbon Partnership Facility, the respective Indigenous peoples' policies of the two institutions apply.[903] As explored before, the World Bank does not pursue a rights-based approach, and until 2018 only required informed consultations with Indigenous peoples. Moreover, the World Bank's safeguards are only relevant for World Bank-funded projects and investments. They usually do not apply to World Bank-funded readiness activities as the Forest Carbon Partnership Facility is not supposed to fund projects or investments on the ground.[904] However, they will become relevant with respect to projects and activities funded by the World Bank's Carbon Fund, which is set up to provide incentive payments to countries in the Global South.

In contrast, the UN-REDD program has adopted FPIC guidelines. It recommends seeking consent in the development of national REDD+ strategies affecting the rights and interests of Indigenous peoples and forest-dependent communities and for projects significantly impacting the land, natural resources, or traditional knowledge of communities.[905] The FPIC requirement is strong: without consent, the territories and resources of the communities in question should not be included in the policy or activity.[906]

Another relevant climate change fund is the Green Climate Fund which has financed low-emission and climate-resilience projects since 2015—and provides funding for all phases of REDD+. In 2018, it adopted an Indigenous Peoples policy, which recognizes the 'principle of free, prior, and informed consent'[907] as a part of the risk management strategy. FPIC needs to be obtained when activities have a significantly negative impact on the cultural heritage of Indigenous peoples, on their territories and natural resources, and for relocations.[908]

Despite these commitments in the context of REDD+, find states have regularly ignored the land rights and consent rights of rural communities in both readiness and implementation activities.[909] According to a meta-study, 'many of the REDD+

[901] Ibid appendix 1.

[902] Forest Carbon Partnership Facility and UN-REDD Programme (2012) Guidelines on stakeholder engagement in REDD+ readiness: With a focus on the participation of Indigenous peoples and other forest-dependent communities.

[903] Ibid paras 6–7; Gover (2017), p. 89.

[904] Savaresi (2013), p. 9; Gover (2017), pp. 91–92.

[905] UN-REDD Programme (2013) Guidelines on free, prior and informed consent, pp. 11, 27.

[906] Ibid p. 30.

[907] Green Climate Fund (2018) Indigenous peoples policy, s III(11)(j).

[908] Ibid ss VII(59), VII(61), VII(63).

[909] Sarmiento Barletti and Larson (2017) p. 5.

projects examined under this review demonstrated a lack of FPIC, and the withholding of information by project implementers'.[910]

The Special Rapporteur on Indigenous Peoples is also concerned about the lack of adequate consultation in the context of renewable energy projects under the Clean Development Mechanism.[911] The Clean Development Mechanism assists developing countries in achieving sustainable development with the assistance of developed countries as part of their Kyoto commitments. Often, projects such as wind parks in the Global South are financed under the mechanism.[912] However, its modalities and procedures do not reference human rights, let alone participation rights.[913]

The Clean Development Mechanism is also the main source of funding for the so-called Adaption Fund, which was created in 2001 under the UNFCCC to finance climate change adaptation projects.[914] Under the Adaptation Fund's social guidelines, the fund shall not support projects with disproportionate adverse impacts on marginalized and vulnerable groups, including Indigenous peoples and tribal groups.[915] Moreover, the UNDRIP is mentioned in relation to core labor rights.[916] The guidance document also calls upon implementing entities to describe 'how the project/program will be consistent with UNDRIP, and particularly with regard to Free, Prior, Informed Consent'[917] throughout the project cycle.

Hence, while the language of consent is increasingly used in climate change law, albeit often in the reduced form common in the field of development law, an even more limited understanding is common with respect to traditional resource rights and protected area designation and management.

2.6.3 *Institutional Autonomy, Gender, and the Environment*

With FPIC only having recently emerged in the field of environmental law, not much engagement with its internal dimension has occurred. Most actors, however, commit to gender equality and particularly the participation of women.

---

[910] Saeed et al. (2017), p. 589.

[911] Olawuyi (2016), pp. 76ff; HRC (2017) Report of the Special Rapporteur on the Rights of Indigenous Peoples, UN Doc A/HRC/36/46, para 92.

[912] Hesketh (2021), p. 548.

[913] Obergassel et al. (2017), p. 56.

[914] HRC (2017) Report of the Special Rapporteur on the Rights of Indigenous Peoples, UN Doc A/HRC/36/46, para 99.

[915] Adaptation Fund Board (approved in November 2013, revised in March 2016) Environmental and social policy, para 14.

[916] Ibid para 18.

[917] Adaptation Fund Board (2016) Guidance document for implementing entities on compliance with adaptation fund environmental and social policy, 12.

Like all UN organizations, the UNESCO has adopted a gender mainstreaming approach.[918] Moreover, the UNESCO Policy on Indigenous Peoples recognizes the particular discrimination that Indigenous women and girls are confronted with.[919] It acknowledges their right to 'full and effective participation in all matters affecting their lives and cultures, taking into account the needs of different groups, as well as their gender'.[920]

The World Heritage Committee's Operational Guidelines also emphasize the need for gender equality in World Heritage processes in various contexts.[921] They call upon member states to ensure the 'gender-balanced participation of a wide variety of stakeholders and rights-holders, including [...] local communities, [Indigenous] peoples [...]'[922] in the identification, nomination, management, and protection of World Heritage sites. In preparing their tentative lists of sites, states shall ensure 'the full, effective and gender-balanced participation of a wide variety of stakeholders and rights-holders'.[923] The same paragraph goes on to encourage states to consult and cooperate in good faith with Indigenous peoples 'through their own representative institutions'[924] to obtain their consent. In relation to the nomination of World Heritage sites, FPIC shall, if appropriate, be obtained 'through, inter alia, making the nominations publicly available in appropriate languages and public consultations and hearings'.[925] Reading the guidelines, one gets the impression that gender and Indigeneity are seen as the foundation for different rights- or stakeholder groups, which are not seen as overlapping.

In the context of the Ramsar Convention, it is recommended to 'encourage active and informed participation of local communities, including Indigenous peoples, and in particular women, in the conservation and wise use of wetlands'[926] and to take into consideration that communities are not homogenous but composed of a variety of different interest groups.[927]

In the framework of the Convention on Biological Diversity, the Mo' otz Kuxtal Guidelines on Prior and Informed Consent remain silent with respect to gender. In contrast, the guidelines on impact assessments acknowledge the vital role of women and youth—particularly women and youth within Indigenous and local

[918] See UNESCO (2014) UNESCO priority gender equality action plan: 2014–2021, para 15.

[919] UNESCO Executive Board (2018) UNESCO policy on engaging with Indigenous peoples, part A para 15.

[920] Ibid part B para 77(b).

[921] UNESCO (2019) Operational guidelines for the implementation of the World Heritage Convention, UN Doc WHC.19/01, paras 15(o), 64, 111(b), 155, 214, 239(j).

[922] Ibid para 12.

[923] Ibid para 64.

[924] Ibid para 64.

[925] Ibid para 123.

[926] Conference of Contracting Parties to the Convention on Wetlands (2002) Guiding principles for taking into account the cultural values of wetlands for the effective management of sites, Resolution VIII.19, para 6.

[927] Ibid p. 6.

communities—in the conservation and sustainable use of biological diversity and the need for the full and effective participation of women in policy-making and implementation'.[928] Indigenous women organizations like the Native Women's Association of Canada have criticized the absence of a stringent approach to including 'Indigenous women, gender diverse and Two-Spirit people'[929] in the implementation of the CBD and in the different guidelines.

The Global Biodiversity Framework requires 'the full, equitable, inclusive and gender-representation and participation in decision-making [...] by Indigenous peoples and local communities, respecting their cultures and their rights over land, territories, resources, and traditional knowledge, as well as by women and girls, children and youth, and persons with disabilities'.[930] Moreover, the framework pursues a gender-sensitive and human rights based approach.[931] This suggests that the Conference of Parties increasingly recognizes the right of Indigenous women to participation.

Similarly, under the OAU Model Law, FPIC shall be obtained, ensuring that women are also involved in decision making'.[932]

The UN-REDD+ Program's FPIC Guidelines stress the right of Indigenous peoples to self-identify, as well as their right to consent through 'their own representative institutions and those representatives chosen by the people themselves in accordance with their own procedures'.[933] Simultaneously, the guidelines note that 'women have the right to equality in the exercise of the rights of Indigenous peoples in both internal and external decision-making processes and institutions'.[934] This approach recognizes the intersection of gender and Indigeneity.

The Green Climate Fund's Indigenous Peoples Policy commits to ensuring that FPIC is obtained through appropriate procedures and, in particular, through representative institutions.[935] It shall be obtained in a 'culturally appropriate manner, in a

---

[928] Secretariat of the Convention on Biological Diversity (2004) Akwé: Kon Voluntary Guidelines for the conduct of cultural, environmental and social impact assessments regarding developments proposed to take place on, or which are likely to impact on sacred sites and on lands and waters traditionally occupied or used by Indigenous and local communities, para 54.

[929] Native Women's Association of Canada. Critical review: Indigenous peoples and local communities and the post-2020 global biodiversity framework development of a fully integrated programme of work on article 8(j) and related provisions within the post-2020 global biodiversity framework. https://www.nwac.ca/assets-knowledge-centre/ecco-nwac-review-of-indigenous-peoples-and-local-communities-and-the-post-2020-global-biodiversity-framework.pdf. Accessed 14 Jul 2023, p. 7.

[930] Conference of the Parties to the Convention on Biological Diversity (2022) Kunming-Montreal Global Biodiversity Framework, CBD/COP/DEC/15/4, Annex Target 22.

[931] Ibid Annex Target 23, para 7(g).

[932] Organization of African Unity (2000) African model legislation for the protection of the rights of local communities, farmers and breeders, and for the regulation of access to biological resources, para 5(1).

[933] UN-REDD Programme (2013) Guidelines on free, prior and informed consent, p. 39.

[934] Ibid p. 39.

[935] Green Climate Fund (2018) Indigenous peoples policy, para 22(a).

local language that is understood by them, and through a process of transparent and inclusive consultations, including with women and youth'.[936]

To conclude, most documents—except for those located at the intersection of the fields of development and human rights law—put little emphasis on respecting customary ways of decision-making. This tendency can be explained by the lack of engagement with the right to culture and the institutional autonomy of communities. Yet, there is an emerging consensus to include Indigenous women in consultation processes.

2.6.4 Emerging Understanding

Claims that 'biodiversity protection and Indigenous peoples' rights represent essentially distinct and incompatible bodies of law'[937] are largely refuted nowadays. Still, while human rights law has certainly influenced transnational environmental law, the latter's purpose is not to enhance human dignity and protect vulnerable groups but to protect the environment. Moreover, since donors like the World Bank regularly fund conservation projects, risk-management approaches are common.[938]

Transnational environmental law underwent some changes concerning the recognition of collective rights-holders and consultation rights. While the emergence of a transnational law protecting the global commons restricted the external sovereignty of states, it paradoxically also enhanced their internal sovereign powers.[939] Indigenous peoples' and communities' rights remained at the field's periphery.[940] Until quite recently, consent was seen as a prerogative of states. Indigenous peoples were considered stakeholders whose participation should be ensured by states.

Under the influence of the field of human rights law, however, FPIC and consultations have increasingly become an issue. Simultaneously, the emergence of the legal identity of *local communities and Indigenous peoples* has contributed to a reduced understanding of FPIC. It does not have the same quality as Indigeneity in human rights law. With local communities' rights lagging behind the rights of Indigenous and tribal peoples, the merging of the two groups constitutes the emergence of a new legal identity.[941] This legal identity is also more of a stakeholder than

---

936 Ibid para 54.

937 See also Barelli (2020) Two opposing commitments? Towards a synchronised protection of biodiversity and indigenous peoples' rights. https://voelkerrechtsblog.org/two-opposing-commitments/. Accessed 10 Aug 2023.

938 Lustig and Kingsbury (2006), p. 407.

939 von Benda-Beckmann and von Benda-Beckmann (1997), p. 2.

940 Razzaque (2019), p. 208; Lixinski (2020) Indigenous power beyond human rights. https://voelkerrechtsblog.org/indigenous-power-beyond-human-rights/. Accessed 5 August 2020.

941 Morgera et al. (2015), pp. 39–41.

a rightsholder group.[942] While some organizations like the UNESCO have begun referencing the UNDRIP and Indigenous peoples' rights, the field does generally not recognize the right to self-determination of groups within the state. Even though, in some instances, their right to culture is recognized, it can be overridden by the higher value of environmental protection.[943] This is also reflected in the Kunming-Montreal Global Biodiversity Framework, which acknowledges the role of Indigenous peoples and local communities as 'custodians of biodiversity'[944] and protects 'the sustainable use [of wild species] by Indigenous peoples and local communities'.[945]

Thus, the coupling of *Indigenous and local communities* marks the emergence of a new (diluted) legal category with fewer rights.[946] Their consultation rights are usually grounded in the principle of multistakeholder approaches, participation, and ideas of community-based natural resource governance. Some Indigenous peoples are concerned about this development and advocate for two separate legal identities.[947] Others understand the culturalization of their claims to land and natural resources as a strategy.[948]

For law-making and the implementation of transnational law, consultations remain the standard. The UN Secretary-General criticizes that 'there exists a significant gap in international environmental law regarding effective participation by non-State actors in international law-making and implementation'.[949]

While intellectual property law was early to recognize the importance of the prior and informed consent or approval of Indigenous and local communities with respect to their traditional resource rights, the scope of this consent is narrow and subject to the discretion of states. In the context of protected area designation and management, FPIC was neglected for a long time. While today development and conservation are increasingly thought of together, FPIC processes remain uncommon. Disko and Sambo Dorough also show that the nomination of many World Heritage sites 'continues to be marked by an exclusion of Indigenous peoples from the decision-making processes affecting them, a lack of respect for their relationship to the land, a

942 See also Coombe and Baird (2015), p. 337.

943 See also Lixinski (2019), pp. 252ff.

944 Conference of the Parties to the Convention on Biological Diversity (2022), Kunming-Montreal Global Biodiversity Framework, CBD/COP/DEC/15/4, Annex para 7(a).

945 Ibid Annex Target 5.

946 Posey (1997), p. 256; Parks et al. (2019), p. 23.

947 Inuit Circumpolar Council (2020) ICC policy paper on 'local communities' chronicles opposition to the undermining and erosion of Inuit rights. https://www.inuitcircumpolar.com/news/icc-policy-paper-on-local-communities-chronicles-opposition-to-the-undermining-and-erosion-of-inuit-rights/. Accessed 17 Jul 2023; HRC (4 Aug 2021), Efforts to implement the United Nations Declaration on the Rights of Indigenous Peoples: Indigenous peoples and the right to self-determination, UN Doc A/HRC/48/75, para 34.

948 Coombe and Baird (2015), p. 349; see also Larsen and Buckley (2018), pp. 87–88.

949 UNGA (2018), Gaps in international environmental law and environment-related instruments: Towards a global pact for the environment. Report of the Secretary-General, UN Doc A/73/419, para 84.

lack of protection of their traditional livelihoods, and disregard for their cultural heritage.'[950]

Even though the language of FPIC is more commonly used, the understanding of FPIC tends to be rather conservative, and the absence of consent remains justifiable by the overarching goal of environmental protection.

Thus, FPIC in environmental law does not fundamentally alter the relationship between the state and Indigenous peoples. Derived from the states' ownership of natural resources, including water, minerals, and, in many places, forests, conservation continues to be seen as states' business.[951] Or, to put it in Lustig's and Kingsbury's words, the field of transnational environmental law continues to apply a 'balancing approach rather than a rights-as-trumps-approach'.[952]

2.7 The Fragmentation of FPIC

Having examined the various coexisting understandings of FPIC, it is evident that FPIC remains an element under negotiation. The use of the phrase FPIC is far from cohesive or stringent in the global time-space.[953] FPIC originates from an Indigenous rereading of positivist international law. It was subsequently appropriated by the field of human rights law. From there, it traveled to the fields of environmental and development law. But also within these fields, several versions of FPIC coexist. Benda-Beckmann thus correctly argues that independent of the location of a sociolegal space, there are 'different understandings and interpretations of human rights by different kinds of social actors'.[954] FPIC remains indeterminate and fragmented.[955]

It is fragmented because it has a different meaning depending on the legal identity. The logic of the field in question determines the legal identity to which FPIC or consultations are attached. Thus, the legal identities created within the different legal fields function as nodal points shaping the element FPIC.[956] They include Indigenous peoples, Indigenous and tribal peoples, peoples, peasants, and Indigenous peoples and local communities. However, the legal identities are not completely fixed in the global time-space even when the same terminology is used. For instance, the legal identity of *Indigenous and tribal peoples* as a rights-holding group in transnational human rights law differs from the legal identity of *Indigenous peoples and local communities* as a stakeholder group in the field of transnational

[950] Disko and Sambo Dorough (2022), p. 518.

[951] Cox and Elmqvist (1997), p. 84.

[952] Lustig and Kingsbury (2006), p. 411.

[953] Jacobsen (2016), p. 290.

[954] von Benda-Beckmann (2009), p. 120.

[955] Mertz (1994), p. 1246.

[956] Laclau and Mouffe (2001), p. 113.

environmental law. Even though they describe the same or at least a very similar social identity, the field's logic alters their meaning and, thereby, the meaning of the relational elements.[957] While the boundaries between the social identities are blurry, the categorization of a group—for instance, as Indigenous or non-Indigenous—has tangible legal consequences. It determines the theoretical underpinning of FPIC, the applicability and meaning of consent, and FPIC's internal dimension.[958]

The field of human rights law grants different rights to minorities, Indigenous peoples, and peasants. Indigenous and tribal peoples have the strongest rights. Yet, even in their case, there is a tendency to derive FPIC from a washed-out version of self-determination that is closer to the right to culture or the collective right to property than to Indigenous sovereignty. Consequently, Indigenous peoples can only dissent under exceptional circumstances. Simultaneously, the lack of an intersectional framework has contributed to the negligence of women's right to self-determination and FPIC.

Minorities have a right to culture under the human rights framework. However, their participation rights are very weak. Simultaneously, the consultation rights of minority women are not well recognized. As for peasants, their legal identity is detached from the right to culture. Therefore, only the right to food sovereignty can be the basis for very limited consultation and participation rights. Their representative institutions are also granted no particular protection. Simultaneously, a stronger emphasis is put on the participation of peasant women, partially because it was a priority to the NGOs involved in the drafting.

The logic of development law strongly differs from human rights law. It tends to attach FPIC or consultation rights to the legal identity of *Indigenous peoples+* resembling the understandings of the ILO C 169 and the Inter-American human rights system. However, Indigenous peoples+ are generally not rightsholders but stakeholders. Simultaneously, FPIC is transformed from a right into a principle or a risk-management tool in the light of the right to culture. FPIC is then about making communities agree to unavoidable development projects.[959] The detachment from the rights framework also means that FPIC procedures are taken out of the communities' hands, and customary institutions and decision-making processes are only respected when they are compatible with the projects' timeframes. This, in combination with the stakeholder logic, makes it easier to accommodate the participation of (Indigenous) women, even though their right to self-determination and institutional autonomy is likely to be discarded as well.

Environmental law has been even more reluctant to incorporate FPIC. State sovereignty over natural resources continues to be a central principle in environ-

[957] Cornell makes a similar observation with respect to the meaning of self-determination. While government agencies use the language of self-determination, they actually mean self-government under the national legal framework (Cornell 2006, p. 10).

[958] See also Mertz (1994), p. 1249.

[959] Merino (2018), p. 140.

mental governance. The creation of the legal identity of *Indigenous peoples and local communities* is a way of circumventing the Indigenous law framework—even though the influence of human rights is growing. Taking Indigeneity away from a group also means that its specific rights vanish.[960] The emerging legal identity is also one that is a stakeholder rather than a rightsholder group. Except for the law of climate finance located at the intersection of environmental and development law, FPIC is either not recognized, only a recommendation, depends on its recognition in the national legislation, or can be overridden by the public interest. The lack of engagement with FPIC also translates into a lack of engagement with its institutional and gender dimension.

Hence, within the different legal fields and based on their logic, legal identities are constructed in a way that enables departing from Indigenous and self-determination-based understandings of FPIC.[961] One of the reasons for FPIC's success in the different fields explored above is that through its focus on the procedural aspects, 'it offers a *lingua franca* that allows for contacts between radically different conceptions of development, nature and human flourishing'.[962] It enables dialogue and does not fundamentally interfere with the economic development and environmental protection model.[963] Yaffe refers to this re-negotiation of FPIC as a 'normative drift'.[964]

The theoretical underpinnings of FPIC prevailing in the global time-space also translate into the lack of an FPIC requirement with respect to international law-making. While under the Indigenous sovereignty paradigm it would be logical to include Indigenous peoples in treaty negotiations, this has not occurred.[965] Even an interpretation of the UNDRIP in the light of a 'contextual-participation-approach'[966] is unlikely to garner widespread support. Under this approach, Indigenous peoples may participate in law-making depending on the circumstances, similar to the sliding scale approach common in human rights law. However, non-state actors primarily have an advisory function, oftentimes depending on the goodwill of states. While NGOs, including Indigenous organizations, can participate in many fora, their participatory rights are 'narrowly defined, qualified, and conditioned'.[967] This is not to say that Indigenous peoples and other non-state actors are powerless in transnational law—quite the contrary is the case.[968] As exemplified by the Working Group on Indigenous Populations that drafted the UNDRIP, Indigenous

---

960 The negation of a group's identity as a way of extinguishing their rights has a long colonial tradition (See also Christie 2005, p. 19).

961 Germann makes similar observations in relation to the right to food (Germann (2009), p. 138).

962 Rodríguez-Garavito (2010), p. 11.

963 Hale (2005), p. 18.

964 Yaffe (2018), p. 3.

965 See also Bayot (2019), pp. 304–305; Lixinski (2019), pp. 101ff.

966 Charters (2010), p. 222.

967 Ebbesson (2007), p. 691.

968 See also Tennant (1994), pp. 51ff.

organizations can yield considerable influence.[969] Another example is the increasing presence of Indigenous representatives in the UN treaty bodies.[970] Yet, these legitimacy-generating modes of engagement are not formally recognized as a right or the expression of their sovereignty or self-determination. The fields of transnational law thus continue to leave little space for Indigenous sovereignty.

Moreover, the separation of identities—may it be in the form of different rights regimes for women and Indigenous peoples or under a stakeholder paradigm—translates into a lack of recognition of the FPIC of women. Some Indigenous groups criticize the 'pan-Indigenous approach'[971] that contributes to the essentialization and homogenization of Indigenous identities and does not leave enough space for the right of Indigenous 'women, gender diverse, and Two-Spririt people'.[972]

Some communities may still be able to navigate the different legal identities and choose the identity and legal framework that best suits their interest. The different versions of FPIC can be 'a means to mediate Indigenous politics with the final aim of obtaining more spaces for self-determination'.[973] However, in many cases, geopolitical interests limit their freedom of choice. If conservation NGOs or donors decide to designate a protected area, they become an *Indigenous people and local community* under environmental law.[974] If the government or companies have economic interests in the area, then the legal identities of development law will be imposed on them, which does not allow for their self-identification. However, some communities—particularly those involved in transnational alliances—will still have the capital and resources to challenge these legal identities, choose their identities, or claim rights that are beyond their legal identity.

References

Adebowale M et al (2001) Environment and human rights: a new approach to sustainable development. IIED

African Development Bank Group (2016) Development and Indigenous peoples in Africa

Aikins JK (2016) Indigenising democracy? Renegotiating the role of Indigenous political authorities in Ghana's Constitution review. In: Dhawan N et al (eds) Negotiating normativity: postcolonial appropriations, contestations, and transformations. Springer, Cham, pp 61–78

969 Barelli (2016), pp. 49–50.

970 Charters (2010), p. 220.

971 Native Women's Association of Canada. Critical review: Indigenous peoples and local communities and the post-2020 global biodiversity framework development of a fully integrated programme of work on article 8(j) and related provisions within the post-2020 global biodiversity framework. https://www.nwac.ca/assets-knowledge-centre/ecco-nwac-review-of-indigenous-peoples-and-local-communities-and-the-post-2020-global-biodiversity-framework.pdf. Accessed 14 Jul 2023 p. 7.

972 Ibid p. 7.

973 Merino (2018), p. 135.

974 See also von Benda-Beckmann (2001), p. 35.

Akermark SS (2005) The World Bank and Indigenous peoples. In: Ghanea N, Xanthaki A (eds) Minorities, peoples and self-determination. Koninklijke Brill NV, Leiden, pp 93–112
Alfredsson G (2005) Minorities, Indigenous and tribal peoples, and peoples: definitions of terms as a matter of international law. In: Ghanea N, Xanthaki A (eds) Minorities, peoples and self-determination. Koninklijke Brill NV, Leiden, pp 163–172
Anaya SJ (2000) Indigenous peoples in international law. Oxford University Press, Oxford
Anaya J (2009) The right to self-determination of Indigenous peoples in the post-Declaration era. In: Charters C, Stavenhagen R (eds) Making the Declaration work: the United Nations Declaration on the Rights of Indigenous Peoples. IWGIA, Copenhagen, pp 184–199
Anderson M (2007) When afro becomes (like) indigenous: Garifuna and Afro-Indigenous politics in Honduras. J Lat Am Caribb Anthropol 12:384–413
Anghie A (1999) Finding the peripheries: sovereignty and colonialism in nineteenth-century international law. Harv Int Law J 40:1–80
Anghie A (2006) The evolution of international law: colonial and postcolonial realities. Third World Q 27:739–753
Ashby Wilson R (2007) Conclusion: Tyrannosaurus lex: the anthropology of human rights and transnational law. In: Goodale M, Engle Merry S (eds) The practice of human rights: tracking law between the global and the local. Cambridge University Press, Cambridge, pp 342–369
Baker SH (2012) Why the IFC's free, prior, and informed consent policy doesn't matter (yet) to Indigenous communities affected by development projects. University of San Francisco Law Research Paper, pp 1–39
Banda F, Chinkin C (2004) Gender, minorities and Indigenous peoples. Minority Rights Group International
Barelli M (2010) The interplay between global and regional human rights systems in the construction of the Indigenous rights regime. Hum Rights Q 32:951–979
Barelli M (2012) Free, prior and informed consent in the aftermath of the UN Declaration on the Rights of Indigenous Peoples: developments and challenges ahead. Int J Hum Rights 16:1–24
Barelli M (2016) Seeking justice in international law: the significance and implications of the UN Declaration on the Rights of Indigenous Peoples. Routledge, London
Barelli M (2018) Free, prior and informed consent in the UNDRIP: Articles 10, 19, 29(2), and 32(2). In: Hohmann J, Weller M (eds) The UN Declaration on the Rights of Indigenous Peoples: a commentary. Oxford University Press, Oxford, pp 247–272
Barker J (2005) For whom sovereignty matters. In: Barker J (ed) Sovereignty matters: locations of contestation and possibility in Indigenous struggles for self-determination. University of Nebraska Press, Lincoln, pp 1–31
Barker J (2006) Gender, sovereignty, and the discourse of rights in native women's activism. Meridians 7:127–161
Barsh RL (1987) Revision of ILO Convention No. 107. Am J Int Law 81:756–762
Barten U (2015) What's in a name: peoples, minorities, Indigenous peoples, tribal groups and Nations. J Ethnopolit Minor Issues Eur 14:1–25
Baxi U (2001) What happens next is up to you: human rights at risk in dams and development. Am Univ Int Law Rev 16:1507–1529
Bayot AB (2019) Free, prior and informed consent in the Philippines: a Fourth World critique. In: Feichtner I et al (eds) Human rights in the extractive industries: transparency, participation, resistance. Springer, Cham, pp 281–310
Beltrán J (2000) Indigenous and traditional peoples and protected areas. IUCN and WWF
Bennett NJ et al (2017) An appeal for a code of conduct for marine conservation. Mar Policy 81: 411–418
Berman PS (2007) Global legal pluralism. South Calif Law Rev 80:1155–1238
Boisson de Chazournes L (2012) Partnerships, emulation, and coordination: toward the emergence of a droit commun in the field of development finance. Int Financ Inst Glob Leg Govern 3:173–188

Bosselmann K (1997) The right to self-determination and international environmental law: an integrative approach. NZ J Environ Law 1:1–42
Bourdieu P (1986) The force of law: toward a sociology of the juridical field. Hastings Law J 38: 805–813
Bourdieu P, Wacquant LJD (1992) The purpose of reflexive sociology (the Chicago workshop). In: Bourdieu P, Wacquant LJD (eds) An invitation to reflexive sociology. Chicago University Press, Chicago, pp 61–216
Brunné J (2022) Consent. Max planck encyclopedia of public international law. https://opil.ouplaw.com/display/10.1093/law:epil/9780199231690/law-9780199231690-e1388?rskey=mfUjDI&result=1&prd=MPIL. Accessed 11 Oct 2023
Bryan J (2012) Rethinking territory: social justice and neoliberalism in Latin America's territorial turn. Geogr Compass 6:215–226
Brysk A (2000) From tribal village to global village: Indian rights and international relations in Latin America. Stanford University Press, Stanford
Burger M, Wentz J (2015) Climate change and human rights. UNEP
Cabrera Ormaza MV, Ebert FC (2019) The World Bank, human rights, and organizational legitimacy strategies: The case of the 2016 environmental and social framework. Leiden J Int Law 32:483–500
Cariño J, Colchester M (2010) From dams to development justice: progress with "free, prior and informed consent" since the World Commission on Dams. Water Altern 3:423–437
Carvosso R (2020) Examining the suitability of the international minority rights regime as an avenue for advancing self-determination claims. Int J Minor Group Rights 27:675–727
Castellino J (2005) Conceptual difficulties and the right to Indigenous self-determination. In: Ghanea N, Xanthaki A (eds) Minorities, peoples and self-determination. Koninklijke Brill NV, Leiden, pp 55–74
Castellino J, Doyle C (2018) Who are "Indigenous peoples"? An examination of concepts concerning group membership in the UNDRIP. In: Hohmann J, Weller M (eds) The UN Declaration on the Rights of Indigenous Peoples: a commentary. Oxford University Press, Oxford, pp 7–37
Castellino J, Gilbert J (2003) Self-determination, Indigenous peoples and minorities. Macquarie Law J 3:155–178
Charters C (2010) A self-determination approach to justifying Indigenous peoples' participation in international law and policy making. Int J Minor Group Rights 17:215–240
Cheyns E, Thévenot L (2019) Interview with Marcus Colchester, founder of the NGO Forest Peoples' programme, on the 'free, prior and informed consent' of communities. La Revue des Droits de l'Homme 16:1–22
Christie G (2005) A colonial reading of recent jurisprudence: Sparrow, Delgamuukw and Haida nation. Windsor Yearb Access Justice 23:17–53
Cittadino F (2020) Incorporating Indigenous rights in the international regime on biodiversity protection: access, benefit-sharing and conservation in Indigenous lands. Brill Nijhoff, Leiden
Claeys P, Edelman M (2020) The United Nations Declaration on the Rights of peasants and other people working in rural areas. J Peasant Stud 47:1–68
Colchester M (2014) Indigenous peoples and protected areas: towards reconciliation. In: Disko S, Tugendhat H (eds) World heritage sites and Indigenous peoples' rights. IWGIA, Copenhagen, pp 39–54
Comaroff J, Comaroff J (1992) Ethnography and the historical imagination. Westview Press, Boulder
Committee on the Rights of Indigenous Peoples (2012) Sofia conference (2012) Rights of Rndigenous peoples. International Law Association
Coombe RJ, Baird MF (2015) The limits of heritage. In: A companion to heritage studies, pp 337–354
Cornell S (2006) Indigenous peoples, poverty and self-determination in Australia, New Zealand, Canada and the United States. Joint Occ Pap Nat Aff 2:1–39

Corntassel J (2008) Toward sustainable self-determination: rethinking the contemporary Indigenous-rights discourse. Alternatives 33:105–132
Corpuz J et al (2006) Indigenous peoples' free, prior, and informed consent in the Convention on Biological Diversity: an overview
Cotterrell R (2008) Transnational communities and the concept of law. Ratio Juris 21:1–18
Cox PA, Elmqvist T (1997) Ecocolonialism and Indigenous-controlled rainforest reserves in Samoa. Ambio 26:84–89
Dann P (2013) The law of development cooperation: a comparative analysis of the World Bank, the EU and Germany. Cambridge University Press, Cambridge
Davis SH (2002) Indigenous peoples, poverty and participatory development: the experience of the World Bank in Latin America. In: Sieder R (ed) Multiculturalism in Latin America: Indigenous rights, diversity and democracy. Palgrave Macmillan, New York, pp 227–251
Davis M (2008) The globalisation of international human rights law, Aboriginal women and the practice of Aboriginal customary law. In: Cain M, Howe A (eds) Women, crime and social harm: towards a criminology for the global age. Hart Publishing, Oxford, pp 137–160
Davis SH (2021) The World Bank and Indigenous peoples. In: Koch-Weser M, Guggenheim S (eds) Social development in the World Bank: essays in honor of Michael M. Cernea. Springer International Publishing, Cham, pp 191–204
de Costa R (2006) A higher authority: Indigenous transnationalism and Australia. UNSW Press, Sidney
de Moerloose S (2020) Indigenous peoples' free, prior and informed consent (FPIC) and the World Bank safeguards: Between norm emergence and concept appropriation. World Comparative Law 53:223–244
de Sousa Santos B (2002) Toward a new legal common sense. Butterworths, LexisNexis, London
Deloria V Jr (1998) Intellectual self-determination and sovereignty: looking at the windmills in our minds. Wicazo Sa Review 13:25–31
Denetdale JN (2006) Chairmen, presidents, and princesses, the Navajo Nation, gender, and the politics of tradition. Wicazo Sa Rev 21:9–28
Diergarten Y (2019) Indigenous or out of scope? Large-scale land acquisitions in developing countries, international human rights law and the current deficiencies in land rights protection. Hum Rights Law Rev 19:37–52
Disko S, Ooft M (2018) The World Heritage and sustainable development policy - a turning point for Indigenous peoples? In: Larsen PB, Logan W (eds) World Heritage and sustainable development: new directions in World Heritage management. Routledge, Abingdon, pp 101–119
Disko S, Sambo Dorough D (2022) "We are not in Geneva on the Human Rights Council": Indigenous peoples' experiences with the World Heritage Convention. Int J Cult Prop 29: 487–530
Disko S et al (2014) World Heritage sites and Indigenous peoples' rights: an introduction. In: Disko S, Tugendhat H (eds) World Heritage sites and Indigenous peoples' rights. IWGIA, Copenhagen, pp 3–39
Doyle CM (2015) Indigenous peoples, title to territory, rights and resources: the transformative role of free, prior and informed consent. Routledge, Abingdon
Dulitzky AE (2010) When Afro-descendants became tribal peoples: the Inter-American Human Rights system and rural black communities. UCLA J Int Law 15:29–82
Ebbesson J (2007) Public participation. In: Bodansky D et al (eds) The Oxford handbook of international environmental law. Oxford University Press, Oxford, pp 681–703
Edelman M, James C (2011) Peasant's rights and the UN system: Quixotic struggle? Or emancipatory idea whose time has come? J Peasant Stud 38:81–108
Eichler J (2019) Reconciling Indigenous peoples' individual and collective rights: participation, prior consultation and self-determination in Latin America. Routledge, Abingdon
Eisenberg A (2020) Consent, resistance and the duty to consult. Int J Minor Group Rights 27:270–290

Ekpere JA (2000) The OAU's model law the protection of the rights of local communities, farmers and breeders, and for the regulation of access to biological resources: an explanatory booklet. Organization of African Unity
Engle K (2010) The elusive promise of Indigenous development: rights, culture, strategy. Duke University Press, Durham
Engle K (2011) On fragile architecture: the UN Declaration on the Rights of Indigenous Peoples in the context of human rights. Eur J Int Law 22:141–163
Engle Merry S (1988) Legal pluralism. Law Soc Rev 22:869–896
Engle Merry S (2003) Human rights law and the demonization of culture (and anthropology along the way). PoLAR Polit Leg Anthropol Rev 26:55–76
Engle Merry S (2005) Human rights and global legal pluralism: reciprocity and disjuncture. In: von Benda-Beckmann F et al (eds) Mobile people, mobile law: expanding legal relations in a contracting world. Ashgate, Aldershot, pp 215–232
Engle Merry S (2006) Human rights & gender violence: translating international law into local justice. The University of Chicago Press, Chicago
Enyew EL (2019) International human rights law and the rights of Indigenous peoples in relation to marine space and resources. In: Allen S et al (eds) The rights of Indigenous peoples in marine areas. Hart Publishing, Oxford, pp 45–68
Errico S (2006) World Bank and Indigenous peoples: the operational policy on Indigenous peoples (o.P. 4.10) between Indigenous peoples rights to traditional lands and to free, prior and informed consent. Int J Minor Group Rights 13:367–390
Errico S (2009) The draft UN Declaration on the Rights of Indigenous Peoples: an overview. In: Anaya J (ed) International human rights and Indigenous peoples. Wolters Kluwer, Austin, pp 63–69
Errico S, Claeys P (2020) Human rights and the commons: exploring approaches to the governance of land and natural resources beyond indigenous peoples' rights. The case of peasants. Int J Minor Group Rights 27:1–33
Estrada A et al (2022) Global importance of Indigenous peoples, their lands, and knowledge systems for saving the world's primates from extinction. Sci Adv 8:1–19
Farran S (2019) Marine protected areas and Indigenous rights. In: Allen S et al (eds) The rights of Indigenous peoples in marine protected areas. Hart Publishing, Oxford, pp 319–340
Filer C et al (2020) The FPIC principle meets land struggles in Cambodia, Indonesia and Papua New Guinea. Land 9:67–88
Flikke R (2014) On the fractured, fragmented and disrupted landscapes of conservation. Forum Dev Stud 41:173–182
Franco J (2014) Reclaiming free, prior and informed consent in the context of global land grabs. Transnational Institute for Hands Off the Land Alliance
Fredericks CF (2017) Operationalizing free, prior, and informed consent. Albany Law Rev 80:429–482
Friedmann M (2003) Autonomy, gender, politics. Oxford University Press, Oxford
Fujita S (2013) The World Bank, Asian Development Bank and human rights: developing standards of transparency, participation and accountability. Edward Elgar, Cheltenham
Germann J (2009) The human right to food: 'voluntary guidelines' negotiations. In: Atasoy Y (ed) Hegemonic transitions, the state and crisis in neoliberal capitalism. Routledge, Abingdon, pp 126–144
Gilbert G (2004) Individuals, collectivities and rights. In: Ghanea N, Xanthaki A (eds) Minorities, peoples and self-determination: essays in honour of patrick thornberry. Martinus Nijhoff Publishers, Leiden, pp 139–162
Gilbert J (2006) Indigenous peoples' land rights under international law: From victims to actors. Transnational Publishers, Ardsley
Göcke K (2010) The case of Ángela Poma Poma v. Peru before the Human Rights Committee: the concept of free, prior and informed consent and the application of the International Covenant on Civil and Political Rights to the protection and promotion of Indigenous peoples' rights. In: von

Bogdandy A, Wolfrum R (eds) Max Planck yearbook of United Nations law. Koninklijke Brill N.V., Leiden, pp 337–370
Golay C (2018) The right to food sovereignty and to free, prior and informed consent. Geneva Academy of International Humanitarian Law and Human Rights
Golay C (2019) Trust and complementarity, ingredients for success. J Peasant Stud:19–25
Goodale M (2009) Surrendering to utopia: an anthropology of human rights. Stanford University Press, Stanford
Goodland R (2004) Free, prior and informed consent and the World Bank group. Sustain Dev Law Policy 4:66–74
Gover K (2017) REDD+, identity law and 'free, prior and informed consent'. In: Gover KA et al (eds) The impact of climate change mitigation on Indigenous and forest communities: international, national and local law perspectives on REDD+. Cambridge University Press, Cambridge, pp 85–86
Green JF, Colgan J (2012) Protecting sovereignty, protecting the planet: State delegation to international organizations and private actors in environmental politics. Governance 26:473–497
Grewal K (2016) Can the subaltern speak within international law? Women's rights activism, international legal institutions and the power of "strategic misunderstanding". In: Dhawan N et al (eds) Negotiating normativity: postcolonial appropriations, contestations, and transformations. Springer, Cham, pp 27–44
Griffiths J (1986) What is legal pluralism? J Leg Plur Unoff Law 18:1–55
Gunn BL (2019) Bringing a gendered lens to implementing the UN Declaration on the Rights of Indigenous Peoples. In: Borrows J et al (eds) Braiding legal orders: implementing the United Nations Declaration on the Rights of Indigenous Peoples. Centre for International Governance Innovation, Waterloo, pp 55–65
Güven AB (2017) The World Bank and emerging powers: beyond the multipolarity–multilateralism conundrum. New Polit Econ 22:496–520
Hale CR (2005) Neoliberal multiculturalism: the remaking of cultural rights and racial dominance in Central America. Polit Leg Anthropol Rev 28:10–28
Hales RJ et al (2012) Indigenous free prior informed consent: a case for self-determination in World Heritage nomination processes. Int J Herit Stud:1–18
Hall S (1996) Introduction: who needs identity? In: Hall S, du Gay P (eds) Questions of cultural identity. Sage, Los Angeles, pp 1–17
Hanna P, Vanclay F (2013) Human rights, Indigenous peoples and the concept of free, prior and informed consent. Impact Assess Proj Apprais 31:146–157
Hannum H (2011) Autonomy, sovereignty, and self-determination. University of Pennsylvania Press, Philadelphia
Haugen HM (2016) The right to veto or emphasising adequate decision-making processes? Clarifying the scope of the free, prior and informed consent (FPIC) requirement. Neth Q Hum Rights 34:250–273
Heinze E (1999) The construction and contingency of the minority concept. In: Fottrell D, Bowring B (eds) Minority and group rights in the new millenium. Martinus Nijhoff, The Hague, pp 25–73
Henrard K (2007) Minority protection mechanisms as means to prevent and settle disputes over sovereignty. In: Jovanovic M, Henrard K (eds) Sovereignty and diversity. Eleven International Publishing, Utrecht, pp 103–130
Heri C (2021) Pushing the boundaries of human rights discourse: peasant right and peasant interests. In: Zyberi G (ed) Protecting community interests through international law. Intersentia, Cambridge, pp 275–306
Hesketh C (2021) Clean development or the development of dispossession? The political economy of wind parks in Southern Mexico. Environ Plan E Nat Space 5:543–565
Heyvaert V, Etty T (2012) Introducing transnational environmental law. Trans Environ Law 1:1–11

Humphreys S, Otomo Y (2016) Theorizing international environmental law. In: Orford A et al (eds) The Oxford handbook of the theory of international law. Oxford University Press, Oxford, pp 797–819

Imai S (2009) Indigenous self-determination and the state. In: Richardson BJ et al (eds) Indigenous people and the law: comparative and critical perspectives. Hart Publishing, Oxford, pp 285–314

International Labour Organization (2019) Implementing the ILO Indigenous and Tribal Peoples' Convention No. 169: towards an inclusive, sustainable and just future. ILO

Iorns CJ (1993) The Draft Declaration on the Rights of Indigenous peoples. Murdoch Univ Electron J Law 1:4–5

IWGIA, Comisión Interamericana de Derechos Humanos (28 Dec 2021) Derecho a la libre determinación de los pueblos Indígenas y tribales

IWGIA et al (2022) Submission to the UN Special Rapporteur on the Rights of Indigenous Peoples for his report to the 77th session of the UN General Assembly

Jacobsen AF (2016) Soft law in participation rights: tools in development. In: Lagoutte S et al (eds) Tracing the roles of soft law in human rights. Oxford University Press, Oxford, pp 273–292

Jaimes Guerrero MA (2003) "Patriarchal colonialism" and Indigenism: implications for Native feminist spirituality and native womanism. Hypatia 18:58–69

Johnston DM (1986) Quest of the six nations confederacy for self-determination. Univ Toronto Law Rev 44:1–32

Jonas H et al (2013) The living convention: a compendium of internationally recognised rights that support the integrity and resilience of Indigenous peoples' and local communities' territories and other social-ecological system. Natural Justice

Joona T (2020) ILO Convention No. 169 and the governance of Indigenous identity in Finland: recent developments. Int J Hum Rights 24:241–256

Jørgensen MW, Phillips L (2002) Discourse analysis as theory and method. SAGE Publications, London

Jovanovic M (2015) Constructing legal personality of collective entities - the case of "peasants". https://papers.ssrn.com/sol3/papers.cfm?abstract_id=2599926. Accessed 10 Aug 2023

Kapstein EB (2018) Governing the global land grab. Global Pol 9:173–183

Keck ME, Sikkink K (1998) Activists beyond borders: advocacy networks in international politics. Cornell University Press, Ithaka

Kemp D, Owen JR (2017) Corporate readiness and the human rights risks of applying FPIC in the global mining industry. Bus Hum Rights J 2:163–170

Khan MT (2016) Normative conflicts in Bangladesh: nature/forest conservation, corporate interests and the politics of co-management. In: Dhawan N et al (eds) Negotiating normativity: postcolonial appropriations, contestations, and transformations. Springer, Cham, pp 225–240

Kingsbury B (1998) "Indigenous peoples" in international law: a constructivist approach to the Asian controversy. Am J Int Law 92:414–457

Kingsbury B (1999) Operational policies of international institutions as part of the law-making process: the World Bank and Indigenous peoples. In: Goodwin-Gill GS, Talmon S (eds) The reality of international law: essays in honour of Ian Brownlie. Clarendon Press, Oxford, pp 323–342

Kingsbury B (2000) Reconstructing self-determination: a relational approach. In: Aikio P, Scheinin M (eds) Operationalizing the right of Indigenous self-determination. Institute for Human Rights, Åbo Akademi University, pp 19–37

Kingsbury B (2001) Reconciling five competing conceptual structures of Indigenous peoples' claims in international and comparative law. Int Law Polit 34:189–250

Koskenniemi M (1994) National self-determination today: problems of legal theory and practice. Int Comp Law Q 43:241–269

Kuokkanen R (2012) Self-determination and Indigenous women's rights at the intersection of international human rights. Hum Rights Q 34:225–250

Kuokkanen R (2016) Indigenous women's rights and international law: challenges of the UN Declaration on the Rights of Indigenous Peoples. In: Lennox C, Short D (eds) Routledge handbook of Indigenous peoples' rights. Routledge, pp 129–145
Kymlicka W (1999) Theorizing Indigenous rights. Univ Toronto Law J 49:281–293
Laclau E, Mouffe C (2001) Hegemony and socialist strategy: towards a radical democratic politics. Verso, London
Ladner KL (2000) Women and Blackfoot nationalism. J Can Stud 35:35–60
Ladner KL (2009) Gendering decolonisation, decolonising gender. Aust Indig Law Rev 13:62–77
LaDuke W (2002) Don't cheapen sovereignty. In: LaDuke W (ed) The Winona LaDuke reader: a collection of essential writings. Voyageur Press, Stillwater, pp 191–195
Laltaika E (2022) Chapter 23 - Indigenous peoples' participation and the management of wetlands in Africa: a review of the Ramsar Convention. In: Dalu T, Wasserman RJ (eds) Fundamentals of tropical freshwater wetlands. Elsevier, pp 711–726
Larsen PB, Buckley K (2018) Approaching human rights at the World Heritage Committee: capturing situated conversations, complexity, and dynamism in global heritage processes. Int J Cult Prop 25:85–110
Lehr AK (2014) Indigenous peoples' rights and the role of free, prior and informed consent. United Nations Global Compact
Lehr AK, Smith GA (2010) Implementing a corporate free, prior, and informed consent policy: benefits and challenges. Foley Hoag
Lenzerini F (2006) Sovereignty revisited: international law and parallel sovereignty. Texas Int Law J 42:155–190
Lenzerini F (2019) Implementation of the UNDRIP around the world: achievements and future perspectives. The outcome of the ILA committee on the implementation of the rights of Indigenous peoples. Int J Hum Rights 23:51–62
Lixinski L (2019) International heritage law for communities: exclusion and re-imagination. Oxford University Press, Oxford
Lobel O (2004) The renew deal: the fall of regulation and the rise of governance in contemporary legal thought. Minn Law Rev 89:343–470
Lustig D, Kingsbury B (2006) Displacement and relocation from protected areas: international law perspectives on rights, risks and resistance. Conserv Soc 4:404–418
MacKay F (2002) Universal rights or a universe unto itself? Indigenous peoples' human rights and the World Bank's draft operational policy 4.10 on Indigenous peoples. Am Univ Int Law Rev 17:527–624
MacKay F (2009) A guide to Indigenous peoples' rights in the International Labour Organization. Forest Peoples Programme
Mamdani M (2012) Define and rule: native as political identity. Harvard University Press, Cambridge
Marauhn T (2007) Changing role of the state. In: Bodansky D et al (eds) The Oxford handbook of international environmental law. Oxford University Press, Oxford, pp 727–748
McCorquodale R (1994) Self-determination: a human rights approach. Int Comp Law Q 43:857–885
McIvor SD (1995) Aboriginal women's rights as "existing rights". Can Women Stud 15:34–38
McKay MC, Benjamin C (2010) A vision for fulfilling the indivisible rights of Indigenous women. In: Hartley J et al (eds) Realizing the UN Declaration on the Rights of Indigenous Peoples: Triumph, hope, and action. Purich Publishing Ltd., Saskatoon, pp 156–168
Merino R (2018) Law and politics of Indigenous self-determination: the meaning of the right to prior consultation. In: Watson I (ed) Indigenous peoples as subjects of international law. Routledge, Abingdon, pp 120–140
Mertz E (1994) Conclusion: a new social constructionism for sociolegal studies. Law Soc Rev 28: 1243–1265
Meskell L (2013) UNESCO and the fate of the World Heritage Indigenous Peoples Council of Experts (WHIPCOE). Int J Cult Prop 20:155–174

Michaels R (2009) Global legal pluralism. Annu Rev Law Soc Sci 5:1–35
Mikaere A (1999) Colonization and the destruction of gender balance in Aotearoa. Nativ Stud Rev 12:1–28
Mombeshora S, Le Bel S (2009) Parks-people conflicts: the case of Gonarezhou national park and the Chitsa community in South-East Zimbabwe. Biodivers Conserv 18:2601–2623
Montón D (2019) We want the Declaration to come to life. J Peasant Stud:40–43
Moreton-Robinson A (2005) Patriarchal whiteness, self-determination and Indigenous women: the invisibility of structural privilege and the visibility of oppression. In: Hocking BA (ed) Unfinished constitutional business?: rethinking Indigenous self-determination. Aboriginal Studies Press, Canberra, pp 61–73
Morgera E et al (2015) Unraveling the Nagoya Protocol: a commentary on the Nagoya Protocol on access and benefit-sharing to the Convention on Biological Diversity. Brill, Leiden
Moyn S (2010) The last utopia: human rights in history. Harvard University Press, Cambridge
Napoleon V (2002) Raven's garden: a discussion about Aboriginal sexual orientation and transgender issues. Can J Law Soc 17:149–171
Napoleon V (2005) Aboriginal self determination: individual self and collective selves. Atlantis 29: 31–46
Napoleon V (2009) Aboriginal discourse: gender, identity, and community. In: Richardson BJ et al (eds) Indigenous peoples and the law: comparative and critical perspectives. Osgoode Readers, Oxford, pp 233–256
Nash JC (2001) Mayan visions: the quest for autonomy in an age of globalization. Routledge, New York
Ndahinda FM (2011) Indigenousness in Africa: a contested legal framework for empowerment of "marginalized" communities. The Hague, T.M.C. Asser Press
Newman D (2020) Interpreting FPIC in UNDRIP. Int J Minor Group Rights 27:233–250
Niezen R (2010) Public justice and the anthropology of law. Cambridge University Press, Cambridge
Obergassel W et al (2017) Human rights and the clean development mechanism: lessons learned from three case studies. J Hum Rights Environ 8:51–71
Olawuyi DS (2016) The human rights-based approach to carbon finance. Cambridge University Press, Cambridge
Ong D (2010) From 'international' to 'transnational' environmental law? A legal assessment of the contribution of the 'Equator principles' to international environmental law. Nord J Int Law 79: 35–74
Oviedo G, Ali MK (2018) The relationship of Indigenous peoples and local communities with wetlands: an initial report. Ramsar Convention Secretariat
Owen JR, Kemp D (2014) 'Free prior and informed consent', social complexity and the mining industry: establishing a knowledge base. Resources Policy 41:91–100
Oyěwùmí O (1997) The invention of women: making sense of Western gender discourses. University of Minnesota Press, Minneapolis
Pahuja S (2007) Rights as regulation: the integration of development and human rights. In: Morgan B (ed) The intersection of rights and regulation: new directions in sociolegal scholarship. Routledge, London, pp 167–191
Parisi L, Corntassel J (2007) In pursuit of self-determination: Indigenous women's challenges to traditional diplomatic spaces. Can Foreign Policy J 13:81–98
Parks L et al (2019) Guidelines and codes on the participation of Indigenous peoples and local communities of the Convention on Biological Diversity: a comparative analysis using natural language processing
Porter RB (2002) The meaning of Indigenous Nation sovereignty. Ariz State Law J 34:75–112
Posey DA (1997) Identifizierung und Respektierung der Grenzen zwischen Indigenen Völkern, traditionellen Bauern und örtlichen Gemeinschaften. In: von Weizsäcker EU (ed) Grenzen-los? Jedes System braucht Grenzen - aber wie durchlässig müssen diese sein? Springer Basel AG, Basel, pp 242–268

Posey DA, Dutfield G (1996) Toward traditional resource rights for Indigenous peoples and local communities. International Development Research Centre, Ottawa
Quane H (2011) The UN Declaration on the Rights of Indigenous Peoples: new directions to self-determination and participatory rights. In: Allen S, Xanthaki A (eds) Reflections on the UN Declaration on the Rights of Indigenous Peoples. Hart Publishing, Oxford, pp 259–288
Raghu P (2018) The prism of expanding peasants' rights: a critical investigation of diverse frames applied to la vía campesina's human rights engagements. Perspect Global Dev Technol 17:327–340
Ramos AR (1999) Cutting through state and class sources and strategies of self-representation in Latin America. Ser Antropol 247:1–22
Razzaque J (2019) A stock-taking of FPIC standards in international environmental law. In: Shelton DL et al (eds) Environmental rights: the development of standards. Cambridge University Press, Cambridge, pp 195–221
Reguart-Segarra N (2019) Business, Indigenous peoples' rights and security in the case law of the Inter-American Court of Human Rights. Bus Hum Rights J 4:109–130
Reyes-García V et al (2022) Recognizing Indigenous peoples' and local communities' rights and agency in the post-2020 biodiversity agenda. Ambio 51:84–92
Richardson BJ (2009) The ties that bind: Indigenous peoples and environmental governance. In: Richardson BJ et al (eds) Indigenous peoples and the law: comparative and critical perspectives. Hart Publishing, Oxford, pp 337–370
Riedel A, Bodle R (2018) Local communities and Indigenous peoples platform - potential governance arrangements under the Paris Agreement. Nordic Council of Ministers
Riles A (2001) The network inside out. The University of Michigan Press, Ann Arbor
Rittich K (2016) Theorizing international law and development. In: Orford A et al (eds) The Oxford handbook of the theory of international law. Oxford University Press, Oxford, pp 820–843
Robbins B (2015) Blue water: a thesis. Oceanamerica(s) 8:47–66
Rodríguez-Garavito C (2010) Ethnicity.Gov: global governance, Indigenous peoples, and the right to prior consultation in social minefields. Indiana J Glob Leg Stud 18:1–44
Rombouts SJ (2014) Having a say: Indigenous peoples, international law and free, prior and informed consent. Wolf Legal Publishers, Oosterwijk
Saeed A-R et al (2017) Are REDD+ community forest projects following the principles for collective action, as proposed by Ostrom? Int J Commons 11:572–596
Salcito K (2020) FPIC at the IFC: how performance standard 7 could better protect Indigenous peoples and uphold human rights. NomoGaia
Salomon S (2017) Self-determination in the case law of the African Commission: lessons for Europe. Law Polit Afr Asia Latin Am 50:217–241
Sambo Dorough D (2020) Perspective on Convention 169, its significance to Inuit and some troubling developments. Int J Hum Rights 24:293–296
Sanders D (1989) The UN Working Group on Indigenous Populations. Hum Rights Q 11:406–433
Sarfaty GA (2005) The World Nank and the internalization of Indigenous rights norms. Yale Law J 114:1791–1818
Sarfaty GA (2007) Doing good business or just doing good: competing human rights frameworks at the World Bank. In: Morgan B (ed) The intersection of rights and regulation. Routledge, London, pp 93–106
Sarmiento Barletti JP, Larson AM (2017) Rights abuse allegations in the context of REDD+ readiness and implementation: a preliminary review and proposal for moving forward. CIFOR
Savaresi A (2013) REDD+ and human rights: Addressing synergies between international regimes. Ecol Soc 18:5–13
Schaaf T, Clamote Rodrigues D (2016) Managing Midas: harmonising the management of multi-internationally designed areas: ramsar sites, world heritage sites, biosphere reserves and UNESCO global geoparks. IUCN
Schade J, Obergassel W (2014) Human rights and clean development. Wuppertal Institute for Climate Environment and Energy

Scheinin M (2005) What are Indigenous peoples. In: Ghanea N, Xanthaki A (eds) Minorities, peoples and self-determination. Koninklije Brill NV, Leiden, pp 3–13

Schilling-Vacaflor A, Flemmer R (2020) Mobilising free, prior and informed consent (FPIC) from below: a typology of Indigenous peoples' agency. Int J Minor Group Rights 27:291–313

Schmidt-Soltau K, Brockington D (2007) Protected areas and resettlement: what scope for voluntary relocation? World Dev 35:2182–2202

Schultz L et al (2011) Participation, adaptive co-management, and management performance in the world network of biosphere reserves. World Dev 39:662–671

Sellheim N (2018) The evolution of local involvement in international conservation law. Yearb Int Environ Law 29:77–102

Shrinkhal R (2014) "Free, prior informed consent" as a right of Indigenous peoples. J Natl Law Univ Delhi 2:54–65

Shrinkhal R (2021) "Indigenous sovereignty" and right to self-determination in international law: a critical appraisal. AlterNative Int J Indig Peoples 17:71–82

Sikkink K (2002) Transnational advocacy networks and the social construction of legal rules. In: Dezalay Y, Garth BG (eds) Global prescriptions: the production, exportation, and importation of a new legal orthodoxy. The University of Michigan Press, Ann Arbor, pp 37–64

Slaughter A-M (2002) Breaking out: the proliferation of actors in the international system. In: Dezalay Y, Garth BG (eds) Global prescriptions: the production, exportation, and importation of a new legal orthodoxy. The University of Michigan Press, Ann Arbor, pp 12–36

Smith A (2005) Native American feminism, sovereignty, and social change. Fem Stud 31:116–132

Snyder F (1999) Global economic networks and global legal pluralism. EUI Work Pap 99:1–30

Snyder E (2014) Indigenous feminist legal theory. Can J Women Law 26:365–401

Socha P (2017) Definitionen und Anerkennung substaatlicher Gruppen im Völkerrecht: Eine Untersuchung der rechtlichen Anwendung völkerrechtlicher Konstruktionen stubstaatlicher kollektiver Identitäten und aktuelle Entwicklungen im Intergovernmental Committee der WIPO. Universitätsverlag Göttingen, Göttingen

St. Denis V (2007) Feminism is for everybody: aboriginal women, feminism and diversity. In: Green J (ed) Making space for Indigenous feminism. Fernwood Publishing and Zed Books, Winnipeg, pp 33–52

Starblanket G (2018) Complex accountabilities: deconstructing "the community" and engaging feminist research methods. Am Indian Cult Res J 42:1–20

Stavenhagen R (2013) Pioneer on Indigenous rights. Heidelberg, Springer

Stimac Z (2022) Indigenous peoples through the Lens of UNESCO Religions 13(10):957–971

Stoll-Kleemann S et al (2010) The role of community participation in the effectiveness of UNESCO biosphere reserve management: Evidence and reflections from two parallel global surveys. Environ Conserv 37:227–238

Suiseeya KRM, Zanotti L (2019) Making influence visible: innovating ethnography at the Paris climate summit. Glob Environ Polit 19:38–60

Suksi M (2008) Personal autonomy as institutional form – focus on Europe against the background of article 27 of the ICCPR. Int J Minor Group Rights 15:157–178

Suksi (2013) Autonomy. Max planck encyclopedia for public international law. https://opil.ouplaw.com/display/10.1093/law:epil/9780199231690/law-9780199231690-e1007?rskey=3jYv80&result=1&prd=OPIL. Accessed 13 Oct 2023

Sunseri L (2011) Being again of one mind: oneida women and the struggle for decolonization. UBC Press, Vancouver

Szablowski D (2011) Operationalizing free, prior, and informed consent in the extractive industry sector? Examining the challenges of a negotiated model of justice. Can J Dev Stud 30:111–130

Tahvanainen A (2005) The treaty-making capacity of Indigenous peoples. Int J Minor Group Rights 12:397–419

Telesetsky A (2017) Legal pluralism - linking law and culture in natural resource co-management and environmental compliance. In: Nafziger JAR (ed) Comparative law and anthropology. Edward Elgar Publishing, Cheltenham, pp 116–132

Tennant C (1994) Indigenous peoples, international institutions, and the international legal literature from 1945-1993. Hum Rights Q 16:1–57

Tennberg M (2010) Indigenous peoples as international political actors: a summary. Polar Record 46:264–270

Thornberry P (1998) Images of autonomy and individual and collective rights in international instruments on the rights of minorities. In: Suksi M (ed) Autonomy: applications and implications. Kluwer Law International, The Hague, pp 97–124

Thornberry P (2002) Indigenous peoples and human rights. Manchester University Press, Manchester

Thürer D, Burri T (2008) Self-determination. Max planck encyclopedia of public international law. https://opil.ouplaw.com/display/10.1093/law:epil/9780199231690/law-9780199231690-e873. Accessed 11 Oct 2023

Tomaselli A (2015) Indigenous peoples and their right to political participation: International law standards and their application in Latin America. Nomos, Frankfurt/Main

Tomaselli A (2020) Political participation, the international labour organization, and Indigenous peoples: Convention 169 'participatory' rights. Int J Hum Rights 24:127–143

Tomlinson K (2019) Indigenous rights and extractive resource projects: negotiations over the policy and implementation of FPIC. Int J Hum Rights 23:880–897

Trask H-K (1996) Feminism and Indigenous Hawaiian nationalism. Signs 21:906–916

Trubek DM, Trubek LG (2007) New governance & legal regulation: complementarity, rivalry, and transformation. Leg Stud Res Pap Ser 1047:539

Trubek DM et al (1994) Global restructuring and the law: studies of the internalization of legal fields and the creation of transitional arenas. Case West Reserv Law Rev 44:407–498

Tsosie R (2010) Indigenous women and international human rights law: the challenges of colonialism, cultural survival, and self-determination. UNCA J Int Law Foreign Affairs 15:187–238

UNESCO et al (2011) Preparing world heritage nominations. UNESCO

UNESCO (2020) Report submitted by UNESCO to the 19th session of the United Nations Permanent Forum on Indigenous Issues (UNPFII). UNESCO

van Genugten W (2015) The World Bank Group, the IMF and human rights: a contextualised way forward. Intersentia, Cambridge

Venne S (2018) How governments manufacture consent and use it against Indigenous peoples. In: Watson I (ed) Indigenous peoples as subjects of international law. Routledge, Abingdon, pp 141–170

Voices of the Earth Congress (1993) Recommendations from the Voices of the Earth Congress: Indigenous peoples, new partners, the right to self-determination in practice

von Benda-Beckmann K (2001) Transnational dimensions of legal pluralism. In: Fikentscher W (ed) Begegnung und Konflikt - eine kulturanthropologische Bestandsaufnahme. Verlag der Bayerischen Akademie der Wissenschaften, München, pp 33–48

von Benda-Beckmann F (2009) Human rights, cultural relativism and legal pluralism. In: von Benda-Beckmann F et al (eds) The power of law in a transnational world: anthropological enquiries. Berghahn Books, New York, pp 115–136

von Benda-Beckmann F, von Benda-Beckmann K (1997) Community based tenurial rights: emancipation or indirect rule. In: von Benda-Beckmann K, Winkler HF (eds) Papers of the xlth international congress "folk law and legal pluralism: societies in transformation". Commission on Folk Law and Legal Pluralism, Ottawa, pp 169–187

Vrdoljak AF (2018) Indigenous peoples, World Heritage, and human rights. Int J Cult Prop 25:245–281

Wainwright J, Bryan J (2009) Cartography, territory, property: postcolonial reflections on Indigenous counter-mapping in Nicaragua and Belize. Cult Geogr 16:153–178

Weiss C (2021) The road to achieving a critical mass of sociologists and anthropologists in the World Bank. In: Koch-Weser M, Guggenheim S (eds) Social development in the World Bank: essays in honor of Michael M. Cernea. Springer International Publishing, Cham, pp 27–40

Wiessner S (1999) Rights and status of Indigenous peoples: a global comparative and international legal analysis. Harv Hum Rights J 12:57–127
Wiessner S (2008) Indigenous sovereignty: a reassessment in light of the UN Declaration on the Rights of Indigenous Peoples. Vand J Transnatl Law 41:1141–1176
Wiessner S (2011) The cultural rights of Indigenous peoples: achievements and continuing challenges. Eur J Int Law 22:121–140
Wilson W (1918) President wilson's address to congress, analyzing German and Austrian peace utterances. https://wwi.lib.byu.edu/index.php/President_Wilson%27s_Address_to_Congress,_Analyzing_German_and_Austrian_Peace_Utterances. Accessed 13 Oct 2023
Xanthaki A (2005) The right to self-determination: meaning and scope. In: Ghanea N, Xanthaki A (eds) Minorities, peoples and self-determination. Koninklijke Brill, Leiden, pp 15–33
Xanthaki A (2019) Culture: Articles 11(1), 12, 13(1), 15 and 34. In: Hohmann J, Weller M (eds) The UN Declaration on the Rights of Indigenous Peoples: a commentary. Oxford University Press, Oxford, pp 273–298
Yaffe N (2018) Indigenous consent: a self-determination perspective. Melb J Int Law 19:1–47
Yupsanis A (2013) Article 27 of the ICCPR revisited - the right to culture as a normative source for minority/ indigenous participatory claims in the case law of the human rights committee. In: Lavranos N, Kok RA (eds) Hague yearbook of international law. Brill Nijhoff, Leiden, pp 359–411
Zumbansen P (2010) Transnational legal pluralism. Comp Res Law Polit Econ 6:3–57

Chapter 3
The National Time-Space: FPIC in the Liberian Fields of Post-Conflict Law-Making

The exploitation of its forests, to a considerable extent, funded Liberia's bloody civil war raging from 1980 to 2003.[1] In response, the UN Security Council in 2001 imposed logging sanctions for the first time in its history. Moreover, many peacebuilders assumed that land conflicts were one of the root causes of the war.[2] After the end of the war, international actors, including US agencies, international and national non-governmental organizations (NGOs), together with the Liberian government, embarked upon post-conflict legal reform processes targeting the forest and land sector.

After the negative experiences with purely top-down peacebuilding and in line with the so-called 'local turn',[3] a hybrid model of peacebuilding was pursued in Liberia that sought to bridge the gap between the *local* and the *global*, emphasizing national ownership. Legal reforms, including various stakeholders, were a central element of the hybrid peacebuilding package. The legislative spaces in which the reforms took place are the fields of the post-war forest sector and land reform. They are primarily national time-spaces, yet they are under the strong influence of global time-spaces.[4]

Different actors competed for the 'monopoly to determine the law'[5] in these legislative spaces.

These actors did not have access to the same (legal) knowledge or the same financial and political means.[6] Their visions of natural resource and land governance and agendas also strongly differed. The two fields were thus characterized by

[1]Some aspects included of this chapter have already been published in shorter form in Roesch (2019).

[2]See also Richards (2005), p. 588; Unruh (2009b), p. 425.

[3]Paffenholz (2015), pp. 858 ff.

[4]de Sousa Santos (2002), p. 85.

[5]Bourdieu (1986), p. 817.

[6]See also Engle Merry (2005), p. 223.

R. Rösch, *Negotiating Norms*, Interdisciplinary Studies in Human Rights 9,
https://doi.org/10.1007/978-3-031-45910-8_3

'different and sometimes contradictory considerations of international institutions [. . .], bilateral donors, United Nations organizations [. . .], and different elements within the government'.[7] Moreover, the two fields were legally pluralistic.[8] Human rights norms coexisted with the project law of donors, Liberian laws, and transnational environmental law.

The transplantation of legal norms is common in post-conflict contexts.[9] FPIC was one of these transplanted human rights norms. While explorations of human rights within national contexts often focus on their implementation or lack thereof, this chapter starts from the assumption that the transplantation of FPIC to Liberia is not so much an issue of (non-) compliance but of norm negotiation and interaction with other normative orders in a given field.[10] Transplanted norms are aligned to the values prevailing in the field. Their accommodation depends on the economic and political conditions as well as the actors within that field.[11] It has been shown in the previous chapter that FPIC as a norm is fragmented in the global time-space and has no fixed meaning. Thus, in norm negotiation processes, different actors can resort to different versions or 'interpretations'[12] of FPIC. As a result of the negotiation and the interaction with other norms, new norms emerge as 'mediations of double movements already taking place in specific national and local contexts'.[13]

After briefly illuminating the pre-war land and natural resource legislation, this chapter examines the negotiation of FPIC in the post-war forest sector and land reforms.

Thereby, it will be explored how legal identities are renegotiated, determining the theoretical underpinning of FPIC, the scope and meaning of the emerging FPIC norm, and FPIC's internal dimension. With respect to the latter, the negotiation of gender roles is common in war-to-peace transitions. Activists and donors often see post-conflict reforms as a window of opportunity for addressing gender inequality.[14] Liberia has particularly been applauded for the role women played in ending the war, the incorporation of gender considerations into the Accra Peace Agreement, and the implementation of the UN Security Council Resolution (UNSCR) 1325 on women, peace and security.[15] It will be explored whether this gender focus also translated into the forest sector and land reforms: could women participate in the legal reform

---

[7] Hellum and Derman (2005), p. 179.

[8] Weilenmann (2009b), p. 157.

[9] See also Suhrke and Borchgrevink (2009), p. 213; Desai et al. (2012), pp. 251–252.

[10] Eg Goodman and Jinks (2004); Risse et al. (2013).

[11] von Benda-Beckmann and von Benda-Beckmann (2007b), p. 65.

[12] Griffiths (2003), p. 46.

[13] Filer et al. (2020), p. 81.

[14] Moran (2010), p. 267.

[15] Aning (1998), p. 17; UNSC (2003), Peace Agreement between the Government of Liberia, the Liberians United for Reconciliation and Democracy, the Movement for Democracy in Liberia and the political parties, UN Doc S/2003/850, annex, arts 16.3.b, 31; Chinkin and Charlesworth (2006), pp. 942, 947; Badmus (2009), pp. 827–828; Press (2010), p. 23; Moran (2012), p. 51.

processes? And how was gender negotiated in relation to forest and land governance?

FPIC first emerged in the Liberian forest sector. The policies, laws, and regulations adopted during the reform of the forestry legislation include the 2006 National Forestry Reform Law, the 2006 National Forest Policy, the 2007 Ten Core Regulations, the 2009 Community Rights Law with Respect to Forest Lands (CRL), and the 2011 Community Rights Law Regulation (CRL Regulation) which was amended in 2017. FPIC is an element of both the Ten Core Regulations and the CRL.

However, the adoption of the forestry legislation was not the end of the story of FPIC in Liberia. Due to the perceived link between land conflicts and the Liberian civil war, a coalition of government actors, donors, and national and international NGOs began reforming the Liberian land legislation.[16] One goal was the legal recognition of customary land rights, which had frequently been disrespected in Liberian history.[17] In 2013, the Liberian Land Commission adopted a Land Rights Policy, which laid the foundation for recognizing customary land rights, and, in 2018, after years of difficult negotiations, the Liberian legislature passed the Land Rights Act (LRA). In 2022, the Land Rights Act Regulations were adopted. Just like the forest legislation, the LRA recognizes the right to FPIC for measures and decisions affecting customary land. The land reform process, which began in 2009 and is not yet completed, constitutes the Liberian field of land reform.

3.1 The Pre-War Land and Natural Resource Legislation

To understand the functioning and values of a field, it is oftentimes instructive to take its history into consideration.[18] Liberia has a unique history. It was settled by American People of Color under the lead of the American Colonization Society but was never officially declared a US colony.[19] It was also the first African state to gain independence in 1847.[20] In the early years of the settlement endeavor, land was acquired by treaties between agents of the American Colonization Society and Indigenous rulers. Later, after the creation of the Liberian state and due to increasing French and British pressure on the Liberian Hinterland, the government expanded its territorial claims, contributing to the gradual extinction of Indigenous sovereignty.[21]

Liberia is characterized by legal plurality and global normative orders coexist with state law, state-sponsored customary law, and customary law.[22] Customary law

[16] Richards (2005), p. 588; Unruh (2009b), p. 425.

[17] Alden Wily (2007), pp. 119 ff.

[18] von Benda-Beckmann and von Benda-Beckmann (2007a), p. 18.

[19] Akpan (1973), p. 236.

[20] Liberian Declaration of Independence (1847) (Republic of Liberia).

[21] Akpan (1973), pp. 220–221; Lyon (1981), p. 225.

[22] Heemann (2020), p. 188.

describes law that is usually not codified. Following the colonization of Liberia, the central government introduced different legal systems for the littoral, which had been settled first, and the Hinterland, which was mainly populated by Indigenous peoples.[23] In the Hinterland, a state-sponsored customary legal system was introduced, in which chieftaincies played an important role.[24] It primarily reflected the settlers' idea of what customary governance was and bore a strong resemblance to the legal systems introduced in other colonized states.[25]

In the twentieth century, also under the influence of Liberia's economic open-door policy, the rule emerged that all land that was not private was public—even though that was never made explicit in the property law.[26] Customary land rights were gradually reduced to rights of use instead of ownership. According to the 1949 Hinterland Regulations, territorial title was vested in the state, while the so-called tribes could use an adequate area of the land for essential activities such as farming.[27] The Regulations' terminology remained vague and did not provide an insight into what essential activities are and how much land would be adequate for these activities. Nevertheless, deeds were not a precondition for this usufruct right and the 'perfect reserve'[28] gave communities 'title to the land against any person or persons'.[29] It is controversial whether that title amounted to ownership. Title in common law jurisdictions is generally only a right or interest in a thing.[30] But it can also be an entitlement to that interest vis à vis other persons. Several persons can have a title to the same thing, even though the strength of their claims may differ. The 1956 Aborigines Law, which replaced the Hinterland Regulations, does not make any reference to title anymore but only speaks of use rights, thus using a weaker language than the Hinterland law.[31] As it was not reprinted in the 1973 revised Code of Laws, it is assumed that instead of the Aborigines law, the Hinterland regulations remained applicable.[32]

---

[23] Under the 1914 Act making regulations governing the Interior Department of the Republic of Liberia. No copy of the Act was accessible to the author (see Boyah et al v Horace (1916) Supreme Court of Liberia. 2 LLR 265; Local Government Law (1982) (Republic of Liberia), ch 1 para 1); Huberich (1947), pp. 1233–1234.

[24] Unruh (2009a), pp. 7–8.

[25] International Crisis Group (2006), p. 7.

[26] Land rights policy (2013) (Land Commission), p. 6; Stevens (2014), p. 265.

[27] Revised laws and administrative regulations for governing the Hinterland (1949) (Republic of Liberia), art 66; Legal rules and regulations governing the Hinterland of Liberia (2001) (Republic of Liberia), art 66(a).

[28] Legal rules and regulations governing the Hinterland of Liberia (2001), art 66(a).

[29] Ibid art 66(a).

[30] Clarke and Kohler (2005), p. 383.

[31] Aborigines law (1956) (Republic of Liberia), ch 2 para 270.

[32] The Aborigines law was part of the 1956 Code of Laws, but not included in the 1973 Code of Laws Revised (see Liberian Code of Laws revised (1973) (Ithaca, New York), p. vii). As the 1973 Code of Laws replaced the 1956 Code and its 1956-7 supplements, the Aboriginal law is no longer in force (see Simpson Jr. 1973, p. xi).

Irrespective of these legal ambiguities, the government increasingly assumed it could freely dispose of the so-called public land and natural resources. According to the Liberian Constitution, mineral resources are held in trust by the government.[33] Moreover, both forest products, save for agroforestry, and wildlife were made the property of the nation.[34]

Customary land rights were frequently disrespected in the granting of concessions, the designation of protected areas, and the sale of public land.[35] By 2014, approximately 42.8% of the Liberian landmass had been granted to investors, straining the relationship between rural communities and the government.[36] In the case of concessions and protected areas, the government generally neither consulted with the communities living on the land nor did it apply the constitutional procedure of expropriations in the public interest (eminent domain), requiring just compensation.[37] However, since the adoption of the 1988 New Wildlife and National Park Law, the Forestry Development Authority (FDA) had to consult with local residents and 'take into account the views of local residents in the administration and management of National Parks and Nature Reserves'.[38] Customary owners were entitled to compensation but no longer had the right to enter the national park without a valid entry permit.[39] In view of the civil wars raging in the following years, it may be doubted whether the FDA actually followed the procedure as enshrined in the law. Conflicts between the FDA and communities over the designation of protected areas persist.[40]

Only the sale of *public land* required a form of community consent. Under the 1956 Public Lands Law, a precondition for the sale of public land and the acquisition of a public land sale deed was a so-called tribal certificate, a hybrid legal concept located between customary and statutory law.[41] Potential buyers of customary land needed to obtain the consent of the *tribal authority* in exchange for a financial token of respect. The *tribal authority* was usually the paramount or clan chief—positions created by the central government that did not, in many places in Liberia, build upon Indigenous institutions;[42] then, the District or County Commissioner had to ensure

[33] Constitution of Liberia (1986) (Republic of Liberia), art 24(a).

[34] An Act adopting the new National Forestry Law (2000) (Republic of Liberia), s 2.1.

[35] Makain and Foh (2009), pp. 16–17, 23, 34.

[36] The Rights and Resources Group (2013), p. 1.

[37] Constitution of Liberia (1986), art 24(a); See also Unruh (2009a), p. 15.

[38] An Act adopting a New Wildlife and National Parks and repealing chapters 1, 2, 3 and subchapter a and c of chapter 4 title 24 of the Natural Resources Law, volume 5 of the Liberian Code of Laws 1956, relating to the conservation of forests, forest reserves, conservation of wildlife and fish resources and national parks (1988) (Republic of Liberia), ch III s 26.

[39] Ibid chs III s 16, IV s 11.

[40] Roesch R (2 Mar 2019) Skype interview with former senior staff member of a Liberian NGO, para 36 ff.

[41] Public Lands Law (1956) (Republic of Liberia), ch 3 para 30.

[42] For example, in theory, the paramount chiefs were elected but had to be approved by the President (Legal rules and regulations governing the Hinterland of Liberia (2001), art 21).

that the land in question was unencumbered.[43] Upon paying the purchasing price to the Bureau of Revenues, the president of Liberia confirmed the application. The customary owners did not get any financial compensation, besides the aforementioned token of respect, for the sale of their land.

In summary, customary land rights were regularly disrespected before and during the Liberian civil war. While use rights were recognized to some extent, the government often ignored these rights in practice. The Liberian Land Commission therefore concluded in 2013 that Liberia had never had a clear land policy; that the land legislation had not significantly been amended in the past 150 years; and that it lagged behind international best practices.[44] In the following, the emergence and negotiation of FPIC in the forest and land sector reform processes will be explored.

3.2 The Liberian Field of Forest Sector Reform: 2003-Today

As shown in the previous chapter, FPIC had existed in the fields of transnational law before it became part of the Liberian legislation. It was vernacularized in Liberia between 2007 and 2009.[45] The following section will explore how FPIC emerged and how it was renegotiated and incorporated into the national legal system. After mapping the field of forest-sector reform, the actors constituting the field will be examined, the negotiation of FPIC in the legal reform, and the emerging understanding of FPIC.

3.2.1 *Mapping the Field of Forest Sector Reform*

Before looking at the renegotiation of FPIC, the question arises: what field are we talking about? The starting point is not the material space of Liberia but the unique sociotemporal situation following the end of the civil war, during which the forest sector reform took place. Even though the field of the legal reforms was a predominantly national time-space, it was also a field over which international peacebuilders and development practitioners yielded considerable influence and assumed a 'quasi-state status'.[46] It thus shows many of the characteristics of what Santos describes as the 'heterogeneous state'.[47] Migdal and Schlichte also argue that the 'weaving of practices by local societies, governments, and international agencies has produced

[43] Public Lands Law (1956), ch 3 para 30.

[44] Land rights policy (2013) (Land Commission), p. 7.

[45] Regulation No 102-07 on forest land use planning (2007) s 61(c)(3).

[46] Weilenmann (2009b), p. 156.

[47] de Sousa Santos (2006), p. 70.

settings far from the image of the state as a coherent, unified actor'.[48] Instead, authority is 'fragmented and contentious'.[49] Hence, the legislative field was not autonomous and the legislation that resulted from it was a consequence of complex 'processes of ordering, conservation, and change'[50] in that field.

The collective habitus of peacebuilding and development professionals considerably influenced the field's logic.[51] In the 1990s, a set of international best practices and programs seeking to re-establish the rule of law in post-conflict societies began to emerge. The goal was not only reconstruction but also the pursuit of a certain vision of social progress.[52] The liberal model of peacebuilding usually focused on 'democratization, democratic government, market-oriented reform, and social inclusion'.[53] However, the Liberian peacebuilding project differed from previous peacebuilding endeavors to some extent. International peacebuilders and development practitioners increasingly took into account the role that natural resources can play in fueling conflicts. The academic literature on the so-called resource curse emerging in the 1990s provided the foundation for doing so.[54]

In 2003, the UN Security Council imposed timber sanctions for the first time in its history, recognizing the impact of 'conflict timber'[55] on the Liberian civil war.[56] Governing natural resources in a way that prevents social conflict became one of the drivers for the post-conflict forest sector reform. Equitable resource governance had two components for the peacebuilders: they sought to bring the Liberian economy back on track by allowing for the commercial use of forest resources, and they wanted to protect the remaining part of the Upper Guinea forest characterized by its outstanding conservation value.[57] While the different actors had different priorities to some extent, there was a general agreement both with regard to the need for reform, as well as the desired outcome—peace.

Hence, after the end of the war, a coalition of different actors endeavored to rebuild the sector and its legal framework from scratch to fill the 'governance vacuum'.[58] The US embassy organized the first workshop for mapping the future of the Liberian forest sector in 2003, which resulted in the elaboration of a

[48] Migdal and Schlichte (2005), pp. 14–15, 33.

[49] Podder (2013), p. 355.

[50] Griffiths (2003), p. 18.

[51] Lenoir (2006), p. 26.

[52] Sannerholm (2007).

[53] Hensell and Gerdes (2012), p. 154.

[54] Beevers (2015).

[55] Rochow (2008), p. 463.

[56] UNSC (2003), Resolution 1521 (2003) adopted by the Security Council at its 4890th meeting, on 22 December 2003, UN Doc S/Res/1521(2003).

[57] Altman et al. (2012), p. 357; Beevers (2015), p. 31.

[58] Beevers (2015), p. 28.

roadmap.[59] The US government also founded the Liberia Forest Initiative and put the US Forest Service in charge of implementing and coordinating it, while the US State Department took the policy lead.[60] Other actors involved in the Liberia Forest Initiative were international organizations like the International Monetary Fund, the World Bank, the United Nations Mission in Liberia (UNMIL), the Food and Agriculture Organization, international conservation organizations, and national players, including the Forestry Development Authority (FDA) and civil society organizations.[61] The organization and implementation of the Liberia Forest Initiative drew from multi-donor coordination experiences in other countries.[62] It was mandated to make the forest sector more accountable by building strong institutions and reforming forest allocation policy and practice to meet international obligations 'including conservation and extractive uses'.[63] After the Liberia Forest Initiative expired in 2007, the negotiation of the forest legislation took place in the newly created Community Forestry Working Group. It was chaired by the Liberian Governance Commission, and its members included two non-governmental organizations (NGOs), the FDA, the USAID-funded Land Rights and Community Forestry Program (LRCFP), and private sector representatives.[64]

The peacebuilding and development logic strongly shaped the field's practice or 'cultural system'[65] as well as its law.[66] However, also state law and what was perceived as customary law influenced the law of the field of the forest sector reform by providing status to some actors—such as parliament or the Forestry Development Authority—and by influencing the field's discourses.[67] Law is understood in the processual sense: it refers to the 'shop floor'[68] rules that are produced by the field and that are generally complied with.[69]

The legislative field's law was strongly informed by international best practices. Experiences made in other geographical contexts and incorporated into the peacebuilders' habitus were largely accepted by the various actors at play.[70] Development logic and the so-called project law thus shaped the legislative field. Weilenmann understands project law as an 'important governance technique'[71]

---

[59] Blundell (2003).

[60] McAlpine et al. (2006), p. 85.

[61] Center for International Forestry Research (2005).

[62] McAlpine et al. (2006), p. 90.

[63] Ibid p. 85.

[64] Roesch R (23 Apr 2018) Skype interview with a former senior staff member of the LRCFP, para 40; Roesch R (19 Dec 2017) Interview with a former senior staff member of a Liberian NGO, Duazon, para 68.

[65] Engle Merry (2005), p. 222.

[66] Falk Moore (1973), p. 728.

[67] See also ibid p. 728.

[68] Griffiths (2003), p. 38.

[69] Falk Moore (1973), p. 722.

[70] Bourdieu (1986), p. 831.

[71] Weilenmann (2009a), p. 41.

working both as a planning instrument and an implementing tool.[72] Project law includes the development project logic—with its strict timelines, focus on measurable results, and its best practices.[73] But it also has what Griffiths calls independent effects: They can occur when countries adopt rules to get access to funding and support while taking little interest in the social effects of these rules.[74] Thereby, project law has both homogenization—by harmonizing practices worldwide—and fragmentation effects—by adding another governance layer.[75]

In particular, the field was characterized by the focus on legal reforms, the dominance of international legal and technical expertise, and the commitment to hybridity and national ownership.

Regarding the first characteristic, it appeared to be common sense that legal reforms would be a crucial component of the peacebuilding project.[76] In the law and development movement, legal systems in the Global South are often perceived as a problem that needs to be fixed.[77] Therefore, donors provide legal advice to governments and assist them in ratifying international treaties and drafting legislation.[78] Legal transplants—norms and concepts originating from another space—are frequently used to reform legal systems *in crisis*. The rationale behind legal transplants is the assumption that what has worked elsewhere may also generate social change in a post-war society.[79] Moreover, project law makes the introduction of legal transplants, model laws, and templates a logical consequence.[80] 'Quick win fixes'[81] with legal experts forging 'legal blue prints all over the globe'[82] are often more attractive than more fundamental participatory reform processes.[83] The international pressure weighing on Liberia to reform its forestry sector also made Liberia join the Extractive Industries Transparency Initiative (EITI), which, uncommonly enough, also covers the forestry sector. Besides that, Liberia signed a Voluntary

[72] Weilenmann (2009b), p. 157.

[73] See also Nichols and Moumin (2016), p. 431.

[74] Griffiths (1979), pp. 354–355.

[75] See also Weilenmann (2009a), p. 39.

[76] UNSC (2003), Resolution 1521 (2003) adopted by the Security Council at its 4890th meeting, on 22 December 2003, UN Doc S/Res/1521(2003), para 10.

[77] Griffiths (1979), p. 350.

[78] Sannerholm (2007), p. 79.

[79] Suhrke and Borchgrevink (2009), p. 213; Desai et al. (2012), pp. 251–252.

[80] von Benda-Beckmann and von Benda-Beckmann (2007b), p. 59.

[81] Pugh (2005), p. 31.

[82] von Benda-Beckmann et al. (2005), p. 19; see also Public International Law & Policy Group (2012) Post-conflict constitution drafter's handbook. https://static1.squarespace.com/static/5900b58e1b631bffa367167e/t/5abe746e6d2a73e4f849cf2d/1522431088444/PILPG_Post-Conflict%2BConstitution%2BDrafter%27s%2BHandbook_Final.pdf. Accessed 11 Aug 2023.

[83] See also Moran (2006), p. 128.

Partnership Agreement (VPA) with the European Union and adopted a national REDD+[84] strategy in 2016.[85]

The second characteristic of the field's law was the faith placed in technical and legal expertise.[86] In many cases, foreign experts draft laws with limited and superficial involvement of national actors.[87] Knowledge of the place where the reforms take place is often only an asset in the hiring of legal consultants, highlighting that technical expertise is valued more than local knowledge.[88] But this happens not only on the legal side of things; conservation and forestry expertise works similarly. Khan observes that 'whether it is "scientific forestry" or "co-management conservation", the Global South is still on the receiving end in terms of implementing biodiversity conservation projects and adopting global forestry discourses'[89] produced in the North.

The third characteristic—hybridity—gave rise to new participatory practices. Since the 1990s, multi-stakeholder processes are increasingly common in peacebuilding.[90] During the early post-war reforms—particularly those targeting the security sector—national ownership and the *local* referred to the National Transitional Government of Liberia, while other actors had limited access to the reforms.[91] Civil society was mainly seen as providing legitimacy to the national owners of the process.[92] In view of the power of the peacebuilders and donors, government actors still complained that the reforms had not been sufficiently 'liberianized'.[93] Later in the process, when the reform of the forest sector took off, national ownership acquired a different meaning. The legal reforms were designed as a participatory process to enhance the legitimacy and effectiveness of the institutions that would be created.[94] The UN Panel of Experts on Liberia proposed a roundtable approach making the drafting process a collaborative effort.[95] This resulted in a legal drafting practice, where it was generally accepted that different actors would

[84] REDD+ is the UN program seeking to combat deforestation.

[85] An Act establishing the Liberia Extractive Industries Transparency Initiative (LEITI) (2009) (Republic of Liberia); Voluntary Partnership Agreement between the European Union and the Republic of Liberia on forest law enforcement, governance and trade in timber products to the european union (2012) OJ L 191; National strategy for reducing emissions from deforestation and forest degradation (REDD+) in Liberia (2016) (Forestry Development Authority).

[86] Bourdieu (1986), p. 828; Sannerholm (2007), p. 81.

[87] Suhrke and Borchgrevink (2009), pp. 213 f.

[88] Autesserre (2014), pp. 69, 72.

[89] Khan (2016), p. 235.

[90] Fuest (2010), p. 7.

[91] Andersen (2006), p. 4.

[92] Leonardsson and Rudd (2015), p. 830.

[93] Andersen (2006), p. 5.

[94] Wallis (2016), p. 362.

[95] UNSC (2003), Letter dated 28 October 2003 from the Chairman of the Security Council Committee established pursuant to resolution 1343 (2001) concerning Liberia addressed to the President of the Security Council, UN Doc S/2003/937, para 160.

Fig. 3.1 Timeline of the Liberian forest sector reform

produce drafts, which would then be commented on by other actors. National actors would also regularly receive input from outside experts, who would come to the country occasionally to provide expertise.[96] While controversies arose between the actors, particularly between NGOs and the government, about whether the other parties followed the rules, the process itself was not questioned. The field's law—in the sense of the rules of the game—was thus quite clear and largely accepted by most actors.[97]

However, the field's practice also underwent some changes over time: The drafting of the laws and regulations at first occurred in the context of strong donor influence, a dire economic situation, and government institutions being largely dysfunctional and donor-dependent.[98] During the reform process, the power of international actors decreased with the consolidation of the FDA and other government agencies. This made the field's law and practice change.

Several laws, regulations, and policies were adopted between 2003 and 2017. Just like many legal reforms in the Global South with heavy international involvement, the forest sector reform was essentially a 'legal laboratory'.[99] Policies were endorsed and then followed by vague 'umbrella acts'.[100] Subsequently, and based on additional experience, implementing regulations 'turn[ed] what is gray into black and white'[101] (see also Fig. 3.1).

The adopted policies were the National Forest Policy and the National Forestry Management Strategy.[102] While not legally binding, they still had a considerable impact on the subsequent legislation. In 2006, the National Forestry Reform Law, which regulates commercial forestry and forest conservation, was adopted and operationalized by the 2007 Ten Core Regulations.[103] In 2009, the Parliament

[96] Roesch R (26 Feb 2018) Interview with a senior staff member of an international human rights organization, Monrovia, para 213.

[97] Falk Moore (1973), p. 743; Griffiths (2003), pp. 23–24.

[98] Roesch R (7 Jun 2018) Skype interview with a lawyer of an international human rights organization, para 102.

[99] Bognitz (2020), p. 205.

[100] McCarthy (2005), p. 158.

[101] Government official, as cited in: ibid p. 158.

[102] National forestry policy and implementation strategy (2006) (Forestry Development Authority); National forest management policy (2007) (Forestry Development Authority).

[103] An Act adopting the National Forestry Reform Law of 2006 (amending the National Forestry Law of 2000, as amended; and amending an Act creating the Forestry Development Authority, as amended) (2006) (Republic of Liberia); Ten Core Regulations (2007).

adopted the Community Rights Law introducing community forestry in Liberia.[104] In 2011, the Community Rights Law Regulations were promulgated and amended in 2017. Moreover, in 2016, the National Wildlife Conservation Law was passed.[105]

3.2.2 Actors in Relation

Actors play a crucial role in the formation of fields.[106] The field's actors can be compared to players in a game: they have different stakes, they invest in the game (at times they compete, at times they cooperate), they subject themselves to the rules of the game, and some of them have trump cards, which may change the rules of the game.[107] Moreover, they can draw from different legal orders.[108] The *situs* of actors within the game, as well as their relation to other actors, determines their power.

In the following, the different actors and their power, stakes, and relations will be explored.[109] The actors constituting the field of forest sector reform included donors, conservationists, non-governmental organizations (NGOs), government actors, and logging industry representatives. It will also be explored who was not part of the field.

Moreover, the discourses used by the different actors will be examined. Some scholars theorize outside influences on the negotiation of norms as 'external normative environments' such as neoliberalism, peacebuilding, and human rights.[110] The use of the term external implies that a clear line can be drawn between external and internal actors. However, such a clear line is neither useful nor realistic. Instead, the actors of the field of post-conflict forest sector reform are simultaneously located in several fields. Particularly the fields of peacebuilding, human rights, and the economic field are worth mentioning in this respect. These multiple positionalities influenced the negotiation of FPIC in Liberia, as actors imported the values and the discourses of the fields in which they were co-located.

Thus, the following will examine the different actors in more detail, their co-location in other fields, their capital, their relationship to other actors, and their vision of communities, the state, and FPIC. It will be shown that, unlike in the global time-space, it is not the collective identity that determines FPIC's meaning but the

---

[104] An Act to establish the Community Rights Law of 2009 with respect to forest lands (2009) (Republic of Liberia); Regulation to the Community Rights Law of 2009 with respect to forest lands, as amended (2017).

[105] An Act adopting the National Wildlife Conservation and Protected Area Management Law of Liberia (2016a) (Republic of Liberia).

[106] Bourdieu and Wacquant (1992a), p. 97.

[107] Ibid p. 98.

[108] See also von Benda-Beckmann (2022), p. 25.

[109] See also Trubek et al. (1994), pp. 416–417.

[110] Krook and True (2010), p. 120.

forest as a space of imagination. The forest, thereby, functions as a nodal point attributing meaning to other elements, such as the state, the community, and, thus, also FPIC.[111]

3.2.2.1 Donors and the Fields of Peacebuilding and Development

Bi- and multilateral donors played a central role in the field of forest sector reform. Some of them are co-located in the field of peacebuilding, while others are in the field of development. Peacebuilding efforts are also usually linked to the broader development agenda.[112] Moreover, some of them are simultaneously located in the field of conservation. The global discourses on human rights, peace, and development legitimized their strong role and 'have become the code for institutionalized involvement of all kinds of externally-rooted agencies that shape states on all continents'.[113] Following the identification of the key actors, their power and the discourses, which they imported, will be explored.

The United Nations (UN), the World Bank, and the US government assumed key roles in the forest sector reform process. In 2004, a UN Panel of Experts began its work monitoring the progress required for lifting the UN timber sanctions. The UN timber sanctions also provided critical leverage to NGOs opting for comprehensive forest sector reform.[114] However, in the law reform itself, the UN played only a minor role. Still, it supported the Liberian government in its objective to attract more foreign direct investment. For example, when students planned to release a report on the negative impacts of foreign direct investment in Liberia during the 2011 presidential campaign, the head of the UN Mission in Liberia urged them to postpone the release until after the elections.[115]

The World Bank equally participated in the forest sector reform. Its activities focused on getting the timber sanctions lifted and the re-establishment of commercial forestry.[116] Moreover, it provided technical and legal expertise.

The most important donor in the forest sector reform may have been the US government. It initiated the Liberia Forest Initiative, in which the United States Agency for International Development (USAID) and the US Forest Service assumed central roles.[117] After the expiration of the Liberia Forest Initiative in 2007, the US Government began funding the Land Rights and Community Forest Program (LRCFP). The goal of the project was to develop and implement a framework for

---

[111] Laclau and Mouffe (2001), p. 112.

[112] Datzberger and Le Mat (2018), p. 62.

[113] Migdal and Schlichte (2005), p. 33.

[114] Eg Kpanan Ayoung Siakor (2017), p. 32.

[115] Mukpo (2018) The tyranny of good intentions. https://africasacountry.com/2018/12/the-tyranny-of-good-intentions. Accessed 19 Jul 2023.

[116] Brottem and Unruh (2009), p. 997; Independent Evaluation Group (2012), pp. 68–69.

[117] Independent Evaluation Group (2012), pp. 6–7.

community forestry.[118] The project was designed by USAID in collaboration with the US Forest Service and had a biodiversity earmark.[119] Therefore, the LRCFP had a conservation-centered vision of community forestry.[120] One of the expected outputs was the 'synthesis of community forestry best practice'[121] in line with the LRCFP's biodiversity conservation objectives. Moreover, Conservation International was made one of the LRCFP's sub-contractors.[122] In 2009, the LRCFP began testing community forestry in four pilot communities located on 'biologically significant'[123] land. The LRCFP also joined the Community Forest Working Group in charge of drafting the Community Rights Law in 2008. It took an active role in the legal reforms and provided continuous advice to the Forestry Development Authority.[124]

The power of donors is linked to the capital they hold.[125] Multi- and bilateral donors had significant economic capital.[126] With the Liberian economy and state institutions dysfunctional and underfunded, donors made considerable funds available to be invested in the forest sector reform.[127] Even though they tended to disguise their interventions as technical assistance, practice shows that donor involvement often goes well beyond that, and they are sometimes close to assuming legislative functions.[128] Thereby, they also had decent cultural capital, as they mastered the rules of the game—or even set them.[129]

Moreover, given the overarching value of the field—peace—donors also had considerable symbolic capital. Symbolic capital is 'any property [. . .] when it is perceived by social agents endowed with categories of perception which cause them to know and recognize it, to give it value'.[130] Reforming the forest sector as a way of ensuring peace endowed the actors with considerable symbolic capital. The peacebuilders further enhanced their legitimacy by stressing the participatory nature of the peacebuilding project. In the discourse of hybrid peacebuilding, local ownership, Indigenous governance, and shared sovereignty are important buzzwords.[131] In most cases, the legal reforms still follow the logic of liberal peacebuilding to a

---

[118] ARD Inc. (2008b), p. 1.

[119] Ibid p. 1; Russell et al. (2011), p. 17.

[120] Russell et al. (2011), p. 44.

[121] ARD Inc. (2008b), p. 5.

[122] Russell et al. (2011), p. 32.

[123] Ibid p. 9.

[124] Land Rights and Community Forestry Program (2008–9).

[125] Bourdieu and Wacquant (1992b), p. 99.

[126] Bourdieu et al. (1994), pp. 5 f.

[127] McAlpine et al. (2006), p. 84; Weilenmann (2009b), p. 156.

[128] See also Kapoor (2008), p. 31.

[129] Davis (2010), p. 206.

[130] Bourdieu et al. (1994), pp. 8 ff.

[131] Graef (2015), p. 82.

considerable extent.[132] The international community remains *de facto* the 'architect/legitimate knower of peacebuilding practice'.[133] This was also the case in Liberia.

Even though the discourse employed by the different actors was not completely homogenous, peacebuilding and development discourse shared certain characteristics. The actors generally (1) had a vision of the forest as an economic resource, (2) did not attempt to fundamentally interfere with the internal dimension of sovereignty, and (3) had a narrow perspective on gender in conflict.

Firstly, Liberia's forests—as the nodal point in the field's discourse—were primarily seen as a source for economic development. In this respect, the grievance and greed theory was popular, according to which economic development would be the best strategy for preventing armed conflicts.[134] The actors of the field envisioned getting the sanctions lifted and establishing a regime of sustainable forest management.[135] The marketization of conflict resources should transform them into peace resources to be used for rebuilding the country.[136] The fact that the reforms targeted the forest sector instead of tackling the more fundamental issue of tenure insecurity demonstrates the prioritization of economic concerns over more fundamental social reforms. Liberian President Ellen Johnson Sirleaf became a strong ally in this respect. She made 'rapid, inclusive and sustainable economic growth'[137] the core of the Liberian Poverty Reduction Strategy that the World Bank mandated. The Liberian forests thus became a potential source of governmental income, enabling development in the long run.

Secondly, the nodal point *forest* determined the meaning of the elements *state* and *community*.[138] From the economic understanding of the forest, a vision of a strong state managing these economic resources was derived. For example, most actors did not question the state's right to grant concessions.[139]

Moreover, even though the actors co-located in the fields of peacebuilding and development tended to be critical of national institutions, they also had a negative perception of rural communities and their culture. Through 'the semiotic construction of culture',[140] it was reified and dismissed as backward: communities' involvement in natural resource governance was seen as unrealistic. The emerging social identity can be described as the *incompetent community*.[141] Thus, the internal sovereignty of the state was not questioned, and communities were not seen as

[132] See also Paffenholz (2015), p. 861; Waldorf (2018), p. 445.

[133] Shepherd (2017a), p. 151.

[134] Eg Bannon and Collier (2003); Pugh (2005), p. 23; Radelet (2007), p. 1.

[135] Independent Evaluation Group (2012), p. 68.

[136] Beevers (2019), p. 188.

[137] Liberia: Poverty reduction strategy paper (2008) (Republic of Liberia), p. 35.

[138] Laclau and Mouffe (2001), p. 112.

[139] Alden Wily (2008), pp. 22–23.

[140] Kapoor (2008), pp. 21, 26.

[141] Eg Pugh (2005), p. 31.

partners or agents but rather as beneficiaries.[142] Benefit-sharing, instead of real community participation, is the method of choice within that paradigm. Community rights and FPIC remained at the margin of the field. For example, one senior staff member of the LRCFP argued that 'FPIC is very much associated with Europe, with the European Union and other European donors',[143] while USAID only saw it as a component of transparency.

Thirdly, gender played an increasing role in peacebuilding processes and development.[144] This was institutionalized with the adoption of the 2000 UN Security Council Resolution 1325 on Women, Peace and Security (UNSCR 1325).[145] UNSCR 1325 is firmly rooted in 'international conflict feminism'[146] and has become 'a central factor in the political economy of conflict contexts'.[147] The 2003 Accra Peace Agreement reflected the spirit of UNSCR 1325. It foresaw the participation of women in the Governance Commission and called upon the transitional government to 'accord particular attention to the issue of the rehabilitation of vulnerable groups or war victims (children, women, the elderly and the disabled)'.[148] The UN Security Council reaffirmed 'the need to address violence against women and girls as a tool of warfare'[149] in Liberia.

Hence, in the peacebuilding discourse, Liberian women were primarily seen as victims of violence.[150] International organizations and NGOs implemented gender-sensitive programs mostly in the context of the judicial and security sector reform, as well as agriculture.[151] Groups not fitting into the women-as-victims paradigm had problems accessing services provided by development organizations. Those included, for example, female combatants, who were largely excluded from programs targeting ex-combatants and child soldiers, but also male non-combatants.[152] The dominance of the social identity of women-victims created a peacebuilding reality, in which 'certain policy initiatives become "thinkable", even necessary, while others are excluded'.[153] With the forest sector reform being located at the

---

[142] Russell et al. (2011), p. 8.

[143] Roesch R (4 Apr 2018) Skype interview with a former senior staff member of the LRCFP and PROSPER, para 126.

[144] Kunz (2016), p. 101.

[145] UNSC (2000), Resolution 1325 (2000) adopted by the Security Council at its 4213th meeting, on 31 October 2000, UN Doc S/Res/1325(2000).

[146] Nesiah (2012), p. 140.

[147] Ibid pp. 140–141.

[148] UNSC (2003), Peace Agreement between the government of Liberia, the Liberians United for Reconciliation and Democracy, the movement for Democracy in Liberia and the political parties, UN Doc S/2003/850, arts 16.3.a, 31.1.a.

[149] UNSC (2003), Resolution 1509 (2003) adopted by the Security Council at its 4830th meeting, on 19 September 2003, UN Doc S/RES/1509(2003), para 11.

[150] Puechguirbal (2005), pp. 3–4; Moran (2010), pp. 263, 268; Shepherd (2017b), pp. 3–5.

[151] Gizelis (2011), p. 528.

[152] Coulter et al. (2008), pp. 21 ff; Fuest (2008), p. 210.

[153] Shepherd (2017b), p. 5.

complex intersection of economic empowerment, local governance, and land tenure, donors and other actors failed to recognize the gender dimension of forestry.[154] Moreover, due to the time pressure caused by the UN sanctions and the focus on foreign direct investment, gender sensitivity was not one of the core concerns during the negotiation of the forest legislation.[155] Nagelhus Schia's and de Carvalho's criticism that 'supply-driven humanitarian and development projects that resonate with donors, at the expense of long-term infrastructure projects'[156] risk reproducing gender-based and other inequalities is thus well-founded. Despite the inherent limitations of the women-victim identity, the integration of this gender perspective helped legitimize the peacebuilding project.[157]

Development and peacebuilding discourse—and their construction of forests as an economic resource, the strong state, incompetent communities, and gender as a non-forest issue—was thus particularly powerful and strongly influenced the field. To some extent, national NGOs and government agencies echoed this discourse or aspects of it.

3.2.2.2 The Field of Conservation

According to Brottem and Unruh, post-conflict Liberia provided a 'window of opportunity to conservationists'.[158] The civil war, which resulted in the collapse of much of Liberia's industrial sector, as well as a continuing lack of infrastructure, contributed to the conservation of considerable forest areas of high biodiversity value. Several actors, including conservation NGOs, the USAID-funded Liberia Land and Community Forestry Program (LRCFP), and some elements within the Forestry Development Authority (FDA), are also co-located in the field of conservation.

Conservation NGOs were heavily involved in the legal reform process.[159] The US-based NGO Conservation International has been active in Liberian forestry for a long time advocating for forest conservation. Already in 2002, it signed a Memorandum of Understanding with the Liberian government pledging to set aside 30% of its forest land as protected areas.[160] This commitment translated into the adoption of the 2003 Act for the Establishment of a Protected Forest Area Network and was also

[154] See also The national gender policy (2009) (Ministry of Gender and Development).

[155] Land Rights and Community Forestry Program (2008) para 3.

[156] Nagelhus Schia and de Carvalho (2010), p. 5.

[157] See also Kunz (2016), p. 99.

[158] Brottem and Unruh (2009), pp. 995–996.

[159] UNEP (2004), pp. 69 ff.

[160] Ibid p. 76.

included in the 2006 National Forestry Reform Law.[161] Moreover, international conservation NGOs gave the National Forest Management Strategy a strong conservation imprint.[162] In relation to the Community Rights Law, conservation NGOs were concerned about the possibility that national forests and protected areas could be restituted to communities.[163] Besides that, the US government took a strong interest in forest conservation and parts of the FDA committed to the conservation agenda, possibly as a way of accessing donor funding and due to the strong international pressure.[164] This corresponds to what Griffiths describes as the independent effects of project law.[165]

Conservation actors had considerable capital in the legal reforms. They derived their legitimacy from the protection of a higher good: the environment. Their legitimacy was enhanced by transnational and national environmental law.[166] Particularly the Convention on Biological Diversity is worth mentioning in this respect. It provides the legal foundation for land use zoning as it calls for the designation of *in situ* conservation areas.[167] Conservationists also had considerable economic capital. The Society for the Conservation of Nature of Liberia and Conservation International piloted the first community forests. Conservation International also helped to build the FDA's conservation department, and the USAID forest projects were operating under a biodiversity earmark.[168]

With respect to the prevailing conservation discourse, conservationists viewed the forest as an *ecological resource* to be preserved. But what did this understanding of the forest mean for the social identities of the *state* and the *community*? Conservationists—as explored in the previous chapter—often envision a strong state protecting the environment.[169] This resonated well with national actors such as the FDA, which used conservation discourse as a way of positioning itself as the legitimate guardian of Liberia's natural resources. It saw the extension of the protected area network as an opportunity for establishing legal control over large land tracts.[170]

---

[161] An Act adopting the National Forestry Reform Law of 2006 (amending the National Forestry Law of 2000, as amended; and amending an Act creating the Forestry Development Authority, as amended) (2006), s 9.1.a.

[162] Lamb et al. (2009), p. 301.

[163] Anonymus source 3 (2008); Roesch R (19 Dec 2017) Interview with a former senior staff member of a Liberian NGO, Duazon, para 128.

[164] Lamb et al. (2009), p. 302; see also Sect. 3.2.2.1.

[165] Griffiths (1979), pp. 354–355.

[166] See also von Benda-Beckmann (2001), p. 38.

[167] Convention on Biological Diversity (adopted 6 Jun 1992, entered into force 29 Dec 1993) 1760 UNTS 69, art 8.

[168] Liberia's national biodiversity strategy and action plan (2004) (National Transitional Government of Liberia), pp. 51–52; McAlpine et al. (2006), p. 87.

[169] Fouladbash (2013) Agroforestry and shifting cultivation in Liberia: Livelihood impacts, carbon tradeoffs, and socio-political obstacles. MSc thesis, University of Michigan, p. 58.

[170] Roesch R (13 Jun 2018) Skype interview with an anthropologist, paras 15 ff.

Simultaneously, conservationists had a more negative perception of the communities and their relationship to the forest. The 'modern conservation lobby'[171] often argues that the creation of people-free protected areas is the only way of halting deforestation.[172] It constructs communities as the primary culprits of deforestation and a fiction of uninhabited land is regularly used as a strategy for illegalizing local forest uses:[173] Areas which are rich in biodiversity must be uninhabited and protected from future community uses.

Thereby, conservationists heavily influenced how local forest uses, including bushmeat hunting, shifting cultivation, and charcoal production, were negotiated in Liberia.[174] The terminology of 'forest fringe communities'[175] adjacent to protected areas, which neglects that customary land usually does not end at the border of protected areas, exemplifies this. Moreover, shifting cultivation was declared to be the greatest threat to biodiversity in Liberia.[176] The term describes the clearing of land for small-holder farming and then leaving it fallow for several years before re-starting the planting cycle. Conservation NGOs, government officials, and representatives of international organizations alike echoed its harmfulness during the legal reform process, even though the causality between shifting cultivation and deforestation is controversial at best.[177] Similarly, small-scale miners in the Sapo National Park were portrayed as 'illegal inhabitants'[178] that had to be evacuated.

Concerning bushmeat hunting, the National Transitional Government of Liberia held in 2004 that 'poverty and ignorance, shifting cultivation, misguided timber exploitation and monoculture plantation development, poaching and lack of land use planning'[179] are the biggest threats to biodiversity in Liberia. The Liberian report to the Convention on Biological Diversity also stresses that poaching could destroy outstanding flora and fauna.[180] According to the National Forestry Policy, between 75 and 85% of all hunting activities target protected or fully protected species, and it suggests prohibiting the hunting of protected wildlife, despite the importance of

---

[171] Fairhead and Leach (1998), p. 46.

[172] DeFries et al. (2005), p. 25; Bennett (2015), p. 143.

[173] See also Lowenhaupt Tsing (2003), p. 30; Brottem and Unruh (2009), p. 999.

[174] Eg USAID (2010) Liberia: Property rights and resource governance. https://land-links.org/wp-content/uploads/2016/09/USAID_Land_Tenure_Liberia_Profile.pdf. Accessed 11 Aug 2023, p. 12.

[175] Eg the country director of Conservation International, as cited in: Fouladbash (2013) Agroforestry and shifting cultivation in Liberia: Livelihood impacts, carbon tradeoffs, and socio-political obstacles. Master of Science MSc thesis, University of Michigan, p. 58.

[176] Liberia's national biodiversity strategy and action plan (2004) (National Transitional Government of Liberia), p. 74; Eba'a Atyi (2018), p. 50.

[177] Center for International Forestry Research (2005), pp. 8, 12, 34, 86, 95; Ickowitz (2006), p. 599.

[178] McAlpine et al. (2006), p. 88.

[179] Liberia's national biodiversity strategy and action plan (2004) (National Transitional Government of Liberia), p. 73.

[180] Republic of Liberia (2014), p. 13.

bushmeat as a source of protein.[181] Moreover, the common use of the term poaching instead of bushmeat hunting is a way of undermining the legitimacy of local practices and cultural ecologies.[182]

Hence, in conservation discourse, communities tended to be portrayed as irrational and unable to sustainably use their forests without guidance from the state or international actors.[183] The construction of the *incompetent community* resembled the social identity prevailing in peacebuilding and development discourse. Local knowledge of forest management and environmental protection was negated. The othering of local practices found expression in statements like the lack of an adequate legal framework has prevented the 'rational exploitation'[184] of forest resources by communities. Many development projects in Liberia thus sought to change century-old agricultural practices.[185] International actors also pushed national authorities towards better protecting existing protected areas.[186]

Simultaneously, scientific forestry becomes the positive antonym enabling environmental protection and serving a greater (or greener) good.[187] The scientification of forestry went hand in hand with the functional territorialization of forests, ie, the designation of forest areas for specific uses based on suitability criteria. However, as Vandergeest notes, 'the classification of land and land use activities by experts using scientific criteria is incompatible with participatory approaches which would recognize and allow for complex on-the-ground arrangements among users'.[188] Human rights and FPIC are thus usually not part of the forestry discourse. For example, a survey by the US Forest Service identified 3.41 million hectares suitable for commercial, 1.14 million hectares for conservation and only 52,000 hectares for community use without taking customary land rights into consideration.[189]

Hence, conservation discourse and particularly its vision of the forest as an *ecological resource*, a strong state, and *incompetent communities* resonated well with a wide range of actors making it particularly powerful.

---

[181] National forestry policy and implementation strategy (2006) (Forestry Development Authority), p. 17.

[182] Eg Liberia's national biodiversity strategy and action plan (2004) (National Transitional Government of Liberia), p. 79; Fauna & Flora International (2019) Liberia. www.fauna-flora.org/countries/liberia. Accessed 19 Jul 2023.

[183] Eg Liberia's national biodiversity strategy and action plan (2004) (National Transitional Government of Liberia), p. 79; Fauna & Flora International (2019) Liberia. www.fauna-flora.org/countries/liberia. Accessed 19 Jul 2023.

[184] Republic of Liberia (2014), p. 23.

[185] Eg Forestry Development Authority (2009), p. 3.

[186] Ibid p. 3.

[187] Fairhead et al. (2012), p. 239.

[188] Vandergeest (1996), p. 171.

[189] National forest management strategy (2007) (Forestry Development Authority), pp. 11–12.

3.2.2.3 NGOs and the Field of Human Rights

The NGO scene is not one cohesive transnational alliance network but rather a conglomerate of multiple networks with differing agendas and power.[190] Both donors and NGOs are simultaneously located within the field of human rights, albeit to varying degrees. Many NGOs also have bonds to the field of development, as they receive funding from donors like the UK Department for International Development and the European Union. This section identifies the key actors co-located in the field of human rights, their power, and their vision of the forest, the state, and communities.

The civil war contributed to the creation of many Liberian NGOs in the 1990s, most of them dealing with emergency situations.[191] Yet civil society in the field of natural resource governance tended to be weak. The main NGOs in the forest sector reform were Green Advocates and the Sustainable Development Institute (SDI). They worked closely together with international human rights organizations.[192]

These actors understood legal drafting as a strategy for norm change.[193] They made community forestry a part of the 'cartographic-legal strategy',[194] which aims to correct historical injustices and/or enable development by recognizing the collective property rights of communities. Already during the Accra peace talks in 2003, NGOs advocated for placing a moratorium on natural resource-related commercial activities.[195] This call was taken up by international organizations and laid the cornerstone for a comprehensive concession review.[196] The US Forest Service also supported the inclusion of national civil society representatives in the drafting of forestry laws.[197] This is in line with many hybridized peacebuilding projects, where international actors welcome the participation of civil society.[198] Yet, the relationship tends to be unequal, with international actors imposing the framework and NGOs being granted the right to participate.[199]

Before the adoption of the Community Rights Law, the SDI, together with an international organization, conducted nationwide consultations with forest communities and tasked an international land tenure specialist with drafting a report on

---

190 See also Carpenter (2007), p. 115.

191 Sawyer (2005), p. 75.

192 Roesch R (26 Feb 2018) Interview with a senior staff member of an international human rights organization, Monrovia, para 213; Roesch R (7 Jun 2018) Skype interview with a lawyer of an international human rights organization, paras 38 ff.

193 Sikkink (2002), pp. 46 ff.

194 Wainwright and Bryan (2009), p. 154.

195 Kpanan'Ayoung Siakor (2011), p. 18.

196 Rochow (2008), pp. 464–465.

197 Roesch R (19 Dec 2017) Interview with a former senior staff member of a Liberian NGO, Duazon, para 28.

198 Weilenmann (2009b), p. 170; Fuest (2010), p. 6.

199 Shepherd (2017a), p. 151.

forest land tenure.[200] This report strongly informed the positions of civil society during the negotiation of the Community Rights Law (CRL). National NGOs also relied on the input of international NGO experts, who continuously provided comments on the different versions of the CRL.[201] Nevertheless, they were regularly divided in their assessment of the legal reforms. While some of them rejected the National Forestry Reform Law for being a 'logging law',[202] others saw it as an important achievement.[203]

National NGOs tend to have limited economic capital. However, they have considerable symbolic capital. They draw legitimacy from human rights discourse and from being seen as the voice of local communities. This confers a grassroots-type of legitimacy to them. Moreover, they tend to have considerable social capital as they have links to donors and international NGOs.[204]

The discourse(s) of international and national NGOs strongly differed from the discourses explored above: They understood forests as forested land owned by rural communities, the state as corrupt, communities as either legitimate guardians of the forest or as incompetent and community rights as more important than women's rights. With forests primarily seen as forested customary land, NGOs' main goal was thus to secure these customary land rights and use the forest sector reform as an interim solution.[205] Simultaneously, and just like many actors in the field of development, NGOs distrusted government agencies and so-called national elites.[206] They portrayed the government as corrupt and intransparent.[207] NGO representatives stressed their problems accessing information from the FDA and placed little trust in the FDA's management of community forests and concessions.[208]

However, NGOs' and INGOs' visions of communities strongly differed. International NGOs and anthropologists tended to portray communities as the guardians of the forest, emphasizing their unique relationship with their land and natural

[200] Alden Wily (2007).

[201] Roesch R (26 Feb 2018) Interview with a senior staff member of an international human rights organization, Monrovia, para 213; Roesch R (7 Jun 2018) Skype interview with a lawyer of an international human rights organization, paras 38 ff.

[202] Roesch R (19 Dec 2017) Interview with a former senior staff member of a Liberian NGO, Duazon, para 52.

[203] Smyle (2012), p. 6.

[204] See also Moran (2010), p. 268.

[205] Roesch R (19 Dec 2017) Interview with a former senior staff member of a Liberian NGO, Duazon, paras 62 ff; Roesch R (23 Apr 2018) Skype interview with a former senior staff member of the LRCFP, para 78.

[206] Beevers (2015), p. 36.

[207] This can be traced back to the role of government agencies in the Liberian civil war and the ongoing corruption and lack of transparency in many agencies (eg ibid p. 36).

[208] Eg Roesch R (4 Jan 2018) Interview with a senior staff member of a Liberian NGO, Monrovia, para 50; Roesch R (2 Mar 2018) Interview with a senior staff member of a Liberian NGO, Duazon, paras 444–447.

resources.[209] They also stressed the positive impact of shifting cultivation on soil fertility and questioned the (mono)causality between deforestation and shifting cultivation.[210] National NGOs, in contrast, drew a less positive picture of communities and their customary governance arrangements, thereby being closer to the fields of development and conservation. Many NGOs feared community-level elite capture. For example, one NGO staff member explained that democratic decision-making and customary governance institutions would be mutually exclusive.[211]

Despite these differing perspectives on the *community* as a social identity, national and international NGOs strongly advocated for community rights and FPIC, and most informants acknowledged that NGOs were the ones introducing FPIC in Liberia.[212] The NGO drafts of the Community Rights Law—also thanks to the work of an international consultant—explicitly referenced the ILO C 169 and the UNDRIP.[213] The 2011 and 2012 NGO complaints against transnational palm oil companies before the Roundtable on Sustainable Palm Oil (RSPO) also made the concept of FPIC more widely known.[214] Moreover, Liberia was a case study for the UN Voluntary Guidelines on the Responsible Governance of Tenure (VGGT), which disseminated the idea of FPIC even more in the national NGO scene.[215]

However, national NGOs generally did not frame FPIC as an Indigenous right, even though they strongly mobilized the dichotomy between urban elites and the rural poor in their work.[216] While the urban-rural distinction overlaps with Indigeneity under human rights law, it lacks the dimension of culture and self-determination. Instead, economic marginalization and collective property rights became the foundation for FPIC. FPIC was thus transformed into a right of rural communities with customary land rights. The ease with which they reframed FPIC as

[209] Lomax (2008), p. 8; Porter-Bolland et al. (2012), p. 9.

[210] Fairhead and Leach (1998), pp. 56–57; Carter (2005), p. 54; Roesch R (13 Jun 2018) Skype interview with an anthropologist, para 100.

[211] Roesch R (2 Mar 2019) Skype interview with a former senior staff member of a Liberian NGO, para 70.

[212] Roesch R (19 Dec 2017) Interview with a former senior staff member of a Liberian NGO, Duazon, para 80; Roesch R (26 Feb 2018) Interview with a senior staff member of an international human rights organization, Monrovia, paras 211 ff; Roesch R (2 Mar 2018) Interview with a senior staff member of a Liberian NGO, Duazon, para 99; Roesch R (21 Mar 2018) Interview with several staff members of a Liberian NGO, Monrovia, para 37; Roesch R (23 Apr 2018) Skype interview with a former senior staff member of the LRCFP, paras 78 ff.

[213] Eg A community rights law with respect to forest lands (2008) (Republic of Liberia), s 3.10.

[214] Those include the 2008 concession with LIBINC/EPO, the 2009 agreement with Sime Darby and the 2010 agreements with Golden Veroleum Liberia (GVL) and Maryland Oil Palm Plantation (MOPP); Letter to RSPO concerning Sime Darby's new planting procedure (2011); Sustainable Development Institute (2013), p. 5.

[215] Roesch R (23 May 2018) Skype interview with an international land tenure expert, para 69; Roesch R (7 Jun 2018) Skype interview with a lawyer of an international human rights organization, para 68.

[216] Eg Roesch R (19 Dec 2017) Interview with the a former senior staff member of a Liberian NGO, Duazon, para 246.

a non-Indigenous right was possibly also influenced by the Roundtable on Sustainable Palm Oil, which applies FPIC to local communities.[217]

Moreover, most civil society actors at the time did not see gender as a forestry issue. They argued that 'there is a bigger struggle to create space for broader citizen participation',[218] making gender equality a 'non-issue'.[219] Simultaneously, NGOs with a gender focus did not take much interest in natural resources.[220] The president of the only Liberian natural resource NGO with a specific gender focus concluded that 'the gender impacts on forest management [were] not adequately understood by [...] all the civil society organizations promoting greater citizen participation'.[221] The civil society's legal drafts also mainly constructed women as one stakeholder group amongst many, including youth, religious, and ethnic groups.[222] They also opposed women's quotas. One of the NGO representatives in the Community Forest Working Group argued that a gender quota for the Community Assembly[223] would have conflicted with a representative approach to community forestry by impairing the right of communities to elect their delegates freely.[224] Hence, unlike in transnational Indigenous law, where quotas could be seen as interfering with Indigenous self-determination and autonomy, NGOs saw quotas as undermining democracy.

Thus, in human rights discourse, forests were redefined as customary land with trees on it. The main goal was to secure those customary land rights. Consequently, NGOs sought to curb the power of the state that had regularly violated customary land rights in the past whilst being more ambiguous with respect to the social identity of the *community*. Even though the NGOs' understanding of FPIC was clearly influenced by human rights law and particularly the UNDRIP, they focused mainly on FPIC in the context of expropriations and did not pursue a broader self-determination-based approach. The construction of the *incompetent community* also enabled neglecting FPIC's institutional autonomy dimension, while the right to FPIC of rural women was also no priority for NGOs.

---

[217]Eg Roesch R (26 Feb 2018) Interview with a senior staff member of an international human rights organization, Monrovia, paras 63 ff; Roesch R (7 Jun 2018) Skype interview with a lawyer of an international human rights organization, para 192; Roesch R (14 May 2018) Skype interview with two staff members of an international environmental law organization, para 28.

[218]Foundation for Community Initiatives (2011), p. 4.

[219]Ibid p. 4.

[220]Massaquoi (2007) Women and post-conflict development: A case study on Liberia. BSc thesis, Massachusetts Institute of Technology, p. 89; Kunz (2016), p. 108.

[221]Weah (2012), p. 2.

[222]Eg the civil society drafts zero, one and three (available upon request).

[223]The highest decision-making body in community forestry that should represent the whole community.

[224]Roesch R (2 Mar 2019) Skype interview with the a former senior staff member of a Liberian NGO, para 64.

3.2.2.4 Government and National Ownership

The government agencies assuming a central position in the reforms were the Governance Commission and the Forestry Development Authority (FDA). However, the government itself also influenced the field. The following sections shed light on the relations between government and other actors, their power, and the discourse prevailing in the field of government.

Astri Suhrke's research on Afghanistan indicates that, in post-conflict contexts, national actors are often no more than string puppets, with local ownership being restricted to ownership of imported ideas.[225] To some extent, this was also the case for Liberia. The FDA had barely any economic capital. Moreover, due to its shady involvement in commercial forestry during the war and afterwards, it possessed only minimal cultural and social capital.[226]

Still, the field of government tried to resist the reforms. Resistance characterizes all fields and practices to varying degrees.[227] The government used a discourse of sovereignty to enhance its capital and to prevent far-reaching reforms. In post-conflict legal reforms, sovereignty is continuously under negotiation in such processes and 'manifested through struggles over ownership'.[228] National ownership, thereby, became an element, ie, a floating signifier with different meanings in the field of government and the field of peacebuilding.[229]

In theory, it was clear from the onset that the Government of Liberia would be in charge of implementing the forestry reform, with international actors only providing funding and technical expertise.[230] However, international actors placed little trust in the willingness and the capacity of government actors to implement the reforms. Participants of the Liberia Forest Initiative expressed concerns that the FDA's core interest was to get the sanctions lifted and to get back to business as usual.[231] The FDA was also seen as completely dysfunctional and unable to effectively handle commercial forestry.[232] Mistrust in the FDA went so far that it was placed under the donor-funded, World Bank-led supervision program Governance and Economic Management Assistance Program (GEMAP) to enhance transparency and combat corruption.[233]

However, the National Transitional Government vigorously tried to prevent more fundamental reforms, and tensions prevailed in its relationship with the

[225] Suhrke (2007), p. 1292.

[226] See also Beevers (2015), p. 37.

[227] Graef (2015), p. 52.

[228] de Carvalho et al. (2019), pp. 4–5.

[229] Laclau and Mouffe (2001), p. 113; Results focused transitional framework, revision april 2005 (2005) (National Transitional Government of Liberia et al).

[230] Lamb et al. (2009), p. 300.

[231] McAlpine et al. (2006), p. 86.

[232] Beevers (2015), p. 37.

[233] USAID (2009), p. 32.

peacebuilders. This changed during Ellen Johnson Sirleaf's presidency. Given Johnson Sirleaf's investment-friendly policies, the discourse of sovereignty was mainly used by her government for pushing through reforms and silencing opponents.[234] For example, community protests against the expansion of the Golden Veroleum Palm Oil Plantation were framed as 'unpatriotic and non-nationalistic'.[235] Responding to the ongoing involvement of civil society, President Johnson Sirleaf also declared that 'some NGOs have sought to become super-national bodies challenging sovereignty even as they themselves lack national and international governance status and rules in transparency and accessibility'.[236] Sovereignty was thus seen as a way of realizing the government's economic interests. This also translated into the field of government's reluctance to embrace community forestry.[237] The fact that the Johnson Sirleaf administration granted several illegal forest concessions just a few weeks before the Community Rights Law (CRL)—recognizing the right of communities to customarily owned forest resources—was adopted is equally symptomatic of the government's prioritization of commercial logging over community rights.[238]

Simultaneously, resistance was growing during the reforms. For instance, members of Parliament inserted provisions in the CRL that granted them the right to participate in community forestry.[239] Moreover, conflicts between the GEMAP and the FDA arose. The FDA criticized the GEMAP and NGOs for paralyzing the logging sector.[240] They even threatened to prosecute the GEMAP controllers for 'economic sabotage'.[241] Moreover, they claimed that civil society participation in the forestry sector was no longer necessary.[242] With the termination of the GEMAP project and increased governmental power, government agencies could resist external reforms to a greater extent. Until now, national ownership remains a concern for the FDA. In 2018, the Managing Director of the FDA called for the restoration of 'FDA's autonomous power, which was deleted or narrowed to semi-autonomy level

[234] The difference in bargaining power between donors and the Liberian government was immense: in 2010/11 the government had an annual budget of 369.4 USD, while UNMIL's budget alone amounted to 524.1 USD (Röhner (2012) UN peacebuilding - light footprint or friendly takeover? PhD thesis, Freie Universität Berlin, p. 185).

[235] Lanier et al. (2012), p. 57.

[236] Johnson Sirleaf (2014) Annual message to the third session of the 53rd national legislature of the Republic of Liberia. https://allafrica.com/view/resource/main/main/id/00080457.html. Accessed 19 Jul 2023, p. 40.

[237] Sustainable Development Institute (2008a), p. 1.

[238] Alden Wily et al. (2010), p. 4.

[239] Land Rights and Community Forestry Program (2008–9), p. 5.

[240] Beevers (2019), pp. 112–113.

[241] Ibid p. 118.

[242] Beevers (2015), p. 36.

during the 2006 National Forestry reform process, which [. . .] has and continues to stall the management dream and vision'.[243]

Unlike in the discourses explored above, the forest as a space of imagination did not function as a nodal point in the field of government.[244] Instead, government actors were quite flexible with respect to their vision of the forest—as long as it functioned to enhance their capital. Forests thus remained an element without a fully fixed meaning.

Even though not all government agencies have the same vision of sovereignty or pursue the same goals, they often have similar understandings of the roles of the state and communities. They tend to envision a strong, sovereign state and place little faith in community forest governance. In this respect, overlaps with development and conservation discourse exist.[245] Consequently, community rights and community forestry were not a priority for the FDA during the reform process, and it had little experience in working with communities.[246] Conservation, in contrast, had a strong international lobby and the FDA has been traditionally titled towards commercial. This was also reflected by the FDA Managing Director's proposal to have three deputy positions within the FDA. Those should be commercial enterprises, administration, and community/conservation.[247] By 2007, the FDA had been restructured, now featuring four technical departments: community, conservation, commercial, and research & development.[248] The three Cs—commercial, conservation, and community forestry—, in theory, should have been designed as interrelated within the FDA.[249] However, the relationship between the departments was characterized by a lack of communication and cooperation.[250] The community department was also flagrantly understaffed compared to the other departments.[251]

Many within the FDA believed that community forestry exceeded the capacity of communities, and similar concerns were voiced by members of the Governance Commission during the legal reforms.[252] In line with that mentality, the FDA and other government agencies were critical of FPIC. Government officials described the commercial forestry regulations and FPIC as impractical, as they did not provide the confidentiality required between the negotiating partners, ie, the state and

[243] Mike Doryen, as cited in: Kwanue (2018) FDA managing director warns VPA partners. Daily Observer. https://allafrica.com/stories/201806180614.html. Accessed 11 Aug 2023.

[244] Laclau and Mouffe (2001), p. 112.

[245] Lomax (2008), p. 19.

[246] Lamb et al. (2009), p. 301.

[247] Blundell (2003), p. 12.

[248] National forest management strategy (2007) (Forestry Development Authority), p. 14.

[249] Smyle (2012), p. 4.

[250] Russell et al. (2011), p. 37.

[251] Smilie and Brownell (2007), p. 10; Lamb et al. (2009), p. 302.

[252] Smilie and Brownell (2007), p. 10; Sustainable Development Institute (2008a), p. 1; Lamb et al. (2009), p. 302; Roesch R (20 Mar 2018) Interview with a former senior staff member of the land commission, Monrovia, para 236.

companies.[253] However, they also underestimated the power of FPIC at the time.[254] This explains why they did not oppose it more strongly.[255] For instance, the FDA drafts did not remove FPIC, but the FDA was still proposing to set aside 'at least 40% of forested areas [...] as community forests',[256] which would have been difficult to reconcile with FPIC as a human right. Later in the negotiations, the FDA began vigorously opposing FPIC. For instance, the sixth draft of the CRL submitted by the FDA to the legislature gives the FDA the right to grant so-called Community Forest Contracts for community lands, removing the explicit FPIC requirement that had been agreed on by all parties in earlier drafts.[257]

Nevertheless, many interviewees working in the administration stressed that FPIC had emerged because the government had granted concessions without involving affected communities.[258] They thus frame FPIC as a right in the context of expropriations. Practice shows, however, that the FDA has either ignored the FPIC or, at best, consulted and informed communities when granting logging concessions.[259] FPIC was thus officially endorsed but not applied in practice.[260]

The FDA also did not take a specific interest in gender considerations. During the negotiation of the CRL, the FDA removed the women's quota for the community forest governance structure in their drafts of the law.[261] Informants equally reported that the inclusion of women quotas regularly meets the resistance of government agencies.[262]

Hence, despite of or as a counterreaction to the heavy influence of transnational actors, many government actors had a vision of internal sovereignty resembling a 'bottomless pit',[263] particularly in relation to environmental regulation and the

---

[253] Kaul and Heuty (2009), p. 61.

[254] Roesch R (7 Jun 2018) Skype interview with a lawyer of an international human rights organization, para 86.

[255] FPIC was much more controversial in the negotiation of the 2018 Land Rights Act, when the potential power of the concept was better understood by government actors and parliamentarians.

[256] Points advanced by the FDA to be considered in the draft of the community rights law (CRL) with respect to forest land (3 June 2008) (available upon request).

[257] Community rights law with respect to forest lands (14 July 2008) (Republic of Liberia), s 5.3; The community rights law of 2008 with respect to forest lands (6 August 2008) (Republic of Liberia), s 5.2.

[258] Roesch R (5 Mar 2018) Interview with staff member of the Liberia Land Authority, Monrovia, para 110; Roesch R (23 Mar 2018) Interview with a former staff member of the Land Commission and current staff member of the Land Authority, Monrovia, para 12.

[259] Lamb et al. (2009), pp. 304–305; Beevers (2019), p. 110; Email from a staff member of an international human rights organization to the author (14 Feb 2019).

[260] Cabrera Ormaza and Ebert (2019), p. 487.

[261] The Community Rights Law with respect to forest lands of 2008 (third draft) (2 July 2008) (Republic of Liberia); The Community Rights Law of 2008 with respect to forest lands (6 August 2008).

[262] Roesch R (4 Jan 2018) Interview with a senior staff member of a Liberian NGO, Monrovia, para 160.

[263] von Benda-Beckmann and von Benda-Beckmann (2007b), p. 70.

governance of natural resources. The dominant vision of community and the state overlapped with the fields of peacebuilding and conservation and resulted in the general reluctance to embrace community rights and FPIC.

3.2.2.5 Logging Industry Representatives

Logging companies participated in the legal reforms while also being located in the economic field. While some of them had made considerable money during the war and possessed economic capital, their reputation had severely suffered. They were hit hard by the UN sanctions and the concession review, which resulted in the cancellation of all existing concessions in 2006.[264] Yet, new companies emerged and got involved in the forest sector reform. They feared that the prioritization of conservation would eventually make commercial logging impossible and advocated for a very streamlined forest legislation.[265] They used their financial means to influence the legal drafting and human rights activists even reported to have been threatened by them.[266]

However, during the drafting of the Community Rights Law (CRL), the Liberia Timber Association, the Association of Liberian Loggers, and the Liberian Business Association formed an interesting alliance with civil society: industry representatives and the NGO Coalition supported the comprehensive version of the CRL with a strong human rights imprint that had been submitted by civil society to Parliament.[267] Logging companies very likely saw community forestry as a way of circumventing the state and entering into more favorable agreements directly with forest communities.[268] They thus shared the negative perception of the state as corrupt and not being able to manage concessions.

3.2.2.6 Participatory Exclusions

The term 'participatory exclusions'[269] describes the exclusion of certain actors under the cloak of participation. While hybrid peacebuilding emphasizes national ownership and the participation of the *local,* the *local* was, in practice, a synonym for government actors and national NGOs.[270] Rural communities, and particularly rural women, could not meaningfully participate in the legal reforms. Little resources were invested in inquiring which local governance institutions had survived the

[264] Forest sector reform, executive order No 1 (2006).

[265] Beevers (2019), p. 93.

[266] Alfred Brownell, as cited in: ibid para 98.

[267] NGO Coalition of Liberia (2008).

[268] See also Global Witness (2018).

[269] Agarwal (2001), pp. 1627 ff.

[270] Paffenholz (2015), pp. 862 f.

colonization of the Hinterland and the civil war and how these institutions continued to govern social relations.[271] Despite calls for community participation, forest-dependent communities were excluded from the legal reform processes to a large extent.[272]

With regard to the 2006 National Forest Policy, public consultations with NGOs, chiefs, county superintendents, and city mayors took place in Robertsport and Tubmansburg, and so-called *local authorities* were also invited to a workshop in Monrovia to review the draft.[273]

During the drafting of the Community Rights Law (CRL), national NGOs received funding from the International Union for Conservation of Nature and the World Bank to hold regional consultation workshops in 2008.[274] The Land Rights and Community Forestry Project (LRCFP) also invited members of their pilot community forests to meetings of the Community Forestry Working Group and the National Benefit-Sharing Trust Working Group.[275] The Community Forestry Working was open to different stakeholders. But all NGO members were based in Monrovia. Moreover, it cannot be assumed 'that civil society organizations represent the population in any given peacebuilding context, nor can it be assumed that civil society actors are able to affect change when they are included'.[276]

Beyond the participation of NGOs, regional consultations were seen as the method of choice for enabling the participation of communities.[277] But do these consultations amount to actual participation? Meaningful participation has three components: attendance, contribution, and engagement.[278] It is possible that people do not have access to the relevant fora, that they may have access but are unable to participate in the discussions, or that they attend and participate but are not being heard.

The consultations on the legal framework were organized as one or two-day non-recurring regional consultations. Most people had no access at all to these consultations simply because of financial constraints and the costs for and duration of transportation.[279] Whether those who managed to participate could actually contribute and engage is difficult to reconstruct. Generally, it may be doubted whether the highly complex and technical details of a law can effectively be

[271] See also Sawyer (2005), p. 58.

[272] See also Beevers (2015), pp. 36–37.

[273] National forestry policy and implementation strategy (2006) (Forestry Development Authority), p. 9.

[274] Community Forest Working Group (Technical Sub-Group) (2008), p. 3.

[275] Russell et al. (2011), p. 41.

[276] Shepherd (2017a), p. 149; Gizelis and Joseph argue that there exists a considerable difference between so-called elite NGOs having access to external funding and more loosely organized community-based organizations (Gizelis and Joseph 2016, p. 547).

[277] Also with respect to the Ten Core Regulations (see Altman et al. 2012, p. 348).

[278] Banks (2007), pp. 114–115.

[279] See also Russell et al. (2011), p. 27.

discussed in such a forum, given the time constraints and high levels of illiteracy in rural areas. Moreover, the bargaining power of communities tends to be very low, so their input is likely disregarded, particularly when the law has already been drafted. Thus, even though FPIC is also relevant in the adoption of legal and administrative measures affecting communities, it was not attempted to meaningfully engage with rural communities. The exclusion of communities was legitimized by development, human rights, and conservation discourse and their construction of the *incompetent community*.

Women are also often excluded from fields of peacebuilding. Liberia and its female peace activists are, however, often cited as a positive counterexample.[280] Yet, women were not present in the formal peace talks, and not a single signatory, lead mediator, or negotiator of the Accra Peace Agreement was female.[281] An absence of women also characterized the forest sector reform process. The two NGO representatives in the Community Forestry Working Group that drafted the Community Rights Law (CRL) were male, the FDA had practically no female staff members at the time, and the LRCFP representative during the drafting of the CRL was a man.[282] A few expat women were working with conservation NGOs and the Governance Commission. Moreover, no evidence exists that the government agencies attempted to grasp the perspectives of rural women in the context of regional or national consultations, and no gender analysis was done during the drafting of the forest legislation.[283]

The lack of women's participation is not surprising given the gendered nature of the Liberian political and economic system. Moran argues that, due to Liberia's colonization, the dichotomy of civilized and native, which is deeply gendered, emerged.[284] It shows overlaps with the urban-rural dichotomy, even though some natives are living in cities and some civilized people in villages.[285] Women are often assigned subsidiary roles in the civilized-urban system, as they do not have the same access to education.[286] Consequently, neither civilized nor native women have easy access to prestigious jobs in the NGO or public sector.[287] Even though Liberia has a

[280] Eg, Gbowee (2019) When women stand together as one: The power of women's grassroots peace movements. https://jia.sipa.columbia.edu/when-women-stand-together-one-power-womens-grassroots-peace-movements. Accessed 19 Jul 2023.

[281] Massaquoi (2007) Women and post-conflict development: A case study on Liberia. BSc thesis, Massachusetts Institute of Technology, pp. 64 ff; Moran (2010), p. 265; Castillo Diaz and Tordjman (2012), p. 5; similar observations were made in other post-conflict states, see Hudson (2009), pp. 294–295.

[282] The LRCFP generally failed to implement a gender-sensitive staffing policy with only two women amongst the 36 Tetra Tech/ARD employees (Russell et al. 2011, pp. 23, 28).

[283] Foundation for Community Initiatives (2011), p. 10; Weah (2012), p. 2.

[284] Moran (1990), pp. 169 ff.

[285] Moran (2006), p. 74.

[286] See also Fuest (1986), p. 4.

[287] Aisha (2005), p. 149; Fuest (2008), pp. 222–223.

history of women who have the education and networks necessary for pursuing political careers, those women did not play a role in the law reform process.[288]

Rural women also face difficulties in accessing fora like regional consultations because of the gendered division of labor, but also because such fora may be perceived as a civilized sphere favoring men. For instance, Fuest notices that illiterate people are often reluctant to join workshops, fearing they may be exposed as 'country people'.[289] With female illiteracy rates considerably higher than those of men, this is particularly a problem for rural women.[290] Women—and even more so rural women—were thus largely excluded from the field of post-conflict forest sector reform.

The social identity of the *incompetent community* prevailing in (parts of) the fields of human rights, conservation, peacebuilding and development thus legitimized not only the exclusion of rural communities and their customary authorities but also the exclusion of rural women. FPIC was not seen as applicable to the forest sector reform even though it strongly impacted the land, natural resources, and culture of rural communities.

3.2.3 A Matter of Negotiation

Having explored the actors constituting the field of the post-conflict forest sector reform, the re-negotiation of FPIC will be explored. Power relations and alliances did not remain stable during the reform process. The field of post-conflict forest sector reform was characterized by 'processes of competition'.[291] Semi-autonomous social fields are not homogenous, with their sub-groups regularly having different interests pursuing different goals.[292]

During the first phase (2003–2007), the actors simultaneously located in the field of peacebuilding and development and, to some extent, conservation were dominant and influenced the National Forestry Policy, the National Forest Management Strategy, the National Forestry Reform Law, and the Ten Core Regulations. The second phase (2007–2011), during which the CRL was adopted, was dominated by the human rights discourse of national NGOs. In the last phase, ranging from 2011 to now, the fields of government, conservation, and development gained influence, reshaping Liberian forestry again and following the logic of the first phase to some

[288] Aning (1998), pp. 7–8; Massaquoi (2007) Women and post-conflict development: A case study on Liberia. BSc thesis, Massachusetts Institute of Technology, p. 38; Moran (2012), p. 59; Fynn Bruey (2018), p. 21.

[289] Fuest (2010), p. 15.

[290] Liberia Institute of Statistics and Geo-Information Services (2013), pp. 37–38.

[291] Falk Moore (1973), p. 743.

[292] See also Griffiths (2003), p. 37.

extent. The hegemonic discourse thus changed in the course of the forest sector reform.

3.2.3.1 2003–2007: Getting the Sanctions Lifted

In 2006, upon recommendation of the Forest Concession Review Committee, the government canceled all existing forest concessions for not complying with the legal requirements.[293] The first step in the Liberian forest sector reform was the adoption of the 2006 National Forestry Policy. It greatly informed the legal reform process, and international observers described it as a 'state-of-the-art quality'[294] document for sustainable forest management.[295] It formalized the 3 Cs—commercial, conservation, and community forestry—that still govern the Liberian forestry regime. The idea behind it is the territorialization of forest land and the zoning of areas for commercial, conservation, and community uses. The model was developed in South Africa in the 1990s.[296]

In 2006, the National Forestry Reform Law was adopted after noteworthy pressure from the UN Security Council.[297] The US-based NGO Environmental Law Institute was in charge of the technical drafting.[298] It was negotiated by a coalition of actors, including the US Forest Service, the Forestry Development Authority (FDA), the two national NGOs Sustainable Development Institute (SDI) and Green Advocates, and the Liberia Timber Association representing logging companies.[299] At the time, no consensus on the community-C could be found.[300] The National Forest Reform Law thus only regulates commercial forestry and conservation. However, it stipulated that within one year, a separate community rights law had to be developed.[301] This provision was inserted after the negotiations

[293] McAlpine et al. (2006), p. 87.

[294] Tissari et al. (2008), p. 48.

[295] National forestry policy and implementation strategy (2006) (Forestry Development Authority), p. 7.

[296] Lamb et al. (2009), p. 300.

[297] Eg UNSC (2005), Letter dated 13 June 2005 from the Chairman of the Security Council Committee established pursuant to resolution 1521 (2003) concerning Liberia addressed to the President of the Security Council, UN Doc S/2005/360, pp. 32 ff.

[298] Altman et al. (2012), p. 346.

[299] Roesch R (19 Dec 2017) Interview with a former senior staff member of a Liberian NGO, Duazon, para 68.

[300] Russell et al. (2011), p. 39.

[301] An Act adopting the National Forestry Reform Law of 2006 (amending the National Forestry Law of 2000, as amended; and amending an Act creating the Forestry Development Authority, as amended) (2006), ch 10.

were stuck to such an extent that national NGOs called for the Senate to reject the law.[302]

The Ten Core Regulations adopted a year later guided the implementation of the National Forestry Reform Law and introduced international best practices for sustainable forest management.[303] They were also drafted by the Environmental Law Institute and then circulated in a so-called 'notice-and-comment rule-making process'.[304] Involved actors included the US Forest Service and the national NGOs Green Advocates and SDI. Twenty-one public meetings were held in 12 counties collecting comments from local authorities and other stakeholders.[305]

In the same year, the FDA published a draft National Forestry Management Strategy to operationalize the Forestry Policy and to uphold the National Forestry Reform Law and its regulations.[306] The National Forest Management Strategy intended to zone the land based on suitability criteria and designate separate areas for commercial, conservation and community use. Yet, the forest land use planning was never fully implemented.[307]

But how about FPIC in this first phase of the forest sector reform? The National Forestry Reform Law, as the first step of the legal reform process, considerably enhanced the FDA's power.[308] It consolidated the state's ownership over forest resources introduced during Charles Taylor's presidency.[309] Under the land legislation at the time, all undeeded customary land was considered public land. The sale of such public land, however, required the consent of the tribal authority.[310] This protection mechanism, as weak as it was, no longer applied to forest lands. Due to the state's ownership of forest resources, the alienation of forest land only required

---

302 Roesch R (19 Dec 2017) Interview with a former senior staff member of a Liberian NGO, Duazon, paras 52–60.

303 Smyle (2012), p. 2.

304 Altman et al. (2012), p. 348.

305 Ibid p. 348.

306 National forest management policy (2007) (Forestry Development Authority), p. 20; Under the National Forestry Reform Law, the FDA's Board of Directors is required to adopt National Forest Policies 'that reflects sound forestry principles and sustainable management of the forests' (s 4.3). It is unclear whether the National Forest Management Policy was ever officially adopted.

307 UNSC (2009), Letter dated 12 December 2008 from the Acting Chairman of the Security Council Committee established pursuant to Resolution 1521 (2003) concerning Liberia addressed to the President of the Security Council, UN Doc S/2008/785, paras 74 ff; Email from a senior staff member of a Liberian NGO to the author (31 January 2019); Email from a staff member of an international human rights organization to the author (14 Feb 2019); Roesch R (2 Mar 2019) Skype interview with a former senior staff member of a Liberian NGO, para 8.

308 See also Lomax (2008), p. 18.

309 An Act adopting the national forestry reform law of 2006 (amending the National Forestry Law of 2000, as amended; and amending an Act creating the Forestry Development Authority, as amended) (2006), s 2.1.

310 Public lands law (Liberian Code of Laws revised) (2000) (Republic of Liberia), ch 3 para 30.

the consent of the FDA under the National Forestry Reform Law.[311] Moreover, the National Forestry Reform Law focuses on the commercial exploitation of forest resources and forest conservation and does not mention FPIC—however, the Ten Core Regulations do.[312] The following sections explore FPIC in commercial forestry, in forest conservation, and FPIC's institutional autonomy and gender dimension.

3.2.3.1.1 FPIC in Commercial Forestry

The Ten Core Regulations introduced FPIC in Liberia—probably thanks to the Environmental Law Institute's drafting team and the fact that it flew under the radar of the FDA. FPIC is mentioned in two contexts: firstly, for land use actions that designate land for commercial uses and, secondly, for the negotiation of the social agreement between companies and communities that is legally mandated for forest concessions.[313] The rights-holders are communities with an interest in the affected forest area.[314] They are required to elect a Community Forest Development Committee to take decisions on their behalf. Thus, the legal identity to which FPIC is attached is that of the *affected community*.

Firstly, Forest Land Use Actions that allow for the commercial use of customary land require the *prior informed consent* of the affected communities' Community Forest Development Committee.[315] The rationale for Forest Land Use Actions is that the forest has been designated for a specific use, ie, commercial, conservation, or community. If the FDA wants to use customary land for a commercial purpose or conservation, it has to issue a land use action and obtain the FPIC of the affected community. This raises the question of how the forests have been territorialized in the first place. While the National Forestry Reform Law prescribes that forest use decisions should be made based on their legal status—potentially including customary law—and suitability criteria, the National Forest Management Strategy fails to incorporate any considerations of land ownership and use.[316] Instead, it proposes

[311] An Act adopting the National Forestry Reform Law of 2006 (amending the National Forestry Law of 2000, as amended; and amending an Act creating the Forestry Development Authority, as amended) (2006), s 8.2.b; see also Alden Wily (2007), p. 244.

[312] Eg Smyle (2012), p. 11.

[313] Regulation No 102-07 on forest land use planning (2007) s 61(c)(3); Regulation No 104-07 on tender, award and administration of forest management contracts, timber sale contracts and major forest use permits (2007) s 22(j)(1).

[314] Regulation No 102-07 on forest land use planning (2007) s 1(a); Regulation No 104-07 on tender, award and administration of forest management contracts, timber sale contracts and major forest use permits (2007) s 2(a).

[315] Regulation No 102-07 on forest land use planning (2007) s 61(c)(3).

[316] An Act adopting the National Forestry Reform Law of 2006 (amending the National Forestry Law of 2000, as amended; and amending an Act creating the Forestry Development Authority, as amended) (2006), s 4.4.b.

forest land use planning based entirely upon suitability considerations.[317] Moreover, as the Liberian forests were never completely zoned, it is unlikely that the provision has been applied.

Secondly, the Ten Core Regulations stipulate that concessions may only be awarded once the Community Forest Development Committee has given its FPIC to the negotiation of a social agreement as required under the National Forestry Reform Law.[318] If the negotiation of the social agreement fails, a satisfactory solution shall be obtained through independent arbitration. In case of the failure to do so, the FDA 'may reconsider'[319] the terms of the concession. In summary, FPIC has to be obtained in the time period after the designation of land for commercial use and the selection of a concession-holder and before the negotiation of the terms of the social agreement.[320] Even when communities dissent, the FDA has the final say. It is thus not surprising that Lamb and her colleagues found no proof for any participatory process in which communities could voice their concerns in a meaningful way.[321] Instead, Community Forest Development Committees were under considerable pressure and had little leverage. They also had no right to consent to the social agreement itself. During the negotiation of the social agreement, the Ten Core Regulations only prescribe one public meeting facilitated and attended by the FDA for communities to 'ask questions about and express views on community rights and benefits under Forest Resource License'.[322] Even these weak consent requirements do not seem to have been implemented in practice: the Liberia Extractive Industries Transparency Initiative criticized the absence of written evidence for these consent processes.[323]

To sum it up, even though FPIC is part of the Ten Core Regulations in the context of state-granted concessions, its scope is extremely limited.[324] It is questionable whether the information provided by the FDA or companies is culturally appropriate and accessible, and the FDA always has the final say. The approach to FPIC is a box-ticking exercise at best.

---

[317] See also Lomax (2008), p. 19.

[318] Regulation No 104-07 on tender, award and administration of forest management contracts, timber sale contracts and major forest use permits (2007) s 22(j)(1).

[319] Ibid s 22(j)(2).

[320] For instance, the volume fee that is part of the social agreement, is only negotiated after FPIC has been obtained (Smyle 2012, p. 7).

[321] Lamb et al. (2009), p. 305; see also Beevers (2019), p. 110; Email from a senior staff member of a Liberian NGO to the author (31 January 2019).

[322] Regulation No 105-07 on major pre-felling operations under forest resources licenses (2007) s 35(a).

[323] Liberia Extractive Industries Transparency Initiative (2013), p. 70.

[324] See also Waugh and Murombedzi (2016), p. 569.

3.2.3.1.2 FPIC in Conservation

According to the National Forestry Reform Law, Liberia shall designate 30% of its forest land as protected areas to implement the Convention of Biological Diversity.[325] Requiring FPIC for the creation of protected areas was envisioned neither by conservation NGOs nor by donors or the government. According to the National Forestry Reform Law, a proposal for the creation of a protected area needs to contain a summary of consultations with affected persons and 'especially the views of local communities'.[326] Thus, communities are just a stakeholder group to be consulted with.

3.2.3.1.3 Institutional Autonomy and Gender

Given the limited understanding of FPIC emerging during this first phase, little thought was dedicated to the FPIC's internal dimension. The Ten Core Regulations introduce Community Forest Development Committees as the institutions to grant consent.[327] Thereby, it does not build upon existing institutions. However, the National Forestry Reform Law provides no information on these committees, and the Ten Core Regulations provide little. It is unlikely that communities have a Community Forest Development Committee in place before the designation of land for commercial use due to the high registration costs.[328] Moreover, according to estimations, half of the country's existing Community Forest Development Committee had not been incorporated by 2016, nine years after the adoption of the National Forestry Reform Law.[329]

With respect to FPIC's gender dimension, only the Ten Core Regulations mention women. Community residents must freely and fairly elect a Community Forest Development Committee, and the Community Forest Development Committees 'must provide a means for all residents that it represents, including women and youth, to have their views heard and considered'.[330] Yet, the participation of women in Community Forest Development Committees is not mandated. In 2012, not a single Community Forest Development Committee had more than 20% female

---

[325] An Act adopting the National Forestry Reform Law of 2006 (amending the National Forestry Law of 2000, as amended; and amending an act creating the Forestry Development Authority, as amended) (2006), s 9.1.a.

[326] Ibid s 9.3.d.

[327] Regulation No 105-07 on major pre-felling operations under forest resources licenses (2007) parts 3, 6.

[328] The Liberia Social Audit also found that in 2008 and 2009, the Community Forest Development Committees had not been fully established yet (Harris et al. 2012–3, p. 10).

[329] Waugh and Murombedzi (2016), p. 572.

[330] Regulation No 105-07 on major pre-felling operations under forest resources licenses (2007) s 62(c); see also s 62(b).

members, and none of the female members assumed one of the key offices within the Community Forest Development Committee.[331]

Moreover, logging concession holders, in the negotiation of the social agreement, shall hold at least one public meeting and 'use best efforts to involve women, youth, and other historically excluded groups in each public meeting'.[332] The FDA, in the validation of the land use actions and the drafting of new regulations, 'shall make its best efforts to include women, youth, and other historically marginalized groups in each local public meeting'.[333] The call for best efforts plainly demonstrates the low priority given to the inclusion of rural women and other marginalized groups.

Hence, in the first phase of the legal reform process, gender considerations were superseded by other concerns. While the field of peacebuilding certainly took an interest in gender equality, the forest sector reform flew under the radar of international gender experts and organizations. Also, NGOs did not focus on gender and forestry. Instead, lobbying to introduce community forestry monopolized all civil society resources. The weak provisions for women and youth participation can very like be attributed to the Environmental Law Institute, which drafted the Ten Core Regulations and also takes an interest in the social dimension of environmental law. The construction of women and youth as vulnerable groups was possibly influenced by the peace- and conflict studies literature, which emphasizes the historical marginalization of women and youth.[334]

The first period of the legal reform process was thus clearly dominated by discourses of development, peacebuilding, conservation, and forestry. International best practices played a central role, which translated into the proposed territorialization of Liberian forest lands and the focus on commercial forestry and conservation. Particularly, the government's commitment to transform 30% of the forests into protected areas reflects the power of conservationists. In contrast, human rights discourse played a very limited role. The main contribution of NGOs was the insertion of the obligation that a Community Rights Law had to be adopted.

The right to FPIC of *affected communities* appears to be even more limited than the conceptions of FPIC circulating in development law. Moreover, even this limited version of FPIC has not been respected in practice.[335] Alden Wily, therefore, concludes that the National Forestry Reform Law did just enough for 'releasing a little of the public pressure that has mounted'[336] and appeasing civil society while envisioning to proceed mainly as before the legal reform.

---

[331] Weah (2012), p. 3.

[332] Regulation No 105-07 on major pre-felling operations under forest resources licenses (2007) s 35(a)(4).

[333] Regulation No 102-07 on forest land use planning (2007) s 62(i).

[334] Eg, Richards (2005).

[335] See also Cabrera Ormaza and Ebert (2019), p. 487.

[336] Alden Wily (2007), p. 239.

3.2.3.2 2007–2011: The Quarrel About Community Rights

In the period following the adoption of the National Forestry Reform Law, community forestry remained highly controversial.[337] The power relations within the field of the post-war forest sector reform changed during the second phase of the reform. International criticism of the government's concession policy and also the FDA's lack of experience with community forestry contributed to the rise of NGOs. The then-managing director of the FDA told civil society that 'you got what you wanted, so we will expect that you will play a big role in developing this'.[338] This is in line with the observation that forest sector reforms often only incorporate Indigenous or minority interests when there is strong social mobilization in the reform process.[339]

The Community Forestry Working Group was the forum where the drafting took place. The starting point of the legal negotiation was the so-called zero draft written by a national and international NGO in December 2007.[340] A World Bank-funded consultant took over the subsequent technical drafting work.[341] Seven regional consultations informed the drafting process.[342] Due to major disagreements between the FDA and donors on the one side, and civil society on the other side, the process took much longer than expected, and the CRL was only adopted in September 2009.

During the drafting of the CRL, two opposed groups emerged with very different views on forest ownership, forest management, and good law-making. One group comprised conservation NGOs, the UN Panel of Experts, the FDA, the USAID-funded LRCFP, and the Governance Commission, which argued that the CRL should not include forest land tenure but should restrict itself to forest resources.[343] Instead, the yet-to-be-founded Land Commission should address the question of land tenure. Moreover, forest management rights should not wholly be given out of FDA's hands. The group also preferred the adoption of a vague law, while the details should be outlined in a separate regulation based on additional experiences with community forestry in Liberia.[344]

The other group consisted of national and international human rights NGOs that pursued a rights-based approach to community forestry. They also advocated for a more detailed draft, as they wanted to curb the power of the FDA.[345] Their drafts

---

[337] Tissari et al. (2008), p. 36.

[338] Roesch R (19 Dec 2017) Interview with a former senior staff member of a Liberian NGO, Duazon, para 106.

[339] Colchester (2006), p. 31.

[340] ARD Inc. (2008b), p. 3.

[341] Roesch R (19 Dec 2017) Interview with a former senior staff member of a Liberian NGO, Duazon, para 132.

[342] Sustainable Development Institute (2008a), p. 1.

[343] Russell et al. (2011), p. 56; Beevers (2019), p. 105.

[344] Roesch R (23 Apr 2018) Skype interview with a former senior staff member of the LRCFP, para 27.

[345] Roesch R (2 Mar 2019) Skype interview with a former senior staff member of a Liberian NGO, para 42.

granted more extensive rights to communities. The NGOs incorporated FPIC already in their zero draft, and its inclusion in the law's final version can be attributed to their strong advocacy.[346] International NGO employees from the Forest Peoples Programme and FERN also advised national NGOs to insist on the introduction of FPIC.[347]

When the two groups could not find a compromise, the LRCFP stepped in and brought the different actors back to the table.[348] A phased approach was agreed upon that foresaw handing over 30% of the forest land to communities and reviewing the process after five years before restituting more land.[349] The FDA, however, started a secret, parallel drafting process. The situation fully escalated when the FDA, without informing civil society, made amendments to the compromise draft that had been submitted to President Johnson Sirleaf. Those changes included the limitation of community participation in large-scale commercial concessions.[350] Consequently, the relationship between civil society and the government deteriorated to the extent that first Green Advocates and then the SDI quit the working group.[351]

The NGOs submitted an alternative draft to Parliament, which was adopted by both chambers. Under the Liberian Constitution, laws passed by parliament need to be transmitted to the president for their approval within 20 days.[352] However, the bill was—very likely for political reasons, after intensive FDA lobbying[353]—never officially transmitted to President Johnson Sirleaf, and the Parliament decided to send the bill back to the FDA to find a compromise between the two camps.[354] The FDA submitted another draft to the Senate, which was adopted in amended form.[355] Subsequently, the LRCFP facilitated another consultative meeting with NGOs and members of Parliament, who managed to agree on a common draft. It entered into

[346] A Community Rights Law with respect to forest lands (zero draft) (2007) (Republic of Liberia), s 4.3.

[347] Anonymus source 1 (2008); A Community Rights Law with respect to forest lands (2008), s 3.10.

[348] Anonymus source 2 (22 September 2008); Roesch R (23 Apr 2018) Skype interview with a former senior staff member of the LRCFP, para 40.

[349] Anonymus source 2 (22 September 2008).

[350] Ibid.

[351] Roesch R (19 Dec 2017) Interview with a former senior staff member of a Liberian NGO, Duazon, paras 166–170; Roesch R (23 Apr 2018) Skype interview with a former senior staff member of the LRCFP, para 44.

[352] Constitution of Liberia (1986), art 35.

[353] See also ARD Inc. (2008a), p. 5; Daygbor. 2008. Liberia: Negotiations to veto community rights act ongoing? The Analyst; Sustainable Development Institute (2008a), p. 2; Sustainable Development Institute (2008b).

[354] Roesch R (2 Mar 2019) Skype interview with a former senior staff member of a Liberian NGO, paras 48 ff.

[355] Land Rights and Community Forestry Program (2008–9), p. 5.

force in September 2009 and was seen as a compromise between the two different positions. It has been described as one of the most progressive laws in the region.[356]

The CRL revokes the National Forestry Reform Law's provision that the government owns all forest resources.[357] Instead, communities own the forest resources located within community forests.[358] Moreover, one of the guiding principles of the CRL is that 'any decision, agreement or activity affecting the status or use of community forest resources shall not proceed without the prior, free informed consent of the said community'.[359] Beyond that, the CRL provides little information on the scope and implementation of FPIC.

Regarding the institutional autonomy dimension of FPIC, even though the law does not spell it out, most experts agree that FPIC is to be granted through the three-tier governance structure as outlined in the CRL, consisting of a Community Assembly, an Executive Committee, and a Community Forest Management Body (CFMB).[360] This imposed governance structure exemplifies the little faith practically all actors placed in the capacities of local communities and their potential contribution towards sustainable and equitable forest governance. Thus, the CRL neglects the institutional autonomy of rural communities.

However, in this second phase, the internal dimension of FPIC and gender issues were discussed to the greatest extent. The civil society drafts, which played a central role in the drafting process, were weak in terms of gender. They enumerated gender as one type of vulnerability amongst many without providing any guidance on how it should be integrated into community forestry. This can be attributed to the fact that other aspects of the law were seen as more critical and that most national NGOs at the time had not developed clear positions on gender yet.[361] Additionally, the key civil society negotiator felt that more far-reaching gender quotas would not have been compatible with their vision of democratic governance institutions.[362]

Moreover, the fields of peacebuilding and development had a limited understanding of gender. Hudson argues that the relationship between the liberal peace project and liberal feminism has contributed to a practice 'where liberalism has become so embedded in mainstream discourses about gender and peacebuilding'[363] that it becomes unchallengeable. This also contributed to the failure to include (rural)

---

[356] Eg, Russell (2009), p. 25; Alden Wily et al. (2010), p. 4; Roesch R (19 Dec 2017) Interview with a former senior staff member of a Liberian NGO, Duazon, paras 180–182.

[357] An Act adopting the National Forestry Reform Law of 2006 (amending the National Forestry Law of 2000, as amended; and amending an Act creating the Forestry Development Authority, as amended) (2006), s 2.1.a.

[358] An Act to establish the Community Rights Law of 2009 with respect to forest lands (2009), s 2.2.a.

[359] Ibid s 2.2.c.

[360] Ibid s 4.

[361] Weah (2012), p. 2.

[362] Roesch R (2 Mar 2019) Skype interview with a former senior staff member of a Liberian NGO, para 64.

[363] Hudson (2017), p. 76.

women in the forest sector reform and to think about the gender dimension of forestry.[364] Thus, the CFMB's weak women's quota was only inserted in the last months of the drafting process and was quite likely supported by the fields of development, human rights, and conservation. One participant held that as quotas were, to some extent, already prescribed by the Ten Core Regulation, it was not a 'point of disagreement'.[365] But the last-minute insertion of the women's quota strongly indicates the low priority it had.

Liberian human rights discourse thus dominated the second phase of the forest sector reform and contributed to the recognition of community ownership of forest resources and FPIC. One international NGO representative describes the phase as 'a very strange hiatus, but also a wonderful moment in some ways because you could do things that you couldn't do now'.[366] Yet, sovereignty, conservation, and development discourse contributed to the adoption of a rather vague law, which had to be concretized later. For this reason, the CRL was even criticized by the NGOs for being an 'anti-community rights law'[367] in view of the strong position of the government actors in community forestry. Moreover, the implementation of the CRL through the FDA remained a major concern for NGOs.[368] In addition, the vision of the *incompetent community* contributed to the emergence of an understanding of FPIC that safeguards neither the institutional autonomy of communities nor women's right to FPIC.

3.2.3.3 2011–2018: Turning Back the Clock

Given the CRL's vagueness, the FDA adopted the CRL Regulation in 2011 to govern its implementation. A Liberian consultant provided the zero draft after two stakeholder workshops.[369] Subsequently, it was discussed in four regional and one national workshop. Yet, it shows astonishing overlap with the Cambodian community forestry degree, and it conflicted with the CRL in several respects.[370] In 2017, the CRL Regulation was amended to eliminate the incoherence between the CRL and its Regulation and to bring it in line with the Constitution. Moreover, in 2016, Liberia passed the National Wildlife Conservation and Protected Area Management

[364] Eg Hudson (2009), pp. 295 ff.

[365] Roesch R (2 Mar 2019) Skype interview with a former senior staff member of a Liberian NGO, para 62.

[366] Roesch R (7 Jun 2018) Skype interview with a lawyer of an international human rights organization, p. 102.

[367] Sustainable Development Institute (2010) Liberia - the promise betrayed. https://sdiliberia.org/sites/default/files/publications/2010_Liberia_The_Promise_Betrayed.pdf. Accessed 11 Aug 2023, p. 19.

[368] Kpanan'Ayoung Siakor (2011), pp. 27 f.

[369] Russell et al. (2011), p. 58.

[370] Sub-decree on community forestry management (2003) (Kingdom of Cambodia); Roesch R (18 Dec 2017) Interview with a senior legal consultant in the forestry sector, Monrovia, para 101.

Law, which regulates the establishment of conservation areas and the management of wildlife.

The CRL Regulation was a significant backlash for the field of human rights, while government actors saw it rather positively in terms of national ownership.[371] According to one NGO staff member, national NGOs failed to sufficiently participate in the drafting.[372] Donors, in contrast, were heavily involved. Some of them even felt that the CRL Regulation should correct the errors of the CRL.[373] Moreover, the FDA became more powerful. Given the overlapping interests with donors, it gained considerable social capital. The drafter of the CRL Regulation also supported the FDA's vision of forestry and was later appointed to be the Chairperson of the Public Procurement and Concession Commission.[374]

The following sections examine how the meaning of FPIC in community forestry and conservation changed during the third phase of the forest sector reform and sheds light on some political developments that also influenced the emerging understanding of FPIC.

While the 2011 Regulation does not mention FPIC, an earlier draft explicitly stated that

> the CRL provides a strong foundation for community participation in forestry matters by providing that "prior, free, and informed consent" of communities is required for all decisions affecting the use of community resources. This right, however, is not absolute and does not override the powers of the [FDA].[375]

This provision, which would effectively have turned FPIC into consultations at best, was removed upon recommendation of the Environmental Law Institute and the LRCFP.

Nevertheless, the CRL Regulation transforms Liberian community forestry into a license system subject to approval by the FDA, leaving little leeway for local knowledge and governance. The forest licenses—so-called Community Forest Management Agreements—expire after 15 years. Only if communities 'meet the technical and legal requirements',[376] the FDA may renew the Community Forest Management Agreement. Thereby, the CRL Regulation clearly departed from the rights-based approach of the CRL.

---

[371] Roesch R (19 Dec 2017) Interview with a former senior staff member of a Liberian NGO, Duazon, para 180.

[372] Roesch R (2 Mar 2019) Skype interview with a former senior staff member of a Liberian NGO, para 76.

[373] Russell et al. (2011), p. 59; Smyle (2012), p. 12.

[374] Roesch R (2 Mar 2019) Skype interview with a former senior staff member of a Liberian NGO, para 76.

[375] Regulations to the Community Rights Law of 2009 with respect to forest lands (draft, 30 June 2011) (2011) ch 6 s 3.

[376] Regulation to the Community Rights Law of 2009 with respect to forest lands, as amended (2017) s 7.6.

Moreover, the 2016 National Wildlife Conservation Law reinforces the state's ownership of wildlife and its commitment to creating 1.5 million hectares of protected areas.[377] Despite using the language of community consent for the designation of protected areas, consent is used as a synonym for consultations. This reflects the continuous power of conservationists.

Besides the legal reforms, some noteworthy political developments took place. Massive negative publicity on the illegality of many logging licenses, as well as the pending Land Rights Act, made the government rethink its concession policy.[378] In 2011, it stopped granting Forest Management Contracts and Timber Sale Contracts, the most common Liberian logging licenses.[379] Subsequently, the FDA started to issue so-called Private Use Permits, for which regulations were lacking. Owners of forest land could grant these licenses to companies.[380] As a result, a high number of collective deeds suddenly appeared. The Private Use Permits covered approximately 23% of the Liberian territory and allowed for any forest use, including the clearance of the forest.[381] International NGOs played a significant role in the revelation of forged deeds and corruption. After a considerable public outcry, President Johnson Sirleaf canceled most of the Private Use Permits.[382]

To date, community forestry is the only way of obtaining a logging license under a so-called Commercial Use Contract, which the owners of a community forest can conclude with third parties.[383] In theory, this could enable the FPIC of communities as they decide whether to enter into such an agreement—or not.

Hence, a considerable shift within commercial logging occurred during the reform process. While the National Forestry Reform Law put the FDA in an extraordinary position of power, the Ten Core Regulations already restricted this power to some extent. The public outrage following the granting of illegal concessions caused the government to overthrow its concession policy completely.[384] This illustrates how the field of human rights can use campaigns to trump the interests of other actors. Donors and conservationists also shared concerns about the FDA's discretionary concession policy and joined forces with NGOs. Despite this common

[377] An Act adopting the National Wildlife Conservation and Protected Area Management Law of Liberia (2016), ss 2.2.1, 5.2.1.

[378] See Global Witness (2017).

[379] An Act adopting the National Forestry Reform Law of 2006 (amending the National Forestry Law of 2000, as amended; and amending an Act creating the Forestry Development Authority, as amended) (2006), ss 5.3, 5.4.

[380] Ibid s 5.6.

[381] Global Witness et al. (2012), p. 1.

[382] Executive order No 44: Protecting Liberian forests by a temporary moratorium on Private Use Permits (2013).

[383] An Act to establish the Community Rights Law of 2009 with respect to forest lands (2009), ch 6.

[384] Eg UNSC (2009), Letter dated 12 December 2008 from the Acting Chairman of the Security Council Committee established pursuant to resolution 1521 (2003) concerning Liberia addressed to the President of the Security Council, UN Doc S/2008/785, para 70; Global Witness (2009); Sustainable Development Institute (2009).

ground, donors supported the FDA in watering down the CRL. This exemplifies the fluidity of alliances.

3.2.4 *FPIC Re-Negotiated*

The emergence of FPIC in Liberia was thus a matter of negotiation in a legally pluralistic constellation with national law, project law, transnational human rights, and environmental law coexisting. Moreover, the field was characterized by shifting alliances and power relations. The result is a fragmented legal framework reflecting the differing agendas, normative orders, and discourses.

The Liberian field of post-conflict law-making was susceptible to the introduction of FPIC for two reasons: being an international norm at a time when little trust was placed in national norms and institutions and a potential tool for avoiding future conflicts based upon the unequal distribution of natural resources.[385] This section explores the emerging understanding of FPIC in relation to (1) the adoption of legal and administrative measures, (2) projects or activities affecting the land and natural resources of communities, and (3) the negotiation of FPIC's institutional autonomy and its (4) gender dimension.

3.2.4.1 Legal and Administrative Measures

The National Forestry Reform Law and its regulations have enhanced public participation in the drafting of forest-related regulations and decision-making.[386] The Ten Core Regulations institutionalized the consultation-based approach to legal drafting and forest land use planning that emerged during the forest sector reform.[387]

Regarding the drafting of Regulations, the FDA is required to hold three regional consultations in English and at least one other language.[388] Attending community members are informed about the content of the regulation and may provide comments. Yet, three workshops for the whole country are inadequate, given the vast areas of forest land in Liberia, the lack of good infrastructure, and the high transportation costs. Even though the FDA shall select the location of the regional consultation based on the proximity to forest lands and ease of transport, the consultation workshops, in practice, remain inaccessible for the majority of forest

385 Rochow (2008), p. 463.

386 An Act adopting the National Forestry Reform law of 2006 (amending the National Forestry Law of 2000, as amended; and amending an Act creating the Forestry Development Authority, as amended) (2006), s 10.1.b(ii).

387 Regulation No 101-07 on public participation in promulgation of regulations, codes, and manuals (2007) s 23.b; Regulation No 102-07 on forest land use planning (2007) s 43.c.

388 Regulation No 101-07 on public participation in promulgation of regulations, codes, and manuals (2007) s 23.

communities, and particularly rural women.[389] The Ten Core Regulations also only require that the FDA 'shall use its best efforts to involve youth, and other historically excluded groups in each regional public meeting'.[390] The drafters thus put a lot of faith in the FDA's willingness and capacity to ensure inclusive consultation processes. Moreover, the FDA makes the final decision about the content of Regulations and only needs to consider communities' comments, even though it has to justify if it decides to ignore them.[391]

For forest land use actions, which are administrative measures, the FDA has to hold local meetings with affected communities to hear their comments, with the FDA making the ultimate decision.[392]

Thus, the participation of communities, as introduced by the Ten Core Regulations, is closer to public participation than to FPIC. While public participation and FPIC overlap, their rationale is different. Under the public participation paradigm, communities are just seen as one stakeholder group amongst many, and the FDA has the right to dismiss their comments. Moreover, public participation is only required for Regulations but not for Statutes. The lack of a lobby for FPIC-based law-making contributed to the neglect of this aspect of FPIC. FPIC in relation to law-making was never seen as a feasible option.

The legal identity of *affected communities* to which FPIC is linked in the Ten Core Regulations helped to legitimize this. Affected communities are only those that are quite specifically affected by a proposed measure. Legislation or measures affecting communities all over Liberia do not create this condition of specific affectedness. Hence, they are no more than a stakeholder group.

3.2.4.2 Land and Natural Resources

It has been shown that FPIC is most commonly discussed in relation to land and natural resources in the global time-space. This was also the case in Liberia. The proposed territorialization of forest land was one of the cornerstones of the forest sector reform process. Basically, three different legal sub-regimes coexist, depending on the designation of the forest for commercial, conservation, or community use. Despite this trifurcation, the boundaries between the legal frameworks ended up being more fluid than envisioned by conservationists and proponents of scientific forestry. In 2018, Liberia had still not adopted a Forest Management Plan.[393] Moreover, the adoption of the Community Rights Law (CRL) had a considerable impact on forest conservation and commercial forestry. With the Liberian government no longer granting logging concessions, commercial forestry

---

389 Ibid s 23.b.5.D.

390 Ibid s 23.b.5.C.

391 Ibid s 23.e.

392 Regulation No 102-07 on forest land use planning (2007) s 62(j) ff.

393 Eba'a Atyi (2018), p. 50.

will only be explored in the context of community forestry, while conservation will be treated both independently and as part of community forestry. This section thus examines FPIC in conservation and community forestry.

3.2.4.2.1 Conservation

Liberia's five national protected areas amount to about 11% of the forested land.[394] In view of Liberia's commitment to designate 30% of its forests as protected areas, the question arises of how this can be reconciled with community forestry and customary land rights.[395] The 2016 National Wildlife Conservation Law provides little guidance on how to resolve overlaps between customary land and proposed protected areas, and regulations are still lacking. The World Bank has been pressuring the FDA to adopt policy guidelines for such overlaps.[396]

The National Wildlife Conservation Law prescribes the procedure for designating protected areas. The FDA shall 'in a transparent and participatory manner and in consultation with communities to be affected'[397] identify potential protected areas 'while taking into account rural communities' needs, rights to community forest lands and forest resources'.[398] To designate the type of protected area—eg, national forest reserve, multiple sustainable use reserve, or national park—the FDA shall consult, amongst others, with forest-dependent communities.[399]

After the identification and designation of a proposed protected area, the FDA shall submit 'a description of the proposed boundaries for the area indicating community awareness and agreement at least in principle'[400] and 'indication of prior, free, informed consent of the community where community forest lands are affected'.[401]

Subsequently, the President of Liberia designates the proposed protected area, and the FDA holds stakeholder consultations and shall 'have in place a community consultation process'.[402] Upon the Parliament's designation of the protected area, the FDA shall fully inform communities about the boundary demarcation of the protected area and prepare the management plans in collaboration with affected

[394] World Bank (2018c), p. 19.

[395] Roesch R (28 Feb 2018) Interview with a senior legal consultant in the forestry sector, Monrovia, paras 155–157.

[396] World Bank (2018b) para 13.

[397] An Act adopting the National Wildlife Conservation and Protected Area Management Law of Liberia (2016), s 5.2.

[398] Ibid s 5.2.

[399] Ibid s 5.3.

[400] Ibid s 5.4.1.1.b.

[401] Ibid s 5.4.1.1.i.

[402] Ibid s 5.4.5.

communities.[403] To finalize the designation of a protected area, the FDA must indicate 'free, prior, and informed consent where community forest lands are affected'.[404] Even though the definition of customary forest land does not include a Community Forest Management Agreement, the FDA requires FPIC only for authorized community forest but not for customary land in general.[405] In these cases, consultations, awareness, and *agreement in principle* appear to be the norm.

3.2.4.2.2 Community Forestry

The CRL introduced community forestry and stipulates that no decision affecting community forests may be taken without the communities' FPIC.[406] By 2018, approximately 130 communities had applied for community forest status. The FDA had approved 36 of those applications with a total size of more than 700,000 ha in late 2018, and at least 12 of them had already entered into commercial use contracts with companies.[407] In 2022, 49 applications had been approved and another 128 communities were still in the authorization process.[408] The World Bank estimates that 3 million hectares of forest land could fall under yet-to-be-issued Community Forest Management Agreements.[409] When exploring the meaning of FPIC, the following questions are relevant: Who are the rights-holders, in which situations does it apply, what does consent mean, and which institutions can give consent?

3.2.4.2.2.1 Rights-holders

Concerning the rights-holders, communities are defined as self-identified and publicly or widely-recognized coherent social groups, who share common customs and traditions, residing in a particular area of land over which they exercise jurisdiction.[410] The statutory recognition of customary tenure is not a requirement for establishing a community forest. However, communities are restricted in the free

[403] Ibid ss 5.7.1.a, 5.9.1.a.

[404] Ibid s 5.4.1.1.i.

[405] Ibid s 1.3. Please note that this has changed with the adoption of the Liberian Land Rights Act in 2018. However, the Land Rights Act will not be examined here as it emerged in a different field.

[406] An Act to establish the Community Rights Law of 2009 with respect to forest lands (2009), s 2.2.c.

[407] World Bank (2018c), pp. 15, 18; Sustainable Development Institute (2019), pp. 2, 3.

[408] Agyeman et al. (2022), pp. 145, 149.

[409] World Bank (2018c), p. 18.

[410] An Act to establish the Community Rights Law of 2009 with respect to forest lands (2009), s 1.3.

designation of their forest land by the requirement that community forests must be between 5001 and 49,000 hectares in size.[411]

In theory, the CRL departs from the zoning approach to forestry based on suitability criteria by allowing for community forestry without any geographical restrictions. Yet, it is unlikely that the FDA would grant community forest status for forest land that is part of a government-granted concession or a protected area.[412] Some exceptions to this rule exist: the FDA has authorized community forests within the Arcelor Metal and the Golden Veroleum Liberia concession areas.[413] A possible explanation for these overlaps is the lack of knowledge of the boundaries of concession areas.[414]

The rights-holder of FPIC is thus a *community forest-owning community* as long as the forest they own has not been earmarked for another use than community forestry. It is thus linked to the collective right to property.

3.2.4.2.2.2 Meaning of FPIC

What impact does the legal identity of the Community Forest-owning Community have on the meaning of FPIC and the situations in which it applies? Regarding the situations which require FPIC, the law refers to acts changing the status or use of forest resources.[415] In principle, FPIC could thus be relevant in two contexts: (1) Communities may decide how they want to use their community forest, and (2) communities have to consent if the government wants to use their community forest in any other way.

Firstly, under the CRL Regulation, the protection of forest land rights is qualified by the need to register as a community forest and to go through the so-called 9 (or 11[416]) steps. Interviews with experts in Liberia suggest that the 11-step procedure for obtaining community forest status is seen as the embodiment of FPIC. Communities can decide how they want to use their forest and codify the

---

[411] Ibid s 2.3. However, the CRL Regulation also contains provisions on smaller and bigger community forestry indicating that FDA in practice does not stick to the size requirement of the CRL.

[412] For instance, the community forests around the East Nimba Nature Reserve, only extend to the buffer zones of the park but not to the park itself (eg Gill (2017) Managing Liberia's forests: Community forestry for social justice. Master thesis, Wageningen University, pp. 36–37); moreover, the 2018 Land Rights Act holds that communities FPIC is not required for customary land that is part of concessions or other licenses or rights previously granted by the government (An Act to establish the Land Rights Law of 2018 (2018) (Liberia), art 33).

[413] Litz (2015), p. 3.

[414] Foster-Turley et al. (2018), p. 96.

[415] An Act to establish the Community Rights Law of 2009 with respect to forest lands (2009), s 2.2.c.

[416] Those additional steps consist of the submission and implementation of a Community Forest Management Plan.

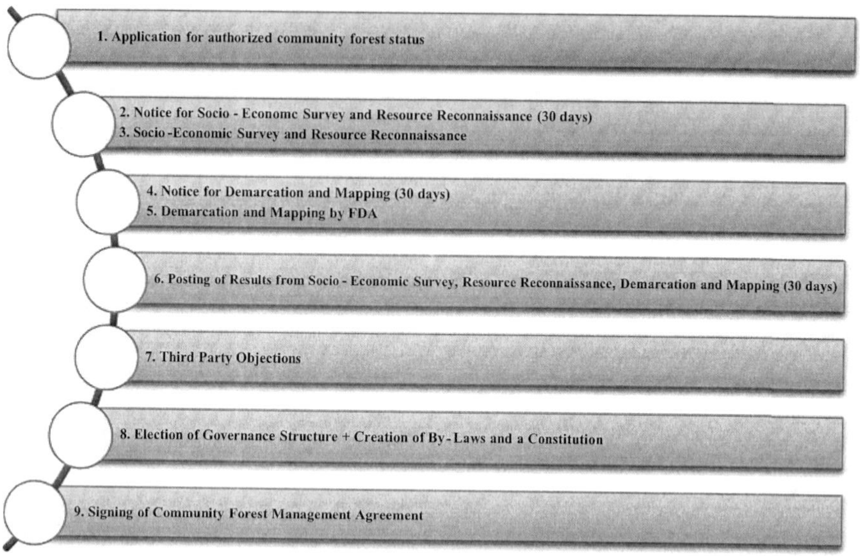

Fig. 3.2 9-step procedure for authorized community forest status

intended forest use.[417] They may, for example, decide to grant a commercial use contract to a logging company or to conserve their forest.

As depicted in Fig. 3.2, these steps include a letter of application, payment of an application fee, repeated posting of notices, a socio-economic resource reconnaissance (SER) survey, mapping and demarcation, creation of a three-tier governance structure,[418] adoption of by-laws and a Constitution, and signing a Community Forest Management Agreement with the FDA.[419] After the 9 steps, a Community Forest Management Plan designating, amongst others, the way the different parcels of the forest may be used has to be adopted and implemented (steps 10 and 11). The procedure not only can take years but is also extremely costly.[420] Moreover, it should be noted that the FDA is in charge of the SER survey, the mapping, the boundary demarcation, and the posting of notices and results. As a result, the self-identification and the identification of customary land are largely taken out of the communities' hands. How communities can decide in practice about the future of their forest land will be explored in the next chapter.

---

[417] Roesch R (28 Feb 2018) Interview with a senior legal consultant in the forestry sector, Monrovia, para 69; Roesch R (15 Jan 2018) Interview with a senior staff member of the FDA, Monrovia, paras 622 ff; see also LTS International (2019a), p. 16.

[418] Consisting of Community Assembly, Executive Committee, and Community Forest Management Body.

[419] Regulation to the Community Rights Law of 2009 with respect to forest lands, as amended (2017) ch 2.

[420] Eg Roesch R (15 Jan 2018) Interview with a senior staff member of the FDA, Monrovia, paras 344 ff.

Secondly, the wording of the CRL suggests that FPIC may also apply in the case of eminent domain—for example, if the government seeks to designate a protected area or grant a concession.[421] According to the 2017 CRL Regulation, the government may terminate Community Forest Management Agreements by exercising its power of eminent domain. While the government now has to follow the constitutional procedure for the taking of land, FPIC as an additional requirement is not mentioned.[422]

To date, no communities have claimed a community forest within an existing protected area. It is also unlikely that communities will do so in the future. According to a Liberian forestry expert, 'most of the [community forest] applications have been triggered by logging companies that would like to be in good relationship with FDA [...] So they have tended to stay away from protected areas'.[423] It is also unlikely that the FDA would (knowingly) approve a community forest application covering part of a protected area. For instance, the community forests around East Nimba Nature Reserve, a type of protected area, only extend to the buffer zones of the park but not to the park itself.[424]

The situation is different for community forest applications overlapping with proposed protected areas, which is more common.[425] In these cases, the FDA has two options. In the first option, communities can decide to use their community forests for conservation. Conservation NGOs and donors often offer communities so-called conservation agreements, including social benefits and/or alternative livelihood activities.[426]

In the second option, the state makes use of its constitutional power of eminent domain. The amended 2017 CRL Regulation holds that the government may make use of its power of eminent domain in relation to community forests, but it has to follow the constitutional procedure for the expropriation of private property.[427] The government must provide the reasons for the expropriation and pay just compensation without delays. Moreover, communities have the right to challenge the government's decision, and the government is obliged to return the land once it does not use it anymore.

Even though the wording of the CRL and the National Wildlife Conservation Law suggest that FPIC applies to expropriations, it is likely that, given the FDA's

421 Constitution of Liberia (1986), art 24(a).

422 Regulation to the Community Rights Law of 2009 with respect to forest lands, as amended (2017) s 7.9.b.

423 Roesch R (2 Mar 2019) Skype interview with a former senior staff member of a Liberian NGO, para 18, see also Chap. 4.

424 Gill (2017) Managing Liberia's forests: Community forestry for social justice. Master thesis, Wageningen University, pp. 36–37.

425 World Bank (2018d), p. 4.

426 Regulation to the Community Rights Law of 2009 with respect to forest lands, as amended (2017) ss 1.2.x, 8,3, 9.2.e; The 2011 Regulation did not contain any reference to such third-party conservation agreements.

427 Ibid s 7.9.a.

understanding of FPIC, this would amount to consultations at best.[428] International experts equally argue that the 'government ultimately always has the right under certain circumstances [to seize the land]'.[429]

At the moment, a coalition of the World Bank, NGOs, donors, and the FDA are trying to build protected areas around community forests while at the same time incentivizing communities to designate their forests for conservation.[430] The World Bank states that it intends to avoid involuntary resettlement and negotiate with communities living within parks to ensure their voluntary consent.[431] Even though, this leaves space for FPIC, both international actors and the FDA are under considerable pressure to meet their conservation goals. Therefore, a forestry expert concludes that

> they [World Bank and their implementing partners] have had extensive consultations, they have had intensive information collection, different surveys, and awareness-raising campaigns, but I think it is fair to say they all stopped short of giving the community the right to veto, basically saying, we don't want a protected area on our land.[432]

Similarly, an anthropologist describes the World Bank consultations in Liberia as 'condescension without any obligation, but it is dressed up as democracy'.[433] In line with the versions of FPIC prevailing in the global fields of development and environmental law, FPIC becomes a method for preventing conflicts and enhancing the legitimacy of projects as long it does not fundamentally interfere with the higher goal of environmental protection. Thereby, it is decontextualized and largely detached from questions of self-determination, autonomy, and culture.

Hence, the *community forest-owning community*, as a legal identity, has a right to property. However, this collective right to property is more limited than the individual right to property. The Community Forest Management Agreement expires after 15 years and has to be renewed.[434] It is thus closer to a license than to the collective right to property in human rights law. Simultaneously, FPIC gets reduced to the 11-step procedure. The subtraction of culture, autonomy, and self-determination from FPIC thus results in FPIC getting a new and more limited meaning.

---

428 This is also the approach pursued by the newly adopted Land Rights Act (An Act to establish the Land Rights Law of 2018 (2018), art 54).

429 Roesch R (28 Feb 2018) Interview with a senior legal consultant in the forestry sector, Monrovia, para 445.

430 Ibid para 157.

431 Government of Liberia (2010) Expansion of the protected area network: Process framework final draft. http://documents.worldbank.org/curated/en/384861468263969138/pdf/RP10960P1145801tlement1ProcessFrmk1.pdf. Accessed 20 Mar 2023, pp. 10–11.

432 Roesch R (2 Mar 2019) Skype interview with a former senior staff member of a Liberian NGO, para 18.

433 Roesch R (13 Jun 2018) Skype interview with an anthropologist, para 15; see also LTS International (2019a), p. 17.

434 Regulation to the community rights law of 2009 with respect to forest lands, as amended (2017) s 7.6.

3.2.4.2.2.3 Institutional Autonomy

As to the *how* of FPIC, it was discussed in the legal reform process whether to build upon existing institutions or whether new and possibly more inclusive structures should be created.[435] Global Indigenous law requires that FPIC needs to be obtained through the 'representative institutions'[436] of Indigenous peoples. In contrast, the CRL and its Regulation stipulate that communities have to establish a Community Assembly as their highest decision-making body.[437] While the CRL defines the Community Assembly as 'the collectivity of resident adult members of aged 18 years and above, representative of gender and all social grouping within the community organized into a body',[438] the CRL Regulation prescribes the election of representatives from each of the constituent towns by secret ballot.[439] The Community Assembly then elects a Community Forest Management Body and an Executive Committee. The CFMB is in charge of the day-to-day activities. The Executive Committee supervises the CFMB and reports to the Community Assembly.[440] It was introduced very late in the drafting process, as the members of Parliament only agreed to pass the law under the condition that they could be members of the governance structure.[441] To avoid their presence in the Community Forest Management Body, the Executive Committee was created.[442]

While the CRL remains silent as to who should grant FPIC, earlier drafts of the CRL explicitly held that the Community Assembly has to give FPIC.[443] It can thus be assumed that FPIC in the Liberian forest sector is realized through the consent of the Community Assembly as the highest decision-making body.

Thus, the lack of engagement with customary land and forest governance in the forest sector reform and the absence of local communities in the reform process resulted in the negligence of customary modes of decision-making. With FPIC being detached from the rights to self-determination and culture, it was possible to deprive it of its institutional autonomy dimension. The field's hegemonic discourse thus transformed the social identity of the *incompetent community* into the legal identity

---

[435] Menzies (2007), p. 132; Meinzen-Dick and Pradhan (2016), p. 540.

[436] United Nations Declaration on the Rights of Indigenous Peoples (2007) UNGA Res 61/295, arts 19, 32(2).

[437] An Act to establish the Community Rights Law of 2009 with respect to forest lands (2009), s 4.1.a.

[438] Ibid s 1.3.

[439] Regulation to the Community Rights Law of 2009 with respect to forest lands, as amended (2017) s 3.4.

[440] An Act to establish the Community Rights Law of 2009 with respect to forest lands (2009), s 4.1.f.

[441] Roesch R (2 Mar 2019) Skype interview with a former senior staff member of a Liberian NGO, paras 66–68.

[442] The EC shall, amongst others, comprise members of the legislature (An Act to establish the Community Rights Law of 2009 with respect to forest lands (2009), s 4.1.c).

[443] Eg, first, second and third draft of the CRL.

of the *community forest-owning community*, whose customary institutions and ways of decision-making can just be replaced.

3.2.4.2.2.4 Gender and Community Forestry

The negotiation of community forestry and FPIC did not center much around customary governance. Similarly, little resources were invested in the participation of women in customary institutions.

According to the CRL, one member of the Community Forest Management Body must be female, while no such requirement exists for the other two bodies.[444] The insertion of the weak women's quota in the last stages of the legal reform reflects the low priority of gender in the process. There is no evident reason why exactly one woman within the Community Forest Management Body should be female. Quotas are generally viewed as compensation for structural obstacles to the participation of certain groups.[445] The rationale is that the descriptive representation of marginalized groups will also improve their substantive representation. It is assumed that a critical mass of members of a marginalized group can make a difference, even when not consciously pursuing a common interest.[446] Evidence from community forestry in South Asia suggests that women quotas in community forests can enhance the effective participation of women and may change gender relations. According to Agrawal, community forests with between 25% and 33% women in the governance structure had a significantly higher share of women speaking in meetings, even though it did not necessarily contribute to more women becoming office-bearers.[447] To achieve that, further training and quotas are necessary. The CRL's women's quota is insufficient for creating a critical mass of women and reflects the half-heartedness with which gender was negotiated. The CRL thus missed not only the opportunity to give statutory recognition to customary governance arrangements but also to integrate women groups and institutions already existing in many places in Liberia.[448]

Moreover, the enumeration of vulnerable groups—including women—as in the Ten Core Regulations and in relation to the Community Assembly membership rests on the assumption that members of these groups have similar experiences.[449] At the same time, it implies that women are one minority group amongst many.[450] This

[444] An Act to establish the Community Rights Law of 2009 with respect to forest lands (2009), s 4.2.a.

[445] Bauer and Britton (2006), p. 7.

[446] Fourth World Conference on Women (1995), Beijing Declaration and platform for action, A/CONF. 177/20(1995) and A/CONF. 177/20/Add. 1(1995); Krook and True (2010), p. 118; Agarwal (2014), p. 2.

[447] Agarwal (2010), p. 108; similar observations on the critical mass have been made in relation to female parliamentarians (see Bauer and Britton 2006, p. 4).

[448] Eg Moran (1990), p. 166.

[449] Krook and O'Brian (2010), p. 255.

[450] See also Puechguirbal (2005), p. 3.

additive approach risks 'to end up reifying identity politics'[451] by implying the existence of homogenous marginal groups.[452] Group identities are only useful when not understanding them as a homogenous group but rather as a positionality describing the 'contours of important patterns of social, political and, and economic inequality'[453] and when considering overlapping identities. It is, however, likely that the lip services paid to the inclusion of women—and other marginalized groups—will not have any practical impacts, particularly in cases when those references are recommendary in character.[454]

Both the quota approach and the inclusivity provisions follow the spirit of the liberal theory of representation. They are reminiscent of the 'add women and stir'[455] approach prevailing in liberal feminism.[456] It assumed that by granting the same rights to women and improving their participation, the problem of gender inequality would be tackled. However, quotas and calls for the representation of marginalized groups tend to have little impact if they are not contextualized and part of a broader and intersectional gender equality scheme.[457] Hence, the absence of women and communities—and especially rural women—makes some of the power relations within the field of the post-conflict forest sector reform evident. It was characterized by 'participatory exclusions',[458] with rural communities—and their rural women—not being present in a meaningful way.

3.2.5 FPIC in the Forestry Sector

The negotiation of community forestry and FPIC took several years, and the outcome is essentially a compromise between competing visions of the forest as a space of imagination.[459] In the hegemonic discourse, it became either an environmental or a commercial resource, while other meanings were located in the field of discursivity and unthinkable.[460]

Based on the forest as a nodal point, the social identities of the community and the state were a lot less controversial than in the global time-space. With respect to communities, the social identity of the *incompetent community* was translated into either the legal identity of the *affected community* or the *community forest-owning*

[451] Hudson (2017), p. 82.

[452] Williams (2000), p. 5.

[453] Ibid p. 6.

[454] Shepherd (2017a), p. 95.

[455] Harding (1995), pp. 296 ff.

[456] Zalewski (1993), pp. 116–117.

[457] Tadros (2010), p. 4.

[458] Agarwal (2001), pp. 1627 ff.

[459] See also von Benda-Beckmann (2001), p. 36.

[460] Jørgensen and Phillips (2002), p. 27.

community. The construction of the incompetent community legitimized their lack of participation in the legal reforms, the lack of engagement with customary governance, and the lack of respect for their right to culture, autonomy, and self-determination.[461]

More controversial was the social identity of the state. While government actors, conservationists, and donors, to some extent, stressed the state's role as the guardian of natural resources, conservationists and donors also doubted the state's capacity to fulfill that function. Only NGOs clearly positioned themselves against the power of the state. Ultimately, the FDA's power was reinforced but controlled by the watchdog activities of NGOs to some extent.

These social and legal identities reflect the power relations at play and strongly impacted the emerging understanding of FPIC.[462] It resulted in the limitation of FPIC to land and natural resources instead of also recognizing the right of communities to participate in legislative processes. Moreover, even in relation to land and natural resources, the Liberian FPIC departs from global Indigenous law; FPIC is not required when the state exercises its prerogative of eminent domain. It is only realized within the 11 steps, during which communities decide how they want to use their forest land. However, these steps do not have their roots in any customary governance arrangements and are incredibly burdensome for most communities. Whether communities can realize this limited form of FPIC also depends on the goodwill of the FDA, which has the power to authorize (or refuse) community forest status. Thanks to civil society pressure, the government no longer grants concessions on customary land and has not made use of its power of eminent domain in the designation of protected areas. Yet, this is a political decision and not reflected in the law.

Moreover, even though the forest legislation ignores the institutional autonomy of communities, it also does not acknowledge the right of rural women to FPIC. The 'trinity of democratization, good governance and women's rights'[463] prevailing in many international peacebuilding projects contributed to a very limited, liberal understanding of gender. It created an understanding of women as victims and built their programs on this perception. In addition to the fields of peacebuilding and development, the Liberian field of human rights failed to acknowledge the gendered dimension of forestry, as it dedicated most of its resources to improving the situation of the *local*, ie, the community, which was seen as the central battlefield in the reform process.

These limitations notwithstanding, the Liberian FPIC and community forestry provide some space for the community-based management of natural resources. They protect customary land rights, and, most noteworthy, they made Liberia the first African country to incorporate FPIC into its national legal system and to operationalize it. This complexity clearly shows that legal transplants are not so

[461] For similar observations see Newberry (2014), p. 310.

[462] Menzies (2007), p. 157.

[463] Kandiyoti (2004), p. 134.

Fig. 3.3 Reform of the Land Sector

much a question of failure/success or (non-)compliance but a matter of negotiation between actors and fields. The field of forest sector reform was characterized by the continuous struggle between the different actors and their fields to impose their vision of forestry. The emerging hegemonic discourse thus created identities and relations in which FPIC as a legal transplant became embedded. The renegotiated FPIC norm thereby follows the field's logic and does not touch upon questions of sovereignty, autonomy, and culture. Instead, it becomes a matter of forest management.

3.3 The Field of the Liberian Land Sector Reform: 2008-Today

The introduction of community forestry was not the end of the story of FPIC in Liberia. Instead, it also became an issue during the land reform that took off in 2008. Voices for reforming Liberia's land legislation became loud very soon after the end of the civil war. Researchers like Unruh and Richards argued that land conflicts, together with the dysfunctionality of local governance structures—privileging elders over youth and women—, had been the root cause of the war.[464] The Poverty Reduction Strategy mirrored that perspective and found that 'communal land and boundary disputes between ethnic and clan groups have historically been a source of interethnic conflicts'.[465]

However, it was easier to get the forest legislation in place than to implement comprehensive land reforms.[466] The high complexity of land sector reforms, particularly in post-war situations characterized by high displacement rates, often makes them a time-consuming and resource-intensive endeavor.[467] Moreover, the logging sanctions contributed to the prioritization of forest over land reforms.

Again, and as shown in Fig. 3.3, the land reform was realized in several steps. In 2008, the Governance Commission launched three regional consultation workshops to flagship the most crucial land tenure issues and sponsored the drafting of the Land Commission Act.[468] The Land Commission was endowed with the mandate to

[464] Richards (2005), p. 588; Unruh (2009b), p. 425.

[465] Liberia: Poverty reduction strategy paper (2008) (Republic of Liberia), p. 55.

[466] Roesch R (23 Apr 2018) Skype interview with a former senior staff member of the LRCFP, para 23.

[467] See also Hellum and Derman (2005), p. 182.

[468] Bruce (2016), pp. 1, 3.

spearhead the land reform process. Subsequently, the Interim Guidelines for the Sale of Public Land were elaborated by the Land Commission and endorsed by President Johnson Sirleaf in 2011.[469] In 2013, the Land Commission issued a Land Rights Policy. While the Land Rights Policy recognizes customary land as one category of land and grants full ownership to communities over their customary land, it does not mention FPIC.[470]

With the Land Commission's mandate expiring in 2014, the Land Authority Act and the Land Rights Act (LRA) were drafted simultaneously. In October 2016, the legislature passed the Land Authority Act, creating the Liberia Land Authority as the successor organization of the Land Commission.[471] However, the adoption of the Land Rights Act (LRA) took much longer than expected. Only in September 2018, under the newly elected Weah government, was it finally passed. In 2019, the Liberia Land Authority published the Land Rights Implementation Strategy.[472] The Liberia Land Authority planned to adopt a series of regulations governing the implementation of the LRA.[473] However, it took them until 2022 to adopt the Land Rights Act Regulations (LRA Regulations).[474]

This chapter first maps the field of the Liberian land reforms. Secondly, it portrays the actors involved in the reform. Thirdly, it explores the negotiation of FPIC during the land reform and, fourthly, the emerging understanding of FPIC.

3.3.1 Mapping the Field of Land Sector Reform

Before exploring the actors of the field and their negotiation of FPIC, the sociotemporal context, the logic, and the law and practices of the field of post-conflict land sector reform will be mapped.

Firstly, regarding the sociotemporal context, the field describes the time following the beginning of the land sector reform process in 2008. Given the persisting question marks surrounding the implementation of the LRA, the field still exists. The field of post-conflict land sector reform is also a legislative and predominantly national field. While it is temporally more distant from the civil war, it was still influenced by the field of peacebuilding, giving it a post-conflict dimension.

Secondly, its logic largely concurs with that of the field of the post-conflict forest sector reform. Its main goal is to improve tenure security. Partly land conflicts were

[469] Interim guidelines and procedures for the sale of public land (2011) (Land Commission).

[470] Land Rights Policy (2013) (Land Commission), pp. 15 ff.

[471] An Act to amend Title 16, Executive Law of the Liberian Codes of Law revised to add thereto a new chapter creating the Liberia Land Authority (2016) (Republic of Liberia).

[472] Liberia Land Rights Act implementation strategy (2019) (Liberia Land Authority).

[473] Land Administration Policy (2015) (Land Commission), p. 54.

[474] Liberia Land Rights Act Regulations (2022) (Liberia Land Authority).

seen as a threat to peace; partly, it was framed as a matter of human rights.[475] Moreover, some actors stressed the importance of tenure security for economic prosperity.[476] And thirdly, what the fields had in common was the focus on international best practices and technical expertise.

However, the legislative practice differed in many respects. Even though participation was still an important principle, roundtable legal drafting became uncommon, and a considerable part of the legal negotiation took place within Parliament. The rules of the game thus differed from the field of the post-conflict forest sector reform, with the field's law being under a stronger influence of the national legal system.[477]

As a first step, the Land Commission embarked upon drafting a Land Rights Policy. Several studies commissioned by donors like the World Bank and USAID played a significant role in that phase.[478] These studies were usually prepared by international consultants who 'own the research tools, record the information, and abstract and summarize according to project criteria of relevance'.[479] A World Bank-funded consultant drafted a report proposing the establishment of three clusters within the Land Commission to lead the land reform process.[480] The Land Commission subsequently endorsed his report.[481]

The Land Rights cluster, composed of a policy task force and a legal drafting team, was in charge of drafting the Land Rights Policy with the participation of government institutions and NGOs.[482] Moreover, consultations took place in all fifteen counties.[483] The draft was subsequently discussed in the Land Rights Working Group featuring NGOs, the Environmental Protection Agency, ministries, and the Women Land Rights Taskforce.[484] After the elaboration of the first draft, six additional county-level consultations took place, and the draft was then validated in a national validation conference.[485] These consultations were largely implemented as a 'listening exercise'.[486]

Following the adoption of the Land Rights Policy, different stakeholders came together to draft the Land Rights Act (LRA). Again, external actors considerably shaped the process. The recommendation to adopt not one Land Law but to strive for

---

475 See also Sects. 3.3.2.1 and 3.3.2.3.

476 See also Sect. 3.3.2.1.

477 Griffiths (1986), p. 38.

478 Eg World Bank (2008); Unruh (2009b); Corriveau-Bourque (2010); Bruce and Kanneh (2011); Namubiru-Mwaura et al. (2012); Scalise and Hannay (2013).

479 Mosse (2001), p. 9.

480 Bruce and Kanneh (2011), pp. 37 ff.

481 Land rights policy (2013) (Land Commission), p. 5.

482 USAID (2012); Land Rights Policy (2013) (Land Commission), pp. 5–6.

483 Land Commission (2010).

484 Roesch R (18 Apr 2019) Skype interview with a senior staff member of the LGSA, para 10.

485 Bruce (2016), p. 6.

486 Ibid p. 14.

several laws which should subsequently be concretized in regulations came from an international World Bank-funded consultant.[487] The Land Commission also endorsed his recommendations.[488]

Departing from the working group approach to legal drafting, the subsequent drafting was delegated to a Land Rights Drafting Team established by the Land Commission's Land Rights Taskforce.[489] One participant in the process held that 'it was clear to him [the World Bank consultant] and everybody else that you don't draft by committee'.[490] NGOs were not part of that team, but staff members from different ministries and particularly the Land Commission. The drafting team appointed a Liberian lawyer to develop a zero draft, which was widely seen as a codification of the Land Rights Policy.[491] The drafting was thus 'mainly done by technicians in Monrovia'.[492] A few consultations were held in a Community Land Rights Task Force composed of government agencies, civil society, and donors.[493] However, apparently, the iterative consultations during the drafting of the Land Rights Policy had contributed to some consultation fatigue among the various stakeholders.[494]

After civil society and other stakeholders approved the first draft, it was submitted to the legislature in July 2014. The Ebola outbreak in 2014 delayed the process. Subsequently, the debates around the law took place mainly within Parliament. The legislature took a much bigger interest in the LRA than in the Land Rights Policy. The Joint Committee on Land, Energy, Environment, and Natural Resources held a public hearing in June 2015, inviting various stakeholders, including the Ministry of Land, Mines and Energy, the FDA, the Land Commission, the Civil Society Organizations (CSO) Council of Liberia, and the Governance Commission.[495] Requests for changes were submitted to the Land Commission, and negotiations took place between the Land Commission and the Ministry of Justice.

As the mandate of the Land Commission expired in the meantime, the Land Commission and the legislature jointly decided that the Land Authority bill, which sought to create a successor organization for the Land Commission, should be prioritized over the Land Rights bill.[496] The Liberia Land Authority should then facilitate the adoption of the Land Rights Act. The Land Authority Act was finally passed in April 2016.[497]

---

[487] Ibid p. 4.

[488] Land Rights Policy (2013) (Land Commission), p. 5.

[489] Bruce (2016), p. 6.

[490] Roesch R (18 Apr 2019) Skype interview with a senior staff member of the LGSA, para 118.

[491] Social Impact Inc. (2018), p. 2.

[492] Roesch R (21 Dec 2018) Skype interview with a Liberian land tenure expert para 60.

[493] Land Administration Policy (2015) (Land Commission), p. 19.

[494] Bruce (2016), p. 14.

[495] Ibid p. 8.

[496] Tetra Tech (2016c), p. 5.

[497] Tetra Tech (2016a), p. 5.

The publication of a Global Witness report on corrupt legislative practices with respect to the granting of concessions contributed to internal conflicts in the House of Representatives and further delays.[498] In May 2017, the United Nations Development Program organized a public consultation in Monrovia and, in July 2017, it facilitated a five-day consultative session in Buchanan.[499] Comments from the May consultation were incorporated into the draft before an updated version was resubmitted to the Senate. However, despite these consultations, the two chambers negotiated a version of the LRA in August 2017, which departed strongly from the earlier drafts.[500] Donors and NGOs kept building up pressure on the government and were willing to accept the weak 2017 version in return for its timely adoption. Nevertheless, the opposition blocked the passage of the law. In September 2018, the LRA was finally adopted.

Hence, while the drafting of the forest legislation was mainly a technical process, the negotiation of the LRA occurred in a more political environment.[501] Public consultations were also uncommon. Instead, the Liberia Land Authority, with donor funding, held awareness workshops, which are less input-oriented than consultations.[502] The field's law and legislative practice thus differed significantly from that of the field of forest sector reform.

3.3.2 *Actors in Relation*

The actors involved in the land sector reform overlapped with those of the forest sector process. They included international organizations, donors and their projects, government actors, and national and international NGOs. Conservationists, in contrast, were less present. Development actors and government agencies still ensured that the land reform would not jeopardize the government's conservation efforts.[503] Communities, again, were largely excluded. Moreover, the alliances and power relations changed over time.

[498] Global Witness (2016) Global witness exposes bribes to top Liberian officials by UK mining company and Varney Sherman. www.globalwitness.org/en/press-releases/global-witness-exposes-bribes-top-Liberian-officials-uk-mining-company-and-varney-sherman/. Accessed 19 Jul 2023.

[499] Tetra Tech (2017c), p. 9.

[500] Draft Land Rights Act (18 August 2017) (Republic of Liberia).

[501] Social Impact Inc. (2018), p. 2.

[502] Eg Tetra Tech (2017b), p. 1.

[503] World Bank (2018c), p. 33.

3.3.2.1 Donors and the Field of Development

Rebuilding or reforming property law systems has become a component of many peacebuilding operations.[504] Donors were concerned about the high number of land disputes in Liberia. UNMIL Deputy Director El Hillo declared that the adoption of a land law was 'cardinal and a cornerstone in the consolidation of peace in Liberia'[505] and would 'augur well for the country's stability and prosperity'.[506] However, the legal reforms were not only seen as necessary for avoiding future conflict by reducing social inequality but also as a precondition for attracting and securing investments.[507] This highlights how the harmonization of property law regimes has become a pillar of the neoliberal economic consensus.[508]

Donors in Liberia had considerable economic, social, and cultural capital, making them powerful actors in the legal reform process. While US agencies dominated the forest sector reform, more donors were involved in the land sector reform. They organized themselves in a Consultative Group on Land, with the UNDP, the World Bank, and USAID being the key actors.[509] Moreover, the Swedish International Development Agency, together with the World Bank, supported the Land Commission and the development of the Land Rights Policy.[510]

The World Bank took a strong interest in the legal reforms, as it was concerned about the negative impacts of insecure tenure on the economy.[511] Under the Land Sector Reform Project, the World Bank funded consultancies to provide guidance for the legal reform process, supported the elaboration of the Interim Guidelines on the Sale of Public Land, and funded most public consultations related to the drafting of the Land Rights Policy.[512] Moreover, in 2017, the Bank's Land Administration Project, which mainly provided institutional support to the Liberia Land Authority, was launched.

The United Nations Development Program (UNDP) also got increasingly involved after the expiration of the UNMIL's mandate in 2018. It facilitated the institutionalization of the Land Authority and the consultations on the LRA.[513] The

---

[504] Meinzen-Dick and Pradhan (2016), p. 525.

[505] UNMIL (2017) UNMIL deputy SRSG urges enactment of Liberia land rights bill. https://unmil.unmissions.org/unmil-deputy-srsg-urges-enactment-Liberia-land-rights-bill. Accessed 19 Jul 2023.

[506] Ibid.

[507] Liberia: Poverty reduction strategy paper (2008) (Republic of Liberia), pp. 67 ff.

[508] de Sousa Santos (2002), pp. 314 ff; de Sousa Santos (2006), pp. 39–40; Bryan (2012), p. 217.

[509] Tetra Tech (2016b), p. 2; Tetra Tech (2016d), p. 3.

[510] Email from a senior staff member of the LGSA to the author (10 April 2019); Liberia Land Rights Act implementation strategy (2019) (Liberia Land Authority), p. 11.

[511] World Bank (2017) para 10.

[512] Interim guidelines and procedures for the sale of public land (2011) (Land Commission), 5; Land Rights Policy (2013) (Land Commission), p. 5; Email from a senior staff member of the LGSA to the author (10 April 2019).

[513] Email from a senior staff member of the LGSA to the author (10 April 2019).

EU was equally involved but mainly provided funding for projects implemented by national and international NGOs.

Moreover, the Land Governance Support Activity (LGSA), funded by USAID from 2015 to 2020, played a vital role in the legal reforms. The LGSA was implemented by the development firm ARD/Tetra Tech.[514] LGSA's mandate had several components, including supporting legal and regulatory reform, developing a customary land rights recognition model, and supporting stakeholder engagement in the sector.[515] Given the duration of the legal reform process, LGSA later shifted its focus from supporting the statutory reform to developing methodologies for the implementation of the Land Rights Policy and the Land Rights bill.[516] The LGSA worked in close collaboration with the Land Commission, using a partnering approach and provided technical advice when necessary.[517] In doing so, it certainly still influenced the legal reforms. Moreover, during the LGSA's second year, the project supported three public consultations on the draft LRA: one with paramount chiefs from all Liberian counties, one with the Women Land Rights Taskforce and the NGO Coalition, and one with legal professionals.[518] Since 2021, a follow-up project—the Liberia Land Management Activity—supports communities in obtaining deeds for their land.[519]

The donors' discourse with respect to the land, the community, and the state was more nuanced than in the forest sector reform. Despite the economic perspective on land, there was still a general agreement that customary land had to be protected against encroachment.[520] As the road for recognizing FPIC had already been paved by the forest legislation, most donors did not oppose its inclusion in the LRA. The World Bank even congratulated the Liberian government for passing the LRA and, thereby, 'recognizing customary community land rights including the right [to] their Free, Prior and Informed Consent [and] [. . .] bolstering women and minority land rights'.[521] Moreover, the FAO and the European Union provided funding for a project for capacity development on FPIC and land acquisitions.[522]

At the same time, some donors had a rather limited understanding of FPIC, reminiscent of the field of development law. One leading expert held that 'government anywhere in the world has the right of eminent domain [. . .] FPIC has got nothing to do with it'.[523]

---

[514] Tetra Tech (2016a), pp. 1–2.

[515] Ibid p. 2.

[516] Tetra Tech (2016d), p. 4.

[517] Tetra Tech (2016a), pp. 2–3.

[518] Tetra Tech (2017b), p. 1.

[519] ECODIT (2022), p. 5.

[520] Liberia: Poverty reduction strategy paper (2008) (Republic of Liberia), pp. 67 ff.

[521] World Bank (2018a), p. 1.

[522] USAID. Land governance programme map & database. https://landgov.donorplatform.org. Accessed 19 Jul 2023.

[523] Roesch R (18 Apr 2019) Skype interview with a senior staff member of the LGSA, para 142.

With respect to the collective identity of the *community*, and unlike in the forest sector reform, more engagement with customary land governance took place during the drafting of the LRA. The LGSA commissioned eight reports related to customary land, addressing issues like land dispute resolution mechanisms, community land governance, and community membership.[524] An extensive 2011 report recommended that land governance authorities should be 'socially legitimate actors with deep knowledge of customary norms and rules'.[525]

Simultaneously, 'women's land rights' were a concern for donors. Potentially this may be attributed to the Sustainable Development Goals, which recognize 'women's equal rights to land ownership'.[526] Donors assumed that women's participation in land governance institutions would have political and economic benefits.[527] Therefore, most of the donor projects had a gender component. For example, the LGSA has a Gender and Land Specialist and a gender component that was mostly implemented by the US-based organization Landesa, which completed, among other things, a gender analysis of the Land Authority and Land Rights bills in 2016.[528] Besides that, the LGSA's Gender and Land Specialist, together with the Women's Land Rights Taskforce, published a Liberian Women Manifesto, including policy recommendations on women's land rights.[529] Yet, the interactions with rural women, like female elders and town chiefs on the bill, were framed as awareness training rather than consultations.[530] Moreover, even though the LGSA was involved in the self-identification of communities, no information on how it gender-mainstreamed these processes could be found.

In the course of the reforms, customary governance and its impact on women were increasingly seen as a problem.[531] A 2012 report recommended that while customary governance arrangements should be respected, the government should 'promote stronger integration of women and youth as governance authorities over land'.[532] The authors suggested introducing quotas to enhance the number of women and youth and contribute to gradual changes in stereotypical and discriminatory behavior.[533] The mid-term assessment of the LGSA found that 'currently chiefs and

---

524 Tetra Tech (2016b), p. 10.

525 Namubiru-Mwaura et al. (2012), p. 109.

526 Food and Agriculture Organization of the United Nations. SDG indicator 5.A.2 - women's equal rights to land ownership. http://www.fao.org/sustainable-development-goals/indicators/5a2/en/. Accessed 19 Jul 2023; see also Committee on World Food Security (2012) Voluntary guidelines on the responsible governance of tenure of land, fisheries and forests in the context of national food security, part 3 para 9.10.

527 Hartman et al. (2018), p. 10.

528 Gender equality and female empowerment policy (2012a) (USAID); Tetra Tech (2016a), p. 6.

529 Tetra Tech (2017a), pp. 12–13.

530 Ibid p. 12.

531 Eg Scalise and Hannay (2013).

532 Namubiru-Mwaura et al. (2012), p. 109.

533 Ibid p. 109.

elders handle land transactions at the local level in an opaque manner, frequently with limited or no involvement by women and youth'.[534]

The gender-land nexus was thus much better recognized than the gender dimension of forestry, and the objective of strengthening women's land rights became common sense within the field of development. Donors could also draw from a much bigger pool of experience with and literature on women-sensitive legal reforms.[535] Yet, the rise of gender went hand in hand with skepticism towards customary land governance. This contributed to the gradual negligence of the cultural dimension of land and land-related decision-making.

To conclude, the identity of the state played a marginal role in the field. As many actors read land as an economic resource or as a potential source of conflict, the recognition and registration of customary land were seen as beneficial. However, the social identity of the community through the land-gender nexus was seen as a discriminatory structure that needed transformation.

3.3.2.2 Government, Parliament, and the Field of Politics

Government agencies and the Parliament were more divided than in the forest sector reform. While the land authorities pursued similar objectives as many donors co-located in the field of development, many members of Parliament opposed the reforms more forcefully and mobilized the discourse of sovereignty to do so.

The Land Commission and the Liberia Land Authority (LLA) are the key governmental actors in the area of land governance in Liberia. In 2009, a law to create the Land Commission was enacted and the Land Commission was put in charge of reforming the land legislation. Upon the expiration of the Land Commission's term, President Johnson Sirleaf created an Interim Land Task Force in March 2016 to fill the institutional gap caused by the delays in the adoption of the Land Authority bill.[536] The main functions of the Interim Task Force were to engage the legislature for the passage of the bill mentioned above, to maintain good donor relations, and to assume the key functions of the Land Commission.

In 2016, the LLA was established. In the drafting of the LRA, the LLA was perceived as not 'taking any strong position',[537] 'but [it] worked between the different partners to find a common language'.[538] International NGOs saw this as an advantage, particularly compared to the investment-driven FDA, even though they were concerned about its weak institutional capacity.[539] The LLA had a keen

[534] Social Impact Inc. (2018), p. 9.

[535] Eg USAID.

[536] Tetra Tech (2016c), p. 2.

[537] Roesch R (21 Dec 2018) Skype interview with a Liberian land tenure expert para 108.

[538] Ibid para 108.

[539] Email from a senior staff member of an international human rights organization to the author (26 November 2018).

interest in the passage of the LRA, as it needed a legal framework for its operations. The then-chairman of the LLA urged the government to pass the LRA as it would grant communities 'the right to use, manage and control the land in line with customary traditional practices and norms, meaning that they will decide what they want to do with their lands, and not anyone else, including the government'.[540] He also criticized the Johnson Sirleaf government for putting 'people in positions who have failed to implement'[541] the respective policies. But also other government actors, including President Johnson Sirleaf, called for the adoption of the law.[542]

Unlike in the forest sector reform, most of the legislative debates took place within Parliament. With the Parliament being less (directly) dependent on donor funding, it had more power. Some government actors and members of Parliament strongly opposed the land sector reform. One reason was personal motives: informants explained that many parliamentarians held tribal certificates[543] awaiting presidential confirmation and were, therefore, concerned about their possible extinction.[544] Similarly, a former staff member of the Land Commission believed that the members of Parliament feared that, under the new LRA, 'if you went to the community now and ask for the piece of land, then all these new ideas of FPIC and all of these things will step in. And the cost of the land is going to be high [compared to] what you would normally pay for public land'.[545]

Members of Parliament used the discourse of national ownership and sovereignty to legitimize their position. They argued that they had been put under pressure by international actors. One Senator held that 'they (Global Witness) know that we are on a verge of passing a law, so they want to get the credit. Liberia is a responsible country and we should be allowed to run our affairs'.[546] Another Senator justified the 2017 amendments to the LRA, restricting customary land rights, by arguing that 'you have international people sponsoring some of these acts because they want things done the right way. But sometimes some of the provisions in the act do not

540 Davis (5 May 2017) Liberia: "Land rights crisis looms". Daily Observer. https://allafrica.com/stories/201705050742.html?fbclid=IwAR0eO4yysqWxEjaWyTTipIz0_BGCW3cjgTJMyL5caaP3lkOr7M_ADEjOlWY. Accessed 11 Aug 2023.

541 Ibid.

542 Johnson Sirleaf (2016) Annual message on the state of the Republic to the fifth session of the 53rd national legislature of the Republic of Liberia, delivered on Monday, January 25, 2016. https://www.mofa.gov.lr/public2/doc/ANNUAL%20MESSAGE%20on%20the%20State%20of%20the%20Nation%20by%20President%20Ellen%20Johnson%20Sirleaf%20-%20Monday,%20January%2025,%202016.pdf. Accessed 11 Aug 2023, p. 3.

543 Tribal certificates are the first step for obtaining a public land sale deed.

544 Roesch R (8 Jan 2018) Interview with a senior staff member of the LGSA, Monrovia, para 152.

545 Roesch R (20 Mar 2018) Interview with a former senior staff member of the Land Commission, Monrovia, para 66.

546 Karmo (29 Aug 2017) Land Rights Act suffers setback at Liberian legislature. https://frontpageafricaonline.com/amp/news/2016news/land-rights-act-suffers-setback-at-Liberian-legislature/. Accessed 11 Aug 2023.

relate to the way we do things in Liberia'.[547] After President Johnson Sirleaf extended the legislative session into 2018 in order to enable, among other things, the adoption of the LRA, a Senator held that 'there should be no urgency in passing of bills'.[548]

Controversies also arose between the FDA and the LLA over the meaning of customary land. The FDA feared that the recognition of customary land as a stand-alone category of land would undermine their ownership of forests and their capacity to manage them.[549] Government and administration were thus divided about the land sector reform.

Like in the forest sector reform, many government actors saw land as an (economic) resource that they needed to control. They had a very broad understanding of the state's sovereignty over land and natural resources. The FDA and other agencies handling concessions held that 'the government does not need FPIC to go on its own land'.[550] It was also commonly argued that, according to the Constitution, the government owns all land within the Liberian territory.[551] Recognizing community ownership was seen as unduly interfering with their right to grant concessions.[552] They thus envisioned more limited customary land rights, and FPIC became a point that met particular resistance.

The Land Commission and the LLA also had a relatively narrow understanding of FPIC similar to that prevailing in the field of development law. Fearing repercussions by concession holders, the Land Commission also made it clear from the onset that existing concessions could not be affected by the LRA.[553] Moreover, the Liberia Land Authority and many donors took the position that 'history is history'[554] and that protected areas should remain protected areas. In terms of FPIC's meaning, the former FPIC expert of the Land Commission described FPIC as 'gathering the key segments of the town, then talk to them the importance of the investment, they have the right to give their view, and they should willingly give up their land'.[555]

Respecting the institutional autonomy of communities contravened the interest of large parts of the field of government, as it would have made FPIC more burdensome. The gender-land-nexus, in contrast, was acknowledged to a greater extent. Both the Land Commission and the Liberia Land Authority took some interest in

547 Roesch R (3 Jan 2018) Interview with a Senator, Monrovia, para 88.

548 Varney Sherman, as cited in: Leroy M. Sonpon (2018) Ellen wants 13 bills enacted before January 13. Daily Observer. https://allafrica.com/stories/201801090503.html. Accessed 11 Aug 2023.

549 Roesch R (18 Apr 2019) Skype interview with a senior staff member of the LGSA, para 64.

550 Roesch R (21 Dec 2018) Skype interview with a Liberian land tenure expert para 104.

551 Ibid paras 94–96.

552 Roesch R (23 Mar 2018) Interview with a Liberian lawyer Monrovia, para 98.

553 Mulbah (2015), pp. 111, 114.

554 Roesch R (18 Apr 2019) Skype interview with a senior staff member of the LGSA, para 84.

555 Roesch R (23 Mar 2018) Interview with a former staff member of the Land Commission and current staff member of the Land Authority, Monrovia, para 36.

gender and women's land rights. Partly this was caused by the Land Commission's Land Dispute Resolution Taskforce being flooded with complaints related to women's land rights.[556] Moreover, the donors' project law and its 'better world-visions'[557]—in which women's land rights are secured—provided a strong incentive to government agencies.

The Land Commission created a land and gender unit, and, for a while, half of the commissioners were women.[558] Upon the recommendation of the LGSA, the Liberia Land Authority equally established a Gender Unit. While the LLA has been susceptible to many of the LGSA's proposals, it also criticized LGSA's 'over-emphasis on women'[559] and suggested focusing on constraints experienced by both genders and particularly the male youth.[560] Just like FDA, the Liberia Land Authority had few women staff members.[561] Consequently, due to the perceived 'lack of gender capacity',[562] the Women's Land Rights Task Force provided advice on gender issues.

Hence, while the land institutions regularly joined forces with the field of development, Parliament resisted the reform attempts to a greater extent. Government actors and Parliament had a different vision of the state and its rights and understood collective property rights as potentially interfering with their prerogatives of sovereignty. FPIC remained contentious: while the land institutions supported the streamlined version of FPIC, it met resistance from other agencies, such as the FDA and some members of Parliament.

3.3.2.3 National and International NGOs and the Field of Human Rights

Again, national and international NGOs, both co-located in the field of human rights, played a central role in the land sector reform. It is also worth noting that the national NGO landscape was considerably more diverse than in the forest sector reform. During the drafting of the LRA, national NGOs formed the NGO Land Rights Working Group.

National NGOs secured comprehensive INGO and donor funding for land projects. In 2009, the Liberian NGO Sustainable Development Institute (SDI), in cooperation with the International Development Law Organization and the US organization Namati, signed a Memorandum of Understanding with the Land

[556] Roesch R (18 Apr 2019) Skype interview with a senior staff member of the LGSA, para 16.

[557] Weilenmann (2009b), p. 168.

[558] Bruce (2016), p. 1; Roesch R (18 Apr 2019) Skype interview with a senior staff member of the LGSA, para 104.

[559] Social Impact Inc. (2018), pp. 23–24.

[560] Roesch R (18 Apr 2019) Skype interview with a senior staff member of the LGSA, para 104.

[561] Tetra Tech (2016b), p. 13.

[562] Tetra Tech (2016d), p. 8.

Commission permitting the SDI to pilot a community land registration process in Rivercess. This first pilot study greatly informed the customary land registration procedure prescribed by the LRA.[563]

Building upon these experiences, Namati and the British Department for International Development introduced a customary land project implemented by the SDI.[564] Between 2015 and 2017, the SDI piloted the customary land registration in 36 clans.[565] The SDI and its partners also explored the impact of community land titling on women's land rights and their participation in land governance.[566]

The Land Tenure Facility played a similarly important role. The project was initiated in 2014 by the Swedish NGO Rights and Resource Foundation and is primarily funded by the Swedish International Development Agency. The SDI also took the lead in the project. Between 2015 and 2017, the Tenure Facility completed a pilot project on community self-identification in 12 communities.[567] Self-identification is the first step in the process of securing land rights. Following the adoption of the LRA, the project worked with 24 communities to improve their tenure security by, among other things, developing a methodology of participatory land and resource mapping. The second phase of the project was led by the NGO Foundation for Community Initiatives, focusing on gender and land and natural governance.[568] The third phase, under the lead of Parley Liberia, supports the fifteen new communities in addition to the 24 original communities.[569]

NGOs, whilst being less directly involved in the negotiation of the LRA, pursued a different advocacy approach in the land sector reform. They had more economic and social capital than in the field of forest sector reform, as they implemented many land rights projects funded by donors. Moreover, they focused more on (social) media campaigns and protests. In this respect, NGOs used a narrative of inclusivity to enhance their legitimacy and symbolic capital. The participation of women's groups was strongly emphasized, and, in the photo documentation of the rallies

[563] Hartman et al. (2016), pp. 11–12.

[564] USAID p. 3.

[565] Ibid p. 4.

[566] Knight et al. (2013), pp. 19–20.

[567] Liberia Land Authority. Community self-identification guide (CSI). https://new.sdiLiberia.org/sites/default/files/2022-12/LLA%20-%20CSI%20Guide.pdf. Accessed 27 Jul 2023, p. 2; The Tenure Facility. Protection of customary collective community land rights in Liberia. https://thetenurefacility.org/projects/protection-of-customary-collective-community-land-rights-in-Liberia/. Accessed 27 Jul 2023.

[568] The Tenure Facility. Strengthening the capacity of Community Land Development and Management Committees (CLDMCs) to implement their mandates (phase 2 extension). https://thetenurefacility.org/projects/protection-of-customary-collective-community-land-rights-in-Liberia-phase-2/. Accessed 27 Jul 2023.

[569] The Tenure Facility. Keeping the promise: Expanding and strengthening community land and forest governance for a sustainable future. https://thetenurefacility.org/projects/keeping-the-promise-expanding-and-strengthening-community-land-and-forest-governance-for-a-sustainable-future/. Accessed 27 Jul 2023.

and protest actions, women are strongly represented.[570] The women in the pictures advocated not only for their right to own land and equal participation in land governance but also FPIC. In addition to women, NGOs stressed the support of other marginalized groups, like the disabled community, in the protests for the passage of the LRA in February 2018.[571]

Besides that, the NGO campaigns created the impression that they were supported by the *communities*.[572] However, this narrative of solid grassroots support of the Land Rights bill contrasts with the representation of these groups within national NGOs and the meetings of the CSO Working Group on Land Rights. While NGOs made some effort to provide a voice to communities, women, or disabled people, this cannot mask the power imbalances between them and those they seek to represent.

Land remains an element without fixed meaning in the Liberian human rights discourse.[573] The causality between land shortage and the outbreak of the civil war is controversial.[574] INGOs tended to contest a general pattern of land shortage.[575] For example, Wily argues that disputes over boundary lines are natural in a post-war context and a move towards tenure security and peace.[576] Liberian NGOs, however, have aligned themselves more with the narrative of the field of peacebuilding and development, constructing land disputes as a severe threat to peace in Liberia.[577] The negative impacts of large-scale concessions are, however, a storyline that NGOs and INGOs agree on.

With respect to the collective identity of the *community*, the Indigenous rights/urban-rural language was mobilized to a greater extent in the land sector reform. For instance, in a video protesting against the 2017 version of the law, Isaiah Dippay of the Farmers Union Network held that 'George Weah is an [Indigenous] son, a country boy'.[578] International projects like the Land Tenure facility also frequently referred to the Indigenous population of Liberia and the need for recognizing and

[570] Liberia Civil Society Working Group on Land Rights Reform (30 May 2018) Facebook post. https://www.facebook.com/LiberiaLandRights/photos/pcb.640527716289540/640524792956499/?type=3&theater. Accessed 27 Jul 2023.

[571] Liberia Civil Society Working Group on Land Rights Reform (8 Feb 2018) Facebook post. https://www.facebook.com/LiberiaLandRights/photos/pcb.586011885074457/586009665074679/?type=3&theater. Accessed 27 Jul 2023.

[572] Eg Altman et al. (2012), pp. 355–356.

[573] Laclau and Mouffe (2001), p. 113.

[574] Alden Wily (2009), p. 31.

[575] Roesch R (20 Mar 2018) Interview with a former senior staff member of the Land Commission, Monrovia, paras 35 ff.

[576] Alden Wily (2009), p. 32.

[577] Knight et al. (2013), p. 37.

[578] Liberia Civil Society Working Group on Land Rights Reform (2018) Join our call. www.facebook.com/LiberiaLandRights/videos/639836446358667/. Accessed 19 Jul 2023.

safeguarding Indigenous land rights.[579] This would have left some space for recognizing the cultural dimension of collective property.

However, women's land rights were also much more on the NGOs' agenda and many donor-funded projects focused on 'women and other vulnerable groups'.[580] Within the Land Rights Working Group, several women's rights NGOs were represented, including the Natural Resource Women Platform and the Women NGO Secretariat of Liberia. In 2016, NGOs called for ensuring the adequate representation of 'women and gender issues within land-related bodies'.[581] They suggested introducing gender quotas within the Liberia Land Authority, stronger involving the Ministry for Gender and Development in the land sector reform, and increasing the number of women on county land boards. Hence, women's land rights were not only seen as an integral aspect of NGO programs relating to land governance but also of the political and administrative sphere.

Like in the field of development, this contributed to the negligence of the institutional autonomy of communities, with traditional decision-makers being seen as undemocratic, corrupt, and patriarchal. The field of human rights thus shared the donors' concerns about elite capture and understood the inclusion of women as a way of ensuring more legitimate and democratic land governance.[582] The emerging social identity is thus equally that of the *discriminatory community* that needs to be transformed.

3.3.2.4 Women's Land Rights Taskforce: Between Development and Human Rights

Another difference compared to the forest sector reform was that a focal point for women's land rights was created. It was located at the intersection of the fields of development, government, and human rights. In 2013, the Ministry of Gender and USAID's Land Policy and Institutional Support Project created the Women's Land Rights Taskforce (WLRTF).[583] The WLRTF facilitated several public consultations on the proposed Land Policy.[584]

---

[579] Eg The Tenure Facility (2018) A visual history of Indigenous peoples' land rights in Liberia. https://thetenurefacility.org/timeline/Liberia/. Accessed 19 Jul 2023.

[580] Knight et al. (2013), pp. 134 ff.

[581] The Civil Society Working Group on Community Land Rights in Liberia (2016) Position statement on the Land Authority Act (LAA) and the Land Rights Act (LRA). www.forestpeoples.org/sites/fpp/files/publication/2016/07/position-statement-laa-lra-2016.pdf. Accessed 19 Jul 2023, p. 4.

[582] Knight et al. (2013), pp. 25, 31.

[583] USAID (2013) Snapshot: Women's Land Rights Task Force established. www.land-links.org/wp-content/uploads/2016/09/USAID_Land_Tenure_LPIS_WLRTF_Snapshot.pdf. Accessed 19 Jul 2023.

[584] Bruce (2016), p. 16.

After the Ebola outbreak, the LGSA, the Liberian government, NGOs, and UN entities reactivated the WLRTF.[585] It was chaired by representatives of the Mano River Women's Network for Peace and the Association of Female Lawyers. The LGSA gender specialist was elected to serve as Secretary-General. Moreover, different ministries appointed task force members.

The WLRTF advocated, among other things, for a gender-sensitive LRA and the participation of women in the land reform processes.[586] It held advocacy meetings with the LLA, conducted a review of the LRA together with the Land Rights Working Group, and lobbied presidential candidates to support their agenda.[587] Members of the WLRTF also participated in meetings of the NGO coalition and helped connect Ministry staff members, civil society, and donor representatives. The existence of the WLFTF exemplifies the central role that women's land rights played in the land reform.

3.3.2.5 Participatory Exclusions

When exploring fields, examining who is not part of the field can also be instrumental: the field's exclusions. Just like in the forest sector reform, consultations with rural communities were the method of choice.

Consultations with communities occurred mainly before and during the drafting of the Land Rights Policy. According to the Land Commission, a 'targeted audience of paramount, clan and town chiefs, district commissioners, public surveyors, land commissioners, women's groups, civil society, and youth organizations'[588] were brought together to collect input. However, the Land Commission could only host a limited number of participants in the consultations where the draft Land Rights Policy was discussed.[589] While the SDI had considered advertising the regional consultations, this idea was dropped due to the fear of alienating the Land Commission. The SDI also criticized the lack of distribution of the draft of the policy.[590] The Land Commission, in turn, attacked the SDI for jeopardizing the process.[591]

Even fewer resources were invested in consultations on the Land Rights bill. Due to the regional consultations during the drafting of the Land Rights Policy and the earlier research on customary land governance, it was assumed that communities had already had the opportunity to provide input.[592] Moreover, some donors argued that

---

[585] Tetra Tech (2016c), p. 16.

[586] Ibid p. 16.

[587] Tetra Tech (2017a), p. 12.

[588] Land Commission (2010), p. 2.

[589] Kaba and Madan (2014), p. 11.

[590] Ibid p. 11.

[591] Roesch R (21 Dec 2018) Skype interview with a Liberian land tenure expert para 60.

[592] See also Roesch R (18 Apr 2019) Skype interview with a senior staff member of the LGSA, paras 37 ff; Roesch R (21 Dec 2018) Skype interview with a Liberian Land tenure expert para 60.

the 'CSO working group has been the voice for communities',[593] making the presence of community representatives at the negotiating table in Monrovia superfluous. As the lead organization, the SDI provided information on the Land Rights bill to community members and collected signatures for a petition. However, they described their efforts as not a systematic 'process to inform community members and solicit their views to be able to inform the Land Rights law'.[594] Consequently, even though national NGOs did not necessarily share the view that they could speak on behalf of communities, this narrative became so dominant that donors widely refrained from actually including community representatives.

Nevertheless, the National Traditional Council, an association of chiefs from all over Liberia, and other rural organizations participated in the civil society protests surrounding the lengthy negotiation of the LRA.[595] Members of the National Traditional Council held that they had endorsed the Land Rights Policy and, therefore, also supported the Land Rights bill.[596] They argued that they were 'disappointed to hear that the House of Representatives spoiled the law that we gave them'.[597] This indicates that some customary leaders felt a sense of ownership over the Land Rights Policy and also the 2014 version of the LRA. They called upon the legislators not to 'sign the bad law that the Lower House passed in August 2017 without consulting [them]'.[598] However, overall, little in-depth engagement took place with those affected by the Land Rights Policy and the LRA.[599]

Moreover, the participatory exclusion of communities also had a gender dimension. During the drafting of the Land Rights Policy, women were recognized as one stakeholder group to be included in the consultations. However, just as in the drafting of the forest legislation, it may be doubted whether they could participate in a meaningful way. The documentation report produced by the Land Commission on the regional consultations just summarizes the responses of each county without clarifying whether controversies arose and which participants took the lead in the discussions.[600] A public surveyor, for instance, very likely has a different perspective on land rights than a women's group. However, as *experts*, they are more likely to be heard in discussions than *non-expert* community members.

---

593 Email from a member of the EU delegation to Liberia to the author (12 November 2018).

594 Roesch R (21 Dec 2018) Skype interview with a Liberian land tenure expert para 68.

595 Mwanza (2018) Liberians plan sit-in to pressure Weah to protect land rights. www.reuters.com/article/us-Liberia-landrights-law/Liberians-plan-sit-in-to-pressure-weah-to-protect-land-rights-idUSKBN1HX33T?fbclid=IwAR0mSEQoUiPmNJylkWrsGtV-43ioNHO3EQJOwf4q3T_S0JRkwJDKCGk7jrA. Accessed 19 Jul 2023.

596 Front Page Africa (10 Dec 2017) Traditional leaders want house version of Land Rights Act rejected by Senate. https://frontpageafricaonline.com/news/2016news/traditional-leaders-want-house-version-of-land-rights-act-rejected-by-senate/. Accessed 11 Aug 2023.

597 Wordorwor Gaye-Tuahn, as cited in: ibid.

598 Wordorwor Gaye-Tuahn, as cited in: ibid.

599 See also Shepherd (2017a), p. 151.

600 Land Commission (2010).

During the drafting of the LRA, the USAID-funded LGSA project sought to incorporate the views of rural women in the drafting of the LRA. For instance, the Gender and Land Rights specialist 'met with female chiefs and elders from five counties to raise awareness on the status of the LRA'.[601] The LGSA also held public dialogues with rural women on the Land Rights and the Land Authority bills in six counties.[602]

Moreover, different women's rights organizations were active in the Women's Land Rights Taskforce, and some of them also participated in the civil society land working group. Women groups also played an important role in the 2017 protests against the watered-down version of the LRA, and a women's group marched on the presidential palace to kick off the campaign.[603] Furthermore, they submitted a petition to Vice President Jewel Howard Taylor to support the 2014 version of the LRA.[604] Despite the stronger presence of women in the land reform, these women were mainly from capital-based NGOs. Again, rural women were—at best—addressed by awareness campaigns without being able to provide much input.

3.3.3 *A Matter of Negotiation*

Just like the forest sector reform, the land reform process went through different phases with shifting power relations and alliances. The main phases will be identified in this section. While it was clear from the onset that one outcome of the reforms should be the protection of customary property rights in rural Liberia, the scope of this collective right to property was highly controversial. The main controversies touched upon (1) overlaps between customary land and (proposed) protected areas, (2) overlaps between customary land and concessions, (3) tribal certificates granted by communities in the past, which had not yet been transformed into public land sale deeds, (4) the reservation of a certain percentage of customary land for government use, and (5) the protection of women's land rights. All of these questions relate to FPIC.

[601] Tetra Tech (2017a), p. 13.

[602] Tetra Tech (2016c), p. 15.

[603] Mwanza (2018) Liberians plan sit-in to pressure weah to protect land rights. www.reuters.com/article/us-Liberia-landrights-law/Liberians-plan-sit-in-to-pressure-weah-to-protect-land-rights-idUSKBN1HX33T?fbclid=IwAR0mSEQoUiPmNJylkWrsGtV-43ioNHO3EQJOwf4q3T_S0JRkwJDKCGk7jrA. Accessed 19 Jul 2023.

[604] Clay Jr. 2018. 'Pass land rights bill'. New Republic Liberia.

3.3.3.1 2009–2015: Under the Radar of Politicians

In the first phase of the land reform, the Land Rights Policy and the Interim Guidelines on the Acquisition of Public Land were endorsed. Moreover, the first two drafts of the LRA were circulated. During that time, most public consultations were held while the negotiations took place mainly in the Community Land Rights Taskforce.

3.3.3.1.1 Interim Guidelines on the Sale of Public Land

In 2011, the Interim Guidelines on the Sale of Public Land were adopted in response to the moratorium placed upon the issuance of Public Land Sale Deeds by President Johnson Sirleaf.[605] They regulated how public land could be sold. Under the Public Lands Law, undeeded customary land was classified as public land and could be sold under the condition that communities issued a so-called tribal certificate.[606] The town or clan chief could issue these tribal certificates, which caused a considerable number of questionable land transactions. The Interim Guidelines, in contrast, required the consent of 'the owner of the land/elder, clan chief, a female representative designated by the women in the affected community(ies), and a youth representative designated by the youth in the affected community(ies)'.[607] If the four authorities were satisfied with the survey, they could issue a public land certificate. However, the moratorium on the sale of public land remained in place.

3.3.3.1.2 Land Rights Policy

In 2013, the Land Rights Policy was adopted. Donors and national and international NGOs considerably shaped it. Informants explained that government agencies, at the time, took little interest in it, allowing for the insertion of customary land-friendly provisions.[608] Although the Land Rights Policy does not mention FPIC, it recognizes customary land as one category of land, similar to private land.[609] However, it also reinforces the government's right to acquire customary land by eminent domain without mentioning FPIC.[610]

---

[605] Bruce and Kanneh (2011), p. 5.

[606] Public Lands Law (1956), ch 3 para 30.

[607] Interim guidelines and procedures for the sale of public land (2011) (Land Commission), p. 8.

[608] Roesch R (21 Dec 2018) Skype interview with a Liberian land tenure expert para 132; Roesch R (18 Apr 2019) Skype interview with a senior staff member of the LGSA, para 12.

[609] Land Rights Policy (2013) (Land Commission), s 6.0.

[610] Ibid s 5.3.

Moreover, the gender-land nexus influenced the Land Rights Policy.[611] It recognized both the institutional autonomy of communities and women's rights to land and participation. National policies and laws should have a 'minimal impact'[612] on customary practices. At the same time, it called for the integration of customary practices and norms 'not in conflict with national land laws, the Constitution, and international legal obligations, including women's land rights'[613] into the statutory legal system.

In addition, it recommended that communities identify their membership and establish management institutions that are 'fully representative and accountable to all community members, including women, youth, and minorities'.[614] The sale and distribution of customary land within the community should also be subject to inclusive decision-making.[615] Management decisions relating to customary land are prohibited if they do not fulfill the requirement of inclusivity.[616]

Thus, neither the Land Rights Policy nor the Interim Guidelines for the Sale of Public Land mention FPIC, but its seed had been planted. The recognition of customary tenure implies that the government cannot just alienate customary land but that it needs to follow the constitutional procedure for expropriations. Still, it was also clear that customary land alienated in the past would neither be restituted nor compensated. While the Land Rights Policy recognizes customary institutions and decision-making, it is closer to the field of human rights law than to an Indigenous sovereignty approach. In the case of a conflict between the right to culture and the right of women, women's rights prevail.

3.3.3.1.3 First LRA Drafts

The drafting team of the LRA considerably built upon the Land Rights Policy. The 2013 draft stipulated that existing concessions remained untouched by the LRA, while the status of designated protected areas was unclear.[617] It also did not include FPIC. Moreover, if land was required for a public purpose, and the owner(s) refused to sell it to the government, the government could institute eminent domain proceedings.[618] However, the 2013 draft departed from the 'women, youth and minority' stakeholder approach and also required the inclusion of 'physically challenged persons' in the context of the community self-identification.[619] The benefits of

[611] Ibid s 2.5.

[612] Ibid s 6.1.3.

[613] Ibid s 6.1.4.

[614] Ibid ss 6.1.5, 6.2.4.

[615] Ibid ss 6.3.3, 7.4.2.

[616] Ibid s 6.3.1.

[617] Draft Land Rights Act (NGO version) (7 Dec 2013) (Republic of Liberia), art 32(4).

[618] Ibid art 27(3).

[619] Ibid art 33(2).

leasing out customary land should be distributed in a way that considers 'women, the physically challenged and minorities',[620] omitting the youth.

The 2014 draft that was submitted to the legislature differed considerably from the draft discussed in 2013. The national NGO scene strongly supported the 2014 version of the law, even though it was concerned about the lack of clarity regarding eminent domain.[621] The draft contained stronger safeguards for customary land. For instance, holders of tribal certificates could only apply for a public land sale deed under the condition that the land had been occupied and developed.[622] Concessions on customary land issued before the adoption of the LRA still remained in force.[623]

The 2014 draft also included FPIC and understood it as a requirement preceding eminent domain; if the government fails to obtain the consent of communities for the establishment of a protected area, it can make use of its right to eminent domain.[624] Moreover, FPIC was required for the extension of existing concessions, contracts, or permits on customary land.[625] The extraction of mineral resources from customary land equally required the FPIC of the community, as well as land lease agreements.[626] The draft did not make any reference to existing protected areas, though.

The draft also considered FPIC's internal dimension and women's participation. Prior to the establishment of the official governance structure, the customary land should be governed by the 'elders, chiefs, traditional leaders, women and youth of that community'.[627] Later, the governance structure should be 'inclusive of a fair number of women, men, youth and other representatives of all other stakeholder groups'.[628] To the extent possible, it should consist of equal numbers of the three stakeholder groups—adult men, adult women, and youth—democratically elected by the three stakeholder groups.[629] Additionally, two representatives of the chiefs and traditional leaders should be members. Any decision by the governing body that denies 'women or children or persons with disability'[630] access to land ownership or use should be null and void. This stakeholder approach was most likely supported by donors and NGOs and departed from the Land Rights Policy's recognition of customary institutions and ways of decision-making.

The documents of this early phase thus reflect the influence of development and Liberian human rights discourse. They also prove that women's rights were an important aspect from the onset of the reform process.

---

620 Ibid art 47(2).

621 Sustainable Development Institute (2015), p. 2.

622 Draft Land Rights Act (3 Jul 2014) (Republic of Liberia), art 47(3).

623 Ibid art 48(1).

624 Ibid art 42(5).

625 Ibid art 48(3).

626 Ibid art 33(5).

627 Ibid art 70(2).

628 Ibid art 35(1)(c).

629 Ibid art 36(4).

630 Ibid art 36(6).

3.3.3.2 2016–2017: The Rise of the Field of Politics

In the second phase of the reform process, the Land Authority Act was adopted, and two LRA drafts were discussed. During this period, the field of politics gained power to the detriment of the fields of human rights and development. This considerably changed the field's law and practice. Most of the negotiations took place within Parliament. Moreover, national NGOs were reluctant to insist on their vision of the law, as they saw the last months of the Johnson Sirleaf administration as a window of opportunity for getting the law passed.[631] They were thus inclined to accept a watered-down version of the law.

3.3.3.2.1 Land Authority Act

The Land Authority Act limited communities' right to customary land. It departed from the prevailing approach that protected areas could be located on any type of land, as stipulated in the early drafts of the LRA. Instead, all protected and proposed protected areas were declared to be government land.[632] Donors and government actors supported a vision of conservation based on *in situ* protected areas in the hands of the government. NGOs, in contrast, objected to this extended definition of government land to no avail.[633]

3.3.3.2.2 2016 LRA Draft

The LRA draft from September 2016 draft minimally weakened the language of the 2014 version. As for the tribal certificates, the 2016 draft was quite similar to the 2014 draft. However, it allowed for the transformation of up to 150 acres of customary land into public land sale deeds for holders of tribal certificates instead of the 25-acre cap of the earlier drafts.[634] Concerning protected areas, it held that the establishment of a protected area on customary land 'must be with the consent of the community and must comply with the procedural and substantive requirements for eminent domain'.[635] This indicates that FPIC was understood as a binding requirement that could not be replaced by the government's exercise of eminent domain.

---

[631] Eg Roesch R (7 Jun 2018) Skype interview with a lawyer of an international human rights organization, para 112.

[632] An Act to amend Title 12, Executive Law of the Liberian Codes of Law revised and to add thereto a new Chapter creating the Liberia Land Authority (2016) (Republic of Liberia), s 3.1.2.

[633] The Civil Society Working Group on Community Land Rights in Liberia (2016) Position statement on the Land Authority Act (LAA) and the Land Rights Act (LRA). www.forestpeoples.org/sites/fpp/files/publication/2016/07/position-statement-laa-lra-2016.pdf. Accessed 19 Jul 2023, p. 2.

[634] Draft Land Rights Act (27 Sep 2016) (Republic of Liberia), art 47(3).

[635] Ibid art 42(6).

However, in line with the Land Authority Act, the definition of government land was extended to also include protected and proposed protected areas as of the effective date of the LRA.[636]

Moreover, it introduced FPIC for the extension of existing concessions. FPIC had to be granted by two-thirds of the entire community, including major decision-makers.[637] The extraction of mineral resources also required FPIC and a lease agreement.[638] Moreover, the participation and consent of communities were prescribed for the promulgation of regulations.[639] Concerning FPIC's internal dimension, it mostly concurred with earlier versions.

3.3.3.2.3 2017 LRA Draft

The September 2017 bill was a major setback for NGOs both in terms of its content and the way it was negotiated. International actors like the USAID-funded LGSA project as well as national NGOs complained that they did not even get a copy of the law from the legislature.[640] They criticized that 'if the work of the legislature is shouldered in secrecy and hidden from the public, it erodes the confidence of the public in the law'.[641]

In terms of its content, the bill severely limited customary ownership. Already the preamble began with the historically inaccurate statement that 'title to and ownership of all the land with the boundaries of Liberia were originally vested in the state'.[642]

Tribal certificates further limited customary ownership. The draft removed the size restriction for tribal certificates and stipulated that 100% of developed land may be transformed into a public land sale deed, as well as 50% of undeveloped land.[643] This provision would have made much bigger portions of customary land susceptible to alienation. Moreover, the representatives added the provision that depending on the amount of available customary land, 30% of customary land should be set aside as public land.[644]

The provision requiring the consent of communities for the extension of concessions was also removed. Communities only had a right to the reversion of their

---

636 Ibid art 2.

637 Ibid art 48(3).

638 Ibid art 33(5).

639 Ibid art 36(10).

640 Roesch R (7 Jun 2018) Skype interview with a lawyer of an international human rights organization, para 112.

641 Constance Teage, as cited in: Senah. 2017. Senate fails to agree with House of Representatives on passage of the Land Rights Act. The Bush Chicken. www.bushchicken.com/senate-fails-to-agree-with-house-of-representatives-on-passage-of-land-rights-act/. Accessed 11 Aug 2023.

642 Draft Land Rights Act (18 Aug 2017), preamble.

643 Ibid art 47(2).

644 Ibid art 37(3).

customary land after the expiration of a concession, but they could not be parties to extended leases.[645] Moreover, protected and proposed protected areas continued to be classified as government land.[646]

Concerning FPIC, 'any interference with or use of the surface of customary land shall require the consent of the community'.[647] Thus, the bill no longer referenced the term FPIC and used the term consent without clarifying its meaning. To designate a protected area on customary land, the government had to consult in good faith with the community. If it failed to reach an agreement, it could exercise its eminent domain prerogative.[648] Consent was thus no longer mandatory in the designation of protected areas.

In addition, several of the references to marginalized groups were removed. The draft still defined community members as residents 'irrespective of age, gender, belief or religious backgrounds'.[649] In relation to the governance body, one representative of each quarter/ward, one woman, and one youth representative should be elected by the three stakeholder groups.[650] The body should be presided over by a chief. Thus, the draft not only strengthened the role of chiefs but also foresaw that both the community as a whole and its governance body must make decisions by consensus. Therefore, the chief, as the representative of the state-sponsored customary legal system, or individual community members could have effectively vetoed any decision of the governance body.[651]

Hence, the second phase of the negotiation was dominated by sovereignty discourse employed by actors co-located in the field of politics, and the draft watered down many of the provisions protecting customary land rights. The language of FPIC was no longer used. Government actors had realized FPIC's power and tried to prevent its inclusion in the law. Several international experts recommended national NGOs to drop the language of FPIC to not jeopardize the whole land reform process.[652] National NGOs, however, decided to insist on FPIC. These debates and the strong external pressure notwithstanding, Parliament failed to adopt the law.

3.3.3.3 2018: Taking it to the Streets

After the presidential election in December 2017, power relations changed again. NGOs launched a major campaign to put the new administration under pressure to pass the law. Among other things, they submitted a petition with 80,000

[645] Ibid art 48.

[646] Ibid art 42(1).

[647] Ibid art 33(4).

[648] Ibid art 42(2).

[649] Ibid art 2.

[650] Ibid art 36(6).

[651] Ibid art 36(7).

[652] Roesch R (23 May 2018) Skype interview with an international land tenure expert, para 71.

signatures.[653] Without civil society's massive campaign, the LRA would probably not have been adopted.[654] Moreover, it has been argued that the United Nations Mission in Liberia (UNMIL), whose mandate expired in March 2018, pressured the government to finally pass the law.[655] The newly elected Vice President Jewel Howard Taylor also supported the cause.[656] On top of that, a first land rights case was submitted to the ECOWAS Court, claiming 500 million USD of compensation from the Liberian government, which may have been another incentive for adopting the law.[657] The field of politics thus lost ground while the overlapping fields of human rights and development became stronger.

In June 2018, a draft preceding the final bill was circulated that departed considerably from the 2017 version and revoked some of its limitations. For example, a maximum of 10% of customary land 'or more at the discretion of the community'[658] could be converted into public land. It also strengthened the rights of communities in relation to the tribal certificates. The draft foresaw a rigid validation process carried out by the LLA involving communities.[659] After the validation process, 100% of the developed land could be transformed into a public land sale deed, while the undeveloped land was subject to negotiations between the certificate holder and the community. For the designation of protected areas on customary land, however, the government retained its right to eminent domain if good faith negotiations with the community failed.[660] It required the FPIC of communities for any interference with or use of the surface of customary land 'subject to the government's constitutional rights to extract all mineral resources'.[661] However, FPIC was not required for extending concessions, and communities only had the right to provide input and concerns during concession reviews and the right to have their land reverted after the expiration of the concession's term.[662]

---

[653] The Tenure Facility (2018) A visual history of Indigenous peoples' land rights in Liberia. https://thetenurefacility.org/timeline/Liberia/. Accessed 19 Jul 2023.

[654] Roesch R (18 Apr 2019) Skype interview with a senior staff member of the LGSA, para 88.

[655] UNMIL (2017) UNMIL deputy SRSG urges enactment of Liberia Land Rights bill. https://unmil.unmissions.org/unmil-deputy-srsg-urges-enactment-Liberia-land-rights-bill. Accessed 19 Jul 2023.

[656] Roesch R (8 Jan 2018) Interview with a senior staff member of the LGSA, Monrovia, para 92.

[657] Dodoo (24 May 2018) "Mandingoes" sue Liberian government for USD 500 million at ECOWAS court. Front Page Africa. https://frontpageafricaonline.com/news/mandingos-sue-Liberian-government-for-us500-million-at-ecowas-court/. Accessed 11 Aug 2023; Dodoo (28 May 2018) Liberia: Campaigner fears more cases at ECOWAS court without 'correct' Land Rights Act. Front Page Africa. https://frontpageafricaonline.com/news/Liberia-campaigner-fears-more-cases-at-ecowas-court-without-correct-land-right-act/?fbclid=IwAR39w9CoLRJAw4DRceG2qfuic9SciYOs8y9IIFYBv03O0BOnICQUgcjbKK4. Accessed 11 Aug 2023.

[658] Revised draft Land Rights Act (25 Jun 2018) (Republic of Liberia), art 37(3).

[659] Ibid art 47.

[660] Ibid art 42(2).

[661] Ibid art 33(3).

[662] Ibid art 48.

Concerning women's land rights, the draft was strongly built upon the earlier ones. Community membership remained independent of age, gender, belief, or religious background, and a person marrying a resident should assume the same status as a resident.[663] Instead of mandating a representative of each quarter and a woman and man representative for the governance structure, it again called for the equal representation of men, women, and youth, democratically elected by their stakeholder group, while also providing for the membership of chiefs.[664]

The draft ultimately adopted mostly aligns with the June 2018 draft. Its content will be explored in the next section. It shows more overlaps with the 2014 draft than the one adopted by the House of Representatives in 2017, and NGOs managed to have many of their suggestions incorporated. Particularly the tribal certificates had been a significant concern for NGOs as well as the community decision-making by consensus, as foreseen by the 2017 draft. With respect to these points, they managed to shape the law considerably.

Other aspects reflect the compromises that had to be found between the different fields and actors. For instance, allowing for the transformation of 30% of customary land into public land was a provision opposed by most actors (national NGOs, the LLA, and international actors). The 10% rule was thus clearly a compromise between the government and everybody else.

Concerning protected areas, the field of human rights could, however, realize its interests to a lesser extent. One reason for this was the synergy between the field of politics and the fields of development and conservation. Given the massive resources invested in the protection of Liberian forests, they felt that the recognition of customary ownership would have undermined the conservation efforts.

As for concessions, government actors were very strong in their position that it was their right to grant concessions before the law's passage and that the law could not be retroactive in scope. Thus, the law that was ultimately passed reflects many of the negotiations and compromises that were made during the drafting process. Generally, it was seen as a big success for the NGOs and indicates that the field's social mobilization and media campaign can indeed shape the outcome of legal reforms. The next section explores the understanding of FPIC in the 2018 LRA. In late 2022, the Liberia Land Authority adopted the Land Rights Act Regulations, which guide the implementation of the LRA. While the drafting history will not be explored, it will be considered with respect to the emerging meaning of FPIC.[665]

---

[663] Ibid art 2.

[664] Ibid art 36(6).

[665] According to NGOs, the negotiation took mainly place behind closed doors and the endorsement came as a surprise to most actors (Roesch R (15 Feb 2023) Informal video call with a senior staff member of a Liberian NGO).

3.3.4 *FPIC Re-Negotiated*

The Land Rights Act was finally adopted in 2018 and recognizes FPIC. The following section examines the emerging understanding of FPIC in the Liberian land sector in the context of legal and administrative measures and land governance.

The LRA, just like the CRL, is a relatively vague law and its implementation will be governed by Regulations. However, it does not prescribe any specific procedure for the adoption of Regulations and it took the Liberia Land Authority more than four years to adopt the LRA Regulations.[666] The LRA Implementation Strategy states that the first year after the adoption of the LRA will be dedicated to public outreach. It has two components: sensitizing communities about their rights under the LRA and active and meaningful community participation in the implementation of the LRA.[667] However, the provision of the 2016 draft of the LRA that had called for the consent and participation of communities for the promulgation of regulations concerning customary land governance has been removed, and the LLA is under no legal obligation to seek their FPIC.[668] Instead, communities may meaningfully participate, which will very likely translate into regional consultations at best. FPIC thus only applies in relation to land governance.

According to the LRA, 'any interference with or use of the surface of Customary land require the Free, Prior and Informed Consent (FPIC) of the Community'.[669] But what does this mean? Who are the rights-holders and in which situations is the consent requirement triggered? In the following section, the scope of FPIC in the LRA will be explored. Moreover, it will shed light on FPIC's institutional autonomy and gender dimension.

3.3.4.1 Rights-holders

FPIC, under the LRA, is tied to the legal identity of the *customary land-owning community.*[670] This raises the question of the meaning of community and customary land. The LRA defines community as a 'self-identifying coherent social group or groups comprising of community members'.[671] A community member is a

> Liberian citizen irrespective of age, gender, belief or religious backgrounds who was (i) born in the Community or (ii) parent(s) was born within a Community; or (iii) who has lived continuously within the Community for at least seven years; or (iv) a spouse of a Community Member both of whom reside in the Community.[672]

---

[666] Liberia Land Rights Act Regulations (2022) (Liberia Land Authority).

[667] Liberia Land Rights Act implementation strategy (2019) (Liberia Land Authority), p. 7.

[668] Draft Land Rights act (27 Sep 2016), art 36(10).

[669] An Act to establish the Land Rights Law of 2018 (2018), art 33(3).

[670] Eg ibid art 2.

[671] Ibid art 2.

[672] Ibid art 2.

Moreover, communities must not exclude a community member from membership in the community, and community members, regardless of 'age, gender, ethnicity, religion and disability',[673] shall have equal rights to the use and management of customary land.[674] These provisions certainly interfere with the institutional autonomy and customary land management of many communities: Land is usually owned by the patriline, while so-called strangers have limited land rights.[675]

The LRA also links FPIC to land ownership. It defines customary land as 'land owned by a Community and used or managed in accordance with customary practices and norms'.[676] The acquisition and ownership of customary ownership are established by (1) deed, (2) by common and long-standing understanding among community members, including land that

> has been used or possessed exclusively or continuously by the Community or some of its members for socio-cultural and economic purposes for a minimum period of fifty (50) years as can be established by oral testimonies of members of the Community and members of neighboring Communities,[677]

and (3) the use or claim of possession through historical activities and ties, as acknowledged by neighboring communities and/or recognized by rules of customary practice.[678]

However, even though the customary right to land arises by 'operation of law based on the proven longstanding relationship between the Individual Community and the Land',[679] communities are obliged to register their land since the passage of the LRA.[680]

With the implementation of the LRA pending, it is not entirely clear what the procedure for registering customary land will look like. Even though the LRA Regulations were adopted in 2022, questions remain particularly with respect to the sequencing of the customary land registration. The Regulations only stipulate that the community self-identification and the community social mapping must precede the confirmatory survey.[681] Moreover, given the fact that the Committee—most likely referring to the Community Land Management and Development Committee—shall participate in the survey, this implies that communities need to have their governance structure in place.[682] The Regulations thus concur with the

673 Ibid art 34(3).

674 Ibid art 34(2).

675 See also next chapter.

676 An Act to establish the Land Rights Law of 2018 (2018), art 2.

677 Ibid art 32(3)(ii).

678 Ibid art 32(3).

679 Ibid art 32(5).

680 Ibid art 11(1).

681 Liberia Land Rights Act Regulations (2022) (Liberia Land Authority), s 11.3.

682 Ibid s 11.7.

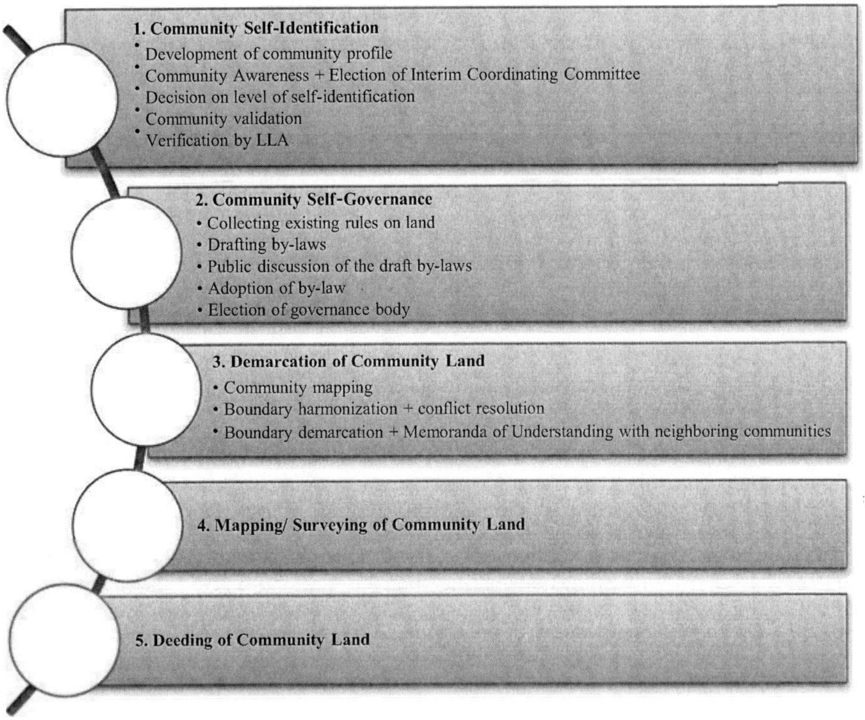

Fig. 3.4 5 step-procedure for customary land registration (The six sub-steps relating to community self-identification and the five sub-steps of community self-governance are based on the Land Tenure Facilities' Self-Identification Guide. The sub-steps relating to the demarcation of customary land are based on SDI's tool)

LLA's Implementation Strategy, adopted in 2019 and based on the LGSA's experiences with their pilot communities.[683] As shown in Fig. 3.4, it foresees five steps:

Concerning the first step—community self-identification—the LRA Regulations provide little details with respect to the sub-steps.[684] However, the Land Tenure Facility's project developed a community self-identification guide based on their work in twelve communities in 2016, which was endorsed by the LLA.[685] The methodology prescribes six sub-steps and requires external facilitators to support communities in the process. The first sub-step is the development of a community profile, which resembles the SER survey under the CRL.[686] This is followed by the raising of community awareness and the creation of an Interim Coordinating

683 Liberia Land Rights Act implementation strategy (2019) (Liberia Land Authority), 10.

684 Liberia Land Rights Act Regulations (2022) (Liberia Land Authority), ss 7.1 ff.

685 Liberia Land Rights Act implementation strategy (2019) (Liberia Land Authority), p. 10.

686 Liberia Land Authority. Community self-identification guide (CSI). https://new.sdiliberia.org/sites/default/files/2022-12/LLA%20-%20CSI%20Guide.pdf. Accessed 27 Jul 2023, pp. 7–9.

Committee in charge of the process, as long as no formal governance structure has been elected.[687] As a third sub-step, the community determines its level of self-identification, ie, whether it wants to organize itself within a smaller town or a bigger clan or district unit. The guidebook calls for the highest degree of participation possible at this step and recommends holding 'separate consultations with sub-groups including women, youth and elders'.[688] Subsequently, the community land area is identified (sub-step four). According to the LRA Regulations, leaders—including women and youth leaders, and members of neighboring communities shall participate in the identification of the community's boundaries.[689] Moreover, concessions, private land claims, and existing forest reserves and conservation shall be identified.[690] If land disputes with neighboring communities arise, the County Land Dispute Resolution Officer shall resolve the conflict.[691] The fifth sub-step is the declaration of identity as a land-owning community. Communities have to discuss and validate the community self-identification process in a participatory meeting.[692] Finally, the LLA has to verify the self-identification process within 90 days and issue a certificate of self-identification.[693]

The second step in the process is the establishment of a governance structure consisting of a Community Land Development and Management Committee (CLDMC). The highest decision-making body is the community itself. Regarding the governance structure, the LGSA has worked on templates for the by-laws defining the roles and responsibilities of the CLDMC.[694]

Steps three and four are the mapping and demarcation of the customary land. The LRA Regulations refer to it as 'community social mapping'.[695] During the drafting of the LRA, it was controversial whether the LLA should be in charge of demarcating customary land. As a compromise, a provision was inserted allowing for communities to enter into stipulations with one or more communities or private persons to determine the boundaries of their customary land.[696]

The SDI, with funding from the British and the Australian government, the Open Society Foundation, and the International Development Law Organization, worked with 20 communities in Rivercess to demarcate and harmonize the boundaries of their customary land.[697] The methodology applied in these pilot communities was

---

687 Ibid, pp. 9–11.

688 Ibid, p. 11.

689 Liberia Land Rights Act Regulations (2022) (Liberia Land Authority), s 7.2.

690 Ibid s 7.3.

691 Ibid s 9.3.

692 Liberia Land Authority. Community self-identification guide (CSI). https://new.sdiLiberia.org/sites/default/files/2022-12/LLA%20-%20CSI%20Guide.pdf. Accessed 27 Jul 2023, pp. 14–15.

693 Ibid pp. 15–16.

694 Liberia Land Rights Act implementation strategy (2019) (Liberia Land Authority), 10.

695 Liberia Land Rights Act Regulations (2022) (Liberia Land Authority), s 10.

696 An Act to establish the Land Rights Law of 2018 (2018), art 9(4).

697 Knight et al. (2013), p. 9.

loosely based on the procedure established by the CRL for forest land and followed the 2010 Interim Guidelines on the Sale of Public Land.[698] The methodology foresees four sub-steps: (1) community mapping, (2) boundary harmonization, including conflict resolution with neighboring communities and boundary tree planting, (3) boundary demarcation, including the signing of Memoranda of Understanding with neighboring communities, and (4) GPS mapping or formal survey.[699] The LRA Regulations highlight that the mapping shall be carried out in a gender-sensitive way, recording the land rights of all community members.[700] Moreover, the mapping shall be based on 'cost-effective methodologies consistent with international survey and mapping standards adapted to the national and community situation'.[701]

Subsequently, the boundaries of community land will be confirmed through a nationwide confirmatory survey to be commenced within twenty-four months after the passage of the LRA. The LLA will bear the costs of the confirmatory survey and mapping.[702] Changes to the confirmatory survey require a 'prior consultation'[703] with the Committee. As of mid-2023, it had not been carried out. While the absence of the survey does not preclude customary ownership, it is a precondition for the alienation of customary land.[704]

The last step—step 5—is the issuance of a deed by the Liberia Land Authority. The LRA Regulations provide more details on the sub-steps. Those include posting notices for 21 days, during which caveats can be lodged.[705] If a caveat is lodged, the County Land Dispute Resolution Officer shall conduct a hearing.[706] Appeals to the Liberia Land Authority's Dispute Resolution Committee are possible.[707] The deed is then issued by the LLA in the name of the community.[708]

3.3.4.2 Meaning of FPIC

As shown in the previous section, FPIC is a right of *communities* with respect to their *customary land*, which they have to register under the LRA. But how and when do communities have the right to consent? Different forms of consent and consultations coexist in the LRA, depending on the type of land. Moreover, some types of land are precluded from community ownership. Deeded private land located on customary

[698] Ibid pp. 48–49.

[699] Ibid p. 60.

[700] Liberia Land Rights Act Regulations (2022) (Liberia Land Authority), s 10.2.

[701] Ibid s 10.2.

[702] Ibid s 11.9.

[703] Ibid s 11.8.

[704] An Act to establish the Land Rights Law of 2018 (2018), art 37(4).

[705] Liberia Land Rights Act Regulations (2022) (Liberia Land Authority), ss 12.1, 12.2.

[706] Ibid s 12.6.

[707] Ibid s 12.7.

[708] Ibid s 13.8.

land and protected areas do not revert to the community.[709] The following sections explore FPIC in relation to (1) (proposed) protected areas, (2) concessions, (3) public land on customary land, (4) tribal certificates, (5) eminent domain, and (6) the governance of customary land.

3.3.4.2.1 (Proposed) Protected Areas

Protected area management was a major controversy during both the forest and land sector reforms. Even though NGOs problematized the impact of the government's conservation policy on communities, the government insisted on retaining control over its protected areas. Both protected and proposed protected areas that have been gazetted as of the effective date of the LRA are classified as government land.[710] State agencies also tend to argue that—given the fact that most of the gazetted proposed protected areas were previously classified as national forests—communities do not have rights to these lands.[711]

Not yet gazetted proposed protected areas have to be negotiated between the FDA and communities.[712] Moreover, it is possible to create new protected areas on customary land, potentially allowing for co-management schemes. However, in 2021, the FDA, with financial support from conservationists and donors, tried to gazette new protected areas on customary land, assuming that the land would then automatically revert to the government.[713]

Moreover, the LRA once had contained provisions that would have allowed for compensation for community land alienated in the past.[714] However, these provisions were removed before the draft was submitted to the legislature. Thus, the LRA legitimizes past land takings without legal safeguards and compensation.[715] In 2022, 475,390 hectares were part of protected areas, while another 776,820 hectares were proposed protected areas.[716]

[709] An Act to establish the Land Rights Law of 2018 (2018), art 46.

[710] Ibid arts 2, 48(4).

[711] LTS International (2019a), p. 17.

[712] An Act to establish the Land Rights Law of 2018 (2018), art 42(1).

[713] Ibid arts 42(1),4(2); Lomax and Warner (2020); Email from a senior staff member of an international human rights organization to the author (3 March 2021).

[714] Litz and Kindberg (2017).

[715] See also Cavanagh (2018), p. 10.

[716] National biodiversity strategy and action plan-ii 2017–2025 (2017) (Environmental Protection Agency), p. 37; Agyeman et al. (2022), p. 58.

3.3.4.2.2 Concessions

The fate of concessions was another one of the most contentious issues during the land reform process. According to the Land Rights Policy, 'the government is responsible for managing concessions on customary land in the public interest'.[717] In line with that, the LRA holds that FPIC is required 'save for concessions, contracts, permits, and other rights previously granted by the Government'.[718]

Upon the expiration of concessions, the customary land reverts automatically to the community.[719] However, in 2013, concessions with a term of more than 25 years covered more than 25% of Liberia's territory.[720] For instance, the 220,000 hectares Sime Darby oil palm is going to expire in 2072.[721] Similarly, the contract with Golden Veroleum Liberia covering 350,000 hectares will remain in effect until 2075.[722] Both concession agreements allow for the extension of the contract. As the provision requiring the FPIC of communities for such extensions has been removed, it is unclear whether the government can still negotiate extensions single-handedly or whether future negotiations will be held directly between communities and companies.

Moreover, given the large-scale alienation of customary land in the past decades and the environmental degradation regularly caused by concessionaires, a sole right to reversion after the expiration of the concession term is a rather conservative approach when not foreseeing any compensation.

The Land Rights Act Regulations provide more clarity with respect to concessions: for new concessions on customary land, a sub-Committee of the Community Land Development and Management Committee shall lead the negotiations on behalf of the community. External experts may support it.[723] Without the FPIC of the community, the concessionaire may not proceed.[724] Moreover, FPIC is needed for the compensation agreement between the community and the concessionaire.[725]

A noteworthy aspect of the Land Rights Act Regulations are the provisions on mineral resources: even though mineral resources remain in the hands of the state, government agencies are obliged to obtain the FPIC of communities for the authorization of mining activities.[726] Moreover, the concessionaire must enter into a land

[717] Land Rights Policy (2013) (Land Commission), s 6.2.2.

[718] An Act to establish the Land Rights Law of 2018 (2018), art 33(3).

[719] Ibid art 2.

[720] Knight et al. (2013), p. 35.

[721] An Act to ratify the amended and restated concession agreement between the Republic of Liberia and Sime Darby plantation (Liberia) inc. (2009) (Republic of Liberia), arts 3(1), 4(1)(c).

[722] An Act to ratify the concession agreement between the Republic of Liberia and Golden Veroleum (Liberia). Inc. (2010) (Republic of Liberia), art 3.1.

[723] Liberia Land Rights Act Regulations (2022) (Liberia Land Authority), s 20.20.

[724] Ibid ss 20.12, 20.13.

[725] Ibid s 20.19.

[726] Ibid s 19.17.

use agreement with the communities, which is a precondition for any mining activities on customary land.[727] This strongly indicates that the government's ownership of mineral resources cannot just trump the communities' land ownership. In that respect, the Regulations go a step beyond the LRA and also the national FPIC Guidelines. According to the final report on the development of national FPIC Guidelines, community consultations in the mining sector are about informing communities and documenting their perspectives and not about consent, as mineral resources belong to the state.[728]

3.3.4.2.3 Public Land

As the government had feared that the recognition of customary land would make them lose access to land, they insisted on including a provision according to which a certain percentage of customary land would be transformed into public land. According to the final version of the LRA, 'a maximum of ten (10) percent of Customary Land in each Community, or an amount of Customary Land at the discretion of the Community, shall be set aside and allocated as Public Land'.[729]

As the LLA did not support this provision, it is unclear how it will implement it.[730] Questions arise particularly in relation to the determination of the size of the land to be set aside, its location, and whether the LLA or the community has the final say in this respect. The wording of the provision suggests that the size of the land to be set aside is only 'at the discretion of the community'[731] when it exceeds 10% of the customary land. The LRA thus could allow government agencies to interfere with customary land rights without FPIC.

3.3.4.2.3.1 Tribal Certificates

Before the adoption of the LRA, all undeeded land was considered to be public land and susceptible to alienation by the government.[732] The use rights of communities were still recognized to some extent, and the granting of a tribal certificate was a precondition for buying *public land*. Tribal certificates were the 'most important instrument used for acquiring public land in the local communities'.[733] The tribal certificates caused many boundary disputes and conflicts because many community

[727] Ibid s 19.18.

[728] LTS International (2019a), p. 27.

[729] An Act to establish the Land Rights Law of 2018 (2018), art 37(3).

[730] Roesch R (18 Apr 2019) Skype interview with a senior staff member of the LGSA, paras 52–54.

[731] An Act to establish the Land Rights Law of 2018 (2018), art 37(3).

[732] Land rights policy (2013) (Land Commission), s 4.0.

[733] Interim guidelines and procedures for the sale of public land (2011) (Land Commission), p. 4.

members felt they had been left out of these land sale decisions.[734] Consequently, President Johnson Sirleaf placed a moratorium on the sale of public land in 2010.[735]

The fate of the pending tribal certificates, which had not yet been transformed into Public Land Sale Deeds, became one of the most controversial points of the land reform process. According to the LRA, pending tribal certificates can be validated within the next 24 months after a rigid validation process 'involving the community'[736] conducted by the LLA. Even though this provision suggests that the LLA is primarily in charge of validating the tribal certificates, it is likely that LLA will take the position that it is the communities' decision whether they want to formalize those certificates or not.[737] If the validation of tribal certificates follows the community self-identification, the designation of community land, and the establishment of a governance structure, this could indeed allow for the FPIC of the community.

However, it is questionable whether these steps can be implemented within 24 months. The LRA Regulations were only adopted in late 2022. They stipulate that 'within six months of the coming of the force of these Regulations, the Authority shall issue detailed Guidelines [...] for the submissions and validation of tribal certificates'.[738] However, that has not happened. Besides a few pilot communities, no systematic attempts had been made to support communities in their land registration.[739] Consequently, there is a risk that communities will have to decide about the future of tribal certificates before mapping their land. Under such conditions, communities can hardly make informed decisions. It is controversial why this time constraint was introduced. On the one side, it may prevent tribal certificate holders from approaching communities and claiming customary land indefinitely. On the other side, some individuals within the LLA apparently have a vested interest in waiving through pending public land sale deeds without due process.[740] However, the delay in the validation of tribal certificates suggests that the LLA intends to wait for the confirmatory survey to be completed.

3.3.4.2.4 Eminent Domain

FPIC is also relevant in relation to eminent domain. The Liberian Constitution provides for the application of the eminent domain prerogative, ie, expropriations in the public interest under the condition of just compensation.[741] Before using its

---

[734] Ibid p. 4.

[735] Bruce and Kanneh (2011), p. 5.

[736] An Act to establish the Land Rights Law of 2018 (2018), art 47.

[737] Roesch R (18 Apr 2019) Skype interview with a senior staff member of the LGSA, para 124.

[738] Liberia Land Rights Act Regulations (2022) (Liberia Land Authority), s 14.1.

[739] Roesch R (24 March 2021) Skype conversation with a staff member of the Liberia Land Authority.

[740] Roesch R (30 May 2019) Skype interview with an anonymous expert.

[741] Constitution of Liberia art 24(a).

right to eminent domain, the government is obliged to make good faith efforts to lease or purchase the land 'by way of negotiations'.[742] Only if no agreement can be reached may eminent domain be exercised. This raises the threshold for expropriations. At the same time, the Liberian state endorses a broad understanding of public purpose, according to which commercial activities may fall under the eminent domain provision.[743] Moreover, eminent domain in Liberia is quite unregulated to date, which is why the LRA Implementation Strategy calls for the adoption of specific legislation clarifying its scope, procedure, and rights of appeal.[744] On top of that, the wording of art 33(3) LRA suggests that customary land susceptible to mineral extraction is generally exempted from the communities' right to give their FPIC.[745] However, the LRA Regulations go a step beyond the LRA: before the commencement of any concession activities, the 'free, prior and informed consent of the community shall be sought'.[746] As for community mining lands, this means that no mining activities may be carried out 'without the free, prior and informed consent with the community'.[747] However, FPIC is defined as the 'consent of the majority'[748] while the LRA requires the consent of 2/3 of the whole community for the alienation of customary land.[749]

Hence, communities have a right to negotiate with the government and to agree to the lease or sale of their customary land. According to the Land Rights Act Regulations, they also have a right to FPIC with respect to the compensation agreement.[750] However, if no agreement on the alienation of customary land can be reached, the eminent domain procedure could be triggered, which does not foresee any additional consultation safeguards for customary land. It is possible that the government will refrain from granting governmental concessions in the future and instead create a framework for commercial use contracts, as in the logging sector.

3.3.4.2.5 Customary Land Management

FPIC certainly applies to the registration of customary land and its management.[751] Situations that require FPIC could be companies approaching communities to obtain

[742] An Act to establish the Land Rights Law of 2018 (2018), art 50(2); see also art 54(2).

[743] See Cummings v Hughes (1968) 19 LLR 18 (Supreme Court of Liberia), p. 20; Land rights policy (2013) (Land Commission), paras 5.3.1.3., 5.3.1.4.

[744] Liberia Land Rights Act implementation strategy (2019) (Liberia Land Authority), pp. 16–17.

[745] An Act to establish the Land Rights Law of 2018 (2018), art 33(3).

[746] Liberia Land Rights Act Regulations (2022) (Liberia Land Authority), s 20.13.

[747] Ibid s 19.17.

[748] Ibid s 20.13.d).

[749] An Act to establish the Land Rights Law of 2018 (2018), art 36(2).

[750] Liberia Land Rights Act Regulations (2022) (Liberia Land Authority), s 20.19.a).

[751] An Act to establish the Land Rights Law of 2018 (2018), art 33(3).

a commercial use contract, conservation NGOs proposing communities to conserve their land, or private persons seeking to lease a portion of customary land. Moreover, it also includes the internal governance of customary land. Even though the recognition of customary land does not depend on the formalization of customary rights, communities are now obliged to register their land.[752]

To conclude, the emerging understanding of FPIC is grounded in the collective right to property of the *customary land-owning community*. These property rights are, however, limited, reducing the number of contexts in which FPIC applies. FPIC neither applies to protected areas nor to existing concessions. Its realization with respect to the designation of public land and new protected areas and the validation of tribal certificates remains unclear. Moreover, the emerging right to FPIC does not interfere with the government's right to eminent domain.

However, FPIC will be realized in the management of customary land. Nevertheless, many management decisions are incumbent upon communities following the customary land registration procedure. Moreover, their land management decisions are also limited by the LRA. They are only allowed to permanently alienate land after 50 years following the effective date of the LRA.[753] They may also only enter into lease agreements if they have adopted by-laws, elected and set up rules for the Community Land Development and Management Committee, developed eligibility requirements for becoming a community member, and developed a land-use management plan.[754] The free choice of communities in registering and managing their customary land is thus quite limited—also compared to owners of private land. Whether FPIC can actually be realized within the registration of customary land is yet to be seen.

3.3.4.3 Institutional Autonomy

During the legal reforms, the question of what legitimate decision-making processes should look like played a much bigger role than in the forest sector reform. The LRA explicitly states that 'any decision taken in respect of Customary Land shall be in accordance with the customs, traditions and practices of the community'.[755]

Nevertheless, the LRA—just like the CRL—does not build upon existing institutions but introduces new ones. The daily activities relating to community land will be carried out by Community Land Development and Management Committees (CLDMCs), which are to be democratically elected by the communities.[756] The CLDMC shall consist of 'equal representation of the three stakeholder groups men,

[752] Ibid arts 11(1), 35(2).

[753] With the exception of residential areas (ibid art 49(3)).

[754] Ibid arts 36, 49(6).

[755] Ibid art 36(8).

[756] Ibid art 35(1)(b).

women and youth'.[757] Chiefs shall be ex-officio members of the CLDMC. The CLDMC has to make decisions by consensus and, among other things, shall render decisions in land disputes relating to community land.[758] Moreover, it has the right to enter into lease agreements for areas smaller than fifty acres.[759]

However, the power of the CLDMCs is limited, and the community members have the highest decision-making authority. The community membership is in charge of making important decisions, including those pertaining to the sale and lease of customary land and they may investigate complaints against CLDMC members.[760] Community decisions need to be made by two-thirds of the whole community.[761] These provisions strongly interfere with customary land governance and the institutional autonomy of the *customary land-owning community*. They indicate that the collective right to property has no cultural dimension under the LRA.

3.3.4.4 Inclusive Governance: The Rise of Women, Men, and Youth

It has been shown that the link between gender and land is better recognized than the link between gender and forestry.[762] However, the so-called gender dimension is usually used as a synonym for women's land rights.[763]

In the field of post-conflict land sector reform, the tendency to construct women as a stakeholder and a marginalized group emerged.[764] Firstly, gender was recognized as a reason for marginalization. However, the different characteristics of identity enumerated in different provisions of the LRA suggest that it was controversial who should qualify as a marginalized group. Mentioned vulnerabilities include gender, youth, religion and belief, ethnicity, disability, and traditional leadership.[765] Concerns about women's land rights were shared by the Land Commission, the Liberia Land Authority, and the fields of human rights and development, while calls for the inclusion of disabled people were mostly voiced by NGOs. Worries about the exclusion of youth were common amongst government, development, and NGO actors, albeit to varying degrees. Given these different priorities and the difficult drafting process, it does not come as a big surprise that the different

757 Ibid art 36(6).

758 Ibid arts 36(5), 36(7).

759 Ibid art 49(4).

760 Ibid art 36(2).

761 Ibid art 36(2).

762 Nichols and Moumin (2016), p. 451.

763 Shepherd (2017a), p. 72.

764 For instance, the SDI divided the communities in separate groups of women, (male) elders and youth for the community mapping (Knight et al. 2013, p. 83).

765 An Act to establish the Land Rights Law of 2018 (2018), arts 34(3), 39(2).

provisions of the LRA have not been harmonized and reference different stakeholder groups.[766]

Secondly, the triad of women-elders-youth emerged: women, (male) youth, and (male) elders made up the three stakeholder groups. It went hand in hand with the idea prevailing in most fields that customary decision-making needed to be reformed to some extent. The category of women-and-youth, as if the two were facing the same marginalization and share the same needs, is on the rise in many parts of Africa.[767] The assumption that the youth is particularly vulnerable emerged after the war in Liberia when a growing number of national and international NGOs started to introduce the youth as a stakeholder group in their consultations and workshops.[768] However, in these workshops, controversies arose about whether participants spoke on behalf of their ethnic group or the youth. Moreover, the understanding of youth is contested. While international experts argued that 35 years would be the age limit for youth and that the youth referred to both men and women, men are either elders or youth in many parts of Liberia.[769] Consequently, the youth stakeholder group is usually male, and every man who does not hold a customary position (ie, elder, zoe,[770] or chief) belongs to it.[771] This example highlights that the stakeholder approach to difference is static and does not take shifting and multiple identities into account. Moran also argues that, in the project law of donors, some kind of gender angle is increasingly the norm, even though gender usually stands for women.[772] Thereby, it is ignored that this type of gender mainstreaming is rooted in Western epistemologies and neglects the complexity of pre-existing gender relations.[773] Assumptions about a 'pre-war gender asymmetry has become all but canonical'.[774]

In terms of land management, the LRA distinguishes between the interim institutions that should support communities in formalizing their land and the land governance institutions to be elected. Before the establishment of the official governance structure, the 'elders, chiefs, traditional decision-makers, women and youth'[775] shall develop and manage the customary land together. Customary decision-makers are thus granted a central role in the registration of customary land. The mention of women and youth gives the impression of being an add-on—to make the group more inclusive—while the main decision-making space would be

766 Roesch R (18 Apr 2019) Skype interview with a senior staff member of the LGSA, para 90.

767 Hudson (2017), p. 79.

768 Fuest (2010), pp. 15 ff.

769 Roesch R (19 Dec 2017) Interview with a former senior staff member of a Liberian NGO, Duazon, para 488.

770 Zoes are local authorities that derive their power from their leadership role in the secret societies common in some parts of Liberia (eg Käihkö 2019, p. 7).

771 Roesch R (18 Apr 2019) Skype interview with a senior staff member of the LGSA, para 108.

772 Moran (2012), pp. 52–53.

773 See also Fuest (1986), p. 15.

774 Moran (2012), p. 63; see also Abramowitz and Moran (2012), p. 124.

775 An Act to establish the Land Rights Law of 2018 (2018), art 69(1).

left to customary authorities. The rationale for this approach was probably to enhance the legitimacy of the land registration process based on NGOs' experiences with community land titling. They found that including elders, youth, and zoes facilitated the solution of boundary disputes and enhanced the legitimacy of the whole project.[776]

However, things change with the establishment of the governance structure. The community becomes the highest decision-making body. Community members are defined as

> a Liberian citizen irrespective of age, gender, belief or religious backgrounds who was (i) born in the Community or (ii) parent(s) was born within a Community; or (iii) who has lived continuously within the Community for at least seven years; or (iv) a spouse of a Community Member both of whom reside in the Community.[777]

The definition was introduced to improve the land tenure situation of strangers, ethnic and religious minorities, and women. As most Liberian communities are patrilocal—meaning it is common for women to move to their husbands' communities—they are sometimes seen as strangers with limited land rights.[778] Even though the fields of human rights and development recognized that access to land varies strongly from community to community and that even within one community the decision to grant someone access to land is frequently made on a case-by-case basis, this definition of community membership clearly reflects the mistrust placed in customary institutions and interferes with Indigenous understandings of belonging.

The Community Land Development and Management Committee (CLDMC), as the institution in charge of day-to-day land management, shall consist of equal representation of the three stakeholder groups—men, women, and youth—who shall be democratically elected.[779] The quota introduced for women is quite high and may allow for the participation of a critical mass of women in the land governance structure. At the same time, the prohibition of remuneration for members of the CLDMC may hinder the participation of (younger) women in the CLDMC.[780] Participation in CLDMC meetings may thus contribute to a loss of income and effectively prevent their participation.

Thus, the stakeholder approach goes hand in hand with the marginalization of customary decision-making. The elders and zoes are replaced by the stakeholder group *men*. While the recognition of youth as a stakeholder group can mean that customary decision-makers will be accommodated within the stakeholder group *men*, the imposition of the three stakeholder groups still interferes with customary land governance arrangements and the right to institutional autonomy of both communities and the rural women within these communities.

---

[776] Knight et al. (2013), p. 67.

[777] An Act to establish the Land Rights Law of 2018 (2018), art 2.

[778] Dodd et al. (2018), p. 42.

[779] An Act to establish the Land Rights Law of 2018 (2018), art 36(6).

[780] Ibid art 36(10).

3.3.4.5 FPIC in the Land Sector

The discourses prevailing in the field of land sector reform contributed to the emergence of quite stable identities. While land has a different meaning for different actors, it does not serve as a nodal point. Instead, the economic understanding and the human rights-based approach to land were reconcilable, likely because most actors additionally linked tenure security to peace. The compatibility and mutual legibility of the discourses were very likely enhanced by the stronger alliances between the fields of human rights and development.

The emerging understanding of FPIC reflects the compromises that had to be found between the different actors. FPIC's scope is rather limited.

The social identity of the *incompetent* and *discriminatory community* legitimized the imposition of new forms of decision-making and institutions. Notably, women's rights served as a legitimization for overhauling customary land governance. The introduction of new land governance institutions also highlights the lack of faith placed by more or less all actors in customary decision-making. This constitutes a point of departure from the early years of peacebuilding, where customary authorities were seen as building blocks of the peace process.[781] The framing of the culture of communities as backward—having caused the civil war and discriminating against women—contributed to the emergence of a version of FPIC that has no cultural dimension. This deculturalization of FPIC enabled *women's land rights* to trump the institutional autonomy of rural communities. The collective identity of the *discriminatory community* contributed to their exclusion from the legal reform process and the prioritization of the female over the local. Simultaneously, it also disrespects the right to self-determination, culture, and institutional autonomy of rural women.

3.4 FPIC Between the Local and the Female

It has been shown that the two fields of forest and land sector reform were characterized by 'multiple, entangled [power relations and spatialities that were] not monopolized by a sovereign state rationality'.[782] The legislative practices were considerably determined by external actors. Santos describes the legal reforms supported by donor agencies in the South as a 'globalized local',[783] as they—through the influence of *international best practices*—leave little space for alternative practices and outcomes. Still, shifting power relations within the fields influenced the practice of the legal reforms, and the *forest* remained a contested

[781] Fuest (2010), p. 26.

[782] Moore (2005), p. 21.

[783] de Sousa Santos (2002), p. 334.

space of imagination, attributing different meanings to the *state*, the *community*, and FPIC.

At first, UN sanctions played an essential role in the forest sector reform, providing critical leverage to donors and NGOs. The peacebuilders' project law dominated the field's practice in a way that considerations of time and cost-effectiveness allowed for little debate and research on customary law and governance. The *local turn* in peacebuilding and the omnipresent language of participation created the illusion of a legal reform process legitimized from below.[784] In reality, communities were never a meaningful part of the legal reforms.

Later, the lack of experience with community forestry, together with the scandals in the logging sector, enhanced the capital of NGOs. NGOs had the chance to assume a lead role in the drafting of the CRL and managed to impose their vision of community forestry to a large extent.

The CRL Regulation, in contrast, reflects the increased power of the government, conservationists, and donors, which placed little trust in the capacity of communities to manage their land. This lack of trust translated into the 11 steps, over-formalizing the procedure for securing customary tenure rights. It leaves no space for customary governance arrangements and local knowledge. Moreover, requirements like the submission of a highly technical Management Plan reflect the influence of scientific forestry. As an expression of 'legal orientalism'[785]—legitimized by the identity of the *incompetent community*—international best practices superseded the living law, institutional autonomy, and knowledge of communities. 'Writing culture'[786]—as controversial as it may be—was not even attempted in Liberia. Instead, 'transnational legal templates'[787] and 'project law'[788] shaped the legal reform process. In this respect, the field's law, with its focus on feasibility and effectiveness, played a central role.

Shifting practices also characterized the field of land reform. While NGOs and development actors were dominant in the early drafting and negotiation phase of the LRA, government actors and parliamentarians later changed the way the law was being negotiated. NGOs were then largely excluded from the negotiation, and development actors mainly provided technical advice. However, NGOs remained powerful players due to their campaigns. Even though one would expect that direct participation in drafting processes grants the highest degree of influence, this was not the case in the land reform processes in Liberia. Instead, the field of human rights managed to realize its vision of customary land governance to a greater extent in the land than in the forest sector reform. Moreover, the high number of active NGOs contributed to more diversity in terms of perspectives and priorities. Land tenure as the cross-cutting issue also contributed to alliances between donors and NGOs,

---

[784] See also Mertz (1994), p. 1251.

[785] Nader (2009), p. 62.

[786] Zerner (2003), p. 4.

[787] von Benda-Beckmann and Turner (2019), p. 12.

[788] Weilenmann (2005), p. 235; von Benda-Beckmann and Turner (2019), p. 13.

whose agendas overlapped to a greater extent than in the forest sector reform. But also, the Land Commission and the LLA aligned themselves more with the field of development and showed less resistance to the legal and institutional reforms. Members of Parliament, the government, and the FDA were more critical of the reforms and used the discourse of sovereignty.

Concerning FPIC, the LRA's understanding concurs largely with that of the CRL. The emerging FPIC norm does not substantively touch upon the state's sovereignty and applies to *customary land-owning communities*. It reflects 'state concerns about societal cohesion and universality'[789] as well as its interest in the accessibility of natural resources. The Liberian FPIC is neither retroactive with respect to protected areas and concessions nor does it interfere with the state's legislative and administrative power or its right to eminent domain. In this respect, both the forest and land legislation are another example of 'territorialisation [that] works 'internally' to fill in state space, unevenly'.[790]

The emerging legal identity—the *customary land-owning community*—does not have a culture that is seen as worth protecting in the emerging hegemonic discourse. As a consequence, FPIC becomes deculturalized and is attached to a limited understanding of the collective right to property. In the CRL, FPIC is supposed to be realized through the acquisition of community forest status, and the LRA equally requires communities to register their customary land. However, the LRA's 5-step procedure could become more community-driven than the CRL's 9-step procedure.

FPIC's institutional autonomy and gender dimensions were negotiated differently in the land and forest sector reforms. While in the forest sector reform, the construction of the *incompetent community* legitimized overriding the institutional autonomy of communities, in the land sector reform, the construction of the *incompetent and discriminatory community* had a similar effect.

In the peacebuilding process, gender and forestry were largely treated as separate issues.[791] The field of peacebuilding focused mainly on the participation of women in the security sector reform and combatting sexual and gender-based violence. So even though the Peace Agreement contained both provisions on natural resources and gender, the different actors failed to think of the two aspects together. The last-minute insertion of a half-hearted women's quota reflects the lack of consideration given to gender dynamics in forestry and dismantles the gender blindness of the different actors. Moreover, the lack of engagement with customary law and governance is eye-catching. Fuest's argument that the peacebuilding machinery (as well as the development industry) was 'caught halfway between a "top-down", liberal peace approach and a (naïve) "bottom-up" approach of local ownership'[792] seems to be accurate. Moran similarly criticizes the blunt rejection of 'legitimate, authoritative

---

[789] Cornell (2006), p. 11.

[790] Wainwright (2008), p. 22.

[791] See also Karuro and Yeung (2016), p. 581.

[792] Fuest (2010), p. 27.

political roles for women'[793] that could have been built upon. The field of forest-sector reform was thus characterized not only by the exclusion and neglect of the *local* but also of the *(local) female*.

The land sector reform process took an entirely different approach to gender by recognizing the connection between gender and land from the beginning. As the Land Commission had been confronted with a considerable number of women's land rights cases, they assumed that there was a link between land and gender relations.[794] The land-gender nexus has also been recognized much more in the fields of peacebuilding and development. As many donor projects had a strong women's land rights component, gender (or better: women's land rights) also became a priority for the national NGOs implementing these projects. Moreover, the higher number of NGOs involved in the reform process and the establishment of the Women's Land Rights Taskforce allowed for the participation of NGOs with a specific focus on women's rights. However, the provisions calling for the participation of women were introduced mainly without asking rural women about their concerns. It is questionable whether the consultations on land tenure, as well as the reports produced by NGOs and international organizations, used methodologies that gave voice to rural women. Thus, the priorities of rural women may not necessarily overlap with those identified by the participants of the drafting process. The stakeholder approach to gender also risks making overlapping and shifting identities invisible. For example, it is likely that conflicts will arise as to whether women can be members of the youth group. In many ways, the actors of the reform process just chose the easiest way; introducing a women's quota is less complicated than an in-depth engagement with women's right to self-determination, culture, and institutional autonomy.[795] While the forest sector reform had already marginalized the *local*, the land reform built upon this tendency. The rise of women's rights—or inclusive decision-making, to put it more broadly—thus contributed to the further decline of customary law and decision-making by portraying it as an alternative, inefficient, and undemocratic legality.[796] The *female*, in this respect, served as a legitimization for transforming the *local*. The overlapping discourses, with their blindness to gender and culture, in effect neglected both the rights of local communities and rural women.[797]

Hence, in many respects, the legal identities of the state and the *customary land-owning community* and their relations, as created by the land and forest legislation, are reminiscent of colonial legalities. In colonial legal systems, it was common that customary law only continued to govern private relations like family life.[798] With

[793] Moran (2012), p. 63.

[794] Roesch R (18 Apr 2019) Skype interview with a senior staff member of the LGSA, para 16.

[795] In the Ghanaian constitutional reform, in contrast, it was attempted to build on pre-existing female leadership institutions that had been neglected during colonialism (Aikins 2016, p. 75).

[796] von Benda-Beckmann et al. (2009), p. 7; see also Abramowitz and Moran (2012), p. 142.

[797] Jørgensen and Phillips (2002), p. 63; see also Moran (2012), pp. 53, 55.

[798] Hellum and Derman (2005), p. 182.

respect to land and natural resources, the law imposed by the colonizers altered or replaced customary law. Both the CRL and LRA follow this type of thinking. If one attempted to categorize the Liberian forest and land legislation and the rationale of FPIC, it comes closest to 'self-administration or self-management'.[799] Pre-existing customary claims to property or sovereignty are dissolved into 'the universal logic of the Western property rights grid'.[800] While this may be the best legal protection communities have had in the past decades in Liberia, it also replaces self-determination claims with more limited property rights (or even less):

> [While] pre-existing Aboriginal interests may be transformed into proprietary, or quasi-proprietary rights, Aboriginal sovereignty is removed from the scene at the point of the assertion of [in the Canadian case] Crown sovereignty replaced with, at most, the notion of 'self-government'[. . .].[801]

The legal and administrative framework remains firmly in the hands of the state while communities have limited leeway in governing their own affairs. FPIC has been renegotiated from a right entwined with notions of Indigenous sovereignty to a right that applies only in very few situations. It no longer refers to the relationship between the state and communities but governs the relations between private parties negotiating the use of customary land. In line with that logic, the emerging FPIC norm is characterized by 'internal exclusion',[802] neglecting the institutional autonomy of communities. A report issued by the Environmental Protection Agency and the Forestry Development Authority also concludes that the Liberian understanding of FPIC 'is not fully compliant with best practice in FPIC implementation'[803]—namely because of the lack of recognition of self-determined decision-making.

Still, the use of the term FPIC re-emphasizes that communities have a legal personality and rights, which may only be infringed upon in exceptional circumstances. Thereby, it alters the relationship between the state and rural communities to some—albeit very limited—extent.

Despite the 'internal legal pluralism'[804] created by the forest and land legislation reflecting the predominantly Western distinction 'settled-wild-divide',[805] a strikingly uniform understanding of FPIC has emerged in the two laws.[806] When the legal negotiation process in a field is concluded, a 'neostandardization'[807] of the norm occurs, followed by a re-pluralization. A strong indication exists that the Liberian national legislation is close to that point.

---

[799] Imai (2009), p. 297.

[800] Zerner (2003), p. 3.

[801] Christie (2005), p. 46.

[802] Eisenberg (2020), p. 279.

[803] LTS International (2019a), p. 16.

[804] de Sousa Santos (2002), p. 95.

[805] Lowenhaupt Tsing (2003), p. 31.

[806] von Benda-Beckmann et al. (2009), p. 4.

[807] von Benda-Beckmann and Turner (2019), p. 13.

Nevertheless, negotiations are still ongoing in some areas. In 2019, the Environmental Protection Agency developed National FPIC guidelines with funding from the World Bank.[808] They explicitly address situations where the government intends to change the tenure status of customary land: either for the creation of protected areas or the granting of concessions.[809] Given the fact that they were endorsed after the adoption of the LRA, this could indicate that the government intends to go back to granting government concessions—instead of promoting commercial use contracts between communities and companies. However, the communication strategy of the National FPIC guidelines reframes FPIC: it is explicitly derived from the right to self-determination, thereby departing from the FPIC guidelines.[810] It also stresses that communities are rights-holders and not only stakeholders—while the National Guidelines mostly refer to stakeholders.[811]

Another political development that may have serious consequences on FPIC as a national legality is the Memorandum of Understanding signed by the Liberian government and the Dubai-based firm Blue Carbon in 2023. Newspapers revealed that the government has committed to granting a concession—featuring exclusive use rights—to the company, covering nearly the totality of Liberian forests and amounting to 10% of the Liberian landmass.[812] The goal is to put the forests under protection for thirty years, generate carbon credits, and sell these on carbon markets or to other governments. Hundred thousands of rural Liberians could lose forest access due to the deal. Yet, according to the Memorandum of Understanding, Blue Carbon and the Liberian government are only obliged 'to apply best efforts to undertake free, prior, and informed consent (FPIC) negotiations with communities in project areas within three months'.[813] This is neither compatible with the Community Rights Law nor with the Land Rights Act.[814] In light of these developments, it becomes evident that FPIC continues to be under negotiation.

---

[808] Azango (2019) Liberia: Government drafts guidelines for free, prior and informed consent. Front Page Africa. https://frontpageafricaonline.com/health/Liberia-government-drafts-guidelines-for-free-prior-informed-consent/. Accessed 11 Aug 2023; LTS International (2019b).

[809] LTS International (2019b), The FPIC process; see also Proforest Initiative Africa (2022), p. 19.

[810] Proforest Initiative Africa (2022), p. 17.

[811] LTS International (2019b) The FPIC Process; Proforest Initiative Africa (2022), p. 20.

[812] Cholo Brooks (17 Jul 2023) IFMCM issues statement on proposed Conservation Agreement between Liberia and Blue Carbon. GNN Liberia. https://gnnliberia.com/ifmcm-issues-statement-on-proposed-conservation-agreement-between-liberia-and-blue-carbon/. Accessed 15 Aug 2023; Mukpo (4 Aug 2023) Massive carbon offset deal with Dubai-based firm draws fire in Liberia. Mongabay. https://news.mongabay.com/2023/08/massive-carbon-offset-deal-with-dubai-based-firm-draws-fire-in-liberia/#:~:text=Liberia%20is%20set%20to%20hand,local%20and%20international%20environmental%20groups. Accessed 14 Aug 2023.

[813] Ibid.

[814] See also Far (31 Jul 2023) Liberia: Six laws Blue Carbon deal would violate explained. Daily Observer. https://www.liberianobserver.com/liberia-six-laws-blue-carbon-deal-would-violate-explained. Accessed 15 Aug 2023.

References

Abramowitz S, Moran MH (2012) International human rights, gender-based violence, and local discourses of abuse in postconflict Liberia: a problem of “culture”? Afr Stud Rev 55:119–146

Agarwal B (2001) Participatory exclusions, community forestry, and gender: an analysis for South Asia and a conceptual framework. World Dev 29:1623–1648

Agarwal B (2010) Does women’s proportional strength affect their participation? Governing local forests in South Asia. World Dev 38:98–112

Agarwal B (2014) The power of numbers in gender dynamics: illustrations from community forestry groups. J Peasant Stud 42:1–20

Agyeman VK et al (2022) Sustainable forest management (SFM) in Liberia - the 4Cs approach. Forestry Development Authority and World Bank Group

Aikins JK (2016) Indigenising democracy? Renegotiating the role of indigenous political authorities in Ghana’s Constitution review. In: Dhawan N et al (eds) Negotiating normativity: postcolonial appropriations, contestations, and transformations. Springer, Cham, pp 61–78

Aisha F (2005) Mainstreaming gender in peace support organizations: the United Nations Mission in Liberia. In: Abogaye F, Bah AMS (eds) A tortuous road to peace: the dynamics of regional, UN and international humanitarian interventions in Liberia. Institute for Security Studies, Pretoria, pp 147–164

Akpan MB (1973) Black imperialism: Americo-Liberian rule over the African peoples of Liberia, 1841-1964. Can J Afr Stud 7:217–236

Alden Wily L (2007) ‘So who owns the forest’ an investigation into forest ownership and customary land rights in Liberia. Sustainable Development Institute and FERN

Alden Wily L (2008) Whose land is it? Commons and conflict states, why the ownership of the commons matters in making and keeping peace. Rights and Resources Initiative

Alden Wily L (2009) Tackling land tenure in the emergency to development transition in post-conflict states: from restitution to reform. In: Pantuliano S (ed) Uncharted territory: land conflict and humanitarian action. Practical Action Publishing, Bourton in Dunsmore, pp 27–52

Alden Wily L et al (2010) The end of the Hinterland: forest, conflict and climate change. Rice +Resource Initiative

Altman SL et al (2012) Leveraging high-value natural resources to restore the rule of law: the role of Liberia Forest Initiative in Liberia’s transition to stability. In: Lujala P, Rustad SA (eds) In high-value natural resources and peacebuilding. Earthscan, London, pp 337–365

Andersen L (2006) Post-conflict security sector reform and the challenge of ownership: the case of Liberia. Danish Institute for International Studies. http://pure.diis.dk/ws/files/84423/lan_postconflict_security_sector_reform.pdf. Accessed 11 Aug 2023

Aning EK (1998) Gender and civil war: the cases of Liberia and Sierra Leone. Civ Wars 1:1–26

ARD Inc. (2008a) Land rights and community forestry program, work plan: 1 November 2008 - 30 September 2009. USAID

ARD Inc. (2008b) Land rights and community forestry programme, work plan: 1 March - 30 September 2008. USAID Liberia

Autesserre S (2014) Peaceland: conflict resolution and the everyday politics of international intervention. Cambridge University Press, Cambridge

Badmus IA (2009) Explaining women’s roles in the West African tragic triplet: Sierra Leone, Liberia, and Cote d’Ivoire in comparative perspective. J Alt Perspect Soc Sci 1:808–839

Banks AM (2007) Challenging political boundaries in post-conflict states. Univ Pa J Int Law 29: 105–168

Bannon I, Collier P (2003) Natural resources and violent conflict: options and actions. The World Bank, Washington D.C.

Bauer G, Britton HE (2006) Women in African parliaments: a continental shift? In: Bauer G, Britton HE (eds) Women in African parliaments. Lynne Rienner Publishers, London, pp 1–30

Beevers MD (2015) Peace resources? Governing Liberia’s forests in the aftermath of conflict. Int Peacekeeping 22:26–42

Beevers MD (2019) Peacebuilding and natural resource governance after armed conflict: Sierra Leone and Liberia. Palgrave Macmillan, Cham

Bennett B (2015) Plantations and protected areas: a global history of forest management. MIT Press, Cambridge; London

Blundell AG (2003) A new environment for Liberia - a road map for the forest sector - outcome of the US embassy workshop on forest sector reform (December 15 & 16, 2003 - Monrovia). USAID

Bognitz S (2020) The legal laboratory in Rwanda: experimentalization and adaptation. In: Seidel K, Elliesie H (eds) Normative spaces and legal dynamics in Africa. Routledge, Abingdon, pp 124–156

Bourdieu P (1986) The force of law: toward a sociology of the juridical field essay. Hastings Law J 38:805–813

Bourdieu P, Wacquant LJD (1992a) An invitation to reflexive sociology. University of Chicago Press, Chicago; London

Bourdieu P, Wacquant LJD (1992b) The purpose of reflexive sociology (the Chicago workshop). In: Bourdieu P, Wacquant LJD (eds) An invitation to reflexive sociology. Chicago University Press, Chicago, pp 61–216

Bourdieu P et al (1994) Rethinking the state: genesis and structure of the bureaucratic field. Sociol Theory 12:1–18

Brottem L, Unruh J (2009) Territorial tensions: rainforest conservation, postconflict recovery, and land tenure in Liberia. Ann Assoc Am Geogr 99:995–1002

Bruce J (2016) A strategy for further reform of Liberia's law on land. Tetra Tech

Bruce JW, Kanneh BN (2011) Reform of Liberia's civil law concerning land: a proposed strategy report, report to the Land Commission

Bryan J (2012) Rethinking territory: social justice and neoliberalism in Latin America's territorial turn. Geogr Compass 6:215–226

Cabrera Ormaza MV, Ebert FC (2019) The World Bank, human rights, and organizational legitimacy strategies: the case of the 2016 Environmental and Social Framework. Leiden J Int Law 32:483–500

Carpenter RC (2007) Setting the advocacy agenda: theorizing issue emergence and nonemergence in transnational advocacy networks. Int Stud Q 51:99–120

Carter J (2005) Liberian communities & the forest. In: Proceeding of the first international workshop on community forestry in Liberia: towards a shared vision and an action frame for community forestry in Liberia. CIFOR, pp 54–57

Castillo Diaz P, Tordjman S (2012) Women's participation in peace negotiations: connections between presence and influence. UN Women

Cavanagh CJ (2018) Enclosure, dispossession, and the green economy: new contours of internal displacement in Liberia and Sierra Leone? Afr Geogr Rev 37:120–133

Center for International Forestry Research (2005) Proceedings of the first international workshop on community forestry in Liberia: towards a shared vision and action frame for community forestry in Liberia

Chinkin C, Charlesworth H (2006) Building women into peace: the international legal framework. Third World Q 27:937–957

Christie G (2005) A colonial reading of recent jurisprudence: sparrow, delgamuukw and haida nation. Windsor Yearb Access Justice 23:17–53

Clarke A, Kohler P (2005) Property law: commentary and materials. Cambridge University Press, Cambridge

Colchester M (2006) Justice in the forest: rural livelihood activities and forest law enforcement. Center for International Forestry Research

Community Forest Working Group (Technical Sub-Group) (2008) Consolidation of comments from proceedings of the CFWG meeting on review of the zero draft of the Community Rights Law (CRL) by technical sub-group

Cornell S (2006) Indigenous peoples, poverty and self-determination in Australia, New Zealand, Canada and the United States. Joint Occas Pap Native Aff 2:1–39

Corriveau-Bourque A (2010) Confusions and palava: the logic of land encroachment in Lofa county, Liberia. Norwegian Refugee Council

Coulter C et al (2008) Young female fighters in African wars: conflicts and its consequences. The Nordic Africa Institute

Datzberger S, Le Mat MLJ (2018) Just add women and stir? Education, gender and peacebuilding in Uganda. Int J Educ Dev 59:61–69

Davis A (2010) Forms of capital and mobility in the political field: applying Bourdieu's conceptual framework to UK party politics. Br Polit 5:202–223

de Carvalho B et al (2019) Everyday sovereignty: international experts, brokers and local ownership in peacebuilding Liberia. Eur J Int Relat 25:1–24

de Sousa Santos B (2002) Toward a new legal common sense. Butterworths; LexisNexis, London; Buenos Aires; Chatswood

de Sousa Santos B (2006) The heterogeneous state and legal pluralism in Mozambique. Law Soc Rev 40:39–75

DeFries R et al (2005) Increasing isolation of protected areas in tropical forests over the past twenty years. Ecol Appl 15:19–26

Desai D et al (2012) Rethinking justice reform in fragile and conflict-affected states: the capacity of development agencies and lessons from Liberia and Afghanistan. World Bank Leg Rev 3:241–262

Dodd M-L et al (2018) Women's land rights in Liberia in law, practice, and future reforms: LGSA women's land rights study. USAID. https://www.land-links.org/wp-content/uploads/2018/03/USAID_Land_Tenure_LGSA_WLR_Study_Mar-16-2018.pdf. Accessed 11 Aug 2023

Eba'a Atyi R (2018) Assessing progress in forest law enforcement and governance in Africa. African Development Bank Group

ECODIT (2022) USAID/Liberia land management activities. Quarterly report submitted January 27, 2022

Eisenberg A (2020) Consent, resistance and the duty to consult. Int J Minor Group Rights 27:270–290

Engle Merry S (2005) Human rights and global legal pluralism: reciprocity and disjuncture. In: von Benda-Beckmann F et al (eds) Mobile people, mobile law: expanding legal relations in a contracting world. Ashgate, Aldershot; Burlington, pp 215–232

Fairhead J, Leach M (1998) Reframing deforestation - global analysis and local realities: studies in West Africa. Routledge, London; New York

Fairhead J et al (2012) Green grabbing: a new appropriation of nature? J Peasant Stud 39:237–261

Falk Moore S (1973) Law and social change: the semi-autonomous social field as an appropriate subject of study. Law Soc Rev 7:719–746

Filer C et al (2020) The FPIC principle meets land struggles in Cambodia, Indonesia and Papua New Guinea. Land 9:67–88

Forestry Development Authority (2009) Liberian forestry brief No 1. http://www.fao.org/forestry/18684-05bb9122a69fe9a03c649a654724ba385.pdf. Accessed 11 Aug 2023

Foster-Turley P et al (2018) Liberia tropical forest and biodiversity analysis. USAID

Foundation for Community Initiatives (2011) Liberia: women rising, women falling - how poor policy formulation and implementation is disempowering women in Liberia

Fuest V (1986) Frauenbezogene Entwicklungsprojekte in Liberia. Liberia Working Group

Fuest V (2008) 'This is the time to get in front': changing roles and opportunities for women in Liberia. Afr Aff 107:201–224

Fuest V (2010) Contested inclusions: pitfalls of NGO peace-building activities in Liberia. Afr Spectr 45:3–33

Fynn Bruey V (2018) Redefining women's roles in international and regional law: the case of pre- and postwar Liberia. In: Shekhawat S (ed) Gender, conflict, peace, and UNSC resolution 1325. Lexington Books, Lanham, pp 21–42

Gizelis T-I (2011) A country of their own: women and peace-building. Confl Manag Peace Sci 28: 522–542

Gizelis T-I, Joseph J (2016) Decoupling local ownership? The lost opportunities for grassroots women's involvement in Liberian peacebuilding. Coop Confl 51:539–556

Global Witness (2009) Liberia posed to hand forests to timber pirates. www.globalwitness.org/en/archive/liberia-poised-hand-forests-timber-pirates/. Accessed 19 July 2023

Global Witness et al (2012) Spoiled: Liberia's private use permits. https://www.google.com/url?sa=t&rct=j&q=&esrc=s&source=web&cd=4&ved=2ahUKEwjM1bXlvvLgAhWC_aQKHdU3Cy0QFjADegQIBxAC&url=http%3A%2F%2Fic.fsc.org%2Fpre-download.gwsamfusadi-2012spolied-liberias-pup.1954.htm&usg=AOvVaw1Yh0JVmjfUDqQkEQrjlkcF. Accessed 11 Aug 2023

Global Witness (2017) Holding the line. https://www.globalwitness.org/en/reports/liberia-holding-line/. Accessed 11 Aug 2023

Global Witness (2018) Power to the people? How companies are exploiting community forestry in liberia. https://www.globalwitness.org/en/campaigns/forests/power-people/. Accessed 11 Aug 2023

Goodman R, Jinks D (2004) How to influence states: socialization and international human rights law. Duke Law J 54:621–703

Graef J (2015) Practicing post-liberal peace-building: legal empowerment and emergent hybridity in Liberia. Palgrave Macmillan, London; New York

Griffiths J (1979) Is law important? N Y Univ Law Rev 54:339–374

Griffiths J (1986) What is legal pluralism? J Leg Plur Unoff Law 18:1–55

Griffiths J (2003) The social working of legal rules. J Leg Plur 2003:1–48

Harding S (1995) Just add women and stir? In: Gender Working Group (United Nations Commission on Science and Technology for Development) (ed) Missing links: gender equity in science and technology for development. Intermediate Technology Publications, Ottawa, pp 295–308

Harris R et al (2012–3) Liberia social audit: assessing the forestry sector. Civil Society Independent Forest Monitors and NGO Coalition of Liberia

Hartman A et al (2016) Evaluation of the community land protection program (CLPP) in Liberia. USAID. https://www.land-links.org/wp-content/uploads/2016/09/CLPP-IE_Baseline-Report_2016-01.pdf. Accessed 11 Aug 2023

Hartman A et al (2018) Community land protection in Liberia: the impact on neocustomary norms and institutions. www.land-links.org/wp-content/uploads/2018/04/Session-01-10-Hartman-603_paper.pdf. Accessed 11 Aug 2023

Heemann L (2020) Living customary law: negotiating spaces for women in traditional communities. In: Seidel K, Elliesie H (eds) Normative spaces and legal dynamics in Africa. Routledge, Abingdon

Hellum A, Derman B (2005) Negotiating water rights in the context of a new political and legal landscape in Zimbabwe. In: von Benda-Beckmann F et al (eds) Mobile people, mobile law: expanding legal relations in a contracting world. Ashgate, Aldershot; Burlington, pp 177–198

Hensell S, Gerdes F (2012) Elites and international actors in post-war societies: the limits of intervention. Int Peacekeeping 19:154–169

Huberich CH (1947) The political and legislative history of Liberia. The Lawbook Exchange, Ltd., Clark, New Jersey

Hudson H (2009) Peacebuilding through a gender lens and the challenges of implementation in Rwanda and Côte d'Ivoire. Secur Stud 18:287–318

Hudson H (2017) Decolonising gender and peacebuilding: feminist frontiers and border thinking in Africa. In: Shepherd LJ (ed) Building peace: feminist perspectives. Routledge, Abingdon; New York, pp 73–88

Ickowitz A (2006) Shifting cultivation and deforestation in tropical Africa: critical reflections. Dev Change 37:599–626

Imai S (2009) Indigenous self-determination and the state. In: Richardson BJ et al (eds) Indigenous people and the law: comparative and critical perspectives. Hart Publishing, Oxford; Oregon, pp 285–314

Independent Evaluation Group (2012) Liberia country program evaluation: 2004-2011. World Bank

International Crisis Group (2006) Liberia: resurrecting the justice system

Jørgensen MW, Phillips L (2002) Discourse analysis as theory and method. SAGE Publications, London; Thousand Oaks, California; New Delhi

Kaba A, Madan G (2014) Walking with villagers: how liberia's land rights policy was shaped from the grassroots. IIED et al

Käihkö I (2019) On liberian secret societies and conflict resolution. Nordic J Afr Stud 28:1–20

Kandiyoti D (2004) Political fiction meets gender myth: post-conflict reconstruction, "democratisation" and women's rights. IDS Bull 34:134–136

Kapoor I (2008) The postcolonial politics of development. Routledge, London; New York

Karuro N, Yeung LH (2016) Integrating gender into post-conflict natural resource management. In: Bruch C et al (eds) Governance, natural resources and post-conflict peacebuilding. Routledge, Abingdon, pp 579–604

Kaul R, Heuty A (2009) Getting a better deal from the extractive sector. Revenue Watch Institute

Khan MT (2016) Normative conflicts in Bangladesh: nature/forest conservation, corporate interests and the politics of co-management. In: Dhawan N et al (eds) Negotiating normativity: postcolonial appropriations, contestations, and transformations. Springer, Cham, pp 225–240

Knight R et al (2013) Protecting community lands and resources: evidence from Liberia. IDLO et al. https://namati.org/wp-content/uploads/2013/01/12-namati-book-complete-lr.pdf. Accessed 11 Aug 2023

Kpanan Ayoung Siakor S (2017) Reforming Liberia's forestry sector: reflections of a civil society activist. Sur File Nat Resour Hum Rights 14:27–35

Kpanan'Ayoung Siakor S (2011) Forest governance and the voluntary partnership agreement: deepening forest sector reform in Liberia. Sustainable Development Institute. https://sdiliberia.org/sites/default/files/publications/2011%20Forest%20governance%20and%20the%20voluntary%20partnership%20agreement.pdf. Accessed 11 Aug 2023

Krook ML, O'Brian DZ (2010) The politics of group representation: quotas for women and minorities worldwide. Comp Polit 42:253–272

Krook ML, True J (2010) Rethinking the life cycles of international norms: the United Nations and the global promotion of gender equality. Eur J Int Relat 18:103–127

Kunz R (2016) Windows of opportunity, troyan horses and the waves of women on the move: de-colonizing the circulation of feminist knowledges through metaphors. In: Bustelo M et al (eds) The politics of feminist knowledge transfer: gender training and gender expertise. Palgrave Macmillan, Houndmills; New York, pp 99–117

Laclau E, Mouffe C (2001) Hegemony and socialist strategy: towards a radical democratic politics. Verso, London; New York

Lamb JN et al (2009) Pursuing community forestry in Liberia. Environ Policy Gov 19:296–308

Land Commission (2010) Land Commission consultations. https://ekmsliberia.info/wp-content/uploads/2019/11/2010_County_Consultation_on_Land.pdf. Accessed 19 July 2023

Land Rights and Community Forestry Program (2008) Comments on draft Community Rights Law (available upon request)

Land Rights and Community Forestry Program (2008–9) Quarterly report excerpts from the USAID Land Rights and Community Forestry Program (available upon request)

Lanier F et al (2012) "Smell-no-taste" the social impact of foreign direct investment in Liberia. Center for International Resolution and Columbia School of International and Public Affairs

Lenoir R (2006) Scientific habitus: Pierre bourdieu and the collective intellectual. Theory Cult Soc 23:25–43

Leonardsson H, Rudd G (2015) The "local turn" in peacebuilding: a literature review of effective and emancipatory local peacebuilding. Third World Q 36:825–839

Liberia Extractive Industries Transparency Initiative (2013) Liberia Extractive Industries Transparency Initiative (LEITI): post award process audit final report
Liberia Institute of Statistics and Geo-Information Services (2013) Demographic and health survey. https://dhsprogram.com/pubs/pdf/fr291/fr291.pdf. Accessed 11 Aug 2023
Litz V (2015) Protected area expansion: a call for restraint. USAID. https://dec.usaid.gov/dec/content/Detail_Presto.aspx?ctID=ODVhZjk4NWQtM2YyMi00YjRmLTkxNjktZTcxMjM2NDBmY2Uy&rID=MjE2NjI2. Accessed 11 Aug 2023
Litz V, Kindberg L (2017) Conflict: the fourth "C" in Liberia's forest management? Africa Biodiversity Collaborative Group. https://abcg.org/files/documents/Conflict%20the%20fourth%20C%20in%20Liberia%27s%20forest%20management.pdf. Accessed 11 Aug 2023
Lomax T (2008) Forest governance in Liberia: an NGO perspective. FERN and IUCN
Lomax T, Warner N (2020) The legal basis for rights-based conservation in Liberia. Forest Peoples' Programme
Lowenhaupt Tsing A (2003) Cultivating the wild: honey-hunting and forest management in Southeast Kalimantan. In: Zerner C (ed) Culture and the question of rights: forests, coasts, and seas in Southeast Asia. Duke University Press, Durham; London, pp 24–55
LTS International (2019a) Development of national guidelines on free prior and informed consent (FPIC): project report. Environmental Protection Agency and Forestry Development Authority
LTS International (2019b) National guidelines on achieving free prior and informed consent (FPIC) with respect to communities and forest resources
Lyon JM (1981) Informal imperialism: the United States in Liberia, 1897–1912. Dipl Hist 5:221–243
Makain JS, Foh MS (2009) Social dimensions of large-scale land acquisition rights in Liberia (1900-2009): challenges and prospects for traditional settlers. Liberian Stud J 33:1–40
McAlpine J et al (2006) Liberia: forests as a challenge and an opportunity. Int For Rev 8:83–92
McCarthy JF (2005) Contesting decentralization: transnational policy narrative and the emergence of volatile socio-legal configurations in Central Kalimantan, Indonesia. In: von Benda-Beckmann F et al (eds) Mobile people, mobile law: expanding legal relations in a contracting world. Ashgate, Aldershot; Burlington, pp 153–176
Meinzen-Dick R, Pradhan R (2016) Property rights and legal pluralism in post-conflict environments: problem or opportunity for natural resource management. In: Bruch C et al (eds) Governance, natural resource, and post-conflict peace-building. Routledge, Abingdon, pp 525–544
Menzies NK (2007) Our forest, your ecosystem, their timber: communities, conservation, and the state in community-based forest management. Columbia University Press, New York
Mertz E (1994) Conclusion: a new social constructionism for sociolegal studies. Law Soc Rev 28: 1243–1265
Migdal JS, Schlichte K (2005) Rethinking the state. In: Schlichte K (ed) The dynamics of states: the formation and crises of state domination. Ashgate, Aldershot, pp 1–44
Moore DS (2005) Suffering for territory: race, place, and power in Zimbabwe. Duke University Press, Durham; London
Moran MH (1990) Civilized women. Cornell University Press, Ithaca; London
Moran M (2006) Liberia: the violence of democracy. University of Pennsylvania Press, Philadelphia
Moran MH (2010) Gender, militarism, and peace-building: projects of the postconflict moment. Annu Rev Anthropol 39:261–274
Moran M (2012) Our mothers have spoken: synthesizing old and new forms of women's political authority in Liberia. J Int Women's Stud 13:51–66
Mosse D (2001) "People's knowledge", participation and patronage: operations and representations in rural development. In: Cooke B, Kothari U (eds) Participation: the new tyranny. Zed Books, London; New York, pp 16–35
Mulbah S (2015) The political economy of land law reform in a post-conflict country: Liberia on the verge of a Land Rights Act. Land Tenure J 15:95–121

Nader L (2009) Law and the frontiers of illegalities. In: von Benda-Beckmann F et al (eds) The power of law in a transnational world: anthropological enquiries. Berghahn Books, New York; Oxford, pp 54–73
Nagelhus Schia N, de Carvalho B (2010) Peacebuilding in Liberia and the case for a perspective from below. NUPI
Namubiru-Mwaura EL et al (2012) Liberia land policy & institutional support (LPIS) project: customary land tenure in Liberia: findings and implications drawn from 11 case studies. USAID. https://www.land-links.org/wp-content/uploads/2016/09/USAID_Land_Tenure_Liberia_LPIS_Synthesis_Report.pdf. Accessed 11 Aug 2023
Nesiah V (2012) Uncomfortable alliances: women, peace and security in Sri Lanka. In: Loomba A, Lukose RA (eds) South Asian feminisms. Duke University Press, Durham, pp 137–161
Newberry D (2014) Why are there cattle in the conservation area? Social barriers to biofuel governance in Brazil. Geoforum 54:306–314
NGO Coalition of Liberia (2008) Government of Liberia recognizes communities' ownership of forests
Nichols SS, Moumin MA (2016) The role of environmental law in post-conflict peacebuilding. In: Bruch C et al (eds) Governance, natural resources and post-conflict peacebuilding. Routledge, Abingdon, pp 429–460
Paffenholz T (2015) Unpacking the local turn in peacebuilding: a critical assessment towards an agenda for future. Third World Q 36:857–874
Podder S (2013) Bridging the 'conceptual–contextual' divide: security sector reform in Liberia and UNMIL transition. J Interv Statebuilding 7:353–380
Porter-Bolland L et al (2012) Community managed forest and forest protected areas: an assessment of their conservation effectiveness across the tropics. For Ecol Manag:1–12
Press RM (2010) Guided by the hand of God!: Liberian women peacemakers and civil war. Rev Faith Int Aff 8:23–29
Proforest Initiative Africa (2022) Liberia national FPIC communications strategy. Republic of Liberia
Puechguirbal N (2005) Gender and peace building in Africa: analysis of some structural obstacles. In: Rodríguez D, Natukanda-Togboa E (eds) Gender and peace building in Africa. University for Peace, Ciudad Colón, pp 1–12
Pugh M (2005) The political economy of peacebuilding: a critical theory perspective. Int J Peace Stud 10:23–42
Radelet S (2007) Reviving economic growth in Liberia. Center for Global Development
Republic of Liberia (2014) Fifth report of Liberia to the Convention on Biological Diversity. https://www.cbd.int/doc/world/lr/lr-nr-05-en.pdf. Accessed 23 Mar 2023
Richards P (2005) To fight or to farm? Agrarian dimensions of the mano river conflicts (Liberia and Sierra Leone). Afr Aff 104:571–590
Risse T, Ropp SC, Sikkink K (2013) The Persistent Power of Human Rights: From Commitment to Compliance, Cambridge University Press, Cambridge
Rochow KWJ (2008) Stuck in stages: the evolving role of enforcement in Liberia forest sector reform. In: Gerardu J et al (eds) 8th international conference on environmental compliance and enforcement. Conference proceedings. Cameron May, INECE Secretariat, London, pp 463–474
Roesch R (2019) A new era of customary property rights? – Liberia's land and forest legislation in light of the Indigenous right to self-determination. Glob Comp Law 52:439–462
Russell D (2009) Mid-term assessment of land rights and community forestry program. USAID Liberia
Russell D et al (2011) Final evaluation of the land rights and community forestry programme (LRCFP). USAID Liberia
Sannerholm R (2007) Legal, judicial and administrative reforms in post-conflict societies: beyond the rule of law template. J Confl Secur Law 12:65–94
Sawyer A (2005) Beyond plunder: toward democratic governance in Liberia. Lynne Rienner Publishers, London

Scalise E, Hannay L (2013) Land policy reform for women in Liberia. Focus on Land in Africa Brief
Shepherd LJ (2017a) Gender, UN peacebuilding, and the politics of space: locating legitimacy. Oxford University Press, Oxford
Shepherd LJ (2017b) Victims of violence or agents of change? Representations of women in UN peacebuilding discourse. In: Shepherd LJ (ed) Building peace: feminist perspectives. Routledge, Abingdon; New York, pp 1–15
Sikkink K (2002) Transnational advocacy networks and the social construction of legal rules. In: Dezalay Y, Garth BG (eds) Global prescriptions: the production, exportation, and importation of a new legal orthodoxy. The University of Michigan Press, Ann Arbor, pp 37–64
Simpson CL Jr (1973) Preface. Liberian Code of Laws revised, adopted by the legislature of the Republic of Liberia and President William R Tolbert, Jr. Cornell University Press, Ithaca, New York, pp xi–xii
Smilie I, Brownell A (2007) Land grabbing and land reform: diamonds, rubber and forests in Liberia. Partnership Africa Canada and Association of Environmental Lawyers of Liberia
Smyle J (2012) Liberia forest sector diagnostic. World Bank
Social Impact Inc. (2018) Activity review: land governance support activity. USAID
Stevens CJ (2014) The legal history of public land in Liberia. J Afr Law 58:250–265
Suhrke A (2007) Reconstruction as modernisation: the 'post-conflict' project in Afghanistan. Third World Q 28:1291–1308
Suhrke A, Borchgrevink K (2009) Negotiating justice sector reform in Afghanistan. Crime Law Soc Change 51:211–230
Sustainable Development Institute (2008a) One step beyond: different viewpoints, one way forward towards recognizing communities' rights with respect to forests
Sustainable Development Institute (2008b) Special edition: so who owns the forest?
Sustainable Development Institute (2009) Who is buying Liberia's forests? https://landmatrix.org/media/uploads/who-is-buying-liberias-forests.pdf. Accessed 19 July 2023
Sustainable Development Institute (2013) Community complaint against equatorial palm oil. www.forestpeoples.org/sites/fpp/files/news/2013/10/Community%20Complain_LiberiaGrandBassaCounty_Oct2013.pdf. Accessed 11 Aug 2023
Sustainable Development Institute (2015) What the people say? Citizens urge government to keep the promise to formalize and protect customary land rights. https://sdiliberia.org/sites/default/files/publications/What%20the%20people%20say%20flyer.pdf?fbclid=IwAR3_an4JV3Rq5H7Js-z50S1_4iZWtqqOkJZG6FQT81lfNmFeh42MGunE8g4. Accessed 11 Aug 2023
Sustainable Development Institute (2019) Practical potential conflict and implementation challenges for the CRL and the LRL
Tadros M (2010) Introduction: quotas - add women and stir? IDS Bull 41:1–10
Tetra Tech (2016a) Land governance support activity annual report (August 2015 - September 2016). USAID
Tetra Tech (2016b) Land governance support activity: quarterly report FY16, Q2 (January-March 2016). USAID
Tetra Tech (2016c) Land governance support activity: quarterly report FY16, Q3 (April-June 2016). USAID
Tetra Tech (2016d) Land governance support activity: quarterly report FY17, Q1 (October-December 2016). USAID
Tetra Tech (2017a) Liberia land governance support activity annual report: year two (October 2016 - September 2017). USAID
Tetra Tech (2017b) Liberia land governance support activity: quarterly report, FY17 Q2 (January-March 2017). USAID
Tetra Tech (2017c) Liberia land governance support activity: quarterly report, FY17 Q3 (April-June 2017). USAID

The Rights and Resources Group (2013) Investments into the agribusiness, extractive, and infrastructure sectors of Liberia. https://rightsandresources.org/wp-content/exported-pdf/countryreportliberiafinal.pdf. Accessed 11 Aug 2023

Tissari J et al (2008) Draft report: World Bank diagnostic trade integration study: wood industry component. FAO. http://www.fao.org/forestry/23514-0844c34823f11a36c65f6587345dc2b1d.pdf. Accessed 11 Aug 2023

Trubek DM et al (1994) Global restructuring and the law: studies of the internalization of legal fields and the creation of transitional arenas. Case West Reserve Law Rev 44:407–498

UNEP (2004) Desk study on the environment in Liberia

Unruh JD (2009a) Catalyzing the socio-legal space for armed conflict: land and legal pluralism in pre-war Liberia. <http://commission-on-legal-pluralism.com/volumes/58/unruh-art.pdf>. Accessed 11 Aug 2023

Unruh JD (2009b) Land rights in postwar Liberia: the volatile part of the peace process. Land Use Policy 26:425–433

USAID (2009) Governance and economic management assistance program (GEMAP): IBI annual report to USAID 2009. https://pdf.usaid.gov/pdf_docs/PDACN298.pdf. Accessed 23 Mar 2023

USAID (2012) Snapshot: Liberia land commission drafts land rights policy. www.land-links.org/wp-content/uploads/2016/09/USAID_Land_Tenure_LPIS_Land_Policy_Snapshot.pdf. Accessed 20 Mar 2023

USAID Gender-sensitive land tenure impact evaluations. www.land-links.org/wp-content/uploads/2016/10/USAID_Land_Tenure_Gender-Sensitive_Impact_Evaluation_Overview.pdf. Accessed 19 July 2023

USAID Land and governance in rural Liberia: results from the community land protection program. www.land-links.org/wp-content/uploads/2016/09/2018-06-19-CLPP-Policy-Brief.pdf. Accessed 19 July 2023

Vandergeest P (1996) Mapping nature: territorialization of forest rights in Thailand. Soc Nat Resour: Int J 9:159–175

von Benda-Beckmann K (2001) Transnational dimensions of legal pluralism. In: Fikentscher W (ed) Begegnung und Konflikt - eine kulturanthropologische Bestandsaufnahme. Verlag der Bayerischen Akademie der Wissenschaften, München, pp 33–48

von Benda-Beckmann K (2022) Trajectories of legal entanglement examples from Indonesia, Nepal, and Thailand. Leg Plur Crit Soc Anal 54:13–30

von Benda-Beckmann K, Turner B (2019) Legal pluralism, social theory, and the state. J Leg Plur Unoff Law:1–20

von Benda-Beckmann F, von Benda-Beckmann K (2007a) Gesellschaftliche Wirkung von Recht: Rechtsethnologische perspektiven. Reimer Verlag, Berlin

von Benda-Beckmann F, von Benda-Beckmann K (2007b) Transnationalisation of law, globalisation and legal pluralism: a legal anthropological perspective. In: Antons C, Gessner V (eds) Globalisation and resistance: law reform in Asia since the crisis. Hart Publishing, Oxford; Portland, pp 53–80

von Benda-Beckmann F et al (2005) Mobile people, mobile law: an introduction. In: von Benda-Beckmann F et al (eds) Mobile people, mobile law: expanding legal relations in a contracting world. Ashgate, Aldershot; Burlington, pp 1–26

von Benda-Beckmann F et al (2009) Introduction: the power of law. In: von Benda-Beckmann F et al (eds) The power of law in a transnational world: anthropological enquiries. Berghahn Books, New York; Oxford, pp 1–32

Wainwright J (2008) Decolonizing development: colonial power and the Maya. Blackwell Publishing, Oxford; Victoria

Wainwright J, Bryan J (2009) Cartography, territory, property: postcolonial reflections on Indigenous counter-mapping in Nicaragua and Belize. Cult Geogr 16:153–178

Waldorf L (2018) Legal empowerment and horizontal inequalities after conflict. J Dev Stud 55: 437–455

Wallis J (2016) How important is participatory constitution-making? Lessons from timor-leste and bougainville. Commonwealth Comp Polit 54:362–386
Waugh J, Murombedzi J (2016) Social benefits in the Liberian forestry sector: an experiment in post-conflict institution building for resilience. In: Bruch C et al (eds) Governance, natural resources, and post-conflict peacebuilding. Routledge, Milton Park, Abingdon, pp 561–578
Weah J (2012) Women and forests in Liberia: gender policy and women's participation in the forest sector of Liberia. Rights+Resources Initiative
Weilenmann M (2005) Project law - normative orders of bilateral development cooperation and social change: a case study from the German Agency for Technical Cooperation. In: von Benda-Beckmann F et al (eds) Mobile people, mobile law: expanding legal relations in a contracting world. Ashgate, Aldershot; Burlington, pp 233–256
Weilenmann M (2009a) Project law - a legal intermediary between local and global communities: a case study from Senegal. Anthropologica 51:39–51
Weilenmann M (2009b) Project law - a power instrument of development agencies: a case study from Burundi. In: von Benda-Beckmann F et al (eds) The power of law in a transnational world. Berghahn Books, New York; Oxford, pp 156–175
Williams MS (2000) Voice, trust and memory: marginalized groups and the failings of liberal representation. Princeton University Press, Princeton
World Bank (2008) Liberia: insecurity of land tenure, land law and land registration in Liberia. http://www-wds.worldbank.org/external/default/WDSContentServer/WDSP/IB/2008/11/23/000333037_20081123230839/Rendered/PDF/461340ESW0P10310Box334099B01PUBLIC1.pdf. Accessed 11 Aug 2023
World Bank (2017) International Development Association project appraisal document on a proposed grant in the amount of SDR 5.0 million to the Republic of Liberia for a Liberia Land Administration Project
World Bank (2018a) Implementation status & results reports, 30 November 2018. http://documents.worldbank.org/curated/en/803981543941178720/pdf/Disclosable-Version-of-the-ISR-Liberia-Land-Administration-Project-P162893-Sequence-No-03.pdf. Accessed 19 July 2023
World Bank (2018b) Liberia Forest Sector Project, fourth implementation support and REDD+ readiness preparation support mission, February 2 - February 9, 2018, aide-memoire
World Bank (2018c) Liberia: country forest note
World Bank (2018d) Republic of Liberia: Liberia Forest Sector Project (LFSP), 5th implementation support mission, April 30-May 11, 2018, aide memoire
Zalewski M (1993) Feminist theory and international relations. In: Bowker M, Brown R (eds) From cold war to collapse: theory and world politics in the 1980s. Cambridge University Press, Cambridge, pp 115–144
Zerner C (2003) Introduction. Moving translations: poetics, performance, and property in Indonesia and Malaysia. In: Zerner C (ed) Culture and the question of rights: forests, coasts, and seas in Southeast Asia. Duke University Press, Durham; London, pp 1–23

Chapter 4
The Local Time-Space: FPIC in the Fields of Community Forestry

The drafting history of the CRL already foreshadowed some of the challenges that the Liberian community forestry project could encounter in practice. While lawyers tend to frame the non-application of a norm as a black-and-white issue of non-compliance, this chapter takes a different angle.[1] It assumes that we find ourselves in a situation of legal plurality, in which norms are renegotiated, adapted, or rejected depending on the circumstances in the relevant field.

While I first considered examining the *community* field, I then realized that the *community* is not a clear-cut concept and that different understandings coexist. Thus, this chapter does not look at the impact of national law on a given rural community, nor does it examine the geographical space of the community forest. Instead, it explores the renegotiation of FPIC in two communities registering their forest land under the Community Rights Law. These forest-owning communities had not existed as a governance unit prior to the introduction of community forestry. Moreover, even though community forests have a material dimension, they will be understood as 'expressive domains of social relations'[2] rather than a geographical unit.

The community forest fields are made up of a relational network of different actors from different scales with different visions of the community and the forest.[3] Thereby, the community forests constitute an 'entangled landscape'[4] in which multiple fields, temporalities, legalities, and configurations of power overlap. Multiple fields overlap in the sense that many of the other actors constituting the field are co-located in other fields. Moreover, even though the field of the community forest is

---

[1] Griffiths (1986), p. 4.

[2] Gururani (2002), p. 240.

[3] Starblanket (2018), p. 7.

[4] Moore (2005), p. 4.

R. Rösch, *Negotiating Norms*, Interdisciplinary Studies in Human Rights 9,
https://doi.org/10.1007/978-3-031-45910-8_4

a primarily local time-space, actors from national and transnational time-spaces are part of it.[5] Examples include donors and national NGOs.

The community forest as a field also has a temporal dimension. It covers the time span between the adoption of the Community Rights Law and today. However, the history of governmental land grabs and the experience of the civil war also influenced the way the different actors approached notions of community, forests, territory, and law.

This chapter first explores the legally pluralistic context in which the operationalization of community forestry takes place, focusing on national and local legalities, and the actors involved in the operationalization of community forestry.

Secondly, the implementation of FPIC in the fields of the Beyan Poye and the Sehzueplay community forest will be analyzed.[6] This includes an examination of the situations in which FPIC applies, the meaning of consent, and the question of who may grant consent. Moreover, the discourses contributing to the emergence of a specific version of FPIC will be explored.

Thirdly, the emerging understanding of FPIC as a local legality will be examined. According to Imai, self-determination in governance arrangements may be realized if the community fully participates in and consents to it, has the power to determine its implementation, and if transparency and accountability are realized within it.[7] Based on these criteria, special attention will be paid to the governance aspect. Who from the community gives consent? To what extent does customary decision-making interfere with the community forest institutions as introduced by the national legislation? And what are the consequences of these overlapping layers of jurisdictions on gender relations within the authorized community forest? Based on this, the emerging understanding of FPIC will be identified and analyzed.

4.1 Community Forestry in (a Legally Pluralistic) Context

To understand the implementation of community forestry and the renegotiation of FPIC, it is crucial to take the different legalities at play into consideration. Unlike in the national time-space, where existing Liberian law was to a large extent discarded while human rights and project law played a central role, several normative orders exist in the community forest field.

Those normative orders include the national forestry legislation and institutions and (state-sponsored) customary law, institutions, and practices. The community forestry framework is determined by the national time-space, which subsequently

---

[5] de Sousa Santos (2002), p. 85.

[6] A few preliminary results of my research in Sehzueplay and Beyan Poye have already been published in Roesch (2021).

[7] Imai (2009), p. 313.

gets embedded in and adapted to local social matrices.[8] This impacted the implementation of community forestry and explains why community forestry in practice differs from community forestry as envisioned in the national time-space. Additionally, donors and NGOs involved in community forestry bring in their own sets of own norms, values, and practices.[9] Moreover, they act as translators of the national legal framework, thereby creating chains of translation.[10]

The community forest is thus characterized by legal plurality with different normative orders applying to the same field.[11] In the following sections, I will first shed light on the living law applicable to land and natural resources. Secondly, the history of state forestry contributing to the emergence of community forestry will be examined. Thirdly, the operationalization of community forestry, including the participating actors, the legal framework, and FPIC will be explored.

4.1.1 Customary Land and Forest Governance

While the years following the civil war have been characterized by fundamental changes in the forestry sector, including the introduction of community forestry, communal forms of forest and land governance have existed for much longer in Liberia.[12] In some places, they also continue to exist under the regulatory radar of the Forestry Development Authority (FDA).[13] Community forestry, as formalized by the 2009 Community Rights Law, has thus not been introduced in a normative vacuum but in a normative space primarily governed by customary law. Customary law often describes law that is not created by the state, usually not codified, and governs the everyday life of communities.[14] It regularly co-exists with other normative orders in a given space. Sometimes, the term customary living law is used to emphasize its processual and fluid nature, as opposed to the customary law codified by the state.[15] However, given the fact that legalities are in constant interaction, it is challenging to draw a clear line between them.[16] State-sponsored customary law often reified what was perceived as precolonial traditions and provided power to certain institutions, which in turn impacted the living law of communities.

What needs to be taken into consideration when thinking about customary law in Liberia is that the creation of the Liberian state in 1847 by freed People of Color

[8] See also Engle Merry (1997), p. 30.

[9] Vanderlinden (2015), p. 155.

[10] Griffiths (2003), p. 47.

[11] Bavinck (2005), p. 811.

[12] See also Russell et al. (2011), p. 51.

[13] E.g. Manvell (2019).

[14] Tobin (2014), pp. 1ff.

[15] Diala (2017), p. 144.

[16] See also Snyder (1981), p. 74.

significantly interfered with customary law, and little is known about pre-colonial land and natural resource governance.[17] The following sections briefly illuminate the colonial interferences with customary land and forest governance and identify some of the characteristics of contemporary customary law whilst acknowledging that literature is scarce and considerable differences may exist between the different parts of Liberia.

4.1.1.1 Colonial Interferences

In most colonized states, the colonizing powers attempted to codify customary law that did not contradict their interests. However, the codified customary law reflected mainly what the colonizers and, in some instances, anthropologists perceived as the law.[18] Customary law was squeezed into legal categories originating from profoundly different legal systems.[19] It was also regularly assumed that customary law was traditional in the sense that it would not change and be adapted to changing circumstances.[20] Thus, the distorted translation of the customary law gave rise to a new body of law sometimes described as state-sponsored customary law, neocustomary law, or official customary law, which strongly interfered with pre-existing normative systems.[21]

Thereby, the Liberian state also altered gender relations. It can be suspected that the codification of customary law in the so-called Hinterland Regulations was essentially 'a conversation of man with man'.[22] Even though female chiefs existed in some regions of Liberia, the introduction or redefinition of the chieftaincy system contributed to less space for the participation of women in many places, including the governance of land.[23,24]

The colonial interference with customary land governance came in different forms. An increasing area of customary land was alienated. While at first, the settlers only bought coastal land and held it in freehold, national and, to some extent, local elites began obtaining deeds in the Hinterland later.[25] A growing area of customary land was permanently alienated and excluded from customary governance. From the

[17] See also ibid., p. 49; Ford (1990) Ethnic relations and the transformation of leadership among the Dan of Nimba, Liberia (ca. 1900–1940). PhD thesis, State University of New York, p. 93; Abasiattai (1992), pp. 108ff.; Oyěwùmí (1997), pp. 146ff.

[18] See also Tamanaha (2008), p. 410.

[19] See also Nader (1965), p. 11.

[20] Mamdani (2012), p. 49.

[21] See also von Benda-Beckmann and von Benda-Beckmann (2007a), pp. 24–25; Diala (2017), p. 146.

[22] Minh-ha (1989), p. vii; Diala (2017), p. 145; Heemann (2020), p. 190.

[23] Moran (1989), pp. 455ff; Oyěwùmí (1997), p. 125; Aikins (2016), p. 65; Nevin (2017).

[24] Bledsoe (1976), pp. 386–87.

[25] Carter (1982), p. 48.

1940s on, the government alienated customary land for large-scale concessions on a much greater scale.[26] In response, communities that had the financial means tried to obtain deeds for their land. However, the costs for obtaining a deed were high, and some customary authorities also rejected the idea of buying their own land back from the government.[27]

Simultaneously, the state-sponsored customary law also was also renegotiated locally, contributing to the emergence of hybrid legalities.[28] For instance, tribal certificates—a letter of consent by the tribal authorities—were formally only the first step towards obtaining a public land sale deed. However, they were usually seen as conveying full private ownership in rural Liberia.[29] Particularly farmers planting cash crops acquired tribal certificates to protect their expenditure in human labor. While the government did not necessarily accept these *deeds*, they still altered customary land governance by establishing strong deed-like claims to particular parcels of land.[30]

Moreover, the government interfered with customary land governance arrangements by introducing and intensifying ethnicized territorialities. Territoriality, unlike tenure, has an element of jurisdiction and is based on a claim over territory vis à vis other groups.[31] Owners of private deeds were no longer under the authority of customary institutions.[32] Moreover, with the imposition of sovereignty, all undeeded land became public land—even though that was never made explicit.[33] The government began forcing communities to cut boundary lines in the forest between the 1930s and 1970s to delimit customary land.[34] The surveying of the land often hardened the previous fluid boundaries between different communities and interfered with customary modes of governance.[35]

Additionally, the government introduced land use planning and the distinction between forests and other land, creating two separate legal regimes.[36] Forests

[26]E.g. Makain and Foh (2009); Beevers (2015), p. 29.

[27]Munive Rincon (2010), p. 12; Corriveau-Bourque (2011) "This land is not for you" post-war land tenure systems in crisis in Central and Northwestern Liberia. MA thesis, McGill University, pp. 100–101.

[28]De Sousa Santos makes similar observations on Pasargada law (de Sousa Santos 2002, p. 155).

[29]Namubiru-Mwaura et al. (2012), pp. 65–66.

[30]This corresponds to my experiences made in communities in Margibi, Grand Bassa, and Nimba where community members did regularly use the terms deed and tribal certificate interchangeably.

[31]McCarthy (2002), p. 85.

[32]Corriveau-Bourque (2011) "This land is not for you" post-war land tenure systems in crisis in Central and Northwestern Liberia. MA thesis, McGill University, p. 103.

[33]Legal Rules and Regulations governing the Hinterland of Liberia (2001) (Republic of Liberia), art 66; Alden Wily (2007), pp. 80ff.

[34]Alden Wily (2007), pp. 164–65.

[35]E.g. Manvell (2019), p. 27.

[36]An Act for the Conservation of the Forests of the Republic of Liberia (1953) (Republic of Liberia); An Act supplemental to "an Act for the Conservation of the Forests of the Republic of Liberia", passed and approved April 17, 1953 (1957) (Republic of Liberia).

became the realm of the state, thereby ignoring that community jurisdiction regularly extends over forests. Historically, community ownership is derived from the principle of 'who came there first, brushed the bush, and made the land arable'.[37] While the practice of forest brushing usually does not extend to primary forest, customary forest governance often mirrors the rules in place for secondary forest and farmland.[38] For example, the different parcels of the Zavey forest in Bong County are managed by the family who owns the land under customary law.[39] The *de facto* expropriation of forest land by the state interfered with customary law without eradicating it. It will be shown that, unless the FDA actively enforced its claim to the forest in question, communities continued to use their forests for hunting, the collection of non-timber forest products, and the harvesting of trees.[40]

Finally, the war had a disruptive effect on forest governance. Logging companies constructed roads in the dense forest during the war, and these roads often attracted ex-combatants-turned-pitsawers later, who depended on a certain road infrastructure to transport their logs and cut even more paths into the forest.[41] As a consequence, many forest areas that used to be inaccessible could suddenly be used. Simultaneously, a growing number of communities realized the economic value of their forests, the rural labor force decreased with more young people moving to the cities, and an increasing number of community members planting trees instead of annual crops.[42] Some authors also argue that compliance with customary rules has decreased after the war.[43]

4.1.1.2 Contemporary Customary Law

Given the strong interference with customary land and forest governance in the past 150 years and the pre-colonial differences in the different parts of Liberia, it is difficult to draw general conclusions about how forests are governed under customary law today. Additionally, it is difficult—if not impossible—to draw a clear line between state-sponsored customary and customary law and institutions as they have interacted in manifold and complex ways.[44] Customary law adapts to changing

---

[37] Corriveau-Bourque (2011) "This land is not for you" post-war land tenure systems in crisis in Central and Northwestern Liberia. MA thesis, McGill University, pp. 100–101; see also Ford (1990) Ethnic relations and the transformation of leadership among the Dan of Nimba, Liberia (ca. 1900–1940). PhD thesis, State University of New York, p. 105.

[38] Namubiru-Mwaura et al. (2012), pp. 52–53.

[39] Manvell (2019), pp. 21ff.

[40] See Sects. 4.2.1 and 4.3.1.

[41] Cheng (2011) Extralegal groups, natural resources, and statebuilding in post-conflict Liberia. PhD thesis, University of Oxford, p. 239; Manvell (2019), p. 15.

[42] Alden Wily (2007), pp. 183–84; Namubiru-Mwaura et al. (2012), p. 65.

[43] Namubiru-Mwaura et al. (2012), pp. 55–56.

[44] See also Bennett (2009), p. 30; Diala (2017), p. 154.

socio-economic circumstances and it is also a matter of perspective: even community members from one community may have different visions of land tenure.[45]

Nevertheless, scholars identify some characteristics observable in different parts of Liberia. Land ownership is not mono-dimensional; layers of ownership and use rights exist on the individual, the household, the extended family, the quarter, and the town level.[46] Rural communities' sense of ownership usually derives from the principle of aboriginality, according to which the original inhabitants have a stronger claim to the land than newcomers.[47] The owners or managers of the land are the descendants of the 'first lineage to settle in the community'.[48] The extended family, and more specifically, the patriline, is the most common means of accessing land for most rural Liberians.[49] For example, for the Gola and Kpelle of Western Liberia, title and property are passed down between household members having an ancestor in common.[50] Family land is often undeeded. Another characteristic of customary tenure is that land may usually not be alienated.[51]

While most communities—whether on the clan, the town, or the family level—feel that they own the land, the right to manage the land is another question and strongly contextual. In many places, elders, Town Chiefs, family heads, or town citizens exercise jurisdiction over land on a case-by-case basis.[52] They may grant farmland to later-comers or 'strangers'[53]—people who do not originate from the patriline.[54] The reciprocal relationship between strangers and landlords is constantly under negotiation, making land access fluid.[55] For example, while strangers are often not allowed to plant so-called live or tree crops, which establish a strong individual claim to the customary land, some communities have departed from that rule.[56]

The relationship between customary and statutory law in Liberia is thus complex. Statutory law has permeated and transformed customary law and governance

[45] See also Bakker (2009), pp. 109–10.

[46] Namubiru-Mwaura et al. (2012), p. 37.

[47] Unruh (2009), pp. 6–7.

[48] Carter (1982), p. 41.

[49] Brown (2017), p. 274.

[50] D'Azevedo (1962), p. 511.

[51] Carter (1982), p. 41; Unruh (2009), pp. 6–7.

[52] Makain (2010), p. 95; Corriveau-Bourque (2011) "This land is not for you" post-war land tenure systems in crisis in Central and Northwestern Liberia. MA thesis, McGill University, p. 78.

[53] Conceptions of strangers vary considerably in the different parts of Liberia depending on the core tenure unit. Moreover, often strangers are not seen as a homogenous group so that obtaining use rights may be easier for some groups than for others (e.g., Alden Wily 2007, pp. 185–86).

[54] Carter (1982), pp. 38, 42–43; Alden Wily (2007), p. 168; Corriveau-Bourque (2011) "This land is not for you" post-war land tenure systems in crisis in Central and Northwestern Liberia. MA thesis, McGill University, p. 84.

[55] Bedert (2016), p. 6.

[56] Corriveau-Bourque (2011) "This land is not for you" post-war land tenure systems in crisis in Central and Northwestern Liberia. MA thesis, McGill University, p. 89.

arrangements, giving rise to hybrid practices. Different layers of law and jurisdiction continue to exist.

4.1.1.3 State Forestry

The central government introduced the distinction between forests and other land. Hence, besides the customary and state-sponsored customary law and its hybrids, state forest governance emerged.

In the 1950s, the central government began enforcing its claim to forest land to a greater extent.[57] It created national forests controlled by the government, which could no longer be used by communities and granted an increasing number of logging licenses, which also played an infamous role in funding the Liberian civil war.[58] Following the civil war and under the influence of the UN logging sanctions, the legal and political framework for logging concessions underwent considerable changes. A concession review resulted in the cancellation of all existing concessions.[59] The 2006 National Forestry Reform Law, which was adopted to get the logging sanctions lifted, foresees four different types of forest concessions: Forest Management Contracts, Timber Sale Contracts, Private Use Permits, and Forest Use Permits.[60] Between 2008 and 2017, the government issued a considerable number of logging concessions, covering 28% of the Liberian forests.[61] Often these concessions did not meet the legal requirements and the Forestry Development Authority could not prove that community consent—which is mandatory for the negotiation of a social agreement—had been obtained.[62]

The Community Rights Law and its regulation created another governance layer—formalized community forestry under the auspices of the Forestry Development Authority (FDA). Community forests have their foundation in the national legal framework, and it has been shown in the previous chapter that the laws and regulations were adopted with little research on customary forest governance and little consultation with rural communities. Following the decision that community forestry would be introduced and that the government would no longer grant Forest Management Contracts and Timber Sale Contracts, companies increasingly approached rural communities and persuaded them to grant so-called Private Use

[57] An Act for the Conservation of the Forests of the Republic of Liberia (1953); An Act supplemental to "an Act for the Conservation of the Forests of the Republic of Liberia", passed and approved April 17, 1953 (1957); Verschuren (1983), paras 28ff.

[58] Gatter (2002), p. 136; UNSC (2003) Resolution 1521 (2003) adopted by the Security Council at its 4890th meeting, on 22 December 2003, UN Doc S/Res/1521(2003).

[59] Forest sector reform, Executive order No 1 (2006).

[60] An Act adopting the National Forestry Reform Law of 2006 (amending the National Forestry Law of 2000, as amended; and amending an Act creating the Forestry Development Authority, as amended (2006) (Republic of Liberia), ch 5.

[61] World Bank (2018a), p. 7.

[62] Liberia Extractive Industries Transparency Initiative (2013), pp. 100, 111–12.

Permits (PUPs). A PUP is a logging license between landowners and companies that allows for any kind of forest use, including clearing the forest, and lacks regulation.[63] In 2012, the government was hit hard by the PUP scandal that attracted considerable national and international attention.[64] The PUPs covered approximately 23% of the Liberian territory, and not a single one complied with the legal framework.[65] In response, the FDA's Board of Directors and President Johnson Sirleaf imposed a temporary moratorium on logging operations under inactive PUPs, which many companies ignored.[66] Moreover, the Senate investigated the issue, the Forestry Development Authority's (FDA) Managing Director was suspended, and President Johnson Sirleaf founded an independent investigative panel.

At the same time, communities began applying for community forest status to secure their customary rights to forest lands under the Community Rights Law (CRL). In 2011 and 2012, the FDA granted 10 Community Forest Management Agreements—five of them were supported by the USAID-funded Land Rights and Community Forestry Program, and five of them were sponsored by the FDA.[67] Following the cancellation of PUPs, the number of community forest applications rocketed upwards.[68] Because of the shortcuts taken in the authorization of some of the FDA-sponsored community forests, President Johnson Sirleaf also issued a moratorium on community forestry, which remained in effect until April 2014.[69]

More delays in the operationalization of community forestry occurred in 2014 when the FDA suddenly declared that communities could not complete the community forest registration process until one of the FDA's pilot sites had been fully approved.[70] Moreover, no community forests would be authorized before the harmonization of the CRL and its Regulation, with the latter not fully complying with the CRL.[71] However, international actors put the FDA under pressure. Consequently, ten community forests were approved in 2017, and another 12 had completed the process and were awaiting the FDA's board approval in January 2018.[72] By 2019, the FDA had authorized at least 38 community forests, and approximately 100 were still in the registration process.[73] In 2022, 49 applications had been

[63] An Act adopting the National Forestry Reform Law of 2006 (amending the National Forestry Law of 2000, as amended; and amending an Act creating the Forestry Development Authority, as amended (2006), ch 5.

[64] Tetra Tech ARD (2012a), p. 2.

[65] Waugh and Murombedzi (2016), p. 576.

[66] Special Independent Investigating Body (2012), p. 8.

[67] Bluyeama, Gba and Zor, Zor, Nitrian, Gibi, Doru, Nimopoh, Neezonnie, Bloquai, Blei; VOCA/VOCA and Pact (2016), p. 4.

[68] Global Witness (2013), pp. 4–5; Tetra Tech ARD (2013c), p. 2.

[69] Keyser (2013), p. 4; Tetra Tech ARD (2015b), p. 42; VOCA/VOCA and Pact (2016), p. 6.

[70] Tetra Tech ARD (2015b), p. 14.

[71] Tetra Tech ARD (2015a), p. 38.

[72] EU FLEGT (2018), pp. 24–25.

[73] Forestry Development Authority (2019) Community forests statistics. https://lbr.forest-atlas.org/dashboard/communityforestsstatistics. Accessed 21 May 2023.

approved and another 128 communities were still in the authorization process—it is likely that the adoption of the Land Rights Act slowed down the authorization of community forests.[74] According to estimations, up to 3 million hectares—23% of the Liberian territory—could be covered by community forests.[75] Formalized community forestry thus impacts customary land and forest governance on a great scale in rural Liberia.

4.1.2 The Operationalization of Community Forestry

As explored in the previous chapter, the legal framework for community forestry was determined at the national level with strong involvement of external actors. Under the forest legislation, communities need to register their forests to receive a Community Forest Management Agreement.[76] Within and subsequent to the registration procedure, FPIC is realized.[77] In the following section, the actors involved in the operationalization of community forestry, the registration procedure—the so-called 11 steps—and the meaning of FPIC in the forest legislation will be briefly outlined.

4.1.2.1 Actors

While this chapter focuses on the local time-spaces of community forestry, these fields are also linked to the national time-space of forest sector reform. Since 2009, different actors have been piloting the implementation of community forestry in different parts of Liberia. Even though not all of these actors were involved in the case studies presented below, their presence and power in the forest sector reform and the operationalization of community forestry also impacted the way community forestry was implemented in other places. The actors constituting the field of community forestry included donors and international organizations, government actors, NGOs, the Community Forest Working Group, customary authorities, and companies.

Thus, the key actors will briefly be presented to identify the different interests and discourses shaping the operationalization of community forestry. Reminiscent of the 3Cs—conservation, commercial, and community forestry—underlying Liberian forestry, Charles distinguishes between three paradigms or worldviews underlying

---

[74] Agyeman et al. (2022), pp. 145, 149.

[75] World Bank (2018b), p. 18.

[76] Regulation to the Community Rights Law of 2009 with respect to forest lands, as amended (2017) s 2.1.

[77] As shown in the previous chapter.

natural resource governance.[78] These include conservation, economic performance, and community welfare. The different meanings of the forest for the different actors will be examined, as well as their relations and power. It will be shown that Liberian community forestry was operationalized in a climate where the forest was mainly seen as either an economic resource or a place of high biodiversity value. Thereby, the forest as a space of imagination functions as a nodal point and determines the meaning of the community and its rights, including FPIC.[79]

4.1.2.1.1 Donors and International Organizations

Donors and international organizations co-located in the field of development were (and continue to be) very powerful actors. Given the limited financial capacities of the national institutions, they assumed a strong role in the implementation of community forestry, providing technical expertise and funding. Forest-owning communities tended to be very interested in cooperating with them. Thus, donors possessed considerable economic and cultural capital.[80] Moreover, with the different donors and, to some extent, also the Forestry Development Authority (FDA) and NGOs working together, they also had a solid amount of social capital, i.e., a network of mutual recognition.[81]

The donors and international organizations involved in the implementation of community forestry had two key priorities: ensuring that Liberia met its obligations under the United Nations Collaborative Program on Reducing Emissions from Deforestation and Forest Degradation (REDD+) program and enhancing transparency in the logging sector. With Liberia becoming a partner country to REDD+, it has committed to protecting its forests. Both the 2006 National Forestry Reform Law and the 2016 REDD+ strategy reflect the Liberian government's commitment to halt deforestation and forest degradation by increasing the percentage of protected forest areas from 3 to 30%.[82] Donors and conservationists hope that, in the long run, the international emission trading system will help to make conservation-based community forestry economically viable.[83]

Moreover, it is assumed that transparency will improve the governance of natural resources.[84] Therefore, several donor-supported projects and regulatory

---

[78] Charles (1992), p. 384.

[79] Laclau and Mouffe (2001), p. 112.

[80] Bourdieu (1986), p. 244.

[81] Ibid, p. 248.

[82] An Act adopting the National Forestry Reform Law of 2006 (amending the National Forestry Law of 2000, as amended; and amending an Act creating the Forestry Development Authority, as amended (2006), s 9.1.a; National strategy for reducing emissions from deforestation and forest degradation (REDD+) in Liberia (2016) (Forestry Development Authority), p. 14.

[83] VOCA/VOCA (2019b), p. 21.

[84] E.g. Overdevest and Zeitlin (2018), pp. 64–65.

approaches—like the Voluntary Partnership Agreement between the European Union and Liberia and the Extractive Industries Transparencies Initiative—aim at increasing transparency in the logging sector.

Donor projects and INGOs involved in the implementation of community forestry also add another layer of law: their project law.[85] This quasi-law includes their internal procedures, rules for the implementation of their programs, and values that guide their operations.[86] It has been shown in the previous chapter that project law can contribute to behavioral changes, particularly in situations with strong power imbalances.[87] In the implementation of community forestry, 'international best practices',[88] i.e., experiences made with community forestry elsewhere, played a significant role. The donors active in the operationalization of community forestry included the United States Agency for International Development (USAID), the World Bank, and the European Union.

Amongst the bilateral donors active in Liberia, USAID has taken the greatest interest in the forest sector reform. It did so by funding three successive community forest projects: the Land Rights and Community Forestry Program (LRCFP), People, Rules, and Organizations Supporting the Protection of Ecosystem Services (PROSPER), and Forest Incomes for Environmental Sustainability (FIFES). As the Land Rights and Community Forestry Program ended before community forestry was operationalized on a greater scale, the focus of this section will be on PROSPER and FIFES. Both were funded under USAID's biodiversity earmark. They were designed and implemented in compliance with USAID's Biodiversity Policy—which seeks to combat the main drivers for biodiversity loss and deforestation—and the USAID Biodiversity Code.[89]

PROSPER ran from 2012 to 2017 with a budget of approximately 9 million USD and sought to introduce, operationalize, and refine a model for the community management of forest resources.[90] It was implemented by the US consulting company Tetra Tech. Due to the biodiversity earmark of their funding, they clearly envisioned community forestry to be a strategy for protecting the Liberian rainforest. This approach limited the activities they could carry out as any activities contributing to forest conversion were excluded.[91]

PROSPER played a key role in shaping the national framework for the implementation of community forestry in Liberia. They supported the drafting of the 2011 CRL Regulation and took the lead in developing strategies for operationalizing

[85] See also von Benda-Beckmann (2001), p. 39.
[86] See also Weilenmann (2009), p. 157.
[87] See also Murray Li (2009), pp. 253–54.
[88] See also Desai et al. (2012), p. 253.
[89] Biodiversity policy (2014) (USAID), pp. 13, 21.
[90] Tetra Tech ARD (2014a), p. 1.
[91] Tetra Tech ARD (2013e), p. 28.

community forestry.[92] Besides that, PROSPER supported eleven communities in Grand Bassa and Nimba throughout the authorization process.[93] Those eleven forests were seen as pilot community forests to potentially become models for other communities in Liberia. PROSPER took the position that FPIC would have to be implemented (1) before the decision to form a forest community is made, (2) before it is authorized, (3) during the development of the Community Forest Management Plan, and (4) before signing a Commercial Use Contract or conservation agreement.[94] Yet, it found the implementation of FPIC challenging. According to the final report, 'the current 9-step process [for registering a community forest] does ensure FPIC, but it is not currently within the means of the FDA to replicate'.[95] Moreover, the project did not take a particular interest in FPIC's institutional autonomy dimension: 'community forestry under the CRL stipulates a model of community management that is transparent, open, and rooted broadly in the community. In this regard, gender and social inclusion have a critical role to play in community forestry in Liberia'.[96]

Before PROSPER's expiration in 2017, the project Forest Incomes for Environmental Sustainability (FIFES) came into being. It sought to create well-developed and sustainable forest-based enterprises and enhance the capacity of the FDA and communities to sustainably manage community forests and their buffer zones.[97] The prime contractor was the US company ACDI/VOCA. FIFES also clearly linked community forestry and conservation. For example, the provision of eco-friendly alternative livelihood opportunities was one of the core aspects of the project.[98] FIFES took over the 11 community forests from PROSPER and planned to support another seven community forests in their authorization process.[99] However, this plan was abandoned when the Trump administration reduced FIFES' budget from 23 to 16 million USD.[100] Because of the biodiversity earmark of FIFES' funding, FIFES could also not support communities in the negotiation of commercial use contracts with companies, contributing to several of their community forests signing unfavorable logging contracts.[101]

Another major actor is the World Bank. In 2014, the Norwegian and the Liberian government signed a 150 million USD contract to promote the improved management of and increased benefit-sharing in forest areas. The program was managed by the World Bank under the Liberia Forest Sector Project, which ran from 2016 to

---

[92] Tetra Tech ARD (2015d), p. 11.

[93] Tetra Tech ARD (2012a), p. 1.

[94] Aldinger (2015a), p. 2.

[95] Tetra Tech ARD (2017), p. 28.

[96] Tetra Tech ARD (2012c), p. 30.

[97] ACDI/VOCA (2019a), p. 1.

[98] ACDI/VOCA (2016b), p. 3.

[99] Ibid, p. 13.

[100] Liberia Strategic Analysis (2018), p. 12.

[101] ACDI/VOCA (2019a), p. 9.

2023. The project was primarily implemented by the Forestry Development Authority (FDA).[102]

As of 2019, the Liberia Forest Sector Project supported 35 applicant community forests in the authorization process.[103] Thereby, it built upon PROSPER's experiences to a considerable extent.[104] Yet, the World Bank's strategy was more pragmatic than that of the USAID-funded projects. It acknowledged that commercial forestry and conservation are not mutually exclusive and that protected areas are only one strategy for meeting Liberia's goals under the UN REDD+ program.[105] Moreover, the Liberia Forest Sector Project did not only implement so-called alternative livelihood projects but also offered 'social service packages'[106] to communities willing to conserve their forest.

Regarding the community forest registration, the World Bank sided with the FDA advocating for a more streamlined approach with less community participation.[107] The project's 'aggressive timeline and work plan'[108] also put the FDA under considerable pressure. It was feared that this could incite them to take shortcuts in the authorization of community forests.

The World Bank also found that its standards on Indigenous peoples did not apply in Liberia and has been reluctant to accept the applicability of FPIC for the project.[109] However, as the donor, the Norwegian government, took the position that for designating at least 30% of the Liberian forest estate as protected areas, it had to be ensured 'that the Free, Prior, and Informed Consent (FPIC) rights of individuals, [Indigenous], forest-dependent and local communities are respected'.[110] Consequently, the World Bank provided funding for the drafting of national FPIC guidelines, which are not publicly available.[111]

Moreover, in 2013, the European Union (EU) and the Liberian government signed a Voluntary Partnership Agreement (VPA) to promote the trade of legal timber. With funding from the British government and the EU, the VPA Support Unit was established in Monrovia to support the various stakeholders in the process. The VPA Support Unit started issuing licenses in 2018. Those licenses verify that the extracted timber complies with the Liberian legislation. The VPA Support Unit also worked on including Community Forest Management Agreements in the VPA's

---

[102] ACDI/VOCA and Pact (2016), p. 17.

[103] World Bank (2019), p. 16.

[104] Foster-Turley et al. (2018), p. 120.

[105] O'Hagan et al. (2020), p. 363.

[106] World Bank (2019), p. 7.

[107] ACDI/VOCA and Pact (2016), p. 16.

[108] Social Impact's Liberia Strategic Analysis (2016), p. 37.

[109] Nketia et al. (2016), p. 23.

[110] Government of the Republic of Liberia and Government of the Kingdom of Norway (2014) Letter of intent on "Cooperation on reducing greenhouse gas emissions from deforestation and forest degradation (REDD+) and developing Liberia's agriculture sector", p. 6.

[111] Nketia et al. (2016), p. 55; LTS International (2019b).

legality matrix.[112] Moreover, the VPA Support Unit collaborated with the USAID-funded forest projects in working out the details of the authorization procedure for community forests.[113]

4.1.2.1.2 Government Actors

Moreover, government actors, which are primarily located in national time-spaces influenced the community forest fields. The key governmental actor in forestry is the Forestry Development Authority (FDA).[114] It implements the community forest authorization procedure and has considerable power in the approval of community forests.[115] Therefore, it has significant juridical and symbolic capital.[116] Yet, its economic capital is minimal and depends on keeping good relations with donors and companies.

After adopting the CRL Regulation in 2011, the FDA was overwhelmed by the high number of community forest applications. PROSPER found the FDA 'to be largely dysfunctional'[117], and it was 'thrown into even greater disarray in 2013',[118] when large-scale irregularities concerning the PUPs were detected. The FDA is ambivalent with respect to the community forestry project. The heavy involvement of PROSPER and other donors contributed to the FDA's perception that community forestry was imposed upon them. For instance, in 2015, the FDA temporarily stopped the registration of PROSPER's pilot forests, as controversies arose as to whether the PROSPER pilots were also FDA pilots.[119] Ultimately, the FDA recognized the PROSPER pilots as FDA pilots and allowed PROSPER to proceed. Moreover, the FDA did not apply all the tools and procedures developed together with PROSPER and the VPA Support Unit.[120]

The underfunding of the community department also remained a major obstacle to the implementation of community forestry. In 2016, the conservation department had an annual budget of 903,967 USD, the commercial department of 588,862 USD, while the community forestry department received only 237,050 USD.[121] The

[112] Roesch R (1 Mar 2018) Interview with a staff member of the VPA support unit, Monrovia, para 223ff.

[113] Tetra Tech ARD (2015d), p. 11.

[114] An Act to establish the Community Rights Law of 2009 with respect to forest lands (2009) (Republic of Liberia), s 3.1.e.

[115] Regulation to the Community Rights Law of 2009 with respect to forest lands, as amended (2017), ch 6.

[116] Bourdieu et al. (1994), p. 9.

[117] Tetra Tech ARD (2013e), p. 1.

[118] Ibid, p. 1.

[119] Tetra Tech ARD (2015b), p. 14.

[120] Social Impact's Liberia Strategic Analysis (2016), p. 37.

[121] ACDI/VOCA and Pact (2016), p. 8.

department also only had one computer (provided by PROSPER), one internet stick, and one phone card, and regularly had to borrow vehicles from the other departments.[122] Moreover, up to 40% (of the 23 staff members) were too old to perform their functions due to the lack of a retirement plan.[123]

These factors contributed to the FDA's inability to process the community forestry applications as foreseen by the legal framework.[124] When PROSPER began supporting the FDA in screening the community forest applications in 2014, 47 had to be canceled for not meeting the criteria.[125] In 2015, after intensive outreach activities, the number of applications increased even more, aggravating the problem.[126] Therefore, debates of streamlining the authorization of community forests in collaboration with the Liberian Forest Sector Project popped up occasionally.[127]

Simultaneously, the FDA has a vested interest in allowing for the commercial exploitation of community forests as it receives a 45% cut of timber sales.[128] It is an open secret that the FDA brokers Commercial Use Contracts—a logging license for community forests—between communities and companies.[129] A senior FDA official also claimed that political and private actors put the FDA under pressure to fast-track the authorization of community forests.[130] Communities, in turn, reported that FDA had pushed them towards signing logging agreements.[131] Therefore, the relationship between the FDA and communities tends to be strained, with many communities having the perception that the FDA is trying to take away their forest resources.[132]

This is also reflected in the FDA's approach to the community forest registration. Ensuring the effective participation of community members is not a priority for them. For instance, they tried to prevent community involvement in the community forest demarcation, as mandated by the CRL, when they developed demarcation tools together with PROSPER.[133] Moreover, their vision of forestry is very technical, and they put little faith in the capacity of communities to manage their forests. When I told a senior FDA officer about my field research, she asked why I wanted to go there, as most communities do not understand what community forestry is about.[134]

---

[122] Ibid, p. 9.

[123] Ibid, p. 9.

[124] Ibid, p. 13; Liberia Strategic Analysis (2018), p. ix.

[125] Tetra Tech ARD (2014a), p. 31.

[126] Tetra Tech ARD (2015b), p. 16.

[127] ACDI/VOCA and Pact (2016), p. 18.

[128] O'Hagan et al. (2020), p. 364.

[129] Liberia Strategic Analysis (2018), p. vii.

[130] ACDI/VOCA and Pact (2016), p. 4.

[131] Tetra Tech ARD (2013b), p. 12; Tetra Tech ARD (2013c), p. 11.

[132] Aldinger (2015a), p. 4.

[133] ACDI/VOCA and Pact (2016), p. 12.

[134] Roesch R (2018) Informal conversation with a senior staff member of the FDA, Monrovia.

Besides the FDA, the Environmental Protection Agency is involved in the implementation of community forestry. It provided input to the authorization procedure.[135] Moreover, it is a member of the Community Forest Working Group, which carried out awareness campaigns on the forest legislation and monitors the registration of community forests.[136]

4.1.2.1.3 National and International NGOs

National NGOs took a big interest in the protection of Liberia's forests after the war. Through their long-time advocacy for community rights, they possess considerable symbolic and cultural capital.[137] Yet their social and economic capital is limited. Moreover, most of them are based in Monrovia, meaning that they mostly supported communities on an ad hoc basis and less regularly than the donor projects. PROSPER also found that the NGOs lacked the resources to carry out their role as defined by the CRL Regulation.[138]

The Sustainable Development Institute, the lead NGO in that area, regularly worked with six community forests in 2018.[139] Women rights NGOs, besides the Foundation for Community Initiatives, were not directly involved in forestry. In 2018, the Foundation for Community Initiatives supported four community forests.[140] Liberian NGOs, together with international NGOs like Client Earth, also cooperate with the National Union of Community Forest Management Bodies, in which members of the governance institutions are organized, to provide training to members of the community forest governance structures.[141]

Compared to human rights NGOs, conservation NGOs have been more active in implementing community forestry, several of them offering conservation agreements to communities willing to preserve their community forests. For example, Conservation International has been piloting such conservation agreements. It had attempted to collaborate with PROSPER. Yet, PROSPER found their approach to conservation agreements too top-down and voiced concerns relating to FPIC.[142] Moreover, Fauna and Flora International was active in Sapo National Park and the East Nimba Nature Reserve and implemented biomonitoring activities in several

135 Tetra Tech ARD (2015a), p. 32.

136 Tetra Tech ARD (2013a), p. 14; Tetra Tech ARD (2013f), p. 1.

137 Bourdieu (1986), p. 244.

138 Tetra Tech ARD (2017), p. 28.

139 Roesch R (2 Mar 2018) Interview with a senior staff member of a Liberian NGO, Duazon, para 407.

140 Roesch R (4 Jan 2018) Interview with a senior staff member of a Liberian NGO, Monrovia, para 76.

141 Roesch R (2 Mar 2018) Interview with a senior staff member of a Liberian NGO, Duazon, paras 275, 283; Roesch R (28 Nov 2018) Skype interview with a lawyer from an international human rights organization, para 5.

142 Tetra Tech ARD (2015c), p. 16.

community forests with financial support from the mining company Arcelor Mittal.[143]

The Liberian NGO Society for the Conservation of Nature in Liberia has been implementing a conservation agreement project in Barconnie in collaboration with Conservation International.[144] It also received EU funding for working with the GolaMa community forests. Together with the Royal Society for the Protection of Birds, it sought to establish a corridor community forest between two proposed protected areas.[145]

Comparing the agenda of the NGOs involved in Liberia, it is eye-catching that while most Liberian NGOs advocate for a rights-based approach to community forestry, including the right to FPIC, international NGOs are located more on the conservation side.

4.1.2.1.4 The Community Forest Working Group

The FDA established the Community Forest Working Group in 2007 to provide input to the drafting of the CRL and PROSPER reactivated it in 2012.[146] PROSPER supported the working group in disseminating information on the new legal framework, focusing on Nimba and Grand Bassa, where PROSPER had its pilot community forests. Later, outreach campaigns funded by PROSPER targeted the other counties. In Southeastern Liberia, the outreach activities were executed by PROSPER, the conservation NGO Society for the Conservation of Nature in Liberia, and the FDA, while the Sustainable Development Institute and the FDA focused on Central Liberia.[147] The fourth campaign covered Sinoe, Gparpolu, and Grand Gedeh.[148]

Moreover, a subcommittee of the Community Forest Working Group has been in charge of vetting community forest applications since 2013.[149] However, the NGO members of the Community Forest Working Group regularly complained about the lack of information they received from the FDA, rendering their work very difficult.[150] For the community forest demarcation, the socioeconomic resource reconnaissance survey, and the election of the governance structure, it was also common

[143] ACDI/VOCA (2016a), p. 13.

[144] Tetra Tech ARD (2016c), p. 14.

[145] ACDI/VOCA (2016a), p. 13.

[146] Tetra Tech ARD (2013f), p. 1.

[147] Tetra Tech ARD (2014b), p. 14.

[148] Tetra Tech ARD (2016b), p. viii.

[149] Tetra Tech ARD (2013a), p. 14.

[150] Roesch R (2 Mar 2018) Interview with a senior staff member of a Liberian NGO, Duazon, para 445.

that representatives of national NGOs were invited.[151] According to an NGO activist, the Community Forest Working Group was no longer in existence in 2021, with the relationship between NGOs and the FDA again having deteriorated.[152]

4.1.2.1.5 Local Authorities

While local authorities may have considerable power within their communities, their power in the field of community forestry tends to be limited. Most of them have little economic capital. Moreover, with most of the other actors involved in the operationalization of community forestry distrusting their capacities, the social, cultural, and symbolic capital they hold in their communities does not necessarily translate into symbolic capital in the field of community forestry.[153] However, they have cultural capital—knowing the place and understanding the relations between the different stakeholders on the ground.[154]

The CRL grants considerable rights to communities. Communities have the authority to manage forest resources located within community forests.[155] However, forest management decisions have to be made by the new forest governance structure while local authorities' involvement is explicitly debarred: 'the Community Assembly shall elect its officers none of whom shall be a sitting government official'.[156] The rationale for this was the fear of elite capture common amongst international experts and national NGOs.[157]

Sitting government officials include those actors that several authors refer to as 'state-sponsored customary'[158] or 'neocustomary':[159] institutions formally recognized or introduced by the government in 1905 to strengthen its grip over the Hinterland.[160] The official hierarchy ranges from the Town Chiefs, the General Town or Zone Chiefs, the Clan Chief, the Paramount Chief, the District

---

[151] E.g. Office of the Deputy Managing Director for Administration of the Forestry Development Authority (15 Sep 2016) Letter from the FDA to the Honorable Sam Narpal Weh.

[152] Roesch R (17 Feb 2021) Informal conversation with an NGO staff member.

[153] Bourdieu (1986), p. 248.

[154] Ibid, p. 243.

[155] An Act to establish the Community Rights Law of 2009 with respect to forest lands (2009), s 2.2.b.

[156] Ibid, s 4.1.b.

[157] Knight et al. (2013), p. 31; Roesch R (2 Mar 2019) Skype interview with a former senior staff member of a Liberian NGO, para 70.

[158] See also Unruh (2009).

[159] Hartman et al. (2018).

[160] Buell (1928), p. 740; Wrubel (1971), p. 191; Brown (1982), p. 481; Alden Wily (2007), pp. 84ff; Namubiru-Mwaura et al. (2012), p. 73.

Commissioner, to the County Superintendent.[161] Officially, the chiefs are elected, but no elections have been held since 1987.[162] District Commissioners and County Superintendents are employees of the Ministry of Internal Affairs and are appointed by the President of Liberia.[163]

In this context, it should be noted that in some parts of Liberia, chiefs already were well-established customary authorities, while in others, they were introduced by the Liberian government. In the northwestern part of Liberia, chiefs had considerable power in relation to the family, labor, and land, while eastern Liberia was characterized by more egalitarian forms of governance.[164] Yet, already with the emergence of slave trade and new trade routes in the nineteenth century, customary governance along those trade routes underwent changes with the emergence of powerful individuals that had access to goods without deriving their power from the patriline.[165] Moreover, even in places where the chieftaincy system existed before, its role changed due to the government's interventions and also the civil war. Generally, the chiefs lack the power they have in other West African states even though they may have considerable symbolic capital.[166] The power of the state-sponsored governance system is thus strongly contextual and also depends on the persons that assume these positions.[167] Nevertheless, the chiefs are excluded from community forestry, while other customary authorities, such as elders or members of the secret societies, can be elected.

4.1.2.1.6 Companies

Companies tend to have considerable economic capital both compared to communities and the FDA. Yet, given the logging sector's inglorious role in the war, their social and symbolic capital is very limited.[168]

At first, most companies assumed that community forestry would only be relevant in relation to conservation, also because of the heavy involvement of conservationists in the reforms.[169] Yet, after several scandals concerning illegal logging concessions that led to the cancellation of many of these licenses, community forestry

[161] Local Government Law (1972) (Republic of Liberia); Legal Rules and Regulations governing the Hinterland of Liberia (2001), arts 10ff.

[162] Legal Rules and Regulations governing the Hinterland of Liberia (2001), arts 21ff; Namubiru-Mwaura et al. (2012), p. 75.

[163] Sawyer (1995), p. 160.

[164] Liebenow (1969), p. 39; Richards et al. (2005).

[165] D'Azevedo (1962), p. 517; Holsoe (1974), p. 164; Lowenkopf (1976), p. 31.

[166] Brown (2017), p. 280.

[167] Namubiru-Mwaura et al. (2012), pp. 73–74.

[168] Bourdieu (1986), p. 248.

[169] ACDI/VOCA and Pact (2016), p. 11.

became the only way of obtaining a logging license. Companies, therefore, put the FDA under pressure to allow for the commercial use of community forests.

The CRL and its regulation provide little information on whether and how companies can and should support communities in registering their community forests. PROSPER recommended that third parties should not be allowed to support communities.[170] The FDA also made this its official position.[171] Yet, it is generally known that the FDA is unwilling or unable to prevent companies from getting involved during the authorization procedure.[172] A high number of community forest applications overlapped with previous logging licenses, indicating the involvement of logging companies in the registration of community forests.[173] Given the financial constraints faced by the FDA's community forest department and also national NGOs, together with the lack of social infrastructure in many rural areas, companies thus have considerable power in the implementation of community forestry.

4.1.2.2 The 11 Steps

After having explored the actors involved in the operationalization of community forestry, this section explores the community forest registration procedure—the so-called 11 steps.

The national forestry legislation requires communities to register their community forests and complete several steps to get the FDA's approval. The FDA officially endorsed a 9-step handbook developed by the USAID-funded PROSPER project based on the CRL Regulation and made it the benchmark for all community forest authorization procedures.[174] Each of the 9 steps has to be approved by the FDA's Board of Directors.[175] More recently, many actors speak of 11 instead of 9 steps, including the adoption and implementation of a Community Forest Management Plan as steps 10 and 11.[176]

As a **first step**, communities have to send a letter of application to the FDA and pay a 250 USD non-refundable fee.[177] The communities themselves decide on

[170] Aldinger (2015b), p. 5.

[171] Roesch R (15 Jan 2018) Interview with a senior staff member of the FDA, Monrovia, para 363.

[172] Global Witness (2018), p. 3; Roesch R (5 Jan 2018) Interview with a staff member of the Liberia Timber Association, Monrovia, paras 117–20; Sustainable Development Institute (2018b), p. 3.

[173] Keyser (2013), p. 3; Aldinger (2015a), p. 1.

[174] Tetra Tech ARD (2015d), p. 11.

[175] Tetra Tech ARD (2015a), p. 32.

[176] Regulation to the Community Rights Law of 2009 with respect to forest lands, as amended (2017) appendix.

[177] Ibid, ss 2.2, 2.4.

the size of the community unit and describe it in the letter of application.[178] The community self-identification thus essentially takes place before the 11 steps. The FDA then screens the applications for, among other things, the 'conservation of the environment and biological diversity'[179] and the 'sustainable use of the forest resources to maintain the forest ecosystem'.[180] Following the application, the FDA usually encourages the community to establish a Community Forest Organizing Committee that takes the lead in the authorization procedure.[181] Subsequently, the FDA sends a notice to the applicant community announcing the posting of the notices for the socioeconomic resource reconnaissance survey (SER survey).

The **second step** is the posting of notices announcing the SER survey. The FDA recommends posting copies of the notice in at least ten public places and prominent areas within the community, as well as in adjacent communities.[182]

The **third step** is the SER survey itself. The SER survey aims to identify the forest resources located in the forest and explores the relationship between the people and the forest.[183] The tool developed for the SER survey by PROSPER and endorsed by the FDA was a hybrid of the FDA's survey tool used in the award of Forest Management Contracts, i.e. large-scale logging concessions, and PROSPER's community profiling tool.[184]

This is followed by the **fourth step**: the posting of notices for the demarcation for 30 days.[185]

The **fifth step** is the preliminary demarcation and mapping of the proposed community forest.[186] With the support of PROSPER, the FDA endorsed a mapping process consisting of three steps: (1) formal communication to the county, district, chiefdom and community leadership and government institutions, (2) preliminary mapping, whereby community representatives support the FDA in collecting waypoints, and (3) verification of the preliminary mapping including retracing the

[178] An Act to establish the Community Rights Law of 2009 with respect to forest lands (2009), s 1.3 (definition community forest land); Regulation to the Community Rights Law of 2009 with respect to forest lands, as amended (2017), s 2.2; Roesch R (16 Mar 2018) Interview with a staff member of the FDA, Tappita, para 77; Roesch R (4 Apr 2018) Skype interview with a former senior staff member of the LRCFP and PROSPER, para 87.

[179] Forestry Development Authority (2014) Application for the granting of authorized community forestry status: Screening form.

[180] Ibid.

[181] Roesch R (15 Jan 2018) Interview with a senior staff member of the FDA, Monrovia, paras 194ff.

[182] Technical Manager of the Community Forestry Department (2014) Letter from the FDA to the Superintendent of Margibi: Re: Notice to conduct socio-economic and reconnaissance survey in the Beyan-Poye community.

[183] Regulation to the Community Rights Law of 2009 with respect to forest lands, as amended (2017), s 2.5.

[184] Tetra Tech ARD (2015d), p. 12.

[185] Regulation to the Community Rights Law of 2009 with respect to forest lands, as amended (2017) s 2.8.

[186] Ibid, s 2.7.

demarcation line with a GPS and interviews with community members.[187] Later, a boundary line is cut in the bush using machetes to mark the boundaries of the community forest.[188]

Then the results of the SER survey and the mapping are posted in the community for 30 days (**step 6**), and third parties may submit complaints (**step 7**). The FDA must examine complaints concerning forest resources within 30 days, while other grievances will be responded to within 90 days by the relevant government agency.[189]

During **step 8**, the community elects its three-tier governance structure and adopts a constitution and by-laws. The FDA requires the election of the governance structure to be fair and free, overseen by the FDA, and validated by at least two civil society organization representatives.[190] Before the election of the governance structure and the adoption of the constitution and the by-laws, the FDA makes applicant communities sign a so-called affidavit of consent to testify that the communities cooperated with the FDA in the authorization process. The FDA introduced the additional requirement to ensure that the applications are authentic and comply with the legal requirements.[191]

The three-tier governance structure consists of the Community Assembly and its Executive Committee and a Community Forest Management Body (CFMB). The Community Assembly is the highest decision-making body.[192] It meets twice per year, approves the budget and management plan, and receives regular reports from the CFMB.[193] According to the CRL Regulation, each settlement must be represented in the Community Assembly.[194] Usually, the FDA asks the communities to elect two representatives per town.[195]

The Executive Committee of the Community Assembly comprises four members of the Community Assembly and members of the legislature from the county in which the forest is located.[196] It organizes the meetings of the Community

---

[187] Tetra Tech ARD (2016c), p. 16.

[188] Boundary brushing was already a common practice in the 1950s when the government, together with donors, attempted to zone the Liberian forests (Holsoe 1954, pp. 14–15)

[189] Regulation to the Community Rights Law of 2009 with respect to forest lands, as amended (2017), s 2.10.

[190] Office of the Deputy Managing Director for Administration of the Forestry Development Authority (15 Sep 2016) Letter from the FDA to the Honorable Sam Narpal Weh.

[191] Beyan Poye Community (2015) Affidavit of consent.

[192] An Act to establish the Community Rights Law of 2009 with respect to forest lands (2009), s 4.1. a.

[193] Regulation to the Community Rights Law of 2009 with respect to forest lands, as amended (2017), s 3.2.

[194] Ibid, s 3.3.

[195] Roesch R (15 Jan 2018) Interview with a senior staff member of the FDA, Monrovia, paras 271ff.

[196] Regulation to the Community Rights Law of 2009 with respect to forest lands, as amended (2017), s 4.1.c.

Assembly, represents the Community Assembly when it is not in session and receives reports from the CFMB.[197]

The five-member CFMB is elected by the Community Assembly and is in charge of managing the day-to-day affairs of the community forest.[198] It shall, among other things, implement the policies of the Community Assembly and Executive Committee, prepare and implement community forestry rules and a Community Forestry Management Plan with the approval of the Executive Committee, and represent the community forest.[199] Unlike the members of the Community Assembly and the Executive Committee, CFMB officers may be remunerated.[200]

In the constitution and by-laws, the community shall, inter alia, outline the necessary qualifications, duration of tenure, and a code of conduct for members of the governance structure.[201] Most communities adopt a template provided by PROSPER with only minimal amendments.[202]

The authorization procedure is completed with the signing of the Community Forest Management Agreement (**step 9**). The FDA verifies that all the steps have been followed by reviewing the documentation. Practice shows that it has a considerable margin of appreciation in doing so. In some instances, the FDA has not only excluded concessions but also proposed concessions from community forest lands.[203] The Community Forest Management Agreement remains in force for 15 years and can be renewed.[204]

This is followed by **step 10**, the adoption of a Community Forest Management Plan.[205] The Community Forest Management Plan determines how forest resources may be used. The CRL Regulation remains silent on its exact content.[206] The USAID-funded Land Rights and Community Forestry Project drafted a 300-page manual on the adoption of a Community Forest Management Plan, which was not seen as implementable by the FDA.[207] The successor project, PROSPER, developed a Community Forest Management Plan manual for conservation purposes, which the FDA amended to also make it applicable to commercial-use community forests. In 2018, the World Bank, under its Liberia Forest Sector Project, funded a process for

[197] Ibid, s 3.7.

[198] An Act to establish the Community Rights Law of 2009 with respect to forest lands (2009), s 4.2.a.

[199] Regulation to the Community Rights Law of 2009 with respect to forest lands, as amended (2017) s 4.7.

[200] Ibid, s 4.8.

[201] An Act to establish the Community Rights Law of 2009 with respect to forest lands (2009), s 4.1.j.

[202] Roesch R (28 Feb 2018) Interview with a senior legal consultant in the forestry sector, Monrovia, para 203.

[203] Tetra Tech ARD (2016c), p. 17.

[204] Regulation to the Community Rights Law of 2009 with respect to forest lands, as amended (2017), s 7.6.

[205] Ibid, s 8.1.

[206] Ibid, s 8.1.

[207] Sustainable Development Institute (2018a), p. 4.

drafting a more streamlined template led by a legal consultant and involving civil society actors, international NGOs, and the FDA.[208]

Staff members of the USAID projects and the FDA take the position that it is necessary to conduct a forest inventory (including a household survey) and to biomonitor the forest to be able to then zone the forest for different purposes based on suitability criteria.[209] Communities may 'request technical assistance from the Authority, institutions, donors, or individuals with skills in community forest management or other relevant technical areas'[210] in doing so. Hence, companies and other actors may support communities in drafting the Community Forest Management Plan.[211] Subsequently, the Community Assembly adopts the Community Forest Management Plan, and the FDA approves it. It shall be reviewed every 5 years.[212]

During **step 11**, the CFMB implements and monitors the Community Forest Management Plan unless it has entered into a contract with a third party that implements the Community Forest Management Plan on its behalf.[213] Communities that have included conservation in their Community Forest Management Plan may enter into conservation agreements with NGOs or donors. If the Community Forest Management Plan allows for the commercial use of the forest, they may sign a Commercial Use Contract with a logging company.[214] The negotiation of such agreements is left to the communities without FDA oversight. The FDA takes the position that it is 'not [its] role to get involved in negotiating the community and company agreement'[215] and that the deal communities get 'depends on [their] negotiation skills'.[216] The European NGO ClientEarth, together with a Liberian law firm and the National Union of Community Forest Management Bodies, developed a Commercial Use Contract negotiation guide to be used by communities.[217]

---

[208] Ibid, p. 5.

[209] Roesch R (16 Mar 2018) Interview with FIFES staff member based in Nimba, Tappita, paras 50–52; Roesch R (16 Mar 2018) Interview with a staff member of the FDA, Tappita, para 407; Roesch R (3 May 2018) Anonymus source 4, para 11.

[210] Regulation to the Community Rights Law of 2009 with respect to forest lands, as amended (2017), s 8.1.

[211] Roesch R (15 Jan 2018) Interview with a senior staff member of the FDA, Monrovia, paras 52–54.

[212] Regulation to the Community Rights Law of 2009 with respect to forest lands, as amended (2017), s 8.2.

[213] Ibid, s 8.3.

[214] An Act to establish the Community Rights Law of 2009 with respect to forest lands (2009), s 6.4.

[215] Roesch R (15 Jan 2018) Interview with a senior staff member of the FDA, Monrovia, para 444.

[216] Ibid, para 126.

[217] Sustainable Development Institute (2018a), p. 6; ClientEarth et al. (2022) Commercial use contracts legal guide: Negotiating and implementing the CUC in Liberia. https://loggingoff.info/wp-content/uploads/2018/08/ClientEarth2022-CommercialUseContractsLegalGuide.pdf. Accessed 3 Aug 2023.

The USAID-funded project Land Governance Support Activity (LGSA) also planned to produce guidelines for the negotiation of Commercial Use Contracts.[218]

4.1.2.3 FPIC

While the authorization procedure is spelled out in much detail, the question arises where and how FPIC is accommodated in community forestry. According to the CRL's guiding principles, 'any decision, agreement, or activity affecting the status or use of community forest resources shall not proceed without the prior, free, informed consent of the said community'.[219] Community forest resources are defined as anything that can be potentially used by humans in a 'community forest, including but not limited to flora, fauna, and micro-organisms'.[220] With community forests being 'forested or partially forested land traditionally owned or used by communities for socio-cultural, economic, and developmental purposes',[221] the authorization of a community forest is not a pre-condition for FPIC. Instead, it may be assumed that FPIC is to be safeguarded throughout the 11 steps. However, it has been shown in the previous chapter that most actors understand FPIC as not applying beyond that (i.e. in the context of expropriations).

While the CRL Regulation defines nine steps for the authorization of a community forest and two more steps for the land-use decision, the eleven steps can be categorized by four core elements:

1. The identification of the community unit. This happens already through the application and is double-checked during the SER survey.
2. The identification of the forest land. The size and location of the forest are indicated through the application and the SER survey and affirmed during the demarcation and boundary mapping.
3. The introduction of a governance structure and governance rules. In this respect, communities have little leeway but have to follow the requirements of the CRL.
4. The forest-use decision. The letter of application often already refers to the intended forest use. Forest uses are also included in the Community Forest Management Agreement. However, only in the Community Forest Management Plan is the decision on how to use the different parts of the forest finalized.[222]

---

[218] ACDI/VOCA (2019a), pp. 15–16.

[219] An Act to establish the Community Rights Law of 2009 with respect to forest lands (2009), s 2.2.c.

[220] Ibid, s 1.3.

[221] Ibid, s 1.3.

[222] The EPA and the FDA understand the implementation of the Community Forest Management Plan as another element requiring FPIC. However, as during the field research, none of the communities had been at that point, it will not be explored (LTS International 2019a, p. 21).

Community members should be fully informed about each of the elements and they should consent freely and prior to any actions being taken. For the community self-identification and the identification of forest land, the decision should be taken by the broader community. In contrast, after the election of the governance structure, when the decision about the use of the forest is made, the Community Assembly, as the communities' highest decision-making body, must give its FPIC. In the following, it will be explored how FPIC is realized within these four elements in two community forests: Beyan Poye and Sehzueplay.

4.2 FPIC in the Beyan Poye Community Forest

The Beyan Poye community forest is located mainly in Margibi County, with overlaps in Bong and Grand Bassa counties. It is one of the authorized community forests that only the FDA supported in its registration. From Monrovia, it is a 2-h drive to Kakata—the capital of Margibi county—on a paved road, and another 1–2-h drive on a dirt road to Worhn, the capital of Gibi District. Worhn is not located within the forest; the primary forest is several walking hours away. In the following sections, the Beyan Poye community's history and relationship to the forest will be illuminated. Subsequently, the actors constituting the field and the renegotiation of FPIC within the four elements of the community forest authorization—community self-identification, identification of forest land, forest governance, and forest use—will be explored.

4.2.1 Beyan Poye and the Forest

To get a better understanding of the field of the Beyan Poye community forest, this section examines the history of the Beyan Poye community and the relationship between community members and the forest. The Beyan community was founded in the late nineteenth century by Gio and Mano migrants from Nimba.[223] In the early twentieth century, settlers from Grand Bassa joined them. Other ethnic groups settling in the region include the Kpelle, Vai, and Lorma in the 1950s. In 1973, the Beyan and Poye communities merged. According to the FDA, the community consists of two clans, the Gbankanaklor and the Gbarfen clan, and Bassa is the main language spoken, followed by Kpelle.[224]

[223] Forestry Development Authority, Social, economic and reconnaissance survey to establish authorized forest community: Field information easy notes, Beyan Poye, p. 5.

[224] Tetra Tech ARD (2012b), p. 8.

According to estimations, 93 towns are located in the Beyan Poye community forest.[225] It takes about twelve hours to walk from Worhn to the most distant towns in the community forests.[226] Most of the towns in the forest are only connected by dirt tracks, and no cars, motorbikes, or bicycles can reach the towns beyond Poie town, which is located at the boundary of the community forest but several hours away from the actual primary forest.

Land governance in Beyan Poye resembles the observations made elsewhere in Liberia and is characterized by legal plurality. A 1912 Public Land Sale Deed covers at least 8000 hectares of Gibi District, and former Liberian President Tubman granted an Aborigines Land Grant Deed covering 26,493 hectares to Chief Vorvor and the elders and citizens of Gibi Chiefdom in 1953.[227]

At the town level, the land is either owned by the citizens or a certain family. In half of the towns that I visited, town inhabitants held tribal certificates or deeds.[228] In Morris town, the 'Singben family owns the land, the father makes decisions about the land'.[229] In Gearwoe Town, the senior elder had a deed for the farmland.[230] I could not verify whether these towns held deeds or tribal certificates. In the case of Poie Town, the Poie family had a tribal certificate.[231]

Land sales are uncommon in Beyan Poye. Either land is seen as inalienable, or no one has ever shown interest in it. Women argued that 'if we want to sell some land, then the word is one [unanimous decision]. But we don't sell land'.[232] The Town Chief of Worhn confirmed this and explained that 'if anybody have their private land and want to give it to somebody or want to sell it, it's not my knowledge because since I took power, it has not come before me'.[233]

Concerning land management, differences between the towns could be observed. In most towns, the elders seem to be primarily responsible for managing the land.[234] This also was the case for the towns with deeded land.[235] However, the elders cannot decide alone. The district chairman explained that 'the first person who owns the

[225] Forestry Development Authority (2007) 4; Tetra Tech ARD (2012b), p. 8.

[226] Roesch R (8 Dec 2017) Interview with a District Commissioner, Worhn, para 46.

[227] Forestry Development Authority (2007), p. 14.

[228] See also Tribal certificate inventory gains momentum. http://necLiberia.org/doc_download/Tribal%20Certificate%20Inventory%20Gains%20Momentum-rvsed_MMP.pdf. Accessed 21 Jul 2023, p. 1.

[229] Roesch R (11 Dec 2017) Focus group discussion with community members from Morris town, Morris Town, para 11.

[230] Roesch R (11 Dec 2017) Focus group discussion with community members from Gearwoe town, Gearwoe, para 9.

[231] Roesch R (12 Dec 2017) Focus group discussion with community members from Poie town, Poie Town, para 10.

[232] Borma M (10 Dec 2017) Focus group discussion with women from Kaiuway town, Kaiuway Town, para 10.

[233] Roesch R (8 Dec 2017) Interview with a General Town Chief, Worhn, para 50.

[234] Similar observations were made by Liebenow (1969, p. 42).

[235] Poie town, Morris town, Gearwoe town.

land is the *elder* who owns the land [...] He is supported by other stakeholders'.[236] In the case of important land decisions, it thus seems to be common that the elders will consult with more community members.[237] Community members also explained that 'strangers can't just come in the town for one person to receive him. They have to gather people'.[238] But also, if the land of a family is particularly affected, the elders will put the person in touch with the family that has a claim to the land.[239] Another informant remembered that '[our family] have their village [...] because thing like the mission, that was [our family land], they put together the elders and give the mission to the white people. That was agreement with the group to give the mission out'.[240] Hence, what the towns have in common is that several stakeholders are involved in important land management decisions.

Customary law very likely does not distinguish between primary forest and farmland, and the forest plays an important role in the lives of the communities living within and nearby it. One elder explained that 'the forest is the first thing in our life'.[241] Statements like 'we were thinking that the forest is for us, but it's for the government'[242] were very common in all of the towns visited. They indicate that customary ownership extends to the forests. Moreover, they illustrate how the government has interfered with customary governance and the relationship between the people and their land. In addition, the war altered the relationship between the communities and the forest. Many community members spent several years in the forest, hiding from the different armed groups.[243]

Forest products were used in all the towns visited. One community member explained that the forest

> was used for hunting, used, people fell those big logs. Because the only means of living here is through farming. Our people used to use the forest, cut down the big trees, plant the bitterballs, because when you plant the bitterballs in the forest, it can geminate and produce pepper and all of that.[244]

---

[236] Roesch R (8 Dec 2017) Interview with Beyan Poye CFMB officer 1, Worhn, para 152; please note that while he uses the language of ownership, he seems to refer to the management or governance of customary land.

[237] E.g. Kaiuway town, Gbarnyou town (Roesch R (8 Dec 2017) Interview with Beyan Poye CFMB officer 2, Worhn, para 118).

[238] Roesch R (12 Dec 2017) Focus group discussion with women from Poie town, Poie Town, para 11.

[239] Roesch R (8 Dec 2017) Interview with Beyan Poye CFMB officer 1, Worhn, para 160.

[240] Roesch R (8 Dec 2017) Interview with a General Town Chief, Worhn, para 2.

[241] Roesch R (11 Dec 2017) Focus group discussion with community members from Gearwoe town, Gearwoe, para 21.

[242] Roesch R (11 Dec 2017) Focus group discussion with women from Morris town, Morris Town, para 23.

[243] Roesch R (8 Dec 2017) Interview with a District Commissioner, Worhn, para 28; Roesch R (2017) Informal conversations with community members in Beyan Poye.

[244] Roesch R (8 Dec 2017) Interview with a District Commissioner, Worhn, para 30.

Those communities deeper in the forest made their farms in the forest, and those living at the fringe of the forest collected rattan or cut wood to build furniture or houses, installed traps, produced charcoal, and collected snails and wild palm nuts.[245]

In 2011, community members granted a Private Use Permit (PUP) to the Nigerian logging company Akewa. The PUP covered more than 22,163 hectares of the forest and was valid for 13 years.[246] The legal basis was the Aborigines Land Grant Deed of Chief Vorvor and the elders and citizens of District Gibi. However, most community members were not aware of any deed.[247]

After the cancellation of the PUP, community members sent a letter of application to the FDA asking for the authorization of their 22,000 ha-community forest in September 2013.[248] The FDA made the Beyan Poye forest a pilot community, supporting it in going through the first 9 steps and, in 2017, it authorized the Beyan Poye community forest.[249] In March 2017, community members and the company Akewa entered into a Commercial Use Contract with a duration of 15 years.[250] The company started its logging operations at the beginning of the rainy season in 2018.

4.2.2 *Mapping the Field: Actors in Relation*

The Beyan Poye community forest is a field comprised of several actors. It is a predominantly local time-space even though it has a multiscalar dimension with several actors active at different scales. The actors constituting the field include the Forestry Development Authority (FDA), the logging company Akewa, NGOs and donors, and customary authorities. However, it was also characterized by participatory exclusions, most notably that of rural women. The following sections explore the capital of each of the different actors, their relations, and their vision of the forest and the community.

[245] Borma M (10 Dec 2017) Focus group discussion with women from Gays Town, Gays Town, paras 42, 47; Borma M (11 Dec 2017) Focus group discussion with women from Gearwoe town, Gearwoe Town, para 22; Roesch R (11 Dec 2017) Focus group discussion with women from Morris town, Morris Town, para 28.

[246] Private Use Permit between the Forestry Development Authority and the People of Gibi District, Margibi County (2011), arts 3, 4; Tetra Tech ARD (2012b), p. 8.

[247] Tetra Tech ARD (2012b), p. 8.

[248] Barnyou (5 Sep 2013) Letter from Sam Barnyou to the FDA: Letter of application: Beyan Poye, p. 1.

[249] Tetra Tech ARD (2015b), p. 14.

[250] Forestry Development Authority (2017) Community Forest Management Agreement between the Beyan Poye Community Forest Management Body and Akewa Group of Companies Liberia Inc.

4.2.2.1 Forestry Development Authority

The Forestry Development Authority is generally a powerful actor, possessing more economic and juridical capital than community members.[251] Following an invitation by the District Commissioner, the FDA visited Beyan Poye on a regular basis since 2009 and assessed the tree species in the forest.[252] It also approved the request for a Private Use Permit (PUP) in 2011. Community members reported that the FDA had put them in touch with the logging company Akewa.[253] After the signing of the PUP, the FDA brokered a social agreement between Akewa and the community.[254]

The FDA also educated the community about community forestry.[255] Community members remembered their first encounter with community forestry as 'the FDA told us that they need the forest'.[256] In 2015, the FDA decided that Beyan Poye would become a pilot community forest.[257] Without consulting with the Community Forest Working Group, the FDA informed PROSPER that they would need to suspend the 9-step procedure in their pilot sites until Beyan Poye had completed the process. At the same time, they expected PROSPER to develop the tools necessary for completing the 9 steps in Beyan Poye. Following lengthy negotiations, including the adoption of a resolution by the Community Forest Working Group, the FDA gave in. The FDA paid for the SER survey.[258] The posting of the SER notices was supported by PROSPER and implemented by four FDA officers.[259] According to an FDA official, the FDA did not get involved in the negotiations between Akewa and the community.[260]

4.2.2.2 Akewa

The Nigerian logging company Akewa possesses considerable economic and social capital—due in part to its good connections with the FDA.[261] It has been active in

[251] Bourdieu et al. (1994), p. 9; Roesch R (10 May 2018) Informal Skype conversation with two staff members of an international NGO.

[252] Roesch R (8 Dec 2017) Interview with a District Commissioner, Worhn, para 46.

[253] Ibid, paras 106, 124.

[254] Tetra Tech ARD (2012b), p. 8.

[255] Roesch R (8 Dec 2017) Interview with Beyan Poye CFMB officer 1, Worhn, paras 27ff.

[256] Roesch R (11 Dec 2017) Focus group discussion with community members from Morris town, Morris Town, para 23.

[257] Tetra Tech ARD (2015b), p. 14.

[258] Technical Manager of the Community Forestry Department (2015) Submission of socio-economic cost estimated for the revised Beyan Poye community forest, p. 1.

[259] Forestry Development Authority and Community Forest Working Group (2014) Report on posting of 30 days notice for socio-economic and reconnaissance survey in Beyan Poye community forest, Worhn, Margibi County, p. 1.

[260] Roesch R (15 Jan 2018) Interview with a senior staff member of the FDA, Monrovia, para 444.

[261] Bourdieu (1986), p. 248.

Liberia for several years. The FDA awarded it a Timber Sale Contract in Grand Bassa in 2010 and the above-mentioned PUP in 2011.[262] Moreover, it signed another Commercial Use Contract in Grand Bassa.[263]

According to the District Commissioner, the first meeting between Akewa and community representatives took place after they had informed the FDA about the commercial value of their forest.[264] Some community members reported that 'Abigail [the CEO of Akewa] called the people from the different towns'[265] to the meeting, where the application letter to the FDA was drafted. Even though it is difficult to reconstruct when and how exactly Akewa got involved during the 11 steps, the interviews strongly indicate that Akewa was continuously present.

As of 2018, Akewa had not paid its outstanding land rental fees but had started its operations.[266] In 2019, a Liberian newspaper reported that Akewa's president was on the run and searched by the Liberia Revenue Authority for submitting a fake tax clearance.[267] In 2020, community members were still complaining about the company's failure to pay its land rental fees.[268] Two years later, the situation had escalated to the extent that community members planned to sue Akewa for neither implementing its social agreement nor paying land rental and harvesting fees.[269]

4.2.2.3 NGOs and Donors

PROSPER found that no NGOs were active in the Beyan Poye on a permanent basis.[270] PROSPER had considered working with the community but refrained due to the PUP and their funding restrictions, which would not have allowed for working

---

[262] Harris et al. (2012-13), p. 25.

[263] Sherman and Harding Giahyue (2022) Akewa: The Nigerian company breaking Liberia's logging laws unpunished. Daily Observer. https://www.Liberianobserver.com/akewa-nigerian-company-breaking-Liberias-logging-laws-unpunished. Accessed 4 Aug 2023.

[264] Roesch R (8 Dec 2017) Interview with a District Commissioner, Worhn, para 108.

[265] Roesch R (10 Dec 2017) Focus group discussion with community members from Gays Town, Gays Town, paras 13–14.

[266] Sustainable Development Institute (2018c), p. 8.

[267] Front Page Africa (2019) Liberia Revenue Authority investigates Akewa Group of Company for parading "fake tax clearance". https://frontpageafricaonline.com/news/Liberia-revenue-authority-investigates-akewa-group-of-company-for-parading-fake-tax-clearance/?fbclid=IwAR2VX_m5jd0bRftxj84xGYRs52rBdXljd97ptOnsd-uNNFEabymejbmhGIs. Accessed 21 Jul 2023.

[268] Giahyue (2019) Liberia: Two communities sign logging contracts, but sector woes loom. Front Page Africa. https://frontpageafricaonline.com/county-news/Liberia-two-communities-sign-logging-contracts-but-sector-woes-loom/. Accessed 21 Jul 2023; Louis et al. (2020), p. 11.

[269] Joint Implementation Committee of the Liberia-EU FLEGT Voluntary Partnership Agreement (2022) Aide memoire: Session of the 9th joint implementation committee, March 21–24, 2022, Monrovia, p. 30; Sherman and Harding Giahyue (2022) Akewa: The Nigerian company breaking Liberia's logging laws unpunished. Daily Observer. https://www.Liberianobserver.com/akewa-nigerian-company-breaking-Liberias-logging-laws-unpunished. Accessed 4 Aug 2023.

[270] Tetra Tech ARD (2012b), p. 8.

with a logging company. They also feared that providing training on the legal framework could trigger intra-community conflicts, as community members could come to realize the illegality of the PUP.[271] However, PROSPER and other donors indirectly influenced the field through their development of many tools for the operationalization of community forestry.

4.2.2.4 Local Authorities

The capital of local authorities is difficult to assess. While their economic capital is mostly low, they often have a good network of contacts, i.e. social capital, at their disposal.[272] External actors, such as companies, depend on their cooperation. Moreover, their symbolic capital—their legitimacy within the community—tends to be high. However, the power imbalances between different community members were striking, and particularly those that already possessed cultural, social, and symbolic capital beforehand could use this capital to gain access to the field of community forestry.[273]

In Beyan Poye, local authorities play a crucial role in land and natural resources governance. The District Commissioner settles intra-town disputes, and the Clan Chief resolves disputes over the use of forest resources.[274] The Town Chiefs handle disputes relating to the use of non-timber forest products and wildlife, while the zoes[275] and elders investigate those relating to farmland. While the elders' power has eroded during and after the war in many parts of the country, this does not seem to apply to Beyan Poye to the same extent.[276]

Beyan Poye has a powerful District Commissioner with good relations with the Paramount Chief, the women leader, and the youth leader.[277] He also holds quarterly meetings with the Town Chiefs in Worhn.[278] Moreover, he had access to the field of post-conflict forest reform and participated in the regional consultation on the CRL in Buchanan.[279] Furthermore, the FDA invited the District Commissioners from different counties on various occasions to hear their perspectives on the law. At one

[271] Ibid, p. 9.

[272] Bourdieu (1986), p. 248.

[273] Ibid, p. 244.

[274] Forestry Development Authority, Social, economic and reconnaissance survey to establish authorized forest community: Field information easy notes, Beyan Poye, p. 36.

[275] Zoes are local authorities that derive their power from their leadership role in the secret societies common in many parts of Liberia (e.g. Käihkö 2019, p. 7).

[276] See also Namubiru-Mwaura et al. (2012), p. 77.

[277] Tetra Tech ARD (2012b), p. 8.

[278] Roesch R (8 Dec 2017) Interview with a District Commissioner, Worhn, para 18.

[279] Ibid, para 28.

of those meetings, the District Commissioner told the FDA to come and visit the district to assess whether they would be eligible for community forest status.[280]

It was also the District Commissioner, together with the Paramount Chief, the women leader, and the youth leader, who applied for the PUP.[281] Moreover, the District Commissioner played an important role in the community forest authorization procedure. He described himself as the 'point man for all of these things [...] running in between FDA, the community, and the citizens, calling meeting, before we reach to the formation of these various assemblies [governance structure]'.[282] Together with the Paramount Chief, he invited representatives from the different towns to the meeting, where the application letter to the FDA was written.[283] The application letter was signed by seven elders, the youth leader, the women leader, the two Clan Chiefs, the Paramount Chief, and the representative of a development association. It was attested to by the District Commissioner.[284]

Local authorities also attempted to become members of the governance structure. In violation of the CRL, the District Commissioner was elected as a Community Assembly and Executive Committee member. The district women leader equally became a member of the Community Assembly but had to step back after she became the General Town Chief of Worhn, and the district youth leader became a CFMB officer. Moreover, many of the Community Assembly members are elders.[285] In the CFMB, in contrast, where literacy is a precondition for being elected, the youth is more strongly represented, and four of the five members identified themselves as youth.[286]

Community members also reported that the elders, the chiefs, and the District Commissioner were involved in the negotiations with Akewa.[287] These observations indicate that powerful local authorities understood the forest from the onset as an economic resource and got involved in the community forest project, either formally or informally.

280 Ibid, para 46.

281 Tetra Tech ARD (2012b), p. 8.

282 Roesch R (8 Dec 2017) Interview with a District Commissioner, Worhn, para 102.

283 Roesch R (8 Dec 2017) Interview with a General Town Chief, Worhn, paras 30–31.

284 Barnyou (5 Sep 2013) Letter from Sam Barnyou to the FDA: Letter of application: Beyan Poye, p. 2.

285 Seven of the 18 CA members, who revealed their position in the community in the attendance sheets, were elders.

286 Roesch R (8 Dec 2017) Informal conversation with CFMB officers in Beyan Poye, Beyan Poye.

287 Roesch R (10 Dec 2017) Focus group discussion with community members from Gays Town, Gays Town, para 13; Roesch R (12 Dec 2017) Focus group discussion with community members from Poie town, Poie Town, para 19.

4.2.2.5 Gendered Participatory Exclusions

In line with findings from other regions, the gender relations in Beyan Poye seem to have changed during and after the war. Disrupting the 'continued coloniality of gender and of power',[288] (educated) women can access political offices like chieftaincy positions more easily now.[289] For example, the General Town Chief of Worhn is a woman. Moreover, the female CFMB officer repeatedly explained that 'since Ellen [former President Ellen Johnson Sirleaf] got in the Chair, she says that if man speaks, woman too should speak also'.[290] This sentiment was shared by other women. One woman from Morris town argued that 'we hear some [get some information]. Because every meeting they have, they have to include women's name'.[291]

In Beyan Poye, women leaders or chairladies and women groups are also well-established institutions. The function of the women's groups and the tasks assumed by the women leader or chairlady differ from town to town. In Gays and Kaiuway town, for instance, the women reported that they had founded a cooperative (kuu[292]) supporting each other in making their farms.[293] Such cooperatives are particularly common when men cannot support them in the family farm work, for example, when they seek wage labor or perform other duties like brushing roads or constructing public buildings.[294] Moreover, women's saving groups (susus) are widespread.[295] Some women's groups also provide financial support to women in childbed, who are sick, or for funeral costs.[296]

Women leaders or chairladies may settle disputes primarily amongst women, and they assume management positions in the women's groups. The war and the influence of external actors have increased their influence. One of them explained that 'when we are talking the case [judicial hearing], the Carter Center [US NGO] tells the elders that the chairlady should come and sit'.[297] Nevertheless, dispute

[288] Aikins (2016), p. 62.

[289] Namubiru-Mwaura et al. (2012), pp. 75–76.

[290] Roesch R (12 Dec 2017) Focus group discussion with women from Poie town, Poie Town, para 16; women in other parts of Liberia made similar statements (see also Tripp 2015, p. 107).

[291] Roesch R (11 Dec 2017) Focus group discussion with women from Morris town, Morris Town, para 30.

[292] See also Liebenow (1969), p. 41.

[293] Borma M (10 Dec 2017) Focus group discussion with women from Gays Town, Gays Town, para 165; Borma M (10 Dec 2017) Focus group discussion with women from Kaiuway town, Kaiuway Town, para 91.

[294] See also Carter (1982), p. 79; Namubiru-Mwaura et al. (2012), p. 68.

[295] E.g. Borma M (10 Dec 2017) Focus group discussion with women from Gays Town, Gays Town, paras 147, 163.

[296] Borma M (12 Dec 2017) Focus group discussion with women from Worhn, Worhn, paras 124–27.

[297] Roesch R (8 Dec 2017) Interview with a General Town Chief, Worhn, para 19.

settlement relating to land and natural resources seems to remain mainly in the hands of men.[298]

During the 11 steps, women were involved to varying degrees. The 11-step documentation and interviews indicate that the district chairlady was actively involved in the community forest authorization procedure.[299] However, the district chairlady usually lives in Worhn. Other women explained: 'We come here from the cassava hamlet [farming village] [. . .] For them to say, this is our chairlady from the hamlet, here's your chair, no way!'[300] Consequently, none of the women from the towns closer to or within the forest had the chance to take a key role in the 11 steps. Unless directly invited, most of them did not attend meetings in other towns: 'the business meeting that you talk, the women's meeting [. . .], here is the Hinterland, you can't go and everybody goes. But the chairlady looks sometimes into it'.[301] Many towns reported that they send their women leaders to meetings in Worhn or that the town elders selected a woman to participate.[302]

Amongst the participants in the SER survey, 31.25% were women. No women participated in the mapping and demarcation of the community forest.[303] As boundary cutting and *brushing roads* are usually seen as men's business, the absence of women from the demarcation and mapping indicates that the gender-based division of labor also translated into community forest registration.[304] However, it is not uncommon for women to have their own farmland.[305] Their lack of participation in the mapping and demarcation increases the risk that their individual land rights are not taken into consideration. Some women also complained about not having been informed about the demarcation: 'We see people, even when it started we were

[298] See also Namubiru-Mwaura et al. (2012), pp. 76, 90.

[299] Roesch R (8 Dec 2017) Interview with a General Town Chief, Worhn, para 4.

[300] Borma M (10 Dec 2017) Focus group discussion with women from Gays Town, Gays Town, para 134.

[301] Ibid, para 118.

[302] Ibid, paras 97, 107; Borma M (10 Dec 2017) Focus group discussion with women from Kaiuway town, Kaiuway Town, para 68; Borma M (12 Dec 2017) Focus group discussion with women from Worhn, Worhn, para 57.

[303] Forestry Development Authority (17 Oct 2015) Attendance sheet mapping; Borma M (10 Dec 2017) Focus group discussion with women from Gays Town, Gays Town, paras 22, 88; Borma M (10 Dec 2017) Focus group discussion with women from Kaiuway town, Kaiuway Town, para 34; Roesch R (11 Dec 2017) Focus group discussion with community members from Gearwoe town, Gearwoe, para 17; Roesch R (12 Dec 2017) Focus group discussion with women from Poie town, Poie Town, para 51.

[304] Mayer (1951), pp. 19–20; Carter (1982), p. 79; Borma M (10 Dec 2017) Focus group discussion with women from Gays Town, Gays Town, para 22.

[305] E.g. some women in Gaerwoe town have individual cassava farms that they run without male support (Borma M (11 Dec 2017) Focus group discussion with women from Gearwoe town, Gearwoe Town, paras 99, 104). Moreover, in nearly all of the towns visited female-headed households existed (e.g. Borma M (10 Dec 2017) Focus group discussion with women from Gays Town, Gays Town, para 173; Roesch R (11 Dec 2017) Focus group discussion with women from Morris town, Morris Town, para 116).

afraid. We say, "But this much noise, where does it come from?" They say they send people, they are cutting this forest. Government sent them!'[306]

Regarding the involvement of women in the governance structure, several community members were aware of the external pressure to include women. CFMB members explained that they introduced a 50% women's quota for the Community Assembly.[307] In reality, this was not the case. The by-laws just require the election of two women into the Community Assembly, and, in 2017, 11.9% of the Community Assembly members were women.[308] According to a 2020 report, the women's percentage had been augmented to 35%.[309]

Not a single woman was elected to the Executive Committee, and just one woman—as required by the CRL—was a CFMB officer. Moreover, the female CFMB officer had not been involved in the community forest registration, lived in Monrovia, and was asked to run because 'they needed a female'.[310] While her lack of experience with community forestry could have undermined her position in the CFMB, a national NGO that invited specifically one male and one female CFMB member from different community forests for training helped her bridge the knowledge gap.[311]

Mobility, formal education, and gender stereotypes were the key reasons for the gendered exclusions in community forestry. Carter notes that rural women tend to be less mobile than men.[312] While it is common for men to move between the different towns regularly, women's farm and care work prevent such mobility. Women from Gearwoe town similarly explained that they do the farm work and pay young men to take their products to the market in Worhn.[313] This is even more the case for elderly women taking care of small children and the ones living in smaller villages.[314] Moreover, a Community Assembly member from Charben held that the two repre-

[306] Borma M (10 Dec 2017) Focus group discussion with women from Kaiuway town, Kaiuway Town, para 38.

[307] Roesch R (9 Dec 2017) Focus group discussion with community members from Wairlii Town, Wairlii Town, para 13; Roesch R (11 Dec 2017) Focus group discussion with community members from Gearwoe town, Gearwoe, para 13.

[308] Beyan Poye Community Forest (2017) Beyan Poye by-laws, art I s 4; Forestry Development Authority (2017) Members of the Community Assembly, Executive Committee, and Community Forest Management Body: Beyan Poye.

[309] Louis et al. (2020), p. 13.

[310] Roesch R (10 Dec 2017) Interview with Beyan Poye CFMB officer 5, Worhn, para 14.

[311] Ibid, para 91.

[312] Carter (1982), p. 112.

[313] Borma M (11 Dec 2017) Focus group discussion with women from Gearwoe town, Gearwoe Town, paras 90–92.

[314] E.g. Borma M (10 Dec 2017) Focus group discussion with women from Kaiuway town, Kaiuway Town, para 106.

sentatives from his town were men 'because they [the women] are scared, they can't walk for 5 h [...] they can feel weak'.[315]

Moreover, class and education may limit the ability of women to become a member of the governance structure.[316] In one town, a woman explained that the chairlady went to one of the meetings because she is 'really the main person. She is the one who runs after the things because she understands English'.[317] Illiteracy also negatively impacts the effective participation of women. One female Community Assembly member complained that she did not receive any documents because of her illiteracy.[318] Consequently, she could also not take the documents back to her town to share them with her fellow residents. Other female Community Assembly members equally depended on the willingness of their male colleagues to explain the documents to them.[319] Moreover, they cannot become members of the Executive Committee and the CFMB without some degree of formal education.[320] Female Community Assembly members also reported being silenced in meetings.[321] Furthermore, the exclusion of women from the governance structure can be exacerbated by the predominantly patrilocal Liberian marriage system: married women are often strangers in their community as they move to their husband's community upon marriage.[322] The other town inhabitants may thus not see them as being able to speak on behalf of the town.[323] At the same time, their loyalty to their community of origin may be questioned as well, meaning that they can represent neither of the two.[324]

In theory, the representative approach to community forestry in Liberia foresees that the town representatives will share the information within their town. However, many women, particularly those from Worhn, complained that the 'top top elders'[325] did not share information with them. Other women, particularly in the more remote towns, held that the elders shared all the information with them. In contrast to these assertions, their level of knowledge was not better than in the towns where women

[315] Roesch R (10 Dec 2017) Interview with Beyan Poye Community Assembly member 2, Kaiuway, para 23.

[316] See also Onzere et al. (2020), p. 33; Agyeman et al. (2022), p. 149.

[317] Roesch R (12 Dec 2017) Focus group discussion with women from Poie town, Poie Town, para 38.

[318] Roesch R (11 Dec 2017) Interview with Beyan Poye Community Assembly member 1, Gearwoe, para 2.

[319] Louis et al. (2020), p. 13.

[320] Beyan Poye Community Forest (2017) Beyan Poye by-laws, arts iii s 1, iv s 1(d).

[321] Louis et al. (2020), p. 15.

[322] Namubiru-Mwaura et al. (2012), p. 40.

[323] Borma M (10 Dec 2017) Focus group discussion with women from Kaiuway town, Kaiuway Town, para 32.

[324] See also Corriveau-Bourque (2011) "This land is not for you" post-war land tenure systems in crisis in Central and Northwestern Liberia. MA thesis, McGill University, p. 95.

[325] Borma M (12 Dec 2017) Focus group discussion with women from Worhn, Worhn, paras 42–44.

complained about being excluded.[326] A possible explanation for this phenomenon is that often dissent within a community is only possible when the grip of customary authorities is loosened.[327] This is very likely the case for Worhn, with its more diverse population, where the women there were particularly vocal in expressing their criticism.

Moreover, the Community Assembly members should also take their constituents' concerns and wishes back into the Community Assembly and speak on behalf of their community. However, a woman from Gays town summarized her experience as 'our big people, they are the discussants. And we, the children, cooperate with them'.[328] In another town, similarly, the women explained that only 'the big people are talking it'.[329]

To summarize, the field of the community forest was constituted by various actors, including the FDA, the company Akewa, and local leaders, while women—besides particularly vocal women leaders—have largely been excluded.

4.2.3 *FPIC in Practice*

Having mapped the field of the Beyan Poye community forest, the question arises of how FPIC was renegotiated. This section explores the realization of FPIC within the four core elements of the community authorization procedure: (1) Community self-identification, (2) identification of community forest land, (3) introduction of the governance structure and rules, and (4) forest-use decision.

4.2.3.1 Community Self-Identification

First of all, the question of the emerging social identity of the *community* will be examined: is it a pre-existing governance unit, is it a conglomerate of towns with forest use rights, or has the community forestry project created a new community? How was the decision to self-identify as a community taken?

The message of community forestry reached Beyan Poye already during the drafting of the CRL.[330] After visiting the Beyan Poye forest, the FDA confirmed

---

[326] E.g. in Wairlii Town, where the women did not know anything about the community forest other that the company has promised to build roads, schools, and a town hall (Borma M (9 Dec 2017) Focus group discussion with women from Wairlii Town, Wairlii Town).

[327] Corriveau-Bourque (2011) "This land is not for you" post-war land tenure systems in crisis in Central and Northwestern Liberia. MA thesis, McGill University, p. 105.

[328] Borma M (10 Dec 2017) Focus group discussion with women from Gays Town, Gays Town, para 91.

[329] Borma M (11 Dec 2017) Focus group discussion with women from Gearwoe town, Gearwoe Town, para 35.

[330] Roesch R (8 Dec 2017) Interview with a District Commissioner, Worhn, para 28.

its eligibility for community forest status in 2009 and asked the community to file an application.[331] However, instead of doing so, the community applied for a Private Use Permit (PUP). According to the PUP application letter submitted by the District Commissioner, the 'citizens of Worhn'[332] requested a PUP.

Following the cancellation of the PUPs, an elder submitted a letter of application on behalf of the 'citizens of the Beyan Poye community in Gibi District'[333] to the FDA in 2013. The SER survey found that the forest was owned by 21 towns.[334] Ten of the towns belong to the Gbarnfen clan and 11 to the Gbarjorkor clan.[335] While the language of clans is used in the SER survey, the interviewees were only referring to the Beyan section and the Poye section when describing the community forest. Moreover, the proximity to Monrovia and the war have contributed to considerable migration in the area. In all towns, several languages are spoken. In most of them,[336] Bassa is the principal language, while in two,[337] it is Kpelle.[338]

However, the map of the Beyan Poye community forest indicates that there are many more settlements within the community forest. PROSPER also found that the Beyan Poye community comprises 93 towns.[339] Moreover, the inclusion of Worhn indicates that the local authorities felt that community forest governance should be a district matter. As the district capital, Worhn is the place where most of the community forest decisions are made. Statements from CFMB members like 'isn't Worhn everybody's big town?'[340] highlight this. One woman in Kaiuway explained, 'everything that happens here, the order where it comes from, is there in the city [Worhn]'.[341] Moreover, most of the actors involved in community forest registration reside in Worhn and the Community Assembly's headquarters is also in Worhn.[342]

[331] Ibid, para 46.

[332] Letter from Amos Boyer to the FDA: Letter requesting a PUP (2010).

[333] Barnyou (5 Sep 2013) Letter from Sam Barnyou to the FDA: Letter of application: Beyan Poye, p. 1.

[334] Resident Country Surveyor Margibi (22 Nov 2010) Letter from the Resident Country Surveyor to the Ministry of Land, Mines and Energy: Verification & reconnaissance survey of 65,445,00 acres of land in Whorhn Gibi District, Margibi County.

[335] Forestry Development Authority, Social, economic and reconnaissance survey to establish authorized forest community: Field information easy notes, Beyan Poye, p. 3.

[336] Worhn, Poye, Woegbar, Sawzon, Tuan Village, Benthol, Gaye Village, Willie, Morris Goevoll, Kaiuway, Saturday, Charben, Targben, Beahn, Nuah, Bodine, Gbassive, Barnyou, Laka.

[337] Kpelle Jacob, Molley.

[338] Forestry Development Authority, Social, economic and reconnaissance survey to establish authorized forest community: Field information easy notes, Beyan Poye, p. 6.

[339] Tetra Tech ARD (2012b), p. 8.

[340] Roesch R (10 Dec 2017) Interview with Beyan Poye CFMB officer 5, Worhn, para 93.

[341] Borma M (10 Dec 2017) Focus group discussion with women from Kaiuway town, Kaiuway Town, para 40.

[342] Forestry Development Authority (2015) Letter receipts log for signing affidavit of consent; Republic of Liberia (2015) Beahn-Poye community affidavit; Beyan Poye Community Forest (2017) Beyan Poye constitution, art v s 6.

Several informants stressed that the whole district supported the creation of the community forest, makes decisions about the community forest, and should benefit from it.[343] Similarly, the SER finding that the Gbarnfen and Gbarjorkor constitute the Beyan Poye community corresponds to the district-level understanding of community; the two clans cover the whole territory of district Gibi, while the community forest does not.[344] On top of that and in violation of the CRL, the District Commissioner was elected as a member of the Executive Committee.[345] Only after complaints by a national NGO was he deposed.[346]

The district-level understanding of community means that the Beyan Poye community is not particularly close-knit. Some interviewees were under the impression that the FDA had 'told the 24 [21] towns to work together'.[347] They argued that 'the citizens together agree to become a community for the community forest. We weren't a community before'.[348] These statements indicate that a new understanding of community has emerged.[349] The fact that the self-identification essentially took place before the letter of application was sent and not questioned later suggests that the decision was made by a few powerful local authorities—possibly together with the FDA and the logging company Akewa—without having informed and obtained the consent of the rest of the community.

4.2.3.2 Identification of Community Land

The second element of the community forest registration is the identification of the customary land. The approximate size of the forest was already included in the letter of application: 22,000 hectares—just like the PUP.[350]

343 Roesch R (8 Dec 2017) Interview with a District Commissioner, Worhn, para 64; Roesch R (8 Dec 2017) Interview with a General Town Chief, Worhn, para 23.

344 Clans of Liberia. https://maps.mapaction.org/dataset/9c665f76-2dfe-4953-88b6-df50369f0ba7/resource/0c7778c8-cf56-4cbb-b56f-d4dbc566a493/download/Liberiaadministrativeoverviewddpv2a3.pdf. Accessed 21 Jul 2023.

345 According to the CRL, no government official must be elected to the EC (An Act to establish the Community Rights Law of 2009 with respect to forest lands (2009), art 4.1.b).

346 Roesch R (9 Dec 2017) Focus group discussion with community members from Wairlii Town, Wairlii Town, para 18.

347 Ibid, para 10.

348 Ibid, para 8.

349 A forestry expert also argued that 'they view [community] in terms of how much benefit in terms of financial can come to them' (Roesch R (2 Mar 2018) Interview with a senior staff member of a Liberian NGO, Duazon, para 209).

350 Barnyou (5 Sep 2013) Letter from Sam Barnyou to the FDA: Letter of application: Beyan Poye, p. 1.

For the demarcation and mapping, three FDA technicians patrolled the community for 4 days in October 2015.[351] However, given the size of the forest, 3 days were by far not enough to cover all boundary lines, let alone to verify the location of the towns within the forest. The attendance sheet also does not indicate which towns were represented in the demarcation. Due to time constraints and technical problems, the map produced was inaccurate. Community members complained that several towns were missing, and the size of the forest was increased from 22,000 to 39,895 hectares, including a part of Bong and Grand Bassa counties.[352] Nevertheless, community members and the FDA were eager to proceed without further delays.[353] The FDA made community representatives sign the affidavit of consent right after the preliminary mapping in December 2015.[354] The validation in January 2016 largely confirmed the first map. While the validation should have resulted in a more detailed map, the second map is even less accurate.[355]

However, the augmentation of the size of the community forest caused the eruption of an 'age-old'[356] land dispute.[357] The problem was aggravated by the fact that, at the time, the Land Authority bill had not been adopted, and the other agencies took the position that as 'foresters, we're not there to solve land issues, we are not the Land Authority that should be solving land issues'.[358] The main contentious issue was the boundary between the counties Margibi, Grand Bassa, and Bong. The community claimed part of the forest in Grand Bassa as part of their community forest and argued that the Farmington River was the boundary. However, the neighboring community in Grand Bassa had been in negotiation with a logging company for the use of that very parcel of land.[359] Following a meeting of the two County Superintendents and county land surveyors, it was decided to shift the eastern boundary line to avoid delays in the authorization of the community forest. The border area was declared to be 'no man's land'.[360]

---

[351] Forestry Development Authority (2015) Report covering the validation and mapping of Beyan Poye community forest, Gibi District, Margibi County, p. 1.

[352] Ibid, pp. 2, 6.

[353] Forestry Development Authority (18 Jan 2016) Internal memorandum: Validation exercise report on the Beahn Poye's community forest, p. 2.

[354] Beyan Poye Community (2015) Affidavit of consent; Forestry Development Authority (2015) Attendance sheet for the signing of the affidavit of consent: Beyan Poye.

[355] Forestry Development Authority (18 Jan 2016) Internal memorandum: Validation exercise report on the beahn poye's community forest, p. 4.

[356] Forestry Development Authority (2015) Report covering the validation and mapping of Beyan Poye community forest, Gibi District, Margibi County, p. 3; Roesch R (15 Jan 2018) Interview with a senior staff member of the FDA, Monrovia, para 299.

[357] Roesch R (5 Mar 2018) Interview with a staff member of the environmental protection agency, Monrovia, para 85.

[358] Ibid, 85.

[359] Roesch R (8 Dec 2017) Interview with a District Commissioner, Worhn, para 72.

[360] Ibid, para 72.

In September 2016, a final map was produced, which shifts the eastern boundary line inwards. Considerable parts of the area located in Grand Bassa were excluded from the community forest, and the new eastern boundary does not follow the landscape but seems to have been drawn with a ruler. Moreover, several of the towns identified by the SER survey cannot be located on the map.

Also in September 2016, the FDA informed the Beyan Poye community that, while the FDA had provided funding for the first four steps of the authorization process, the community itself would have to finance the demarcation.[361] The FDA estimated that it would cost 2310 USD.

The results of the mapping were posted in September 2016, and in December 2016, the FDA confirmed that no third-party objections had been raised.[362] However, the results of the mapping did not reach all towns. For instance, community members from Poie town remembered that the map had only been posted in other towns.[363] In Morris town, complaints were raised that as the map was only explained in Worhn at the big meeting, the details of the meeting were not transmitted to them, and they could not read the map.[364]

Community members were also under the impression that the contours of the community forest had been proposed by the FDA. The District Commissioner explained that the FDA told them 'how much hectares makes a community forest and we were even able to even go a little beyond that'.[365] This implies that the FDA has been asking the community to designate a sufficiently big area or even proposed the demarcation itself.

The mapping and demarcation were thus conducted in a context where the FDA did not have the time and resources to identify and map all the towns within the forest. The FDA also did not consult with community members from all towns in the forest, and it is possible that it suggested the size and location of the community forest. Consequently, nobody knows how much farmland is located within the community forest area. Only a portion of the community forest area is primary forest, while other parts are secondary forest and farmland. Community members—other than the key stakeholders—had no say in the identification of community land.

---

[361] Office of the Managing Director of the Forestry Development Autority (5 Sep 2016) Letter from the FDA to the District Commissioner: Confirmation steps 1–4.

[362] Planning Officer of the Forestry Development Authority (12 Dec 2016) Letter from the planning officer to the Managing Director of the FDA: Memorandum: No third party objection to SER survey and preliminary demarcations results.

[363] Roesch R (12 Dec 2017) Focus group discussion with community members from Poie town, Poie Town, 15; Roesch R (12 Dec 2017) Focus group discussion with women from Poie town, Poie Town, para 55.

[364] Roesch R (11 Dec 2017) Focus group discussion with community members from Morris town, Morris Town, para 15.

[365] Roesch R (8 Dec 2017) Interview with a District Commissioner, Worhn, para 50.

4.2.3.3 Community Forest Governance

The third element of the community forest authorization is the election of a governance structure and the adoption of governance rules in the form of a constitution and by-laws.

In December 2016, the FDA organized a meeting to elect the governance structure and adopt the by-laws and a constitution.[366] The election of the governance structure was facilitated by an FDA officer together with an NGO representative. Two representatives from each of the 21 towns participated in the constitutive meeting of the governance structure. The towns selected their representatives without FDA support.[367] The FDA confirmed the delegates as members of the Community Assembly.[368] The Community Assembly subsequently elected four Executive Committee and five CFMB officers.

However, in practice, the issue of representation is more complex. Not only the exclusion of most towns located within the forest from the community forest project but also the size differences between the towns raise questions. For example, Tuan Village has three, Benthol and Gaye Village have 20, and Worhn, as the district capital, has 5000 inhabitants.[369] Still, in theory, the 21 towns have the same number of votes in the community forest governance structure.

Moreover, even though each of the 21 towns is supposed to have two delegates, some towns complained of not having any representatives,[370] and two Community Assembly members reported to represent several towns.[371] For instance, the Community Assembly members from Charben Town declared that they also represent Chaplim Town, Neoda Town, Saturday Town, and Hardtime Village.[372] Some of the Community Assembly members apparently also represent towns that are not amongst the 21 identified by the SER survey.[373] Whether this confusion can be traced back to the distinction between towns—settlements that are permanently inhabited—and (farming) villages or the exclusion of most towns from the gover-

[366] Forestry Development Authority (2017) Field report from Community Assembly elections in Beyan Poye community forest held in Worhn town, Margibi County, pp. 1–2.

[367] Ibid, p. 1.

[368] Ibid, p. 3.

[369] Forestry Development Authority, Social, economic and reconnaissance survey to establish authorized forest community: Field information easy notes, Beyan Poye, p. 8.

[370] E.g. Gays Town (Roesch R (10 Dec 2017) Focus group discussion with community members from Gays Town, Gays Town, para 9).

[371] E.g. Kaiuway town (Roesch R (10 Dec 2017) Focus group discussion with community members from Kaiuway, Kaiuway, para 14).

[372] Roesch R (10 Dec 2017) Interview with Beyan Poye Community Assembly member 2, Kaiuway, para 17.

[373] E.g. Gbaygbar.

nance structure is unclear.[374] Yet, some community members were clearly unhappy about how they were represented.[375]

On top of that, many members of the governance structure do not permanently live in the community forest area. One reason for this is the requirement of formal education for the Executive Committee and the CFMB members. To become an Executive Committee member, it is explicitly required to be able to speak and write simple English.[376] Members of the CFMB must not only be literate and speak English but also have graduated from high school.[377] The requirement of formal education prevents the participation of the community members living within the forest who struggle to access schools. Moreover, mobility requires a certain degree of economic capital. Hence, the community members with economic and cultural capital often do not permanently live in their community of origin. I heard several times that Community Assembly members were not available to talk to me because they were in Wohrn or Monrovia.[378] Moreover, most CFMB members did not live in the community forest area. The Beyan Poye Constitution stipulates that in case of the absence of qualified candidates residing within the forest-owning community, the Executive Committee may 'authorize non-residents to serve on the CFMB'.[379] Two of the five CFMB members live permanently in Monrovia, while one resides in Worhn and one in Poie Town, several hours away from the primary forest. While four have their towns of origin within the forest, their socio-economic situation and level of education strongly differ from that of the average community members.[380] Due to their access to wage labor, they also do not depend on farmland to the same extent.

Hence, even though community members regularly mentioned the affectedness by potential logging activities and forest ownership, this did not translate into the governance structure. Instead, mobility, education, and the framing of community forestry as a district enterprise contributed to the exclusion of ordinary community members from the project, particularly those permanently living within the forest. This is even more the case for women from within the forest—their lack of access to formal education, language barriers, the weaker attachment to their town of residence caused by the patrilocal marriage system, the gendered division of labor, stereotypes concerning their physical strength, and their limited mobility made community forestry inaccessible for most of them.

---

[374] See also Alden Wily (2007), p. 160.

[375] E.g. Gays Town.

[376] Beyan Poye Community Forest (2017) Beyan Poye by-laws, art iii s 1.

[377] Ibid, art iv s 1.

[378] E.g. Roesch R (11 Dec 2017) Focus group discussion with community members from Gearwoe town, Gearwoe, para 13; Roesch R (12 Dec 2017) Focus group discussion with community members from Poie town, Poie Town, para 10.

[379] Beyan Poye Community Forest (2017) Beyan Poye constitution, art vii s 2.

[380] See also Louis et al. (2020), p. 11.

Moreover, irregularities occurred in relation to the Community Forest Management Agreement. It was signed by a person claiming to be the chief officer of the CFMB whilst not even being a member of the governance structure.[381] This indicates not only that the FDA has not been capable of adequately monitoring the formation of the governance structure, but also that interactions with pre-existing authorities and forms of decision-making occurred that are hard to understand for outsiders.

4.2.3.4 Forest-Use Decision: 'The Cow Business'

This section explores how the forest-use decision was made. The decision to use the forest commercially went hand in hand with the prohibition of local forest uses.

Strong indicators exist that the decision to opt for the commercial exploitation of the forest was made well before the application. In the memory of many community members, no clear line is drawn between the PUP and the authorization of the community forest—probably because the same persons spearheaded the two processes, and the logging company Akewa was the partner in both cases.[382]

In 2011 or 2012, when PROSPER considered working with the Beyan Poye community, community members told them that 'as much as we want to preserve, we want our area now for commercial purpose, so at least that can get we few lines of streets, and roads and then at least we can get the benefits'.[383] So the decision to opt for commercial logging had already been made at that point.

After the cancellation of the PUP and during the 11-step procedure, community members were aware of Akewa's continuous interest in a Commercial Use Contract.[384] As Akewa had already commenced its logging operations in 2011, the NGO Sustainable Development Institute suspected that the community had just applied for the Community Forest Management Agreement to allow the company to resume its logging activities.[385] Moreover, the application letter states 'the proceed derived from the extraction of the forest resources will be equally shared in the communities',[386] indicating that the application was driven by the hope for the commercial exploitation of the forest. During the boundary mapping, when problems arose with

---

[381] Forestry Development Authority (2017) Community Forest Management Agreement between the Beyan Poye Community Forest Management Body and Akewa Group of Companies Liberia Inc.

[382] E.g. Roesch R (11 Dec 2017) Focus group discussion with community members from Gearwoe town, Gearwoe, para 14.

[383] Roesch R (8 Dec 2017) Interview with a District Commissioner, Worhn, para 70.

[384] Ibid, paras 114ff.

[385] Sustainable Development Institute (2018c), p. 3.

[386] Barnyou (5 Sep 2013) Letter from Sam Barnyou to the FDA: Letter of application: Beyan Poye, p. 1.

regard to the accuracy of the map produced by the FDA, community members were also eager to not delay the authorization process 'as they [were] yearning for an investor to come in their area',[387] making them agree to the loss of considerable forest areas to the neighboring counties.

Following the signing of the Community Forest Management Agreement in February 2017, the CFMB signed a Commercial Use Contract with Akewa in March 2017. The signing ceremony was an event that—unlike the nine steps—most community members remember vividly as the 'cow business':[388] an event where the women slaughtered a cow.[389]

The Commercial Use Contract grants Akewa the right to use the entire community forest area for a duration of 15 years, and the contract may be renegotiated after 5 years. However, the agreement will be put on hold in the case of force majeure and so-called 'interruptions'[390] of Akewa's operation. In the case of a dispute between the community and Akewa, the parties shall resolve their dispute with the aid of the FDA and, if necessary, third-party mediation or arbitration.[391] The agreement cannot be revoked by any party—unless Akewa fails to commence its operations within 1 year following the signing of the agreement.[392]

In terms of social benefits, Akewa will have to build a motor road between Worhn and the Farmington River with concrete bridges and maintain it.[393] Moreover, it shall construct wooden bridges and 13 latrines and hand pumps.[394] As Akewa only has to build two of them per year, many towns will have to wait several years before the construction begins, and most towns will be left empty-handed.[395] Akewa's obligation to provide education scholarships is not restricted to the forest-owning towns, but they may be granted to deserving students from the whole district, reflecting the district-level understanding of the *community*.[396]

The construction of the forest as a commercial resource caused the extinction of customary forest use rights. According to the community forest by-laws, community

387 Forestry Development Authority (18 Jan 2016) Internal memorandum: Validation exercise report on the Beahn Poye's community forest, p. 2.

388 Borma M (12 Dec 2017) Focus group discussion with women from Worhn, Worhn, para 94.

389 The cow business may have been so noteworthy because cows are extremely rare in Beyan Poye: according to the SER survey, only two cows live in the area (Forestry Development Authority, Social, economic and reconnaissance survey to establish authorized forest community: Field information easy notes, Beyan Poye, p. 15).

390 Forestry Development Authority (2017) Community Forest Management Agreement between the Beyan Poye Community Forest Management Body and Akewa Group of Companies Liberia Inc., para 31.

391 Ibid, para 25.

392 Ibid, paras 28, 30, 32.

393 Ibid, para 4.

394 Ibid, para 4.

395 Ibid, paras 8, 9.

396 Ibid, para 11.

members commit an offense by illegally entering the community forest.[397] The CFMB is obliged to protect the forest from 'encroachers, illegal sawyers, intruders and/or trespassers'.[398] The Community Forest Management Agreement stipulates that the CFMB must inform the FDA and 'if possible, halt any ongoing illegal activities'.[399] Moreover, it has to investigate the matter and submit a report to the Executive Committee, which may impose fines or other sanctions.[400]

According to the Commercial Use Contract, the CFMB also must refrain from farming in the concession area.[401] It may be assumed that the prohibition to farm within the forest applies to both the CFMB and the rest of the community. At the same time, Akewa 'shall respect the rights of Beyan Poye community, in carrying out and preserving its traditional practices in conformity with applicable customary laws including animals, plants, medicinal plant sites, hunting'.[402] Moreover, Akewa shall not 'encroach on existing cash crops or cause destruction to the same'.[403] However, Akewa only has to negotiate with the owners of cash crops growing outside of the concession area, strongly indicating that cash crops within the concession area may be destroyed by the company without any compensation.[404] Akewa also has the right to construct security gates at all the entrances to the community forest to 'protect [the concession area] against the interference of illegal chainsawing and unauthorized people'.[405] Community members reported that, since 2017, security guards have prevented them from entering the forest.[406]

According to the Community Rights Law, Commercial Use Contracts may only be signed once a Community Forest Management Plan has been adopted and implemented.[407] In the FDA's records, no indication could be found that the Beyan Poye community has submitted a Community Forest Management Plan. CFMB members argued that they had not granted Akewa the right to log in the

---

[397] Beyan Poye Community Forest (2017) Beyan Poye by-laws, art v s 2.a.

[398] Forestry Development Authority (2017) Community Forest Management Agreement between the Beyan Poye Community Forest Management Body and Akewa Group of Companies Liberia Inc., para 2.

[399] Ibid, s 3.2.h.

[400] Beyan Poye Community Forest (2017) Beyan Poye by-laws, art v s 3.

[401] Forestry Development Authority (2017) Community Forest Management Agreement between the Beyan Poye Community Forest Management Body and Akewa Group of Companies Liberia Inc., para 3.

[402] Ibid, para 18.

[403] Ibid, para 22.

[404] Ibid, para 22.

[405] Ibid, para 15 (exempted from this rule are the movement of citizens and road users).

[406] Roesch R (10 Dec 2017) Focus group discussion with community members from Kaiuway, Kaiuway, para 21.

[407] An Act to establish the Community Rights Law of 2009 with respect to forest lands (2009), ss 6.4.c.-e.

whole community forest but that some areas had been set aside as a reserve.[408] However, it is unlikely that the forest has been properly zoned in the short period of about 4 weeks between the Community Forest Management Agreement and the Commercial Use Contract. Moreover, the forest size in the Community Forest Management Agreement and the Commercial Use Contract is identical, indicating that no part of the community forest has been designated for non-commercial uses.

Hence, under the Beyan Poye community forest framework, local forest uses became fully illegalized. The CFMB and the Executive Committee are put in charge of investigating and sanctioning violations of the no-forest-use-policy. However, it is likely that the CFMB will face challenges in the enforcement of the policy. Community members explained that the forest had been used until very recently, and it may be assumed that the community members living within the forest still use their farmland.[409] This indicates that community members have retained some space for counter-practices or acts of resistance. While most community members support the Commercial Use Contract, they were not fully informed, and—in view of the heavy external pressure—it is unclear whether the governance structure's decision can be seen as free.

4.2.4 *Consent without Alternatives*

Hence, the emerging understanding of FPIC in Beyan Poye is narrower than the conceptions of FPIC in the national legislation and transnational law. Local authorities played a more vital role than envisioned by the national legislation. Simultaneously, they were under tremendous pressure to allow for the commercial exploitation of the forest. Time constraints, together with the lack of funding, made free and informed decision-making a challenge. Moreover, the language of FPIC—and community rights, for that matter—disappeared from the scene.

But how did that happen? The idea of consultations or consent became embedded in development discourse. This legitimized the transformation of FPIC from a right to an economic benefit-sharing and participation concept. Development discourse's construction of the forest as an economic resource determined the meaning of the other elements.[410] Those elements included the forest use, the relationship between the community and the forest, and their participation in community forestry. The main discursive strands were thus the construction of forests as an economic resource and economic development as a necessity, the social identity of the

[408] Roesch R (8 Dec 2017) Interview with Beyan Poye CFMB officer 2, Worhn, paras 40–46; Roesch R (10 Dec 2017) Interview with Beyan Poye CFMB officer 4, Worhn, paras 40–44.

[409] Roesch R (8 Dec 2017) Interview with Beyan Poye CFMB officer 2, Worhn, para 126; Roesch R (10 Dec 2017) Interview with Beyan Poye Community Assembly member 2, Kaiuway, para 53; Borma M (11 Dec 2017) Focus group discussion with women from Gearwoe town, Gearwoe Town, para 22.

[410] Laclau and Mouffe (2001), p. 113.

community that should benefit from the forest, local forest uses as unsustainable and backward, and commercial forestry as a pre-condition for forest ownership.

4.2.4.1 Roads in Exchange for the Forest

Corriveau-Bourque shows that development discourse is regularly used for asserting control over space and legitimizing land encroachment.[411] The first strand of the hegemonic discourse in the field of the Beyan Poye community forest is the construction of the forest as an economic resource while portraying development as being without alternatives.[412]

It was used by decision-makers and ordinary community members alike. A community member from Worhn described her encounter with the FDA as 'they say if we give them the forest, they will give us road [. . .] they will fix hand pump [. . .] They will make our road from here into the forest'.[413] Often suffering is evoked as a legitimization for the urgent need for development. One woman explained, 'everyone of us agrees to it really [. . .] The suffering is too much. The walking is a battle!'[414] Another one held that 'we suffer a lot. So if they talk about making our road, we say, some of us say, we agree [. . .] Then for us, there we stop. What is our authority?'[415] According to Munive, roads have widely become a symbol of peace and development in many places in Liberia, 'holding the promise of future connectivity'.[416] The prospect of getting a road thus provides the justification for the extinction of forest use rights, and resistance becomes difficult in light of the prospect of development.

Additionally, the unspoken promise of *civilization* made some community members embrace the agreement with Akewa. The interpreting CFMB members told community members several times that Akewa would employ their husbands and that they would no longer have to do farm work.[417] This narrative was echoed by community members in some cases: some claimed that 'we will not make farm again',[418] others argued that 'we will be saved. If my child works [. . .] I know that I will eat'.[419] This ideal is, however, in stark contrast to the pride many of the women

---

[411] Corriveau-Bourque (2010), pp. 40–41.

[412] Dunlap makes similar observations with respect to the normalization of development in Juchitán (Dunlap 2018, p. 102).

[413] Borma M (12 Dec 2017) Focus group discussion with women from Worhn, Worhn, para 34.

[414] Borma M (9 Dec 2017) Focus group discussion with women from Wairlii Town, Wairlii Town, para 49.

[415] Borma M (12 Dec 2017) Focus group discussion with women from Worhn, Worhn, para 55.

[416] Munive (2017), p. 286.

[417] Roesch R (11 Dec 2017) Focus group discussion with women from Morris town, Morris Town, para 84.

[418] Ibid, para 89.

[419] Borma M (10 Dec 2017) Focus group discussion with women from Kaiuway town, Kaiuway Town, para 85.

took in their agricultural businesses. Some women even announced that they plan to expand their agricultural business once the roads have been built, as they can transport their rubber and other goods more easily to the market in Worhn.[420] Wage labor as a principal outcome of the Commercial Use Contract was also only brought up in these towns, where the interpreting CFMB members explicitly asked about it. This indicates that most community members do not intend to fundamentally change their mode of living but that the narrative of civilization is mostly employed by the field's elites.

These examples show how the promise of development is instrumentalized to justify the alienation of customary land in different ways: by using the language of suffering, which extinguishes any alternatives to commercial forestry, and by linking development to modernity and civilization.

Indeed, the development discourse is so dominant that the 11 steps just become a minor stumbling block on the road to development. When asked about the 11 steps, most informants just provided information about the social benefits promised to them.[421] Even the members of the governance structure had very limited knowledge of the legal framework and the various documents they had adopted.

However, while the need for development is persuasive, many community members expressed dissatisfaction with Akewa. They feared—very likely because of the government's previous concession policy—that once the company starts extracting logs from the forest, it will not keep its promise of building roads and realizing the other social benefits.[422] Moreover, some community members strongly felt that they (should) have a say in the implementation of commercial logging. When a CFMB member told them that when 'they will be breaking down some of your houses, you shall not get angry',[423] community members responded that 'where the road is to pass through, we the land's people will show it [where the road is to be built]. Houses will not be broken down'.[424]

Despite the hegemony of the discourse of development, it is not uncontested. In this respect, different understandings of development prevail between ordinary community members and the stakeholders and members of the governance structure.

4.2.4.2 Creating a New Community

From the construction of the forest as an economic resource follows the second strand of the discourse: the social identity, which potentially has a right to FPIC. In

[420] Borma M (11 Dec 2017) Focus group discussion with women from Gearwoe town, Gearwoe Town, para 77.

[421] E.g. Borma M (12 Dec 2017) Focus group discussion with women from Worhn, Worhn, para 34.

[422] Borma M (10 Dec 2017) Focus group discussion with women from Gays Town, Gays Town, para 91.

[423] Ibid, para 63.

[424] Ibid, para 65.

Beyan Poye it is noteworthy that actually not one but two communities emerged: the 21 towns constituting the forest-owning community and the district. Generally, for commercial logging to be economically viable, a certain concession size is necessary.[425] It was thus clear from the onset that the forest-owning community needed to claim jurisdiction of a considerable forest area, precluding a self-identification, for example, at the town level.

It is unclear how the 21 towns were selected. They quite obviously do not have the same kind of relationship to the forest. Bigger towns like Worhn and Poie are several walking hours away from the primary forest. Worhn is not even located within the community forest area. While residents of the two towns may have used the forest economically or for cultural purposes, they very likely have not done so to the same extent as the residents living within the forest. This sentiment was shared by several informants.[426] For instance, the General Town Chief of Worhn explained that 'the whole district [owns the community forest]. But the affected area, where the forest is, the people there have more care over it than the people on this side'.[427] It is thus likely that the 21 towns were selected for being able to establish jurisdiction over the whole forest area.

Besides that, a district-level understanding of community emerged. It has been shown that the District Commissioner played a central role in the authorization of the community forest, much of the decision-making takes place in Worhn as the district capital, and the informants repeatedly stressed that the whole district needed to benefit from the community forest. While, for instance, the District Commissioner acknowledged the existence of affected areas, he also stated that 'anything, any resource from that particular area, it will also be passed on for district development'.[428]

Hence, the more central community unit is the district. Development discourse gave the community a new meaning: it evolved from *the community owning the forest* to *the community that should benefit from it*, which is the district.

4.2.4.3 'They Told Us to Not Use the Forest Anymore': Local Forest Uses as Unsustainable

The third discursive strand targets local forest use rights. Based on the construction of the community *that should benefit from the forest,* any forest activities that could

[425] E.g. Roesch R (28 Feb 2018) Interview with a senior legal consultant in the forestry sector, Monrovia, para 77.

[426] E.g. Borma M (10 Dec 2017) Focus group discussion with women from Kaiuway town, Kaiuway Town, para 32.

[427] Roesch R (8 Dec 2017) Interview with a General Town Chief, Worhn, para 25.

[428] Roesch R (8 Dec 2017) Interview with a District Commissioner, Worhn, para 34.

reduce the value of the forest as an economic resource get located in the field of discursivity and become unthinkable.[429]

In all towns visited, community members declared that 'they told us to not use the forest. It should be used to benefit us by using it only for logging [. . .] We want to protect the forest so that nobody works there'.[430] One woman explained that 'they say in the forest no one should make farm there. Because a time will come, where people will come to take things [i.e. logs] from the thick forest'.[431]

While in several towns, informants stated that the no-forest-use-policy was introduced a 'long time ago',[432] others held that they were informed in 1997,[433] 2004,[434] 2005[435], 2009,[436] or 2014.[437] It is likely that, in the early years of the forest sector reform, the FDA recommended communities not degrade the forest anymore.[438] Sometime around the adoption of the CRL in 2009, the District Commissioner spread the rule that community members could not use the forest. He invited the Environmental Protection Agency and the FDA to teach the community about the need to protect the forest and started criminalizing the use of forest resources by community members.[439] It is also likely that the FDA and Akewa reinforced the prohibition when Akewa obtained the Private Use Permit. Women from Gays Town reported that a boundary line was cut at that time, and they were told not to use some of their farmland anymore.[440] This indicates that the no-forest-use-policy was not imposed at one specific point in time but that external actors kept pressuring the local population to refrain from using forest resources since the end of the war to preserve the forest's economic value.

---

[429] Jørgensen and Phillips (2002), p. 27.

[430] Roesch R (12 Dec 2017) Focus group discussion with community members from Poie town, Poie Town, paras 13, 14.

[431] Roesch R (11 Dec 2017) Focus group discussion with women from Morris town, Morris Town, para 19.

[432] Borma M (10 Dec 2017) Focus group discussion with women from Kaiuway town, Kaiuway Town, para 21.

[433] Roesch R (9 Dec 2017) Focus group discussion with community members from Wairlii Town, Wairlii Town, para 20.

[434] Roesch R (12 Dec 2017) Focus group discussion with community members from Poie town, Poie Town, para 13.

[435] Borma M (10 Dec 2017) Focus group discussion with women from Kaiuway town, Kaiuway Town, para 23.

[436] Roesch R (11 Dec 2017) Focus group discussion with community members from Gearwoe town, Gearwoe, para 21.

[437] Roesch R (10 Dec 2017) Interview with Beyan Poye Community Assembly member 2, Kaiuway, para 54.

[438] Borma M (10 Dec 2017) Focus group discussion with women from Kaiuway town, Kaiuway Town, para 23.

[439] Roesch R (8 Dec 2017) Interview with a District Commissioner, Worhn, para 56.

[440] Borma M (10 Dec 2017) Focus group discussion with women from Gays Town, Gays Town, paras 26–32.

The construction of local forest uses as unsustainable as opposed to the construction of development as a modern necessity justified the extinction of customary tenure rights. Among community members, it translated into two different narratives: the narrative of ignorance and the narrative of powerlessness.

The narrative of ignorance was regularly used by the educated and geographically mobile key actors. Statements like 'they were just damaging the forest. [. . .] Because we have some knowledge from school [. . .] and we say, "in the future, you can still use the young bush, you can still get rice. So we should not damage that tree. Because in the future it will benefit us."'[441] were common. Similarly, the community forest application states that farming activities of the past have 'greatly affected our forest estate'.[442] In a few cases, the narrative of ignorance was echoed by ordinary community members. In Weirlii town, community members explained that 'we didn't understand that we couldn't just use the forest'.[443] A woman described her experience as 'they send [. . .] many lessons [. . .] because for us to get money business'.[444] What follows from this logic is that members need to be educated to refrain from their *unsustainable* forest uses. The no-forest-use-policy, which prohibits any forest use other than company-run commercial forestry, became the norm. Customary land uses, in contrast, were transformed into a form of land encroachment.

Such narratives are, however, in stark contrast to the experiences of ordinary community members. Many felt that they were already the owners of the land. Instead of securing their land rights, community forestry has rather limited or extinguished them—without them having a considerable say in it. Thus, narratives of disempowerment were more common and the phrase 'they told us to not use the forest anymore'[445] was a recurring theme in all the towns visited. However, the identity of *them* varies. Informants sometimes referenced 'the government and the radio',[446] the FDA,[447] Akewa,[448] or 'people from the city'.[449] External interests in the forest thus take priority over customary tenure rights: 'they say [. . .] they should

[441] Roesch R (8 Dec 2017) Interview with a District Commissioner, Worhn, para 30.

[442] Beyan Poye Community (20 Jun 2014) Letter from the Beyan Poye community to the FDA: Letter of application Beyan-Poye community.

[443] Roesch R (9 Dec 2017) Focus group discussion with community members from Wairlii Town, Wairlii Town, para 20.

[444] Borma M (10 Dec 2017) Focus group discussion with women from Kaiuway town, Kaiuway Town, para 62.

[445] Roesch R (12 Dec 2017) Focus group discussion with community members from Poie town, Poie Town, para 13.

[446] Roesch R (9 Dec 2017) Focus group discussion with community members from Wairlii Town, Wairlii Town, para 20.

[447] Borma M (12 Dec 2017) Focus group discussion with women from Worhn, Worhn, para 34.

[448] Roesch R (10 Dec 2017) Focus group discussion with community members from Kaiuway, Kaiuway, para 11.

[449] Roesch R (11 Dec 2017) Focus group discussion with women from Morris town, Morris Town, para 15.

not make farm there, because the farm then is in the same tree, because it is the tree they're wanting'.[450] The sense of disempowerment goes so far that some community members fear repercussions if they continue to use the forest: 'if we be doing [continue to use] this forest, a storm will be coming'.[451] A sense of disempowerment also prevails in relation to the company Akewa. A member of the Community Assembly admitted that they did not inform the company that they needed a part of the forest for farming, as they were afraid that the company could reconsider the investment.[452] Moreover, I was asked many times when the company would start building the roads. Community members are thus neither aware of the details of the Commercial Use Contract nor the company's timeframe.[453]

The narrative of ignorance and the narrative of powerlessness have a common outcome. From the narrative of ignorance follows that local forest uses have to be prohibited, while the narrative of powerlessness highlights that community dwellers have no other option but to respect that prohibition if they want their economic situations to improve.

4.2.4.4 Commercial Forestry as a Pre-Condition for Forest Ownership

The fourth strand of the field's discourse portrays commercial forestry as a precondition for forest ownership. International experts working on community forestry repeatedly stressed that the decision to go through the 11 steps is often a strategic one, as communities know that it is a way of preventing land encroachment.[454] Indeed, those with important roles in the community employed similar narratives. The General Town Chief of Worhn argued that 'the community forest is for us, we own it. If people want it from us, we [. . .] we all come together to agree for it'.[455] Similarly, the District Commissioner explained that

> since this president took over, Madam Ellen Johnson Sirleaf, we have now from, you know, bottom to top approach. That means if you are a miner or logging company or whatever business you want to do in the interior areas or the rural areas, you first start with the people, discuss with the people, get their views and other views. Then, of course, the information from there will go up. That means the people have consented, the people agreed. But before

[450] Roesch R (10 Dec 2017) Focus group discussion with community members from Gays Town, Gays Town, para 44.

[451] Roesch R (11 Dec 2017) Focus group discussion with women from Morris town, Morris Town, para 15.

[452] Roesch R (10 Dec 2017) Interview with Beyan Poye Community Assembly member 2, Kaiuway, para 56.

[453] E.g. Roesch R (11 Dec 2017) Focus group discussion with community members from Gearwoe town, Gearwoe, para 22.

[454] E.g. Roesch R (4 Apr 2018) Skype interview with a former senior staff member of the LRCFP and PROSPER, para 82.

[455] Roesch R (8 Dec 2017) Interview with a General Town Chief, Worhn, para 23.

then, it used to be direct information from there come straight to the people. [...] Whether you liked it or not, it did happen.[456]

According to a CFMB member, the non-forest-use-policy enabling commercial forestry is a precondition for forest ownership: 'We started to preserve our forest to be able to take ownership of it'.[457]

Hence, community forestry and the commercial use of community forestry are constructed to be preconditions for securing customary forest rights. Thereby, the scope of FPIC is considerably reduced as it no longer has a cultural or autonomy dimension but simply entails the right to consent to development as a *fait accompli* and benefit from the forest as an economic resource.

4.3 FPIC in the Sehzueplay Community Forest

The second field of community forestry is located in Sehzueplay in Southern Nimba. Sehzueplay was supported by two successive USAID-funded projects. Peoples, Rules, and Organisations Supporting the Protection of Ecosystem Resources (PROSPER) was active in Sehzueplay from 2012 to 2017, and Forest Incomes for Environmental Sustainability (FIFES) ran from 2015 to 2021.

To get to Sehzueplay from Monrovia, it takes about 4 h on a paved road to reach Ganta. Ganta and Sehzueplay are connected by a dirt road that is only accessible during the dry season. It takes another 2 h by car to reach Sehzueplay. Seven towns belong to the Sehzueplay community forest: Graie town, Zuolay, Volay, Sehyee Village, Kenpea, Zeonghn, and Korlay. A dirt road connects them, and, unlike in Beyan Poye, they are all located outside of the community forest area. Sehzueplay has approximately 25,000 inhabitants.[458]

This section explores the relationship between the community and the forest and its history, the actors constituting the field of the Sehzueplay community forest, the realization of FPIC in the registration of the community forest, and the field's discourse determining FPIC's meaning.

4.3.1 *Sehzueplay and the Forest*

Just like Beyan Poye, the field of the Sehzueplay community forest is a predominantly local time-space. It consists of the USAID-funded projects, the FDA, local authorities, the logging company Opulence, and other community members.

---

456 Roesch R (8 Dec 2017) Interview with a District Commissioner, Worhn, para 24.

457 Roesch R (10 Dec 2017) Interview with Beyan Poye CFMB officer 4, Worhn, para 34.

458 Sehzueplay Community Forest (2017) Sehzueplay Community Forest Management Plan, p. 3.

However, the history of Sehzueplay and its relationship to the forest is different from that of Beyan Poye. It is characterized by a stronger grip of the central government on the forest. Before its recognition as a community forest, the forest was part of the 58,000-hectares Big Gio national forest.[459] Following an aerial survey supported by USAID, the predecessor of the FDA introduced national forests in 1953 to be owned and administered by the government.[460]

The Big Gio national forest stretched across three districts—Doe, Boe-Quilla, and Kparblee—and the largest portion of the forest fell in the Doe district, where three clans are located: Gblor, Gbear, and Sehzueplay.[461] After the war, the government classified it as an unallocated Forest Management Contract, which is a potential large-scale timber concession.[462] In 2011, the Doe community received a Private Use Permit (PUP) covering 79,263 hectares.[463] The PUP investigation report found that most community members were not aware of the PUP and its underlying deed, and the committee managing the PUP had its business address in Monrovia. Later, the Land Commission found that the deed had been forged.[464] In 2013, the government canceled the PUP.

In the same year, the communities surrounding the Big Gio forest decided to opt for separate community forest status: Sehzueplay, Boe-Quilla, Gbear-Gblor, and Kparblee. The Sehzueplay community forest comprises 6890.[465] In 2017, the community granted a Commercial Use Contract to the US logging company Opulence. Under unclear circumstances, the agreement with Opulence was canceled and the Sehzueplay community entered into a CUC with the Universal Forestry Corporation in 2020.[466] The Universal Forestry Cooperation is alleged to have launched its logging operations without the necessary logging permit.[467]

Community members in Sehzueplay have not used the forest as much as the Beyan Poye community. It is estimated that the communities have lived at the fringe of the forest for around 200 years.[468] Some informants argued that before the government took control of the forest in 1952, it was used by community members.[469] However, due to the FDA's control over the national forest, existing

---

[459] Sachtler (1968), p. 1.

[460] United States Operations Mission to Liberia (1961).

[461] Roesch R (9 Mar 2018) Interview with Sehzueplay CFMB officer 4, Zeonghn.

[462] Vogt (2012), p. 7.

[463] Private Use Permit contract between the Forestry Development Authority & the People of Doe's Chiefdom (2011) (Forestry Development Authority), s 1 art 5.

[464] Tetra Tech ARD (2014c), p. 11.

[465] Tetra Tech ARD (2016c), p. 2.

[466] ACDI/VOCA (2020), p. 13.

[467] Harding Giahyue (2022) Liberia: Inside Minister Cooper Kruah's illegal logging deals. Daily Observer. https://www.liberianobserver.com/liberia-inside-minister-cooper-kruahs-illegal-logging-deals. Accessed 4 Aug 2023.

[468] Sehzueplay Community Forest (2017) Sehzueplay Community Forest Management Plan, p. 18.

[469] Roesch R (12 Mar 2018) Interview with a Zone Chief, Graie, para 44.

customary ownership claims were largely extinguished. Some community members still used the national forest for hunting. However, they risked getting arrested by the FDA's forest guards.[470] The surrounding communities thus look back at a history of 'being mapped',[471] contributing to the extinction of their tenure rights.

During the war, the FDA no longer had the capacity to control the forest, and community members went into hiding in the forest.[472] Others—also strangers, i.e. people from other communities—began using the forest for farming. Moreover, population growth increased the pressure on the forest.[473] The continuing presence of some community members and strangers in the forest still causes conflicts within the community.

Most community members have a weak sense of ownership of the community forest, and they often referred to the community forest as the government or national forest.[474] Farming activities usually take place outside of the forest. Most families' have their farmland in so-called native reserves[475] surrounding the towns where they live. It is common that they hold tribal certificates for these reserves.[476] Hence, while some community members have used the forest for hunting and farming, it did not occur to the same extent as in Beyan Poye.[477]

4.3.2 *Mapping the Field: Actors in Relation*

The actors constituting the field of the Sehzueplay community forest also differ from those in Beyan Poye. Notably, the strong presence and power of first PROSPER and later FIFES influenced the operationalization of community forestry and the negotiation of FPIC. The field was thus constituted of the Forestry Development Authority (FDA), PROSPER and FIFES, local authorities and other community members,

---

[470] Roesch R (12 Mar 2019) Interview with a former FDA staff member, Graie, para 8.

[471] Offen (2003), p. 384.

[472] Sehzueplay Community Forest (2017) Sehzueplay Community Forest Management Plan, p. 18.

[473] Roesch R (11 Mar 2018) Focus group discussion with women from Kenpea, Kenpea, para 11.

[474] E.g. Roesch R (10 Mar 2018) Focus group discussion with women from Zuolay, Zuolay, para 101; Johnson G (12 Mar 2018) Focus group discussion with women from Graie, Graie, paras 16ff.

[475] Native or tribal reserves describe land that could be used by community members for essential activities, as recognized by the Hinterland Regulations.

[476] Roesch R (10 Mar 2018) Focus group discussion with community members from Zuolay, Zuolay, para 4; Roesch R (11 Mar 2018) Focus group discussion with community members from Kenpea, Kenpea, para 4; Roesch R (11 Mar 2018) Focus group discussion with community members from Zeonghn, Zeonghn, para 4; Roesch R (12 Mar 2018) Focus group discussion with community members from Graie, Graie, para 4; Roesch R (12 Mar 2019) Interview with a former FDA staff member, Graie, paras 88–90; Roesch R (13 Mar 2018) Focus group discussion with community members from Korlay, Korlay, para 5; Roesch R (14 Mar 2018) Focus group discussion with community members from Sehyee village, Sehyee Village, para 4.

[477] Roesch R (12 Mar 2018) Focus group discussion with community members from Graie, Graie, para 16.

and the US logging company Opulence. It was also characterized by gendered participatory exclusions.

4.3.2.1 Forestry Development Authority

The FDA was a powerful actor in the field of the Sehzueplay community forest. Due to its cooperation with the USAID projects, it had considerable social capital and also more economic capital.[478] However, it also strongly depended on PROSPER and FIFES. Moreover, the CRL Regulation enhanced its symbolic capital.[479]

Due to the Big Gio forest's status as a national forest, the FDA has been more present in Sehzueplay than in Beyan Poye in the past. Until the civil war, forest guards constantly controlled the forest 'to keep the artificial boundaries clear, to keep out farmers and to control hunters'.[480] Nevertheless, the FDA most likely never managed to entirely prevent community members from entering the forest even though forest rangers brought so-called perpetrators to court and burned down villages in the forest.[481] Moreover, in a few cases, the FDA made concessions to communities and legalized farmland located within the boundaries of the national forest, like in the case of Niloco village or the native reserve of Volay.[482]

PROSPER strongly supported the FDA during the community forest registration because the FDA lacked the infrastructure and economic means.[483] Still, various informants stressed that the FDA took the lead during the 9 steps.[484] While many elements within the FDA understood the forests as an economic resource, they also depended on the USAID funding and supported USAID's biodiversity goals. There were thus different visions of forestry coexisting within the FDA.

4.3.2.2 PROSPER and FIFES

PROSPER and FIFES had considerable economic, symbolic, cultural and social capital.[485] PROSPER, together with the FDA, decided to work in Sehzueplay. It identified potential pilot communities in Nimba, Bong, Margibi, Grand Bassa, and

[478] Bourdieu (1986), p. 248.

[479] See also Bourdieu et al. (1994), p. 9.

[480] Sachtler (1968), p. 1.

[481] Roesch R (9 Mar 2018) Interview with Sehzueplay CFMB officer 4, Zeonghn, para 276; Roesch R (12 Mar 2019) Interview with a former FDA staff member, Graie, para 30; Roesch R (14 Mar 2019) Interview with Sehzueplay Community Assembly member 4, Sehyee Village, para 60.

[482] Roesch R (12 Mar 2019) Interview with a former FDA staff member, Graie, para 44.

[483] Roesch R (4 Apr 2018) Skype interview with a former senior staff member of the LRCFP and PROSPER, para 95.

[484] E.g. Roesch R (16 Mar 2018) Interview with a former PROSPER staff member, Tappita, para 142; Roesch R (16 Mar 2018) Interview with a staff member of the FDA, Tappita, para 51.

[485] Bourdieu (1986), p. 248.

Lofa in coordination with other donors.[486] The selection criteria were, amongst others, the conservation value of the forest, governance capacity, tenure security, and logistical considerations.[487] Ultimately, PROSPER focused on Grand Bassa and Nimba. The activities in Sehzueplay were coordinated through the Tappita office in Southern Nimba.[488] Community mobilizers were continuously located in Sehzueplay to support the community in completing the 11 steps. However, according to community members, the mobilizers were replaced several times, and, most of the time, only one mobilizer was present.[489]

PROSPER viewed the forest primarily as an ecological resource. It strongly emphasized the link between biodiversity conservation and community forestry.[490] Their biodiversity threat analysis highlighted that shifting cultivation, bushmeat hunting, chain-saw logging, and artisanal mining constituted the most significant threats to the forest.[491] Based on the analysis, PROSPER took the position that offering so-called alternative livelihood opportunities could be a way of incentivizing communities to refrain from shifting cultivation in the forest. It introduced oil palm nurseries, a crop diversification group, and a bee-keeping group in Sehzueplay.[492] PROSPER also assumed that, as long as no by-laws of the community forest were adopted, hunting would be banned.[493] Therefore, it attempted to introduce goat and cane rat breeding. Both pilot projects were not successful.[494] Moreover, according to community members, none of the groups established by PROSPER were still active in 2018.[495]

FIFES came in in 2015 when the community forest already had its governance structure in place. The project promoted the conservation of the forest and alternative livelihood projects outside of the forest. According to a local FIFES staff member, 'those negatively affected from the forest demarcation should be able to get a better sustainable livelihood opportunity'.[496] Thus, the project did not question that some community dwellers lost their customary farmland but sought to provide alternative

486 Tetra Tech ARD (2012b), pp. 3–4.

487 Ibid, p. 21.

488 Tetra Tech ARD (2013d), p. 2.

489 Roesch R (9 Mar 2018) Interview with Sehzueplay CFMB officer 4, Zeonghn, paras 56–58.

490 E.g. Tetra Tech ARD (2013e), p. 28.

491 Tetra Tech ARD (2015b), p. 8.

492 Ibid, p. 25; Tetra Tech ARD (2016a), pp. 24, 29.

493 Tetra Tech ARD (2015b), p. 25.

494 Tetra Tech ARD (2015a), pp. 53–54.

495 Roesch R (16 Mar 2018) Interview with a former PROSPER staff member, Tappita, para 276; Roesch R (20 Mar 2018) Interview with FIFES staff member based in Nimba 2, Monrovia, para 18; on the limits of agricultural training see also Newberry (2014), p. 313.

496 Roesch R (20 Mar 2018) Interview with FIFES staff member based in Nimba 2, Monrovia, para 32.

livelihood activities as a form of compensation.[497] In total, there existed 11 enterprise groups in Sehzueplay.[498]

Even though the Sehzueplay community forest decided not to opt for conservation, FIFES continued its work there until the expiration of the project in 2021.[499]

4.3.2.3 Local Authorities

Just like in Beyan Poye, local authorities or *stakeholders* were strongly involved in the authorization of the community forest. However, their capital changed during the registration process. Generally, it can be assumed that most of them had limited economic capital but considerable cultural and symbolic capital grounded in their local knowledge and legitimacy.[500] With the election of the governance structure, their influence waned.

The Private Use Permit (PUP) had already been brokered by the District Commissioner at the time, and the District Commissioner and the chiefs played an important role in the division of the Big Gio forest between the four communities.[501] The first steps of the community forest registration also strongly built on the involvement of the community *stakeholders*. For instance, before the SER survey, the FDA first officially informed the Statutory Superintendent in Tappita before distributing copies to all Town Chiefs, Commissioners, and the Clan Chief.[502] Moreover, the chiefs, the Commissioner, and the Superintendent were well-represented in the SER survey, with 47% of the participants being members of the local governance system.[503]

Besides involving the stakeholders, PROSPER introduced a Community Forest Organizing Committee, a Peace Committee, and a Community Awareness Team in Sehzueplay to facilitate the registration of the community forest.[504] The Community Awareness Team played an important role in the posting of notices during the 11 steps. The Community Forest Organizing Committee was in charge of leading the community through the first steps.[505] Both of them strongly contributed to the dissemination of the conservation message during the authorization process.[506]

---

497 Roesch R (16 Mar 2018) Interview with FIFES staff member based in Nimba, Tappita, para 24.

498 ACDI/VOCA (2018), p. 5; Roesch R (20 Mar 2018) Interview with FIFES staff member based in Nimba 2, Monrovia, para 38.

499 Roesch R (16 Mar 2018) Interview with FIFES staff member based in Nimba, Tappita, para 78.

500 Bourdieu (1986), p. 243.

501 Special Independent Investigating Body (2012), p. 131.

502 PROSPER (2015) Sehzueplay recipients of SER notice.

503 Forestry Development Authority (2015) Attendance sheet, SER survey Sehzueplay, 1–3 June 2015.

504 Tetra Tech ARD (2015a), p. 28.

505 Tetra Tech ARD (2013e), p. 13.

506 Social Impact's Liberia Strategic Analysis (2016), p. 29.

Moreover, the members of the Peace Committees received conflict management training to settle inter and intra-community conflicts. Yet PROSPER's evaluation found that the flow of information from the Community Forest Organizing Committee and the other institutions to the broader community did not work well. Most community members were not aware of the function of the Community Forest Organizing Committee and the 11 steps.[507]

Moreover, with the election of the governance structure, new institutions emerged. The CRL prevents government officials, including chiefs, from becoming members of the governance structure.[508] Therefore, few influential community members were elected to the governance structure.[509] Some of them complained about their limited access to information:

> After step 3 now, they say they have the CFMB [. . .], and we were isolated from their general meetings. So all of what they discuss there about this forest now, what frustrated us is that those who we appointed for them to be CFMB, did not come from there in the meeting to tell us what was unfolding.[510]

PROSPER's insistence on following the legal requirements thus contributed to the decline of the local authorities' symbolic capital, and they could no longer legitimately speak on behalf of the community.

Simultaneously, the members of the governance structure felt very strongly that the community forest was in their hands now. According to one Community Assembly member, the stakeholders may participate 'as observers but they are not higher in decision-making'.[511] Nevertheless, the District Commissioner was still involved by trying to enforce the prohibition to use the forest with the help of the community police.[512] Several community members reported that the District Commissioner—just like before the war—had ordered to burn down villages in the buffer zone to evict the people living there.[513] But also the Clan Chief and other chiefs were supporting the no-forest-use-policy and, for instance, offered money to the community dwellers living in the forest to make them leave.[514]

The company also cooperated with local authorities to convince the community to enter into an agreement with them: they appointed the Zone Chief of Graie Town as

[507] Ibid, p. 25.

[508] An Act to establish the Community Rights Law of 2009 with respect to forest lands (2009), s 4.1. b.

[509] Roesch R (20 Mar 2018) Interview with FIFES staff member based in Nimba 2, Monrovia, para 162.

[510] Roesch R (10 Mar 2019) Interview with a former Town Chief, Zuolay, para 14.

[511] Roesch R (13 Mar 2018) Interview with Sehzueplay Community Assembly member 10, Korlay, para 126.

[512] Roesch R (10 Mar 2018) Focus group discussion with women from Zuolay, Zuolay, para 193.

[513] Roesch R (14 Mar 2019) Interview with Sehzueplay Community Assembly member 4, Sehyee Village, para 60; Roesch R (20 Mar 2018) Interview with FIFES staff member based in Nimba 2, Monrovia, paras 98ff.

[514] Roesch R (12 Mar 2019) Interview with a former FDA staff member, Graie, para 116.

their local coordinator, an unpaid position that he accepted in the hope of getting a salaried job once the logging operations begin.[515]

Another existing institution was the so-called Doe Forest Management Association, that had received the PUP for the Big Gio forest. Members of the body continued to be indirectly involved in the community forestry process. For instance, one member mobilized community people against the community forest project for infringing upon their customary land rights.[516] Moreover, the community's lawyer, that pushed the community towards signing a Commercial Use Contract, had been the chairman of the same association.[517]

So despite the governance structure having a strong sense of ownership of the community forest project, (state-sponsored) customary decision-makers continue to be indirectly involved in the management of the forest. This illustrates the complex interactions between different legalities and institutions of land and forest governance.

4.3.2.4 Opulence

Opulence is a US-registered logging company. At the time of the negotiation with the Sehzueplay community forest, it had not been awarded any other logging license in Liberia. According to the FDA, it was supported by the US Embassy, which demanded information about different community forests from the FDA.[518] Thus, it possessed both economic and social capital.[519]

The national coordinator traveled the whole country to find potential community forests. Community members explained that Opulence approached them before the 9 steps had been completed.[520] In 2017, Opulence obtained two Commercial Use Contracts for the neighboring community forests Sehzueplay and Gblor.[521]

4.3.2.5 Gendered Participatory Exclusions

Unlike in Beyan Poye, women leaders and women groups are a more recent phenomenon in Sehzueplay. According to the Clan Chief, the Johnson Sirleaf

---

515 Roesch R (7 Mar 2018) Interview with a staff member of Opulence, Monrovia, para 72; Roesch R (12 Mar 2018) Interview with a Zone Chief, Graie, paras 137ff.

516 Roesch R (10 Mar 2018) Interview with a former member of the Doe Forest Development Committee, Zuolay, para 4.

517 Roesch R (19 Mar 2018) Interview with Sehzueplay EC member 3, Monrovia, para 136.

518 Roesch R (15 Jan 2018) Interview with a senior staff member of the FDA, Monrovia, para 94.

519 Bourdieu (1986), p. 252.

520 Roesch R (9 Mar 2018) Interview with Sehzueplay CFMB officer 4, Zeonghn, para 174; Roesch R (10 Mar 2018) Interview with Sehzueplay Community Assembly member 13, Zuolay, para 104.

521 Roesch R (7 Mar 2018) Interview with a staff member of Opulence, Monrovia, para 58.

administration and the international NGO Concern had introduced women leaders and youth leaders after the war.[522] Moreover, she explained that 'after the war, the Justice and Peace Commission of the Catholic church came to us, explained to us how to do government work and why you need to have women leader'.[523] Another informant argued that decentralization has contributed to their introduction in Sehzueplay.[524] A woman from Graie confirmed that there were no women leaders before the war and argued that 'people have negative thinking about women leaders'.[525] However, women's groups appear to have a more long-standing history. In some towns, women groups support each other;[526] in others, women have saving clubs,[527] or they farm collectively.[528]

Despite their Gender Integration Plan, PROSPER (and FIFES) faced problems ensuring the participation of women in the establishment of the community forest and also internally. The number of female employees in the Tappita office was very low.[529]

During the first 9 steps, PROSPER recommended that at least three of the seven Community Forest Organizing Committee members should be women, which was accepted by the community.[530] Ensuring the participation of women in the SER survey and mapping was more challenging. PROSPER stressed that women, elders, and youth should be represented in the mapping and demarcation, and the Gender Integration Officer facilitated several consultative dialogues on the role of women and youth in the SER survey and the demarcation.[531] In practice, only 20.1% women participated in the SER survey.[532] 24% of the participants in the community forest demarcation training were women. However, very few women participated in the

[522] Tetra Tech ARD (2012c), pp. 23–24; Roesch R (9 Mar 2018) Interview with the Paramount Chief of Doe Chiefdom, Zeonghn, paras 38–40; Johnson G (15 Mar 2018) Focus group discussion with women from Zeonghn, Zeonghn, para 271.

[523] Roesch R (10 Mar 2018) Interview with a Clan Chief, Volay, para 29.

[524] Roesch R (15 March 2018) Informal conversation with a FIFES staff member based in Nimba, Graie.

[525] Roesch R (12 March 2018) Informal conversation with a woman from Graie town, Graie.

[526] Roesch R (11 Mar 2018) Focus group discussion with women from Kenpea, Kenpea, para 132.

[527] Johnson G (10 Mar 2018) Focus group discussion with women from Volay, Volay, para 230; Johnson G (13 Mar 2018) Focus group discussion with women from Korlay, Korlay, para 100.

[528] Johnson G (13 Mar 2018) Focus group discussion with women from Korlay, Korlay, paras 101, 104.

[529] Tetra Tech ARD (2014b), p. 24.

[530] Tetra Tech ARD (2014c), pp. 4–5; Roesch R (11 Mar 2018) Interview with a former Community Forest Organizing Committee member, Kenpea, para 52.

[531] Tetra Tech ARD (2015a), pp. 28–29.

[532] Forestry Development Authority (2015) Attendance sheet, SER survey Sehzueplay, 1–3 June 2015.

demarcation and mapping itself.[533] Just like in Beyan Poye, many women felt that 'they selected men to go with them. We didn't take part in that'.[534]

Similarly, in the stakeholder workshop preceding the formation of a Community Assembly, only 18% of women participated.[535] PROSPER recommended that each town should elect one man and one woman into the Community Assembly.[536] According to Sehzueplay's constitution, one of the three representatives per town shall be a woman, thereby introducing a women's quota of 33%.[537] Despite this tangible commitment to the participation of women, the towns did not elect the number of women as required by the constitution: just three women are among the 21 Community Assembly members, with none of them being elected to the Executive Committee.[538] Moreover, as legally required, just one woman became a member of the CFMB. Women also did also not participate in the negotiation of the Commercial Use Contract with Opulence.[539]

Most women in Sehzueplay have very limited knowledge about the community forest.[540] PROSPER also found that women had less access to information about 'the community forest governance bodies, the forest community authorization process, the objective of the process, or how the community will manage its forest once it is authorized'[541] and FIFES' midterm evaluation concludes that most women in the 11 community forests felt less capable than men to speak out on community forest governance issues.[542]

One reason for their lack of participation could be that, when meetings were scheduled, certain community members—the so-called stakeholders—were specifically invited. While others could go to the meeting as well, some women explained that they did not go to meetings for which they had not been invited: 'the [Community Assembly] then, the men, they didn't want we come. We can't come'.[543]

---

533 Tetra Tech ARD (2013b), p. 28.

534 Johnson G (15 Mar 2018) Focus group discussion with women from Zeonghn, Zeonghn, para 110; see also Roesch R (10 Mar 2018) Focus group discussion with community members in Volay, Volay, para 9; Johnson G (10 Mar 2018) Focus group discussion with women from Volay, Volay, paras 93–98; Johnson G (12 Mar 2018) Focus group discussion with women from Graie, Graie, paras 56–58.

535 Tetra Tech ARD (2013c), p. 31; Tetra Tech ARD (2014d), p. 10.

536 Tetra Tech ARD (2014c), pp. 4–5.

537 Sehzueplay Community Forest (2016) Sehzueplay authorized forest community constitution Nimba County, art VI s 2.B.

538 Forestry Development Authority (2017) Sehzueplay CFMBs, Executive Committee and Community Assembly.

539 E.g. Johnson G (13 Mar 2018) Focus group discussion with women from Korlay, Korlay, para 86; Johnson G (15 Mar 2018) Focus group discussion with women from Zeonghn, Zeonghn, para 222.

540 Johnson G (12 Mar 2018) Focus group discussion with women from Graie, Graie, paras 70–77.

541 Social Impact's Liberia Strategic Analysis (2016), p. 21.

542 Liberia Strategic Analysis (2018), p. 9.

543 Johnson G (10 Mar 2018) Focus group discussion with women from Volay, Volay, para 128.

Moreover, their lack of spare time and high workload—including farm work, care work, and, in many cases, market-related activities—contributed to them not attending meetings.[544] One woman explained that 'when they call meeting, the women no can't come. So the men can do it'.[545] For many women, mobility is also an issue, as men are often more mobile and can attend meetings in other towns more easily.[546] In addition, PROSPER observed that when women attended meetings, they were often too shy to talk.[547]

The absence of women may have been exacerbated by FIFES' approach to women's participation. FIFES' gender efforts focused on the introduction of so-called WORTH ('WORTH', i.e., Women Saving Resources Together) groups.[548] However, the WORTH groups are not linked to community forest governance.[549]

Moreover, FIFES sought to address the lack of knowledge about the community forestry framework by providing continuous training and support to the governance structure.[550] Due to the low number of women in the governance bodies, few women could benefit from these training opportunities.[551] Hence, while FIFES sought to emphasize their gender angle—i.e. most of the success stories in their reports are about women[552]—the mid-term evaluation found no evidence of a positive impact on women. Instead, 'FIFES' assistance to [community forest] governance has not increased the knowledge and access to information required for women or youth to exert influence on CFMBs' decisions'.[553] Moreover, FIFES' Gender and Youth advisor was dismissed in late 2017 after the budget was cut.[554]

Nevertheless, a narrative of gender inclusiveness was very common amongst members of the governance structure and FDA staff.[555] For instance, one local FDA staff member explained that the Community Forest Organizing Committee in

[544] Johnson G (13 Mar 2018) Focus group discussion with women from Korlay, Korlay, paras 3–9; Johnson G (15 Mar 2018) Focus group discussion with women from Zeonghn, Zeonghn, paras 306–14; Roesch R (16 Mar 2018) Interview with a former PROSPER staff member, Tappita, para 294; Roesch R (20 Mar 2018) Interview with FIFES staff member based in Nimba 2, Monrovia, para 187.

[545] Johnson G (10 Mar 2018) Focus group discussion with women from Volay, Volay, para 125.

[546] Roesch R (20 Mar 2018) Interview with FIFES staff member based in Nimba 2, Monrovia, para 187.

[547] Roesch R (16 Mar 2018) Interview with a former PROSPER staff member, Tappita, para 282.

[548] ACDI/VOCA (2018), p. 15; Roesch R (20 Mar 2018) Interview with FIFES staff member based in Nimba 2, Monrovia, para 48.

[549] Liberia Strategic Analysis (2018), p. 13.

[550] ACDI/VOCA (2017b), p. 16.

[551] ACDI/VOCA (2019a), p. 8.

[552] E.g. ACDI/VOCA (2017d), pp. 20–1; ACDI/VOCA (2019a), pp. 19–20.

[553] Liberia Strategic Analysis (2018), p. viii.

[554] ACDI/VOCA (2016a), p. 4.

[555] Roesch R (11 Mar 2018) Interview with a former Community Forest Organizing Committee member, Kenpea, para 44.

Sehzueplay was 'gender-balanced'.[556] When asked whether gender-balanced meant that 50% of the members were women, he responded that 'men were more, women were less'.[557] Another example of this understanding is the FDA's standard letter announcing the SER survey: it asks the clan chief to mobilize 26 persons from the community from all towns and villages and 'to include at least one woman'.[558] It is thus assumed that the participation of one or a few women would enable the integration of the perspective of women.

However, several women were quite angry about the way community forestry was implemented. One woman from Graie town complained that 'they say nothing. They can't tell us. [They take] their sitting fees over there, when [they come back] they go in their various houses then'.[559] In Volay, they argued that 'we only heard about logging company coming in the forest. How they coming, how it will be, we don't know, because we are not part of it. So when they actually sign, they must let us know, so that we can face it. We are part of the forest'.[560]

Moreover, in contrast to the lack of women's participation in forest governance, women in all towns declared that they could participate in the governance of the land and that the men could not make any land decisions without consulting with them.[561] For example, women from Kenpea explained that 'when women are not among them [. . .] they will send the crier to go round on the motorbike'.[562] Women's participation may be more well-established at the town level, while in the Sehzueplay community forest, as a new jurisdictional entity, legitimate mechanisms for women's participation are lacking.[563] The low degree of participation left women particularly vulnerable with respect to the negative effects of the community forest project.[564] It also indicates that in places where legitimate women's representatives are not well-established, development projects' empowerment strategies and imposed women's quotas produce little results. Mama describes this type of development feminism as

556 Roesch R (16 Mar 2018) Interview with a staff member of the FDA, Tappita, para 123.

557 Ibid, para 125.

558 Office of the Managing Director of the Forestry Development Autority (23 Oct 2014) Letter from the FDA to the Honorable Rebecca Gbar: Re: Conduct of social economic and reconnaissance survey (SER) and posting of notices for demarcation of designated community forest.

559 Johnson G (12 Mar 2018) Focus group discussion with women from Graie, Graie, para 93.

560 Roesch R (10 Mar 2018) Focus group discussion with women from Zuolay, Zuolay, para 112.

561 Roesch R (11 Mar 2018) Focus group discussion with women from Kenpea, Kenpea, paras 148–60; Johnson G (13 Mar 2018) Focus group discussion with women from Korlay, Korlay, para 129; Johnson G (14 Mar 2018) Focus group discussion with women from Sehyee, Sehyee Village, paras 151–60; Johnson G (15 Mar 2018) Focus group discussion with women from Zeonghn, Zeonghn, paras 296–300; see also Abramowitz and Moran (2012), p. 124.

562 Roesch R (11 Mar 2018) Focus group discussion with women from Kenpea, Kenpea, para 162.

563 Moran also explains that women can enforce their rights within customary or through the use of customary institutions in Southwestern Liberia (Moran 2012, pp. 55–56).

564 Social Impact's Liberia Strategic Analysis (2016), p. 22.

> gender inventions, in which gender is applied as a depoliticized, technical device, leading perhaps to more statistical data on women, gender analysis denuded so that it ceases to challenge the patriarchal power of the development industry, and instead "adds value" to existing meta-narratives.[565]

The field of the Sehzueplay community forest was thus characterized by gendered participatory exclusions.

4.3.3 *FPIC in Practice*

Following the identification of actors involved in the community forest authorization process, the emerging FPIC norm will be explored in the following section. This includes an examination of FPIC in the community self-identification, the identification of community land, the election of the governance structure and the adoption of governance rules, and the forest-use decision.

4.3.3.1 Community Self-Identification

The first element of the community forest registration is the determination of the community unit. Just like in Beyan Poye, the identification of the community unit was challenging in Sehzueplay and took place before the community applied for community forest status. The process took about 3 years and was heavily supported by PROSPER.[566] Due to the size of the Big Gio forest, it was decided to divide it between different clans: the Gblor and Gbear clans would establish one community forest together, while the Sehzueplay clan would manage the rest of the forest within Doe district.[567] In April 2013, the Sehzueplay clan 'comprising of six towns'[568] submitted their letter of application to the FDA.[569] However, the SER survey found that the community forest was owned by seven towns.[570]

While donors took the position that the clan system has a high degree of legitimacy and is, therefore, the appropriate community unit for governing the forest, the situation on the ground is actually more complex.[571] In most areas of Liberia, the notion of clans refers to the national government's administrative division of rural

[565] Mama (2004), pp. 122–23.

[566] Roesch R (16 Mar 2018) Interview with a former PROSPER staff member, Tappita, para 94.

[567] Tetra Tech ARD (2013e), p. 17.

[568] Ibid, p. 13.

[569] Sehzueplay Clan (1 Apr 2013) Letter from the Sehzueplay clan to the FDA: Letter of application for authorized forest community status.

[570] Forestry Development Authority, Socio-economic and resource reconnaissance survey result: Sehzueplay.

[571] ACDI/VOCA and Pact (2016), p. 14.

Liberia and not a kinship unit.[572] While in some areas of Liberia, clans did exist as kinship-based governance units, these units have been superseded by the central government's Hinterland policies and understandings of customary governance. For example, in the 1950s and 1960s, many communities were eager to claim clan status for the benefit of having their own Clan or Paramount Chief, prompting the government to introduce stricter rules for the recognition of clans.[573] In the post-war era, the number of clans in Nimba County rocketed upwards: in 1984, it had 34 clans, 73 in 2007, and 74 in 2014.[574] Local sources also confirmed that the clan system in Southern Nimba was introduced by the central government. A former District Commissioner explained: 'Before we were no clan, only in Grand Gedeh, they have the authority'.[575]

Sehzueplay, as a (loose) jurisdictional entity comprising of several towns, already existed in the 1970s.[576] It was part of the Doe clan, which is mentioned in anthropological sources from the 1940s.[577] Doe is now an administrative district and Sehzueplay received clan status in 2004.[578]

However, it was also controversial whether the seven towns owning the Sehzueplay community forest correspond to the clan unit. A few community members argued that the whole Sehzueplay clan manages the Sehzueplay community forest.[579] Other community members took the position that the Sehzueplay community forest-owning community does not correspond to the Sehzueplay clan.[580] Only the Northern towns are in charge of a parcel of the Big Gio forest, while the Southern towns manage the Little Gio forest and are not part of the Sehzueplay community forest.[581] Moreover, when asked about how and when the seven towns work together, community members explained that they only collaborate when a logging company seeks to exploit the forest.[582] Similarly, according to a local FDA officer, a customary relationship to the forest—a requirement for obtaining community forest status—means that a community has 'a common goal [that] has an impact on the forest'.[583] Thus, a functional understanding of community has emerged that does not

---

572 Liebenow (1969), p. 44; Clapham (1976), p. 73; Sawyer (1992), p. 358; Sawyer (2005), p. 161.

573 Jeanette Carter, as cited in: Alden Wily (2007), p. 85.

574 Hasselmann (1978), p. 1; Alden Wily (2007), p. 223; Liberia Institute of Statistics and Geo-Information Services (2014).

575 Roesch R (12 Mar 2019) Interview with a former FDA staff member, Graie, para 172.

576 Hasselmann (1978), pp. 39ff.

577 Schwab (1947), p. 25.

578 Riddell et al. (1971), p. 160; Liberia Institute of Statistics and Geo-Information Services (2014); Forestry Development Authority, Socio-economic and resource reconnaissance survey result: Sehzueplay, p. 1.

579 Roesch R (9 Mar 2018) Interview with Sehzueplay CFMB officer 4, Zeonghn, para 26.

580 See also Roesch R (9 Mar 2018) Interview with a former District Commissioner, Zuolay, para 88.

581 Roesch R (10 Mar 2018) Interview with a Clan Chief, Volay, paras 16–8.

582 Roesch R (12 Mar 2019) Interview with a former FDA staff member, Graie, para 122.

583 Roesch R (16 Mar 2018) Interview with a staff member of the FDA, Tappita, para 81.

correspond to existing customary understandings of forest ownership and governance.

Considerations of affectedness (i.e., whether communities lose farmland or are affected by potential logging operations) played a certain, albeit limited, role in this respect; Sehyee village was granted special status and became one of the seven towns. According to the Executive Committee's chairman, it is just

> a little village, a bullock between Boe-Quilla [neighboring community forest and district] and Sehzueplay. So because it is in the buffer zone, they consider it be a community. So they have three [Community Assembly members] from there [. . .] [even though] it is a village of Graie.[584]

This appears odd, as unlike most of the other towns, Sehyee's farmland was not negatively affected by the community forest demarcation, and other villages located right next to the forest were excluded from the 11 steps procedure.[585] While it is difficult to reconstruct how the decision was made to include Sehyee and have the community forest governed by the seven towns, the confusion about the meaning of Sehzueplay indicates that with the authorization of the community forest, a new territorial unit has emerged.

Community members also argued that the towns were the most important community unit before the war.[586] It will be shown that several towns have lost farmland in the implementation of community forestry. Thereby, it is noteworthy that the towns not negatively affected by the demarcation largely approved the community forest project, while community members from the affected towns were more critical. Even community members that were not personally affected criticized community forestry when people from their town lost farmland.[587] This indicates that there is a high degree of solidarity at the town level but not in the community forest unit. The big community unit thus risks silencing the voices of those negatively affected by community forestry.

Hence, the emerging community was probably the result of different actors pursuing different interests at the time. While some certainly saw the governability of the forest as a priority and envisioned a smaller community unit, other actors, like the FDA, deemed larger forests to be preferable for sustainable forest management or the economic exploitation of the forest.[588] Retrospectively, these competing visions often get masked, and the community identification is declared to be a community decision.[589] A strong narrative of community self-identification thus varnishes competing visions of community and forestry. The outcome is a new territorial unit that seeks to draw from the perceived legitimacy of the clan as a kinship unit,

[584] Roesch R (19 Mar 2018) Interview with Sehzueplay EC member 3, Monrovia, para 20.

[585] E.g. Niloco, Marwien Village, and Jerry Kpanien village (see also Roesch R (20 Mar 2018) Interview with FIFES staff member based in Nimba 2, Monrovia, para 164).

[586] Roesch R (12 Mar 2019) Interview with a former FDA staff member, Graie, para 128.

[587] E.g. community members in Volay and Zuolay.

[588] See also Sect. 4.2.3.2; Russell et al. (2011), p. 50.

[589] Roesch R (16 Mar 2018) Interview with a staff member of the FDA, Tappita, para 67.

but which is actually grounded in functionality considerations and colonial territorialities.

4.3.3.2 Identification of Community Land

Closely linked to the community identification is the identification of the community's forest land—the second element of the community forest authorization procedure. The decision to divide the Big Gio forest between the different districts and the clans within was also made before the 11 steps. The local PROSPER team leader explained that

> we talk like three years, have consultation with the community before going into the issue of the demarcation [...] We have several meetings with Doe district, several meetings with Kparblee, several meetings with Boe-Quilla, several meetings with Sehzueplay.[590]

The demarcation and mapping were highly technical processes, with the FDA taking the lead. One member of the Community Assembly explained that the 'map is being drawn by the FDA and PROSPER. So the map is done that we are expected to follow'.[591] Some community members even feared that PROSPER or the FDA would take their land.[592] Thus, most community members had little sense of ownership.

The basis for the demarcation was the preliminary map produced during the SER survey, which was harmonized with existing maps.[593] PROSPER provided Geospatial Information System (GIS) training to the community members involved in the demarcation.[594] Mixed teams with representatives from the different towns then demarcated the boundaries between their respective community forests.[595] PROSPER's focus in the boundary demarcation process was on the boundaries shared with the other clans, while the boundary between the forest and the community was not the subject of many discussions.[596] Instead, everybody assumed that the 1952 boundary line separating the national forest from the community's farmland would remain in place. Community members also regularly referred to it as the 'traditional boundary'.[597]

However, conflicts arose during the boundary cutting.[598] As the 1952 boundary line had been overgrown during the war, the Land Commissioner had approved

[590] Roesch R (16 Mar 2018) Interview with a former PROSPER staff member, Tappita, para 94.

[591] Roesch R (9 Mar 2018) Interview with a former District Commissioner, Zuolay, para 50.

[592] Roesch R (9 Mar 2018) Interview with Sehzueplay CFMB officer 4, Zeonghn, para 84; Roesch R (10 Mar 2018) Interview with a Clan Chief, Volay, para 90.

[593] Roesch R (16 Mar 2018) Interview with a staff member of the FDA, Tappita, para 205.

[594] Roesch R (9 Mar 2018) Interview with Sehzueplay CFMB officer 4, Zeonghn, para 84.

[595] Tetra Tech ARD (2016b), p. 16.

[596] Roesch R (16 Mar 2018) Interview with a former PROSPER staff member, Tappita, para 168.

[597] Roesch R (12 Mar 2019) Interview with a former FDA staff member, Graie, para 126.

[598] ACDI/VOCA (2019a), p. 10.

public land sales within the boundaries of the forest.[599] PROSPER and the FDA also found that community members did not know the location of the 1952 line.[600] Community members had thus used land located behind the boundary line. They asked the FDA to move the boundary line 600 m inwards to ensure that the towns could still access their farmland.[601] However, members of the Community Forest Organizing Committee—likely under the influence of the FDA—took the position that if 'we go deeply into the forest, we'll be losing management'[602] and that they needed to identify at least 9000 hectares.[603] Following a lengthy negotiation process involving the FDA and PROSPER, they decided to move the boundary 200 m inwards to exclude some of the community farmland.[604]

The maps were posted in the various towns and their quarters. According to a Community Awareness Team member, they also explained them to community members.[605] While in some towns,[606] information about the demarcation was provided, community members from other towns argued that they had not been (well) informed.[607] For example, one community member complained that 'they can [only] come to tell us the simple meaning of the poster. The big problem today is that [...] people did not come down to tell us the importance. They left everything undone!'[608]

When FIFES, the FDA, and community members embarked upon the cleaning of the boundary line in 2017, community members from the three communities still complained that the demarcation line encroached upon their farmland.[609] FIFES had to continuously engage in conflict resolution activities and concluded that PROSPER had not sufficiently ground-truthed the demarcation coordinates. A conflict

[599] Roesch R (10 Mar 2018) Interview with a Clan Chief, Volay, para 90; Roesch R (11 Mar 2018) Interview with a former Community Forest Organizing Committee member, Kenpea, paras, 128, 178; Roesch R (12 Mar 2018) Interview with a forest guard commander, Graie, para 18.

[600] Roesch R (16 Mar 2018) Interview with a former PROSPER staff member, Tappita, para 170.

[601] Doe Sehzueplay Clan (16 Aug 2016) Letter from the Doe Sehzueplay Clan to the FDA: MoU.

[602] Roesch R (12 Mar 2018) Interview with a Zone Chief, Graie, para 44.

[603] See also Roesch R (10 Mar 2018) Interview with a Clan Chief, Volay, para 90.

[604] Roesch R (11 Mar 2018) Focus group discussion with women from Kenpea, Kenpea, paras 61–63; Roesch R (11 Mar 2018) Interview with a former Community Forest Organizing Committee member, Kenpea, para 130.

[605] Roesch R (12 Mar 2018) Interview with a former member of the community awareness team, Graie, paras 142–44.

[606] Roesch R (11 Mar 2018) Focus group discussion with community members from Zeonghn, Zeonghn, para 7; Johnson G (14 Mar 2018) Focus group discussion with women from Sehyee, Sehyee Village, para 59.

[607] Johnson G (10 Mar 2018) Focus group discussion with women from Volay, Volay, paras 41, 85; Roesch R (11 Mar 2018) Focus group discussion with community members from Kenpea, Kenpea, para 7; Roesch R (14 Mar 2018) Focus group discussion with community members from Niloco (Graie), Niloco, para 7.

[608] Roesch R (10 Mar 2019) Interview with a former Town Chief, Zuolay, para 96.

[609] ACDI/VOCA (2019a), p. 18.

with neighboring communities was resolved in 2019, while conflicts within the Sehzueplay community were still lingering.[610]

4.3.3.3 Community Forest Governance

The third element of the community forest registration is the election of the community forest governance structure and the adoption of governance rules. The election procedure in Sehzueplay differed from that in Beyan Poye. The FDA, with support from PROSPER, held elections for the Community Assembly in each of the seven towns.[611] The three candidates with the most votes were sent as delegates to the so-called Community Assembly establishment forum. At the establishment forum, the delegates decided on the composition of the Community Assembly—including a women's quota—and elected the Executive Committee. Moreover, they set criteria for the selection of the CFMB members. Based on these criteria, the Executive Committee members proposed five CFMB candidates to the Community Assembly, which elected them. The Community Assembly representatives, the Executive Committee, and the CFMB were elected for 5 years, and their mandate may be renewed once.[612]

While each town has three Community Assembly members, the different towns are not evenly represented in the Executive Committee and CFMB. Graie (including Sehyee village) and Zeonghn have three representatives each in the Executive Committee or the CFMB, while Kenpea and Volay have no representatives. According to informants, neither the affectedness by the loss of farmland nor the number of inhabitants of the different towns were much discussed. Instead, 'it was a decision of the Community Assembly who they felt that they want to elect and that how they elect them'.[613] PROSPER also supported the community in drafting its constitution and by-laws. However, PROSPER's templates for the constitution and by-laws were hardly amended.[614]

The relationship between the three governance bodies is subject to some confusion; most members of the governance structure understand that the CFMB is in an exceptional position of power.[615] For example, members of the governance structure did not feel that the Community Assembly must provide a mandate for the CFMB to

610 ACDI/VOCA (2019b), p. 23.

611 Tetra Tech ARD (2017), p. 22.

612 Sehzueplay Community Forest (2016) Sehzueplay authorized forest community constitution Nimba county, art IV s 2.C.

613 Roesch R (19 Mar 2018) Interview with Sehzueplay EC member 3, Monrovia, para 20.

614 Sehzueplay Community Forest (2016) Sehzueplay authorized forest community constitution Nimba county; Sehzueplay Community (2016) Sehzueplay authorized community forest by-laws.

615 Roesch R (19 Mar 2018) Interview with Sehzueplay EC member 3, Monrovia, para 32.

negotiate with an investor.[616] Instead, the Community Assembly should only approve the agreement. Moreover, the CFMB determines how and where the social benefits, like the construction of schools, are realized.[617] One woman, therefore, worried that 'if the people [Opulence] agree to give something to the community and you ask the CFMB: you agreed there? We not know much. We not know, we will still be in poverty'.[618] Others stressed that the Community Assembly is the highest decision-making body.[619]

It was controversial amongst community members how well the flow of information within the governance structure and from the governance structure to the broader community worked. PROSPER pursued the strategy that 'if the leaders are educated in the CRL to the extent that it can affect their behaviors, then they can educate their constituencies and govern justly'.[620] Members of the CFMB felt that they informed the Community Assembly in a comprehensive and regular way, and some Community Assembly members shared that feeling.[621] Others complained about a lack of information.[622] They were particularly dissatisfied that they had not received copies of most of the important documents. The Community Assembly's work was also impaired by their lack of funding—if FIFES did not call for meetings, they had to pay for their own transportation, rendering additional meetings very difficult.[623] PROSPER's final evaluation concluded that knowledge was more condensed among those community members closer to the governance structure or PROSPER.[624] FIFES found that even the knowledge of the governance structure

[616] Roesch R (13 Mar 2018) Interview with Sehzueplay CFMB officer 1, Village nearby Zuolay, para 32.

[617] Roesch R (11 Mar 2018) Interview with Sehzueplay Community Assembly member 8, Kenpea, para 86–87.

[618] Roesch R (10 Mar 2018) Focus group discussion with women from Zuolay, Zuolay, para 147.

[619] Roesch R (14 Mar 2018) Interview with Sehzueplay EC member 4, Sehyee Village, para 26.

[620] Tetra Tech ARD (2015b), p. 9.

[621] Roesch R (10 Mar 2018) Interview with Sehzueplay Community Assembly member 5, Volay, para 26; Roesch R (14 Mar 2018) Interview with Sehzueplay Community Assembly member 14, Sehyee Village, para 78.

[622] Roesch R (10 Mar 2018) Interview with Sehzueplay Community Assembly member 3, Volay, para 40; Roesch R (13 Mar 2018) Interview with Sehzueplay CFMB officer 1, Village nearby Zuolay, para 88; Roesch R (13 Mar 2018) Interview with Sehzueplay CFMB officer 2, Korlay, paras 40–42; Roesch R (13 Mar 2018) Interview with Sehzueplay Community Assembly member 12, Korlay, para 50; Roesch R (14 Mar 2018) Interview with Sehzueplay Community Assembly member 14, Sehyee Village, paras 170, 185–86.

[623] Roesch R (9 Mar 2018) Interview with Sehzueplay CFMB officer 3, Zeonghn, para 130; Roesch R (3 May 2018) Anonymus source 4, para 27.

[624] Social Impact's Liberia Strategic Analysis (2016), p. 25.

was meager.[625] FIFES, therefore, focused on getting the CFMB functional and improving the flow of information to the broader governance structure.[626]

The Community Assembly members, in turn, felt that they had forwarded all the relevant information to the community members in their towns.[627] While community members in Sehzueplay generally knew more about the 11 steps and the community forest than in Beyan Poye, the satisfaction with the work of the governance structure greatly varied between the towns that had or had not lost farmland. In Korlay and Sehyee village, for example, where people could keep their native reserves, most people were satisfied with the work of their representatives.[628] In contrast, women in Volay complained that 'during PROSPER time [the 9 steps], that only the big people, not us, the town chiefs, they used to go for the meeting. But when they came, the only thing they can tell is, say we not go in the forest, we not go in the forest. That only thing!'[629] But also, in bigger towns like Graie, community members were dissatisfied with the information they received. According to one woman, 'when the person there [the Community Assembly member], you say: please, come from the workshop. Nothing'.[630] One man from Zuolay explained that 'they didn't tell our people, they conceal information',[631] while another one felt that 'what [PROSPER] says is, when the CFMB go for the workshop, their duty is to come distribute information from the workshop to the people. But none of them did it'.[632] Moreover, the smaller villages at the fringe of the forest were completely cut off from any information.[633]

625 Roesch R (20 Mar 2018) Interview with FIFES staff member based in Nimba 2, Monrovia, para 76.

626 Roesch R (20 Mar 2018) Interview with FIFES staff member based in Nimba 2, Monrovia, paras 82–86.

627 Roesch R (10 Mar 2018) Interview with Sehzueplay Community Assembly member 3, Volay, para 38; Roesch R (10 Mar 2018) Interview with Sehzueplay Community Assembly member 13, Zuolay, para 132; Roesch R (11 Mar 2018) Interview with Sehzueplay Community Assembly member 7, Kenpea, para 64; Roesch R (11 Mar 2018) Interview with Sehzueplay Community Assembly member 8, Kenpea, para 75; Roesch R (13 Mar 2018) Interview with Sehzueplay Community Assembly member 12, Korlay, para 96; Roesch R (14 Mar 2018) Interview with Sehzueplay Community Assembly member 14, Sehyee Village, para 190.

628 Johnson G (13 Mar 2018) Focus group discussion with women from Korlay, Korlay, para 63; Roesch R (14 Mar 2018) Focus group discussion with community members from Sehyee village, Sehyee Village, para 14; Johnson G (14 Mar 2018) Focus group discussion with women from Sehyee, Sehyee Village, paras 163–66.

629 Johnson G (10 Mar 2018) Focus group discussion with women from Volay, Volay, para 56; see also ibid., para 45.

630 Johnson G (12 Mar 2018) Focus group discussion with women from Graie, Graie, para 86.

631 Roesch R (10 Mar 2018) Interview with a former member of the Doe forest development committee, Zuolay, para 13.

632 Roesch R (10 Mar 2019) Interview with a former Town Chief, Zuolay, para 102.

633 Roesch R (14 Mar 2018) Interview with community members from Marwien Village, Marwien Village, para 6; Roesch R (14 Mar 2018) Focus group discussion with community members from Niloco (Graie), Niloco, paras 9, 11.

One Community Assembly member justified the poor information flow with the 'problem [that] when you call for meeting, sometimes it can be hard for everybody to go, so you not get anybody as one [i.e., the whole community] to meet'.[634] Particularly the community members spending most of their time in their farm villages, and women had problems attending meetings with Community Assembly members.[635]

Hence, a quite centralized understanding of forest governance has emerged in Sehzueplay, and the flow of information from the CFMB to the governance structure and the broader community remains a challenge. This may have been reinforced by the USAID-funded projects, which focused on getting the governance structure operational. Moreover, the lack of recognition of the institutional autonomy in the legislative framework resulted in a new governance structure. As it did not build upon existing institutions and rules, its functioning and legitimacy is limited. However, given the restrictions set by the forestry legislation, communities could do nothing but consent to the new institutions and rules.

4.3.3.4 Land-Use Decision

The differing visions of forestry prevailing among the different actors impacted the land-use decision as the fourth element of the community forest registration. The land-use decision had a substantial impact on the relationship between the community and the forest.

Essentially, forests can have three functions: they can be an economic resource, an ecological resource, or they can have a social welfare function—as reflected in the forest legislation's 3 Cs.[636] When the Sehzueplay community began cooperating with PROSPER, it committed to conserving its forest.[637] Yet, Sehzueplay's Community Forest Management Agreement grants the community the right to use the forest for conservation or the sustainable extraction of timber.[638] According to a FIFES field facilitator and a Community Assembly member, the majority of community members were only aware of the commercial use and the conservation option of the forest, but not that the forest could also be used by the community.[639] Several

[634] Roesch R (10 Mar 2018) Interview with Sehzueplay Community Assembly member 13, Zuolay, para 142.

[635] Roesch R (10 Mar 2018) Focus group discussion with women from Zuolay, Zuolay, para 40.

[636] Charles (1992), p. 384.

[637] Sehzueplay Clan (1 Apr 2013) Letter from the Sehzueplay clan to the FDA: Letter of application for authorized forest community status.

[638] Forestry Development Authority (2017) Community forest management agreement between the Forestry Development Authority and the people of Sehzueplay community, Doe administrative district, Nimba county, s 1.1.c.

[639] Roesch R (13 Mar 2018) Interview with Sehzueplay CFMB officer 1, Village nearby Zuolay, para 134; Roesch R (20 Mar 2018) Interview with FIFES staff member based in Nimba 2, Monrovia, para 94.

community members argued that PROSPER had only told them about conservation while the FDA informed them about the commercial use option.[640]

After signing the Community Forest Management Agreement, the problem became evident that the Community Forest Management Body (CFMB) did not acquire sufficient funds for maintaining the community forest.[641] Most community forest boundaries had become overgrown and needed to be cleared again. Also, drafting a Community Forest Management Plan exceeded the capacities of the CFMB. While FIFES had planned to support the community in the drafting, the project struggled with delays. The governance structure was, therefore, increasingly under pressure to generate income from the forest. One member of the CFMB explained that 'just nothing was given to us [by PROSPER and FIFES], at least to encourage us to really take care of the forest. And then, all the time, they say they invested 15 million [USD], and the community is benefitting nothing'.[642] Similarly, an influential member of the Executive Committee asked: 'How do you expect us to keep the forest here, when you are not empowering us with money to say "look, this is an amount of money, keep it in the bank and preserve the forest"'.[643] In response, community members increasingly saw commercial logging as the only viable solution. They took the position that 'as a CFMB officer, it is your responsibility to go and lobby and for company'.[644] The CFMB was thus under pressure to look for an investor.[645] However, as the highest decision-making body, the Community Assembly never officially provided a mandate to the CFMB to do so.[646]

At the same time, the US logging company Opulence was present and expressed its interest in entering into an agreement with the community.[647] Opulence staff members reinforced the discourse that conservation would not help the community in any way: 'FIFES goes in there, and the more forest FIFES has to manage, to not touch [but] does FIFES build one road? It Doesn't do anything to impact the lives of Liberians'.[648]

---

640 Roesch R (9 Mar 2018) Interview with Sehzueplay CFMB officer 3, Zeonghn, paras 50ff; Roesch R (9 Mar 2018) Interview with Sehzueplay CFMB officer 4, Zeonghn, para 182; Roesch R (11 Mar 2018) Interview with a former Community Forest Organizing Committee member, Kenpea, para 38. Only one community member remembered that PROSPER had also informed them about the commercial use option (Roesch R (9 Mar 2018) Interview with Sehzueplay Community Assembly member 9, Zeonghn, paras 59–60).

641 ACDI/VOCA (2018), p. 18.

642 Roesch R (9 Mar 2018) Interview with Sehzueplay CFMB officer 4, Zeonghn, para 182.

643 Roesch R (19 Mar 2018) Interview with Sehzueplay EC member 3, Monrovia, para 166.

644 Roesch R (12 Mar 2018) Interview with a Zone Chief, Graie, para 210.

645 Roesch R (9 Mar 2018) Interview with a former District Commissioner, Zuolay, para 122; Roesch R (12 Mar 2018) Focus group discussion with community members from Graie, Graie, para 16.

646 Roesch R (13 Mar 2018) Interview with Sehzueplay CFMB officer 1, Village nearby Zuolay, para 40.

647 Roesch R (9 Mar 2018) Interview with Sehzueplay CFMB officer 4, Zeonghn, para 174.

648 Roesch R (7 Mar 2018) Interview with a staff member of Opulence, Monrovia, para 82.

The District Commissioner apparently facilitated a secret meeting between members of the governance structure and Opulence during the community forest registration, also inviting the chiefs and the Superintendent.[649] Moreover, Opulence met with members of the governance structure right after the signing of the Community Forest Management Agreement in Monrovia in 2017.[650] However, at that point, no agreement was reached, and when Opulence entered the forest to obtain more information about the available tree species without the consent of the CFMB, the then-CFMB chairman fined them.[651]

Nevertheless, in June 2017, he signed a Memorandum of Understanding (MoU) with Opulence. According to community members, Opulence told the CFMB chairman and secretary that they had 2 weeks for the community to probate the MoU and, after that, it would be legally binding.[652] The FDA takes the position that MoUs may be signed once the Community Forest Management Agreement has been obtained but that they are not legally binding.[653] Irrespective of the MoU's legal status, the members of the governance structure never received a copy of the MoU, and the deadline for probation expired.[654] Many Community Assembly members felt offended and decided to dismiss the CFMB chairman and secretary. Most members of the governance structure portrayed it as a unanimous decision.[655] A few informants, however, argued the dismissal was controversial and that the Executive Committee's chairman had used the opportunity to increase his own power and the number of representatives from his town. The new CFMB Secretary is from the same town as the Executive Committee's chairman and was not elected by the Community Assembly—as required by Sehzueplay's Constitution—but appointed by the Executive Committee's chairman.[656]

After the dismissal of the two CFMB members, the Executive Committee's chairman took over and consulted with Opulence and the community's lawyer in Monrovia and Opulence.[657] According to the chairman, both the company and the

[649] Roesch R (9 Mar 2018) Interview with Sehzueplay CFMB officer 4, Zeonghn, para 242; Roesch R (20 Mar 2018) Interview with FIFES staff member based in Nimba 2, Monrovia, para 116.

[650] Roesch R (13 Mar 2018) Interview with Sehzueplay CFMB officer 2, Korlay, paras 60ff.

[651] Roesch R (11 Mar 2018) Interview with Sehzueplay Community Assembly member 7, Kenpea, para 84; Roesch R (13 Mar 2018) Interview with Sehzueplay CFMB officer 1, Village nearby Zuolay, para 38.

[652] Roesch R (13 Mar 2018) Interview with Sehzueplay CFMB officer 1, Village nearby Zuolay, para 98; Roesch R (19 Mar 2018) Interview with Sehzueplay EC member 3, Monrovia, para 34.

[653] Roesch R (15 Jan 2018) Interview with a senior staff member of the FDA, Monrovia, para 96.

[654] Roesch R (13 Mar 2018) Interview with Sehzueplay CFMB officer 1, Village nearby Zuolay, para 42.

[655] Roesch R (10 Mar 2018) Interview with Sehzueplay EC member 2, Graie, para 62.

[656] Roesch R (14 Mar 2019) Interview with Sehzueplay Community Assembly member 4, Sehyee Village, para 158; Roesch R (20 Mar 2018) Interview with FIFES staff member based in Nimba 2, Monrovia, para 114.

[657] Roesch R (13 Mar 2018) Interview with Sehzueplay CFMB officer 1, Village nearby Zuolay, para 16.

lawyer argued that the MoU was legally binding, and that the community had to sign a Commercial Use Contract with Opulence. An Opulence staff member explained that 'the two people are the officials that you people entrusted and put into office. Whatever they did here, it means that the community forest did it'.[658] Moreover, the lawyer warned them about the 'consequences on the Liberian government'[659] and that if the community opted out of the MoU, the 'people will cry in my knee, that no work, company have to come, and I went and cancel it',[660] which could have interfered with his prospects in the 2017 national election. Members of the governance structure also complained that the lawyer was so busy during the election time that he could not adequately take care of the matter.[661] He was appointed Minister of Posts and Telecommunications after the elections.[662]

Consequently, members of the governance structure felt that they had no other chance but to continue the negotiation.[663] A few days after the dismissal of the CFMB chairman and secretary, the CFMB continued to negotiate with Opulence. They received a draft Commercial Use Contract from Opulence and held a Community Assembly meeting in Zuolay to discuss the social benefits.[664] While the company took a few of their proposals into consideration, it ignored others.

In December 2017, 3 months after the signing of the MoU, the CFMB signed a Commercial Use Contract with Opulence.[665] The CFMB chairman read the agreement to the community members, but they did not have the opportunity to look at the

658 Opulence Staff member, as cited in: Roesch R (19 Mar 2018) Interview with Sehzueplay EC member 3, Monrovia, para 44; see also Roesch R (7 Mar 2018) Interview with a staff member of Opulence, Monrovia, para 120.

659 Lawyer of the Sehzueplay community, as cited in: Roesch R (19 Mar 2018) Interview with Sehzueplay EC member 3, Monrovia, para 56.

660 Lawyer of the Sehzueplay community, as cited in: ibid., para 74.

661 Roesch R (9 Mar 2018) Interview with Sehzueplay CFMB officer 4, Zeonghn, para 226.

662 After the cancelation of the Commercial Use Contract, the same lawyer signed a logging contract with the community in violation of the forest legislation (Harding Giahyue (2022) Liberia: Inside Minister Cooper Kruah's illegal logging deals. Daily Observer. https://www.Liberianobserver.com/Liberia-inside-minister-cooper-kruahs-illegal-logging-deals. Accessed 4 Aug 2023). In 2023, he was dismissed as a Minister due to his misconduct (Newa. 2023. Ex-Minister leaves government with a trail of illegal acts. The Dailight. https://thedaylight.org/2023/06/15/ex-minister-leaves-government-with-a-trail-of-illegal-acts/. Accessed 4 Aug 2023).

663 Roesch R (11 Mar 2018) Interview with Sehzueplay Community Assembly member 2, Kenpea, para 22; Roesch R (13 Mar 2018) Interview with Sehzueplay CFMB officer 2, Korlay, paras 104–106; Roesch R (14 Mar 2018) Interview with Sehzueplay EC member 4, Sehyee Village, para 68; Roesch R (10 Mar 2018) Interview with Sehzueplay Community Assembly member 5, Volay, para 52.

664 Roesch R (9 Mar 2018) Interview with Sehzueplay CFMB officer 4, Zeonghn, paras 208ff; Roesch R (19 Mar 2018) Interview with Sehzueplay EC member 3, Monrovia, para 96.

665 Roesch R (20 Mar 2018) Interview with FIFES staff member based in Nimba 2, Monrovia, para 124.

agreement, nor could they discuss it with the company.[666] According to a Community Assembly member, 'the chairman, to force us, at the time, there was no discussion, that we go through before signing the paper'.[667] Another Community Assembly member complained that 'there was not enough time. Because the thing there, it was hurry, hurry. So the way the people came and talked to us, there was time. But for the signing of the document, it was just fast'.[668] Moreover, apparently, when some community members voiced concerns about some provisions, the chairman silenced them, and they felt that if 'the majority says yes [...], we all agree'.[669] Opulence apparently also promised the Executive Committee's chairman that the members of the governance structure would get a so-called signing fee worth 4000 USD, which provided a strong incentive for waiving through the document.[670]

The Commercial Use Contract remains in effect for 14 years upon its signing and covers the whole community forest. The negotiated land rental and stumpage fees are relatively low, the social obligations of Opulence are often vague, and the community commits to supporting Opulence in the maintenance of roads and to providing building materials for free.[671] On top of that, the community members remain in charge of the costly boundary cleaning, which has to be done twice a year to ensure that the boundaries do not overgrow.[672]

The degree to which the FDA was involved in the communities' decision to opt for the commercial use of the forest is subject to speculation. According to FIFES staff and community members, employees from the FDA headquarters were involved in the negotiation, and local FDA staff 'does not have so much power to stop anything'.[673]

The decision to grant a Commercial Use Contract also fundamentally questioned the relationship between the community and FIFES. The community felt that FIFES did not have the right to interfere with their decision on how to use the forest and that

---

[666] Roesch R (10 Mar 2018) Interview with Sehzueplay Community Assembly member 5, Volay, para 48; Roesch R (11 Mar 2018) Interview with Sehzueplay Community Assembly member 2, Kenpea, para 68.

[667] Roesch R (13 Mar 2018) Interview with Sehzueplay Community Assembly member 12, Korlay, para 62; see also Roesch R (13 Mar 2018) Interview with Sehzueplay Community Assembly member 6, Korlay, para 40.

[668] Roesch R (10 Mar 2018) Interview with Sehzueplay Community Assembly member 5, Volay, para 48.

[669] Roesch R (10 Mar 2018) Interview with a former member of the Doe forest development committee, Zuolay, para 70; Roesch R (11 Mar 2018) Interview with Sehzueplay Community Assembly member 2, Kenpea, para 44.

[670] Roesch R (10 Mar 2019) Interview with a former Town Chief, Zuolay, para 180; Roesch R (19 Mar 2018) Interview with Sehzueplay EC member 3, Monrovia, paras 108ff.

[671] Republic of Liberia (2017) Third party forest management agreement between Sehzueplay Community Forest Management Body and Opulence logging company, ss 3, 5, 7.5.

[672] Sehzueplay Community Forest (2017) Sehzueplay Community Forest Management Plan, p. 18.

[673] Roesch R (16 Mar 2018) Interview with FIFES staff member based in Nimba, Tappita, para 116; see also Roesch R (19 Mar 2018) Interview with Sehzueplay EC member 3, Monrovia, para 56.

they only needed the approval of the FDA.[674] At the same time, they were still hoping for FIFES to continue supporting the community forest.[675]

The Community Forest Management Plan was adopted after the Commercial Use Contract with Opulence had been signed, thereby violating the CRL.[676] Community members strongly felt that they were not capable of meeting the FDA's expectations:

> The CFMB, we didn't have any funding. So even if you wrote the [Community Forest Management Plan] the best to your ability, if you carry it to FDA, it will be condemned [. . .] So the company can be the best person to speak the English they want to hear.[677]

Therefore, it was drafted by Opulence and adopted by the Community Assembly.[678] Most members of the governance structure could never read it.[679]

The Community Forest Management Plan reinforces the commercial earmark of the community forest.[680] Generally, it remains vague and does not zone the forest. Local forest uses are not permitted.[681] However, it speaks of determining quotas for the use of forest resources by community members under a license granted by the CFMB without clarifying the type of forest resources, the relevant forest areas, and the volume of those quotas.[682] Moreover, the Community Forest Management Plan obliges the CFMB to enforce the no-forest-use-policy and calls for the designation of forest guards to ensure that no one *illegally* uses natural resources in the forest or its buffer zone.[683] In 2019, FIFES was in the process of supporting the governance structure to revise the Community Forest Management Plan, which may result in the zoning of the forest and the designation of different use areas.[684]

Overall, few discussions about the commercial use of the forest and the Commercial Use Contract took place in the Community Assembly and the broader community.[685] Except for the meeting where the two CFMB members were dismissed and the one where the Commercial Use Contract draft was negotiated,

---

674 Roesch R (9 Mar 2018) Interview with Sehzueplay CFMB officer 4, Zeonghn, para 142.

675 Roesch R (11 Mar 2018) Interview with Sehzueplay Community Assembly member 2, Kenpea, para 26.

676 Republic of Liberia (2017) Third party forest management agreement between Sehzueplay Community Forest Management Body and Opulence logging company, s 4.

677 Roesch R (19 Mar 2018) Interview with Sehzueplay EC member 3, Monrovia, para 156.

678 Roesch R (9 Mar 2018) Interview with Sehzueplay CFMB officer 4, Zeonghn, para 194; Roesch R (13 Mar 2018) Interview with Sehzueplay CFMB officer 1, Village nearby Zuolay, para 144.

679 Roesch R (13 Mar 2018) Interview with Sehzueplay CFMB officer 1, Village nearby Zuolay, para 148; Roesch R (13 Mar 2018) Interview with Sehzueplay Community Assembly member 6, Korlay, para 32; Roesch R (13 Mar 2018) Interview with Sehzueplay Community Assembly member 10, Korlay, para 62.

680 Sehzueplay Community Forest (2017) Sehzueplay Community Forest Management Plan, p. 1.

681 Ibid, p. 18.

682 Ibid, pp. 20ff.

683 Ibid, p. 21.

684 ACDI/VOCA (2019b), p. 17.

685 E.g. Roesch R (9 Mar 2018) Interview with Sehzueplay Community Assembly member 1, Zeonghn, para 72.

no extra meetings were held.[686] Many Community Assembly members had only seen Opulence representatives at the signing ceremony, while others reported having attended two or three meetings.[687] The only community members having copies of the Commercial Use Contract were the CFMB and the Executive Committee's chairman.[688] Most community members were unaware of the details of the agreement.[689] Particularly the more remote towns faced the problem that community members could not afford to go to meetings and, therefore, had little to no access to information.[690] In Volay town, community members declared that they 'don't know about any negative impacts [of logging], but [we] also don't sit with them [the decision-makers]'.[691]

Following the signing of the Commercial Use Contract, the dissatisfaction with Opulence has grown. Community members complained that Opulence had distributed a lower signing fee than promised and that the community should finance the boundary cleaning.[692] Moreover, unresolved land disputes overshadowed the contract.[693]

While members of the governance structure regularly framed the Commercial Use Contract as a mistake and emphasized their lack of options, most community members saw it in a less negative way. They hoped for the improvement of their economic situation.[694] Community members mentioned the creation of jobs and the construction of roads, bridges, and a school.[695] Women were especially interested in

[686] Roesch R (14 Mar 2019) Interview with Sehzueplay Community Assembly member 4, Sehyee Village, para 178.

[687] Roesch R (9 Mar 2018) Interview with Sehzueplay Community Assembly member 9, Zeonghn, para 86; Roesch R (10 Mar 2018) Interview with Sehzueplay Community Assembly member 13, Zuolay, para 108; Roesch R (13 Mar 2018) Interview with Sehzueplay Community Assembly member 6, Korlay, paras 35–36; Roesch R (13 Mar 2018) Interview with Sehzueplay Community Assembly member 10, Korlay, para 68; Roesch R (14 Mar 2019) Interview with Sehzueplay Community Assembly member 4, Sehyee Village, paras 118–22.

[688] Roesch R (13 Mar 2018) Interview with Sehzueplay Community Assembly member 10, Korlay, para 82; Roesch R (14 Mar 2019) Interview with Sehzueplay Community Assembly member 4, Sehyee Village, para 150.

[689] Roesch R (11 Mar 2018) Focus group discussion with women from Kenpea, Kenpea, paras 81–84.

[690] Roesch R (14 Mar 2018) Focus group discussion with community members from Sehyee village, Sehyee Village, para 13.

[691] Roesch R (10 Mar 2018) Focus group discussion with community members in Volay, Volay, para 15.

[692] Roesch R (19 Mar 2018) Interview with Sehzueplay EC member 3, Monrovia, para 116.

[693] Roesch R (10 Mar 2018) Interview with Sehzueplay Community Assembly member 3, Volay, para 62.

[694] Ibid, para 58; Johnson G (13 Mar 2018) Focus group discussion with women from Korlay, Korlay, para 58; Johnson G (15 Mar 2018) Focus group discussion with women from Zeonghn, Zeonghn, paras 168–83.

[695] E.g. Johnson G (14 Mar 2018) Focus group discussion with women from Sehyee, Sehyee Village, paras 78–82.

providing food or laundry services to the workers to be able to better sustain their families.[696] A few women also hoped to be employed by the company but feared that 'because some of us are not educated, they will not take us. We will just be here suffering'.[697]

Moreover, several women claimed that they would stop the company's activities if it failed to compensate them for destroyed crops.[698] Similarly, one CFMB member declared that if 'nothing is done for us [by Opulence], we evict them'.[699] Thus, the Commercial Use Contract is not seen as set in stone but as an arrangement subject to renegotiation if necessary. These differing understandings of the (legal) quality of the agreement between the community and the company are common in many consultation processes across the world. Rodríguez-Garavito describes them as the 'miscommunication effect',[700] which may contribute to conflicts in the future. The ultimate use of the forest is not fully settled yet.

As explored above, most actors involved in the operationalization of community forestry took an interest either in commercial forestry or forest conservation. In both cases, local forest uses have limited space, causing the emergence of a no-forest-use-policy just like in Beyan Poye. According to community members, it was the FDA that told them not to enter the forest anymore.[701] When the FDA noticed during the demarcation that many community members were living in the forest, they told them to leave.[702] PROSPER also attributed the 'strict protection message'[703] to the FDA.

PROSPER's and FIFES' position on local forest uses is more ambiguous. Leading PROSPER staff members argued that it was never PROSPER's intention to prevent communities from using their forests.[704] They even saw the constitutions and by-laws created in many community forests as unenforceable and unrealistic and assumed that communities codified what they thought 'PROSPER wants to hear'.[705] However, they also saw farming within community forests as a major problem and considered relocating and compensating farmers.[706] Moreover, local PROSPER

[696] Johnson G (13 Mar 2018) Focus group discussion with women from Korlay, Korlay, paras 96, 98.

[697] Johnson G (10 Mar 2018) Focus group discussion with women from Volay, Volay, para 98.

[698] Ibid, paras 207–11; Roesch R (11 Mar 2018) Focus group discussion with women from Kenpea, Kenpea, paras 112–14.

[699] Roesch R (9 Mar 2018) Interview with Sehzueplay CFMB officer 3, Zeonghn, para 148.

[700] Rodríguez-Garavito (2010), pp. 33ff.

[701] Roesch R (13 Mar 2018) Focus group discussion with community members from Korlay, Korlay, para 10.

[702] Roesch R (12 Mar 2018) Interview with a forest guard commander, Graie, para 16.

[703] Tetra Tech ARD (2013e), p. 15.

[704] Roesch R (4 Apr 2018) Skype interview with a former senior staff member of the LRCFP and PROSPER, para 82.

[705] Tetra Tech ARD (2013e), p. 15.

[706] Tetra Tech ARD (2013c), p. 14; Roesch R (9 Mar 2018) Interview with Sehzueplay CFMB officer 3, Zeonghn, para 44; Johnson G (14 Mar 2018) Focus group discussion with women from Sehyee, Sehyee Village, para 9.

staff members supported the no-forest-use policy during the 11 steps as they were concerned about the negative impact of shifting cultivation on the forest ecosystem.[707] To some extent, PROSPER was thus divided about the use of the forest. It is possible that PROSPER staff on the ground promoted a stricter conservation message than intended by the headquarters in Monrovia.

Similarly, international experts linked to FIFES argued that it was not the project's intention to ban local forest uses but that it would still be a 'best practice'[708] to not use the forest during the 11 steps. Just like the local PROSPER staff members, FIFES staff members based in Nimba held that 'automatically nobody can go there for now until the biomonitoring [element of the Community Forest Management Plan] is completed'.[709] It is thus possible that FIFES wanted to be on the safe side, meeting USAID's biodiversity requirements, and pushed communities towards enforcing the no-forest-use policy.[710]

Local leaders adopted this position and, according to an informant, the District Commissioner made the decision that the community members living in the forest should be evicted after the demarcation.[711] They were, however, struggling to enforce the policy.[712] Therefore, FIFES supported the training of forest guards.[713] Every town appointed two volunteers to patrol the forest once per week and report to the CFMB.[714] Some community members also reported that the CFMB fined community dwellers farming in the buffer zone surrounding the community forest.[715] However, a forest guard complained that the community members in the forest did not take them seriously.[716] Community members continued to use forest resources, and members of the governance structure explained that the conflict was a 'legal battle'[717] and that the violators needed to be brought to justice.[718] If

[707] Roesch R (9 Mar 2018) Interview with Sehzueplay CFMB officer 3, Zeonghn, para 44; Johnson G (14 Mar 2018) Focus group discussion with women from Sehyee, Sehyee Village, para 9.

[708] Roesch R (3 May 2018) Anonymus source 4, para 15.

[709] Roesch R (16 Mar 2018) Interview with FIFES staff member based in Nimba, Tappita, para 170; see also Roesch R (20 Mar 2018) Interview with FIFES staff member based in Nimba 2, Monrovia, para 94.

[710] Roesch R (3 May 2018) Anonymus source 4, para 17.

[711] Roesch R (20 Mar 2018) Interview with FIFES staff member based in Nimba 2, Monrovia, para 102.

[712] Roesch R (12 Mar 2019) Interview with a former FDA staff member, Graie, para 32ff; Roesch R (12 Mar 2018) Interview with a former member of the community awareness team, Graie, para 80.

[713] Roesch R (9 Mar 2018) Interview with a former District Commissioner, Zuolay, para 42.

[714] Roesch R (12 Mar 2018) Interview with a forest guard commander, Graie, paras 30, 36, 42.

[715] Roesch R (10 Mar 2018) Interview with Sehzueplay Community Assembly member 3, Volay, para 110.

[716] Roesch R (12 Mar 2018) Interview with a forest guard commander, Graie, paras 56–58.

[717] Roesch R (19 Mar 2018) Interview with Sehzueplay EC member 3, Monrovia, para 132.

[718] Roesch R (12 Mar 2018) Interview with a forest guard commander, Graie, para 46.

communities fail to comply with their Management Plan, they risk losing their community forest.[719]

It can thus be summarized that the Sehzueplay community forest project, to some extent, constitutes a continuation of pre-war land alienation. The policing of local forest uses before the war extinguished customary land rights to a great extent and made community people accept that the forest belongs to the government.[720] The community forest project has a similar effect. Given the strong pressure on the community, it may be doubted thatthey could make a free and informed decision.

After the authorization of the Sehzueplay community forest, another issue concerning the community forest came to light: the buffer zone. Buffer zones are 'best management practices'[721] in forestry and conservation and delimit forest zones used for different purposes.[722] Under the Liberian Code of Forest Harvesting Practices, buffer zones need to be designated around watersheds, local use areas, and protected areas.[723] The forest legislation, however, does not mandate the creation of buffer zones for community forests. During the first 9 steps, the FDA had suggested creating a 3 m-buffer strip around the forest to prevent community members from entering it. However, PROSPER cautioned against the idea, and there exists no indication that it was introduced in Sehzueplay.[724]

In contrast, the FIFES project makes explicit reference to buffer zones: it seeks to enhance the 'capacity of Government of Liberia (GoL) institutions and rural communities to sustainably manage and benefit from community forest (CF) and buffer zone natural resources'.[725] FIFES also reported that the Sehzueplay CFMB has 'agreed to set aside areas along [community forest] boundaries that will be managed as protective zones to the [community forest]. The width of the buffer is yet to be determined'.[726] It is thus likely that FIFES—with the support of the FDA—pushed community members towards introducing a buffer zone.[727] This corresponds to the memory of several community members, who held that a leading staff member of FIFES had given them training on buffer zones.[728] Moreover, the community forests without FIFES' support generally do not have buffer zones.

---

719 Roesch R (16 Mar 2018) Interview with a former PROSPER staff member, Tappita, para 182.

720 Roesch R (12 Mar 2019) Interview with a former FDA staff member, Graie, paras 30–32.

721 Roesch R (3 May 2018) Anonymus source 4, para 33.

722 Cittadino (2020), pp. 317–18.

723 Code of forest harvesting practices (2017), s 2.5.1.

724 Email from leading PROSPER staff member to the author (11 November 2019).

725 ACDI/VOCA (2017a), p. 4.

726 Ibid, p. 26.

727 Roesch R (14 Mar 2018) Interview with Sehzueplay EC member 4, Sehyee Village, para 60; Roesch R (3 May 2018) Anonymus source 4, para 33.

728 Roesch R (10 Mar 2018) Focus group discussion with community members from Zuolay, Zuolay, para 12; Roesch R (12 Mar 2018) Focus group discussion with community members from Graie, Graie, para 10.

Community members were unsure at what point the buffer zone was introduced. In a 2017 report, the buffer zone surrounding community forest area is mentioned for the first time.[729] Furthermore, FIFES and FDA staff and an international forestry expert took the position that it had been demarcated after the Community Forest Management Agreement had been signed.[730] They emphasized that the size was the decision of the community.[731] In Sehzueplay, a 3 km buffer zone[732] was introduced.[733] Some members of the governance structure argued that the FDA had proposed the width of 3 km.[734] Yet, according to an FDA officer, the standard buffer zone is 500 m.[735]

Regarding the function of the buffer zone, a local FDA officer took the position that the buffer zone could be used for farming by community members, but they should not do so as the greater area is a biodiversity habitat: 'the purpose of the buffer zone is to protect the forest, it is almost like a defense for the forest'.[736] FIFES was also concerned about the 'tremendous logging pressure'[737] in the buffer zone. A local FIFES staff member argued that buffer zones are necessary to protect watersheds and biodiversity and that the CFMB could not allow for farming in the buffer zone because then even more community members would encroach upon the community forest.[738] This was echoed by members of the governance structure.[739] One Executive Committee member explained that 'if you have people in buffer zone, they will be leaving from there to go in the forest'.[740]

During the demarcation of the buffer zone, conflicts between the FDA and community members arose. The District Commissioner, the Community Assembly, and the CFMB instructed people to leave the buffer zone, and many of them moved

[729] ACDI/VOCA (2017c), p. 13.

[730] Roesch R (20 Mar 2018) Interview with FIFES staff member based in Nimba 2, Monrovia, paras 181; Roesch R (3 May 2018) Anonymus source 4, para 31.

[731] Roesch R (12 Mar 2018) Interview with a Zone Chief, Graie, para 74; Roesch R (16 Mar 2018) Interview with a staff member of the FDA, Tappita, para 243; Roesch R (16 Mar 2018) Interview with FIFES staff member based in Nimba, Tappita, para 180.

[732] Community members were unsure about the width of the buffer zone, with some of them suggesting that it was 3 miles, 3 km or 300 m. FIFES staff members took the position that it is 3 km.

[733] Roesch R (19 Mar 2018) Interview with Sehzueplay EC member 3, Monrovia, para 176.

[734] Roesch R (10 Mar 2018) Interview with Sehzueplay Community Assembly member 3, Volay, para 86; Roesch R (14 Mar 2018) Interview with Sehzueplay EC member 4, Sehyee Village, para 60.

[735] Roesch R (16 Mar 2018) Interview with a staff member of the FDA, Tappita, para 257.

[736] Ibid, para 241.

[737] ACDI/VOCA (2017c), p. 12.

[738] Roesch R (16 Mar 2018) Interview with FIFES staff member based in Nimba, Tappita, paras 198, 216.

[739] Roesch R (11 Mar 2018) Interview with a former Community Forest Organizing Committee member, Kenpea, para 132.

[740] Roesch R (14 Mar 2018) Interview with Sehzueplay EC member 4, Sehyee Village, para 58.

back from their farming villages into the main towns.[741] Community members, in contrast, rejected the buffer zone as the tribal or native reserves of several towns were located within it. Tribal reserves, under the pre-Land Rights Act legislation, refer to land that communities could use for essential activities.[742] Communities had use rights for these reserves. In Sehzueplay, the government granted some of the reserves as compensation to the communities that were affected by the 1952 boundary line separating the national forest from the farmland or that did not have enough farmland.[743] The native reserves had been used for planting eddoes, rubber trees, cocoa, plantains, and oil palm.[744]

Besides Zeonghn and Sehyee village, all towns reported that some or most of their community members were affected.[745] Community members repeatedly explained that they lost their 'old area',[746] and that 'no big tree here, that only [in the] Doe [community forest], but they take everything from us'.[747] One old man explained: 'the village in which I was born on this side, that the village we're talking about, you see my gray hair, where I was born, today they said I should leave it. This is very impossible'.[748]

While in some towns, community members who had previously farmed in the buffer zone could access alternative farmland, no free farmland was available in other places.[749] Volay town, for instance, is located less than 3 km from the community forest, and community members from Volay argued that 'the old land [was] right [here at] our village, that there was the boundary. So we got no place to make farm!'[750]

741 Roesch R (10 Mar 2018) Interview with Sehzueplay EC member 2, Graie, para 138.

742 Stevens (2014), p. 255.

743 Roesch R (10 Mar 2018) Focus group discussion with women from Zuolay, Zuolay, para 22; Roesch R (10 Mar 2019) Interview with a former Town Chief, Zuolay, para 24; Roesch R (12 Mar 2019) Interview with a former FDA staff member, Graie, para 44; Roesch R (14 Mar 2018) Focus group discussion with community members from Niloco (Graie), Niloco, para 4.

744 Johnson G (10 Mar 2018) Focus group discussion with women from Volay, Volay, para 224; Roesch R (14 Mar 2018) Focus group discussion with community members from Niloco (Graie), Niloco, para 4.

745 Roesch R (10 Mar 2018) Focus group discussion with community members from Zuolay, Zuolay, para 6; Roesch R (11 Mar 2018) Focus group discussion with community members from Kenpea, Kenpea, para 4; Roesch R (12 Mar 2018) Focus group discussion with community members from Graie, Graie, para 4; Roesch R (13 Mar 2018) Focus group discussion with community members from Korlay, Korlay, para 6.

746 Roesch R (10 Mar 2018) Focus group discussion with women from Zuolay, Zuolay, para 2.

747 Johnson G (10 Mar 2018) Focus group discussion with women from Volay, Volay, para 71.

748 Roesch R (10 Mar 2018) Interview with a former member of the Doe forest development committee, Zuolay, para 34.

749 E.g. Roesch R (10 Mar 2019) Interview with a former Town Chief, Zuolay, para 50; Roesch R (10 Mar 2018) Interview with Sehzueplay Community Assembly member 3, Volay, para 104.

750 Johnson G (10 Mar 2018) Focus group discussion with women from Volay, Volay, para 32.

Community members, including members of the Community Assembly, informed the CFMB about the issue to no avail.[751] They also brought the issue to FIFES' attention.[752] A FIFES staff member admitted that he did not know about the number of people affected by the loss of their native reserves, as nobody collected data on the number of farms in the buffer zone before or during the demarcation.[753] Most importantly, in the eyes of many community members, they were 'appealing to FDA that they should at least, [. . .] the old, old farming area, that that they should give it back to them, so that they will be able to eat from there'.[754] Yet, the local FDA officer argued that they were not aware of any problems.[755] The fact that even Community Assembly members appealed to the FDA rather than calling a Community Assembly meeting strongly indicates that the Community Assembly was not involved in the decision about the buffer zone and felt that it was beyond its competence.

Moreover, it contributed to the feeling amongst many community members that their land had been alienated by PROSPER or FIFES.[756] For instance, one woman argued that 'we didn't think that they [PROSPER] would come and get our land [. . .] They take some of ours and add it on their own'.[757] This again illustrates the low level of ownership that the members of the Community Assembly and ordinary community have over the community forest project.

The creation of the buffer zone constituted a considerable extension of the jurisdiction of the governance structure by adding roughly 6000 hectares to the 6890 hectares of the community forest without any indication of community consent. FIFES' mid-term evaluation also found that the restrictive forest rules contributed to degraded livelihoods. The alternative livelihood activities offered by FIFES were less productive than the shifting cultivation within the forest and the buffer zone.[758] Community members complained that they could no longer access their cassava, rice, cocoa, and plantain farms. This had negative consequences not only

[751] Roesch R (10 Mar 2018) Interview with Sehzueplay Community Assembly member 3, Volay, para 92.

[752] Roesch R (14 Mar 2018) Focus group discussion with community members from Niloco (Graie), Niloco, para 4.

[753] Roesch R (16 Mar 2018) Interview with FIFES staff member based in Nimba, Tappita, para 208.

[754] Roesch R (10 Mar 2018) Interview with Sehzueplay Community Assembly member 3, Volay, para 80; see also Roesch R (10 Mar 2018) Interview with a Clan Chief, Volay, para 96; Roesch R (10 Mar 2019) Interview with a former Town Chief, Zuolay, para 18; Roesch R (10 Mar 2018) Interview with Sehzueplay Community Assembly member 11, Graie, paras 33–36; Roesch R (14 Mar 2018) Focus group discussion with community members from Niloco (Graie), Niloco, para 4.

[755] Roesch R (16 Mar 2018) Interview with a staff member of the FDA, Tappita, para 299.

[756] Roesch R (10 Mar 2018) Focus group discussion with women from Zuolay, Zuolay, para 22.

[757] Johnson G (10 Mar 2018) Focus group discussion with women from Volay, Volay, para 62.

[758] Liberia Strategic Analysis (2018), p. 8.

on the availability of local food products but also contributed to reduced household incomes and undermined the legitimacy of the community forest project.[759]

4.3.4 *FPIC Between Conservation and Development*

The emerging understanding of FPIC differs from the understandings of FPIC in the transnational space and from the FPIC as envisioned in the national forestry legislation. It is a complete departure from the rights-based understanding of FPIC. The emerging FPIC is neither grounded in the right to self-determination nor in the right to culture or land. Instead, FPIC gets embedded in technical forest management to the point that the language of FPIC and community rights is no longer used. Following the correct procedure is more important than building community consensus and providing a space for inclusive deliberation. When confronted with protests, members of the governance structure regularly argued that the 11 steps had been followed and the community members in question had failed to submit their complaints in time.[760] Therefore, nothing could be done about their land claims. Most community members, in contrast, see community forestry as just another external program. They have a very limited sense of ownership, feeling that they could not meet the legal requirements on their own and are thus in a position of dependency on external actors like Opulence, the FDA, and PROSPER or FIFES.

To understand how this version of FPIC and forestry has emerged, the hegemonic discourse underlying community forestry in Sehzueplay will be explored. It revolves around the understanding of the forest as an ecological resource, which functions as a nodal point determining the meaning of elements such as FPIC and the community.[761] However, it will be shown that in an interdiscursive encounter with development discourse, the meaning of the forest as an ecological resource changed, also incorporating the commercial use of the forest.[762] Moreover, it drew from legal discourse. The prevailing discourse had four main strands: a fiction of uninhabited land is applied to reject customary land claims, customary land alienation is justified with conservation, and commercial logging is constructed to be a form of forest conservation. In addition to these three discourse strands, a fourth has emerged that is less obvious and more common amongst important community stakeholders: community forestry as a way of reinforcing and extending community jurisdiction.

[759] Ibid, p. 15.

[760] Roesch R (10 Mar 2018) Interview with Sehzueplay EC member 1, Graie, para 56; Roesch R (14 Mar 2018) Interview with Sehzueplay EC member 4, Sehyee Village, para 48.

[761] Laclau and Mouffe (2001), p. 112.

[762] Jørgensen and Phillips (2002), p. 73.

4.3.4.1 The Fiction of the Uninhabited Forest

The fiction of the uninhabited forest is common in forestry and conservation discourse as well as in legal discourse. When donors and the government began measuring the Liberian forest cover in the mid-twentieth century, they assumed that high-density forests were uninhabited and wild.[763] This assumption was based on the understanding of local farming practices as inherently in conflict with forest conservation—where communities live the forest inevitably gets destroyed.[764] The fiction of the uninhabited forest played a major role in Sehzueplay. For instance, a representative of Opulence argued that 'the forest that we are talking about has not been used. Because [it would] be destroyed and busy, there won't be any wood for anybody to go there and get it'.[765]

The fiction of the uninhabited forest also informed the first 9 steps when it was decided that only deeded land should be singled out from the community forest.[766] Members of the Community Forest Organizing Committee concluded there were no people (legitimately) living in the forest, as nobody approached the FDA with their deed.[767] Thereby, they drew from legal discourse and its 'claims to legitimacy and a higher morality'[768] for legitimizing the community forest project.[769] Specifically, from a narrow, centralistic understanding of the law: only tenure arrangements recognized by the state are legitimate while claims based on customary law are not.[770]

The fiction of the uninhabited forest and legal discourse laid the foundation for the illegalization of people living in and using the forest. In this respect, it was often emphasized that people had only moved into the forest during the war or that they were strangers that had exploited the FDA's lack of control over the forest during the war and refuse to leave now.[771] Those resisting the no-forest-use policy were framed as 'stubborn'[772] or 'violators'.[773] Moreover, their actions were constructed as being harmful to the community. A member of the CFMB argued that 'the forest is not for

[763] See also Sect. 4.1.1.3; Lowenhaupt Tsing (2003), pp. 28–29.

[764] This assumption is widespread in many (colonized) countries where environmental policies are now failing (Richardson (2009), p. 338).

[765] Roesch R (7 Mar 2018) Interview with a staff member of Opulence, Monrovia, para 178.

[766] Roesch R (10 Mar 2018) Interview with a Clan Chief, Volay, para 90; Roesch R (12 Mar 2018) Interview with a Zone Chief, Graie, para 44; Roesch R (16 Mar 2018) Interview with a former PROSPER staff member, Tappita, 184.

[767] Roesch R (12 Mar 2018) Interview with a Zone Chief, Graie, para 44.

[768] von Benda-Beckmann et al. (2009a), p. 22.

[769] See also Bourdieu et al. (1994), p. 9.

[770] See also Tobin (2014), pp. 29ff.

[771] Roesch R (9 Mar 2018) Interview with a former District Commissioner, Zuolay, para 4.

[772] Roesch R (9 Mar 2018) Interview with Sehzueplay CFMB officer 4, Zeonghn, para 278.

[773] Roesch R (10 Mar 2019) Interview with a former Town Chief, Zuolay, para 36.

one person',[774] highlighting that the use of forest resources by just a few community people is seen as unfair.[775] Other community members also held that those still using the forest were greedy and just went into the forest because of the good soil quality, even though they had enough farmland near their towns.[776]

4.3.4.2 Justifying Land Alienation with Conservation

A second discourse strand justifies the alienation of customary land with the need to protect the forest. Due to the presence of PROSPER and FIFES, a strong conservation discourse exists in Sehzueplay. Within this conservation discourse that constructs the forest as an *ecological resource,* local forest uses—particularly shifting cultivation—are seen as the main driver for land scarcity and conflicts.[777] Moreover, the negative carbon balance of local agricultural practices is emphasized.[778] PROSPER's outreach campaign furthermore took a critical stance towards bushmeat hunting and local chainsaw logging.[779] From this follows a vision of community forestry that effectively protects the forest from the community.[780]

Many community members echoed this conservation discourse. At a 2014 citizens' meeting in Zuolay, the community agreed that all farmers and settlers needed to clear the forest.[781] One former Community Awareness Team member explained that they told people that 'we should not farm in the forest [. . .] Because the forest helps us to get good water. And there are some animals in the forest that we have to maintain for our children to benefit tomorrow'.[782]

In this respect and similar to the findings from Beyan Poye, the narrative of ignorance was very common both among members of the governance structure and other community members.[783] Community members and officials alike declared that

774 Roesch R (13 Mar 2018) Interview with Sehzueplay CFMB officer 2, Korlay, para 164.

775 Roesch R (12 Mar 2018) Interview with a former member of the community awareness team, Graie, para 22.

776 Roesch R (9 Mar 2018) Interview with a former District Commissioner, Zuolay, para 8; Roesch R (12 Mar 2018) Focus group discussion with community members from Graie, Graie, para 8; Johnson G (12 Mar 2018) Focus group discussion with women from Graie, Graie, para 67; Roesch R (12 Mar 2018) Interview with a former member of the community awareness team, Graie, para 72; Roesch R (12 Mar 2018) Interview with a Zone Chief, Graie, paras 230ff.

777 Roesch R (16 Mar 2018) Interview with FIFES staff member based in Nimba, Tappita, para 226.

778 Ibid, para 238.

779 Tetra Tech ARD (2015a), pp. 13ff.

780 Roesch R (16 Mar 2018) Interview with a staff member of the FDA, Tappita, para 241.

781 Tetra Tech ARD (2014b), p. 37.

782 Roesch R (12 Mar 2018) Interview with a former member of the community awareness team, Graie, para 20.

783 Roesch R (9 Mar 2018) Interview with Sehzueplay CFMB officer 3, Zeonghn, paras 42, 44; Roesch R (13 Mar 2018) Interview with Sehzueplay Community Assembly member 10, Korlay, para 4.

'prior to PROSPER [...], they had little or no environmental awareness'.[784] Traditional farming practices such as hunting, shifting cultivation, and upland rice farming are framed as backward and unsustainable.[785] Farming is seen as 'destroying the forest'.[786] One woman defined the community forest as the forest 'that is being protected from the things of the community'.[787] Another woman argued that 'during our days, we used to go in the forest and spoil it, because we go to spoil the trees, because we cut down the trees, no use!'[788] One man explained that 'so that we gain from them [PROSPER], those days our parents did not know about it before'.[789] The conservation discourse thus justifies the imposition of the no-forest-use policy.

4.3.4.3 Re-Defining Conservation

In the early stages of the application process, everybody assumed that the community would decide to conserve its forest.[790] However, during the 9 steps, the discourse changed in an interdiscursive encounter—the prevailing conservation discourse met development discourse, changing the order of the discourse.[791] With conservation and development discourses having a very similar understanding of the community and FPIC, the merging of the two discourses was possible.

The discourse change occurred through the portrayal of the commercial use option as a necessity, and the meaning of conservation was redefined as also including the commercial exploitation of the forest. Similar to Beyan Poye, the forest was increasingly framed as an *economic resource* from which the community should benefit. However, benefitting does not mean that the forest is a communally used and managed resource but rather a collective source of income. To put it in the words of a CFMB member, 'we agree to work with [Opulence] because [...] for 50 years or a decade, we've been conserving this forest. But the community cannot

[784] Social Impact's Liberia Strategic Analysis (2016), p. 28; see also Roesch R (12 Mar 2018) Interview with a Zone Chief, Graie, para 44; Johnson G (14 Mar 2018) Focus group discussion with women from Sehyee, Sehyee Village, para 34.

[785] Social Impact's Liberia Strategic Analysis (2016), p. 25.

[786] Roesch R (11 Mar 2018) Focus group discussion with women from Kenpea, Kenpea, para 17.

[787] Johnson G (12 Mar 2018) Focus group discussion with women from Graie, Graie, para 23.

[788] Johnson G (13 Mar 2018) Focus group discussion with women from Korlay, Korlay, para 22.

[789] Roesch R (9 Mar 2018) Interview with Sehzueplay Community Assembly member 9, Zeonghn, para 58; see also ibid., para 32.

[790] E.g. Sehzueplay Clan (1 Apr 2013) Letter from the Sehzueplay Clan to the FDA: Letter of application for authorized forest community status.

[791] Jørgensen and Phillips (2002), p. 73.

benefit nothing'.[792] Moreover, just like in Beyan Poye, it was repeatedly stressed that the community urgently needed roads, clinics, and schools.[793]

Commercial logging was redefined as a form of forest conservation. Many community members did not see any contradiction between the two forest uses: 'If there is no forest, there is no good life. Because there we have drinking water from, cold breeze and we use the forest to [. . .] generate money. We live on it'.[794] Others argued that 'some of the wildlife they saw, their children can't see it. So they want to preserve it for those things to come back. As their children go to school, then at least investment will help [us]'[795] and 'when PROSPER came, they told us that the forest is important for the future of the children. The log, the animals that in the forest, nobody should make farm in the forest. If you make farm, you damage the log, the logs will build the country. That is the future of the children'.[796] Community members thus drew from both conservation and development discourses. Notably, they gave a new, broader meaning to conservation—one that includes the generation of income for the community. The emerging discourse sees no contradiction between commercial forestry and forest conservation. This discursive strand made the conservation discourse more powerful and helped legitimize the eviction of community members from the forest.[797]

4.3.4.4 Reinforcing and Extending Community Jurisdiction

Community forestry is also a matter of jurisdiction and control. Community jurisdiction in this respect is not only enforced externally, i.e., vis à vis strangers, neighboring community forests, and the central government, but also within the community. Already the letter of application states that 'the illegal claim of forest land is posing a serious threat to the forest'.[798]

With respect to the external dimension, community members repeatedly stressed their historically difficult relationship with the central government. The government had taken forest resources without informing and compensating them.[799] One

[792] Roesch R (9 Mar 2018) Interview with Sehzueplay CFMB officer 4, Zeonghn, para 182.

[793] E.g. Roesch R (10 Mar 2018) Focus group discussion with community members in Volay, Volay, para 14; Johnson G (13 Mar 2018) Focus group discussion with women from Korlay, Korlay, para 98; Johnson G (14 Mar 2018) Focus group discussion with women from Sehyee, Sehyee Village, para 80.

[794] Roesch R (10 Mar 2018) Interview with Sehzueplay EC member 2, Graie, para 6.

[795] Johnson G (13 Mar 2018) Focus group discussion with women from Korlay, Korlay, para 18.

[796] Roesch R (14 Mar 2018) Focus group discussion with women from Sehyee village, Sehyee Village, para 9.

[797] Roesch R (14 Mar 2018) Interview with Sehzueplay EC member 4, Sehyee Village, para 38.

[798] Sehzueplay Clan (1 Apr 2013) Letter from the Sehzueplay Clan to the FDA: Letter of application for authorized forest community status.

[799] Roesch R (10 Mar 2018) Focus group discussion with women from Zuolay, Zuolay, para 2; Roesch R (10 Mar 2018) Interview with Sehzueplay Community Assembly member 5, Volay, para

woman explained that 'during before, the forest, it was not in the hand of the community, so the good thing [about community forestry] is, that the forest to rest in the hand of the community, to manage their own forest'.[800] Moreover, when asked about what they know about the community forest, some community members made statements like 'so that how the community and the forest, they were one. To take care of the forest. Community forest is for the community'.[801] The authorization process is thus seen as a way of reconciling the community and the forest and establishing jurisdiction over it.

The establishment of jurisdiction is tied to the introduction of a physical boundary delimiting the forest. Some community members explained that they 'were happy [about the demarcation] because other people used to come in [. . .] and make farm, leaving their own area. So for them to make the survey for everybody to know that area was fine'.[802] Moreover, the overgrown forest boundaries were seen as the main reason for *illegal* people remaining in the forest, ignoring the orders of the community stakeholders.[803]

Establishing jurisdiction over the forest is also seen as a way of strengthening customary governance internally. Several community members complained that the chiefs and elders had lost power and the people in the forest ignored their orders.[804] In their view, if the elders are empowered, they can better defend the communities' tenure rights against strangers and other *illegal* forest users. However, not only customary decision-makers but also the community forest governance structure is struggling to establish its authority. In 2018, the CFMB met with the community members living in the forest and threatened to prosecute them if they did not leave.[805] The fear of losing legitimacy and authority resulted in the claim that if the governance structure tolerated the activities of some community members in the forest, this would contribute to all community members flooding the forest.[806] The community forest project has thus become a tool for reinforcing and—as in the case of the buffer zone—extending community jurisdiction both internally and externally.

8; Roesch R (11 Mar 2018) Focus group discussion with women from Kenpea, Kenpea, para 28; Johnson G (13 Mar 2018) Focus group discussion with women from Korlay, Korlay, para 25.

800 Roesch R (14 Mar 2018) Focus group discussion with women from Sehyee village, Sehyee Village, para 24.

801 Roesch R (10 Mar 2018) Interview with Sehzueplay EC member 1, Graie, para 22.

802 Johnson G (13 Mar 2018) Focus group discussion with women from Korlay, Korlay, para 48.

803 Roesch R (10 Mar 2018) Interview with Sehzueplay EC member 2, Graie, para 124; Roesch R (13 Mar 2018) Interview with Sehzueplay CFMB officer 1, Village nearby Zuolay, para 124.

804 Roesch R (9 Mar 2018) Interview with a former District Commissioner, Zuolay, para 4.

805 Roesch R (14 Mar 2018) Interview with Sehzueplay EC member 4, Sehyee Village, para 46.

806 Ibid, para 40.

4.4 Situating the Findings: FPIC Re-Negotiated

Natural resource policies often interfere with local time-spaces.[807] These interferences may cause local contestations or the adaptation of the policies. Having explored the operationalization of community forestry in two local time-spaces, the emerging understanding of FPIC will be explored. This includes an examination of the rights-holders of FPIC, its meaning, and its enforceability.

4.4.1 Rights-Holders: A New Understanding of Community?

Generally, the CRL is relatively vague in terms of the legal identity to which it attaches FPIC: the *community forest-owning community*. In theory, the concept of the community only gets filled with meaning in the local fields, and communities can decide whether and how they want to identify. A community could thus be a family, a village, a town, a clan, a district, or any other unit.

However, the identity of the community is indirectly determined by national legalities. The right to FPIC is qualified by the legal requirement to register the community forest—which is both costly and time-intensive. Without registering the customary forest lands, the forest resources would remain in the hands of the government.[808] In this respect, the FDA remains in an extraordinary position of power as it decides about the eligibility of the applications for community forest status. Given the license approach introduced by the CRL Regulation, FPIC is thus more grounded in a lease agreement than in the collective right to property; the Community Forest Management Agreements expire after 15 years and may be renewed if the community meets all technical and legal requirements.[809] The CRL Regulation thus created the legal identities of *communities currently registering their forest land* and *authorized forest communities*, which have a right to FPIC.[810]

4.4.2 Meaning of FPIC

The CRL Regulation as a national legality also determines in which situation FPIC applies. It does not interfere with the government's right to eminent domain, and not all land is susceptible to being registered as a community forest.[811] As examined in

[807] See also Agrawal and Gibson (1999), p. 639.

[808] However, this may change once the Land Rights Act is being implemented.

[809] Regulation to the Community Rights Law of 2009 with respect to forest lands, as amended (2017), s 7.6.

[810] Ibid, s 1.2.c.

[811] E.g. concessions and protected areas; ibid, s 7.9.b.

the previous chapter, most actors—including the FDA and donors—take the position that FPIC is mainly realized within the 11 steps.[812]

However, due to previous conflicts between the FDA and communities, the FDA has shown some willingness to negotiate with communities located in or nearby protected areas.[813] Moreover, the FDA no longer grants logging concessions.[814] The government's fear of conflicts and negative publicity has provided a strong incentive to widen the scope of FPIC in practice.

Still, the scope of FPIC in Liberia is quite limited. Communities have to accept the state's strong internal sovereignty in return for the—very limited—protection of their tenure rights or, more accurately, their right to benefit from their forests.[815] The forests remain within the regulatory sphere of the FDA.[816] The FDA conducts the SER survey, during which the community unit is confirmed, takes the lead in the mapping and demarcation, and has the power to reject applications.[817] Still, a—albeit slight—power shift from the state to the new collective identity took place and the FDA can no longer freely dispose of the forests.

The language of FPIC and human rights was used neither in Sehzueplay nor in Beyan Poye. Nobody had heard of FPIC and neither the FDA nor PROSPER and FIFES had a rights-based understanding of community forestry. As both communities relied upon these actors for information, they equally adopted an understanding of the forest as an ecological or commercial resource. Still, the resistance against the alienation of native reserves and the destruction of crops indicates that the community forest framework has failed to fully supersede local legalities. The following sections explore the realization of FPIC in the community self-identification, the identification of the forest, forest governance, and the land-use decision.

4.4.2.1 Community Self-Identification

The community identity emerging in both local time-spaces—Sehzueplay and Beyan Poye—is strongly shaped by development and conservation discourse and the forest as a nodal point. The forest, as a space of imagination, was either constructed to be an *ecological or a commercial resource*. The emerging collective

[812] Aldinger (2015a), p. 2; Roesch R (15 Jan 2018) Interview with a senior staff member of the FDA, Monrovia, paras 622ff; Roesch R (28 Nov 2018) Skype interview with a lawyer from an international human rights organization, para 41.

[813] Roesch R (28 Feb 2018) Interview with a senior legal consultant in the forestry sector, Monrovia, para 155.

[814] An act adopting the national forestry reform law of 2006 (amending the national forestry law of 2000, as amended; and amending an act creating the Forestry Development Authority, as amended) (2006), ss 5.3, 5.4.

[815] See also Wainwright and Bryan (2009), p. 163.

[816] Regulation to the Community Rights Law of 2009 with respect to forest lands, as amended (2017), s 6.1.

[817] Ibid, ss 6.2.a., 6.2.b.

identity is that of a *community that should benefit from the forest.* It needs to claim jurisdiction over an area big enough for commercial logging. The meaning of the forest thus strongly impacts the community self-identification.

Moreover, in both cases, the community unit was influenced by colonial territorialities and the administrative division of the Hinterland. In Beyan Poye, a district-level understanding of community has emerged. It has been impossible to reconstruct how the decision about which towns would be part of the community forest was made. Notably, a large number of towns, particularly those located deep within the forest, have been formally excluded, while the district capital, which is far away from the forest, plays an important role.

In Sehzueplay, in contrast, PROSPER invested considerable time and resources in the community self-identification. It was assumed that the clan would be the most legitimate community unit. The community stakeholders played a crucial role in the community self-identification but it is unclear whether consent was obtained beyond the stakeholders.

Hence, the *customary land-owning community* as a legal identity included in the CRL did not translate into a social identity shaped by local legalities.[818] Instead, it is a new hybrid identity merging the collective identities as set by the forest legislation, colonial territorialities (i.e., the clan or the district), and a functional understanding of the community as a group of beneficiaries.[819] While communities may have had some say in the process, their decision-making capacity was heavily limited by imposed legalities and discourses.

4.4.2.2 Identification of Community Land

The collective identity of the *community that should benefit from forest resources* already implies a certain forest size necessary to enable commercial forestry. Nevertheless, the size difference between the Beyan Poye and Sehzueplay forests is remarkable.

In Beyan Poye, the size of the forest seems to have been determined by the previous Private Use Permit. The boundaries of the community forest were not ground-truthed in any way, and nobody attempted to single out farmland from the community forest area. Sehzueplay, just like the other PROSPER forests—the smallest one with 240 hectares and the biggest one with 10,707 hectares—is much smaller than the ones with only FDA support.[820] Yet, community people did not feel like owners of the forest land. Because of the government's clear delimitation of the forest and the native reserves in the past, customary land governance did no longer extend to the forest. However, conflicts emerged, particularly in relation to the buffer zone and the native reserves located behind the forest's 1952 boundary line.

[818] Mertz (1994), p. 1248.

[819] von Benda-Beckmann and von Benda-Beckmann (1997), pp. 4–5.

[820] Tetra Tech ARD (2016a), pp. 1–2.

The experiences of the two communities are reminiscent of the experiences of the Awas Tingni community in Nicaragua, whose consultation and property rights came at the price of 'an unprecedented involvement of the state and of neoliberal development institutions in the community's internal affairs'[821] and, most notably, the determination of the boundaries of their land. Drawing boundaries as a way of regaining a degree of autonomy from the state—i.e., drawing a 'counter-map'[822]—failed in both cases. Instead, commercial and conservation discourse and imposed legalities determined the meaning of community and community land. The actors constituting the field made the forests an imagined social space harnessed for pursuing their own goals.[823]

Moreover, in both cases, women were excluded from the map-making endeavor, as boundary cutting is considered to be men's work. It is a risk of the cartographic-legal strategy that meaningful participation gets replaced by the participation of a few, often male and educated, key stakeholders.[824] The absence of women from mapping processes contributes to gendered imaginations of space in which the land and natural resources owned and used by women tend to be neglected.[825]

4.4.2.3 Forest Governance

The governance of community forests has two dimensions: the introduction of a governance structure and the adoption and implementation of forest governance rules. Generally, national legalities leave little space for the institutional autonomy of communities.

The first component of forest governance refers to the forest governance institutions. In Beyan Poye, it was challenging to shed light on the functioning of the governance structure. Several members of the governance structure claimed to be from towns within the forest but lived in the district capital or Monrovia. Moreover, some towns complained about not having any representatives in the Community Assembly. Hence, there exists a strong indication that the forest governance practice differed from the community's constitution and by-laws.

In Sehzueplay, community forestry was strongly detached from customary governance to prevent elite capture. PROSPER made sure that formal elections were held in each of the towns.[826] Joining the governance structure was particularly attractive for younger, mobile men hoping for wage labor. Informally, local authorities still had power over the community forest project, as illustrated by the

---

[821] Hale (2005), p. 16.

[822] Said (1996), p. 28.

[823] McCarthy (2005), p. 156; Wainwright and Bryan (2009), p. 161.

[824] Wainwright and Bryan (2009), p. 162; Altamirano-Jiménez and Parker (2016), p. 93.

[825] Wainwright (2008), pp. 257–58.

[826] See also Sect. 4.3.3.3.

negotiation with Opulence and the enforcement of the no-forest-use-policy.[827] Confusion about the relationship between the governance bodies persisted and culminated in the Commercial Use Contract with Opulence. While information on the community forest was disseminated to a greater extent than in Beyan Poye, most community members—and particularly women—still felt excluded.

Confusion and problems regarding the governance structure appear to be the norm rather than the exception in community forests all over Liberia. These conflicts take place both within the governance structure and between the governance structure and local authorities.[828] They occur in community forests without external support and those that collaborated with the USAID-funded projects and the World Bank.[829] While these tensions and conflicts are a natural reaction to another imposed layer of jurisdiction, it also fundamentally questions whether the new governance structure, while undermining the cultural autonomy of communities, is well-placed to make decisions that may fundamentally impact the lives of rural communities.

The virtual absence of women from the governance structure was eye-catching in both Sehzueplay and Beyan Poye. It also corresponds to the observations made in other formal and informal community forests.[830] In 2015, women made up less than 25% of participants in forest governance activities.[831] Moreover, the presence of women does not necessarily contribute to actual and meaningful participation.[832] The gendered division of labor, together with the lack of formal education, were the main reasons for the low participation of women.[833] Both in the national and the local time-spaces related to community forestry, the perception is widespread that the CRL's requirement to have at least one woman in the CFMB means that there must be exactly one woman.[834] In 2018, not a single CFMB in Liberia had a female chief officer.[835] The low number of women exemplifies that despite the efforts of the USAID-funded projects, gender inequalities remained in place (or deteriorated), and Sehzueplay did even worse in terms of women's participation than Beyan Poye. The focus of PROSPER and FIFES on women's savings groups instead of providing knowledge on forest governance may even have exacerbated gender stereotypes. This corresponds to the observations made by Gururani:

---

[827] See also Menkor. 4 Dec 2018. Gio national forest under threat reveals District Commissioner Dekruah. Liberian Observer.

[828] World Bank (2019), p. 5.

[829] Tetra Tech ARD (2014a), pp. 27–28; Tetra Tech ARD (2016a), p. 19; ACDI/VOCA (2017a), p. 26.

[830] Onzere et al. (2020), p. 32.

[831] Malpani (2015), p. 3.

[832] Ibid, p. 3; Louis et al. (2020), p. 14.

[833] Malpani (2015), pp. 2–3.

[834] Social Impact's Liberia Strategic Analysis (2016), p. 33.

[835] Forestry Development Authority (2018) Authorized community forest governance structure membership listing,

> [Despite] this attention and hundreds of thousands of aid dollars committed to "gendering" environment and development debates, as well as the implementation of "gender-sensitive" policies, rural women continue to unequally bear the burden of producing livelihood and facing extreme hardships. This incongruity between the heightened attention paid to women in both research and policy circles and its virtual non-effect in practice can be attributed mainly to the conceptual limitations that have overlooked the situated practices and local histories that constitute relations of both nature and gender.[836]

The introduction of a new community unit—which, unlike town-level land governance, had no mechanisms for women's participation in place—and the negligence of communities' institutional autonomy contributed to the exclusion of women from community forestry.

The second component of forest governance is the adoption of management rules for the forest. In Liberia, rules on the governance of the forest are part of the constitution and by-laws, and the CFMB may adopt rules regulating the use of the forest resources 'with the involvement of community members and approval of the Executive Committee'.[837] In both community forests, PROSPER's templates for the constitution and by-laws were adopted with minimal amendments. As the forest governance structure has no roots whatsoever in customary governance, this is not surprising, and the same observation has been made in other community forests.[838] The free decision-making capacity of the governance bodies was thus limited by imposed governance rules, and it was not even attempted to codify pre-existing forest use rules.

Thus, community forestry, in this respect, clearly prioritized forestry best practices over culture.

4.4.2.4 Land-Use Decision

The construction of the *forest as an ecological or commercial resource* and the *community that should benefit from the forest* effectively transformed FPIC in the right to approve commercial logging.

In Beyan Poye, the decision to ban local forest uses and grant a Commercial Use Contract was most likely taken long before the community applied for a community forest.[839] A few powerful individuals were the drivers of the community forest project. Nevertheless, most community members approved the decision to contract with Akewa. This indicates that the indirect participation of local authorities contributed to the relatively high legitimacy of the community forest project.

---

[836] Gururani (2002), p. 240.

[837] Regulation to the Community Rights Law of 2009 with respect to forest lands, as amended (2017), s 4.7.c; see also An Act to establish the Community Rights Law of 2009 with respect to forest lands (2009), s 4.2.c.

[838] Roesch R (28 Feb 2018) Interview with a senior legal consultant in the forestry sector, Monrovia, para 203.

[839] See also Sect. 4.2.3.4.

The Sehzueplay community had originally committed to conserving the forest. Later, the governance structure emancipated itself from the conservation agenda of the USAID-funded projects. Yet, they were not free from external and internal pressure. Community members were calling for investments, and important community stakeholders and Opulence pushed them towards the commercial use option. The way the decision to opt for the commercial use of the forest was made, did not comply with the forest legislation. Neither the governance structure nor the broader community were adequately informed before the decision was made. FIFES' evaluation also concluded that 'the CFs are unprepared to negotiate fair, technically sound logging agreements, or monitor and enforce compliance by logging companies within the terms of such agreements'.[840] Moreover, the buffer zone controversy indicates that community forestry practice departed from the national legislation. Under the CRL, such an important decision would have to be approved by the Community Assembly, which most likely never happened. While most community members approved logging in the forest—also because of the weak sense of ownership over the forest—and hoped for economic opportunities, they strongly disagreed with the loss of their farmland and felt that their voices were not being heard. The buffer zone thus interfered with customary property rights and undermined the legitimacy of the community forest project.

Given the strong external pressure on communities and the lack of even the most basic social infrastructure like schools, health care, and roads, the scope of the emerging FPIC norm is extremely narrow, with some choices being unthinkable from the onset.

4.5 Consenting to Development

Recalling Imai's three criteria of self-determined governance, it becomes evident that Liberian community forestry does not enable self-determination, nor does it protect collective property rights or the right to culture. If communities do not participate in the community forestry program, they risk losing their land.[841] Community forestry in Liberia thus reflects 'a tactical engagement with a hegemonic understanding of a space—territory—carried out under conditions hardly of their choosing that in and of itself offers little hope for justice'.[842]

The local time-space is, to a considerable extent, determined by national legalities. The CRL Regulation grants extensive power to the FDA in the 11 steps process. Communities on their own cannot fulfill the requirements established by the CRL

[840] Liberia Strategic Analysis (2018), p. viii.

[841] The situation is different now with the adoption of the 2018 Land Rights Act, which provides other avenues for securing customary land rights.

[842] Bryan (2012), p. 220; see also Colchester and Ferrari (2007), p. 20.

Regulation and feel that they do not speak the right language.[843] Nadasdy makes similar observations in land management processes in the Yukan and describes the outcome as biased, with communities being forced to speak the language of the state or science.[844] Just like in many other countries, substantive discussions have been replaced by procedural talk in the implementation of FPIC.[845]

However, not only do national legalities impact the local time-spaces, but they are also under the influence of the fields of development and conservation, whose actors have considerable economic, cultural, and symbolic capital. Conservation and development discourses alter the social meaning of the forest from a place imbued with cultural meaning to an economic or ecological resource.[846] This meaning of the forest strongly limits FPIC by locating other meanings of the forest and forest uses in the field of discursivity.[847] The community unit and the size of community forests are determined by the forest as a nodal point.[848] The fields' discourses also created new social identities: the community that should benefit from forest resources, perpetrators, and companies as the providers of development. Moreover, conservation and development discourse share a vision of forest management precluding local forest uses.[849] If communities do not manage their resources in the right way, they become illegalized.[850] Thereby, the forest legislation is 'characterized by patterns of obligation and concepts of justice and ideal behavior that are foreign and even incomprehensible to the local community'.[851] Community forestry is an attempt to 'effectively transform their imagined community into a well-controlled and bounded space'.[852] It invades Indigenous spaces and transforms them.[853] The power of these discourses is reflected by the fact that of the 49 authorized community forests, five have committed to conserving their forests, while 42 have granted commercial use contracts to third parties.[854]

In this context, the space for FPIC considerably shrinks, and rights talk completely disappears from the scene. The national legality—together with the strong development and conservation discourse—filtered the logic of human rights out of FPIC and significantly altered its meaning.[855] The negligence of the

[843] Roesch R (19 Mar 2018) Interview with Sehzueplay EC member 3, Monrovia, para 156.

[844] Nadasdy (2003), p. 263.

[845] Rodríguez-Garavito (2010), p. 11.

[846] See also Gururani (2002), p. 240.

[847] Jørgensen and Phillips (2002), p. 27.

[848] See also Tetra Tech ARD (2015c), p. 16; Global Witness (2018), p. 10; Roesch R (13 Jun 2018) Skype interview with an anthropologist, paras 19–21.

[849] See also Lowenhaupt Tsing (1993), pp. 154–55.

[850] See also von Benda-Beckmann (2001), p. 38.

[851] Engel (1980), p. 430.

[852] von Benda-Beckmann et al. (2009b), p. 9.

[853] See also Ramos (1999), p. 9.

[854] Agyeman et al. (2022), p. 149.

[855] von Benda-Beckmann and von Benda-Beckmann (2007b), pp. 63–64.

institutional autonomy of communities further undermines the legitimacy of community forestry, turning it into another imposed program.[856] In both forests, attempts to include women in forest management have largely failed. Given the dismissal of customary land and forest governance, the relevant actors missed an opportunity to build upon existing women's organizations or land governance practices including women.[857] Thus, community forestry 'undermine[s] [women] as active producers of knowledge that participate in complex socio-environmental community processes'.[858]

In light of the very narrow, less-than-property-based understanding of FPIC in the two Liberian community forests, it could be argued that FPIC, in practice, is not a matter of renegotiation but non-compliance.[859] Ordinary community members had little space within the formal community forest project to have their voices heard, felt excluded from the authorization process, and had a strong sense of powerlessness. An anthropologist, therefore, describes the community forestry project as an attempt 'to empower powerless communities which then have to take on all the problems the state should have with poor governance and a capitalist industry'.[860]

However, community members retained some—albeit small—spaces of resistance outside of or at the fringe of the community forest field. The forests continue to have other social meanings: they are places historically owned, they were places of protection during the war, and they are places of legitimate agricultural production.[861] These contradictory social meanings of the forest contributed to a 'social mediation'[862] of the forest as an ecological or commercial resource.

'Everyday acts of resistance'[863] include the continuous use of the forests and the high degree of dissatisfaction with the governance structure, the FDA, PROSPER/FIFES, and the companies. Local authorities' involvement in the forest governance also shows that community forestry in practice differs from community forestry as envisioned by the national legislation.[864] The widespread non-compliance with the new forest governance rules is very likely a symptom of the breaking through of pre-existing norms of forest governance.[865] Falk Moore similarly argues that existing social arrangements, in many cases, are stronger than new laws adopted on the national level.[866] Moreover, the high number of angry women in both community forests complaining about the lack of information and participation

[856] See also Cornell (2006), pp. 13–14.
[857] See also Imai (2009), p. 311.
[858] Altamirano-Jiménez and Kermoal (2016), p. 4.
[859] Griffiths (1986), p. 4.
[860] Roesch R (13 Jun 2018) Skype interview with an anthropologist, para 11.
[861] See also Gururani (2002), p. 238.
[862] Mertz (1994), p. 1248.
[863] Ewick and Silbey (2003), p. 1329.
[864] E.g. Tetra Tech ARD (2013b), p. 14.
[865] Telesetsky (2017), p. 120.
[866] Falk Moore (2000), p. 58.

also indicates that contestation and renegotiation processes are ongoing. Liberian women are known to use protests and collective mobilization as forms of resistance.[867] These acts of resistance are indicative of the absence of legitimate consent and could become the enabler for a more self-determined form of FPIC.[868]

It is yet to be seen whether communities will manage to shape the practice of FPIC within the very limited space that the national legal framework grants them. The pluralistic legal context and the hegemonic discourse, in combination with the major power imbalances between the actors in the field, certainly make community forestry prone to conflicts.[869] In any case, FPIC, as an element of community forestry, remains subject to renegotiation. It is an 'unfinished debate with no clear winner'.[870] Particularly the implementation of the 2018 Land Rights Act may reshuffle the cards. It pursues an approach to customary land rights that is more strongly informed by human rights, specifically recognizing the collective right to property. Hence, it may strengthen the position of communities and broaden the scope of FPIC in the long run.

References

Abasiattai MB (1992) The search for independence: new world blacks in Sierra Leone and Liberia, 1787-1847. J Black Stud 23:107–116

Abramowitz S, Moran MH (2012) International human rights, gender-based violence, and local discourses of abuse in postconflict Liberia: a problem of "culture"? Afr Stud Rev 55:119–146

ACDI/VOCA (2016a) First quarterly report: January 1, 2016 - 31 March 2016. USAID

ACDI/VOCA (2016b) Forest incomes for environmental sustainability (FIFES), FY16 quarterly report: April - June 2016. USAID

ACDI/VOCA (2017a) Forest incomes for environmental sustainability (FIFES), annual report: November 6, 2016 to November 5, 2017. USAID

ACDI/VOCA (2017b) Forest incomes for environmental sustainability (FIFES), FY2017 quarterly report, October-December 2016. USAID

ACDI/VOCA (2017c) Forest incomes for environmental sustainability, FY2017 quarterly report: January 2017 - March 2017. USAID

ACDI/VOCA (2017d) Forest incomes for environmental sustainability, FY2018 first quarterly report: October - December 2017. USAID

ACDI/VOCA (2018) Forest incomes for environmental sustainability, FY2018 quarterly report: January - March 2018. USAID

ACDI/VOCA (2019a) Forest incomes for environmental sustainability, FY2019 quarterly report: October - December 2018. USAID

ACDI/VOCA (2019b) FY19 fourth quarter & annual report: October 1, 2018 - September 30, 2019. USAID

ACDI/VOCA (2020) Forest incomes for environmental sustainability FY20 annual report. October 1, 2019 - September 20, 2020

[867] Moran (1989), p. 444.

[868] See also Eisenberg (2020), p. 273.

[869] Cf Gezelius and Hauck (2011), p. 462.

[870] See also Kidder (1979), p. 300.

ACDI/VOCA, Pact (2016) Rapid analysis of barriers to the formation of community forestry in Liberia. USAID
Agrawal A, Gibson CC (1999) Enchantment and disenchantment: the role of community in natural resource conservation. World Dev 27:629–649
Agyeman VK et al (2022) Sustainable forest management (SFM) in Liberia - the 4Cs approach. Forestry Development Authority and World Bank Group
Aikins JK (2016) Indigenising democracy? Renegotiating the role of Indigenous political authorities in Ghana's constitution review. In: Dhawan N et al (eds) Negotiating normativity: postcolonial appropriations, contestations, and transformations. Springer, Cham, pp 61–78
Alden Wily L (2007) 'So who owns the forest' an investigation into forest ownership and customary land rights in Liberia. Sustainable Development Institute and FERN
Aldinger P (2015a) The importance of free, prior and informed consent: strategies for realization. USAID
Aldinger P (2015b) The role of third parties in establishing forest communities. USAID
Altamirano-Jiménez I, Kermoal N (2016) Introduction: Indigenous women and knowledge. In: Altamirano-Jiménez I, Kermoal N (eds) Living on the land: Indigenous women's understandings of place. AU Press, Edmonton, pp 3–18
Altamirano-Jiménez I, Parker L (2016) Mapping, knowledge, and gender in the Atlantic coast of Nicaragua. In: Kermoal N, Altamirano-Jiménez I (eds) Living on the land: Indigenous women's understandings of place. AU Press, Edmonton, pp 85–106
Bakker L (2009) The Sultan's map: arguing one's land in Pasir. In: von Benda-Beckmann F et al (eds) Spatializing law: an anthropological geography of law in society. Ashgate, Farnham, pp 95–114
Bavinck M (2005) Understanding fisheries conflicts in the South: a legal pluralist perspective. Soc Nat Resour 18:805–820
Bedert M (2016) Dissertation summary: Of strangers and secrets: Continuity and change in the articulation of belonging in contemporary Liberia. Max-Planck-Institute for Social Anthropology, p 6
Beevers MD (2015) Peace resources? Governing Liberia's forests in the aftermath of conflict. Int Peacekeeping 22:26–42
Bennett TW (2009) Re-introducing African customary law to the South African legal system. Am J Comp Law 57:1–31
Bledsoe C (1976) Women's marital strategies among the Kpelle of Liberia. J Anthropol Res 32: 372–389
Bourdieu P (1986) The forms of capital. In: Richardson JG (ed) Handbook of theory and research for the sociology of education. Greenwood Press, New York, pp 241–258
Bourdieu P et al (1994) Rethinking the state: genesis and structure of the bureaucratic field. Sociol Theory 12:1–18
Brown D (1982) Politics as rituals: rules as resources in the politics of the Liberian Hinterland. Afr Polit 81:479–497
Brown D (2017) Social dimensions of land rights reform in Liberia: some unresolved issues and policy dilemmas. Dev Policy Rev 35:270–279
Bryan J (2012) Rethinking territory: social justice and neoliberalism in Latin America's territorial turn. Geogr Compass 6:215–226
Buell RL (1928) The native problem in Africa. The Macmillan Company, New York
Carter JE (1982) Liberian women: their role in food production and their educational and legal status. USAID and Government of Liberia
Charles AT (1992) Fishery conflicts: a unified framework. Mar Policy 16:379–393
Cittadino F (2020) Incorporating Indigenous rights in the international regime on biodiversity protection: access, benefit-sharing and conservation in Indigenous lands. Brill Nijhoff, Leiden
Clapham C (1976) Liberia and Sierra Leone: an essay in comparative politics. Cambridge University Press, London

Colchester M, Ferrari MF (2007) Making FPIC work: challenges and prospects for Indigenous peoples. Forest Peoples Programme

Cornell S (2006) Indigenous peoples, poverty and self-determination in Australia, New Zealand, Canada and the United States. Jt Occ Pap Nat Affairs 2:1–39

Corriveau-Bourque A (2010) Confusions and palava: the logic of land encroachment in Lofa County, Liberia. Can J Dev Stud 31:27–48

D'Azevedo WL (1962) Common principles of variant kinship structures among the Gola of Western Liberia. Am Anthropol 64:504–520

de Sousa Santos B (2002) Toward a new legal common sense. Butterworths, LexisNexis, London

Desai D et al (2012) Rethinking justice reform in fragile and conflict-affected states: the capacity of development agencies and lessons from Liberia and Afghanistan. World Bank Leg Rev 3:241–262

Diala AC (2017) The concept of living customary law: a critique. J Leg Plural Unoff Law 49:143–165

Dunlap A (2018) "A bureaucratic trap:" free, prior and informed consent (FPIC) and wind energy development in Juchitán, Mexico. Capital Nat Social 29:88–108

Eisenberg A (2020) Consent, resistance and the duty to consult. Int J Minor Group Rights 27:270–290

Engel DM (1980) Legal pluralism in an American community: perspectives on a civil trial court. Am Bar Found Res J 5:425–454

Engle Merry S (1997) Legal Pluralism and Transnational Culture: The Ka Ho'okolokolonui Kanaka Maoli Tribunal, Hawai'i, 1993, In: Wilson RA (ed) Human Rights, Culture & Context, Pluto Press: London, pp. 28–48

EU FLEGT (2018) Liberia - EU FLEGT Voluntary Partnership Agreement, aide memoire, sixth meeting of the joint implementation committee. https://flegtvpafacility.org/wp-content/uploads/2022/05/6-Liberia-JIC-aide-memoire-annexes.pdf. Accessed 12 Aug 2023

Ewick P, Silbey S (2003) Narrating social structure: stories of resistance to legal authority. Am J Sociol 108:1328–1372

Falk Moore S (2000) Law as process: an anthropological approach. LIT, Hamburg

Forestry Development Authority (2007) Forest data

Foster-Turley P et al (2018) Liberia tropical forest and biodiversity analysis. USAID

Gatter W (2002) Zur Geschichte Liberias. Forstliche Entwicklungshilfe 80:131–136

Gezelius SS, Hauck M (2011) Toward a theory of compliance in state-regulated livelihoods: a comparative study of compliance motivations in developed and developing world fisheries. Law Soc Rev 45:435–470

Global Witness (2013) Avoiding the riptide: Liberia must enforce its forest laws to prevent a new wave of illegal and destructive logging contracts. https://cdn.globalwitness.org/archive/files/global%20witness%20-%20avoiding%20the%20riptide%20-%207%20June%2013.pdf. Accessed 12 Aug 2023

Global Witness (2018) Power to the people? How companies are exploiting community forestry in Liberia. https://www.globalwitness.org/en/campaigns/forests/power-people/. Accessed 11 Aug 2023

Griffiths J (1986) What is legal pluralism? J Leg Plural Unoff Law 18:1–55

Griffiths J (2003) The social working of legal rules. J Leg Plural 2003:1–48

Gururani S (2002) Forests of pleasure and pain: gendered practices of labor and livelihood in the forests of the Kumaon Himalayas. Gend Place Cult 9:229–243

Hale CR (2005) Neoliberal multiculturalism: the remaking of cultural rights and racial dominance in Central America. Polit Leg Anthropol Rev 28:10–28

Harris R et al (2012–13) Liberia social audit: assessing the forestry sector. Civil Society Independent Forest Monitors and NGO Coalition of Liberia

Hartman A et al (2018) Community land protection in Liberia: the impact on neocustomary norms and institutions. www.land-links.org/wp-content/uploads/2018/04/Session-01-10-Hartman-603_paper.pdf. Accessed 11 Aug 2023

Hasselmann K-H (1978) Spatial development through central place organization in Nimba County/ Liberia. University of Liberia, Monrovia
Heemann L (2020) Living customary law: negotiating spaces for women in traditional communities. In: Seidel K, Elliesie H (eds) Normative spaces and legal dynamics in Africa. Routledge, Abingdon
Holsoe T (1954) Forestry opportunities in the Republic of Liberia. Foreign Agricultural Service and Forest Service (United States Department of Agriculture)
Holsoe SE (1974) The manipulation of traditional political structures among coastal peoples in Western Liberia during the nineteenth century. Ethnohistory 21:159–167
Imai S (2009) Indigenous self-determination and the state. In: Richardson BJ et al (eds) Indigenous people and the law: comparative and critical perspectives. Hart Publishing, Oxford, pp 285–314
Jørgensen MW, Phillips L (2002) Discourse analysis as theory and method. SAGE Publications, London
Käihkö I (2019) On Liberian secret societies and conflict resolution. Nord J Afr Stud 28:1–20
Keyser C (2013) Promoting transparency and accountability in the community forest management process through multistakeholder groups. USAID
Kidder RL (1979) Toward an integrated theory of imposed law. In: Burman SB, Harell-Bond BE (eds) The imposition of law. Academic Press, New York, pp 289–306
Knight R et al (2013) Protecting community lands and resources: evidence from Liberia. IDLO et al. https://namati.org/wp-content/uploads/2013/01/12-namati-book-complete-lr.pdf. Accessed 11 Aug 2023
Laclau E, Mouffe C (2001) Hegemony and socialist strategy: towards a radical democratic politics. Verso, London
Liberia Extractive Industries Transparency Initiative (2013) Liberia Extractive Industries Transparency Initiative (LEITI): post award process audit final report
Liberia Institute of Statistics and Geo-Information Services (2014) Population by county, district, clan and sex, Liberia 2008
Liberia Strategic Analysis (2018) Forest incomes for environmental sustainability midterm performance evaluation. USAID
Liebenow G (1969) Liberia: the evolution of privilege. Cornell University Press, Ithaka
Louis E et al (2020) A report of high level findings from research on women's participation in forest governance bodies in Nimba, Grand Bassa and Margibi counties. Landesa and Foundation for Community Initiatives
Lowenhaupt Tsing A (1993) In the realm of the diamond queen: marginality in an out-of-the-way place. Princeton University Press, Princeton
Lowenhaupt Tsing A (2003) Cultivating the wild: honey-hunting and forest management in southeast Kalimantan. In: Zerner C (ed) Culture and the question of rights: forests, coasts, and seas in Southeast Asia. Duke University Press, Durham, pp 24–55
Lowenkopf M (1976) Politics in Liberia. Hoover Institution Press, Stanford
LTS International (2019a) Development of national guidelines on free prior and informed consent (FPIC): project report. Environmental Protection Agency and Forestry Development Authority
LTS International (2019b) National guidelines on achieving free prior and informed consent (FPIC) with respect to communities and forest resources
Makain JS (2010) Land tenure practices: challenges and prospects of conservation farmers in Bong County and greater Monrovia. Liberian Stud J 35:78–102
Makain JS, Foh MS (2009) Social dimensions of large-scale land acquisition rights in Liberia (1900-2009): Challenges and prospects for traditional settlers. Liberian Stud J 33:1–40
Malpani S (2015) Participation of women in community forests. USAID
Mama A (2004) Demythologising gender in development: feminist studies in African contexts. IDS Bull 35:121–124
Mamdani M (2012) Define and rule: native as political identity. Harvard University Press, Cambridge

Manvell A (2019) Community forestry in Liberia: how Liberia's forest resources can benefit more from their timber resources in small forest reserves. FERN

Mayer KR (1951) Forest resources of Liberia. United States Department of Agriculture and United States Department of State

McCarthy JF (2002) Power and interest on Sumatra's rainforest frontier: clientelist coalitions, illegal logging and conservation in the alas valley. J Southeast Asian Stud 33:77–106

McCarthy JF (2005) Contesting decentralization: transnational policy narrative and the emergence of volatile socio-legal configurations in Central Kalimantan, Indonesia. In: von Benda-Beckmann F et al (eds) Mobile people, mobile law: expanding legal relations in a contracting world. Ashgate, Aldershot, pp 153–176

Mertz E (1994) Conclusion: a new social constructionism for sociolegal studies. Law Soc Rev 28: 1243–1265

Minh-ha TT (1989) Women, native, other: writing postcoloniality and feminism. Indiana University Press, Bloomington

Moore DS (2005) Suffering for territory: race, place, and power in Zimbabwe. Duke University Press, Durham

Moran MH (1989) Collective action and the "representation" of African women: a Liberian case study. Fem Stud 15:443–460

Moran M (2012) Our mothers have spoken: synthesizing old and new forms of women's political authority in Liberia. J Int Women's Stud 13:51–66

Munive J (2017) Roads ad imaginary for employing idle youth in the post-conflict Liberian state. In: Højbjerg CK et al (eds) Politics and policies in upper guinea coast societies: change and continuity. Palgrave Macmillan, New York, pp 271–290

Munive Rincon J (2010) Ex-combatants, returnees, land and conflict in Liberia. Danish Institute for International Studies

Murray Li T (2009) The law of the project: government and 'good governance' at the World Bank in Indonesia. In: von Benda-Beckmann F et al (eds) Rules of law and laws of ruling: on the governance of law. Ashgate, Farnham, pp 237–256

Nadasdy P (2003) Hunters and bureaucrats: power, knowledge and Aboriginal-state relations in the Southwest Yukon. UBC Press, Vancouver

Nader L (1965) The anthropological study of law. Am Anthropol 67:3–32

Namubiru-Mwaura EL et al (2012) Liberia land policy & institutional support (LPIS) project: Customary land tenure in Liberia: Findings and implications drawn from 11 case studies. USAID. https://www.land-links.org/wp-content/uploads/2016/09/USAID_Land_Tenure_Liberia_LPIS_Synthesis_Report.pdf. Accessed 11 Aug 2023

Nevin TDL (2017) In search of the historical Madam Suakoko: Liberia's renowned female Kpelle chief. J West Afr Hist 3:1–38

Newberry D (2014) Why are there cattle in the conservation area? Social barriers to biofuel governance in Brazil. Geoforum 54:306–314

Nketia SK et al (2016) Liberia forest sector project: environmental and social management framework. World Bank and Forestry Development Authority

O'Hagan R et al (2020) Community forestry in Liberia: progress and pitfalls. In: Nikolakis W, Innes JL (eds) The wicked problem of forest policy: a multidisciplinary approach to sustainability in forest landscapes. Cambridge University Press, Cambridge, pp 354–375

Offen KH (2003) Narrating place and identity, or mapping Miskitu land claims in Northeastern Nicaragua. Hum Organ 62:382–392

Onzere SN et al (2020) Who's governing community forests? Gendered participation in Liberian forest management. World Resources Institute and Clark University

Overdevest C, Zeitlin J (2018) Experimentalism in transnational forest governance: Implementing European Union Forest Law Enforcement, Governance and Trade (FLEGT) Voluntary Partnership Agreements in Indonesia and Ghana. Regul Gov 12:64–87

Oyěwùmí O (1997) The invention of women: making sense of Western gender discourses. University of Minnesota Press, Minneapolis

Ramos AR (1999) Cutting through state and class sources and strategies of self-representation in Latin America. Sér Antropol 247:1–22

Richards P et al (2005) Community cohesion in Liberia: a post-war rapid social assessment. World Bank

Richardson BJ (2009) The ties that bind: Indigenous peoples and environmental governance. In: Richardson BJ et al (eds) Indigenous peoples and the law: comparative and critical perspectives. Hart Publishing, Oxford, pp 337–370

Riddell JC et al (1971) Clan and chiefdom maps of the ma (mano) and da (gio). Liberian Stud J 4: 157–162

Rodríguez-Garavito C (2010) Ethnicity.Gov: global governance, Indigenous peoples, and the right to prior consultation in social minefields. Indiana J Glob Leg Stud 18:1–44

Roesch R (2021) Under the disguise of participation: community forestry as a new form of land rush in Liberia. In: Cochrane L, Andrews N (eds) The transnational land rush in Africa: a decade after the spike. Springer International Publishing, Cham, pp 139–172

Russell D et al (2011) Final evaluation of the land rights and community forestry programme (LRCFP). USAID Liberia

Sachtler M (1968) General report on national forest inventory in Liberia. German Forestry Mission to Liberia in Cooperation with the Bureau of Forest and Wildlife Conservation

Said EW (1996) Peace and its discontents: essays on Palestine in the Middle East peace process. Vintage Books, New York

Sawyer A (1992) The emergence of authority in Liberia: tragedy and challenge. ICS Press, San Francisco

Sawyer A (1995) Proprietary authority and local administration in Liberia. In: Wunsch JS, Olowu D (eds) The failure of the centralized state: institutions and self-governance in Africa. Westview Press, Boulder, pp 148–173

Sawyer A (2005) Beyond plunder: toward democratic governance in Liberia. Lynne Rienner Publishers, London

Schwab G (1947) Tribes of the Liberian Hinterland. The Museum, Cambridge

Snyder FG (1981) Colonialism and legal form: the creation of "customary law" in Senegal. J Leg Plural Unoff Law 13:49–90

Social Impact's Liberia Strategic Analysis (2016) Performance evaluation of people, rules, and organizations supporting the protection of ecosystem resources ("PROSPER"). USAID

Special Independent Investigating Body (2012) Report on the issuance of Private Use Permits. https://static1.squarespace.com/static/599cd9d303596eabe91eb655/t/59b013b14c0dbf55424d26fc/1504711663500/aSIIB+Report+on+PUPsb.pdf. Accessed 12 Aug 2023

Starblanket G (2018) Complex accountabilities: Deconstructing "the community" and engaging feminist research methods. Am Indian Cult Res J 42:1–20

Stevens CJ (2014) The legal history of public land in Liberia. J Afr Law 58:250–265

Sustainable Development Institute (2018a) Community forestry in Liberia: community forest management plan processes and draft template for commercial use contract negotiations in community forest operations. https://loggingoff.info/wp-content/uploads/2018a/08/Final-report_Com-Forestry-Worksop-June6-7.pdf. Accessed 21 Jul 2023

Sustainable Development Institute (2018b) The Sewacajua community forest: The need to strengthen rule of law in the community forestry sector in Liberia. https://loggingoff.info/wp-content/uploads/2018b/04/FINAL-SDI-briefing-05.pdf. Accessed 21 Jul 2023

Sustainable Development Institute (2018c) What do communities want? A rapid assessment of local preferences for community-owned forest enterprises. https://sdiLiberia.org/sites/default/files/publications/SDI%20Brief%2006%20Final_March%202018_compressed.pdf. Accessed 30 July 2019

Tamanaha BZ (2008) Understanding legal pluralism: past to present, local to global. Sidney Law Rev 30:375–411

Telesetsky A (2017) Legal pluralism - linking law and culture in natural resource co-management and environmental compliance. In: Nafziger JAR (ed) Comparative law and anthropology. Edward Elgar Publishing, Cheltenham, pp 116–132
Tetra Tech ARD (2012a) People, rules, and organizations supporting the protection of ecosystem resources (PROSPER): first quarterly report (final), 1 June - 30 September 2012. USAID
Tetra Tech ARD (2012b) Preliminary site assessment report. USAID
Tetra Tech ARD (2012c) USAID/PROSPER gender integration plan. USAID
Tetra Tech ARD (2013a) People, rules, and organizations supporting the protection of ecosystem resources (PROSPER), fifth quarterly report (final), 1 July - 30 September 2013. USAID
Tetra Tech ARD (2013b) People, rules, and organizations supporting the protection of ecosystem resources (PROSPER), fourth quarterly report (final), 1 April - 30 June 2013. USAID
Tetra Tech ARD (2013c) People, rules, and organizations supporting the protection of ecosystem resources (PROSPER), third quarterly report (final), 1 January - 31 March 2013. USAID
Tetra Tech ARD (2013d) People, rules, and organizations supporting the protection of ecosystem resources (PROSPER): second quarterly report (final). USAID
Tetra Tech ARD (2013e) People, rules, and organizations supporting the protection of ecosystem resources, annual report. FY2013. USAID
Tetra Tech ARD (2013f) Public outreach and awareness-building approaches: first annual campaign on community forestry. USAID
Tetra Tech ARD (2014a) Annual report, FY2014: people, rules, and organizations supporting the protection of ecosystem resources. USAID
Tetra Tech ARD (2014b) People, rules, and organizations supporting the protection of ecosystem resources (PROSPER), eighth quarterly report, 1 April - 30 June 2014. USAID
Tetra Tech ARD (2014c) People, rules, and organizations supporting the protection of ecosystem resources (PROSPER), seventh quarterly report, 1 January - 31 March 2014. USAID
Tetra Tech ARD (2014d) People, rules, and organizations supporting the protection of ecosystem resources (PROSPER), sixth quarterly report, 1 October - 31 December 2013. USAID
Tetra Tech ARD (2015a) Annual report, FY2015. USAID
Tetra Tech ARD (2015b) People, rules, and organizations supporting the protection of ecosystem resources (PROSPER), 11th quarterly report, 1 January - 31 March 2015. USAID
Tetra Tech ARD (2015c) People, rules, and organizations supporting the protection of ecosystem resources (PROSPER), 12th quarterly report, 1 April - 30 June 2015. USAID
Tetra Tech ARD (2015d) People, rules, and organizations supporting the protection of ecosystem resources (PROSPER), tenth quarterly report, 1 October - 31 December 2014. USAID
Tetra Tech ARD (2016a) People, rules, and organizations supporting the protection of ecosystem resources (PROSPER), quarterly report, FY16 q2, 1 January - 31 March 2016. USAID
Tetra Tech ARD (2016b) People, rules, and organizations supporting the protection of ecosystem resources (PROSPER), quarterly report, FY16 q3, 1 April - 30 June 2016. USAID
Tetra Tech ARD (2016c) Peoples, rules, and organizations supporting the protection of ecosystem resources (PROSPER), quarterly report, FY16 q1, 1 October - 31 December 2015. USAID
Tetra Tech ARD (2017) People, rules, and organizations supporting the protection of ecosystem resources (PROSPER): Liberia PROSPER final report. USAID
Tobin B (2014) Indigenous peoples, customary law and human rights: why living law matters. Routledge, Milton Park
Tripp AM (2015) Women and power in postconflict Africa. Cambridge University Press, Cambridge
United States Operations Mission to Liberia (1961) Third report on forestry progress in Liberia: 1951-1959. International Cooperation Administration
Unruh JD (2009) Catalyzing the socio-legal space for armed conflict: Land and legal pluralism in pre-war Liberia. http://commission-on-legal-pluralism.com/volumes/58/unruh-art.pdf. Accessed 11 Aug 2023
Vanderlinden J (2015) Postface. J Leg Plural Unoff Law 47:151–157

Verschuren J (1983) Conservation of tropical rain forest in Liberia: recommendations for wildlife conservation and national parks. IUCN
Vogt M (2012) Biodiversity assessment report. USAID
von Benda-Beckmann K (2001) Transnational dimensions of legal pluralism. In: Fikentscher W (ed) Begegnung und Konflikt - eine kulturanthropologische Bestandsaufnahme. Verlag der Bayerischen Akademie der Wissenschaften, München, pp 33–48
von Benda-Beckmann F, von Benda-Beckmann K (1997) Community based tenurial rights: emancipation or indirect rule. In: von Benda-Beckmann K, Winkler HF (eds) Papers of the xlth international congress "folk law and legal pluralism: Societies in transformation". Commission on Folk Law and Legal Pluralism, Ottawa, pp 169–187
von Benda-Beckmann F, von Benda-Beckmann K (2007a) Gesellschaftliche Wirkung von Recht: Rechtsethnologische Perspektiven. Reimer Verlag, Berlin
von Benda-Beckmann F, von Benda-Beckmann K (2007b) Transnationalisation of law, globalisation and legal pluralism: a legal anthropological perspective. In: Antons C, Gessner V (eds) Globalisation and resistance: law reform in Asia since the crisis. Hart Publishing, Oxford, pp 53–80
von Benda-Beckmann F et al (2009a) Introduction: the power of law. In: von Benda-Beckmann F et al (eds) The power of law in a transnational world: anthropological enquiries. Berghahn Books, New York, pp 1–32
von Benda-Beckmann F et al (2009b) Space and legal pluralism: an introduction. In: von Benda-Beckmann F et al (eds) Spatializing law: an anthropological geography of law in society. Ashgate, Farnham, pp 1–30
Wainwright J (2008) Decolonizing development: colonial power and the Maya. Blackwell Publishing, Oxford
Wainwright J, Bryan J (2009) Cartography, territory, property: postcolonial reflections on Indigenous counter-mapping in Nicaragua and Belize. Cult Geogr 16:153–178
Waugh J, Murombedzi J (2016) Social benefits in the Liberian forestry sector: an experiment in post-conflict institution building for resilience. In: Bruch C et al (eds) Governance, natural resources, and post-conflict peacebuilding. Routledge, Milton Park, pp 561–578
Weilenmann M (2009) Project law - a power instrument of development agencies: a case study from Burundi. In: von Benda-Beckmann F et al (eds) The power of law in a transnational world. Berghahn Books, New York, pp 156–175
World Bank (2018a) Liberia forest sector project, fourth implementation support and REDD+ readiness preparation support mission, February 2 - February 9, 2018, aide-memoire
World Bank (2018b) Liberia: country forest note. https://documents1.worldbank.org/curated/en/233271527176589175/pdf/Liberia-Country-Forest-Note.pdf. Accessed 12 Aug 2023
World Bank (2019) Republic of Liberia: Liberia forest sector project (LFSP) mid term review mission, May 13-19, 2019, aide memoire
Wrubel TP (1971) Liberia: the dynamics of continuity. J Mod Afr Stud 9:189–204

Chapter 5
Conclusion: FPIC's Journeys

This book has traced the journeys of the right to free, prior and informed consent (FPIC) through different fields at different scales. It has been shown that the transplantation of norms is a norm negotiation process. Norm negotiation processes take place in specific fields. In this respect, legal anthropology has proven useful, particularly its understanding of socio-legal fields as relational networks characterized by power relations, discourses, and overlapping legalities. Fields are not closed systems. Instead, they are 'constituted in interaction with social forces that extend both in space and time'.[1]

Actors use discourses as a strategy for effecting norm change and pushing through their vision of the law. Notably, the construction of social identities—of the community, the state, or the forest—determines FPIC's meaning. These social identities are translated into legal identities, consolidating a certain version of FPIC. Whether actors can shape the field's hegemonic discourse and its identities depends on their power derived from their symbolic, social, cultural, and economic capital.[2]

While interdiscursivity, i.e. encounters between different discourses, is often understood to result in a situation where different discourses seek to disqualify each other, this book has shown that interdiscursive encounters between discourses with overlapping values and identities can also contribute to the consolidation of a particular version of the law.[3]

With FPIC being a relatively new right, it has been shown that the negotiation processes are ongoing and that FPIC remains in a state of fragmentation. To grasp the different versions of FPIC, three characteristics of FPIC were identified and examined in different fields: First, the rights- or stakeholders of FPIC. Discourses create collective identities to which FPIC is attached. These identities determine the theoretical concept underlying FPIC and particularly the relationship between the

[1] Grosz-Ngaté (1997), p. 16; see also Falk Moore (1973), p. 722.

[2] Bourdieu and Wacquant (1992), p. 119.

[3] Ibid, p. 119; see also Smart (1989), pp. 4.

R. Rösch, *Negotiating Norms*, Interdisciplinary Studies in Human Rights 9,
https://doi.org/10.1007/978-3-031-45910-8_5

collective identity and the state. Second, the content of FPIC and the situations in which it applies. And, third, FPIC's internal dimension, including the recognition of its institutional autonomy dimension and women's right to FPIC.

5.1 FPIC in Global Time-Spaces

Originally, consent as a concept of international law has been appropriated by Indigenous peoples, aligned with their understandings of sovereignty, and made part of their legal struggle. The recognition of FPIC in transnational human rights law was a major success for the Indigenous movement. However, it also came at a price: its alignment to the values of the field of human rights law, which does not fundamentally interfere with the sovereignty of states. It recognizes only a narrow Indigenous right to self-determination and the collective right to property from which FPIC can be derived.

Subsequently, it was transplanted to other global legal fields such as transnational environmental law and transnational development law. However, in all these fields, different versions of FPIC exist. FPIC's meaning depends on the legal identity that owns it. The relevant collective legal identities include Indigenous peoples, peoples, tribal peoples, and local communities. The categorization of a group has tangible consequences for FPIC's meaning. However, the identities created by the law are not completely fixed but depend on the legal sub-field in which they are situated. For instance, the legal identity of *Indigenous and tribal peoples* in human rights law differs from the stakeholder group of *Indigenous peoples and local communities* in transnational environmental law. Even though they describe the same kind or at least a very similar social identity, the legal identities differ and, thereby, also the meaning of FPIC.

In human rights law, *Indigenous and tribal peoples* have the strongest rights, while FPIC is not part of the peasant and minority rights framework. Yet even under Indigenous law, FPIC is usually derived either from a washed-out version of self-determination that is closer to the right to culture than to the recognition of Indigenous sovereignty or from the right to property (in conjunction with the right to culture). Consequently, Indigenous peoples can only dissent in very exceptional circumstances. Moreover, the entanglement of culture and FPIC contributes to the recognition of the institutional autonomy of Indigenous peoples (to some extent) while there remains a lack of engagement with Indigenous women's right to self-determination, culture, and FPIC.

The logic of development law strongly differs from that of human rights law. It tends to attach FPIC or consultations to the legal identity of *Indigenous peoples+*. However, Indigenous peoples+ are generally not rightsholders but stakeholders. Simultaneously, FPIC is transformed from a right into a principle. It is about nodding through development projects.[4] The detachment from the rights framework and the lack of recognition of communities' right to culture also means that FPIC procedures are taken out of the communities' hands. However, the stakeholder approach makes it easier to accommodate women as a stakeholder group.

Transnational environmental law has been reluctant to recognize FPIC. State sovereignty continues to be a central principle in natural resource management. The creation of the legal identity of the stakeholder group *Indigenous peoples and local communities* is a way of negating the applicability of the Indigenous law framework. Except for the law of climate change, located at the intersection of environmental and development law, FPIC is usually either not recognized, only a recommendation, or can be overridden by the state. Even though FPIC is not explicitly tied to the right to culture, and the institutional autonomy of communities is generally not recognized, the Indigenous women's right to FPIC also remains underrecognized.

Generally speaking, FPIC remains indeterminate and fragmented. Within the different legal fields, legal identities are constructed in a way that allows for departing from the self-determination-based understanding of FPIC. FPIC enables dialogue while leaving the sovereignty of the state intact. While this made the culture-property-nexus very persuasive for a wide range of actors, it also gave rise to an understanding of FPIC that does not alter international and national power relations.

5.2 FPIC in National Time-Spaces

The second chapter explored the renegotiation of FPIC in two national time-spaces and how it was accommodated and renegotiated in the quite exceptional Liberian post-war context. In 2007, FPIC was made part of the Liberian forestry legislation and, in 2018, it was incorporated into the Land Rights Act.

Following the end of the Liberian civil war, the UN logging sanctions triggered fundamental reforms in the Liberian forest sector and contributed to the emergence of the field of post-conflict forest sector reform. The legal reform process was at first characterized by a practice of multi-stakeholder legal drafting, including government actors, NGOs, conservationists, company associations, and donors. The so-called *local turn* in peacebuilding and the omnipresent language of participation created the illusion of a legal reform process legitimized from below.[5] In reality, development best practices determined the field's legislative practice, and communities could not participate in a meaningful way.

[4] Merino (2018), p. 140.

[5] See also Mertz (1994), p. 1251.

Later, the lack of experience with community forestry, together with the scandals in the logging sector, enhanced the capital of NGOs. They had the chance to assume a lead role in the drafting of the Community Rights Law introducing community forestry. The subsequent regulations governing the implementation of the CRL were, however, shaped more by the agenda of donors and government, which shared a common interest in foreign direct investment and placed little trust in the capacity of communities to manage their forests. The social identity of the *incompetent community* prevailing in most discourses within the field contributed to the disrespect of FPIC's cultural and institutional autonomy dimension, while gender and the rights of rural women were also generally not seen as a forestry matter.

Shifting practices also characterized the field of land sector reform. While development actors played a central role in the early drafting and negotiation phase of the LRA, later, the negotiations took place mainly within Parliament. However, in the final phase of negotiation, NGOs greatly enhanced their symbolic capital by launching major public campaigns, contributing to the passage of the Land Rights Act in 2018.

Concerning FPIC, the land legislation largely concurs with the forest legislation. The emerging FPIC norm does not substantively touch upon the state's sovereignty. FPIC is linked to the registration of forest or customary land. The Liberian FPIC is neither retroactive with respect to protected areas and concessions nor does it interfere with the state's legislative and administrative power and its right to eminent domain. However, depending on its operationalization, the procedure for registering customary land could allow for the greater accommodation of community rights than the procedure for authorizing a community forest, which government actors dominate.

With respect to FPIC's institutional autonomy dimension, the different ways in which gender and customary decision-making were negotiated in the two fields are noteworthy. In both fields, the social identity of the *incompetent community* emerged, whose culture was not seen as worth protecting. Therefore, nobody questioned the introduction of new governance institutions. However, women's rights were negotiated in very different ways. The actors co-located in the field of development played a central role in this. Right after the civil war, the peacebuilding project had a gender angle. However, this gender angle focused mainly on gender-based violence and targeted *women-victims*. Consequently, the forest sector was not seen as a gender issue. The land-gender nexus, in contrast, is well-recognized in the fields of peacebuilding and development. As many of the donor projects had a gender dimension, it also became a priority for the national NGOs implementing the projects. Consequently, the land legislation includes a strong women's quota for land governance institutions, which could, in principle, enable the participation of a critical mass of women. Yet, the rise of inclusive decision-making also contributed to the further decline of local legalities and land governance. Women's rights served as a legitimization for undermining communities' institutional autonomy instead of building up on existing institutions that may have ensured the participation of women. The overlapping discourses with their blindness to both gender and culture thus risk marginalizing both local communities and the women within these communities.[6]

While the forest and land legislation may be the best legal protection communities have had in the past decades in Liberia, it also replaces self-determination claims with property rights or even less. Communities are recognized as rightsholders as long as they submit to the statutory legal framework and state authorities. FPIC has been reduced to a right that applies only in exceptional circumstances. The emerging understanding of FPIC was shaped by a hegemonic discourse based on the social identities of the *incompetent and discriminatory community* and the *strong sovereign state*, leaving the state essentially in charge of managing its land and natural resources.

5.3 FPIC in Local Time-Spaces

Under the forest legislation, FPIC is to be realized in and after the authorization of community forests. The fourth chapter thus explored the norm negotiation processes in two predominantly local time-spaces: the fields of the Beyan Poye and the Sehzueplay community forest. Customary forest land is only protected if communities follow the steps determined by forest legislation. Communities need to self-identify, determine the boundaries of their land, elect their governance institutions, adopt governance rules, and decide how they want to use the forest.

However, not only national and local legalities shape the fields of community forestry. Through the presence of NGOs, the Forestry Development Authority, and donor projects, they are also under the influence of project law and development and conservation discourse. Even though these external actors pursued different goals, they shared a negative perception of local forest uses and forest governance. Their discourses contributed to the construction of the forest as a commercial or environmental resource.[7]

The forest as a space of imagination determined the meaning of the community, of the material forest, and of FPIC. The identity of the customary land-owning community—created by the forest legislation—was transformed into the social identity of the *community that should benefit from forest resources*. This new community was quite big, influenced by colonial legalities, and not rooted in customary law and land governance. Moreover, the commercial or conservation-based understanding of the forest strongly impacted the identification of customary forest land. Both companies and conservationists preferred the designation of larger tracts of forests. Therefore, communities agreed to claim large parcels of customary land, irrespective of the customary boundaries.

---

[6] Jørgensen and Phillips (2002), p. 63.

[7] See also Gururani (2002), p. 231.

Forest governance, in contrast, was determined by national legalities. The community governance structure is not rooted in customary governance. Yet, in both community forests, local authorities yielded influence over the operationalization of community forestry. This exemplifies that the national legalities did not replace local forest governance but contributed to the emergence of new hybrids. In contrast, most community members, particularly those living within the forest and rural women, felt excluded from the decision-making processes. The external actors also missed an opportunity to build upon existing women's organizations or land governance practices.[8]

The forest-use decision was, in both cases, already taken before the community forest registration was launched. Communities were only aware of the conservation or commercial use option. However, most community members did not object to the commercial use of the forest per se but rather to the lack of information and participation.

Hence, in both community forests, FPIC is no longer a matter of rights. Development and conservation discourses extinguished FPIC's cultural dimension and transformed it into the principle that community members may consent to development and benefit from it while other forest uses become unthinkable.[9] However, community members retained little spaces of resistance at the fringe of the community forest project. The forests continue to have other social meanings outside of the hegemonic discourse. This is exemplified by the continuous use of the forests. Moreover, the high number of angry women in both community forests complaining about their lack of information indicates that contestation and renegotiation processes are ongoing.

Moreover, the 2018 Land Rights Act, which pursues an approach to customary land rights more strongly informed by human rights, will likely impact community forestry in the future. Community forests will become a type of customary land.[10] Thereby, the Land Rights Act may broaden the scope of FPIC.

5.4 And Beyond?

Law produced in global time-spaces is often considered the progressive benchmark against which everything else is measured. The fields explored in this book challenge this type of thinking.

Firstly, FPIC highlights the some of the risks inherent in mainstreaming emancipatory concepts. With FPIC's cultural and self-determination dimension being sidelined in most fields, great danger lies in legitimizing projects or programs—particularly when the procedure for obtaining FPIC itself constitutes a violation of

[8] See also Imai (2009), p. 311.

[9] See also Jørgensen and Phillips (2002), p. 27.

[10] An Act to establish the Land Rights Law of 2018 (2018) (Liberia), art 43.

customary ways of decision-making.[11] Once FPIC—or some version of it—has been obtained, it is difficult, if not impossible, to challenge the project.[12] Shrinkhal also argues that FPIC is thwarted when understood solely as a contract while communities 'are not made capable of understanding the nitty-gritties of the contract law'.[13] Moreover, the lack of an intersectional lens in relation to FPIC risks resulting in the extinction of both the institutional autonomy of communities and the rights of women within these communities. Instead of only constructing a dichotomy between Indigenous and collective rights, it should be acknowledged that women have a right to FPIC, too, and that communities and their institutions can also be a source of women's participation.[14]

Secondly, what is lacking in the literature on legal transplants and normative change is the engagement with complex power relations, discourses, and legal plurality. The law is a site of power struggles and tends to reflect the interests of powerful actors. FPIC as a norm, whose meaning remains controversial, exemplifies the struggle between different actors, discourses, and legalities. In this respect, not only power relations matter but also the question of who can access fields in which norms are negotiated. If communities cannot participate in legal reforms that greatly affect them, their discourses and legalities remain excluded. However, often, consent processes take place in contexts of 'cultural disconnect, internal exclusion, epistemic injustice, hegemonic and identity-based subordination'.[15] But while participation is surely not the panacea for all problems, exclusion most certainly isn't either.

Thirdly, fields are inhabited by discourses that shape the identities within the field and, thereby, also the meaning of the law. Discourses can not only stabilize norms, but they can also be a tool for changing the law through strategic interdiscursivity or self-identification practices. Fields and their practices can be changed through 'negotiating discourses'.[16] The capacity to engage with discourses depends on the capital someone holds, as evidenced by the two fields of community forestry. The law and FPIC thus remain fluid and subject to change.

On a practical level, this means that actors with a vision of social justice participating in norm negotiation processes—and scholars alike—should question their own construction of the world and the *reality* underlying and created by the law. They need to broaden their understanding of what the law is to be able to value local knowledge and legalities. The hierarchical, racialized thinking related to global, national, and local legalities needs to be deconstructed. Practices of resistance based on local legalities—like the ongoing use of the forests—should be

[11] Kapoor (2008), p. 66; see also Brilman (2018), p. 60.

[12] See also Brilman (2018), p. 72; Dunlap (2018), p. 93.

[13] Shrinkhal (2014), p. 64.

[14] See also McIvor (1995), p. 36; Napoleon (2005), p. 37; Starblanket (2018), p. 12.

[15] Eisenberg (2020), p. 281.

[16] Kapoor (2008), p. 54.

understood as resistance of 'creative agents, capable of subverting authority in positive and unanticipated ways'.[17]

Fourthly, this book questions the conception that the law is black and white and that there exists the *human right to FPIC* that is then implemented or not. Instead, it highlights some of the struggles underlying the emergence of relatively stable norms and shows that FPIC has, in most cases, not reached that tipping point. Simultaneously, legal transplantations are not straightforward, and they are not one-way processes.[18] The adoption of the United Nations Declaration on the Rights of Indigenous Peoples and the United Nations Declaration on the Rights of Peasants and Other People Working in Rural Areas highlights that knowledge and norm transfers occur in different ways and across different scales.[19] FPIC's journey also exemplifies the power of transnational alliances, which manage to set norms in the transnational field and import it to different scales.

Moreover, in the past years, Indigenous peoples—particularly in the Americas—began adopting so-called autonomous FPIC Protocols.[20] In these protocols, they codify their rules of engagement, drawing also from national and global legalities to avoid having consultation procedures imposed upon them by the state or companies.[21] Indigenous peoples in the Philippines also organized protests against culturally inappropriate government-set consultation guidelines and developed alternatives.[22] In sub-Saharan Africa, these developments have not remained unnoticed: for example, the Ogiek and Endorois have adopted Biocultural Protocols in which FPIC features prominently.[23] New initiatives to develop FPIC Protocols are underway.[24] It is possible and desirable that these new FPIC hybrids will influence the understanding of FPIC in other fields, making more actors recognize FPIC's self-determination dimension in the long run. Hence, Engle Merry is right in her assertion

[17] Ibid, pp. 132–33; see also Bhabha (1994), p. 193; Eisenberg (2020), p. 273.

[18] Brysk (2000), p. 288; von Benda-Beckmann and Turner (2019), p. 13.

[19] Klug (2005), p. 278.

[20] HRC (10 Aug 2018), Free, prior and informed consent: A human rights-based approach. Study of the Expert Mechanism on the Rights of Indigenous Peoples, UN Doc A/HRC/39/62, para 57; HRC (4 Aug 2021), Efforts to implement the United Nations Declaration on the Rights of Indigenous Peoples: Indigenous peoples and the right to self-determination, A/HRC/48/75, para 28; IWGIA and Comisión Interamericana de Derechos Humanos (28 Dec 2021), paras 297ff.

[21] Doyle et al. (2019), p. 9; Papillon and Rodon (2020), pp. 319–20; Schilling-Vacaflor and Flemmer (2020), p. 306.

[22] Lightfoot (2020), pp. 4–5.

[23] Endorois Peoples (2019) Endorois peoples' biocultural protocol: Sustainable biodiversity resource management for access and benefit sharing and protection from threats to culture. http://archive.abs-biotrade.info/fileadmin/media/Knowledge_Center/Pulications/BCPs/Endorois-Peoples-Biocultural-Protocol.pdf. Accessed 23 May 2023; Ogiek Community (2021) Ogiek community bio-cultural protocol (OC-BCP). https://ogiekpeoples.org/index.php/download/ogiek-community-bio-cultural-protocol/?wpdmdl=6190&refresh=646cbf30aac8a1684848432. Accessed 23 May 2023.

[24] Alvarado (2022), p. 57.

that 'the local appropriates and transforms the global for its own needs'.[25] FPIC's journeys are far from being over.

References

Alvarado LJ (2022) Study on consultation and free, prior and informed consent with Indigenous peoples in Africa. IWGIA

Bhabha HK (1994) The location of culture. Routledge, London

Bourdieu P, Wacquant LJD (1992) The purpose of reflexive sociology (the Chicago workshop). In: Bourdieu P, Wacquant LJD (eds) An invitation to reflexive sociology. Chicago University Press, Chicago, pp 61–216

Brilman M (2018) Consenting to dispossession: the problematic heritage and complex future of consultation and consent of indigenous peoples. Colum Hum Rights Law Rev 49:1–72

Brysk A (2000) From tribal village to global village: Indian rights and international relations in Latin America. Stanford University Press, Stanford

Doyle C et al (2019) Free prior and informed consent protocols as instruments of autonomy: laying foundations for rights based engagement. Institut für Ökologie und Aktions-Ethnologie

Dunlap A (2018) "A bureaucratic trap:" free, prior and informed consent (FPIC) and wind energy development in Juchitán, Mexico. Capital Nat Social 29:88–108

Eisenberg A (2020) Consent, resistance and the duty to consult. Int J Minor Group Rights 27:270–290

Engle Merry S (2000) Crossing boundaries: ethnography in the twenty-first century. Polit Leg Anthropol Rev 23:127–133

Falk Moore S (1973) Law and social change: The semi-autonomous social field as an appropriate subject of study. Law Soc Rev 7:719–746

Grosz-Ngaté M (1997) Introduction. In: Grosz-Ngaté M, Kokole OH (eds) Gendered encounters: Challenging cultural boundaries and social hierarchies in Africa. Routledge, London, pp 1–22

Gururani S (2002) Forests of pleasure and pain: gendered practices of labor and livelihood in the forests of the Kumaon Himalayas. Gend Place Cult 9:229–243

Imai S (2009) Indigenous self-determination and the state. In: Richardson BJ et al (eds) Indigenous people and the law: comparative and critical perspectives. Hart Publishing, Oxford, pp 285–314

IWGIA, Comisión Interamericana de Derechos Humanos (28 Dec 2021) Derecho a la libre determinación de los pueblos indígenas y tribales

Jørgensen MW, Phillips L (2002) Discourse analysis as theory and method. SAGE Publications, London

Kapoor I (2008) The postcolonial politics of development. Routledge, London

Klug H (2005) Hybrid(ity) rules: creating local law in a globalized world. In: Dezalay Y, Garth BG (eds) Global prescriptions: the production, exportation, and importation of a new legal orthodoxy. The University of Michigan Press, Ann Arbor, pp 276–305

Lightfoot S (2020) Indigenous laws and governance in Indigenous self-developed FPIC protocols. http://fnemc.ca/wp-content/uploads/2015/07/Sheryl-Lightfoot-Expert-Paper-Indigenous-Legal-Framework.pdf. Accessed 20 Mar 2023

McIvor SD (1995) Aboriginal women's rights as "existing rights". Can Women Stud 15:34–38

Merino R (2018) Law and politics of indigenous self-determination: the meaning of the right to prior consultation. In: Watson I (ed) Indigenous peoples as subjects of international law. Routledge, Abingdon, pp 120–140

[25] Engle Merry (2000), p. 129.

Mertz E (1994) Conclusion: a new social constructionism for sociolegal studies. Law Soc Rev 28: 1243–1265

Napoleon V (2005) Aboriginal self determination: individual self and collective selves. Atlantis 29: 31–46

Papillon M, Rodon T (2020) The transformative potential of Indigenous-driven approaches to implementing free, prior and informed consent: lessons from two Canadian cases. Int J Minor Group Rights 27:314–335

Schilling-Vacaflor A, Flemmer R (2020) Mobilising free, prior and informed consent (FPIC) from below: a typology of Indigenous peoples' agency. Int J Minor Group Rights 27:291–313

Shrinkhal R (2014) "Free, prior informed consent" as a right of indigenous peoples. J Natl Law Univ Delhi 2:54–65

Smart C (1989) Feminism and the power of law. Routledge, London

Starblanket G (2018) Complex accountabilities: deconstructing "the community" and engaging feminist research methods. Am Indian Cult Res J 42:1–20

von Benda-Beckmann K, Turner B (2019) Legal pluralism, social theory, and the state. J Leg Plural Unoff Law 50:1–20